OUR
REASONABLE
FAITH

HERMAN BAVINCK

LATE PROFESSOR OF THEOLOGY, FREE UNIVERSITY
OF AMSTERDAM

Translated from the Dutch edition, *Magnalia Dei*, by
HENRY ZYLSTRA

ISBN: 0-8010-0513-2

Library of Congress Catalog
Card Number: 56-11128

Distributed by
Westminster Discount Book Service
P. O. Box 125-H
Scarsdale, NY 10583

Photolithoprinted in Korea

PREFACE

Those who are at all familiar with the history of the Reformed churches of the Netherlands — that is, of the *Gereformeerde* as distinguished from the *Hervormde kerken* — will know that among the heirs of the *Afscheiding* of 1834 and the *Doleantie* of 1886 no two names are held in such esteem as the names of Abraham Kuyper and Herman Bavinck. They were heroic figures of giant accomplishment in Christian endeavor. Their career at roughly the same time at the end of the last and the beginning of this century must be regarded as a special favor of God for the benefit of historic Christianity in both Europe and the new world.

The two men, who in time came to be mentioned so often in one breath as co-stalwarts of the Reformed cause in Holland, have often been compared and contrasted. Somebody put the difference between them in this way: "In Kuyper we have an example of scintillating genius, in Bavinck an example of clear-headed talent." The Rev. J. H. Landwehr, Bavinck's first biographer, reports another contrast: Bavinck was an Aristotelian, Kuyper a Platonic spirit. Bavinck was the man of the clear concept, Kuyper the man of the fecund idea. Bavinck worked with the historically given; Kuyper proceeded speculatively by way of intuition. Bavinck's was primarily an inductive mind; Kuyper's primarily deductive." The two men complemented each other in the renascence of Calvinist vitality in nineteenth century Dutch life and thought.

Herman Bavinck was born on December 13, 1854. The centennial of his birth was widely celebrated in the Netherlands in 1954, and the nature and scope of his contributions were appreciatively reviewed. Bavinck was born in the town of Hoogeveen in the province of Drenthe. His people originally came from the county or earldom of Bentheim. His father, the Rev. Jan Bavinck, was a minister of the churches which in 1834 had in the interest of maintaining purely the tradition of historic Christianity separated from the State Church of Holland.

The young Bavinck achieved distinction as a student in the gymnasium at Zwolle and then went to the Theological School of his church at Kampen. Here he remained for but a year. He chose then to go to Leiden for his further theological training. Leiden gave him at least two things: a respect for substantial scholarship, and an acquaintance at first hand with the liberally affected modern theology. Both lessons served

5

him well. The ideal of solid theological scholarship for orthodox Reformed Christianity stood high in his life throughout his career. And his intimate acquaintance with the newer religious thought both deepened his Calvinist convictions and fitted him for a profession of theology realistically addressed to the problems of the time.

In 1880 he graduated from Leiden, having done a dissertation on the ethics of Ulrich Zwingli. He served as minister of the church at Franeker for a year, and was then appointed Professor of Dogmatics at the Theological School of Kampen. The subject of his inaugural address, "The Science of Holy Divinity" (*De Wetenschap der Heilige Godgeleerdheid*, 1882), fascinated him all his life. During the decade of his arduous study and effective teaching at Kampen, Bavinck three times received the offer of a professorship in theology at the Free University of Amsterdam. He accepted it only after the third offer, and only after he could satisfy his conscience (see his brochure *Decline or Accept* [*Blijven of Heengaan*], Kampen, 1902 that he was not harming the integrity of theological education in his church. It was when Abraham Kuyper exchanged a professor's portfolio at Amsterdam for a Minister's portfolio in the government at the Hague that Bavinck became Kuyper's successor at the Free University.

Bavinck was primarily the theologian, the dogmatician. His *magnum opus* is the four volumes of his *Reformed Dogmatics* (*Gereformeerde Dogmatiek*). It was the fruit of his Kampen effort, appearing first during the years 1895-1901, and then, in revised form, in 1906-1911 and later. One volume of this work, *The Doctrine of God,* edited and translated by Dr. W. Hendriksen, was published in Grand Rapids in 1951. The present volume, *Our Reasonable Faith,* given out in 1909 as the *Magnalia Dei* (*The Wonderful Works of God*), is a compendium or synopsis of the four-volume *Dogmatics. Our Reasonable Faith* is less technical, less exclusively professional, more popularly intended than the *Dogmatics,* and is more fully supported by Scriptural reference and annotation, but it is, like the larger work, a book of basic Christian dogma. It presents clearly and in fine perspective the fundamental doctrines of Biblical teaching.

Some have said that Bavinck was more the philosopher than the theologian. It is true that his theology exhibits the discipline of the trained and informed philosopher. But what Bavinck wanted first of all to be in his dogmatics was the Scriptural theologian. It is as Landwehr said: "Just as Calvin gathered his thoughts out of Scripture, so Bavinck was always dipping into the Bible for his ideas, and was being guided by Scripture in his systematization of them." Moreover, in his profession of theology he was not the detached spectator non-committally looking in on the reality of religion. In his Amsterdam inaugural address, *Religion and Theology* (*Godsdienst en Godgeleerdheid,* 1902), he said:

> Religion, the fear of God, must therefore be the element which inspires and animates all theological investigation. That must be the pulsebeat of the science. A theologian is a person who makes bold to speak about God because he speaks out of God and through God. To profess theology is to do holy work. It is a priestly ministration in the house of the Lord. It is itself a service of worship, a consecration of mind and heart to the honor of His name.

It was thus that Bavinck conducted his profession. His former student, Landwehr, reports how things went in the classroom: The lecture, he says, became a sermon, as the professor was stirred by the truth. And most of his biographers record the words he uttered during his final illness: "Now my scholarship avails me nothing, nor my dogmatics: it is only my faith can save me." In that statement he was not disparaging a life of scientific theological effort but simply indicating the right order of importances.

When Dr. J. C. Rullman submitted his article on Bavinck to the *Christelijke Encyclopaedie* in 1925 he felt that he could hardly do better towards characterizing Bavinck's work than to quote from Bavinck's colleague at the Free University, Dr. W. J. Geesink. The quotation is useful here also. Dr. Geesink wrote — he was, of course, using the Dutch:

> As professor, Bavinck would have ranked high on any university faculty. His tremendous erudition and his wide reading became richly expressive in the classroom. A keenly penetrating scholar, he had a gift for discovering problems, and when he discovered one he could convey it to his audience in unencumbered terms. If he had a solution to it, he shared the solution also, never hurriedly but with deliberateness and calm. And if he did not yet have a solution, his scholarly integrity kept him from palming off one which was illusory, and in which one term of the problem was satisfied at the cost of annihilating the other. And, what with his respect for logic and his thorough discipline at school, he knew far too well the dangers of irrationalism not to acknowledge that there are some problems that cannot be solved.
>
> As theologian and dogmatician by profession, Bavinck went back to Calvin for his Reformed theology. By doing this, and by taking account also, though not without criticism and reservation, of modern scholarship and science, he helped liberate Reformed theology from the hardening and ossification it had undergone since about 1750 . . . . Like Augustine, whom he placed in the van of all thinkers before and after the fourth century, he looked to a

philosophy of revelation for an answer to the problems of life and the world — for an answer, be it said, that would satisfy both the heart and the mind.

Bavinck wrote an impressive number of substantial works in the areas of religion and theology, philosophy and applied ethics, and, especially too, psychology and the theory of education. The bibliography of his published work, which includes besides full length volumes the many inaugural, rectoral, and other academic addresses which he gave, but which does not include his busy journalistic work, runs to some sixty items in Landwehr's tabulation. In the province of religion and theology, the following publications deserve mention in addition to the *Reformed Dogmatics* and *Our Reasonable Faith*. In 1888 he gave out his little timeless classic on ecumenicity entitled *The Catholicity of Christianity and the Church* (*De Katholiciteit van Christendom en Kerk*). In 1894 there followed a definitive lecture on a theme first delineated by Calvin, and also greatly developed by Abraham Kuyper, namely, *Common Grace* (*De Algemeene Genade*). His beautiful meditations in *The Sacrifice of Praise* (*De Offerande des Lofs*, 1901) had gone into the sixth edition by the time of his death, and were translated into English and published in this country in 1922. A sort of companion volume, *The Assurance of Faith* (*De Zekerheid des Geloofs*), was published in the same year. Important, too, are his rectoral address of 1911 entitled *Modernism and Orthodoxy* (*Modernisme en Orthodoxie*), and his *Calling and Regeneration* (*Roeping en Wedergeboorte*) of 1903.

Among his more philosophically oriented books are the Princeton Stone Lectures, delivered in 1908 and published in English the next following year as *The Philosophy of Revelation,* the *Present Day Ethics* (*Hedendaagsche Moraal*, 1902,) and the two philosophical lectures of 1904 entitled *Christian Philosophy* (*Christelijke Wetenschap*) and *The Christian World and life View* (*Christelijke Wereldbeschouwing.*) A theme which occupied Bavinck again and again and to which he devoted some of his ripest reflection was that of the interrelationship of religion and learning. No institution of orthodox higher Christian education ought to ignore his many publications on this subject: *Religion and Divinity* (*Godsdienst en Godgeleerdheid,* 1902), *Education and Theology* (*Opleiding en Theologie,* 1896). *The Office of Doctor or Professor of Theology* (*Het Doctorenambt,* 1899), *Learning and Philosophy* (*Geleerdheid en Wetenschap,* 1899), *The Authority of the Church and the Freedom of Science* (*Het Recht der Kerken en de Vrijheid der Wetenschap,* 1899), and *The Theological School and the Free University* (*Theologische School en Vrije Universiteit,* 1899).

It was during the later years of his professional life that Bavinck became expressive in those two further provinces of life and thought, namely, applied ethics and morally grounded psychology. To the first category of interest belong such works as *The Role of Woman in Modern Society* (*De Vrouw in de Hedendaagsche Maatschappij*, 1918), *The Christian Family* (*Het Christelijke Huisgezin*, 1908), *The Imitation of Christ in Modern Life* (*De Navolging van Christus in het Moderne Leven*, 1918), *The Problem of War* (*Het Problem van den Oorlog*, 1915), and *Christianity, War, and a League of Nations* (*Christendom, Oorlog, Volkenbond*, 1920). The last named work reminds us how far into the problems of our century Bavinck's interest extended. Indeed, it must be said that he had a fine "sense of his own age." This accounts in part for his pronounced concern with psychology and the principles of education. In 1915 came the treatise *On the Sub-Conscious* (*Het Onbewuste*), in 1897 *The Principles of Psychology* (*Beginselen der Psychologie*), and in 1920 the *Biblical and Religious Psychology* (*Bijbelsche en Religieuse Psychologie*). His major work in the theory of education is the *Pedagogical Principles* (*Paedagogische Beginselen*, 1904). It is no wonder that this area of his achievement should have attracted considerable attention. Dr. Cornelius Jaarsma's *The Educational Philosophy of Herman Bavinck* (Grand Rapids, 1935) and L. Van der Zweep's *De Paedagogiek van Bavinck* (Kampen, n. d.) are representative of it.

Herman Bavinck twice visited America, first in 1892 when he was invited by the Alliance of Reformed Churches Holding the Presbyterian System to address that body meeting in Toronto on the subject: "The Influence of the Protestant Reformation on the Moral and Religious Conditions of Peoples and Nations"; and next in 1908 when he demonstrated by his Stone Lectures at Princeton that he deserved to be named with Kuyper, Warfield, Hodge, and Orr as outstanding among modern Calvinist theologians. In practical political life he was far less active than Kuyper, his bent being for political philosophy rather than for politics. He was, however, a member of the Upper House, representing South Holland in the States General from the year 1911 on. His best services in this capacity were given as consultant and advisor in education. The translation of his works into English has been fitful and scattered. Thus far only *The Sacrifice of Praise, The Kingdom of God, The Philosophy of Revelation,* and the little treatise *Evolution* have appeared. *Our Reasonable Faith* is, accordingly, an important addition. There has as yet been no definitive biography. Three precursors to it have, however, been written. The first is J. H. Landwehr's *In Me-*

moriam of 1921, the next Dr. V. Hepp's *Dr. Herman Bavinck* of the same year — the promised second volume sequel to this was never produced — and the third is A. B. W. Kok's *Herman Bavinck* of 1945. A quantity of Dutch periodical studies have gone to the analysis of Bavinck's ideas. In this country we have had, besides Dr. Jaarsma's book, also the unpublished doctoral dissertion for Princeton of Dr. Anthony Hoekema on Bavinck's doctrine of the Covenant.

It can be said that in the whole of his apology for Scriptural Reformed Christianity Bavinck had four opposing influences in mind, two of them outside and two of them inside the pale of the Reformed faith. The two outside influences were modern religious liberalism and Roman Catholicism. The two inside influences were a moribund formal orthodoxy, on the one hand, and an evasive pietism, on the other. He spoke often and eloquently against all of these forces. Note, for example, with what feeling and with what perspective he advocated the world involvement of a universal Calvinism instead of the world flight of a sectarian pietism:

> We may not be a sect. We may not want to be one, and we cannot be one, except by a denial of the absolute character of the truth. Indeed, the kingdom of heaven is not of this world. But it does demand that everything in this world serve it. It is exclusive and jealous, and it will indulge no independent or neutral kingdom of the world alongside of itself. Naturally, it would be much easier to leave this age to its own ways, and to seek our strength in a quiet withdrawal. No such rest, however, is permitted to us here. Because every creature is good, and nothing is to be refused, if it be received with thanksgiving, since all things are sanctified by the Word of God and prayer, therefore the rejection of any creature were ingratitude to God, a misjudgment or under-evaluation of His goodness and His gifts. Our warfare may be conducted against sin alone. No matter how complicated the relationships may be, therefore, in which the confessors of Christ are placed in this time, no matter how serious, difficult, and virtually insurmountable the social, political, and especially the scientific problems may be, it were faithlessness and weakness in us proudly to withdraw from the struggle, perhaps even under the guise of Christian motivation, and to reject the culture of the age as demonic.

That is one of the notes which Bavinck liked to sound in his defense of the faith. He sounded it in the address entitled *The Catholicity of Christianity and the Church*. It is a representative statement. "The faith," he went on, "has the promise of victory over the world." Dr. Hepp very appropriately wrote at the conclusion of his biography of Bavinck these words:

> What he once said of Calvin, holds also for him: Posterity "can find no better way to honor their pioneer and guide than to confess with heart and mouth: Of Him, and through Him, and to Him are all things. To Him be the glory forever."

August, 1955   Henry Zylstra

CONTENTS

OUR
REASONABLE
FAITH

I

Man's Highest Good

God, and God alone, is man's highest good.

In a general sense we can say that God is the highest good of all His creatures. For God is the Creator and sustainer of all things, the source of all being and of all life, and the abundant fountain of all goods. All creatures owe their existence from moment to moment solely to Him who is the one, eternal, and omnipresent Being.

But the idea of the highest good usually includes the thought that this good is also recognized and enjoyed as such by the creatures themselves. And that is of course not the case for inanimate and for non-rational creatures. The inanimate ones have only an existence, and have no principle of life at all. Other creatures, such as the plants, have a principle of life in them, but are devoid of any awareness. The animals, it is true, have received in addition to their existence and their life a kind of awareness, but it is an awareness which can take note only of the visible and sensuous things around them. They are aware of earthly but not of heavenly things; they are aware of the actual, the pleasant, and the useful, but they have no notion of the true, the good, and the beautiful; they have a sensuous awareness and a sensuous desire, but they are therefore also satisfied by the sensuous and cannot penetrate through to the spiritual order.

For man the case is quite different. He is a creature who, right from the beginning, was created after God's image and likeness, and this Divine origin and Divine kinship he can never erase or destroy. Even though he has, because of sin, lost the glorious attributes of knowledge, righteousness, and holiness which lay contained in that image of God, nevertheless there are still present in him "small remains" of the endowments granted him at creation; and these are enough not merely to constitute him guilty but also to testify of his former grandeur and to remind him continually of his Divine calling and heavenly destiny.

In all his thinking and in all his work, in the whole life and activity of man, it becomes apparent that he is a creature who cannot be satisfied with what the whole corporeal world has to offer. He is indeed a citizen of a physical order of affairs, but he also rises above this order to a supernatural one. With his feet planted firmly on the ground, he raises his head aloft and casts his eye up in a vertical look. He has knowledge of things that are visible and temporal, but he is also aware of things that are invisible and eternal. His desire goes out to the earthly, sensuous, and transient, but it goes out also to heavenly, spiritual, and everlasting goods.

Man shares his sensuous awareness and his sensuous consciousness with the animals. But over and above those qualities he was endowed with an understanding and a reason which enable him to think and to raise himself up out of a world of sensuous images to a world of incorporeal thoughts and to the realm of eternal ideas. Man's thinking and knowing, although bound to his brain, are nevertheless in their essence quite entirely a spiritual activity, far transcending the things he sees with his eye and handles with his hand. By means of such thought he establishes his connection with a world which he cannot see and touch but which is just as actual and which possesses more of essential reality than does the corporeality of the earth. What he is really seeking for is not a tangible reality, but spiritual truth, a truth which is one, eternal, and imperishable. His understanding can find rest only in such an absolute Divine truth.

Just so, too, man shares his sensuous desire with the animal. Consequently he feels the need for food and drink, for light and air, for work and rest, and he is dependent upon the whole earth for his physical existence. But, quite above this level of desire, he received a will, which, guided by his reason and conscience, reaches out to other and higher goods. The pleasant and the useful, although they have their value in their place and at their time, do not satisfy him; he requires and seeks a good which does not become good because of circumstances, but which is good in and through and for itself, an unchanging, spiritual, eternal good. And his will, again, can find its rest only in such a highest, absolute, Divine goodness.

Both of these, the reason and the will, have, according to the representation of the Holy Scriptures, their roots in the heart of man. Concerning that heart, the author of the Proverbs says that it must be kept with all diligence, for out of it are the issues of life (4:23). Even as the heart in the physical sense is the point of origin and the propelling force of the circulation of the blood, so also it is spiritually and ethically the source of the higher life in man, the seat of our self-consciousness, of our relationship to God, of our subservience to His law, in short, of our whole spiritual and moral nature. Hence all of our rational and volitional life has its point of origin in the heart and is governed by it.

Now we learn from Ecclesiastes 3:11 that God has set the world in the heart of man. God makes everything beautiful in His time, He makes everything happen at the right moment, at the moment He has fixed for it, so that history in its entirety and in its parts corresponds to the counsel of God and exhibits the glory of that counsel. And God has placed man in the midst of this world totality, and has set the times in man's heart, in order that he should not rest in the external, visible manifestations but should instead seek out and come to know the eternal thoughts of God in the temporal course of nature and of history.

This *desiderium aeternitatis,* this yearning for an eternal order, which God has planted in the heart of man, in the inmost recesses of his being, in the core of his personality, is the cause of the indisputable fact that everything which belongs to the temporal order cannot satisfy man. He is a sensuous, earthly, limited, and mortal being, and yet he is attracted to the eternal and is destined for it. It is of no profit to a man that he should gain wife and children, houses and fields, treasures and property, or, indeed, the whole world, if in the gaining, his soul should suffer loss (Matt. 16:26). For the whole world cannot balance the scale against the worth of a man. There is no one so rich that he can by any means redeem the soul of his brother, nor give to God a ransom for him; the redemption of the soul is too precious for any creature to achieve (Ps. 49:7-9).

* * * * *

As it happens, there are many who are perfectly willing to grant this so long as only sensuous pleasures and earthly treasures are involved. They readily acknowledge that such things cannot satisfy man and do not correspond to his high destiny. But they judge quite differently when the so-called ideal values — science, art, culture, the service of the true, the good, and the beautiful, the living for others, and the aspiration to serve what is called humanity — enter into the picture. But these things, too, belong to the world of which the Scriptures say that it and all its desirableness pass away (1 John 2:17).

Science, knowledge, learning is certainly a good gift, coming down as it does from the Father of lights, and therefore to be highly prized.

When Paul calls the wisdom of the world foolishness with God (1 Cor. 3:19), and when he elsewhere warns against philosophy (Col. 2:8), he has in mind that false and vainly imagined wisdom which has not acknowledged the wisdom of God in His general and special revelation (1 Cor. 1:21) and has become vain in all its imaginations (Rom. 1:21). But for the rest Paul and the Holy Scriptures in their entirety raise knowledge and wisdom to a very high plane of importance.

It could not be otherwise. For the whole Bible affirms that God alone is wise, that He has perfect knowledge of Himself and of all things, that by wisdom He established the world, that He makes its manifold riches known to the church, that in Christ are hid all the treasures of wisdom and knowledge, and that the Spirit is the Spirit of wisdom and knowledge searching out the deep things of God (Prov. 3:19; Rom. 11:33; 1 Cor. 2:10; Eph. 3:10; and Col. 2:3). A book which proceeds out of thoughts like those cannot put a low estimate on knowledge, nor can it despise philosophy. On the contrary, wisdom is better than rubies, and all the things that may be desired are not to be compared to it (Prov. 13:11); it is the gift of Him who is the God of knowledge (Prov. 2:6 and 1 Sam. 2:3).

But what the Scriptures require is a knowledge which has the fear of God as its beginning (Prov. 1:7). When it severs its connection with that principle it may still, under false pretenses, bear the name of knowledge, but it will gradually degenerate into a worldly wisdom which is foolishness with God. Any science, philosophy, or knowledge which supposes that it can stand on its own pretensions, and can leave God out of its assumptions, becomes its own opposite, and disillusions everyone who builds his expectations on it.

It is easy to understand this. For, in the first place, science or philosophy always has a special character about it and can become the portion of only the few. These select ones, who can devote their whole lives to the discipline of learning, can traverse only a small part of its terrain, and they remain strangers to the rest. Whatever satisfaction knowledge can give, therefore, it can never, because of this special and limited character, satisfy the general deep needs which were planted in human nature at creation, and which are therefore present in everybody.

In the second place, philosophy, whenever after a period of decay it enters upon a period of revival again, always begins with an extraordinary and exaggerated expectation. At such a time it lives in the hope that by means of continued serious investigation it will solve the riddle of the world. But always after this young over-excitement the old disillusionment enters in. So far from decreasing, the problems increase as the study proceeds. What seemed to be self-evident proves to be a new mystery, and the end of all knowledge is then again the sad and sometimes despairing confession that man walks about on the earth in riddles, and that life and destiny are mysteries.

And, in the third place, it is well to remember that philosophy or science, even though it could arrive at much more certainty than it is now able to achieve, would still leave the heart of man unsatisfied. For knowledge without virtue, without a moral basis, becomes an instrument in the hands of sin for conceiving and executing greater evil, and then the head that is filled with knowledge enters into the service of a depraved heart. In this sense the Apostle writes: Though I have the gift of prophecy, and understand all mysteries, and all knowledge, and have not love, I am nothing (1 Cor. 13:2).

The same holds true of art. Art, too, is a gift of God. Just as the Lord Himself is not truth and holiness alone but also glory, and one who spreads the beauty of His name abroad over all His works, so it is He, too, who by His Spirit equips the artists with wisdom and understanding and knowledge in all manner of workmanship (Ex. 31:3 and 35:31). Art is therefore in the first place an evidence of man's ability to do and to make. This ability is spiritual in character and it gives expression to his deep longings, his high ideals, and his insatiable craving for harmony. Besides, art in all its works and ways conjures up an ideal world before us, in which the discords of our existence on earth are purged in a gratifying harmony. Thus a beauty is disclosed which in this fallen world had been obscured by the wise but is discovered to the simple eye of the artist. And because art thus paints for us a picture of an other and higher reality, it is a comfort in our life, it lifts the soul up out of consternation, and fills our hearts with hope and joy.

But, though it is much that art can accomplish, it is only in the imagination that we can enjoy the beauty which art discloses. Art cannot close the gulf between the ideal and the real. It cannot make the *yonder* of its vision the *here* of our present world. It shows us the glory of Canaan from a distance, but it does not usher us into the better country nor make us citizens of it. Art is much, but it is not everything. It is not, as a man of distinction in its domain once called it, the holiest and noblest thing, the one and only religion and the one and only salvation of man. Art cannot reconcile for sin. It cannot cleanse us of our pollution. And it is not able even to dry our tears in the griefs of life.

As for culture, civilization, humanitarianism, the life of society, or whatever one may call it, that, too, cannot be denominated the highest good of man. No doubt we have some right to speak of a kind of progress in humanitarian ideas, and of a development in philanthropy. When we compare how the poor and the sick, the miserable and the destitute, the widows and the orphans, the insane and the imprisoned were frequently dealt with in former ages with the way in which they are very generally treated now, we certainly have cause for happiness and gratitude. A spirit of tenderness and mercy has come up which seeks out the lost and has compassion upon the oppressed. But right alongside of this our present time shows us such a fearful pageantry of gruesome vice, of mammonism, prostitution, alcoholism, and like abominations, that we are embarrassed to answer the question whether we are moving forwards or backwards. At one moment we are optimistic, but the next we are plunged into deep pessimism again.

Be that as it may, this much is sure, that if the life of service for humanity, of love for the neighbor, is not rooted in the law of God, it loses its force and its character. After all, the love for one's neighbor is not a self-vindicating thing which comes up quite spontaneously and naturally out of the human heart. It is a feeling, rather, and an action, and a service, which require tremendous will-power and which must be constantly maintained against the formidable forces of self-concern and of self-interest. Moreover, such love of the neighbor frequently gets little support from the neighbor himself. People generally are not so lovable that we should naturally, without exertion and struggle, cherish and love them as we do ourselves. Indeed, the love for the neighbor can maintain itself only if on the one hand it is based on, and laid upon us, by the law of God, and only if on the other hand that same God grants us the desire to live uprightly according to all His commandments.

*   *   *   *   *

The conclusion, therefore, is that of Augustine, who said that the heart of man was created for God and that it cannot find rest until it rests in his Father's heart. Hence all men are really seeking after God, as Augustine also declared, but they do not all seek Him in the right way, nor at the right place. They seek Him down below, and He is up above. They seek Him on the earth, and He is in heaven. They seek Him afar, and He is nearby. They seek Him in money, in property, in fame, in power, and in passion; and He is to be found in the high and the holy places, and with him that is of a contrite and humble spirit (Isa. 57:15). But they do seek Him, if haply they might feel after Him and find Him (Acts 17:27). They seek Him and at the same time they flee Him. They have no interest in a knowledge of His ways, and yet they cannot do without Him. They feel themselves attracted to God and at the same time repelled by Him.

In this, as Pascal so profoundly pointed out, consists the greatness and the miserableness of man. He longs for truth and is false by nature. He yearns for rest and throws himself from one diversion upon another. He pants for a permanent and eternal bliss and seizes on the pleasures of a moment. He seeks for God and loses himself in the creature. He is a born son of the house and he feeds on the husks of the swine in a strange land. He forsakes the fountain of living waters and hews out broken cisterns that can hold no water (Jer. 2:13). He is as a hungry man who dreams that he is eating, and when he awakes finds that his soul is empty; and he is like a thirsty man who dreams that he is drinking, and when he awakes finds that he is faint and that his soul has appetite (Isa. 29:8).

Science cannot explain this contradiction in man. It reckons only with his greatness and not with his misery, or only with his misery and not with his greatness. It exalts him too high, or it depresses him too far, for science does not know of his Divine origin, nor of his profound fall. But the Scriptures know of both, and they shed their light over man and over mankind; and the contradictions are reconciled, the mists are cleared, and the hidden things are revealed. Man is an enigma whose solution can be found only in God.

II

The Knowledge of God

God is the highest good of man — that is the testimony of the whole Scriptures.

The Bible begins with the account that God created man after His own image and likeness, in order that he should know God his Creator aright, should love Him with all his heart, and should live with Him in eternal blessedness. And the Bible ends with the description of the new Jerusalem, whose inhabitants shall see God face to face and shall have His name upon their foreheads.

Between these two moments lies the revelation of God in all its length and breadth. As its content this revelation has the one, great, comprehensive promise of the covenant of grace: I will be a God unto thee, and ye shall be my people. And as its mid-point and its high-point this revelation has its Immanuel, God-with-us. For the promise and its fulfillment go hand in hand. The word of God is the beginning, the principle, the seed, and it is in the act that the seed comes into its full realization. Just as at the beginning God called things into being by His word, so by His word He will in the course of the ages bring into being the new heaven and the new earth, in which the tabernacle of God shall be among men.

That is why Christ, in whom the Word became flesh, is said to be full of grace and truth (John 1:14).

He is the Word which in the beginning was with God and Himself was God, and as such He was the life and the light of men. Because the Father shares His life with Christ and gives expression to His thought in Christ, therefore the full being of God is revealed in Him. He not only declares the Father to us and discloses His name to us, but in Himself He shows us and gives us the Father. Christ is God expressed and God given. He is God revealing Himself and God sharing Himself, and therefore He is full of truth and also full of grace. The word of the promise, I will be a God unto thee, included within itself from the very moment in which it was uttered, the fulfillment, I am thy God. God gives Himself to His people in order that His people should give themselves to Him.

24

In the Scriptures we find God constantly repeating His declaration: I am thy God. From the mother-promise of Genesis 3:15 on, this rich testimony, comprehending all blessedness and all salvation whatsoever, is repeated again and again, be it in the lives of the patriarchs, in the history of the people of Israel, or in that of the church of the New Testament. And in response the church throughout the ages comes with the endless varieties of its language of faith, speaking in gratitude and praise: Thou art our God, and we are Thy people, and the sheep of Thy pasture.

This declaration of faith on the part of the church is not a scientific doctrine, nor a form of unity that is being repeated, but is rather a confession of a deeply felt reality, and of a conviction of reality that has come up out of experience in life. The prophets and apostles, and the saints generally who appear before us in the Old and New Testament and later in the church of Christ, did not sit and philosophize about God in abstracted concepts, but rather confessed what God meant to them and what they owed to Him in all the circumstances of life. God was for them not at all a cold concept, which they then proceeded rationally to analyze, but He was a living, personal force, a reality infinitely more real than the world around them. Indeed, He was to them *the* one, eternal, worshipful Being. They reckoned with Him in their lives, they lived in His tent, walked as if always before His face, served Him in His courts, and worshipped Him in His sanctuary.

The genuineness and depth of their experience comes to expression in the language they used to express what God meant to them. They did not have to strain for words, for their lips overflowed with what welled up out of their hearts, and the world of man and nature supplied them with figures of speech. God was to them a King, a Lord, a Valiant One, a Leader, a Shepherd, a Savior, a Redeemer, a Helper, a Physician, a Man, and a Father. All their bliss and well-being, their truth and righteousness, their life and mercy, their strength and power, their peace and rest they found in Him. He was a sun and shield to them, a buckler, a light and a fire, a fountain and a well-head, a rock and shelter, a high refuge and a tower, a reward and a shadow, a city and a temple. All that the world has to offer in discrete and sub-divided goods was to them an image and likeness of the unfathomable fulness of the salvation available in God for His people. Hence it is that David in Psalm 16:2 (according to a telling translation) addresses Jehovah as follows: Thou art my Lord; I have no higher good than Thou. Thus also Asaph sang in Psalm 73: Whom have I in heaven but Thee? And there is none upon earth that I desire beside Thee. My flesh and my heart may fail, but God is the strength of my heart, and my portion forever. For the saint, heaven in all its blessedness and glory would be void and stale without God; and when he lives in communion with God he cares for nothing on earth, for the love of God far transcends all other goods.

Such is the experience of the children of God. It is an experience which they have felt because God presented Himself to them for their enjoyment in the Son of His love. In this sense Christ said that eternal life, that is, the totality of salvation, consists for man in the knowledge of the one, true God and of Jesus Christ whom He has sent.

It was an auspicious moment in which Christ spoke those words. He stood at the point of crossing the brook Kidron in order to enter the garden of Gethsemane and to suffer the last struggle of His soul there. Before He proceeds to that point, however, He prepares Himself as our High Priest for His passion and death, and He prays the Father that the Father may glorify Him in His suffering and after it, so that the Son in turn may glorify the Father in giving out all those blessings which He is now about to achieve by His obedience unto death. And when the Son prays in this way, He knows of nothing to desire except that which is the Father's own will and good pleasure. The Father has given Him power over all flesh in order that the Son should give eternal life to as many as the Father has given Him. Such eternal life consists of nothing other than the *knowledge* of the one, true God and of Jesus Christ who was sent to reveal Him (John 17:1-3).

* * * * *

The knowledge of which Jesus speaks here obviously has its own peculiar character. It is different from all other knowledge that can be obtained, and the difference is not one of degree but of principle and essence. This becomes apparent at once when we begin to compare the two kinds of knowledge with each other. The knowledge of God of which Jesus spoke differs from the knowledge of created things in its origin and object and in its essence and effects.

It differs, first of all, in its origin, for it is wholly owing to Christ. It can be said in a certain sense that we get all of our other knowledge by reason of our own insight and judgment, by our own effort and study. But as for this knowledge of the one true God, we, like children, must let Christ give it to us. It is nowhere to be found outside of Him, neither in schools of learning nor among philosophers of distinction. Christ alone knew the Father. He was with God in the beginning, lay in His bosom, and saw Him face to face. He Himself was God, the brightness of God's glory and the express image of His person, the Father's own, only-begotten, and beloved Son, in whom was all His pleasure (Matt. 3:17; John 1:14; and Heb. 1:3). Nothing in the being of the Father is hidden from the Son, for the Son shares the same nature, the same attributes, and the same knowledge. No one knows the Father except the Son (Matt. 11:27).

And this Son has come to us and has declared the Father to us. He has revealed the name of His Father to men. To that end He became flesh and appeared upon earth: that He might give us to know Him that is true (1 John 5:20). We did not know God and took no interest in a knowledge of His ways. But Christ caused us to know the Father. He was not a philosopher, a scholar, or an artist. His work was to reveal the Father's name to us. This He did, completely, throughout His life. He revealed God in His words, in His works, in His life, His death, His person, and in all that He was and did. He never said or did a thing except what He saw the Father doing. It was His meat to carry out the Father's will. Whoever saw Him saw the Father also (John 4:34; 8:26-28; 12:50; and 14:9).

He is dependable in His revelation of God, because He is Jesus Christ who was *sent*. He received the name of Jesus from God Himself because He was to save His people from their sins (Matt. 1:21). And He is called Christ because He is the Anointed of the Father, elected and qualified for all His offices by God Himself (Isa. 42:1 and Matt. 3:16). He is the Sent One because He did not, like so many false prophets and priests, come in His own name, raise Himself up, and take credit for Himself. Indeed not, but because the Father so loved this world that He gave His only-begotten Son that whosoever should believe on Him should not perish but have eternal life, therefore He was *sent* (John 3:16).

Those, then, who accept and believe on Him are given the right and are qualified to bear the name of children of God (John 1:12). They are born of God, they share the Divine nature, they know God in the sight of Christ His Son. No man knows the Son but the Father, neither does any man know the Father except the Son, and he to whom the Son will reveal Him (Matt. 11:27).

In the second place, the knowledge of God differs from all other knowledge in point of its *object*. As for other knowledge, it may particularly in our time be ever so broad in scope, still it revolves around the creature, is limited to the temporal, and can never find out the Eternal. True, there is a revelation of God's eternal power and godhead in the works of nature also. But the knowledge of God which is derived from that source is slight, obscured, mingled with error, and besides is not valued highly. For men, knowing God from nature, have not glorified or praised Him as God, but have become vain in their imaginings, and changed the glory of the incorruptible God into an image made like the creature. The world is a concealment as well as a revelation of God (Rom. 1 :20-23).

But here in this high-priestly prayer, the One who comes to the fore is One who lets such other knowledge go and who dares to speak instead of the *knowledge of God!* God as the object of human knowledge, who can fathom that? How can man know God, the Infinite and Incomprehensible, who can be measured by neither time nor eternity, in whose presence the angels cover their faces with their wings, who lives in unapproachable light, and whom no man has seen nor can see? How can such an One be known by man, whose breath is in his nostrils, and who is less than nothing and less than vanity? How should he know God whose best knowledge is a thing of shreds and patches? For all his knowledge *about,* what has he knowledge *of?* What does he know of things in their origin, essence, and purpose? Is he not ringed round with mystery on every hand? Is he not always standing on the boundaries of the unknown? And is it to be supposed then that such a man, poor, weak, erring, and benighted, should know God, the high, holy, alone-wise, and almighty God?

It is beyond our grasp, but Christ who has seen the Father and declared Him to us speaks of it. We can depend upon Him and His witness is true and worthy of all acceptation. And if you, O man, want to know who God is, do not ask the wise, the Scribes, the disputers of this age, but look upon Christ and hear His word! Say not in your heart: Who shall ascend into heaven or who shall go down to the deep? For the word is very near you, the word which Christ proclaims. He Himself is the Word, the perfect revelation of the Father. As *He* is, such is the Father — just so righteous and holy and full of grace and truth. At His cross the full content of the faith of the Old Testament is unfolded: Gracious and merciful is the Lord God, longsuffering and abundant in goodness. He does not deal with us according to our sins, nor reward us according to our iniquities. For as the heaven is high above the earth, so great is His mercy toward them that fear Him. As far as the east is from the west, so far has He removed our transgressions from us. As a father pities his children, so the Lord pities them that fear Him (Ps. 103 :8-13). And seeing the glory of Christ in the mirror of His word, we cry out in rapture: We know Him because He first knew us; we love Him because He first loved us (1 John 4:19).

Such origin and content determines also the peculiar *essence* of the knowledge of God.

In the verse from the highpriestly prayer referred to above, Jesus speaks of a knowledge which is not mere *information* but is instead a real *knowing*. There is a big difference between the two. To get some information from books about a plant, or an animal, or a person, a country or a people is not yet to have direct personal knowledge of such a subject. Such information is simply based on somebody else's description of a matter. In this sense, information is an affair of the head only. But real knowing includes an element of personal concern and involvement and an activity of the heart.

Now it is true that a description can be found in the Word of the knowledge of God which Christ has given, and so it is possible to have information about God which differs essentially from the real knowing of God which Jesus meant. Hence a kind of knowledge of the will of the Lord unaccompanied by a preparation of the heart for doing that will is possible (Luke 12:47-48). Men can cry out, Lord, Lord, and yet not have access to the kingdom of heaven (Matt. 7:21). There is a faith, like that of the devils, which does not give way to love but rather to fear and trembling (James 2:19). There are hearers of the word who do not want to be doers of it and who will therefore be beaten with double stripes (James 1:22).

When Jesus speaks in this connection of the knowledge of God, He has in mind a knowledge which is similar in kind to the knowledge which He Himself possesses. He was not a theologian by profession, nor was He a doctor or professor in divinity. But He knew God by direct, personal sight and insight; He saw Him everywhere, in nature, in His word, in His service; He loved Him above all else and was obedient to Him in all things, even in the death on the cross. His knowing of the truth was all of a piece with His doing of it. The knowledge and the love came together.

Indeed, to know God does not consist of knowing a great deal about Him, but of this, rather, that we have seen Him in the person Christ, that we have encountered Him on our life's way, and that in the experience of our soul we have come to know His virtues, His righteousness and holiness, His compassion and His grace.

That is why this knowledge, in distinction from all other knowledge, bears the name of the knowledge of faith. It is the product not of scientific study and reflection but of a childlike and simple faith. This faith is not only a sure knowledge but also a firm confidence that not only to others, but to me also, remission of sins, everlasting righteousness and salvation are freely given by God, merely of grace, only for the sake of Christ's merits. Only those who become as little children shall enter the kingdom of heaven (Matt. 18:3). Only the pure of heart shall see the face of God (Matt. 5:8). Only those born of water and of the Spirit can enter the kingdom (John 3:5). Those who know His name will put their trust in Him (Ps. 9:10). God is known in proportion to the extent that He is loved.

If we understand the knowledge of God in such a way, it need occasion no surprise that its operation and *effect* is nothing less than eternal life. True, there seems to be little relationship between knowledge and life. Does not the Ecclesiast say truly: In much wisdom is much grief; he that increaseth knowledge increaseth sorrow; of making many books there is no end; and much study is a weariness of the flesh (Eccles. 1:18 and 12:12)?

Knowledge is power — so much we can understand, at least to a certain extent. All knowing is a triumph of the spirit over matter, a subjection of the earth to the lordship of man. But that knowledge should be life — who can understand that? And yet, even in the natural order, the depth and riches of life are increased by knowledge. The more comprehensive the awareness, the more intense the life. The inanimate creatures do not know, and they do not live. When consciousness develops in the animals, their life also gains in content and scope. The richest life among men is the life of him who knows the most. What, indeed, is the life of the insane, the naive, the simple, the underdeveloped? It is poor and limited compared with that of the thinker and poet. But, whatever difference may be noted here, it is only a difference of degree. Life itself is not changed by it. And such life, whether in the most distinguished scholar or in the simplest working-man, must necessarily end in death, for it is fed only by the limited sources of this world.

But this knowledge that Christ speaks of is not that of a creature but of the one, true God.

If the knowledge of visible things can enrich life, how much more will the knowledge of God make for life? For God is not a God of death and of the dead, but of life and the living. All those whom He recreated after His image and restored to His fellowship are by that fact raised above the level of death and mortality. He that believes on me, said Jesus, though he were dead, shall live, and whoever lives and believes in me shall never die (John 11:25-26). Knowing God in Christ brings with it eternal life, imperturbable joy, and heavenly blessedness. These are not merely effects, but the knowing of God is itself immediately a new, eternal, and blessed life.

In accordance with this teaching of the Holy Scriptures the Christian church determined the character of that body of knowledge or science which from old times has been called Theology or Divinity. Theology is the science which derives the knowledge of God from His revelation, which studies and thinks into it under the guidance of His Spirit, and then tries to describe it so that it ministers to His honor. And a theologian, a true theologian, is one who speaks out of God, through God, about God, and does this always to the glorification of His name. Between the learned and the simple there is only a difference of degree. Both have one Lord, one faith, one baptism, one God and Father of all, who is above all, and through all, and in you all. But unto every one of us is given grace according to the measure of the gift of Christ (Eph. 4:5-7).

In this spirit, Calvin began his Genevan Catechism with the question, What is the chief end of man? And the answer came, clear and resounding: To know God by whom he was created. In the same way the Westminster Catechism began its lessoning with the question: What is the highest and chief end of man? And it gave a brief and rich reply: To glorify God and enjoy Him perfectly unto all eternity.

III

General Revelation

If it is true that man can have knowledge of God then this fact pre-supposes that God on His part voluntarily chose to make Himself known to man in some way or other.

We cannot credit a knowledge of God to ourselves, to our own dis-covery, investigation, or reflection. If it were not given us by an act of free and unobliged favor, there would be no possibility that we could ever achieve it by an exertion of our own efforts.

Where the knowledge of created things is concerned, the situation is somewhat different. Even though in the achievement of such knowl-edge we are absolutely dependent upon God, still at the time of the creation He charged man with the task of subduing and having dominion over the whole earth, and He equipped him for this task and gave Him the interest to do it. Man stands above nature. He can take the measure of natural phenomena, study them, and, to a certain extent, he can artistically cause things to come into being. He can, so to speak, force nature to disclose herself and to discover her secrets.

Still, this ability, too, is limited in all kinds of ways and on every hand. As science penetrates deeper and deeper into phenomena and approaches the essence of things, it sees the mysteries increase and itself hemmed in on all sides by the unknowable. They are not a few who are so deeply convinced of the limitations of human knowledge that they feel like saying, We do not know, and sometimes like adding, And we shall never know.

If such a limitation of human knowledge already becomes apparent in the study of inanimate nature, it naturally becomes the more con-spicuous in the study of living, animated, and rational creatures.

For in this area we come into contact with realities which we cannot push around arbitrarily. They stand before us in their objectivity, and can be known by us somewhat in so far as they correspond to what we find in ourselves. Life, consciousness, feeling and perception, understanding and reason, desire and will, these do not lend themselves to dismemberment and re-assembling. They are not mechanical but organic in their nature; we have to take them as they present themselves, and have to respect them in their mysterious nature. To dismember life is to kill it.

This holds most true of the nature of man himself. For, although it is true that he is a physical being and to that extent cannot escape our perception, it is his external manifestation that we perceive. Behind that manifestation lurks a mysterious life which has but a very imperfect and inadequate expression in its external form. To a limited extent, too, man has the ability to conceal the inner side of his nature from others. He can so control his facial expression that not a muscle betrays what is going on inside him; he can employ language to hide his thoughts; and he can in his actions assume an attitude which is in conflict with what he is within. And, even though we are dealing with a person of integrity who despises all such subtleties of deception, we must, in order to know him, depend very largely upon what he, on his own part, chooses to disclose. True, he sometimes does this unwittingly; he has no absolute control over himself, and he often betrays himself without intending to. All the same, he must by his life, by his words and deeds, whether with or without his will, come out into the open and so express the mystery of his personality, if we are to know him somewhat as he is. Knowledge of a person is possible only if he involuntarily or consciously and deliberately reveals himself to us.

Such considerations lead us to a right understanding of the conditions under which alone a human being can be said to have knowledge of God. God is the absolutely independent One, the perfectly sovereign One. He is dependent upon us in no single respect, but we, both as we are naturally and as we are rationally and morally, are absolutely dependent upon Him. Hence we have no control and no power over Him at all. We have no way to make Him the object of our study and reflection. Except He lets Himself be found, we cannot seek Him. Except He give Himself, we cannot accept Him. Moreover, God is invisible. He dwells in unapproachable light so that no man has ever seen Him or can see Him. If He keeps Himself concealed or hidden, we simply cannot bring Him inside the pale of our physical or spiritual perception; and without any kind of perception, no knowledge of course is possible. Finally, to mention no more, God is the Almighty One. He has not only His creatures but Himself also in perfect control. Although we human beings are always revealing ourselves more or less, be it wittingly or otherwise, God reveals Himself only to the extent that He wills to do so, and only because He wills it. There can be no such thing as an involuntary manifestation of God, taking place, so to speak, outside the sphere of His consciousness and freedom.   God controls Himself perfectly, and He reveals Himself only to the extent of His good pleasure.

Knowledge of God is possible therefore only on the basis of a revelation from God's side. A knowledge of God is available to man only when, and in so far as, God freely chooses to reveal Himself.

*   *   *   *   *

This self-disclosure of God is usually designated by the term *revelation*. Scripture uses various verbs for it, such as appearing, speaking, commanding, working, making known, and the like. These indicate that the revelation does not always take place in the same way, but that it comes in various forms. As a matter of fact, all of the works of God, whether of word or deed, are constituent parts and elements of the one, great, comprehensive, and always continuing revelation of God. The creation, maintenance, and rule of all things, the calling and leading of Israel, the sending of Christ, the pouring out of the Holy Spirit, the inscripturation of the Word of God, the sustaining and propagation of the church, and the like, are altogether ways and forms by which a revelation of God comes to us. Each of them tells us something of God. In this sense, everything that is, and everything that happens, can and ought to lead us up to the knowledge of Him, Whom to know is life eternal.

This revelation, whether it be general or special, has the following characteristics.

In the first place, it always comes from *God Himself* acting in His freedom. In this, as in all things else, He is absolutely sovereign, and He acts with perfect freedom and deliberation. True, there are some who repudiate the confession of a personal, self-conscious God, and yet speak of a revelation of God. But this is to give a meaning to the word which is in conflict with its usual significance. From the point of view of those whose deity is only an impersonal, unconscious, almighty force, it may be possible to speak of an involuntary manifestation of that force, but not of any real revelation, for that is an idea which assumes the perfect consciousness and freedom of God. Every revelation worthy of the name proceeds from the idea that God exists personally, that He is conscious of Himself, and that He can make Himself known to creatures. Our human knowledge of God has its basis and point of origin in the knowledge which God has of Himself. Except there be self-consciousness and self-knowledge in God no knowledge of God is possible for man. Anyone who denies this must come to the unreasonable conclusion either that no knowledge of God is possible at all, or that God achieves self-consciousness only in man, and that were to put man in God's place.

Scripture teaches something quite different. Although it is unapproachable, God's dwelling is *light;* He knows Himself perfectly and He can therefore reveal Himself to us. No man knows the Son except the Father; neither does any man know the Father except the Son, and he to whom the Son will reveal Him (Matt. 11:27).

In the second place, every revelation which proceeds from God is *self*-revelation. God is the origin and He is also the content of His revelation. This holds true of the highest revelation, which has come to us in Christ, for Jesus Himself says that He has revealed the name of the Father to men (John 17:6). The only begotten Son, which is in the bosom of the Father, has declared God to us (John 1:18). But the same is true of every other revelation which God has given of Himself. All of the works of God in nature and grace, in creation and in regeneration, in the world and in history teach us something of the incomprehensible and worshipful being of God. They do not all do it in the same way and to the same extent; there is infinite difference among them. The one work tells of His righteousness and the other of his mercy; from the one His almighty power shines out, and from the other His Divine wisdom.

But all together, and each to its own extent, they declare the mighty works of God to us, and acquaint us with His virtues and perfections, with His being and His self-differentiations, with His thought and word, and with His will and His good pleasure.

In this connection, we must never forget of course that the revelation of God, irrespective of the richness of its content, is never to be thought of as being identical with the self-knowledge of God. The self-knowledge or self-consciousness of God is just as infinite as His being and is from its very nature, therefore, not subject to the apprehension of any creature. The revelation of God in His creatures, both objectively in the works of His hand and subjectively in the consciousness of His rational creatures, can comprise, always, only a small part of the infinite knowledge which God has of Himself. And not only we human beings on earth, but the saints and the angels in heaven also, and even the Son of God in His human nature, have a knowledge of God which is different in principle and essence from the self-knowledge of God. All the same, the knowledge which God has shared in His revelation, and which can be obtained by rational creatures from that revelation, limited and finite as it is and will in all eternity remain, is nevertheless a real and sound knowledge. God reveals Himself in His works to be such as He is. From His revelation we learn to know Him. Hence there can be no rest for man until he rises above and beyond the creature to God Himself. In the study of revelation our concern must be a concern to know God. Its purpose is not to teach us certain sounds and to speak certain words. Its primary purpose is to lead us through the creatures to the Creator and to cause us to rest in the Father's heart.

In the third place, the revelation which proceeds from God, and which has God as its content, also has God as its purpose. This revelation is of Him and through Him, and it is *to* Him also; He has made all things for Himself (Rom. 11:36 and Prov. 16:4). Although the knowledge of God, which is shared in His revelation, is and remains essentially different from His own self-knowledge, it is nevertheless so rich, so broad, and so deep that it can never be wholly absorbed in the consciousness of any rational creature. The angels far exceed man in point of understanding, and they do always look upon the face of the Father who is in heaven (Matt. 18:10), but they nevertheless desire to look into the things which are reported to us by them that have preached the Gospel (1 Peter 1:12). And as people think more and more deeply into the revelation of God they are the more impelled to cry out with Paul: O the depth of the riches both of the wisdom and knowledge of God! How unsearchable are His judgments, and His ways past finding out (Rom. 11:33)! Revelation, therefore, cannot have its final purpose in man; in part it passes him by and soars on beyond him.

It is true that man has an important place in revelation. It is directed to mankind in order that they should seek the Lord, if haply they might feel after Him, and find Him (Acts 17:27), and the Gospel must be preached to all creatures so that, believing, they might have eternal life (Mark 16:15-16 and John 3:16, 36). But this cannot be the final and highest purpose of revelation. God cannot rest in man. Rather, it belongs to man to know and serve God, in order that he, together with and at the head of all creatures, should give God the honor due Him for all His works. In His revelation, whether it passes through man or alongside of him, God is preparing Himself praise, glorifying His own name, and spreading out before His own eyes in the world of His creatures His excellences and perfections. Because revelation is of God and through God, it has its end and purpose also in His glorification.

This whole revelation, which is of God and through Him, has its mid-point and at the same time its high-point in the person of Christ. It is not the sparkling firmament, nor mighty nature, nor any prince or genius of the earth, nor any philosopher or artist, but the Son of man that is the highest revelation of God. Christ is the Word become flesh, which in the beginning was with God and which was God, the Only-Begotten of the Father, the Image of God, the brightness of His glory and the express image of His person; who has seen Him has seen the Father (John 14:9). In that faith the Christian stands. He has learned to know God in the person of Jesus Christ whom God has sent. God Himself, who said that the light should shine out of the darkness, is the One who has shined in His heart in order to give the light of the knowledge of the glory of God in the face of Jesus Christ (2 Cor. 4:6).

* * * * *

But from this high vantage point the Christian looks around him, forwards, backwards, and to all sides. And if, in doing so, in the light of the knowledge of God, which he owes to Christ, he lets his eyes linger on nature and on history, on heaven and on earth, then he discovers traces everywhere of that same God whom he has learned to know and to worship in Christ as his Father. The Sun of righteousness opens up a wonderful vista to him which streches out to the ends of the earth. By its light he sees backwards into the night of past times, and by it he penetrates through to the future of all things. Ahead of him and behind the horizon is clear, even though the sky is often obscured by clouds.

The Christian, who sees everything in the light of the Word of God, is anything but narrow in his view. He is generous in heart and mind. He looks over the whole earth and reckons it all his own, because he is Christ's and Christ is God's (1 Cor. 3:21-23). He cannot let go his belief that the revelation of God in Christ, to which he owes his life and salvation, has a special character. This belief does not exclude him from the world, but rather puts him in position to trace out the revelation of God in nature and history, and puts the means at his disposal by which he can recognize the true and the good and the beautiful and separate them from the false and sinful alloys of men.

So it is that he makes a distinction between a *general* and a *special* revelation of God. In the general revelation God makes use of the usual run of phenomena and the usual course of events; in the special revelation He often employs unusual means, appearances, prophecy, and miracle to make Himself known to man. The contents of the first kind are especially the attributes of power, wisdom, and goodness; those of the second kind are especially God's holiness and righteousness, compassion and grace. The first is directed to all men and, by means of common grace, serves to restrain the eruption of sin; the second comes to all those who live under the Gospel and has as its glory, by special grace, the forgiveness of sins and the renewal of life.

But, however essentially the two are to be distinguished, they are also intimately connected with each other. Both have their origin in God, in His sovereign goodness and favor. The general revelation is owing to the Word which was with God in the beginning, which made all things, which shone as a light in the darkness and lighteth every man that cometh into the world (John 1:1-9). The special revelation is owing to that same Word, as it was made flesh in Christ, and is now full of grace and truth (John 1:14). Grace is the content of both revelations, common in the first, special in the second, but in such a way that the one is indispensable for the other.

It is common grace which makes special grace possible, prepares the way for it, and later supports it; and special grace, in its turn, leads common grace up to its own level and puts it into its service. Both revelations, finally, have as their purpose the preservation of the human race, the first by sustaining it, and the second by redeeming it, and both in this way serve the end of glorifying all of God's excellences.

* * * * *

The content of both revelations, not that of the special only but that of the general also, is contained in Holy Scripture. General revelation, although derived from nature, is nevertheless taken up in Scripture, for, without it, we human beings, because of the darkness of our understanding, would never have been able to read it out of nature. As it is, Scripture sheds a light on our path through the world, and puts into our hand a true reading of nature and history. It makes us see God where we would otherwise not have seen Him. Illumined by it, we behold God's excellences spread abroad in all the works of His hands.

Creation itself, taught by Scripture, demonstrates the revelation of God in nature. For creation is itself an act of revelation, the beginning and first principle of all later revelation. If the world had eternally stood alone, or had eternally stood alongside of God, it could not have been a revelation of Him; in the second instance, such a world would eternally have been an impediment to God in His revelation of Himself. But whoever, together with the Scriptures, holds to the creation of the world, confesses thereby that God reveals Himself in the whole of that world. Every work testifies of its maker, the more so in proportion to the extent that it can in a peculiar sense be called the product of its maker.

Because the world in an absolute sense is the work of God, and owes both its nature and its being, at the beginning and ever after, to its Maker, every creature manifests something of God's excellences and perfections. So soon as the revelation of God in nature is denied or is, for example, limited only to the heart or the feeling of man, the danger threatens that the creation of God will be unacknowledged, that nature will be said to be ruled by another power than that which rules in the human heart, and that in this way, whether openly or covertly, polytheism will again be introduced into human thought. Scripture, by teaching creation, by that fact holds to the revelation of God and at the same time to the unity of God and the unity of the world.

Moreover, Scripture teaches not only that at the beginning God called the world into being, but also that this world is continuously, from moment to moment, sustained and governed by that same God. He is infinitely exalted above the world not only, but He also dwells in all His creatures in his almighty and omnipresent power. He is not far from every one of us, for in Him we live, and move, and have our being (Acts 17:27-28). The revelation which comes to us from the world, therefore, is not merely a reminder of a work of God which He accomplished long ago: it is a testimony also to what God now, in these our times, wills and does.

When we lift up our eyes on high, we see not only who has created these things, and brings out their host by number, but we also observe that He calls them all by names, by the greatness of His might, because He is strong in power, and because not one of them is missing (Isa. 40:25). The heavens declare the glory of God, and the firmament shows His handiwork (Ps. 19:1). He covers Himself with light as with a garment; He stretches out the heavens like a curtain; He lays the beams of His chambers in the waters, makes the clouds His chariot, and walks upon the wings of the wind (Ps. 104:2-3). Mountains and valleys are established in the place He has founded for them, and He waters them from His chambers (Ps. 104:8, 13). He satisfies the earth with the fruit of His works, causes the grass to grow for the cattle, and the herb for the service of man; He brings forth food out of the earth, and wine that makes the heart of man glad (Ps. 104:13-15). Being girded with power, He sets fast the mountains by His strength, and stills the noise of the seas (Ps. 65:6-7). He feeds the birds of the air, and clothes the grass of the field with glory (Matt. 6:26-30). He makes His sun to rise on the evil and on the good, and He sends rain on the just and the unjust (Matt. 5:45). He makes man a little lower than the angels, and crowns him with glory and honor, and gives him dominion over the works of His hands (Ps. 8:5-6)!

Moreover, God carries out His counsel and establishes His work in history as well as in nature. He made of one blood all nations of men to dwell on all the face of the earth (Acts 17:26). He destroys the first human race in the flood, and at the same time preserves it in the family of Noah (Gen. 6:6-9). At the tower of Babel he confuses the language of men and disperses them over the face of the earth (Gen. 11:7-8). And when the Most High divided to the nations their inheritance, and separated the sons of Adam, He determined the times appointed before, and the bounds of their habitation, according to the number of the children of Israel (Deut. 32:8 and Acts 17:26). Although He chose the children of Israel to be the bearers of His special revelation, and permitted the heathen nations to walk in their own ways (Acts 14:16), nevertheless He did not neglect them nor leave them to their own fate. On the contrary, He did not leave Himself without a witness, in that He did good, granting rain from heaven, and fruitful seasons, and filling their hearts with food and gladness (Acts 14:17). That which may be known of God became manifest in them, for God showed it to them (Rom. 1:19), in order that they should seek the Lord, if haply they might feel after Him, and find Him (Acts 17:27).

By this general revelation God preserved the peoples and led them to the dispensation of the fulness of times that He might gather together in one all things in Christ, both the things which are in heaven and the things which are in earth (Eph. 1:10). Out of all nations, and kindreds, and people, and tongues He gathers His church (Rom. 11:25; Eph. 2:14ff.; and Rev. 7:9), and prepares for that end of the world in which the nations of them that are saved shall walk in the light of the city of God, and all the kings and peoples of the earth shall bring their glory and honor into it (Rev. 21:24-26).

In the science of theology men have tried to arrange all these witnesses in nature and history to the existence and being of God, and to classify them into groups. So it comes about that we sometimes speak of six evidences for the existence of God.

In the first place, the world, be it ever so mighty and comprehensive, is nevertheless continually testifying of itself that it is confined to the forms of space and time, that it is temporal, accidental, and dependent in character, and that it requires, therefore, an eternal, essential, independent being as the final cause of all things. This is the cosmological argument.

In the second place, the world in its laws and ordinances, in its unity and harmony, and in the organization of all of its creatures, exhibits a purpose which it would be ridiculous to explain on the basis of chance, and which therefore points to an all-wise and omnipotent being who with an infinite mind has established that purpose, and by his almighty and omnipresent power seeks to achieve it. This is the teleological argument.

In the third place, there is in the consciousness of all men some sense of a supreme being, above whom nothing higher can be conceived, and thought of by all as self-existent. If such a being did not exist, the highest, most perfect, and most inevitable idea would be an illusion, and man would lose his confidence in the validity of his consciousness. This is the ontological argument.

The fourth argument is corollary to the third: man is not merely a rational but also a moral being. He feels in his conscience that he is bound to a law which stands high above him and which requires unconditional obedience from him. Such a law presupposes a holy and righteous law-giver who can preserve and destroy. This is the moral argument.

To these four arguments, two others are usually added, derived from the similarity or correspondence of peoples and of the history of mankind. It is a remarkable phenomenon that there are no peoples or nations without religion. A few scholars have argued that this is not so, but they have been proved mistaken more and more by historical investigations. There are no atheistic tribes or peoples. This phenomenon is of great importance, for the absolute universality of this religious sense puts us before a choice of one of two positions: either that on this point mankind generally is suffering from a stupid superstition, or else that this knowledge and service of God, which in distorted forms makes its appearance among all peoples, is based on God's existence.

In the same way the history of mankind, when seen in the light of Scripture, exhibits a plan and a pattern which point back to a governance of all things by a supreme being. It is true that this idea is confronted by all sorts of objections and difficulties in the life both of individuals and of nations. But it is all the more remarkable, therefore, that anyone who makes a serious study of history proceeds on the assumption that history is something in which thought and plan are evident and makes it his task to discover these and set them forth. History and the philosophy of history are based on faith in the providence of God.

All of these so-called "evidences" are not enough to compel a man to believe. As a matter of fact, science or philosophy has very few evidences capable of accomplishing that. It may be that in the formal sciences, such as mathematics and logic, this is possible; but the moment we make contact with actual phenomena in nature, and even more in history, our argumentations and conclusions as a general rule are subject to all kinds of misgivings and objections. In religion and ethics, in law and aesthetics, even more hinges on the attitude of the investigator as to whether or not he is subject to conviction. The fool can, all testimony to the contrary, still say in his heart, There is no God (Ps. 14:1), and the heathen, although they knew God, did not glorify Him and were not thankful (Rom. 1:21). The arguments for the existence of God named above are not directed to man as a logically ratiocinative creature merely, but to man as a rational and moral being. Their appeal is not solely to his analytical and ratiocinative mind, but also to his heart and feeling, his reason and conscience. As such they have their worth, strengthening the faith and establishing the bond of connection between the revelation of God *outside* of man and the revelation *in* man.

* * * * *

After all, the revelation of God in nature and in history could have no effect upon man if there were not something in man himself that responded to it. The beauty of nature and art could not give man any pleasure unless he have a feeling for beauty in his bosom. The moral law would find no responsive chord in him if he did not himself acknowledge the voice of conscience within him. The thoughts which God by His Word has embodied in the world would be incomprehensible to him if he were not himself a thinking being. And so too the revelation of God in all the works of His hands would be quite unknowable to man if God had not planted in his soul an inerasible sense of His existence and being. The indisputable fact is, however, that God Himself has added to the external revelation in nature an internal revelation to man. The historical and psychological investigations of religion disclose again and again that religion cannot be explained except on the basis of such an increated sense. Always the investigators return at the end of their study to the proposition they repudiated at its beginning, namely, that man is at bottom a religious creature.

Scripture leaves no doubt about it whatever. After God had made all things, He created man, and created him immediately in His image and after His likeness (Gen. 1:26). Man is God's offspring (Acts 17:28). Even though, like the lost son in the parable, he has fled his paternal home, still, even in his most distant straying, he cherishes a memory of his origin and destination. In his profoundest fall he still retains certain small remains of the image of God after which he was made. God reveals Himself *outside* of man; He reveals Himself also *within* man. He does not leave Himself without witness in the human heart and conscience.

This revelation of God is not to be regarded as a second, entirely new revelation, supplementing the first. It is not an independent source of knowledge apart from the other. It is rather a capacity, a susceptibility, a drive to find out God in His works and to understand His revelation. It is a consciousness of the Divine in us which enables us to see the Divine outside of ourselves, just as the eye enables us to detect light and color, and the ear equips us to take notice of sounds. It is, as Calvin called it, a sense of Divinity, or, as Paul described it, an ability to see the invisible things of God, namely, his eternal power and godhead, in the visible things of creation.

When we try to analyze this increated sense of Divinity, we find that it consists of two elements. In the first place, a sense of absolute dependency is characteristic of it. Underneath the mind and will, underneath our thought and action, there is in us a self-consciousness which is interdependent with our self-existence and seems to coincide with it. Before we think, before we will, we *are*, we *exist*. We exist in a *definite* way, and in indissoluble unity with this existence we have a *sense* of existence and a sense of existing *as* we are. And the core of this near-identity of self-existence and self-consciousness is the feeling of dependency. In our inmost selves, we are immediately — without benefit of reasoning, that is, and prior to all reasoning — conscious of ourselves as created, limited, dependent beings. We are dependent *upon* everything around us, upon the whole spiritual and material world. Man is a "dependent" of the universe. And, further, he is dependent, *together with* other created things, and dependent this time in an absolute sense, on God, who is the one, eternal, and real being.

But this sense of Divinity has a further constituent element. If it were nothing but a feeling of absolute dependency, and for the rest left the being whose power caused this feeling to remain quite indefinite, then it would be a feeling which would lead man to impotent revolt or to stoical, passive resignation. But this sense of Divinity has in it a sense of the nature of that being on whom man feels himself to be dependent. It is a sense of a higher and an absolute power, but not of a blind, mindless, imperturbable, and impassive force, equivalent to fate or necessity. Rather, it is a sense of a supreme power which is also perfectly righteous, wise, and good. It is a sense of the "eternal Power" but also of the "Godhead," that is, of the absolute perfection of God. Hence it is that this feeling of dependency does not carry discouragement and despair in its wake, but rather prompts man to religion, to serving and honoring the Godhead. In other words, the dependency of which man is conscious over against the Divine being, is of a very special kind. It has in it the element of freedom and it tends towards free actions. It is the dependency not of a slave, but of a son, be it of a lost son. "The sense of Divinity," therefore, as Calvin wrote, "is at the same time the seed of religion."

IV

The Value of General Revelation

In determining the value of general revelation, one runs the great danger either of over-estimating or of under-estimating it. When we have our attention fixed upon the richness of the grace which God has given in His special revelation, we sometimes become so enamored of it that the general revelation loses its whole significance and worth for us. And when, at another time, we reflect on the good, and true, and beautiful that is to be found by virtue of God's general revelation in nature and in the human world, then it can happen that the special grace, manifested to us in the person and work of Christ, loses its glory and appeal for the eye of our soul.

This danger, to stray off either to the right or to the left, has always existed in the Christian church, and, each in turn, the general and the special revelation have been ignored or denied. Each in turn has been denied in theory and no less strongly in practice. At the present time the temptation to do injustice to the general revelation is not so strong as it was in past ages. So much the stronger, however, is the temptation, assaulting us from all sides, to limit the special revelation to ever narrower confines, to the person of Christ, for instance, or, worse yet, to deny it altogether and to make it a part of general revelation.

We must be on guard against both of these one-sidednesses; and we shall be best advised if, in the light of Holy Scripture, we take a look at the history of mankind and let it teach us what people owe to general revelation. It will then become apparent to us that although, in the light of this revelation, men have in some directions achieved a great deal, their knowledge and ability in other ways have been limited by unavoidable boundaries.

When the first man and woman have transgressed the commandment of God in Paradise, their punishment does not follow immediately nor in full force. They do not die on the self-same day they have sinned, but remain alive; they are not sent into hell, but instead find themselves entrusted with a task on earth; their line does not perish: they receive the promise of the seed of the woman. In short, a condition now sets in which God had known and which God had established, but which man

44

had not been able to anticipate. It is a condition which has a very special character. It is one in which wrath and grace, punishment and blessing, judgment and long-suffering are mingled with each other. It is the condition which still exists in nature and among men and one which comprehends the sharpest of contrasts within itself.

We live in a strange world, a world which presents us with tremendous contrasts. The high and the low, the great and the small, the sublime and the ridiculous, the beautiful and the ugly, the tragic and the comic, the good and the evil, the truth and the lie, these all are heaped up in unfathomable interrelationship. The gravity and the vanity of life seize on us in turn. Now we are prompted to optimism, then to pessimism. Man weeping is constantly giving way to man laughing. The whole world stands in the sign of humor, which has been well described as a laugh in a tear.

The deepest cause of this present state of the world is this: because of the sin of man, God is continually manifesting His wrath and yet, by reason of His own good pleasure, is always again revealing His grace also. We are consumed by His anger and yet in the morning we are satisfied by His mercy (Ps. 90:7, 14). His anger endures but a moment, in His favor is life; weeping may endure for a night, but joy comes in the morning (Ps. 30:6). Curse and blessing are so singularly interdependent that the one sometimes seems to become the other. Work in the sweat of the brow is curse and blessing at once. Both point to the cross which at one and the same time is the highest judgment and the richest grace. And that is why the cross is the mid-point of history and the reconciliation of all antitheses.

This condition set in immediately after the fall, and, during the first period, that is, until the call of Abraham, it had a very special character. The first eleven chapters of the book of Genesis are extremely important: they constitute the point of departure and the foundation of the whole of world history.

* * * * *

What deserves attention immediately is that general and special revelation, although distinguished, do not stand in isolation alongside of each other, but rather in constant interrelationship, and that both of them are directed to the same people, that is, to mankind as it then existed. Special revelation was then not yet given to a few individuals, nor limited to a single people, but was distributed among all who were then alive. The creation of the world, the forming of man, the history of paradise and of the fall, the punishment for sin, and the first announcement of

God's grace (Gen. 3:15), as well as public worship (Gen. 4:26), the beginnings of culture (Gen. 4:17), the flood, and the building of the tower of Babel — these all are treasures which mankind has carried along as part of its equipment in its journey through the world. Hence it need cause no surprise that traditions of these events, be it often in very distorted forms, turn up among various peoples of the earth. The history of mankind has one common beginning and is built up on a broad common basis.

Nevertheless, in despite of this oneness and commonness, a schism soon developed among men. The cause of it was religion, the relationship in which men stood to God. The service of the Lord was very simple still. There was no possibility of a public worship such as we know it so long as mankind consisted simply of a few families. Nevertheless the service of God existed from the beginning in the form of sacrifices and prayers, the presentation of gifts, and the consecration to God of the best that there was (Gen. 4:3-4). Scripture does not tell us how men came to bringing such sacrifices, and the interpretations of scholars of the origin of sacrifices differ widely in our day. But what is clear is that those first sacrifices came up out of a sense of dependency upon God and of gratitude to Him, and that they were symbolical in character. They were intended as an expression of human consecration and surrender to God. What mattered was not the gift as such, but the disposition of the giver expressed in the gift. In point both of disposition and gift, Abel brought a more excellent sacrifice than Cain (Heb. 11:4), and was therefore regarded with favor by the Lord. But from the very beginning there was division among the children of Adam, a division between the righteous and the godless, between martyrs and murderers, between the church and the world. And, even though after Cain's commitment of murder God still has a care for him, seeking him out and admonishing him to conversion, and letting favor accrue to him instead of judgment (Gen. 4:9-16), still the breach was not healed. The schism worked its way through and culminated for the time being in the separation of the Cainites and the Sethites.

* * * * *

In the circle of the Cainites, unbelief and apostasy thereupon increased by leaps and bounds and from generation to generation. It is true that they did not reach the point of idolatry and the service of images; Scripture makes no mention whatever of the existence of these among men before the flood. These forms of false religion are not original, but the product of later development, and they are an evidence of a religious sense which the Cainites suppressed in their hearts. The Cainites did not give themselves up to superstition but to unbelief. They came to the point of practically, if not theoretically, denying the existence and revelation of God. They lived and acted as though no God existed; they ate and drank, married and were given in marriage, just as it will be at the coming of the Son of man (Matt. 24:37-38). And they threw their energies into culture and sought their salvation in that (Gen. 4:17-24). Rejoicing in a long life running sometimes to hundreds of years (Gen. 5:3ff.), possessing rich gifts and titanic physical strength, and boasting of the power of their sword (Gen. 4:23-24), they imagined that their own arm could save them.

In the generations of Seth, it is true, the knowledge of God and the worship of God were purely preserved for a long time. In fact, we read that in the days of his son Enos men began to call upon the name of the Lord (Gen. 4:26). That does not mean that men began to worship God with sacrifices and prayers at that time, for this had been done before. We read of sacrifices in connection with Cain and Abel, and although nothing is said of prayers, these no doubt constituted a part of the service of God from the beginning, for without prayer no service of God is conceivable. Indeed, the offer of the sacrifice is itself an embodied prayer and is always and everywhere accompanied by prayer. Nor does the expression used in Genesis 4:26 mean to say that at this time men first began to call upon God by the name of Lord; for, apart from the question of whether the name of Jehovah was then already known, the nature of God expressed in that name was not revealed by the Lord until He revealed it to Moses, and that was much later (Ex. 3:14). Most likely what is meant by this calling on the name of the Lord is that at this time the Sethites separated themselves as a group from the Cainites, that they held public gatherings for the confession of the Lord's name, and that they thus publicly and unitedly, in distinction from the Cainites, testified of their loyalty to the worship of God. Their prayers and offerings were no longer made individually alone but were an expression also of a unified group witness. In proportion to the extent that the Cainites surrendered to a worship of the world and sought their salvation there, the Sethites committed themselves to God and called on His name in prayer and thanksgiving, in preaching and confession, in the midst of an evil generation.

By means of this public preaching a call to repentance was continually extended to the descendants of Cain. This went on even when religious and moral decadence set in among the Sethites and these too began to mingle with the world. Enos' grandson was called Mahalaleel (Gen. 5:15), which means "the praise of God." Enoch walked with God (Gen.

5:22). Lamech, at the birth of his son Noah, gave expression to his hope that this son would comfort them in the matter of their work and the toil of their hands, because of the ground which the Lord had cursed (Gen. 5:29). And Noah himself finally came as a preacher of righteousness (2 Peter 2:5), and proclaimed to his contemporaries the Gospel of salvation through the Spirit of Christ (1 Peter 3:19-20).

But such saints as these came to be more and more an exception. Sethites and Cainites inter-married and begot children which even surpassed those of earlier generations in physical prowess (Gen. 6:4). The corruption of mankind was rampant, the imagination of men's hearts was evil from their youth on up, and the earth was filled with violence through them (Gen. 6:5, 12-13 and 8:21). Even though God in His long-suffering still granted a postponement of one-hundred twenty years (Gen. 6:3 and 1 Peter 3:20), and although in the preaching of Noah He pointed to an avenue of escape, nevertheless ancient mankind moved on to its doom and finally perished in the waters of the flood.

*   *   *   *   *

After this terrible judgment, from which Noah and his family to the extent of eight souls were spared. a dispensation sets in which in many ways differs from that before the flood. The flood as the Scriptures delineate it was a unique event in the history of mankind which has its parallel only in the world-conflagration of the last days (Gen. 8:21ff.). This flood is like to a baptism which condemns the world and rescues the believers (1 Peter 3:19-20).

The new dispensation was introduced by the conclusion of a covenant. When, after the flood, Noah builds an altar and offers sacrifices to God upon it, voicing as these do the gratitude and prayer of his heart, then the Lord says to Himself that He will never again let such a judgment come upon the earth, and that He will introduce a fixed order into the course of nature. The consideration on this occasion is that the imagination of man's heart is evil from his youth (Gen. 8:21). These words are strikingly similar to and yet are remarkably different from those of Genesis 6:5 where we read that every imagination of the thoughts of man's heart was only evil continually. The words used in Genesis 6:5 are in consideration of the *extirpation*, those of Genesis 8:21 are in consideration of the *preservation*, of the earth. In the first instance the emphasis falls on the wicked deeds in which the corrupt heart of ancient mankind came to expression; in the second instance the stress is on the evil nature which always continues in man, also in post-diluvian man.

It seems therefore as if the Lord in these last words wishes to say that He knows what to expect of His creatures if he were to leave them to their own devices. Then the heart of man, which always remains the same, would again burst out in all kinds of gruesome sins, would constantly provoke Him to wrath, and move Him to destroy the world another time. And this He does not want to do. Hence He will now lay down fixed laws for man and nature, prescribe an established course for both, by which to limit and hem them in. All this takes place in the covenant which God sets up with His creation after the flood, and which is therefore called the covenant of nature.

Now it is true that, in a broad sense, this covenant also came up out of the grace of God. All the same it differs in principle from what is generally called the covenant of Grace and is established with the church in Christ. For this covenant of nature rests upon the consideration that the heart of man is evil and remains evil from his youth on up. It has as its content the restoration of the blessing, given at creation, of fruitfulness and dominion over animals (Gen. 9:1-3, 7), and to that end carries with it a commandment against the taking of life (Gen. 9:5-6). This covenant is set up with Noah, the ancestor of the second race of man, and in him it is set up with the whole of mankind, indeed, with the whole of creation, animate and inanimate alike (Gen. 9:9ff.). This covenant is sealed with a natural manifestation, the rainbow (Gen. 9:12ff.), and its purpose is to circumvent a second judgment such as the flood, and to guarantee the continuing existence of mankind and the world (Gen. 8:21-22 and 9:14-16).

* * * * *

Thus the life and existence of man and the world comes to rest on a different and a firmer basis.

That basis is no longer the act of creation and the law of creation; it is rather a new and special act of God's mercy and long-suffering. It is not by reason of His creation ordinances, which man, after all, transgressed, that God is obligated to grant man His life and existence. It is rather by this covenant that He obligates Himself to maintain the creation despite its fall and rebellion. From this time on the maintenance and government of the created world no longer rest upon a sheer decision of the will but upon covenant obligation. By the terms of this covenant God owes it to Himself to sustain the world and its life. In this covenant, He gave His name and honor, His truth and faithfulness, His word and promise to His creatures as a pledge of their continued existence. The ordinances governing man and the world are therefore firmly fixed in a covenant of grace made with the whole of nature.[1]

This covenant of nature calls an entirely different order of affairs into being than that which existed before the flood. The tremendous natural forces which formerly operated, and which were also at work in the flood itself, were curbed. The terrible monsters among living creatures which lived in the earlier time perished now. The tremendous catastrophes which formerly shook the whole cosmos gave way to a regular course of events. The span of human life was shortened, man's strength was diminished, his nature was mellowed, he was chastened to the requirements of a society and placed under the discipline of government. By this covenant bans and restrictions were laid upon nature and man. Laws and ordinances appeared everywhere. There were dams and dikes now to hold back the stream of iniquities. Order, measure, and number came to be the characterizing earmark of creation. God curbs the wild animal in man and so gives him the opportunity to develop his gifts and energies in art and science, in state and society, in work and calling. Thus God fulfills the conditions which make *history* possible.

* * * * *

Once more, however, this history is interrupted by the intervening hand of God in the confusion of tongues at Babel. After the flood mankind first lived in the land of Ararat, in the Armenian highlands, and there Noah became a husbandman (Gen. 9:20). As the people grew in number, a part of them spread out along the Tigris and Euphrates rivers towards the east and so came into the plains of Shinar or Mesopotamia (Gen. 11:2). Here they settled down and very soon, as they increased in wealth and power, hit upon the plan of building a high tower to make a name for themselves and prevent the dispersion of mankind. In defiance of the command of God to multiply and have dominion over the whole earth, they made it their ideal by means of an external centrum to maintain unity and to bind the whole of mankind together in a world kingdom which should find its strength in might, and in the glorification of man all its purpose and endeavor. For the first time in history the idea arises here of concentrating and organizing against God and His kingdom the whole of mankind in all its strength and wisdom, and in all its art, and science, and culture. It was an idea which arose again and again later on, whose realization has been the goal of all kinds of allegedly great men in the course of the ages.

---

1. Gen. 8:21-22; Job 14:5-6 and 26:10; Ps. 119:90-91 and 148:6; Isa. 28:24ff.; Jer. 5:24; 31:35-36 and 33:20, 25.

Hence it becomes necessary for God to intervene, and to make this effort at the establishment of a world empire impossible for good and all. This He does by the confusion of tongues, for up to this time there had been but one language. Just how, and within what period of time, this confusion took place we are not specifically told. But what it involved was that people physiologically and psychologically differed from each other, began to see and to name things differently, and that in consequence they were divided into nations and peoples, and that they dispersed themselves in all directions over the whole earth. It should be remembered, too, that this confusion of language was prepared for already by the break-up into tribes and families of the descendants of the sons of Noah (Gen. 10:1ff.) and by the migration of the descendants of Noah from Armenia to Shinar (Gen. 11:2). The whole idea of a tower of Babel would not have arisen if the threat and fear of dispersion had not already long and seriously presented itself.

In this way Scripture explains the coming into being of nations and peoples, and of tongues and languages. And, indeed, the astonishing division of mankind is a singular and inexplicable fact. People who come from the same two parents, have the same spirit and the same soul, and share the same flesh and blood, such people come to stand over against each other as strangers. They do not understand each other, and cannot communicate with each other. Moreover, mankind is divided into races who challenge each other's existence, are determined to destroy each other, and live, century in and century out, in cold or open warfare. Race instinct, sense of nationality, enmity, and hatred, these are the divisive forces between peoples. This is an astonishing punishment and a terrible judgment, and cannot be undone by any cosmopolitanism or leagues of peace, by any "universal" language, nor by any world-state or international culture.

If ever there is to be unity among mankind again, it will not be achieved by any external, mechanical rallying around some tower of Babel or other, but by a development from within, a gathering under one and the same Head (Eph. 1:10), by the peacemaking creation of all peoples into a new man (Eph. 2:15), by regeneration and renewal through the Holy Spirit (Acts 2:6), and by the walking of all people in one and the same light (Rev. 21:24).

The unity of mankind which can only be restored by an internal operation, beginning within and working out, is therefore a unity which in the internal operation of that first confusion of tongues was basically disturbed. The spurious unity was radically upset in order that room might be made for the true unity. The world-state was shattered in order that the Kingdom of God should come into existence on earth.

From this time on, therefore, the nations separate and are dispersed over the face of the earth. And out of all these nations, Israel is chosen to be the bearer of the revelation of God. General and special revelation, interrelated until now, are separated for a while to find each other again at the foot of the Cross. Israel is segregated in order to walk in the ways and ordinances of God, and the Lord lets the other nations go in their own ways (Acts 14:16).

* * * * *

We ought not, of course, to interpret this in such a way that God had no care at all for these nations and that he left them entirely to their own fate. Such a thought is in itself unreasonable, for God is the Creator, Sustainer, and Ruler of all things, and nothing exists or happens without His almighty and omnipresent strength.

Moreover, Scripture repeatedly speaks of something quite the opposite of God's neglect of the other peoples. When the Most High divided to the nations their inheritance, when He separated the sons of Adam, He set the bounds of the people according to the number of the children of Israel (Deut. 32:8). In the apportionment of the earth God reckoned with Israel and allotted a territory to them which corresponded to their number; but He also gave the other nations their inheritance, and established their boundaries. He made the whole race of man of one blood, and laid it down that they should not all live in one place, but on the whole face of the earth; for He did not create the earth in vain: He formed it to be inhabited (Isa. 45:18). Accordingly He also plotted out the times which had previously been fixed for the duration of the various peoples and the boundaries of their dwelling. The span of life and the dwelling place of all nations are determined by His counsel and assigned by His providence (Acts 17:26).

Although in times past He suffered the heathen to walk in their own ways, nevertheless He did not leave Himself without witness, but did good to them, giving them rain from heaven, and fruitful seasons, and filling their hearts with food and gladness (Acts 14:16-17). He caused His sun to shine on the evil and on the good, and He sent rain on the just and on the unjust (Matt. 5:45). By His revelation in nature and history He sent out His voice to the hearts and consciences of all (Ps. 19:1). From the very creation of the world on, God manifested His invisible things by the things that were made, namely, His eternal power and Godhead (Rom. 1:19-20). Although the heathen nations received no law, as the people of Israel did, and in the concrete sense therefore have no law, they nevertheless show by sometimes doing what is commanded by the law that in their moral nature they are a law to themselves, and have the law written in their hearts. And this is confirmed by the consideration that the voice of conscience which follows upon their deeds and the thoughts which arise in them either accuse them or excuse them (Rom. 2:14-15).

The religious and moral sense of the Gentiles therefore proves that God continued to have a care for them. By the Word which was with God in the beginning and which was God, all things were made, and the life and the light of men was in that Word; their being and their consciousness, their existence and their understanding were owing to that Word, not only in point of origin and principle but in this sense also that as time went on they were continuously sustained by the Word of God. For the Word of God is not only the maker of all things: it remained in the world as the sustainer and ruler of everything. As such it gave men their life and by way of consciousness, reason, and understanding enlightened every man that came into the world (John 1:3-10).

* * * * *

History puts its confirming seal upon this testimony of the Scriptures. In the circle of the Cainites all kinds of inventions and enterprises began to thrive soon after the fall (Gen. 4:17ff.), and the people who settled in the plains of Shinar after the flood soon achieved a high level of culture. According to Genesis 8:12 Nimrod, a son of Cush, the son of Ham, was the founder of the kingdom of Babel. Scripture speaks of him as a mighty hunter before the Lord because, by his unusual physical strength, he destroyed the predatory beasts, made the plains of Shinar safe for habitation, and moved and enticed people to make this area their dwelling place. In this way he built various cities, Babel, Erech, Accad, and Calneh, all in the plains of Shinar. And from that point he penetrated through to the land of Asshur and laid the foundations there for the cities of Nineveh, Rehoboth, Calah and Resen.

According to the Scriptures therefore the oldest inhabitants of Shinar were not Shemites but Hamites, and the recent science of Assyriology, which busies itself with cuneiform writings excavated in Assyria, confirms this, inasmuch as it also teaches that Shinar was originally inhabited by a tribe of the Sumerians which cannot be reckoned as a part of the Shemites. What happened is that this early population of Shinar was later overrun by a migration of Shemites. These then retained their own language, it is true, but took over the culture of the Sumerians and themselves became merged with it to constitute the later Chaldeans. Specifically the Shemitic element became dominant when Hammurabi, the city-king of Babel, perhaps the same as the Amraphel of

Genesis 14:1, raised Babel to the status of a capital city and made the whole of Shinar subservient to him. The 10th chapter of Genesis gives expression to the same thought, for, although in verse 11 we read that Nimrod the Hamite went to the land of Asshur and founded cities there, verse 22 tells us that Asshur, that is, the people living in Asshur, is related to Arphaxad, Lud, and Aram, and is to be reckoned among the descendants of Shem.

The quality of the civilization which we find in the land of Shinar, in so far as science and art, morality and jurisprudence, commerce and industry are concerned, reached a height which, the more we come to know it from excavations, fills us with amazement. Just how and when it arose, we do not know; but the general idea that the farther we go back the coarser and more barbarous the peoples we encounter will be is totally discredited by it. So long as we do not entertain all kinds of fantastic notions about the uncivilized state of the so-called "primitive" peoples, and, guided by *history*, we try to penetrate through to the past, we are confirmed in the idea of the Scriptures that the oldest period of Noahite humanity, what with the initiative of such men as Nimrod, stood at a very high level of culture.

Moreover, this civilization did not remain confined to the land of Shinar. As mankind spread out more and more after the confusion of tongues, they settled widely separated parts of the earth. Thus some of the tribes were farther and farther removed from the center of culture and civilization, seeking their homes in the wild and inhospitable stretches of Asia, Europe, and Africa. It is no wonder that these tribes and peoples, living their isolated lives, cut off from all commerce with other nations, and wrestling always with a wild and undisciplined nature, remained on the level of culture at which they began, or, in some instances, even fell below it. Such peoples we speak of in historical studies as "primitive peoples," or "uncivilized peoples," but such designations are really misleading and inaccurate. For, among all these peoples, we find the characteristics and properties which are the basic elements of civilization. They are all human as distinguished from natural beings; they all have consciousness and will, reason and understanding, family and community, tools and ornaments.

Further, there is so much difference among these nations that it would be impossible to point out the boundary between the "civilized" and the "uncivilized" peoples. There is a remarkable difference in culture among the bush-folk of South Africa, the population of Polynesia, and the Negroid races. Irrespective, however, of how they differ, they have a common fund of ideas, traditions — concerning the flood, for instance — of memories and hopes. These point to the common origin.

All this is even more true of the so-called "civilized" peoples, the Indians and Chinese, the Phoenicians and Egyptians. The foundations of the world-picture, the *Weltanschauung,* which we find among all these peoples, are the same as those which are called to our attention by the excavations in the land of Shinar. This is the origin of all culture, the cradle and nursemaid of mankind. It was from central Asia that mankind spread out; and from this center mankind took along with it those elements of culture which are common to civilized peoples, and which each of them independently and in its own way brought to further development. The ancient culture of Babylon, what with its writing, its astronomy, its mathematics, its calendar, and the like, is still the basis upon which our culture is built.

*   *   *   *   *

Nevertheless, when we review this whole history of civilization from a religio-moral point of view, we get from it a deep sense of dissatisfaction and disillusionment. The Apostle Paul has said of it that the Gentiles, knowing God from His general revelation, nevertheless did not glorify Him as God nor were thankful to Him, but became vain in their imaginations, and their foolish heart was darkened. Professing themselves to be wise, they became fools, and changed the glory of the uncorruptible into an image made like to corruptible man, and to birds, and fourfooted beasts, and creeping things (Rom. 1:21-23). An impartial historical investigation of the religions of various peoples leads to the same conclusion. One can, with the aid of a false philosophy, study the various forms of religion, and arrive at a nebulous essence of religion in the feelings of mankind, and so blink at the seriousness of St. Paul's conclusion. But the fact remains for all that: mankind on the long road of its civilization has not glorified God nor been thankful to Him.

Even among those earliest of inhabitants in the plains of Shinar we encounter this worship of the creature instead of the Creator. According to some, the idea at the basis of the religion of the Babylonians, like that at the basis of other religions, is still the idea of the oneness of God, and no doubt such a conception of the Deity must have existed before it could be applied to creatures. As a matter of fact, however, religion among the Babylonians consisted of a glorification of all kinds of creatures. These were regarded as gods. How this transition from the service of the one, true God to the glorification of creatures took place, we cannot, in the absence of historical data, make out.

But it is an unproved and arbitrary assumption to say that religion developed out of polydemonism (the glorification of all kinds of souls

and spirits: fetishism, animism, and totemism) by way of polytheism
(the glorification of all kinds of gods) into monotheism (the glorification of one god). Nowhere do we see that such a development has tak-
en place. Israel is a unique exception. But what history does teach
again and again is that men can fall from a confession of one God to the
glorification of many gods: we witness it in the history of Israel, in the
history of many Christian churches, and also in the time in which we
ourselves are living. When belief in the one God is abandoned, all kinds
of polytheistic ideas and superstitious practices soon follow after.

Moreover, there is by no means such a big difference between "higher" and "lower" religions, between the religions, that is, of the so-called
civilized and uncivilized peoples, as is usually alleged. The same ideas
and practices, be it in modified form, recur among all Pagan peoples;
and these ideas and practices live on in their various forms also among
Christian nations. What with the decay of the Christian religion in modern circles, these same ideas and practices are revived there also.

Which are these ideas and practices? First of all, there is idolatry
and the worship of images. These exist among all peoples. Idolatry
means putting something else in the place of the one, true God, or alongside of Him, and placing one's trust in that. Sometimes these substitutes
are creatures, the firmament, for instance, with its sun, moon, and stars,
as in the Babylonian religion, which is therefore properly called an astral
religion; sometimes these are the heroes, geniuses, or great men, conceived of as a sort of intermediate being, half-way between gods and
men, such as were worshipped among the Greeks, for instance, and
among others; sometimes they are the forefathers who, after their
death, have passed on to a different and higher state of being, and these,
as in the Chinese religion, become the chief object of glorification; sometimes, again, these idolatrous substitutes for God are some one or other
of the animals, a steer, a crocodile, or the like, as in the religion of
Egypt; or — to specify one more type — sometimes they are souls
and spirits, conceived of as temporarily or permanently dwelling in all
kinds of animate or inanimate creatures, and thus constituting an object of worship in the religions both of civilized and uncivilized peoples.

Irrespective, however, of what form the idolatry may take, it represents always a worship of the creature instead of the Creator. The distinction between God and the world is lost. The holiness of God, that
is, His distinction from, and His absolute transcendence of, every creature — it was that which was lost to the Gentiles.

In the second place, all kinds of false ideas about man and the world
accompany such idolatry. Among the Gentiles, religion is not something independent, and standing by itself, but is intimately interrelated

with all of life, with state and society, with art and science. Nowhere do we find a religion which consists merely of attitudes and states of feeling. Religion, which is the relationship of man to God, governs all other relations also, and therefore implies a definite view of man and the world, and of the origin, essence, and purpose of all things. The religious ideas which accompany a belief in the gods have a bearing always on the past and the future. There are reminiscences of Paradise and expectations for the future in all religions, and there are ideas about the origin and the future of man and the world. There are notions of a golden age which existed in the beginning, followed by ages of silver, and iron, and clay, and there are notions of an immortality of man, of life after death, and of a judgment which in the end will accrue to all, and of a differing status for the just and the unjust at that time. In the several religions these various ideas are variously emphasized. The Chinese religion looks to the past and consists of ancestor-worship; the Egyptian religion looked to the future, busied itself with the dead, and was in fact a religion of death. But in all the religions, in some more, in some less, these elements have their place.

All these religious representations have this in common that they mingle the component of truth with all sorts of error and folly. The line between Creator and creature has been erased, and therefore the boundary between world and man, soul and body, and heaven and hell has nowhere been rightly drawn. At every turn the physical and the moral, the material and the spiritual, the earthly and the heavenly have been confused and mingled with each other. In the absence of a sense of the holiness of God there is the corresponding absence of a sense of sin. The world of paganism does not know God, it does not know the world and man, and it does not know sin and misery.

In the third place, all the religions of the nations are characterized by the effort to achieve salvation by an exertion of human strength. Idolatry leads naturally to a self-willed religion. When the worship of the one true God is abandoned, and there is no longer an objective, truly historical revelation to appeal to, man tries to compel the gods or spirits he has invented to reveal themselves. Idolatry is always accompanied by superstition, fortune-telling, and magic. Divination, or the *mantic,* is the name given to the effort on one's own part, or with the help of diviners, fortune-tellers, priests, oracles, and the like, and by means of astrology, the interpretation of dreams, and other devices, to come to know the will of the gods. And magic is the name given to the effort by means of formalistic prayers, free-will sacrifices, flagellations, and similar practices, to make the will of the gods serviceable to oneself.

Naturally these things, too, are variously manifested. Nevertheless they all have their place in the several religions and they constitute a necessary component in Gentile religion. It is man who is the central figure and who seeks to earn his salvation. In none of these religions is the real nature of redemption (reconciliation) and of grace understood.

* * * * *

Although such a sketch serves to characterize pagan religions in general, modifications have taken place in some of them which deserve our deliberate attention and a separate, though brief, consideration. When on the one hand the religion of a people loses its character in all kinds of gross and uncouth forms of superstition and divination, and on the other hand the culture or civilization develops apace, a conflict is bound to occur. And out of that conflict, doubtless under the providence of God, those men are born who try for a reconciliation and attempt to lift the religion out of its profound degeneration. Such a man was Zarathustra who lived in Persia, probably prior to the seventh century before Christ. Such was Confucius in the China of the sixth century before Christ. And such were Buddha in the India of the fifth century before Christ and Mohammed in the Arabia of the seventh century after Christ. And there have been many others, not all of them known by name.

There can be no difference of opinion about the fact that the religions founded by these men are in many respects greatly superior to the tribal religions in which they were brought up. Hypotheses of evolution and of degeneration are, both of them, in religion as in every other area of culture, very one-sided, and they are inadequate to account for the plenitude of manifestations evident in all this, at least to account for them by any one formulation. Periods of flowering and of decay, of revival and relapse are constant in the history of all peoples and in all provinces of life.

Moreover, it cannot be said that these men were deliberate deceivers, instruments or agents of Satan. They were earnest men, and in their own souls they wrestled with the conflict which arose between the tribal or popular faith and their own enlightened consciousness. By the light which was granted them they tried for a better way towards obtaining a true happiness.

All the same, though this must be acknowledged, these reformation-religions remain different only in degree and not in kind from the idolatries of the people. True, these men cut off the wild branches from the tree of false religion. But they did not uproot it. Zarathustra in his preaching stressed the contrast between good and evil, but he conceived of this contrast as being not merely ethical but also and primarily physical in character. Hence he was forced to distinguish between a good God and an evil God, and so to create a dualism which extended into everything, into the natural, human, and animal worlds, and which had the practical effect of mutilating life. *Confucianism* was a state-religion compounded out of religious elements other than its own and combining within itself the worship of nature gods and of ancestors. *Buddhism* was at first really no religion at all but rather a philosophy which postulated suffering as the source of evil, and existence as the source of suffering, and which therefore recommended abstinence, the numbing of the consciousness, and the annihilation of being as the way of salvation. And Mohammed, who knew Judaism and Christianity, and who by way of his ardent belief in an impending judgment which, he was convinced, would certainly accrue to his materialistically minded contemporaries, arrived at the confession of a single God, did indeed effect a religious and moral reformation. But in his personal life the preacher of religion gave way more and more to the statesman and law-giver, and the religion which he founded left no room for fellowship between God and man, for it understood neither the cause of the separation nor the way to reconciliation. For *Mohammedanism* the salvation of heaven consists of a total satisfaction of sensual desires.

* * * * *

When, therefore, we review the whole terrain of general revelation, we discover, on the one hand, that it has been of great value and that it has borne rich fruits, and, on the other, that mankind has not found God by its light. It is owing to general revelation that some religious and ethical sense is present in all men; that they have some awareness still of truth and falsehood, of good and evil, justice and injustice, beauty and ugliness; that they live in the relationship of marriage and the family, of community and state; that they are held in check by all these external and internal controls against degenerating into bestiality; that, within the pale of these limits, they busy themselves with the production, distribution, and enjoyment of all kinds of spiritual and material things; in short, that mankind is by general revelation preserved in its existence, maintained in its unity, and enabled to continue and to develop its history.

Despite all this, however, the truth remains, as St. Paul put it, that the world by wisdom has not known God in His wisdom (1 Cor. 1 :21). When Paul ascribes wisdom to the world, he means what he says in full seriousness. In the light of general revelation the world has gathered together a treasure of wisdom, of wisdom, that is, concerning the things of this earthly life. But this wisdom of the world constitutes the world the less excusable, for it proves that mankind did not lack such gifts of God as mind and reason, rational and moral ability. The wisdom of man demonstrates that man because of the darkness of his mind and the hardening of his heart has not used the gifts which were given him aright.

The light shined in the darkness, it is true, but the darkness did not comprehend it (John 1:5). The Word was in the world, but the world did not know Him (the Logos) (John 1:10). In all its wisdom the world did not know *God* (1 Cor. 1:21).

V

The Manner of Special Revelation

The inadequacy of general revelation demonstrates the necessity of special revelation.

But this necessity must be understood correctly. It does not mean that God was obligated or forced, either internally by reason of His being or externally because of circumstances, to reveal Himself in a special way. All revelation, and especially that which comes to us in Christ through the Scriptures, is an act of God's grace, a free dispensation of His will, and a token of His undeserved and perpetually forfeited favor. Hence we can speak of the necessity or indispensability of special revelation only to the extent that such a revelation is indissolubly connected with the purpose which God Himself has appointed for His creation. If it is God's good pleasure to restore a sin-devastated creation, and to re-create man after His own image and cause him to live once more in the eternal blessedness of heaven, then a special revelation is necessary. For such a purpose general revelation is inadequate.

As a matter of fact, it is not even this purpose first of all which makes a special revelation necessary. For when we come to see and acknowledge the inadequacy of general revelation for this destiny of the world and of man, we see also that we owe even this conviction to special revelation. By nature we consider ourselves and our abilities, the world and its treasures, enough for our salvation. The pagan religions are not an exception to this rule, but a confirmation of it. It is true that they all speak of priests, soothsayers, oracles, and the like, and appeal to these as the bearers of a special revelation. And this fact in itself is strong evidence for the thesis that general revelation is inadequate, and that everyone in his heart feels the need for a different and more intimate revelation of God than that which nature and history give him. But these special revelations to which paganism appeals clearly demonstrate also that man, who has lost the fellowship with God, cannot understand His revelation in nature either, and that he is one, therefore, who in his groping after God follows his own ways. These remove him farther and farther from the knowledge of truth and lead him into ever deeper captivity to the service of idolatry and unrighteousness (Rom. 1:20-32).

The special revelation of God, consequently, is necessary also for a right understanding of His general revelation in nature and history, and in heart and conscience. We need it to purge the pure content of general revelation of all kinds of human error and so to evaluate that revelation at its just worth. It is when we go by the light of the Scriptures that we first come to recognize that general revelation has a rich significance for the whole of human life, and that nevertheless it is in all its richness insufficient and inadequate for the achievement of the proper end of man.

If, therefore, in the interest of clear insight and a good order of treatment, we spoke first of general revelation and its insufficiency in order now to proceed to a treatment of special revelation, this mode of approach ought not to be construed as though in dealing with that other we set special revelation to one side, paying no attention to its content all the while. On the contrary, this special revelation guided us also in that earlier discussion and shed its light upon our approach to the problem.

Hence, in this study of special revelation which follows now we do not propose to conduct a so-called pre-suppositionless investigation. We shall not, as the doubters of our day do, go through the gamut of the various religions in order to find out whether these give us the special revelation of God which our heart tells us it requires. The fact that we have learned to know the false religions as being false, and that we have learned to know the idolatry and image worship, the sorcery and divination, the unbelief and the superstition, irrespective of whether these come in coarse or in refined forms as being sinful — this fact we owe to the special revelation which is granted us in Christ. We should therefore be deliberately putting out the light which enlightens us if we were to set special revelation to one side or take no account of it even temporarily and in a methodological sense. To do that would be to prove that we love the darkness rather than the light lest our thoughts and deliberations should be made manifest (John 3:19-21).

General revelation, it is true, can to a certain extent demonstrate the need for and the necessity of a special revelation. It can point to many strong grounds for the possibility of such a revelation. For, if one does not go along with materialism and pantheism in practically denying *all* revelation, if, instead, one still really believes in the existence of a personal God who has made the world, who has given man an immortal soul and destined him for eternal salvation, and who still sustains and rules all things by His providence, then there is no fundamental reason any longer for arguing against the possibility of a special revelation. Creation *is* revelation, a very special, absolutely supernatural, marvelous revelation. Whoever accepts the idea of creation acknowledges in principle the possibility of all further revelation, even that of the Incarnation. But, whatever general revelation may contribute to the case for the *necessity* and the *possibility* of a special revelation, it can say nothing about its *reality* because this rests entirely on a free gift of God. The reality of special revelation can be demonstrated only by its own existence. It is only by its own light that it can be seen and acknowledged.

* * * * *

This special revelation, in which God spoke to us first by way of the prophets and thereupon through the Son (Heb. 1:1), and which we do not accept in consequence of argument and evidence but in childlike faith, does indeed stand in continuous relationship to general revelation but is at the same time essentially distinguished from it. This distinction or difference comes out, as we indicated in passing before but must now develop further, especially in the *manner* in which it takes place, in the *content* which it comprehends, and in the *purpose* at which it aims.

The *manner* in which special revelation takes place is not always the same but differs in terms of the means which God employs for it. Hence, too, it is characterized by such various names as: appearing, revealing, showing, making known, proclaiming, teaching, and the like. The designation *speaking* is especially provocative. The Scriptures also employ this word for the works of God in creation and providence. God said: Let there be light; and there was light (Gen. 1:3). By the word were the heavens made, and all the hosts of them by the breath of His mouth (Ps. 33:6). He speaks and it is done; He commands and it stands fast (Ps. 33:9). The voice of the Lord is upon the waters, it speaks in the thunder, breaks the cedars, causes the wilderness to tremble, puts the enemy to flight and destroys him (Ps. 29:3-9 and 104:7; Isa. 30:31 and 66:6). All of these works of God in creation and providence can rightly be called a *speaking* or *saying* for the reason that God is a personal, conscious, thinking being, who brings all things into existence by the word of His power, and who thus puts thoughts into the mind of man which man, as His image and likeness, can read and understand. God most certainly has something to say to man in His works.

There is very little disagreement about this voice of God in the works of His hands. Many who deny a special revelation are nonetheless fond of speaking of a revelation of God in creation. Among those who do so there is, however, considerable difference. Some find this revelation for the most part in nature, others in history and its famous men, and still others in the history of religions and the leaders of the various faiths. Moreover, the one will tend to emphasize the revelation which comes to man from the outside, be it in nature or history, and the other stresses that which takes place in man himself, in his heart and mind and conscience. More and more the thought is gaining ground in our day that religion and revelation are intimately related, in fact, that both have the same content and are really but the two sides of one and the same matter. Revelation is then regarded as the divine, and religion as the human, element in the relation of God and man. The idea is that God reveals Himself to man to the extent of man's religion, and man possesses so much of religion as God reveals to him of Himself.

This idea has its roots, however, in that pantheism which identifies God and man, and hence identifies also revelation and religion. Those who adhere to this view can hardly speak of any real revelation of God, not even in nature and history, or in the world and man. For revelation, when rightly understood, assumes, as we remarked earlier, that God is conscious of Himself, that He knows Himself, and that therefore He can, according to His good pleasure, share a knowledge of Himself with His creatures. On the pantheistic basis the personality, the self-awareness and self-knowledge, and therefore also the reasonable will of God are denied. On that basis God is no more than the essence and energy of all things and in all things. At best, consequently, pantheism can speak only of an unconscious and involuntary manifestation or working of God. Such a manifestation or working of God would not then be one that presented the mind of man with thoughts, ideas, or knowledge of God, but one which at best could only excite particular moods, affections, or attitudes in the heart of man. Man would then have to take these and, in complete independence and freedom, and in proportion to the extent of his culture and education, embody them in words Practically this is to make of religion in mankind and in individual man a process by means of which God becomes aware of Himself and gets to know Himself. God, then, does not speak to man, nor reveal Himself to man. It is man, rather, who reveals God to Himself.

If this pantheistic line of thought still makes use of the terms *revelation, voice* of God, and the like, it takes them not from its own philosophy, for they have no place there, but from that other world and life view which comes from the Scriptures. Hence, also, it falsifies these terms. Scripture calls even general revelation a *speaking* of God, for it proceeds from the idea that God really has something to say in that revelation and that He says it. Hence Scripture also holds to the idea that God and man are distinct in kind, and that religion and revelation are distinct in kind also. For if God has His own thought and if He knows Himself, and if He has given expression to that thought to a greater or lesser extent in His works, then the possibility remains real that man because of his darkened mind misunderstands those thoughts of God, and becomes vain in his imaginings. In that event, religion could so little be the other side of revelation as to become in fact a guilty and erring misrepresentation of it.

* * * * *

By interpreting the general revelation of God as it does, and by calling it the speech or voice of God in the now designated sense, the Scripture keeps the way open for a further and more essential or proper *speaking* on God's part in His special revelation. The whole Scripture presents God to us as a being who is perfectly conscious of Himself, as a being who can think and therefore speak. We remember the question asked in Psalm 94:9: He that planted the ear, shall He not hear? He that formed the eye, shall He not see? That question could, in accordance with the sense and meaning of the Holy Spirit, be supplemented by this other one: He who knows Himself perfectly, should He not be able to convey a knowledge of Himself to His creatures? Whoever were to deny this possibility were by that token denying not only the God of regeneration but also the God of creation and providence, as Scripture reveals Him to us. Just so, whoever understands the voice or speech of God in general revelation in the good, that is, in the Scriptural, sense loses the right to raise basic objections to the voice of God in special revelation. For God can reveal Himself in a special way because He does it in a general way. He can speak in a proper sense because He can speak in a metaphorical sense. He can be the Re-Creator because He is the Creator of all things.

The great difference between this *speaking* on God's part in the general revelation and that in His special revelation is that in the first God leaves it to man to find out His thoughts in the works of His hands, and that in the second He Himself gives direct expression to those thoughts and in this form offers them to the mind of man. In Isaiah 28:26 we read that God instructs the plowman, teaching him how he is to do his work. But this instruction does not come to the plowman in writing, in so many words, nor in the form of lessons at school; it is a teaching, rather, which is contained and expressed in all the laws of nature, in the character of air and of soil, of time and place, of grain and corn. What the plowman must do is conscientiously to get to know all those laws of nature, and in this way to learn the lesson which God teaches in them. In this effort he is liable to mistake and error, but when in the end he has come to appropriate this teaching, he must thank God for it, from whom all things come, and who is great in counsel and great in deed.

In general revelation such objective teaching is adequate to its purpose. What God intends by it is to provoke man to seek Him, to feel Him out and find Him (Acts 17:27), and, not finding Him, yet be without excuse (Rom. 1:20). But in His special revelation God has compassion upon man who strays about and cannot find Him. In it, God seeks man out and Himself tells man who and what He is. He does not leave it to man to deduce and infer from a group of facts who God is. He Himself tells man in so many words: Here and such am I. True, in special revelation also God makes use of the facts in nature and history to reveal Himself in His various excellences. And those facts, which are often miracles, are not mere supplement or addendum but an indispensable element *in* revelation. They are never sheer facts, however, whose interpretation is left to us. Instead they are surrounded on all sides by the very word of God. They are preceded by this word, accompanied by it, and followed up by it. The central content of the special revelation is the person and work of Christ. This Christ is heralded and described centuries before in the Old Testament, and, once He has appeared and has accomplished His work, He is again interpreted and explained in the writings of the New Testament. The special revelation, consequently, follows a line which leads to the Christ, but parallel with it and in connection with it, it leads also to the Scriptures, the Word of God.

For this reason special revelation can in a much more proper sense be called a *speaking* than general revelation, though that, too, can rightly be so designated. The first verse of the epistle to the Hebrews comprises the whole revelation of God, both of the old and of the new Testament, that of the prophets and that of the Son, in that one term: *speaking*. But it immediately adds that this revelation came at many times and in various manners. The first expression, "at sundry times," means to say that revelation did not come perfect and complete at one moment, but that it came by way of many successive events and therefore ran the gamut of a long history. And the second expression, "in divers manners," means to say that the various divine revelations were not all given in the same way, but that, taking place at different times and places, they happened also in different ways and came in various forms.

*　*　*　*　*

At many points in the Holy Scriptures[1] we simply read that the Lord appeared, said, commanded, and the like, and find no comment at all on

---

1. For example, Gen. 2:16 and 18; 4:6; 6:13; 12:7; and 13:14.

the manner in which this took place. Other texts, however, also shed some light on the manner of the revelation, and these enable us to distinguish between two kinds of means which God employed for the purpose of His revelation.

To the first kind belong all those means which have an external and objective character. Through them, so to speak, God comes to man from without, appears to man, and speaks to him. Thus He often appears to Abraham, Moses, to the people of Israel on Mount Sinai, above the tabernacle and in the holy of holies, and in pillars of cloud or fire as tokens of His presence.[2] At other times He announces what He has to say by means of angels,[3] especially by means of the Angel of the covenant who bears His name in him (Ex. 23:21). Further, He makes use of the lot for the purpose of revealing Himself to Israel (Prov. 16:33), or of the Urim and Thummim (Ex. 28:30). A few times He speaks with an audible voice,[4] or Himself writes His law on the tables of testimony (Ex. 31:18 and 25:16).

The miracles are also to be reckoned with this group of the means of revelation. In the Scriptures the miracles take a large and important place. In our time they have been subjected to heavy attack from all sides. It were effort wasted to try to defend the miracles of Holy Scripture against those who have rejected the Scriptural view of life and the world. For, if God does not exist — and such is the thesis of atheism and materialism — or if He has no proper, personal, independent existence, being merely one with the world — as pantheism maintains — or if, after creation, He withdrew from the world and left it to its own ways — as deism holds — then it is self-evident that miracles are impossible. And if the *impossibility* of miracles is evident from the beginning, no argument about their *reality* is necessary.

But Scripture has quite another idea of God and of the world, and also of the relationship which exists between them. In the first place, it teaches that God is a conscious, willing, and omnipotent being, who called the whole world with all of its energies and laws into existence, and who, in doing so, by no means expended the fulness of His powers. He retains and possesses within Himself an infinite plenitude of life and strength. Nothing is too wonderful or hard for Him (Gen. 18:14); with Him all things are possible (Matt. 19:26).

Besides, the Scriptural view does not regard the world as a unit whose several parts are all of the same nature and the same substance, exhibiting difference only in the forms of their manifestation. Rather it

---

2. Gen. 15:17; Ex. 3:2; 13:21; 19:9; and 33:9; Lev. 16:2, and elsewhere.
3. Gen. 18:2 and 32:1; Dan. 8:13; Zech. 1:9ff.; Matt. 1:20, and elsewhere.
4. Ex. 19:9; Deut. 4:33; 5:26; Matt. 3:17; and 2 Peter 1:17.

regards the world as an organism whose members, while belonging to the whole, are all endowed with different properties and charged with different functions. In the one world there is room for several kinds of beings, which, though they are all sustained and governed by the same divine power, nevertheless differ from each other in their nature. This rich world comprises matter and spirit, body and soul, earth and heaven. It contains inorganic and organic, inanimate and animate, non-rational and rational creatures, minerals and plants and animals, human beings and angels. And within the being of man there is a distinction again between his head and his heart, his reason and his conscience, his concepts and his affections. All these different spheres in one and the same world depend on different energies and abilities, and operate according to different laws. True, all things are inter-dependent with each other, as are the members of the body. All the same each part has its own place and function in the whole.

In the third place, the Scriptures teach that God and the world, although they are different from each other, are never separated. God has indeed a unique, perfect, independent existence in Himself, but He is not segregated from the world; on the contrary, we live and move and have our being in Him (Acts 17:28). He is of course the Creator who at the beginning called all things into being; but He is and remains also the owner, the possessor, the King and Lord who by His omnipotent and omnipresent power sustains and rules all things. He is the first cause of all things, not only in their beginning but also continuously thereafter. The secondary causes through which He works differ from each other; but the first cause of all creatures is and remains God and God alone.

If in these basic concepts we agree with Holy Scripture and so take our stand on the solid ground of theism, we have no basis at all from which to cast doubt upon the possibility of miracles or to attack that possibility. For, on that basis, every phenomenon of nature and history is a deed and a work of God, and is in that sense a miracle. The so-called miracles are nothing but a special manifestation of that same divine power which works in all things. This power is operative in various ways, makes use of different means (secondary causes) according to different laws, and therefore with varying results. It has been said, and that not unjustly, that for the stone it is a wonder that the plant can grow, for the plant it is a wonder that the animal can move about, for the animal it is a wonder that man can think, and for man it is a wonder that God can raise up the dead. If it be true that God, by his omnipresent and omnipotent power works through all creatures as His means, why should He not be able to work in a different way with that same power — a different way, that is, from that which is familiar to us in the normal course of nature and history. Miracles are not a violation of natural laws. For these laws are fully acknowledged in Scripture, even though they are not classified and formulated there. Thus, for example, according to Scripture, the laws of all nature are firmly fixed by the covenant of nature which God made with Noah (Gen. 8:22). But, just as man subdues the earth by his reason and will, and governs and controls nature by means of his culture, so God has the power to make this created world serviceable to the carrying out of His counsel. What the miracles prove is that it is not the world but the Lord that is *God*.

* * * * *

All this would have required no argument or contention if man had not fallen. In that event, man would have known God and acknowledged Him from the works of His hands. Without entering upon the question of whether there would have been miracles if there had been no sin, we can let it suffice to remark here that, if there had been miracles then, they would have been of a different nature and would have had a different purpose. For the miracles which actually have taken place and which Scripture reports have their own peculiar character and purpose.

In the Old Testament, judgment and redemption go hand in hand as accompaniments of the miracles. Thus the flood is a means of destroying the godless generation of that time, and at the same moment a means of preserving Noah and his family in the ark. The miracles grouped around the persons of Moses and Joshua — the plagues of Egypt, the crossing of the Red Sea, the law-giving on Sinai, the invasion and conquest of Canaan — have as their purpose the judgment of the enemies of God and of His people, and the establishment of a secure home for His own people in the land of the promise. The miracles which come later, and at the center of which the person of Elijah bulks large, take place in the time of Ahab and Jezebel, a time when paganism threatened to suppress the worship of Jehovah entirely, and they reach their high point on Carmel where the struggle between Jehovah and Baal is decided.

All the miracles of the Old Testament have the common earmark that, negatively, they spell judgment for the godless nations, and, positively, they create and preserve a place among the people of Israel for the continuing revelation of God. In this they achieve their purpose that, over against all idolatry and worship of images, the God of the covenant, the God of the people of Israel is known and recognized as God: See now that I, even I, am He, and there is no god with Me: I kill, and I make alive; I wound, and I heal: neither is there any that can deliver out of My hand (Deut. 32:39 and 4:35; Isa. 45:5, 18, and 22). And when this purpose has been achieved, there follows quickly the full revelation in the person of Christ.

This person of Christ is itself a miracle, in its origin, in its essence, in its words and works. It is *the* miracle of world history. Consequently, the miracles which He performs have their own peculiar nature. In the first place, He Himself, during His life on earth, does many miracles: those in which He demonstrates His power over nature (changing the water into wine, feeding the multitude, subduing the storm, walking on the sea, and the like); those in which He demonstrates His power over the consequences of sin, that is, over illness, disease, and the calamities of life; and those, finally, in which He demonstrates His power over sin itself, that is, over its guilt and its pollution, and over the domination of Satan (the forgiving of sins, and the expulsion of Satan and of evil spirits). The uniqueness of the person of Christ comes to expression in these three kinds of miracles. But for one exception, namely the cursing of the fig tree, all the miracles of Jesus are redemptive in kind. He did not come into the world to condemn the world, but to save it (John 3:17). In His miracles, too, He is active as prophet, priest, and king; in them also He does the work which the Father has placed upon Him (John 4:34; 5:36; and 9:4).

This person of Christ is manifested even more clearly in the miracles which were done, not by Him but *in* Him and *with* Him. In those especially we see who and what He is. The supernatural conception, His miraculous life and death, His resurrection, ascension, and being seated at the right hand of God, these all are most peculiarly redemptive miracles. They prove, far better even that the works which He performed, His absolute power over sin and all its consequences, over Satan and Satan's whole dominion. And they illustrate, more fully than those other works, that this power of the person of Christ is a redemptive, a regenerative, power, which will gain the final victory only in the new heaven and the new earth.

The miracles which were performed in the apostolic time by the first witnesses can be characterized as the works of the exalted Christ (Acts 3:6 and 4:10). They were necessary in order to demonstrate that Jesus, who had been rejected by the world, had been nailed to the cross and put to death, and was regarded as dead — that this Jesus was still *alive* and that He had all power in heaven and also upon the earth. The miracles of the Old Testament showed that Jehovah was God and that there was none beside Him. The miracles of the New Testament show that Jesus Christ, the Nazarene, whom the Jews have crucified, has been raised of God and placed at His right hand as Prince and Savior (Acts 4:10; 5:30 and 31). When this end has been achieved, when a church has been planted in the world, a church which believes and confesses this revelation of the Father in the Son through the communion of the Holy Spirit, then the visible and external miracles cease, but the spiritual miracles of regeneration and conversion continue in the church until the fulness of the Gentiles is come and all Israel is saved. At the end of the ages, according to the Scriptures, there will come the further miracles of the appearance of Christ, the raising of the dead, the judgment, the new heaven and earth.

The end and object of all revelation, and of the miracles in that revelation, is the restoration of fallen mankind, the re-creation of the world, and the acknowledgment of God as God. Hence the miracles are not a strange and singular element in revelation, nor an arbitrary addendum to it. Rather, they are a necessary and indispensable component of revelation. They are themselves revelation. God makes Himself known to men in all His excellences and perfections by means of word and deed.

* * * * *

To this first group of means, all external and objective in character, a second kind must be added. To it belong all those means which are subjective, which take place inside of man, in which God speaks to man, not from without, but within.

The first place among this kind is taken by the unique revelation which came to Moses as the mediator of the Old Testament. It is described as a revelation in which the Lord spoke to Moses face to face, as a man speaks with his friend (Ex. 33:11).

Moses' role in the Old Testament was a special one. He stood high above the prophets. God spoke to him, not by means of a vision, but by direct discourse. Moses saw God, not as in a dream, but directly: he saw His similitude, His form, not His being or His face, but the afterglow of Him when the glory of the very God had passed by (Num. 12:8 and Ex. 33:18-23).

To this kind of means belong also the dream (Num. 12:6 and Deut. 13:1-6); the vision, that is, a state of being in which the physical eye is closed to the external world and the eye of the soul is opened to the divine things (Num. 12:6 and Deut. 13:1-6); and especially the inspiration of the human mind by the Spirit of God.[1] This last means of revelation occurs frequently in the Old Testament also, but there it is always

---

1. Num. 11:25-29; 2 Sam. 23:2; Matt. 16:17; Acts 8:29; 1 Cor. 2:12; and 2 Peter 1:21.

represented as an operation of the Spirit which comes upon the prophet from above and but for a moment. But in the New Testament, after the Holy Spirit has been poured out, inspiration becomes more common as a means of revelation not only but also takes on a more organic and permanent character.

These two kinds of the means of revelation can be classified under the names of *manifestation* and *inspiration*. In doing so, we should remember, however, that *manifestation* by no means consisted merely of deeds. It included thoughts and words also. We should remember also that the *inspiration* here intended differs both from the activity of the Spirit which the prophets and apostles enjoyed in recording revelation in written form (the inspiration of the Scriptures) and from that internal illumination which is the portion of all believers.

VI

The Content of Special Revelation

Having taken note of the several ways in which the special revelation came to men, we proceed now to the consideration of its *content*. As in the study of the general revelation, so in this we shall do best briefly to review the history of special revelation. In this way — and without separate treatment — its *purpose* will also become clear.

Special revelation did not begin with Abraham. It set in immediately after the fall. Hence it is of some importance to notice that Abraham was the son of Terah, who was a descendant in the eighth generation of Shem. And of Shem we read that Jehovah was his God and would remain so (Gen. 9:26). It was in the family of Shem, as in that of Seth before the flood, that the knowledge of God was preserved longest and in its purest state. Hence, when the Lord calls Abraham, He does not present Himself as a different God but as the same God whom Abraham already knew and confessed. After all, we know from other passages in Scripture also, namely in those which tell of Melchizedek (Gen. 14:18-20), that the knowledge of the true God had not entirely been lost. Besides, we are told concerning the Philistine king, Abimelech, and concerning the children of Heth in Hebron, and concerning the Pharaoh of Egypt that they acknowledged and honored the God of Abraham.[1]

After the confusion of tongues and the division of mankind, unbelief did not grow apace among men, but superstition and idolatry did. So it was in Egypt (Ex. 18:9-12), in Canaan (Gen. 15:16 and 18:1ff.), and in Babylonia. Even among the descendants of Shem the true religion had given way to idolatry. According to Joshua 24:2 and 14-15, Israel's fathers, Terah the father of Abraham, Nahor, and Haran served other gods when they lived on the other side of the river. And from Gen. 31:19, 34 and 35:2-4 we learn that Laban had special household gods and that he honored them. Laban accordingly is called an Aramaian, a Syrian (Gen. 31:20 and Deut. 26:5).

In order to prevent mankind from falling into superstition and unrighteousness, the covenant of nature with Noah from being broken,

---

1. Gen. 20:3; 21:22; 23:6; 26:29; 40:8; 41:16 and 38-39.

and God's purpose for mankind from being frustrated, God now takes a different course of action with Abraham. He cannot again destroy the children of men in a general flood. But, leaving the other peoples to walk in their own ways, He can set up a covenant with one person, and in that person with one people, and so by way of that covenant pursue His promise and fulfill it. And then, when the fulfillment has come, He can again include all mankind within its blessings. The temporary segregation of a people becomes the means to a permanent unification with all mankind.

In Abraham, accordingly, a new epoch begins in the history of revelation. That part of this revelation which accrues to the patriarchs is indeed accommodated to what went before and absorbs the earlier revelation into itself, but it is also enhanced now and developed further. It is very important, consequently, to understand this new revelation in its own charteristic quality. It is the more important because the revelation to Abraham and hence the religion of Abraham is definitive for that which came to Israel and therefore constituted the essence of the religion of Israel.

In our time many have obstructed the way to a right understanding of the essence of Israel's religion. In the first place they refuse to credit the period of the patriarchs as having any historical value, and regard Abraham, Isaac, Jacob, and the others, as demigods or heroes, such, for instance, as are celebrated in the Iliad of Homer. Next, they conceive of the religion of Israel as having its origin in a base, pagan form of religion, such as animism, fetishism, ancestor worship, polydemonism, or polytheism. And, in the third place, they try to point out that the essence of Israel's religion, as in the time of the prophets it later came to be, particularly in the eighth century before Christ, consisted of an ethical monotheism: that is, the acknowledgment of one God who is an omnipotent but also a just and good being.

This modern conception of the Old Testament is to be regarded as an effort to explain the whole religion of Israel, and that of other peoples, on purely natural bases as a slow and gradual development taking place without benefit of special revelation. However, all Scripture is opposed to such a view and punishes the modern conception by the failure of its effort to understand aright either the origin or the nature of Israel's religion.

It is not by this route that the origin of Israel's religion can be found. It is not true that the prophets come each time again with a new and different godhead. They preach the word always in the name of the same God who is the God of Abraham, Isaac, and Jacob, the God of their fathers, the God of Israel, and whom the people are by the terms of the covenant obliged to serve and to worship. Many who feel the weight of this consideration turn back from the prophets to Moses and regard him as the real founder of the religion of Israel. But Moses, too, did not appear, and could not appear, in the name of a strange, unknown Godhead. In that event he would not have found response among the people. Instead he accommodated himself to the people and to their history, and he summoned them to their exodus from Egypt in the name and at the command of that God who was the Faithful One, who had covenanted with the patriarchs, and who now came to substantiate His promise. Indeed, a serious reflection on the origin of Israel's religion compels us to go along with Scripture to the period of the patriarchs.

We must go back to this period if we want to come to understand the essence and nature of Israel's religion. This essence certainly does not lie in the so-called ethical monotheism. True, the religion of Israel also included this element. It held that God was the one, omnipotent, righteous, and holy being. But the religion of Israel is not definitively characterized by that. This element was rather the assumption than the content of it. The heart and core of that religion was something else. It was this: that God who is one, eternal, righteous, and holy had bound Himself in covenant to be *Israel's* God.

* * * * *

That is the way the Apostle Paul understood it. In Romans 4 (with which Gal. 3:5ff. is to be compared), Paul asks what is the characteristic thing that Abraham received of God. And, by way of appeal to Genesis 15:6, he answers his question. He says that this characteristic thing does not lie in works but in the righteousness of faith, in other words, in the grace of the forgiveness of sins, in the unmerited favor of God, even as David later thought of the forgiveness of sins as constituting the blessedness of the sinner.

In addition the Apostle argues that this great gift of grace was not given Abraham when he was under the circumcision but long before (Gen. 15:6), and that the institution of circumcision which followed fourteen years later (Gen. 17) assumed the righteousness of faith and served as a sign and seal of that. Consequently the forgiveness of sins, and so the whole of salvation, is independent of the law and of its demands. The same holds true of the universal scope of this favor: it is not by the law, but long before the law and in independence from the law, that the promise came to Abraham assuring him that he would be the father of many nations and heir to the world.

The whole argument of the Apostle leans on the history of the Old Testament itself. The thing that stands in the foreground of that history is this: not what Abraham knows about God and does for God, but what God gives to Abraham. First, it is God who seeks Abraham out, and calls him, and leads him to Canaan. Second, it is He who promises that He will be a God to him and to his seed. Third, God promises Abraham that, all expectations to the contrary, he will have a posterity, will become the father of a great nation, and that this nation will have Canaan as its inheritance. Fourth, God says that in his posterity Abraham will be a blessing to all the nations of the earth. And, fifth, God draws up this promise in the pledge of a covenant, seals it with the sign of circumcision, and, after Abraham's trial of faith, confirms it with an oath.[1]

All of these promises together constitute the content of the revelation of God to Abraham. Center and core of them all is the one, great promise: I will be thy God, and the God of thy people. These promises extend through the people and the land of Israel to the Christ, and in Christ to all mankind and to the whole world (Rom. 4:11ff.). Not law, but gospel; not demands, but promise: that is the core of revelation. And, from the human side, the thing that corresponds to that is faith and the conduct or walk of faith (Rom. 4:16-22 and Heb. 11:8-21). For a promise cannot become ours except by faith, and faith expresses itself in righteous conduct (Gen. 17:1). Abraham is the example of believing faith, Isaac of a meek faith, and Jacob that of a fighting faith.

It is in the history of the patriarchs that the nature and the calling of the people of Israel is already described for us. While the nations of the earth are walking in their own ways, and are developing what was given them in general revelation, a creative act of God (Gen. 18:10; Deut. 32:6; and Isa. 51:1-2) called a people into being out of Abraham. Like him this people must live by faith, must acknowledge that it owes the land of its inheritance not to its own strength but to God's grace. And it can achieve a blessed domination over the surrounding peoples only when, like Isaac, it faithfully remembers the promise of the salvation of the Lord, and only when, like Jacob, it militantly abides the fulfillment of that promise. No human calculations or deliberations can promote the fulfillment, any more than human weaknesses and sins can hinder it. For God is He who gives and fulfills the promise. Even while He punishes sin, He makes it minister to the carrying out of His purpose. And Israel, like Jacob, comes to share in that promise and blessing of the Lord only when, refined by suffering, broken in strength, it

---

1. Gen. 12:1-3,7; 13:14-17; 15:1ff. and 17-21; 17:1ff.; 18:10; and 22:17-19.

achieves the victory solely through the struggle of faith and prayer. I will not let Thee go, except Thou bless me (Gen. 32:26 and Hos. 12:4).

* * * * *

This promise *remains* the content of all succeeding revelations of God in the Old Testament. It is elaborated, of course, and developed. And this promise also remains the core and essence of the religion of Israel. True, the conclusion of the Covenant on Sinai and the legalistic dispensation which God instituted then mark the beginning of another epoch. But in order to understand the nature of Israel's religion and the economy of the Old Testament, we must be deeply impressed by the conviction that the promise, previously given to Abraham, was not obliterated by the later dispensation of law.

This again the Apostle Paul expressly teaches us.

In Galatians 3:15ff., Paul compares the promise made to Abraham and to his seed with an agreement or rather with a testament which, once it has been confirmed, no man dare annul. The same holds for the promise of God to Abraham and for all the advantages contained in it. The promises are a free dispensation of God. They were so to speak, deeded by God to Abraham and his seed, and therefore they must sometime by virtue of God's direction be put into the hands of that seed. Not all of the peoples who issued from Abraham according to the flesh are to be reckoned among this favored posterity. His offspring by Hagar and Keturah (Gen. 17:20 and 25:2) are not among them. For Scriptures do not speak of "seeds," that is, of many generations or peoples, but only of a seed, of a generation, which should come forth out of Jacob. And that is the seed, the generation, the people that should be born from the son of the promise, from Isaac, and which should issue in Christ as the seed pre-eminent.

When God deeded His properties of salvation to Abraham and his seed in the promise by way of a testament, this action implied that those properties should sometime belong to Christ, that they should be his ownership and possession, and that they would be given out by Him to the church gathered out of all the world. Consequently that promise, given to Abraham by way of a testament, that is, without dependence upon any human condition, solely by God's sovereign dispensation, could not be annulled by a later supplementary law. If that had happened, God would have annihilated His own promise, His own doing, His own testament, and His own oath.

There are, after all, only two possibilities: we either receive the benefits included in the promise out of the promise or we receive them out of the law, by grace or by merit, through faith or through works. It is certain that Abraham received the righteousness of faith from the promise, even before the circumcision was instituted; that the Israelites in the time of the patriarchs, and in Egypt, for hundreds of years consequently, received that same benefit solely in virtue of the promise, for the law was not yet; and that God gave the promise to Abraham and his seed up to and including Christ, in whom it came to all mankind, and that God therefore gave it as an eternal covenant, confirmed with a precious oath (Gal. 3:17 and Heb. 6:13ff.). If all this be true, then it is impossible that the law, which God gave to Israel at a later date, could have abolished His promise.

* * * * *

If this be so, however, the question becomes the more important: Why did God then give the law to Israel? In other words, what is the meaning and importance of that dispensation of the covenant of grace which began with the law, and what is the nature or essence of the religion of Israel? That question was important in Paul's day, and is no less important in our time.

There were some in the days of the Apostles who looked for the essence of the religion of Israel in the law, and who therefore required that the Gentiles come to Christianity by way of Israel, that is, by way of the circumcision and the maintenance of the law.

And there were others who despised the law, who ascribed it to a lower god, and who considered it as representing a lower religious position. Nomism and anti-nomism were both present at the time, representing diametrically opposite extremes.

In our time the same attitudes are present, though the names given it and the forms it takes be different. Some find the essence of Israel's religion in ethical monism, that is to say, in the acknowledgment that God is a holy God, who demands only that we keep His commandments; these find the essence of Christianity in this same thing, and so the distinction between the two is lost: the enlightened Jew and the enlightened Christian confess the very same religion. Others, however, look down from the heights of the spiritual freedom upon the base, narrow-minded, stuffy, and legalistic Judaism; these entertain no ideal higher than that of emancipating mankind from the hands of the Jew. They trace all evil back to Judaism, and look for all good in the Indo-European race. Semitic and anti-Semitic spirits thus oppose each other, and yet, as extremes, they often meet in one and the same error.

For Paul the problem of the meaning and intention of the law was so important that he returned to the consideration of it again and again in his letters. His solution to the problem is as follows.

First, the law is something that was added to the promise, something that came later and was not connected with it originally. Many years passed after the promise before the law was proclaimed. And when it did come, it was of a temporary and transient character. Although the promise, or the covenant of grace, is eternal, the law lasted only up to the time when the true seed of Abraham, namely, the Christ, should appear, in whom the promise eventuated, and who had to receive the content of the promise and distribute it (Rom. 5:20 and Gal. 3:17-19).

Second, this temporary and transient character of the law comes to expression already in its origin. True, the law has its origin in God, but He did not give it directly and immediately to the people and to each member of that people. All kinds of mediating devices were present. From God's side, the law was given by means of angels, amid thunder and lightning, in a dark cloud, with the voice of a trumpet exceeding loud.[2] And from the side of the people, who were full of fear and who had to remain standing at the foot of the mountain, Moses was called up to serve as mediator, to speak with God, and to receive the law.[3] It is not so for the promise. The promise was not conveyed by angels, but was given us by the very Son of God. And, as for our side, we designated no one to serve as mediator for us, to accept the law for us. In Christ all believers personally come to share in that promise (John 1:17 and Gal. 3:22, 26).

Third, inasmuch as it comes from God, the law is holy, and righteous, and good, and spiritual; it is in no sense the occasion or cause of sin, even though sin makes the law its occasion. As a matter of fact, the law is in itself not without energy and strength, for it is a law unto life; it is without this energy and strength only in man because of man's sinful flesh. But all this is not to gainsay that the law differs from the promise not merely in degree but also in kind. True, it is not opposed to the promise, nor in conflict with it, but it is not of the promise and of the faith. Hence it cannot be that the law was given to disannul the promise. Different from the promise in nature, the law also has a different purpose.[4]

Fourth, that special purpose, which is proper to the law, and for which God gave the law, has a two-fold character. In the first place, it

---

2. Ex. 19:16-18; Heb. 12:18; Acts 7:38,53; and Gal. 3:19.
3. Ex. 19:21ff. and 20:19; Deut. 5:22-27 and 18:16; Heb. 12:19; and Gal. 3:19-20.
4. Rom. 7:7-14; 8:3; and Gal. 3:17, 21.

was added to the promise because of the transgressions (Gal. 3:19), that is, to make the transgression more severe. True, there was sin before the giving of the law also (Rom. 15:12-13). But that sin was different; it was not "transgression" in the sense that Paul speaks of it in distinction from sin in general. As in Adam, however, who received a command on the keeping of which the issue of life or death depended (Rom. 5:12-14), so also in Israel which was to inherit life or death in the way of obedience or disobedience, sin takes on a different character.

This sin, being sin against a law to which the issue of life or death was attached, became a "transgression." It took on the character of a broken covenant, a placing oneself outside of and over against the peculiar relationship which God had established in His covenant of works with Adam and in His Sinaitic covenant with Israel. Where there is no such law, sin remains sin, it is true, but there is no "transgression" proper (Rom. 4:15). The sins of the Gentiles are certainly sins, but they are not a breaking of the covenant as they are for Israel; and being without such a law as God gave to Israel, the Gentiles are condemned also without that law (Rom. 2:12).

In Israel sins could become transgressions again precisely because Israel received a law from God which was accompanied by the promise of life and the threat of death. It was the law, therefore, which, so to speak, made this possible. To this extent, consequently, Paul can say that the Sinaitic law, although it is holy and absolutely not the cause of sin, nevertheless has been added to the promise to increase the "transgressions," that it is the strength of sin and awakens desire, that sin takes occasion by the commandment to become transgression, that without such a law, sin is asleep and dead, and that the law makes the offence to abound — offense, that is, not in the sense of sin in general, but in the sense of those special sins which are of the nature of a misstep, fall, or breach of covenant.[5] But, inasmuch as the law carries all this in its wake, it necessarily also arouses wrath, that is, it threatens Divine punishment, pronounces judgment upon all men and upon all their deeds, justifies none but places all under the curse, subjecting all to the wrath of God.[6] Hence, if in the Old Testament there are people who have received the forgiveness of sins and eternal life, they owe that not to the law but to the promise.

However, in connection with this negative purpose, the increase of transgressions and the aggravation of judgment, the law also takes on a positive purpose. For, precisely by giving sin the character of transgression, of covenant breaking, of faithlessness, precisely by making all

5. Gal. 3:19; Rom. 5:13, 20; 7:8; and 1 Cor. 15:56.
6. Rom. 3:19-20; 4:15; Gal. 3:10-11,12.

sin, also the secret desire of the heart, to appear as sin, that is, as being
in conflict with the law of God, and therefore deserving of His wrath
and the curse of death (Rom. 3:20; 7:7; and 1 Cor. 15:56) — precisely
by so doing the law makes clear the necessity of the promise, and proves,
that if the justification of the sinner is to be possible, some other righteousness than that based on the law and the works of the law must be
made available (Gal. 3:11). So far from being opposed to the promise,
therefore, the law serves precisely as the means in God's hand to bring
the promise constantly nearer to its fulfillment. The law put Israel under restrictions, as a prisoner is put under restraint and denied the freedom of movement. Like a "pedagogue" the law took Israel by the hand,
accompanied her always and everywhere, and never for a moment left
her out of its sight. As a guardian and supporter, the law maintained
a strict watch over Israel in order that Israel might learn to know and
to love the promise in its necessity and its glory. Without the law, so
to speak, the promise and its fulfillment would have come to nothing.
Then Israel would quickly have fallen back into paganism, and would
have lost both her revelation of God with its promise and her own religion and her place among the nations. But now the law has fenced
Israel in, segregated her, maintained her in isolation, guarded her
against dissolution, and has thus created an area and defined a sphere
in which God could preserve His promise purely, give it wider scope,
develop it, increase it, and bring it always closer to its fulfillment. The
law was serviceable to the fulfillment of the promise. It placed everybody under the wrath of God and under the sentence of death, it comprehended everybody within the pale of sin, in order that the promise,
given to Abraham and fulfilled in Christ, should be given to all believers,
and that these all should attain to the inheritance as children (Gal. 3:21
and 4:7).

*   *   *   *   *

When we take this vantage point of the Apostle Paul, we get a de-
lightfully illuminating view of the revelation of God in the Old Testament, of the religion of Israel, of the significance of the law, of history
and prophecy, of the psalms and the wisdom books.

With the coming of Moses a really new period enters into the revelation of God and the history of Israel. But just as the revelation given
to Abraham does not break off the earlier announcements of God, but
rather absorbs and continues them, so the dispensation of God's grace
under the law continues the dispensation of God's grace *before* the law.
The law, which was added to the promise, did not render the promise
of no effect or obliterate it, but rather took the promise up into itself in

order to be of service to the development and fulfillment of it. The promise is the main thing; the law is subordinate. The first is the goal; the second is the means. It is not in the law, but in the promise, that the core of the Revelation of God and the heart of Israel's religion lies. And because the promise is a promise of God, it is not a hollow sound but a word full of power, which is the expression of a will bent on doing all that pleases God (Ps. 33:9 and Isa. 55:11). Therefore this promise is the propelling force of Israel's history until it gets its fulfillment in Christ.

Just as, according to Isaiah 29:22, Abraham is redeemed from the land of the Chaldees by the calling of God, and after that by God's free dispensation receives the promise of the covenant, so Israel was first led of the Lord to Egypt and placed in bondage to the Pharaohs, in order thereafter to be redeemed from this misery and as a people to be taken up into the covenant of God at Mount Sinai. These three events, the bondage in Egypt, the emancipation from this bondage by God's strong hand and outstretched arm, and the conclusion of the covenant at Sinai, are the foundation of Israel's history and the pillars on which its religious and ethical life rest. They are events which live on in the memory from generation to generation, are constantly referred to in the histories, the psalmody, and the prophecy, and they cannot, even by the most radical criticism, be denied their historical reality.

Moreover these significant events afford the proof that the law was not given, and could not have been given, to annul the promise. On the contrary, when God appears to Moses in the burning bush, calling him to his office, it is not as a strange, unknown God that He makes his appearance, but as the God of Abraham, the God of Isaac, and the God of Jacob, a God who has seen the oppression of His people, and heard their cry, and who, because He is Jehovah, meaning the Faithful One, now condescends to fulfill His promise and to rescue His people from the misery of bondage (Ex. 3:6ff.). Israel is accordingly not to become the people of God for the first time at Horeb, nor to be accepted as His people on the basis of the law. Israel is His people already and by virtue of the promise, and it is by virtue of that same promise that Israel is now to be redeemed out of its misery. Misery and redemption precede the law-giving at Sinai. And just as Abraham, redeemed by his calling, and having received the promise of God in childlike faith, is in terms of that promise bound to a holy walk before the face of God (Gen. 17:1), just so Israel, having been freed from the bondage of Israel through God's strong arm, is admonished and bound by God at Sinai to a new obedience. The law which came to the people by way of Moses was a law of gratitude; it came in the wake of the redemption, and assumed and rested in the promise. In His strength God guided His people to the lovely habitation of His glory (Ex. 15:13). He bore his people up on the wings of eagles, bringing them to Himself (Ex. 19:4 and Deut. 32:11-12). Hence, too, the law is introduced with the preamble: I am the Lord thy God which have brought thee out of the land of Egypt, out of the house of bondage (Ex. 20:2 and Deut. 5:6).

But this covenant relationship now requires a more specific order of obedience.

In the patriarchal period, when only a few families shared in the blessing of the promise to Abraham, there was no need for a more specific regulation; and in Egypt, when the people sighed in bondage, there was no opportunity for it. But now Israel was redeemed; it became a free and independent people living in its own land. If in these new circumstances also it was to remain a people, a nation, of God, the covenant of grace would have to take on the form of a national covenant, and the promise, in order to maintain itself and further develop itself, would have to make use of the assistance of the law.

This was the more necessary because Israel — so Paul represents it — was still a child. It had gone through a hard school in Egypt, and had by its experience of bondage received a deep sense of dependency, a deep awareness of the need for help and support. But Israel was not immediately ready for independence. All of the wisdom and meekness of Moses was required (Num. 12:3) to provide the indispensable leadership for such a people, both at the exodus from Egypt and in the wilderness. Again and again this Israel is called a stiff-necked people because it will not bow to the commandment of God (Ex. 32:9; 33:3; 34:9; Deut. 9:6, and the like). In the wilderness and also later on in Canaan, Israel constantly exhibits the nature of a child. This people was not a sensible and rational people; it lacked the self-awareness, the probing spirit, the philosophical mind, the power of abstract thought. And all the more, consequently, it was a people of feeling and emotion.

Consequently Israel was on the one hand very receptive to all kinds of impressions, susceptible to a world of feelings, and therefore uncommonly well qualified for the influence of earthly and heavenly powers; in this respect they were formed by God Himself to be the receiver and bearer of His revelation. This side of the Israelitish character confronts us in the Scriptures in all those men and women of God, who, honored with the call of the Lord, have only one humble and childlike response: Here am I, speak Lord, for Thy servant, Thy handmaid, heareth — be it done unto me according to Thy word! They accept the word of the Lord, and they keep it and preserve it in their heart. But, on the other hand, Israel was, as we are told in Exodus 32:8, disposed to "turn aside quickly from the way," inclined to stray, unsteadfast, capricious, temperamental, wayward, easily deflected by some person or incident, passionate, hating with a burning hatred, and loving with a deep, tender, and more than motherly love; now grieving unto death and the next moment leaping up to heaven for joy; never having the Occidental calm but always aflame with an Oriental passion; fond of peppery foods such as garlic and onion (Num. 11:5), of lentils (Gen. 25:34) and savoury meat (Gen. 27:14ff.), and enamored of brilliant colors, gorgeous clothes, perfumes, and precious stones (Josh. 7:21 and Isa. 3:18ff.), and of all that sparkles and beams in the sun. Da Costa and Heine are both sons of Israel.

Such a people had to be placed under the guardianship and discipline of the law if it was to carry out its calling by means of the promise to be a blessing to all the generations of the earth. And the nature of the law corresponds to this need.

In the first place, the law does not come out of the promise or out of the faith, but was added to the promise, and serves, not to annul the promise but to pave the way for its fulfillment. In modern times there are many who try to reverse the roles of law and promise. They speak not of the law and the prophets, but of the prophets and law, and they propound the view that the laws in the books of Moses did not come up until centuries after Moses and to a considerable extent even after the Exile. In this view one can recognize so much of good that it was indeed not the law that was the main thing in God's revelation and in the religion of Israel. The promise preceded it, held the highest place, and the law was its means. Hence it is quite possible that the law of Moses was later reviewed by secondary or tertiary editors, and that it was in this way enriched by means of interpolations or addenda brought on by the circumstances of the time. For the law in its totality had a temporal and transient character. Already in the Book of Deuteronomy Moses had modified various points. Nevertheless, the view suggested above, that prophecy preceded the law, runs counter to the facts, to the nature of the law, to the nature and function of prophecy, and also to sound reasoning. There certainly can be no dispute about the fact that Israel had its temple, priests, sacrifices, and the like, long before the eighth century B. C., and that for this purpose quite as much as for social and political life, laws and regulations were necessary. A religion without a *cultus* and without ritual and regulation is unthinkable anywhere, particularly in antiquity and in Israel. Besides, the objection that there is no room for such a written law, with so rich a content, as is recorded from Exodus to Deuteronomy, in the time of Moses, loses all its force since the discovery of the law of Hammurabi, a man who lived 2,250 years before Christ and who reigned over Babel for fifty-five years.

In the second place, the content of the law is in agreement with the purpose for which God gave it. In order to determine its worth, we must not compare it with the laws that are in force in Christian states today. For, even though the Mosaic law, especially in its principles, continues significant even now, we know that God Himself intended it as a temporary code, and that in the fulness of time, when it had reached its fulfillment, it was abandoned because of its weakness and uselessness.

In the same way, the comparison of the law of Israel with that of ancient peoples, of Babel, for instance, may not be the criterion of judgment. Such a comparison has its uses, of course, calls our attention to all kinds of points of similarity and difference, and so can help us to understand the Mosaic law somewhat better in some instances. But Israel was a peculiar people, set apart by God, and had its own destiny to carry out, namely, to be the bearer of the promise. Therefore Israel had to live its own kind of life also with a view to this purpose.

Looking at the law of the Lord given to Israel from this point of view, we distinguish the following characteristic features:

First: It is a law which is religious through and through. Not only in some of its parts, as in that which regulates the public worship, for instance, but in its entirety, that is, in its ethical, civic, social, and political prescriptions, it is religious also. Above the whole law are the words: I am the Lord thy God who have lead thee out of the house of bondage. The law is not based on an abstract monotheism, but upon an historical relationship between God and His people, a relationship created by God Himself. It is a covenantal law and it regulates the life of Israel as Israel must live it according to the requirements of the promise. He is the lawgiver in all of the commandments, and for His sake all of them must be kept. The whole law is permeated by the thought: Jehovah first loved you, sought you out, redeemed you, took you up into His covenant; hence you must love the Lord with all your heart, and with all your soul, and with all your strength (Deut. 6:5 and 10:12). This is the first and great commandment (Matt. 22:37 and 38).

Second: It is a law which is moral through and through. Three distinguishable parts are usually discovered in it: the moral, the civic, and the ceremonial laws. This is a good classification. But in making these distinctions we must not forget that the whole law is inspired and sustained by moral principles. The application of those moral principles to particular instances often differs from the application we should make in our time. Jesus Himself said that Moses permitted giving a writing of divorcement to a married woman because of the hardness of their hearts (Matt. 19:8). But the spirit which permeates the Mosaic law is the spirit of love. Thou shalt love thy neighbor as thyself (Lev. 19:18). That is the second commandment, like unto the first (Matt. 22:39), and therein the whole law is fulfilled.[7] This love proves to be such a mercy to the weak and oppressed, to the poor, the strangers, the widows, the orphans, to men-servants and maid-servants, to the deaf, the blind, the aged, and the like, as no other law of antiquity knows it. It has been rightly said that Israel's moral code was written from the viewpoint of the oppressed. Israel never forgot that it had been a stranger and a servant in Egypt.

Third: The law of Israel is a holy law, and this characteristic is by no means limited to that part of it which specifically bears the name of the law of holiness (Lev. 17-26). Again there is no law of which memory remains from antiquity which conceives of sin so deeply and profoundly as *sin*. This sin is designated by various names. It is called offence, guilt, falling away, rebellion, and it is always thought of as in the last analysis being committed against God, against the God of the covenant. Hence sin always has the character of "transgression," of covenant-breaking. There is, however, forgiveness for all those sins, but not in the sense that Israel is to achieve this forgiveness by its good works or by its sacrifices. For the forgiveness comes by the promise; it is a benefaction, not of the law, but of the gospel; it is not earned by sacrifices, but is received in childlike humility through faith.[8]

But these same texts, which declare so powerfully the free grace of God, are remarkable for immediately adding the judgment that God will in no way hold the guilty guiltless, that he will visit the iniquity of the fathers upon the children up to the third and fourth generation. The one does not conflict with the other. Precisely because Jehovah forgives the sins of His people out of sheer grace by way of the promise, He desires that this people, having received so great a good through grace, shall also walk in the way of that covenant. And if Israel does not do so, God, according to the nature of the sin committed, takes one of three courses. In some instances the law in its sacrifices opens up the possibility of reconciliation again. If so the offence has no further civic consequences. In other instances, the law lays down one or another civic penalty, sometimes even, though comparatively rarely, the penalty of death. And in a far greater number of instances God retains the visitation for Himself and then comes to the people with His judgments, pestilences, exile, and the like. And these three measures which God maintains over against His people in the event of transgression, do not annul

---

7. Rom. 13:8; Gal. 5:14; and 1 Tim. 1:5.
8. Ex. 33:19; 34:6,7,9; and Num. 14:18-20.

the promise and do not achieve it, but are solely the means by which God fulfills His promise to His people, and vouchsafes his faithfulness, even in days of apostasy and offense.

Of all the generations of the earth, the Lord has known Israel alone; *therefore* He punishes it for all its iniquities.

Fourth: Finally, the Mosaic law is also a law of liberty. It both assumes and grants a large measure of freedom. This becomes apparent immediately from the remarkable fact that the people, on its part, voluntarily acquiesces in the covenant of God and voluntarily takes His law upon itself. God does not impose Himself and His covenant upon His people, but even invites them to a voluntary acquiescence.[9] Besides, the law does not interfere with existing rights and relations, but assumes and acknowledges those. Before the lawgiving on Sinai, after all, Israel had organized itself more or less. It was, for instance, genealogically subdivided into households, families (groups of households), generations, and tribes, and was therefore patriarchally organized. Each of these four subdivisions of the people had its own head or representative. And all of these people's representatives, called elders or princes, together constituted the assembly of Israel (Josh. 7:14). Some assemblies of these elders had already taken place in Egypt (Ex. 4:29 and 3:16ff.), and they were gathered frequently after the exodus to hear the words of the Lord (Ex. 19:7), to pass on proposals presented by Moses (Deut. 1:22-23), or themselves to present propositions to Moses (Deut. 1:22-23). In addition to these assemblies of elders, the people of Israel had two further types of officials: first, the "officers" who regulated affairs pertaining to the civic order, and who were active already in Egypt;[10] and, second, the "judges," whom Moses introduced to assist him in matters of law.[11] Later these judges, like the officers, had to be designated in all cities by the choice of the elders.

In this organization of the people, the household constituted the point of departure and the basis. Even today the household stands in a position of high honor among the Jews. And because the household occupied so important a place in Israel, the wife too was more honored than among any other ancient people. The question which is determinative in this matter — as has rightly been observed — is whether the man was regarded primarily in Israel as a member of the family, be it husband, son or brother, or primarily as citizen or warrior. The last was true for Greece and Rome, and the result was that woman was pushed back and was regarded as inferior. But in Israel the man was regarded first of all as

---

9. Ex. 19:8; 24:3,7; Deut. 5:27; and Josh. 24:15-25.
10. Ex. 5:6,10,14,19; Num. 11:16; Deut. 1:15; 16:18, and Josh. 23:2.
11. Ex. 18:21,23; and Deut. 1:13ff.

a member of the family, and his task was first of all to care for the family. As such he did not stand over against or high above the wife, but beside her. She, together with him laid claim to the respect and love of the children (Ex. 20:2) and she was in her own right deserving of the praise of her husband (Prov. 12:4 and 31:10ff.).

*   *   *   *   *

This entire patriarchal-aristocratic form of government existed in Israel even before it was acknowledged and confirmed by the law. A good many of the laws have reference to marriage and serve to maintain the holiness of this state of life and to protect the household. Other regulations protect the patriarchal form of government from the order of the priesthood and from the kingship. The elders, the officers, and the judges are distinguished from the priests and Levites. It was only in the highest court of justice that the priests also had a seat,[12] inasmuch as a good explanation of the law — a task assigned to the priests[13] — was very important for the weighty decisions taken at that level.

In the whole of its political order Israel was at opposite poles from a hierarchy. Just so, too, there was no room for despotism after the law. When Israel was later to desire a king from God, and to receive one (1 Sam. 8:7), that king was not to be a king after the fashion of the kings of the other peoples; he was to be bound by God's law, and be the executive of His will (Deut. 17:14-20). For in the final analysis God was the King, even as He was the Law-Giver and the Judge of Israel.[14] This came to expression in the fact that as a general rule He pronounced sentence by means of the judges, who had to be strictly impartial in their judgments, were not to be respecters of persons, and had to make their judgments solely according to the norm of the law. It came to expression further in the fact that in special cases He made His will known by means of the lot, of the urim and thummim, and through the prophets. And it came to expression most strongly of all in the fact that in the case of many transgressions He retained the meting out of punishment for Himself. A great many of the prescriptions of the law were not rules in the sense that each of them was assigned a particular penalty in the event of violation, but simply strong admonishments and warnings. They were directed at the conscience and therefore left a high degree of freedom to Israel. The types of punishment, too,

---

12. Deut. 17:8-13; 19:17 and 18.
13. Lev. 10:8-11; Ezek. 7:26; 44:23; and Jer. 18:18.
14. Ex. 15:18; 19:6; Num. 23:21; Deut. 33:5; Judges 8:22ff.; 1 Sam. 8:7; Isa. 33:22; Ps. 44:5; 68:25, and the like.

were limited, consisting mainly of beatings, and in the case of weighty violations (blasphemy, idolatry, sorcery, cursing of parents, murder, and adultery) of death by stoning. There was no mention at all of inquisition, the rack, detention, exile, forfeiture of property, burning at the stake, death by gallows, and the like. If Israel walked in the way of the covenant, the people would receive rich blessings from the Lord; but if it did not obey His voice, it would be visited by His curse and receive all kinds of calamity (Deut. 28:29).

From these characteristic features of the law the *purpose* for which God gave it to Israel becomes evident. The Lord defines this purpose Himself when, at the conclusion of the covenant at Sinai, He has Moses tell the people of Israel that, if they hear His voice and keep His covenant, they among all peoples will be His own, a kingdom of priests and a holy nation (Ex. 19:5, 6). To be the nation chosen by God from all the peoples of the earth, Israel must establish itself in the way of the covenant. For Israel was not chosen for its merits or desert, but according to God's sovereign love and His oath to the fathers (Deut. 7:6-8). And Israel did not receive this gracious privilege in order to spurn the nations and exalt itself high above them, but rather to be a kingdom of priests who have a priestly task to carry out towards the nations, to bring them the knowledge of the service of God, and only in this way to reign over the nations. This calling Israel can fulfill and will carry out only if it is itself a holy nation, if as a people it consecrates itself entirely to the Lord, hears His voice, and walks in His covenant.

This holiness to which Israel is called does not yet have the full, deep sense which it receives in the New Testament. It comprehends not only the moral, but, as becomes especially clear from the law of holiness in Leviticus 17:26, it includes also the ceremonial holiness. What we must observe, however, is that the moral and the ceremonial parts of the law do not stand over against each other. They are rather two sides of one and the same matter. Israel is a holy people when, both internally and externally, in faith and conduct, it lives in accordance with all the laws of moral, social, and ceremonial import given to the people at Sinai. And if this people — as the Lord knew — failed in its faithfulness to its calling, and should throughout its history again and again become guilty of disobedience and falling away, the Lord would certainly visit heavier punishment upon it than upon any other people of the world. Only, at the end of the visitation, the Lord would again return to his people and have compassion upon them, would circumcise their hearts and the heart of their children, in order that they might love the Lord their God with all their heart and all their soul (Deut. 4:29-31 and 30:1ff.). He cannot leave His people to their own ways, for He must be concerned about His own name and honor over against the enemies (Deut. 32:26ff.). Despite Israel's unfaithfulness, and through it, the Lord must establish His own faithfulness, the integrity of His word, the unchangeableness of His counsel, and the steadfastness of His covenant. He must demonstrate that He is God and that there is no other God beside Him (Deut. 32:39). Thus the law ends in the promise, just as it began there. It returns to its point of departure.

* * * * *

It is from the vantage point, then, of the covenant that Scripture views the whole history of Israel. The purpose of Scripture in the historical books of the Old Testament is not to present an exhaustive and unified account of all the fortunes of the people of Israel, nor to trace out the causal connection between all the events. What Scripture describes in those books instead is the progress of the kingdom of God. Whatever has little or no relevance to that is but briefly mentioned or ignored altogther. And, correspondingly, it lingers long on whatever is of significance to that kingdom. In its history of Israel Scripture wants to teach us who and what God is for His people. It is with some propriety, therefore, that the historical writings concerning Israel in Scripture have been called the diary or day-book of Jehovah. As it were, the Lord makes an entry each day to record what His experiences and His cares for Israel have been.

In the early period, when the people still lived under the impact of the mighty works of God, they remained faithful to His law. By those deeds Jehovah had so manifestly proved Himself to be the one true God. (Ex. 6:6 and 18:18) that the people thought of no other gods. When they heard the word of the Lord from the mouth of Moses they all responded as with one voice: All that the Lord has spoken, we will do.[15] Later also, when Israel had received Canaan as its inheritance and was confronted by the hoary Joshua with the choice of whom it would serve, Israel was almost overbearing in its answer: God forbid that we should forsake the Lord, to serve other gods (Josh. 24:16 and Judges 2:7).

But when Joshua and the eldest of the people, they who had witnessed God's mighty deeds, had died, and another generation arose that knew not the Lord nor His work which he had done for Israel, the people fell away from the Lord, the God of their fathers, who had led them out of Egypt, and they followed after other gods, the gods of the surrounding nations (Judges 2:6-13). True, Israel was not productive in idolatry. It did not create its own false religion, but instead either took over the

---

15. Ex. 19:8; 24:3,7; and Deut. 5:27.

gods of the heathen, or proceeded to serve the Lord in the form of images such as the heathen used. In Egypt and in the wilderness the people fell into the Egyptian worship of idols;[16] later, in Palestine, they became guilty of worshipping the Canaanite, Phoenician (Baal, Ashera, Astarte), and Assyrian (fire- and star-) gods.[17] Continually Israel violated the first and second commandments, and in so doing violated the foundations of the covenant.

As early as the days of the judges, those heroes of the people of the law, the history of Israel was a matter of apostasy, punishment, and consequent fear, on the one hand, and of rescue and blessing on the other (Judges 2:11-23). It was a period of confusion, during which the various tribes lost the vision of the national cause, each engaging in its own politics, and every man doing what was right in his own eyes (Judges 17:6 and 21:25). True, an end was put to that state of affairs by Samuel and by the institution of the kingship. But after Solomon the national unity was totally broken, and ten tribes separated themselves from the royal house of David. Jeroboam made this political division a religious one also by setting up a special shrine at Dan, introducing the worship of images, and by abolishing the legitimate priesthood. Thus he became the king who "caused Israel to sin." The history of the kingdom of Ephraim during two and a half centuries became the history of progressive falling away from Jehovah. Prophecy raised its voice in vain, and the culmination was the captivity of the ten tribes. Judah, it is true, was highly privileged above Israel in that it was continuously governed by the royal house of David, and in that it remained in possession of the authorized sanctuary and the legitimate priesthood. All the same, in this realm too, despite the many reformations owing to pious kings, the apostasy and godlessness finally became so great that judgment had to come. Approximately 140 years after the kingdom of Israel, Judah also lost its independent existence.

But this unbroken apostasy of the people of Israel should not blind us to the fact that God throughout the centuries preserved a remnant among them according to the election of His grace. There was a core in Israel which remained true to the covenant of Jehovah. Even in the dark days of Elijah there were seven thousand that had not bowed the knee to Baal. These were the pious, the righteous, the faithful, the destitute, the poor, or however else they may be designated in the Psalms, and they continued putting their confidence in the God of Jacob, and did not deal falsely with His covenant. They yearned for God as the hart longs after the springing brooks; they preferred His temple to any

---

16. Ex. 16:28; Josh. 24:14; and Ezek. 20:7,13.
17. Judges 10:6; 2 Kings 21:3,5,7; 23:5-15; Jer. 7:24-31; Ezek. 20:21 and 22:3.

other dwelling; they pondered His law and clung to His promises. To them the law was no burden but a delight; they rejoiced in it all day. They repeated the words of Moses and said that the keeping of this law would prove to be wisdom and understanding in the eyes of the nations. For when the people heard the ordinances of the law, they were to cry out: Surely this great nation is a wise and understanding people. For what nation is there so great, that hath statutes and judgments so righteous as all this law, which I set before you this day (Deut. 4:6-8).

As the times became more burdensome, this remnant clung the more firmly to the promise. God would not abandon the work of His hands. For the sake of His name and His fame He could not break the covenant which He had in sovereign favor concluded with the fathers. And out of their circle God called out those men who as prophets, psalmists, and sages declared the word of God and unfolded the meaning of the promise in ever clearer accounts. Out of the depths of their calamity, they raise their heads aloft. By the light of the Spirit of the Lord they see into the future, and they prophesy of the new day, the day of David's Son and Lord, of the stem of Jesse, of Immanuel, the Branch of righteousness, the Servant of the Lord, the Angel of the Covenant, of the new covenant and of the out-pouring of the Holy Spirit. The Old Testament begins, after the fall, with the promise of the seed of the woman (Gen. 3:15), and it ends with the announcement of the coming of the Angel of the Covenant (Mal. 3:1).

* * * * *

After the Captivity, too, there remained such a remnant in Israel (Mal. 3:16). By that Captivity, as a matter of fact, the people as a people were purged, were permanently deflected from idolatry and the worship of images, and were placed under the firm discipline of the law by Ezra and Nehemiah. This state of affairs brought new dangers in its wake. There developed a Scriptural scholasticism which peered itself blind in scrutiny of the letter of the law and had no eye at all for the essence and spirit of the old covenant. Sects sprang up, such as those of the Pharisees, the Sadducees, and the Essenes, who by an arbitrary treatment of the divine revelation substituted a fleshly for a spiritual Israel. Nevertheless, also in the four hundred years which elapsed between Malachi and John the Baptist, God's leading of His people went on. After the Exile Israel never again enjoyed a full-fledged political independence. It passed from one might to another and became successively subject to Persia and Media, to Macedonia and Egypt, to Syria and to Rome. It was a servant in its own land (Neh. 9:36-37).

But this political subjection worked some good. Israel began more and more to reflect on its own character and calling, it took pride again in its spiritual possession of the divine revelation, thought of this as its peculiar privilege, and it gave the greatest possible care to the collection and preservation of that revelation. Further, this consciousness of its spiritual privileges became so real to Israel that not only was its character formed by it, but it was also enabled by it to maintain its national independence under heavy persecution. Israel has suffered and been oppressed as no other people of the world.

Both in Palestine and outside it, Israel remained itself. In its Old Testament it had a treasure richer than all the wisdom of the Gentiles. It formed a cosmopolitan community having Jerusalem as its capital. In its synagogues it offered the idolatrous nations the spectacle of a religion without an image or altar, without sacrifice and priesthood. It preached everywhere the oneness and integrity of Israel's God, and it carried in its bosom the ineradicable hope of a glorious future which would also be a blessing to the nations. Thus it paved the way for Christendom among the heathen peoples. And inside itself, by God's grace, those many faithful were preserved, who, like Simeon and Anna, and so many others, awaited the redemption of Israel in quiet expectation. Mary, the mother of the Lord, is the most glorious example of these saints. In her Israel achieves her destiny: that is, to receive the highest revelation of God in childlike faith, and to keep it. Behold the handmaid of the Lord: be it unto me according to thy word! (Luke 1:38).

* * * * *

Thus the whole revelation of the Old Testament converges upon Christ, not upon a new law, or doctrine, or institution, but upon the person of Christ. A person is the completed revelation of God; the Son of Man is the own and only-begotten Son of God. The relationship of the Old and New Testament is not like that of law and gospel. It is rather that of promise and fulfillment (Acts 13:12 and Rom. 1:2), of shadow and body (Col. 2:17), of image and reality (Heb. 10:1), of shaken and unshaken things (Heb. 12:27), of bondage and freedom (Rom. 8:15 and Gal. 4). And since Christ was the real content of the Old Testament revelation (John 5:39; 1 Peter 1:11; and Rev. 19:10), He is in the dispensation of the new covenant also its capstone and crown. He is the fulfillment of the law, of all righteousness (Matt. 3:15 and 5:17), of all promises, which in Him are yea and amen (2 Cor. 1:20), of the new covenant which is now established in His blood (Matt. 26:28). The people of Israel itself, with all its history, its offices and institutions, its temple and its altar, its sacrifices and ceremonies, its prophecy, psalmody, and wisdom teaching, achieves its goal and purpose in Him. Christ is the fulfillment of all that, first of all in His person and appearance, then in His words and works, in His birth and life, in His death and resurrection, in His ascension and sitting at the right hand of God.

If, then, He has appeared, and has finished His work, the revelation of God cannot be amplified or increased. It can only be clarified by the apostolic witness, and be preached to all nations. Since the revelation is complete, the time is now come in which its content is made the property of mankind. Whereas in the Old Testament everything led up to Christ, in the New Testament everything is derived from Him. Christ is the turning point of times. The promise, made to Abraham, now comes to all nations. The Jerusalem which was below gives way to the Jerusalem which is above and is the mother of us all (Gal. 4:26). Israel is supplanted by the church out of all tongues and peoples. This is the dispensation of the fulness of times, in which the middle wall of partition is broken down, in which Jew and Gentile is made a new man, and in which all is gathered together under one head, namely, Christ (Eph. 1:10 and 2:14-15).

And this dispensation continues until the fulness of the Gentiles is come and Israel is saved. When Christ has gathered His church, prepared His bride, accomplished His kingdom, He will give it to the Father in order that God may be all in all (1 Cor. 15:28). I will be thy God, and ye shall be my people: that was the content of the promise. This promise is brought to its perfect fulfillment in the new Jerusalem in Christ, through Him who was and who is and who is to come (Rev. 21:3).

VII

The Holy Scriptures

Our knowledge of revelation, both the general and the special, comes to us from the Holy Scriptures.

It is important to understand the relationship between these two: revelation and Scripture. On the one hand, there is an important difference between them. Revelation, for instance, preceded the recording of it by a long way in many instances. Thus, although there certainly was revelation before Moses, there was no Scripture. Moreover, such revelation often contained much more than was later recorded in writing. The books of the prophets, for example of such a prophet as Amos, are often but a short summary of what they spoke to their contemporaries by word of mouth. Many prophets of the Old Testament and many apostles of the New Testament — and they were all channels of special revelation — left no written record behind. And we are even expressly told of Jesus that He did many other signs, so numerous that if every one should be written the world itself could not contain the books (John 20:30; 21:25). And, conversely, God may have revealed something to His prophets and apostles as they wrote which they did not know before the time of writing, and could not therefore have preached to others beforehand. Such is, for instance, at least for a part, true of the revelation which John received on Patmos concerning the future.

Scripture is therefore not the revelation itself, but the description, the record, from which the revelation can be known. However, when one calls Scripture the record of revelation, he must be on guard against another error. After all, there are those who not only distinguish between revelation and Scripture, but also separate and segregate the two. These acknowledge that God was active in a special way in the revelation which precedes the Scripture; but for the rest they hold that the recording of the revelation was entirely left up to the persons writing it, and that this took place quite outside the pale of God's special providence. Scripture according to this view remains a record of revelation, but an incidental and defective one. The result is that we must at the cost of great difficulty probe the Scriptures to see which parts of them do, and which do not, belong to special revelation. On this basis a big distinction is made between the Word of God and the Holy Scriptures. It is a point of view which leads to the expression that the Holy Scripture *is* not the Word of God but that the Word of God is *contained* in the Holy Scripture.

Such a view of the matter is in itself very unlikely. For, in addition to interpreting the relationship between word and Scripture very mechanically, it also forgets the fact that when God wanted to give a special revelation, which, in the seed of Abraham, was appointed for all mankind in Christ, He also had to take special steps to preserve it in its pure state and to make that revelation generally available. The written word differs from the spoken in these respects that it does not die upon the air but lives on; it is not, like oral traditions, subject to falsification; and that it is not limited in scope to the few people who hear it, but is the kind of thing, rather, which can spread out to all peoples and to all lands. Writing makes permanent the spoken word, protects it against falsification, and disseminates it far and wide.

However, we do not need to linger longer on this human argumentation. The view that special revelation is of God but that Scripture came into being apart from His special care is directly against the testimony of Scripture itself. It repeatedly and emphatically declares that as *Scripture* also it is the Word of God. True, Scripture is to be distinguished from the revelation that precedes it, but it is not to be separated from that revelation. Scripture is not a human, incidental, arbitrary, and defective supplement to revelation but is itself a component part of revelation. In fact, Scripture is the rounding out and the fulfillment, the cornerstone and the capstone of revelation.

* * * * *

In order to feel the force of this, one must note the following clear self-attestations in Scripture.

First, God frequently charges His prophets not merely to proclaim the revelation by word of mouth, but to set it down in writing also. In Exodus 17:14 Moses receives the command from the Lord to write the account of the struggle and victory against Amalek — a battle which was of tremendous importance for Israel — as a memorial into the book of the redemptive deeds of God. In Exodus 24:3, 4, 7 and 34:27 Moses is charged with the duty of writing down the laws and statutes according to which God had made His covenant with Israel. And when Israel has come to the end of its straying about in the wilderness and has arrived over against Jericho in the fields of Moab, we are expressly told that Moses reported the journeys of the children of Israel according to the commandment of the Lord (Num. 32:2). Besides, it is specifically said of the song which Moses sings in Deuteronomy 32, that it is to be written out and taught to the children of Israel, so that later, in days of apostasy, it may stand as a witness against them (Deut. 31:19, 22). Similar commands to record the revelation received are also given to the prophets in their time.[1] Even though such commands refer to but a small part of Scripture, they emphasize nevertheless that God, who demands that no man add to or detract from His words (Deut. 4:2; 12:32; and Prov. 30:6), has also devoted special care to the written record of His revelation.

In the second place, Moses and the prophets are themselves perfectly aware of the fact that they are to proclaim the Word orally not only, but in writing also. Moses is called to his task in a special way, called, that is, to be a leader to the people of Israel (Ex. 3). But the Lord also speaks to him face to face as a man speaks to a friend (Ex. 33:11), and acquaints him with all His statutes and ordinances. Again and again, and as preamble to each particular law, there are the words, "And the Lord spake," "Then the Lord said," and the like (Ex. 6:1, 10, 13 and so on). In the books of Moses, as, indeed, in the whole of Scripture, the entire giving of the law is ascribed to the Lord. He showed His word to Jacob, His statutes and His judgments to Israel. He did not deal so with any other nation, and as for His judgments, others have not known them (Ps. 147:19, 20 and 103:7). The prophets, too, are aware of the source of their prophecy. They know that the Lord has called them,[2] and that they have received their revelation from Him.[3] What Amos says was the conviction of them all: Surely the Lord God will do nothing, except He have revealed His secret to His servants the prophets (Amos 3:7; compare Gen. 18:17). But they also know that when they write they are proclaiming the Lord's word, and not their own. Just as Moses did in recording the laws, so the prophets often introduced their specific prophecies with the formulas "thus saith the Lord," "the word of the Lord came to me," or the "vision," "word," or "burden" of the Lord.[4]

In the third place, there is the witness of the New Testament. It is true that Jesus and the apostles repeatedly quote speeches from the Old Testament under the name of Moses, Isaiah, David, and Daniel (Matt. 8:4; 15:7; 22:43; and 24:15). No less often, however, they make use

---

1. Isa. 8:1; 30:8; Jer. 25:13; 30:2; 36:2; Ezek. 24:2; Dan. 12:4; and Habak. 2:2.
2. 1 Sam. 3; Isa. 6; Jer. 1; Ezek. 1-3; Amos 3:7-8 and 7:15.
3. Isa. 5:9; 6:9; 22:14; 28:22; Jer. 1:9; 3:6; 20:7-9; Ezek. 3:16,26,27; Amos 3:8, and the like.
4. Isa. 1:1; 2:1; 8:1; 13:1; Jer. 1:2; 4:11; 2:1; Ezek. 1:1; 2:1; 3:1; Dan. 7:1; Amos 1:3,6,9, and other places.

of such introductory phrases as "It is written" (Matt. 4:4), or "the
Scripture hath said" (John 7:38), or "the Holy Ghost saith" (Heb.
3:7), and the like. By this method of reference they clearly indicate
that the Scripture of the Old Testament, although made up of various
parts and originated by various authors, nevertheless is an organic whole
also in its written form, whose author is God Himself. Nor do Jesus
and His apostles give indirect expression to this merely. They also say
so directly in the plainest of words. Jesus declares that the Scripture
cannot be broken — that is to say, robbed of its authority (John 10:35);
and He declares further that He personally has not come to destroy the
law and the prophets but to fulfill them (Matt. 5:17 and Luke 6:27).
The apostle Peter writes that the word of prophecy is sure and trust-
worthy and a light upon our path. It is that because the Scripture which
is contained in the Old Testament does not rest upon a personal prediction and interpretation of the future, for no prophecy of the Scripture
is of any private interpretation; for the prophecy did not come in the
old time by the will of man, but holy men of God spoke as they were
moved by the Holy Ghost (2 Peter 1:19-21; *cf.* 1 Peter 1:10-12). In
this same sense Paul testifies that the Holy Scriptures which together
constitute the Old Testament can make us wise unto salvation, if we
search and read them by means of faith, the faith that is in Christ Jesus.
For each and every Scripture included in those Holy Scriptures are
given by inspiration of God, and they are for that reason profitable for
doctrine, for reproof, for correction, and for instruction in righteousness
(2 Tim. 3:16).

In the fourth place, as for the Scriptures of the New Testament itself, it can be said that although Jesus Himself did not leave a document
of writing behind Him, He chose, called, and qualified His apostles to
go into the midst of the world, particularly after His departure, to be
His *witnesses.*[5] He equips them for this task by giving them special
graces and powers,[6] and more specifically He endows them with the
Holy Spirit who will bring all things which Jesus has told them to their
remembrance (John 14:26), guiding them into all truth, also the truth
about things to come (John 16:13). Really, therefore, it is not the
apostles themselves who witness of Jesus; it is the Holy Spirit who
testifies in them and through them of Jesus (John 15:26-27). Just as
the Son has come to glorify the Father, so the Holy Spirit comes to
glorify the Son, and, to this end, the Spirit receives from the Son all
that He speaks and does (John 16:14).

_____

5. Matt. 10:1; Mark 3:13; Luke 6:13; 9:1; and John 6:70.
6. Matt. 10:1,9; Mark 16:15ff.; Acts 2:43; 5:12; Rom. 15:19; and Heb. 2:4.

The apostles were to bring their witness of Christ to their contemporaries and fellow-countrymen not only, living as they were in Jerusalem, Judea, and Samaria, but to all creatures and to the ends of the earth.[7] In this mandate to go out to the whole world is contained the command to testify of Jesus *scripturally* also, although the apostles are not told to do so directly. But if the promise which came to Abraham was also to accrue to mankind in Christ, it could not arrive at this purpose unless it was recorded in writing and thus preserved for all times and distributed to all peoples. Accordingly the apostles were so guided in their mission work by the Holy Spirit that they almost naturally reached for the pen, and by means of epistles and letters witnessed to the fulness of grace and truth which had appeared in Christ Jesus. Not only in their oral preaching, but also in their writings, it was their clearly perceived purpose to unfold the truth which God had revealed in Christ and by His Spirit had made known to them.

Matthew writes the book of the generation, that is of the history, of Jesus Christ, the Son of David (Matt. 1:1). Mark tells how the Gospel began with Jesus Christ, the Son of God, and took its point of origin in Him (Mark 1:1). Luke wants by means of a careful investigation and orderly account to give assurance to Theophilus concerning the things which are most surely believed in the circle of the saints on the basis of the testimony of the apostles (Luke 1:1-4). John writes his Gospel in order that we may believe that Jesus is the Christ, the Son of God, and that, believing, we may have life in His name (John 20:31); and in his first letter he also says that he declares that which he has seen and heard and looked upon, and which his hands have handled, of the Word of life. This he does in order that we may have fellowship with the apostles, and with the Father and with His Son Jesus Christ (1 John 1:1-3). Paul is persuaded not only that he has been called to be an apostle by Jesus Christ Himself (Gal. 1:1), and that he has received his Gospel from Him by revelation,[8] but also that by word of mouth and pen he is proclaiming the Word of God.[9] He goes so far as to say that whoever preaches any other gospel is accursed (Gal. 1:8). And, just as all the apostles connect eternal life or eternal death with the acceptance or rejection of their preaching, so the Apostle John in the last chapter of his Revelation threatens all those who add to the prophecy of these books or detract from it with a heavy punishment (Rev. 22:18-19).

* * * * *

---

7. Matt. 28:19; Mark 16:15; and Acts 1:8.
8. Gal. 1:12; Eph. 3:2; 1 Tim. 1:12.
9. 1 Thess. 2:13; 2 Thess. 2:15; 3:14; 1 Cor. 2:4,10-13; and 2 Cor. 2:17.

The particular activity of the Holy Spirit by means of which the recording of revelation took place is generally given the name of *inspiration* (2 Tim. 3:16). Some light is shed on the nature of this inspiration by comparisons borrowed from nature and by specific explanations in Scripture itself. In general it is true that a human being is capable of taking the thoughts of others up into his mind, and of being guided by others in his thinking. All instruction and education is based on this ability, as are all science and all knowledge. Such communication of thought from one to another usually takes place by way of means, whether they be signs or gestures, spoken or written words. When we are thus being influenced by someone else's thoughts, we usually study them deliberately and intentionally, and often at the cost of considerable exertion. Thus we try to make the other person's ideas and thoughts a part of our own spiritual life. But the phenomena of hypnotism, suggestion, and the like, prove that without any self-activity on our part, another person's ideas and thoughts can be introduced into our consciousness, can be imposed upon us, and can command our will and action. In this way people can be changed into passive instruments who simply carry out the will of the hypnotist. Both the Scriptures and experience teach that in this way a human being is susceptible also to influences and powers of evil spirits; in such cases the person no longer speaks and acts for himself, but is governed by the evil spirit in his thought and conduct. In Mark 1:24, for example, it is the unclean spirit who speaks through the possessed man and who recognizes Jesus as being the Holy One of God.

Another phenomenon which can serve to shed light on the nature of the inspiration of the Holy Spirit is the so-called inspiration of artists. All great thinkers and poets have learned by experience that they owe the best and most beautiful of their productions not to their own exertion but to suddenly invading flashes of insight. Naturally such an experience does not exclude the preliminary investigation and reflection. Genius does not make effort and industry unnecessary.

But even though in such cases study is as a general rule the indispensable condition of such inspirational experiences, the insight which results is not the logical consequence or ripe fruit of the study. Operative in men of genius there is always a secret power which is not susceptible to logical calculation. In writing to his sister, Nietzsche said of this secret power: "You have no idea how powerful such inspirations are; they fill one with a passionate ecstacy of mind, one feels transported and quite beside himself, one hears nothing and sees nothing — one simply accepts. The thought comes to one like lightning. Everything happens involuntarily, as though borne in upon one in a storm of freedom, independence, power, and divinity. Such is my experience of inspiration."

Certainly if manifestations of this kind take place even in the normal life of people and of artists, there can be no basis for attacking the influence of God on the thinking and volition of his creatures. By means of His Spirit God is operative in His creation, being present in it.[10] And of these creatures it is man most particularly who was made by the breath of the Almighty and by the Spirit of God.[11] In Him we live, move, and have our being (Acts 17:28). Our thinking and willing and doing, even in their sinful course, take place under the rule of God, and nothing happens outside the counsel of His will (Eph. 1:11). The king's heart is in the hand of the Lord as the rivers of water; He turns it to whatever He wills (Prov. 21:1). The ways of man are before the eyes of the Lord, and He ponders all his goings (Prov. 5:21; 16:9; 19:21: and 21:2). And, in a quite different and much more intimate way, God by His Spirit dwells in the hearts of His children. By that Spirit He brings them to the confession of Christ as their Lord (1 John 4:3), makes them know the things that are given them of God (1 Cor. 2:12; 1 John 2:20; 3:24; and 4:6-13), grants them the gifts of wisdom and knowledge (1 Cor. 12:8), and works in them both to will and to do of His good pleasure (Phil. 2:13).

Obviously all these influences of the Spirit of God upon the world and the church are not identical with the inspiration which came to the prophets and apostles, but they can serve all the same as a clarification and explanation. If it be true that not in name only but in very deed also there is such a thing as an indwelling and operation of the Spirit of God in all creatures, and if that same Spirit in a different and special sense dwells in the children of God, then there is no ground at all for regarding the special activity which is called *inspiration* as impossible or improbable. At the same time, however, it is very necessary to discern the distinction between the operation of the Spirit of God in the world and the church on the one hand, and that in the prophets and apostles on the other. This distinction becomes very apparent when we compare Romans 8:14 with 2 Peter 1:21. In the first of these, Paul says that as many as are *led* by the Spirit of God are children of God; but in the second, Peter declares that the holy men of God, that is, the prophets, were *moved* by the Holy Spirit, and so gave rise to prophecy. The leading of the Spirit is the portion of all believers and consists of an illumination of the mind, and of a governing and direction of the will and the inclinations; by reason of this influence the mind and will receive the knowledge and the power and the desire to do what pleases God. But the "moving" of the Spirit was granted only to the prophets and

---

10 Gen. 1:3; Ps. 33:6; and Ps. 104:30.
11. Job 33:4 and Ps. 139:1-16ff.

apostles and consisted of an excitation and provocation to make the revelation of the will of God which they had received known to men.

The special character of this inspiration is indicated further by the recurring formula of the New Testament, in referring to the Old, namely, that what is said in the Old was spoken *of* the Lord *by* the prophet (Matt. 1:22; 2:15, 17, 23; 3:3; 4:14, and the like). The Greek uses an expression for this formula which designates the Lord as the source or origin of what is said, and which designates the prophets as the means or *agents* of what is being said. This distinction is the more sharply evident where we read that God spoke *through the mouth* of His prophets.[12] The truth which Scripture teaches in this matter is therefore this truth: that God, or His Spirit, is really the speaker of His word, but that in giving expression to it He has made use of the prophets and apostles as his agents.

*   *   *   *   *

We should, however, be misunderstanding Scripture entirely if we were to infer from these indications that the prophets and apostles were mere passive agents, mentally and volitionally inactive, and serving the Holy Spirit merely as a sort of speaking-tube. For it is true not only that God always honors His own work and never deals with His rational creatures as if they were not rational, but the Holy Spirit also patently contradicts any mechanical idea of inspiration. For, although the prophets were moved, or driven, by the Holy Spirit, they *themselves* also spoke (2 Peter 1:21). The words which they put into writing are again and again referred to as *their* words.[13] In several instances, we read that they were prepared for the office, set apart and equipped for it (Jer. 1:5; Acts 7:22; and Gal. 1:15). And, just as they do in receiving the word, so also in writing down the revelation, they remain altogether self-conscious; their own activity is not suppressed by the moving of the Spirit but is lifted up, energized, and purged. They themselves make diligent investigations (Luke 1:3), they recall and reflect upon the revelation which they have received at an earlier date,[14] they make use of historical sources,[15] some of them, the Psalmists, for instance, find the materials for their song in their own experience, and in all the writings of which the Bible is composed the personal disposition of the writer, the peculiar quality of his character, his personal development and education, his own language and style — these all come to expression in each and all of the many writers. The study of the Scriptures teaches

12. Luke 1:70; Acts 1:16; 3:18; and 4:25.
13. Matt. 22:43,45; John 1:23; 5:46; Rom. 10:20; and the like.
14. John 14:26 and 1John 1:1-3.
15. Num. 21:14; Josh. 10:13, and the like.

us not only the *one* word of God; it acquaints us also with the different persons who wrote them. What a difference there is between the books of the Kings and the Chronicles, between Isaiah and Jeremiah, between Matthew and Luke, between John, and Peter, and Paul!

* * * * *

Such a conception of inspiration as is here suggested permits us also to do full justice to the human side of the Holy Scriptures. The Bible did not come down to us, complete and whole, in an instant of time. It grew up gradually. The Old Testament, as we have it, comprises thirty-nine books: five of them are legal books, twelve are historical (from Joshua to Esther), five are poetical (from Job to the Song of Solomon), and seventeen are prophetical. Such an order is not of course chronological, for many historical books, for example those of Ezra, Nehemiah, and Esther are of a much later date than many of the poetical and prophetical books, and among the prophetical books many of the shorter ones, such as Joel, Obadiah, Amos, and Hosea, are older than the longer books of Isaiah, Jeremiah, Ezekiel, and Daniel. The order is based on the nature of the content, not on chronology. And the genesis of all these books took place gradually, in the course of many centuries, amid very differing circumstances, and by means of the labor of very different men.

In the science of theology there is a special branch which occupies itself with the investigation of the circumstances under which a particular book of the Bible came into existence, by whom it was written, to whom it was addressed, and the like. Because of the abuse which was made of this branch of study, it got a bad name. We must all at one time or another have heard that "higher criticism" has systematically torn page after page out of the Bible. But the abuse of a thing does not make its use an evil. If we are to understand the Scriptures in their totality and in their parts, it is of great importance to know exactly how gradually the Bible came into being and under what circumstances each of its books arose. On the long run such knowledge can only benefit the interpretation of the Word of God. We learn from it that the inspiration of the Spirit of God entered deeply and broadly into the life and thought of the holy men of God.

For centuries, that is, until Moses' time, there was no Scripture, no written record of the Word of God. At least we have no knowledge of any such record. It is by no means impossible, of course, that something like a written report of some word or event was made before Moses' time, some word or event, that is, which was very important for the history of the special revelation, and which, then, was later taken up and preserved by Moses in his books.

It is not so long ago that the assertion of such a possibility would have been called a piece of folly. For it was then supposed that the art of writing was not known in Moses' day. But, by reason of the discoveries made in Babylonia and Egypt, we are now better informed, and we know, not merely that the art of writing was known long before Moses, but also that much use was made of it.

We have knowledge of events and of laws which were set down in writing. The writing took place hundreds of years before Moses. Hence it is not at all unreasonable to make the claim that Moses, before his historical writing and issuance of the law, made use of older written sources. The account of Genesis 14, for instance, might very well rest upon a written tradition.

But we cannot know this as a certainty, and in general we can therefore say that before Moses there was no inscripturated word of God. There was of course a word of God, for special revelation began immediately after the fall, and hence there was in this sense also such a thing as a canon, that is, a rule of faith and life. Mankind was at no time without the Word of God. Always, from the very point of origin, man has been in possession, not only of the general revelation of God in nature and conscience, but of special revelation in word and history also. But that word of God was not immediately written down; it was orally transferred in the families and generations, being passed on from the parents to the children. In that ancient time when the population of the earth was limited, when people still enjoyed the blessing of long life, when blood-relationship, a sense of family, and respect for the past meant so much more than they do in our time, this form of continuity was sufficient for the pure preservation and the extension of the Word of God.

Later on, however, when people began to spread out over the face of the earth, and when they fell into all kinds of idolatry and superstition, the oral tradition was not enough. It is Moses who begins the recording of the Word of God. It may be that there were written reports which he took up and included; as was said, we do not know this as a certainty, though the likelihood of it increases when we consider that only in a very few passages is mention made in the so-called five books of Moses of any writing being done by Moses himself.[16] Hence it is quite possible that various portions of the five books of Moses were in part extant before his time, and also that they were revised by Moses himself, or by others at Moses' behest, or that, later on, after Moses' death, some of them were edited in his spirit and manner, and added

---

16. Ex. 17:14; 24:4, 7; 34:27; Num. 33:2; and Deut. 31:9, 22.

to the already extant portions. This last possibility was generally accepted in earlier periods in regard to the report of Moses' death (Deut. 34), but it should be extended to include also the addenda and like portions, such as are found in Gen. 12:6b; 13:7; 36:31b, and the like. This is to take nothing away from the Divine authority of the Word, and is a possibility which is not at all contradicted by the recurrent Scriptural expression: the law, or the book *of Moses*.[17] For the five books of Moses remain the book or the law of Moses, even though some parts were derived by him from other sources, were set down at his behest by his officers, or were edited in his spirit by those who came after. Paul too did not as a general rule write his letters himself, but had them written by another hand (1 Cor. 16:21). And the book of Psalms is sometimes ascribed in its entirety to David because he is the founder of psalmody, and this is done even though a number of the Psalms are not those of David but are of other authors.

* * * * *

On the basis of this Mosaic law-giving, that is, on the basis of the covenant of God, which God concluded with the patriarchs, which He confirmed for Israel at Sinai, and which He ordained in the law of Moses, there arose in the later history of Israel, under the leading of the Holy Spirit, a threefold holy literature: psalmody, prophecy, and the "wisdom" literature. These special gifts of the Holy Spirit were conjoined with the natural gifts which are peculiar to the Semitic race, and particularly to the people of Israel, but they transcend these natural gifts and are charged with a calling in the service of the Kingdom of God and for the benefit of all mankind.

Prophecy begins with Abraham,[18] and is carried on by Jacob,[19] Moses,[20] and Miriam,[21] but comes into its own particularly in Samuel and after him, and it accompanies the history of Israel until a considerable while after the captivity. The books of the prophets are divided in the Hebrew Old Testament into two great groups, the "earlier" and "later" prophets. The first group comprises the books of Joshua, Judges, Samuel, and Kings. The reason for designating these books as the earlier is that they were written by prophets and that they tell of prophets who preceded the later prophets of the Scriptures.

17. 1 Kings 2:3; 2 Kings 14:6; Mal. 4:4; Mark 12:26; Luke 24:27,44; and John 5:46-47.
18. Gen. 18:17; 20:7; see also Amos 3:7 and Ps. 105:15.
19. Gen. 49.
20. Num. 11:25; Deut. 18:18; 34:10; and Hosea 12:13.
21. Ex. 15:20 and Num. 12:2.

In other words, there were many more prophets in Israel than the four great ones, and the twelve small ones, whose books are preserved in the Bible. The historical books mentioned above are full of the names of prophets and sometimes include lengthy descriptions of their activities. They tell of Deborah, Samuel, Gad, of Nathan, Ahiah, Semiah, of Azariah, Hanani, of Jehu, the son of Nanani, of Eliah, Eliza, Hulda, and of Zachariah, the first martyr of the prophets in the kingdom of Judah, and of many others, some of them not named (2 Chron. 25, for example). Nothing from the hand of these figures has come to us in written form. Sometimes we read, even, of schools of the prophets,[22] where many sons or disciples of the prophets together addressed themselves to spiritual exercises and the theocratic duties. Very probably the prophetical writing of history came up out of these schools, and this, of course, in such books as Joshua, Judges, and the like. In the books of the Chronicles especially there are several references to the historical writings of prophets.[23]

The prophets, whose activities are described in the historical books, are often described in our times as prophets in *deed* as distinguished from the later prophets in *word*. This distinction is permissible if only we remember that all of the prophets, the later as well as the earlier, were prophets of the *word*. All spoke and all witnessed; the original Hebrew points to this fact very probably (Ex. 4:16 and 7:1), and the fundamental characteristics of prophetic teaching are contained already in the witness of the oldest prophets. But there are two respects in which the prophets of the earlier period are distinguished from those of the later. In the first place, they limited their view to the internal exigencies of the people of Israel, and do not yet include other peoples in the pale of their perspective; and in the second place, they pay more attention to the present than to the future. Their word of admonishment and threat has in the main an immediate and practical purpose. It is the period in which, during and for some time after the reigns of David and Solomon, the hope is still entertained that Israel is going to keep the covenant of God and walk in His ways.

But when, in the ninth century before Christ, Israel gradually becomes involved in the foreign polity of surrounding peoples, and in despite of its own calling and destiny lets itself become so involved, then the prophets include the surrounding peoples in their perspective also. They no longer expect the perfect fulfillment of the promises of God in the apostate present. Instead they look for it in the Messianic future, a future which God Himself must bring to pass. Standing on their watch-

---

22. 1 Sam. 10:5-12; 19:19ff.; 2 Kings 2:3,5; 4:38,43; and 6:1.
23. 1 Chron. 29:29; 2 Chron. 9:29; 20:34, and the like.

towers, these later prophets look out over the whole length and breadth of the earth, and point to the signs of the times not as they themselves read them but according to the light of the Holy Spirit.[24] They measure the situations in Israel, whether religious, ethical, political, or social, as well as Israel's relations with other peoples such as Edom, Moab, Asshur, Chaldea, and Egypt against the touchstone of the central covenant in which Jehovah stands over against His people. And all of them, each according to his own nature, in his own time and his own way, preach what in essence is the same word of God: they proclaim Israel's sins and God's punishment for sins; they comfort the people of the Lord with the immutability of His covenant, the promise of His faithfulness, the forgiveness of all their unrighteousnesses; and they direct every eye to the joyous future, in which God under the rule of a king of the house of David will extend His dominion over Israel and over all peoples.

So the word which they preach in the name of God takes on a significance which goes far beyond the time in which it is spoken. That word no longer has its limit and its purpose in the Israel of the old day; instead it has a content and bearing extending to the ends of the earth, and it can come to its fulfillment only in mankind itself. And now the word of prophecy is committed to writing. From the ninth century B.C. on, that is, from the days of Joel and Obadiah, the prophets begin to put the content of their prophecy down in writing, sometimes expressly at God's behest.[25] They do this with clearly indicated purpose that their word may remain until the last day, unto all eternity (Isa. 30:8) and that it may be acknowledged by later generations in its authenticity (Isa. 34:16).

* * * * *

The *psalmody* runs a parallel course with the prophecy. It, too, is of ancient date. Song and music were greatly loved in Israel.[26] Songs devoted to various subjects are preserved for us in the historical books. There is the song of the sword (Gen. 4:23-24), the song of the well (Num. 21:17-18), the song of the conquest of Heshbon (Num. 21:27-30), the song of the passage of the Red Sea (Ex. 15), the song of Moses (Deut. 32), the song of Deborah (Judges 5), the song of Hannah (1 Sam. 2), the lament of David upon the death of Saul and Jonathan (2 Sam. 1) and his lament for Abner (2 Sam. 3:33-34), and the book of Jasher (Josh. 10:13 and 2 Sam. 1:18) which seems to have contained many songs. Further, many songs are reported in the books of

---

24. 1 Peter 1:4 and 2 Peter 2:20-21.
25. Isa. 8:1; Hab. 2:2; and Isa. 36:3.
26. 1 Sam. 18:7; 2 Sam. 19:35; Amos 6:5, and others.

the prophets: for example, the song of the vineyard in Isaiah 5, the song in mockery of the fallen king of Babylon in Isaiah 14, the psalm of Hezekiah in Isaiah 38, the prayer of Jonah in Jonah 2, the song of praise of Habakkuk, and others besides. Many of these songs are closely related to the Psalms: the transition from the one to the other is hardly perceptible. There is a close relationship, too, between psalmody and prophecy. This is apparent even in the form. Both of them come up out of a powerful inspiration of the Holy Spirit, both take into their purview the whole world of nature and history, both regard all things in the light of the Word of God, both issue in the proclamation of the kingdom of the Messiah, and both make use of the language and form of poetry. When the poet of the psalms is led into the mysteries of the will and counsel of God, he becomes a seer, and when the soul of the prophet is refreshed by the promises of God his prophecy is lifted to the plane of poetry (1 Chron. 25:1-3). Asaph is called a seer (2 Chron. 29:30) and David in Acts 2:30 is called a prophet.

But there is of course a difference between the two. The poetry of the Psalms was prepared for by the song of Miriam, the song of Moses (Deut. 32), and the psalm of Moses (Ps. 90), but it reached its flowering, after the revival of the service of Jehovah under Samuel, in the psalms of David, the sweet singer of Israel (2 Sam. 23:1). The Davidic psalmody comprises the fundamental forms according to which the later psalmody of Solomon, Jehoshaphat, Hezekiah and that of the period during and after the captivity was exercised. At the end of Psalm 72 the psalms of David are all designated as prayers. And that is the characteristic that is peculiar to all psalms. They differ a good deal among each other. Some of them are songs of praise and thanksgiving, some of plaint and supplication. Some of them have the quality of hymns, some of elegy, and some are prophetic-didactic in kind. There are psalms which celebrate God's works in nature and psalms which celebrate His works in history. They treat of the past, of the present, and often also of the future. But there is always present in them that basic structure of prayer. That is characteristic of them all. If in the case of prophecy, the Holy Spirit seizes upon someone, controlling and moving him, in the case of psalmody that same Spirit leads the poet into the depths of his own spiritual life. A personal spiritual state is always the occasion for his song. But such a state of the soul has always been formed and molded by the Spirit of the Lord.

David would not have been the sweet singer of Israel if he had not been the man of striking character and rich life experiences that he was. And it was his state of mind, or state of soul, rather, in all of its variations of grief and anxiety, temptation and drive, persecution and rescue, and like experiences, which are the strings on which are played the melodies of the objective words and deeds of God in nature and history, in institutions and preaching, in judgment and redemption. It is the harmony of God's objective revelation and His subjective leading which is voiced in the song, and which is sung as in the presence of God, dedicated to His honor, which calls upon all creatures to join in the paean of praise, which keeps on singing until all that is in heaven and on earth picks up its chords, and which is, therefore, for all ages and for all generations, the richest expression of the deepest experiences that the human soul has felt. The psalms teach us to say what goes on in our hearts in connection with His revelation in Christ through the Spirit. Because of this significance these psalms were uttered by the Psalmists not only, but were also placed on the lips of the church of all ages.

* * * * *

To the prophecy and psalmody must be added the *chokma,* that is, the art of proverb, or the wisdom literature. This too has its basis in natural endowments, as becomes apparent from the fable of Jotham (Judges 9:7ff), the riddle of Samson (Judges 14:14), the parable of Nathan (2 Sam. 12), the conduct of the woman of Tekoah (2 Sam. 14), and the like. But this wisdom literature got its dedicated character especially from Solomon[27] and was then continued in the Proverbs of other wise men (Prov. 22:17ff.) and in the books of Job, Ecclesiastes, the Song of Solomon, and so on until after the captivity. Prophecy discloses the will of God as it comes out in the history of Israel and the other peoples; psalmody gives expression to the echo which the carrying out of God's will in the souls of his saints gives out; and the proverb or wisdom literature relates that will of God to practical life and conduct. This wisdom literature, too, rests on the foundation of Divine revelation; its point of departure is that the fear of the Lord is the beginning of wisdom (Prov. 1:7). But this kind of literature does not relate that revelation to the history of the peoples, or to subjective soul-experience, but instead makes it applicable to ordinary, daily life, the life of man and woman, parents and children, friendship and society, business and profession. It does not operate on the high plane of prophecy; nor does it see so far. It does not explore so profoundly as psalmody. But it pays attention to all the vicissitudes of life — experiences under which people tend despairingly to succumb — and raises people up again above the level of those experiences. This it does by faith in the righteousness of God's providence. Thus the Proverb literature

27. 1 Kings 4:29-34,

takes on a general human significance, and, under the leading of the Holy Spirit, is preserved for all ages.

The revelation, the law, the will of God, principially set forth in the books of Moses, completes itself in the days of the Old Testament in the preaching of the prophet, the song of the singer, the maxims of the sage. The prophet is the head, the singer the heart, the sage the hand.

The prophetic, priestly, and kingly offices have fulfilled their calling in this way under the Old Dispensation. And in Christ this invaluable treasure of holy literature has become the common property of the world.

* * * * *

Just as the promise culminates in the fulfillment, so the Scripture of the Old Testament culminates in that of the New. The one is incomplete without the other. It is only in the New that the Old Testament is revealed, and the New is already in core and essence contained in the Old. The relationship is like that of pedestal and statue, lock and key, shadow and body. The designations Old and New Testament first had reference to the two dispensations of the Covenant of Grace which God gave to his people before and after Christ.[28] Later the terms were transferred to the two bodies of writing which constitute the description and interpretation of those two dispensations of the covenant. In Exodus 24:7, the law, which was the pronouncement or declaration of God's covenant with Israel, is called the book of the covenant (compare 2 Kings 23:2), and in 2 Corinthians 3:14 Paul already speaks of a reading of the old testament — a reference naturally to the books of that testament. In accordance with these examples the word *Testament* gradually came to be used for the writings or books contained in the Bible and which give an interpretation of the old and new dispensation of grace.

Just as the Old, so the New Testament is composed of various books. It comprises five historical books (the four Gospels and the Acts of the apostles), twenty-one doctrinal books (the epistles or letters of the apostles), and one prophetical book (the Revelation of St. John). And, although the thirty-nine books of the Old Testament came into existence during a period of more than a thousand years, the twenty-seven books of the New Testament were all written in the second half of the first century of our Christian era.

The Gospels have first place in the New Testament. The order again is not chronological but material. Even though many of the Letters of the Apostles are earlier, the Gospels are placed first because they treat of the person and work of Christ which constitute the basis of all later

---

28. Jer. 31:31ff.; 2 Cor. 3:6ff.; and Heb. 8:6ff.

apostolic effort. The word Gospel or Evangel at first had the altogether general meaning of a pleasant, joyous message. In the days of the New Testament it came to be used for the good tidings proclaimed by Jesus the Christ (Mark 1:1). Only later did ecclesiastical writers such as Ignatius, Justinius, and others, use it to refer to the books or written records containing that joyous message of Christ.

There are four such Gospels in the New Testament. They do not, of course, contain four different evangels or good tidings, for there is but one Gospel, the Gospel of Jesus Christ (Mark 1:1 and Gal. 1:6-8). But that one Gospel, that one good tiding of salvation has been exhibited in four different ways, by four different persons, from four different points of view, and in four different forms. This idea of the matter comes to good expression in the superscriptions over the four books in our present Bibles: The Gospel *according to* Matthew, *according to* Mark, and the like. The thought was that in the four Gospels the one Gospel, the one image of the person and work of Christ, was being described, be it from various sides. Hence in the ancient church the four evangelists were compared to the four cherubim of the Revelation 4:7: Matthew was thought of as the man, Mark as the lion, Luke as the calf, and John as the eagle. This was done because the first Evangelist described Christ as He was in His human manifestation, the second as He was in His prophetic, the third as He was in His priestly, and the fourth as He was in His divine nature.

Matthew, who was the same as the publican Levi, chosen by Christ for the office of Apostle (Matt. 9:9; Mark 2:14; and Luke 5:27), originally wrote his Gospel, according to Irenaeus, in the Aramaic language, in Palestine, about the year 62 A. D., and specifically for the Jews and the Jewish Christians of Palestine, in order to demonstrate to them that Jesus was truly the Christ, and that all the prophecies of the Old Testament were fulfilled in Him (Matt. 1:1).

Mark was the son of Mary (Acts 12:12), who very probably had her own house in Jerusalem (Acts 1:13 and 2:2). Mark was at first in the service of Paul, later also in that of Peter (1 Peter 5:13), and, according to tradition, he was invited by the Christians at Rome to give an account of the beginning of the Gospel of Jesus Christ (Mark 1:1). The invitation was extended, it is said, because, having sojourned at Jerusalem and gone about with Peter, he was well-informed about the subject. He responded to the invitation in Rome, presumably, in about the years 64-67.

Luke, the beloved physician, as Paul calls him (Col. 4:14), may have come from Antioch. He belonged to the church at that place early, as early as the year 40. He was a travelling companion and fellow-worker with Paul, and remained loyal to him to the end (2 Tim. 4:11). He wrote a history book, not of the life and work of Christ only (in his Gospel), but also of the first spreading out of the Gospel in Palestine, Asia Minor, Greece, and Rome (in the Acts of the Apostles). He wrote the second of these in approximately the years 70-75, and addressed it to a certain Theophilus, a person of some status, who had an interest in the Gospel.

These three Gospels are closely related to each other. They are based on the tradition which lived on concerning Jesus' teaching and life in the circles of the first disciples. The fourth Gospel is different in kind. John, the disciple whom Jesus loved, remained in Jerusalem after Jesus' ascension, and he, together with James and Peter, was one of the three pillars of the church (Gal. 2:9). Later he left Jerusalem, and towards the end of his life he arrived at Ephesus as the successor to Paul. From there, under the emperor Domitian, he was banished to the island of Patmos in the year 95-96, and he died in the year 100 as a martyr. John was not a man to take an important part in missionary effort. He is not the founder of new churches, but instead throws his energies into the preservation of existing churches through a pure knowledge of the truth. A different situation had gradually developed for the church towards the end of the century. The struggle about the relationship of the Christian church to Israel, the law, and the circumcision was over. The church was taking an independent stand in the matter of the Jews, and was penetrating further and further into the Graeco-Roman world. There it came into contact with other spiritual currents, particularly with Gnosticism. And so it is John's purpose to lead the church safely past these dangers from the anti-Christian world, from the tendency, that is, to deny the incarnation of the Word (1 John 2:22 and 4:3). Over against this anti-Christian trend, John in his writings, all of which date from the years 80 to 95, draws the full image of Christ as the Word become flesh. In his Gospel, John indicates that Christ was this in His sojourn on the earth, and in his letters he indicates that Christ is still the incarnate Word in the church now. And in the Revelation, John indicates that He will be that in the future also.

All of the writings of the New Testament referred to thus far have under the guidance of the Holy Spirit been prompted by an historical occasion. And this is true also of the writings of Paul and Peter, of James and Jude. After the ascension of Jesus, and after the persecution of the church at Jerusalem, the apostles did more than go out to preach the Gospel to Jews and Gentiles; they also remained with the congregations they had founded, continuing in fellowship and sojourn with them. They received oral or written reports concerning the spiritual condition of those churches, were interested in their growth, and they bore the care of all the churches in their apostolic hearts (2 Cor. 11:28). Hence they felt called, if possible, to visit the churches personally, or, if that were impossible, then by means of epistles or letters to admonish or comfort the churches according to their needs, to warn or encourage them, and by all these means to lead them more deeply into the truth which is unto salvation.

Just as their apostolic work generally, so this scriptural effort of theirs, constituting as it did an historical, organic, an essential part of that apostolic work, was basic and foundational for the Christian church. The Gospels and Letters of the apostles, are, like the books of the prophets, "occasional" pieces of writing. But at the same time they extend far beyond the temporal and local concerns of the churches of that day, being directed at the church of all ages.

The whole Scripture, although it was historically wrought, is, as Augustine said, a letter sent by God out of heaven to His church on earth. And, so far from supposing that the "historical investigation" of the genesis of the books of the Bible — apart from the abuse that can of course be made of such study — should do violence to the Divine character of Scripture, we can see that such study is peculiarly fitted to teach us the marvelous ways by which God has brought His work of art into being.

* * * * *

Such a glance at the origin of the books of the Bible does not of course exhaust the study of the Bible. It merely begins it. Gradually a whole cluster of sciences have grown up around the Bible: the purpose of all of them is better to understand the meaning of the Scriptures. It must suffice here to say only a few things about these further studies.

In the first place, we know that each book, besides having had its individual origin, eventually took its place in a collection or *Canon,* that is, a list or group of writings which constitute the rule of faith and life. Such a "collection" had already taken place within the pale of a single book: the Psalms and Proverbs, for instance, stem from various persons, and were gradually collected into a body of writing. Later, the several books were collected into one and called the Bible. We must not suppose, however, that the church made this Canon, or granted canonical authority to the writings of the prophets and apostles. Rather, those writings, from the moment they were composed, were immediately authoritative in the church and operated there as the rule of life and faith. The Word of God, unwritten at first and written later, does not derive its authority from men, not even from the authority of believers, but from God, who watches over it and brings about the acknowledgment of it.

Later on, when the number of prophetic and apostolic books increased, and when other writings grew up alongside of them which were not written by prophets and apostles, but which allegedly were so written or were accepted as such in some circles, then it became necessary for the church to distinguish the true canonical books from the false, alleged, apocryphal, or pseudo-epigraphical books, and to draw up a list of the true ones. That took place for the books of the Old Testament before Christ as well as for those of the New Testament in the fourth century after Christ. There is a special science whose work it is to investigate this matter and to shed light on the canonicity of the Bible.

In the second place, it deserves notice that the original manuscripts written by the prophets and apostles themselves have without exception been lost. We have only copies of them. The oldest of these for the Old Testament date from the ninth and tenth centuries, and for the New Testament from the fourth and fifth century after Christ. In other words, centuries separate the original manuscripts from the extant copies. During this period of time the text underwent a history and was subjected to lesser or greater changes. For example — just to mention one aspect of this complex matter — there were no vowel or punctuation markings in the original Hebrew manuscripts, and these were introduced into the copies only centuries later. The division into chapters, such as we are used to now, first took place at the beginning of the thirteenth century, and the division into verses dates from the sixteenth century. For these, and such like considerations, a special science is necessary which makes use of every helpful means to "establish" the original text and to present it as the basis for exegesis.

In the third place, we should note that the Old Testament is written in Hebrew and the New Testament in Greek. The moment, therefore, that the Bible was distributed among people who did not understand these languages, a translation became necessary. As early as the third century before Christ a beginning was made with the translation of the Old Testament into the Greek. And later the translation of the Old and New Testament into many ancient and — after a while — into many modern languages continued. After the revival of Missions to the Heathen in the nineteenth century this work of translation was again energetically pursued and now Scripture in part or in its entirety is available in more than four hundred languages. The study of these translations, too, especially those of old time, is very important for a proper understanding of Holy Scripture. For every translation, after all, is really a kind of interpretation.

In the fourth place, finally, a tremendous amount of care and effort has been devoted to the interpretation of Holy Scripture. This has gone on from the days of the ancient Jews, throughout the centuries, and not the least in our own time. And even though it is true that every exegete has his private slant, and that much of the interpretation has been biased, nevertheless the history of the interpretation of Scripture points to remarkable progress, a progress to which each century has contributed its share. In the final analysis it is God Himself who, often by way of human error, maintains His Word and causes His thoughts to triumph over the wisdom of the world.

VIII

Scripture and Confession

There was in the time of the apostles and thereafter no dearth of difference about the essence of Christianity, and about its relationship to Jew and Gentile. The more remarkable therefore is the unanimity with which Scripture has been accepted as the Word of God in the whole Christian church.

This is true in the first place of the Old Testament. In the teaching of Jesus and the apostles constant mention was made of it. The Old Testament was appealed to again and again. Quite imperceptibly, and as though it were the most natural thing in the world, the authority of the Old Testament of the Jewish church passed over, in the teaching of Jesus and the apostles, into the Christian church. The Gospel took the Old Testament along and could not have been accepted and acknowledged without it. After all, the Gospel is the fulfillment of the promises of the Old Testament. Without it, the Gospel hangs suspended in the air. The Old Testament is the pedestal on which the Gospel rests, and the root out of which it came forth. Wherever the Gospel found an entrance, there the Scriptures of the Old Testament were, immediately and without any opposition, appropriated as the Word of God. In other words, there was no such thing as a New Testament church without a Bible; from the very beginning that church was in possession of the law, the psalms, and the prophets.

To these the apostolic writings were soon added. In part these were writings, such as the Gospels and the general epistles, intended for the whole church. In part, like some of the epistles, they were addressed to specific churches — at Rome, at Corinth, at Colosse, and other places.

It is natural enough that all of these writings, having come from apostles and apostolic persons, in high repute from the very beginning in the Christian churches, were read aloud in the gatherings. and that they were sometimes sent to other churches for reading also. Thus, for example, the apostle Paul himself asks that the letter he is sending to the church at Colosse be sent on to the church at Laodicea, and that they at Colosse also take notice of the letter he had sent out of Laodicea, that is, very probably the letter to the church at Ephesus (Col. 4:16). And in 2 Peter 3:15-16 Peter makes mention not only of a letter which his readers have but recently received from Paul, but also speaks of other letters of Paul which teach the same doctrine as that which Peter himself presents, but which are sometimes difficult to understand and susceptible to being distorted by untutored and unstable people. We are not entitled to infer, of course, that at this time there was a "collection" of Paul's letters; but what we may infer is that the writings of Paul were known in a much larger circle than in the local churches to which each had been addressed. Naturally, too, the churches of that first period got their knowledge of the Gospel for the most part from the apostles and their disciples.

But when these died and their preaching broke off, the writings of the apostles naturally became more and more valuable. From testimony coming to us from the middle of the second century we know that the Gospels, and later also the Epistles or Letters, were regularly read in the assembly of believers, were appealed as evidence of some truth or other, and were placed on one line of authenticity with the books of the Old Testament. Towards the end of the second century, the writings of the New Testament, together with those of the Old, were regarded as "the whole Scripture," as "the foundation and pillar of the faith," as *the* Holy Writ, and were regularly read in the religious services (Irenaeus, Clement of Alexandria, and Tertullian). It is true that concerning some of the writings (Hebrews, James, Jude, 2 Peter, 2 John and 3 John, the Revelation of John, as well as certain books later judged apocryphal) there remained for a long time a difference of opinion as to whether they ought or ought not to be reckoned with the Holy Scriptures. But in this matter, too, there gradually came to be more clarity and unanimity. The generally acknowledged writings were gathered together under the name of *Canon* (meaning *rule of the truth of faith*), and they were registered and established as such at the Synod of Laodicea in the year 360, at Hippo Regius in Numidia in the year 396, and at Carthage in the year 397.

These Scriptures of the Old and New Testaments constitute the foundation of prophets and apostles on which all Christian churches, in fellowship with each other, take their stand or claim to take their stand. In their official confessions, all churches have acknowledged the Divine authority of those Scriptures and have appropriated them as a reliable rule of faith and life. There has never been a difference or conflict about this point of dogma in the Christian churches. Formerly the attack on Scripture as the Word of God came from the outside, from such pagan philosophers as Celsus and Porphyrus in the second century; inside Christendom such an attack does not appear until the eighteenth century.

* * * * *

Now the church has not received this Scripture from God in order simply to rest on it, and still less in order to bury this treasure in earth. On the contrary the church is called to preserve this Word of God, to explain it, to preach it, apply it, translate it, spread it abroad, recommend it, and defend it — in a word, to cause the thoughts of God, laid down in Scripture, to triumph everywhere and at all times over the thoughts of man. All of the work to which the church is called is the effort at, and the ministration of, the Word of God. It is a service of this Word of God when it is preached in the assembly of believers, is interpreted, and applied, when it is shared in the signs of the covenant, and is maintained in discipline. And in a larger sense much more is part and parcel of this service of the Word: this, for example, that in our own hearts and lives, in our profession and business, in house and field and office, in science and art, in state and community, in works of mercy and missions, and in all spheres and ways of life, this Word be applied, worked out, and made to rule. The church must be the pillar and ground of truth (1 Tim. 3:15): that is to say, a pedestal and foundation bearing up the truth and maintaining and establishing it over against the world. When the church neglects and forgets this, the church is remiss in its duty and undermines its own existence.

As soon as the church becomes lax in this its duty, there soon develops a difference of opinion concerning the meaning of the Word of God. Even though the Holy Spirit has been promised to the church and given to it as the Guide into all truth, this does not imply that the church was in its entirety or in its parts fitted out with the gift of infallibility. Even in the churches of the apostolic period various heresies came up which had their point of origin either in paganism or in Judaism. Throughout the ensuing ages these are the two reefs on which the church continually threatens to run aground, and these it must, with the utmost vigilance and care, seek to avoid.

Against such heresies, whether to the right or to the left, the church is obliged to speak out resolutely and clearly, and to state what is the truth vouchsafed to it by God Himself in His Word. The church does this by its lesser and greater assemblies (synods), in which it establishes what according to its conviction must be held as divine truth and thus as a teaching of the church on some particular point or other. Thus the truth laid down in Scripture leads, on the part of all those who believe and embrace it, to a *confession*, a *creed*. Confession is the obligation of all believers and is also the dictate of their own hearts; the person who truly believes with his whole heart and soul cannot but confess, that is, testify to the truth that has made him free, and to the hope that has been planted in his heart by that truth.[1] Thus every believer and every church — if the testimony of the Holy Spirit be present there — confesses that the Word of God is the truth. And as the errors and heresies grow subtler and subtler, the church is the more compelled to take careful account of the truth it confesses and to state its creed in definite and unambiguous terms. Naturally, the oral confession by force of circumstance becomes also a written confession.

There have been those, we know, who have objected on various grounds to the formulation and maintenance of such an ecclesiastical confession. The Remonstrants of the Netherlands, for instance, held that a confession violated the exclusive authority of Scripture, and the freedom of conscience, and that it impeded the growth in knowledge. These objections are, however, based on misunderstanding. The function of the confessions or creeds is not to push the Scriptures into the background, but rather to maintain them and to protect them against individual caprice. So far from violating the freedom of conscience, they support it over against all sorts of heretical spirits who seek to lead weak and uninformed souls astray. And, finally, the confessions do not impede a growth in knowledge but keep it in the right course of development, and they are themselves to be checked and revised against the Holy Scriptures as the only norm of faith. Such examination and review can take place at any time, though it must be done in warranted and legitimate ways.

The apostolic creed (the twelve articles) is the oldest of the Christian creeds. It was not formulated by the apostles themselves, but it came into existence as early as the beginning of the second century. It developed out of the baptismal command of Matthew 28:19. Originally it was somewhat shorter than it is now, but basically it was the same. It was a short summary of the great facts on which Christianity rests, and as such it continues to be the common ground and unbreakable bond of unity of all Christendom. To this apostolic creed four further confessions have been added, all of them of an ecumenical (*i.e.*, general) character, and all of them accepted by many churches. These are: the creed of the Council of Nicea in 325; the creed which in Article IX of the Reformed *Confession of Faith* is called the Nicean Creed, but which,

---

1. Matt. 10:32; Rom. 10:9-10; 2 Cor. 4:13; 1 Peter 3:15; and 1 John 4:2-3.

although it has absorbed the Creed of Nicea into itself, is really an expansion of the creed and came into existence considerably later; the creed of the Council of Chalcedon in 451; and, finally, the creed mistakenly designated the Creed of Athanasius.

In all of these confessions the doctrine concerning Christ and the Trinity are set forth. Those were the points at issue during the first centuries. What think ye of the Christ? — that was the all-important question which, on the basis of the Word of the Lord, the church had to answer for itself and to maintain over against the whole world.

To the Jewish side of the issue went all those persons who were willing to recognize Jesus as a man, a man sent by God, a man endowed with unusual gifts, animated by the prophetic spirit, mighty in deeds and words, but, for the rest, no more than a man. And, from the pagan side, there came those who were willing to recognize in Jesus a son of the gods, a Divinity who came from heaven and who, like the angels of the Old Testament, manifested himself for a little while on the earth in a shadow-body. But these were unwilling to confess Him as the Only-Begotten of the Father who had become flesh. Over against these two heresies, the church, following in the line of Scripture, has to maintain on the one hand that Christ was the very, only-begotten Son of God, and on the other hand that He truly came into the flesh. And this was the confession of its belief which the church made in its creeds after a long struggle of definition. It rejected, together with the apostle John, all anti-Christian teaching which denied that the Son of God came into the flesh (1 John 2:18, 22 and 4:2,3). Thus the Christian church, by the formulation and affirmation of such creeds, maintained the essence and the heart, the very peculiar character, of the Christian religion. And that is why the councils and synods in which these confessions came into existence are of such great and fundamental importance for the whole of Christendom. In the facts of Christianity, which the apostolic confession summarizes, and in the doctrine of the person of Christ and of the triune being of God, there is an agreement in the Christian churches which binds them all together as a unit over against Judaism and Paganism. This is a unity which may not, because of the sorry divisions which separate them, be forgotten or ignored.

Out of this common basis, however, there soon developed all kinds of differences and divisions. The exercise of discipline led to the separation of the Montanists in the second half of the second century, of Novatianism in the middle of the third century, and of Donatism in the fourth century. Much more serious was the schism which gradually developed between the church of the East and that of the West. Many causes contributed to it. First of all, there was the aversion to each other of the

Greeks and the Latins, the continuing tension between Constantinople and Rome, the struggle for supremacy between the patriarchs and the pope. To this were added many lesser differences in point of doctrine and worship. The most important of these was the confession of the Greek church that in the being of God the Holy Spirit did not proceed from the Father *and the Son,* as the West taught, but only from the Father. The separation, which had taken place periodically for brief intervals, became permanent in 1054. The church of the East, which prefers to think of itself as the Orthodox church because as it supposes it has remained more loyal to the teaching of the early church, suffered great losses by way of the formation of sects (the Armenian Christians, the Nestorians in Syria, the Thomas-Christians of Persia, the Monophysite-Jacobites in Syria, the Coptics in Egypt, and the Maronites in Lebanon) and also because of Mohammedanism which in 1453 gained the dominance in Constantinople. At the same time, however, the Eastern church made an important gain in the conversion of the Slavs, and continues to exist as the orthodox church in Greece, Turkey, Russia, and in certain smaller countries such as Bulgaria, Yugoslavia, and Roumania.

* * * * *

In the West the Catholic Church, under the leadership of the bishops of Rome, spread itself out farther and farther in the course of the centuries. A period of rest, privilege, and prestige followed upon the conversion of the Emperor Constantine and upon a long period of persecution and hatred. And although the secularization of the church gained ground by leaps and bounds, the church from the time of Constantine's conversion up to the Reformation nevertheless achieved much. Just as during the first centuries, the church resisted and conquered Paganism, so, later also, it worked hard for the conversion of the nations and the civilization of Europe, maintained the great truths of Christianity and the independence of the church with a commendable firmness, and cooperated effectively in the development of a Christian art and science. Irrespective, however, of these great merits, it cannot be denied that in its spreading out and ascendancy of power, the church moved in directions that were not pointed out by the original, apostolic Christianity. And this became apparent in especially three ways.

In the first place the Catholic Church raised *tradition* more and more to the plane of an independent rule of faith, standing next to, and sometimes even over against, the Holy Scriptures. A quantity of Roman doctrines and usages, such as the mass, celibacy for the religious, the canonization of the saints, the immaculate conception of Mary, and the like, cannot be proved or supported by any text of Scripture. Nevertheless, such doctrines and practices are maintained on the basis of "tradition." Concerning this tradition, it is alleged that it may comprise only that which "has been believed everywhere, always, and by everybody," but in the final analysis it is the pope who determines whether something is tradition or not.

Thus the whole relationship of the Scriptures and the Church has been changed about by Rome. Scripture is not indispensable but merely useful to the church, but the church is indispensable to Scripture. For Scripture has no authority except as the church grants it such authority by declaring it worthy of belief. Scripture is thus held to be obscure in itself and to require the church to make it clear; it does not have precedence over nor constitute the foundation of the church: rather the church has precedence over it and constitutes the basis on which the Scripture rests. Even though the prophets and apostles received the gift of inspiration, the pope also, when speaking "ex cathedra" in his papal office receives the special support of the Spirit and is thus infallible. The church is sufficient in itself, and could, if need were, get along without Scripture, and is the one, true, and perfect mediator of salvation. The church is also the possessor and distributor of the benefits of grace contained in the sacraments. The church is *the* means of grace, the state and the kingdom of God on earth.

In the second place, the Catholic Church, if it has not altogether lost the heart of the Gospel, that is, the free grace of God, the justification of sinners by faith alone, has mingled it nevertheless with very impure component parts, and so has confused the distinction between the law and the Gospel. This distortion of the original Gospel occurred already in the early centuries. But later it developed apace and got official approbation. In the struggle between Augustine and Pelagius, a struggle which still continues, the Roman church, particularly after the Reformation, has more and more aligned itself, not in name merely but in deed also, with Pelagius. True, God grants the *ability* to man who hears the Gospel to turn right about face from sin and self to God and grace and to persevere in this conversion. But the willing and persevering themselves are man's own contribution. By means of good works, therefore, he must earn his admittance to the kingdom of heaven.

Those good works fall into two classifications for the Roman church: the works of keeping the regular commandments as they apply to everyone; and the works aimed at satisfying the counsels added to the law by Christ (celibacy, poverty, and obedience). The first way is a good way, but the second is better and more difficult, although it is shorter and safer also. The first way is intended for the lay people, and the second for the religious — the monks and the nuns. Whoever walks in this way of good works will receive from the church, by way of the sacraments, always so much grace as he has deserved. Finally, if he perseveres to the end, he will arrive — not at the time of his conversion or of his death, and only after years of suffering in purgatory — in the kingdom of heaven.

In the third place, the Catholic Church soon began making a distinction between clergy and laity. It is not the believers in general but the clergy who are in the proper sense the priests. And in this clerical status various further classifications have been made.

In the New Testament the names *elder* and *bishop* are interchangeable designations for the same office-bearers. But as early as the second century this unity was overlooked: the bishop was raised high above the level of deacons and elders (presbyters, priests) and gradually came to be regarded as a successor to the apostles and preserver of the tradition. These bishops have canons, priests, and chaplains as their inferiors and archbishops, patriarchs, and finally the pope as their superiors. And this entire, far-flung ecclesiastical hierarchy culminates in the pope who, at the Vatican Council of Rome in 1870, was officially declared infallible. He is the "father" (Pope: papa) of the whole church, the "chief priest," the successor to Peter, the vice-gerent of Christ, the highest legislative and judicial authority, and the one who, with the help of a large college of officers (cardinals, prelates, procurators, notaries, and the like), governs the whole church.

These errors, which took their point of departure in slight deviations from the right course, grew worse and worse in the course of the ages. They have developed, and continue now to develop in such a direction that the old Christian, catholic church is always more and more becoming the Ultramontanist, Roman (*i. e.*, inseparably subjected to the church at Rome), and Papal church, in which Mary, the mother of Jesus, and the pope as the substitute for Christ force the person and work of Christ more and more into the background.

The three heresies or errors named above represent a curtailment of the prophetic, priestly, and kingly office of Christ and a violation of it.

* * * * *

This corruption of the church did not develop without energetic and constantly renewed efforts to counteract it. In the Middle Ages especially there was no dearth of persons and tendencies aimed at introducing improvement. But all of these movements had little success at that time. Some of them left off with little practical effect. Some of them were forcibly suppressed and smothered in blood. Against the Reformation of the sixteenth century, too, these means of suppression and annihilation were applied, but at that time they did not succeed. The times were then ripe for a reformation. The church was at such a low spiritual and ethical level that it was no longer trusted even by its own people. There was a widespread sense everywhere that this kind of thing could not go on, and a yearning for something to happen; and a good many people, in Italy for instance, fell into mocking religion and Christianity and into complete unbelief. What would have happened to the church without the Reformation is hard to conceive of. It was a blessing also to the Roman church, and continues to be so to this day.

The Reformation was not the only tremendous movement which that new time proclaimed. It was preceded, accompanied, and followed by other movements, each of them as important in its sphere as the Reformation. The discovery of the art of printing and the discovery of gunpowder, the rise of the middle class, the discovery of America, the renascence of literature and art, the new natural science and philosophy — all of these important movements and events were evidences of the reawakening of self-consciousness and of the transition of the Middle Ages to the new time.

And the Reformation, although it proceeded from its own principle and directed to its own end, was borne and supported by all of these movements.

Moreover — and this is by no means the least important consideration — the Reformation in its opposition to the Roman church addressed itself to the root of the trouble. It was not satisfied with an improvement of the external forms but insisted that the cause of the corruption be removed. For that it needed a firm point of departure, a reliable norm or criterion, and a positive principle. The Reformation found this, in contrast to the traditions of the Roman church, in the *word* of Christ which it held to be worthy of acceptation in itself and for its own sake, necessary for the life and well-being of the church and also quite self-sufficient and clear. The Reformation found this, over against the good works to which Rome attached the salvation of man, in the *work* of Christ which it held to be perfect and in need of no human completion. And, finally, the Reformation found this, over against the pope who claimed to be the infallible representative of Christ, in the *Spirit* of Christ poured out upon the church and leading the children of God into all truth.

The Reformation did not find this positive principle by way of scientific investigation and reflection, but by way of the experience of the guilt-oppressed heart which found reconciliation and forgiveness at last in the free grace of God. The Reformation was not a philosophical or scientific movement. It was religious and moral in character. As always happens in the event of schism and separation, many identified themselves with the movement prompted by impure and ignoble motives. But those at the heart and core of the Reformation were the weary and heavy laden who were languishing under the Roman yoke, and who had now found rest for their souls again at the feet of the Savior.

This experience of the forgiveness of sins was enough for Luther. It was enough for him that he had found "a gracious God." True, from this new vantage point which he had taken he looked out more freely and widely over the whole world than did the Roman Christian to whom the natural had always had the quality of the profane. But, resting entirely in justification, which he had obtained by faith alone, he left all that was secular — art and science, state and society — to carry on by itself. The Lutheran Reformation limited itself to the restoration of the preaching office. When it had found in Scripture the answer to the question: How is man saved? it desisted from all further effort.

For Zwingli and Calvin, who took hold of the Reformation in Switzerland, the work only began at the point where it had broken off for Luther. They too came to the point of reformation, not by way of rational argument, but by way of the experience of sin and grace, guilt and reconciliation. This experience was their point of departure, but it was not their resting place, nor the end of their way. They penetrated further, both forwards and backwards. Behind the grace of God which comes to expression in the pardon of guilt, there lies the sovereignty of God, the infinite and worshipful being of God in all of His excellences and perfections. They saw that if God was sovereign in the work of salvation, He was sovereign always and everywhere — in creation as well as in re-creation. If He had become King in the heart of man, He had become that also in his head and hand, in the home and office and field, in state and society, in art and science. The question, How is man saved? did not suffice, but had to be led back to another, higher, deeper, and all-comprehensive one: How is God to have His due of glory? Hence, for Zwingli, and even more for Calvin, the work of reformation had only begun when they had found peace of heart in the blood of the cross. The whole world lay open before them, so to speak, not in order to be left to its own devices but to be penetrated and hallowed by the word of God and by prayer. They began in their immediate environment by addressing themselves to the church and city where they lived. They restored not only the office of preaching but also the worship service and the church discipline; they reformed not merely the religious life of Sunday but also the civic and social life of the days of the week. They reformed not merely the private life of the citizen but also the public life of the state. From that point their reformation spread to other lands and places. The Lutheran Reformation limited itself mainly to Germany and Denmark, Sweden and Norway. But the Reformation of Calvin found admittance in Italy and Spain, Hungary and Poland, Switzerland and France, Belgium and The Netherlands, England and Scotland, and in the United States and Canada. If it had not been counteracted, thrust back, and destroyed by the counter-reformation of the Jesuits in many countries, it would have put an end to Rome's world dominion for good and all.

* * * * *

Such conquest was not, however, permitted it. From the very beginning the Reformation was attacked by the Roman church. At the Council of Trent, Rome deliberately and consciously pitted herself against the Reformation, and thereafter it moved on in the direction it had taken there. Moreover, the Reformation weakened itself by internal division and endless disputes. Alongside of it, even as early as the sixteenth century, Socinianism and Anabaptism put in their appearance. Both of these proceeded out of the same basic idea: that is, the incompatible conflict between nature and grace. Hence they sacrificed either grace to nature, or nature to grace. This same opposition between creation and re-creation, the human and the divine, reason and revelation, earth and heaven, humanity and Christendom — or however one may wish further to designate the terms of the contrast — continued active later on also, and continues active to this day. The separations and schisms of the sixteenth century were not the only ones. Each succeeding century increased the number of them. The seventeenth century gave rise to Remonstrantism in the Netherlands, Independentism in England, and Pietism in Germany. To these in the eighteenth century were added Herrnhuttism, Methodism, and Swedenborgianism, and in that same century all churches were overrun by the flood of Deism. After the French Revolution at the beginning of the nineteenth century a powerful religious revival took place in both the Roman and the Protestant churches. Nevertheless the separations continued. Darbyism, Irvingism, Mormonism, Spiritism, and all sorts of other sects, fell like so many fragments from churches that were themselves often weakened and consumed by an inner spirit of doubt and indifference. And, outside of the churches, the might of monism, be it in materialistic or pantheistic form, organized its forces for a final, deadly assault upon the whole Christian religion.

It would seem therefore that all hope for the unity and universality of the church of Christ is lost . . . . There is, however, one comfort — Christ gathers His own from all nations and kindreds and peoples and tongues. He will bring them all and they shall hear His voice. And they shall be *one* fold, one flock, and *one* Shepherd (John 10:16).

IX

The Being of God

Thus far we have been discussing the nature of the revelation which God has granted us in His grace, and we have given some account of how that revelation came into existence, and how, under the formative leadership of the creeds and confessions, we have come to know it. It remains now to set forth the content of that revelation, and to point out in systematic fashion what we owe to that revelation in mind and heart, in point both of knowledge and life. If, so to speak, we have, in what has been said so far, been looking at the edifice of revelation from the outside, and have some idea of its architectonics, we shall now enter into the sanctuary itself to take a full look at the treasures of wisdom and knowledge contained there and laid out for our eyes to feast on.

It needs no contending that we can develop the rich content of this revelation in various ways, and can let its various parts pass in review before us in different patterns. We do not have to discuss each of these ways and orders of treatment. We limit the discussion to two methods in which the content of Christian doctrine can be treated, and frequently is.

In the first place, we can go straight to the Christian who, with a true faith in his heart, has taken up the content of revelation into himself, and then ask him in what way he has arrived at the knowledge of the truth, of what points this knowledge consists, and what fruit this knowledge has contributed to his thought and life. This is the point of view which our *Heidelberg Catechism* takes. The speaker in that Catechism is the Christian. He gives a comprehensive and clear account of what in life and in death is his only comfort and of the various points which it is necessary to know if one is to live and die blessedly in this comfort. This is a beautiful method of treatment, and it deserves the warmest commendation in a practical handbook of theology. It is a method which has many advantages: it relates the truth immediately to the whole of Christian life, safeguards against academic argument and idle speculations, and in its approach to every doctrine points out directly what is its value for the mind and heart. What benefit and comfort does it give you to believe all this? That I am justified before God in Christ and am an heir of eternal life.

But there is also another major order according to which the truths of the faith can be treated. We are not limited to the method of turning to the Christian and asking him to say what he believes. We can also put ourselves in the position of the Christian, and then try to give ourselves and others an account out of Scripture of the content of our faith. In that way we do not let the development of our confession be determined by the questions which are directed to us about it.

According to this second method we ourselves set forth positively the content of our faith. Our concern is then not so much to follow the order in which we arrived at the knowledge of the truth. Instead we try to trace out what order is objectively present in the truths of the faith themselves, how these are related to each other, and what the governing principle of them all is. This is the order followed in the Reformed *Confession of Faith*. In that Confession, too, the Christian is the speaker, but he does not wait for questions to be put to him; instead he himself explains the content of his faith. He believes with his heart and confesses with his mouth what God has to say to the churches in His Word and through His Spirit.

These two methods of treatment do not of course stand in diametrical opposition to each other. Rather the one completes and fills out the other, and both are of great value. For the Reformed churches and also for the Reformed Christian Schools it is an invaluable privilege that we possess the Confession of Faith alongside of the Catechism, and the Catechism alongside of the Confession of Faith. What these together give us is the objective and subjective, the theological and the anthropological. These are thus intermingled and head and heart are reconciled by them. Thus the truth of God becomes a blessing both for our mind and our life.

That these two methods of setting forth the content of revelation are not opposed to each other, but rather complement and balance each other, is abundantly proved by the fact that, not in the Catechism only but in the Confession also, it is the Christian who is speaking. In both it is the Christian not in isolation but in fellowship with all his brothers and sisters. It is the church, the body of believers, which expresses itself in them. We *all* believe with the heart and confess with the mouth — such are the opening words of the Confession, so it continues, and so it ends. It is a true Christian Confession containing the summary of the doctrine of God and *of the eternal salvation of souls*.

These two, the doctrine of God and the doctrine of the eternal salvation of souls, are not two independent doctrines which have nothing to do with each other, but are, rather, inseparably related to each other. The doctrine of God is at the same time a doctrine of the eternal salvation of souls, and the second of these also includes the first. The knowledge of God in the face of Jesus Christ His Son, this is eternal life (John 17:3).

This knowledge of God is different in kind but not in degree from the knowledge which we obtain from daily life or from the school. It is a peculiar kind of knowledge. It differs in principle, object, and effect from every other kind of knowledge, as we pointed out in Chapter Two above. This knowledge is a matter of head and heart both. It does not make us more "learned," at least not in the first place, but it makes us wiser, better, happier. It makes us *blessed* and gives us *eternal* life, hereafter, indeed, but here and now also. The three things which it is necessary for us to know have not as their end only this, that we should sometime *die* blessedly. It is their end also that we should immediately, from that moment on, *live* blessedly.

He that believes on the Son *has* everlasting life (John 3:16). Blessed *are* the pure in heart: they are that already on earth, be it that this is because of the promise that they shall see God hereafter (Matt. 5:8). For they are saved by hope (Rom. 8:24).

* * * * *

Once we have received the principle of eternal life in our hearts we cannot but long always to know more of Him who granted us that life. More and more we come to look up to Him who is the fountain of our salvation. From the comfort which we enjoy in our hearts, and from the benefit and fruit which the knowledge of God spells for our own selves and our lives, we always go back to the worship of the Eternal Being. And then we always come more certainly to the sense that God does not exist for us but that we exist for Him. We are not indifferent to our salvation, but this salvation is a means to His glory. The knowledge of God gave us life, but the life that was given leads us back to the knowledge of Him. In God we find all our well-being and all our glory. He becomes the object of our worship, the theme of our song, the strength of our life. From God, through God, and unto God are all things — that becomes the choice of our hearts and the watchword of our work. We ourselves and all creatures round about us become means unto His glory. The truth which at first we love especially because it gave us life, thereupon becomes more and more dear to us because of itself, because of what it reveals to us concerning the Eternal Being. The whole doctrine of faith, in its entirety and in its parts, becomes a proclamation of the praise of God, an exhibit of His excellences, a glorification of His name. The Catechism leads us to the Confession of Faith.

However, when we try to reflect somewhat upon what it means that we poor, weak, sinful creatures know *God* who is the Infinite One and the Eternal One, then a deep reverence and holy shyness grips our feelings. Is it really true, we feel then, that in the darkened mind of a guilty human being some light can fall from Him whom no man has seen, who dwells in unapproachable light (1 Tim. 6:16), who is pure light and in whom there is no darkness at all (1 John 1:5)?

There have been many, and there are some still, who have given a negative reply to this question. But this denial of the knowableness of God can come from two very different attitudes of mind. Nowadays this skeptical temper is the result of a purely rationalistic, abstractly scientific sort of argument.

It is said that the knowledge which is available to the human mind is limited to the empirically observable phenomena, and it is then argued that it is a contradiction to hold, on the one hand, that God has personality, mind, and will, and, on the other, to maintain that He is nevertheless infinite, eternal, and absolutely independent.

To this we can readily reply that in very fact there can be no knowledge of God in the mind of man, unless God, whether in a general way in nature and history, or in a special way in His Son, has revealed Himself. If, however, God has so revealed Himself, it follows naturally enough that He can be known to that same extent to which He has done the revealing. But if one were to maintain that He in no way and by no means has revealed Himself, the implication would be that the world has eternally existed alongside of God and independent of Him, and that He could not reveal Himself in it and through it. And the further implication of that would be that we ought never again to speak about God, since this word would be but a hollow sound, having no ground or basis in reality. The so-called agnosticism (the doctrine of the unknowableness of God) turns out in practice to be identical with atheism (the denial of the existence of God).

But this denial of the knowableness of God can also spring from a deep sense of one's own littleness and nothingness and from a deep feeling, combined with that, of God's infinite greatness and overwhelming majesty. In this sense, the acknowledgment that we know nothing, that knowledge is too wonderful for us, has been the confession of all saints. In the fathers and teachers of the church the statement is often found that, in reflecting upon God, they could in the final analysis say much better what God is not than what He is. Calvin somewhere admonishes his readers not to try in their own strength to wrest God's secrets from Him, inasmuch as these mysteries far transcend our frail capacities for knowledge. And the poets, Vondel, for instance, and Bilderdijk, have often sung of this all-surpassing greatness of God.

Although this humble confession of God's sublime majesty and of human littleness can, in a certain sense, be called a denial of the knowability of God, still it would seem that, in the interest of avoiding misunderstanding, and in accordance with Holy Scripture, we ought to make a distinction between God's knowableness and His fathomableness. For there is certainly no book in the world which to the same extent and in the same way as the Holy Scripture supports the absolute transcendence of God above each and every creature and at the same time supports the intimate relationship between the creature and his Creator.

*   *   *   *   *

On the very first page of the Bible the absolute transcendence of God above His creatures comes to our attention. Without strain or fatigue He calls the whole world into existence by His word alone. By the word of the Lord were the heavens made, and all the host of them by the breath of His mouth (Ps. 33:6). He speaks and it is done; He commands and it stands fast (Ps. 33:9). He does according to His will in the army of heaven, and among the inhabitants of the earth. And none can stay His hand, or say unto Him, what doest Thou (Dan. 4:35)? The nations are as a drop of a bucket, and are counted as the small dust of the balance: behold, He taketh up the isles as a very little thing. And Lebanon is not sufficient to burn, nor the beasts thereof sufficient for a burnt offering. All nations before Him are as nothing, and they are counted to Him as less than nothing, and vanity. To whom then will you liken God? or what likeness will you compare unto Him (Isa. 40:15-18). For who in the heaven can be compared unto the Lord? who among the sons of the mighty can be likened unto the Lord (Ps. 89:6). There is no name by which He can truly be named: His name is wonderful.[1] When God speaks to Job out of the thunder and displays the magnitude of His works before him, Job humbly bows his head, and says: Behold, I am vile. What shall I answer Thee? I will lay my hand upon my mouth (Job 40:4). God is great, and we know Him not (Job 36:26). Such knowledge is too wonderful for us. It is high. We cannot attain unto it (Ps. 139:6).

---

1. Gen. 32:29; Judges 13:18; and Prov. 30:4.

Nevertheless, this same sublime and exalted God stands in intimate relationship with all His creatures, even the meanest and smallest. What the Scriptures give us is not an abstract concept of God, such as the philosopher gives us, but puts the very, living God before us and lets us see Him in the works of His hands. We have but to lift up our eyes and see who has made all things. All things were made by His hand, brought forth by His will and His deed. And they are all sustained by His strength. Hence everything bears the stamp of His excellences and the mark of His goodness, wisdom, and power. And among creatures only man was created in His image and likeness. Only man is called the *offspring* of God (Acts 17:28).

Because of this intimate relationship, God can be named in the terms of His creatures, and He can be spoken of anthropomorphically. The same Scripture which speaks in the most exalted way of God's incomparable greatness and majesty, at the same time speaks of Him in figures and images which sparkle with life. It speaks of His eyes and ears, His hands and feet, His mouth and lips, His heart and bowels. It ascribes all kinds of attributes to Him — of wisdom and knowledge, will and power, righteousness and mercy, and it ascribes to Him also such emotions as joy and grief, fear and vexation, zeal and envy, remorse and wrath, hatred and anger. It speaks of His observing and thinking, His hearing and seeing, His remembering and forgetting, smelling and tasting, sitting and rising, visiting and forsaking, blessing and chastising, and the like. It compares Him to a sun and a light, a fountain and a spring, a rock and a shelter, a sword and buckler, a lion and an eagle, a hero and a warrior, an artist and builder, a king and a judge, a husbandman and a shepherd, a man and a father. In short, all that can be found in the whole world in the way of support and shelter and aid is originally and perfectly to be found in overflowing abundance in God. Of Him the whole family in heaven and earth is named (Eph. 3:15). He is the Sun of being and all creatures are His fleeting rays.

It is important, therefore, in this matter of the knowledge of God, for us to keep a firm hold on both of these groups of statements concerning the Divine being and to do justice to each of them. For, if we sacrifice the absolute transcendence of God above all of His creatures, we fall into polytheism (the pagan religion of many gods) or pantheism (the religion in which everything is God), two false religions which, according to the lesson of history, are closely related to each other and easily pass from the one into the other.

And if we sacrifice the close relationship of God to His creatures, we go aground on the reef of deism (belief in God without benefit of revelation) or of atheism (the denial of the existence of God), two religions which, like those others, have numerous characteristics in common with each other.

Scripture clings to both groups of characteristics, and Christian theology has followed in its wake. God actually does not have a name according to which we can truly name Him, and He names Himself and lets us name Him with many, many names. He is the infinitely Exalted One, and at the same time the One who lives along with all His creatures. In a certain sense all of His attributes are such as cannot be shared, and in another sense they are such as can all be shared. We cannot fathom this with our mind. There is no such thing as an adequate concept of God. There is no one who can give a definition, a delimitation, of God that is adequate to His being. The name which fully expresses what He is cannot be found. But the one group of characteristics outlined above does not conflict with the other. Precisely because God is the High and Exalted One, and lives in eternity, He also dwells with those who are of a contrite and humble Spirit (Isa. 57:15). We know that God did not reveal Himself in order that we should draw up a philosophical concept of God from His revelation, but in order that we should accept Him, the true, living God, as our God, and should acknowledge and confess Him. These things are hidden from the wise and prudent, but they have been revealed to babes (Matt. 11:25).

The knowledge which we get of God by way of His revelation is therefore a knowledge of faith. It is not adequate, in the sense that it is not equivalent to the being of God, for God is infinitely exalted above all His creatures. Such knowledge is not purely symbolical either — that is to say, couched in expressions which we have arbitrarily formed and which do not correspond to any reality; instead this knowledge is ectypal (ectype: an impression, as in printing) or analogical (analogy: correspondence or similarity in form) because it is based on the likeness and relationship which, notwithstanding God's absolute majesty, nevertheless exists between God and all the works of His hand. The knowledge which God grants us of Himself in nature and in Scripture is limited, finite, fragmentary, but it is nevertheless true and pure. Such is God as He has revealed Himself in His Word and specifically in and through Christ; and He alone is such as our hearts require.

* * * * *

The effort to take account of all the data of Holy Scripture in its doctrine of God, and to maintain both His transcendence of and His relationship to the creature, led the Christian church to make a distinction very early between two groups of the attributes of the Divine being. These two groups were variously designated from the early church on. The Roman church still prefers to speak of negative and positive attributes, the Lutheran of quiescent and operative attributes, and the Reformed churches of incommunicable and communicable attributes. At bottom, however, this division amounts to the same thing in all of these churches. The purpose for each of them is to insist on God's transcendence (His distinction from and His elevation above the world) *and* on God's immanence (His community with and His indwelling in the world). The Reformed names of incommunicable and communicable attributes do better justice to this purpose than the names which the Catholics and the Lutherans employ. The insistence on the first group of attributes saves us from polytheism and pantheism; and the insistence on the second group protects us against deism and atheism.

Even though all of our designations for these attributes are inadequate, there is no convincing objection to continuing to use the Reformed terms. What we must then do, however, is to remember that the two groups of incommunicable and communicable attributes do not stand alongside of each other in total separation. But the force of the distinction must not be lost either, and the thrust of that distinction is that God possesses all of His incommunicable attributes in an absolute way and to an infinite and therefore incommunicable degree. It is true that God's knowledge, wisdom, goodness, justice, and the like, have certain characteristics in common with those same virtues in His creatures, but they are peculiar to God in an independent, immutable, eternal, omnipresent, simple — or, in a word, in an absolutely Divine way.

We as human beings can make a distinction between the being and the attributes of people. A human being can lose his arm or his leg, or, in a state of sleep or illness, lose consciousness, without ceasing to be human. But in God this is impossible. His attributes coincide with His being. Every attribute is His being. He is wise and true, not merely, good and holy, just and merciful, but He *is* also wisdom, truth, goodness, holiness, justice, and mercy. Hence He is also the source and fount of all the attributes of man. He *is* everything that He *possesses* and is the source of everything that creatures possess. He is the abundant source of all goods.

* * * * *

Among the incommunicable attributes of God those excellences or virtues are meant which demonstrate that all that is in God exists in

Him in an absolutely Divine way, and is therefore not susceptible to being shared by creatures. This group of attributes affirms the absolute exaltedness and incomparableness of God, and has its fullest expression in the name Elohim, or, God. True the name *god* is also applied to creatures in the Bible. The Holy Scriptures make mention not merely of the idols of the heathen as gods, as for instance they do in forbidding us to have any other gods before Him (Ex. 20:3): they also designate Moses as a God for Aaron (Ex. 4:16) and for Pharaoh (Ex. 7:1), and speak of the judges among men as gods (Ps. 82:1 and 6); and Christ appeals to this designation of the Psalms in His own self-defense (John 10:33-35).

But this usage of language is derived, imitative. The name of God originally and essentially belonged to God alone. It is with that name that we always associate an idea of a being who is personal, indeed, but who is also a power raised high above all creatures and eternal in kind.

It is as such that He possesses the incommunicable attributes. They are peculiar and proper to Him alone, are not found in creatures, and cannot even be shared with creatures. For all creatures are dependent, changeable, composite, and subject to time and space. But God is *independent,* in the sense that He is determined by nothing and everything else is determined by Him (Acts 17:25 and Rom. 11:36). He is *unchangeable* so that He eternally remains the same, and all variableness and turning are owing to the creature and the relationship in which the creature places himself over against God (James 1:17). He is *simple,* not composite, wholly free of all compounding of spirit and matter, thought and extent, being and properties, reason and will, and like components, and all that He *has* also *is* pure truth and life and light.[2] He is *eternal* in that He transcends time and yet penetrates every moment of time with his eternity (Ps. 90:2). And He is *omnipresent* in that He transcends all space and yet bears up every point of space by His almighty and ever-present strength.[3]

In modern times there are quite a few observers who deny all religious worth to these incommunicable attributes and see in them nothing but metaphysical abstractions. But quite the opposite is proved by the fact that any sacrifice of these distinctions immediately opens the door to pantheism and polytheism.

If God is not held to be independent and unchangeable, eternal and omnipresent, simple and free from compositism, He is pulled down to the level of the creature and is identified with the world in its totality

---

2. Ps. 36:9; John 5:26; and 1 John 1:5.
3. Ps. 139:7; Acts 17:27 and 28.

or with one of its powers. Hence the number of those is constantly increasing who exchange the God of revelation for an immanentistic world-force or who prefer to confess a polytheism rather than the one true God. It is clear that the *oneness* and *unity* of God is directly connected with the incommunicable attributes.[4] God is the one God and the only God only if no one and no thing can be what He is alongside of Him or under Him. And only if He is independent and unchangeable, eternal and omnipresent can He be the God of our unconditional faith, of our absolute trust, and of our perfect salvation.

* * * * *

Meanwhile it remains true that we need more than these incommunicable attributes. What good would it do us to know that God was independent and unchangeable, eternal and omnipresent, if we had to do without the knowledge that He was compassionate and gracious and very merciful? It is true that the incommunicable attributes tell us about the *way* in which all that is in God exists in Him; but they leave us in the dark about the *content* of the Divine Being. This is not true of the communicable attributes. They tell us that this God who is so infinitely exalted and sublime nevertheless also dwells in all His creatures, is related to all His creatures, and possesses all those virtues which in a derived and limited way are also proper to His creatures. He is not only a God afar off but is also a God nearby. He is not only independent and unchangeable, eternal and omnipresent, but also wise and mighty, just and holy, gracious and merciful. He is Elohim not only but also Jehovah.

Just as the incommunicable attributes come to expression well in the name Elohim, meaning God, so the communicable attributes come into their own in the name Jehovah. The derivation and the original significance of this name is not known to us. Very probably it existed for some time before the time of Moses — as would seem to be suggested by the proper name Jochebed, but God did not yet at that time make Himself known to His people by this name. He reveals Himself to Abraham as El-Shaddai, God the Almighty (Gen. 17:1 and Exod. 6:2), who subjects all the forces of nature and makes them serviceable to grace. But now that hundreds of years have passed by and God seems to have forgotten His covenant with the fathers and His promise to them, then He makes Himself known to Moses as Jehovah, that is, as the God who is the same as He who appeared to the fathers, who is faithful to His covenant, who fulfills His promise, and who, throughout

---

4. Deut. 6:4; Mark 12:29; and John 17:3.

the centuries, remains Himself over against His people. The meaning of Jehovah now becomes: I am that I am (I shall be what I shall be) and the name designates God's unchangeable faithfulness in His relationship to Israel. Jehovah is the God of the covenant who, according to His sovereign love, has chosen His people and made them His own. Thus, while the name Elohim, God, points to the eternal Being in His sovereign elevation above the world, the name Jehovah, Lord, affirms that this same God has voluntarily revealed Himself to His people as a God of holiness, grace, and faithfulness.

The whole religious struggle in Israel and in aftertimes up to our own time is essentially concerned with this question of who God is. The heathen, and many philosophers of early and later date say that Jehovah is only the God of Israel — a national, limited, and minor God. But Moses and Elijah and all the prophets, and Christ and all His disciples, take an opposite position and maintain that the *Lord* alone, who entered into covenant with the fathers and the people of Israel, is the one, eternal, and true God, and that there is no other God beside Him (Isa. 43:10-15 and 44:6). Therefore Jehovah is really God's true, characteristic name (Isa. 42:8 and 48:12). The God of the covenant who so condescendingly comes down to His people, and who dwells with those who are of contrite and humble spirit, is at the same time the High and Lofty One (Isa. 57:15).

The two kinds of attributes are therefore not in conflict with each other. We might say that the first serve to illumine and reinforce the others. Consider, for example, the love of God. We would not be permitted to speak of it, nor could we speak of it, if the attribute which men call love were not in a sense an impression (ectype), image, or likeness of the love that is present in God. There should be a certain correspondence between the Divine and the human love, or else all of our thinking and speaking of the love of God were a hollow sound. But this similarity is by no means an identity. The purest and strongest love among men is but a very weak reflection of the love which is in God. And that teaches us to understand the incommunicable attributes. From them we learn that in God love far transcends the love of creatures. For the love in God is independent, unchangeable, simple, eternal, and omnipresent. It does not depend upon us, nor is aroused by us, but flows, free and pure, from the depths of the Divine being. It knows no variation, neither falls nor rises, appears nor disappears, and there is not even the shadow of turning about it. It is not merely a property of the Divine being alongside of other properties or attributes, and never gets into conflict with these others, but it also coincides with the Divine Being Himself. God is love, He Himself, wholly and perfectly, and with His whole being. This love is not subject to time and space, but stands above it, and comes down out of eternity into the hearts of the children of God. Such a love is absolutely reliable. Our souls can rest in it in every need, including death itself, and if such a God of love be for us, who can be against us? And the same can be said of all of the communicable attributes. There is in God's creatures a faint likeness of the knowledge and wisdom, the goodness and grace, the righteousness and holiness, and of the will and the power which are proper to God. All that is transient is an image. The things that are seen came into being out of the things that are not seen (Heb. 11:3). But all those attributes are present in God in an original, independent, unchangeable, simple, and infinite way. The *Lord* alone is God, and it is He that has made us to be His people, the sheep of His flock (Ps. 100:3).

The communicable attributes are so numerous that it is impossible to sum them all up here and to describe them. If we should want to treat of them adequately, we should have to make use of all those names and images and comparisons which the Holy Scriptures use to give us some idea of who and what God is for His creatures and, specifically, for His people. For Scripture, as we indicated in passing, ascribes such organs of the body as eyes and ears, hands and feet, and the like, to God. It transfers such human awarenesses, emotions, passions, decisions, and actions to Him. It refers to Him with the names of such offices and vocations as are found among human beings, calling Him king and lawgiver and judge, warrior and hero, husbandman and shepherd, and man and father. It calls upon the whole of the organic and inorganic world to help make God real to us, and compares Him with a lion, an eagle, a sun, a fire, a fount, a shield, and so on. And all of these ways of speaking are an effort to help us know God and to leave a deep impression of the all-sufficiency of His being. We human beings need the whole outside world for our spiritual and physical existence. For we are poor and weak in ourselves and we own nothing. But all this that we need, according to soul and body, for time and eternity is without exception available to us — original, perfect, infinite — in God. He is the highest good and the overflowing fountain of all goods.

The first thing that the Holy Scripture wants to give us, in its use of all those descriptions and names of the Divine Being, is an ineradicable sense of the fact that Jehovah, the God, who has revealed Himself to Israel and in Christ, is the very, the true, and the living God. The idols of the heathen and the idols (pantheistic and polytheistic, deistic and atheistic) of the philosophers, are the work of men's hands: they cannot speak nor see, they cannot hear, nor taste nor go. But the God of Israel is in heaven and He does all that He desires. He is the one God (Deut. 6:4), the true God (John 17:3), and He is the ever-living God.[5] People want to make God a dead God so that they may treat Him as they please. But the message of the Scripture is this: That is wrong. God exists. He is the true God, and He *lives,* now and in eternity. And it is terrible to fall into the hands of the living God (Heb. 10:31).

As such a *living* God, who is pure life and the fountain of all life (Ps. 36:9 and Jer. 2:13), He is also *Spirit* (John 4:24), without body, even though all kinds of physical organs are ascribed to Him (Deut. 4:12, 16). Hence no image, likeness, or similitude can be made of Him (Deut. 4:15-19). He is invisible.[6] As Spirit He has *consciousness,* perfect knowledge of Himself (Matt. 11:27 and 1 Cor. 2:10), and in and through Himself He also has perfect knowledge of everything that is to be or happen in time, no matter how hidden or small it may be.[7] As Spirit He has *will,* and by means of it He does all that pleases Him (secret will or counsel),[8] and determines what must be the governing norm of our conduct (revealed will or commandment).[9] And as Spirit, finally, He has *power,* by means of which, notwithstanding any and all opposition, He executes what He has planned and because of which nothing is impossible to Him.[10]

But this knowledge or consciousness, this will and power, are not arbitrary: they are in all their parts ethically determined. This comes to expression in the *wisdom* which in the Holy Scripture is ascribed to God,[11] and by means of which He arranges and directs all things according to the purpose which He has set for them at creation and re-creation.[12] And this moral reality comes to further expression in the *goodness* and *grace,* on the one hand, and in the *holiness* and *justice,* on the other, which are attributed to God. He is not merely the All-wise and the All-mighty: He is also the All-good and the Alone-good (Matt. 5:45), and He is perfect and the source of all that is good in creatures (Ps. 145:9). This goodness of God spreads itself out over the whole world (Ps. 145:9 and Matt. 5:45), but varies according to the objects on which it is directed, assuming, as it were, various forms. It is called *longsuffering* or forbearance when it is manifested to the guilty (Rom.

---

5. Deut. 5:26; John 3:10; Dan. 6:27; Acts 14:15; 2 Cor. 6:16; 1 Tim. 3:15 and 6:17.
6. Ex. 33:20; John 1:18; 6:46; and 1 Tim. 6:16.
7. Isa. 46:10; Jer. 11:20; Matt. 10:30 and Heb. 4:14.
8. Ps. 115:3; Prov. 21:1; and Dan. 4:35.
9. Deut. 29:29; Matt. 7:21 and 12:50.
10. Gen. 18:14; Jer. 22:37; Zech. 8:6; Matt. 19:26; and 1 Tim. 6:15.
11. Prov. 8:22-31; Job 28:20-28; Rom. 16:27; and 1 Tim. 1:17.
12. Ps. 104:24; Eph. 3:10; and Rom. 11:33.

3:25), *grace* when it is manifested to those who receive the forgiveness of sins (Eph. 2:8), and *love* when God, out of grace towards His creatures shares Himself with them (John 3:16 and 1 John 4:8). It is called *loving-kindness* or mercy when this goodness of God is manifested to those who enjoy His favor,[13] and *good will* or *good pleasure* when the emphasis falls on the fact that the goodness and all its benefits are a free gift.[14]

* * * * *

God's holiness and justice go hand in hand with this goodness and grace of God. God is called the Holy One, not only because He is exalted above every creature as creature, but especially because He is apart from all that is sinful and impure in the world. And therefore He requires that His people, which out of free grace He elected to be His own, be holy,[15] and He sanctifies Himself in that people through Christ (Eph. 5:26-27), even as Christ sanctified Himself for them in order that they, too, might be sanctified in the truth (John 17:19). And the *righteousness* and justice of God is closely related to His holiness. For, as the Holy One, He can have no fellowship with sin. He hates sin (Ps. 45:7 and Job 34:10), rages against it (Rom. 1:18), is jealous of His honor (Ex. 20:5), and He can, therefore, in no sense hold the guilty guiltless (Ex. 25:5 and 7). His holy nature requires also that outside of Himself, in the world of creatures, He keep righteousness in force, and, without respect of persons reward everyone according to his works (Rom. 2:2-11 and 2 Cor. 5:10). Nowadays there are those who try to make themselves and others believe that God pays no attention to the sinful thoughts and deeds of men. But the true, the living God, whom Scriptures present to us, thinks very differently about this. His wrath is kindled terribly against native and actual sins, and He wants to punish them both temporally and eternally by way of a righteous judgment (Deut. 27:26 and Gal. 3:10).

But He not only punishes the godless according to His justice. For it is the remarkable teaching of Scripture that it is according to this same justice that He grants salvation to the saints. True, those saints are in themselves sinners also and no better than the others. But while the ungodly conceal their sins or gloss them over, the saints acknowledge them and confess them. This is the distinction between them. Although they are *personally* guilty and impure, they are, so far as the cause is concerned on the side of God and against the world. They can therefore

---

13. Gen. 39:21; Num. 14:19; Isa. 54:10; and Eph. 2:7.
14. Matt. 11:26; Luke 2:14; Luke 12:32; and 2 Thess. 1:11.
15. Ex. 19:5 and 6; Lev. 11:44-45; and 1 Peter 2:9.

appeal to the promise of the covenant of grace, to the truth of His word, to the righteousness which God Himself has accomplished in Christ.

In terms of that righteousness, we might even boldly though reverently say, God is obligated to forgive the sins of His people and to grant them eternal life.[16] And if God often lets His people wait for Him, and tries their faith for a long while, there follows upon it their perfect redemption, and so the *integrity* and *faithfulness* of God is demonstrated the more gloriously.[17]

The Lord will perfect that which concerns His people, for His mercy endures forever (Ps. 138:8). The Lord is merciful and gracious, long-suffering and abundant in goodness and truth.[18]

Some trust in chariots and some in horses, but we will remember the name of the Lord our God.[19] For this God is our God for ever and ever; He will be our guide even unto death (Ps. 48:14). He is a *blessed* and *glorious* God (1 Tim. 6:15 and Eph. 1:17). And blessed is the people whose God is the Lord (Ps. 33:12).

---

16. Ps. 4:2; 7:10; 31:2; 34:22; 35:24; 51:16; 103:17; and 1 John 1:9.
17. Gen. 24:27; 32:10; Josh. 21:45; 2 Sam. 7:28; Ps. 57:3; and Ps. 105:8.
18. Ex. 34:6; Ps. 86:15; 103:8; and 145:8.
19. Ps. 20:7; Jer. 9:23; 1 Cor. 1:31; and 2 Cor. 10:17.

X

The Divine Trinity

The Eternal Being reveals Himself in His triune existence even more richly and vitally than in His attributes. It is in this holy trinity that each attribute of His Being comes into its own, so to speak, gets its fullest content, and takes on its profoundest meaning. It is only when we contemplate this trinity that we know who and what God is. Only then do we know, moreover, who God is and what He is for lost mankind. We can know this only when we know and confess Him as the Triune God of the Covenant, as Father, Son, and Holy Spirit.

In considering this part of our confession, it is particularly necessary that a tone of holy reverence and childlike awe be the characteristic of our approach and attitude. For Moses it was an awful and unforgettable hour when the Lord appeared to him in the desert in the flame of fire coming from the bramble bush. When Moses looked upon that burning fire, which burned but did not consume, from a distance, and when he wanted to hasten to the spot, the Lord restrained him and said: Draw not nigh hither: put off thy shoes from off thy feet, for the place whereon thou standest is holy ground. And when Moses heard that he feared greatly, hid his face, and was afraid to look upon God (Ex. 3:1-6).

Such a holy respect suits us also as we witness God revealing Himself in His word as a Triune God. For we must always remember that as we study this fact, we are not dealing with a doctrine about God, with an abstract concept, or with a scientific proposition about the nature of Divinity. We are not dealing with a human construction which we ourselves or which others have put upon the facts, and which we now try to analyze and logically to dismember. Rather, in treating of the Trinity, we are dealing with God Himself, with the one and true God, who has revealed Himself as such in His Word. It is as He said to Moses: I am the God of Abraham, Isaac, and Jacob (Ex. 3:6). So He reveals Himself to us also in His Word and manifests Himself to us as Father, Son, and Spirit.

It is thus that the Christian church has always confessed the revelation of God as the Triune God, and accepted it as such. We find it in the Twelve Articles of the Apostles' Creed. The Christian is not in that creed saying just how he thinks about God. He is not there giving out a notion of God, nor saying that God has such and such attributes, and that He exists in this and that wise. Instead, he confesses: I believe *in* God the Father, and *in* Jesus Christ His only-begotten Son, and *in* the Holy Spirit: I believe in the Triune God. In confessing this the Christian gives expression to the fact that God is the living and the true God, that He is God as Father, Son, and Spirit, the God of His confidence, to whom he has wholly surrendered himself, and upon whom he rests with his whole heart. God is the God of his life and his salvation. As Father, Son, and Spirit, God has created him, redeemed him, sanctified him, and glorified him. The Christian owes everything to Him. It is his joy and comfort that he may believe *in* that God, trust Him, and expect everything from Him.

What the Christian goes on to confess about that God is not summarized by him in a number of abstract terms, but is described, rather, as a series of deeds done by God in the past, in the present, and to be done in the future. It is the deeds, the miracles, of God which constitute the confession of the Christian. What the Christian confesses in his creed is a long, a broad, and a high history. It is a history which comprises the whole world in its length and breadth, in its beginning, process, and end, in its origin, development, and destination, from the point of creation to the fulfillment of the ages. The confession of the church is a declaration of the mighty deeds of God.

Those deeds are numerous and are characterized by great diversity. But they also constitute a strict unity. They are related to each other, prepare for each other, and are interdependent. There is order and pattern, development and upward movement in it. It proceeds from creation through redemption to sanctification and glorification. The end returns to the beginning and yet is at the same time the apex which is exalted high above the point of origin. The deeds of God form a circle which mounts upward in the form of a spiral; they represent a harmony of the horizontal and the vertical line; they move upwards and forwards at the same time.

God is the architect and builder of all those deeds, the source and the final end of them. Out of Him and through Him and to Him are all things. He is their Maker, Restorer, and Fulfiller. The unity and diversity in the works of God proceeds from and returns to the unity and diversity which exist in the Divine Being. That Being is one being, single and simple. At the same time that being is threefold in His person, in His revelation, and in His influence. The entire work of God is an unbroken whole, and nevertheless comprises the richest variety and change. The confession of the church comprehends the whole of world history. In that confession are included the moments of the creation and the fall, reconciliation and forgiveness, and of renewal and restoration. It is a confession which proceeds from the triune God and which leads everything back to Him.

Therefore the article of the holy trinity is the heart and core of our confession, the differentiating earmark of our religion, and the praise and comfort of all true believers of Christ.

It was this confession which was at stake in the warfare of the spirits throughout the centuries. The confession of the holy trinity is the precious pearl which was entrusted for safekeeping and defense to the Christian church.

* * * * *

If this confession of the trinity of God takes such a central position in the Christian faith, it is important to know on what ground it rests and from what source it has flowed into the church. They are not a few in our time who hold that it is the fruit of human argument and academic learning and who, accordingly, regard it as of no value for the religious life. According to them the original Gospel, as it was proclaimed by Jesus, knew nothing about any such doctrine of the trinity of God — that is, nothing about the term itself nor about the reality to which the term was intended to give expression. It was only — so the argument goes — when the original and simple Gospel of Jesus was brought into relationship with Greek philosophy and was falsified by it that the Christian church absorbed the person of Christ in His Divine nature, and eventually also the Holy Spirit into the Divine Being. And so it came about that the church confessed three persons in the one Divine being.

But the Christian church itself has always had quite a different idea about that. It saw in the doctrine of the trinity no discovery of subtle theologians, no product of the wedding of Gospel and Greek philosophy, but a confession rather which was materially concluded in the Gospel and in the whole Word of God — a doctrine, in short, which was inferred by Christian faith from the revelation of God. In answer to the question, Since there is but one Divine Being, why do you speak of the Father, the Son, and the Holy Spirit?, the Heidelberg Catechism gives a brief and conclusive answer: Because God has so revealed Himself in His Word (Question 25). The revelation of God is the firm ground on which this confession of the church also rests. It is the source out of which this doctrine of the one, holy, catholic, Christian church has grown and been built up. God has thus revealed Himself. And He has revealed Himself thus, that is, as a triune God, because He exists in that way; and He exists in this way because He has so revealed Himself.

The Trinity in the revelation of God points back to the Trinity in His existence.

This revelation did not happen in a single moment. It was not presented and perfected in a single point of time. Rather, this revelation has a long history, spread out over the centuries. It began at the creation, continued after the fall in the promises and deeds of grace which accrued to Israel, and reached its apex in the person and work of Christ, in the pouring out of the Holy Spirit, and the establishment of the church. It maintains itself now throughout the centuries, and over against all opposition, in the ineradicable witness of Scripture and in the rock-firm confession of the church. Because the revelation has had this long history, there is progress and development also in the confession of God's triune existence. God undergoes no change, remaining always the same. But in the progress of revelation, He makes Himself always clearer and more glorious to people and to angels. As His revelation continues, our knowledge grows.

* * * * *

When, in the days of the Old Covenant, God begins to reveal Himself, the thing that stands in the foreground is certainly the unity, the oneness, of God.

For, due to the sin of man, the pure knowledge of God had been lost; the truth, as Paul profoundly says, was held in unrighteousness. Even that which can be known of God in the things that He has made was made vain by their imaginations and was darkened by the foolishness of their hearts. On every hand mankind fell into idolatry and the worship of images (Rom. 1:18-23).

Hence it was necessary that the revelation begin with an emphasis upon the unity of God. It seems to cry out to mankind: The gods before which ye bow are not the true God. There is but one true God, namely, the God who at the beginning made the heaven and the earth (Gen.1:1 and 2:1), the God who made Himself known to Abraham as God the Almighty (Gen. 17:1 and Ex. 6:3), the God who appeared to Moses as Jehovah, as the I-Am-that-I-Am (Ex. 3:14), and the God who, out of sovereign favor, chose the people of Israel, and called them, and accepted them in His covenant (Ex. 19:4 ff.). First of all, therefore, the revelation had as its content: Jehovah alone is Elohim, the LORD alone is God, and there is no other God beside Him.[1]

---

1. Deut. 4:35,39; Josh. 22:22; 2 Sam. 7:22; 22:32; 1 Kings 18:39; Isa. 45:5,18, 21; and elsewhere.

For the people of Israel, too, the revelation of the oneness of God was desperately necessary. Israel was surrounded on all sides by heathen and by heathen who at all times tried to tempt it into apostacy and unfaithfulness to the Lord; moreover, right on up to the captivity a great part of the people of Israel felt themselves attracted to the pagan idolatry and image worship, and again and again fell into the practice of them despite the proscription of the law and the warning of the prophets. Therefore, God Himself placed the emphasis on the fact that He, the Lord, who was now appearing to Moses and who wanted to redeem His people through Moses, was the same God who had made Himself known to Abraham, Isaac, and Jacob as the Almighty God (Ex. 3:6 and 15). When He gave His law to Israel He wrote above it as its preamble: I am the Lord thy God, which have brought thee out of the land of Egypt. And in the first commandment, and the second, He strictly forbade all idolatry and worship of images (Ex. 20:2-5). Because the Lord our God is one God, Israel must love Him with its whole heart, its whole soul, and all its strength (Deut. 6:4-5). The Lord alone is Israel's God and therefore Israel may serve only Him.

Nevertheless, despite the fact that the oneness of God is so strongly emphasized, and, as it were, constitutes the first article of Israel's basic law, the distinctions within that unity of the Godhead come to light also as in that revelation His fulness of Being progresses. The very name which is usually employed for designating God in the original Hebrew has a certain significance here. For this name, *Elohim,* is in plural form, and therefore, although it does not, as was formerly generally supposed, designate the three persons of the divine Being, it does, in its character as an intensive plural, point to the fulness of life and of power which are present in God. It is, no doubt, in connection with this same fact, that God sometimes, in speaking of Himself, uses a plural referent, and by this means makes distinctions within Himself that bear a personal character (Gen. 1:26-27; 3:22; and Isa. 6:8).

Of greater significance is the teaching of the Old Testament to the effect that God brings everything in His creation and providence into being by His Word and Spirit. He is not a human being, who, at the cost of great difficulty and exertion, makes something else out of the materials He has at hand. Instead, simply by the act of speaking, He calls everything into being out of nothing.

In the first chapter of Genesis we are taught this truth in the loftiest way possible, and elsewhere, too, it is expressed most gloriously in word and song. He speaks, and it is done; He commands, and it stands fast (Ps. 33:9). He sends out His word, and melts the morsels of ice (Ps. 147:18). His voice is upon the waters, shakes the wilderness, causes the hills to skip like a calf, and discovers the forests (Ps. 29:3-10).

Two truths are contained in this exalted account of God's works: the first is that God is the Almighty One who has but to speak and all things leap into being, whose word is *law* (Ps. 33:9) and whose voice is *power* (Ps. 29:4); and the second is that God works deliberately, and not without forethought, and carries out all His works with the highest wisdom. The word which God speaks is power, but it is also the vehicle of thought. He has made the earth by His power, He has established the world by His wisdom, and has stretched out the heavens by His discretion (Jer. 10:12 and 51:15). He has made all His works in wisdom: the earth is full of His riches (Ps. 104:24). This wisdom of God did not come to Him from outside Himself, but was with Him from the beginning. He possessed it as the principle of His way, before His works of old. When He prepared the heavens, set a compass upon the face of the deep, established the clouds above, strengthened the fountains of the deep, then wisdom was already there, brought up alongside of Him, daily his delight, and rejoicing always before Him (Prov. 8:22-31 and Job 20:20-28). God rejoiced in the wisdom with which He created the world.

Alongside of this word and wisdom the Spirit of God as the Mediator of the creation makes His appearance. Just as God at one and the same time *is* wisdom and *possesses* it, so that He can share it and can exhibit it in His works, so He Himself is Spirit in His being (Deut. 4:12, 15) and He possesses Spirit, that Spirit by which He can dwell in the world and be always and everywhere present in it (Ps. 139:7). Without anyone having been His counsellor, the Lord by His Spirit brought everything into being (Isa. 40:13 ff.). At the beginning that Spirit moved upon the face of the waters (Gen. 1:2), and He remains active in all that was created. By that Spirit God garnishes the heavens (Job 26:13), renews the face of the earth (Ps. 104:30), gives life to man (Job 33:4), maintains the breath in man's nostrils (Job 27:3), gives him understanding and wisdom (Job 32:8), and also causes the grass to wither and the flower to fade (Isa. 40:7). In short, by the Word of the Lord were the heavens made, and all the host of them by the Breath of His mouth (Ps. 33:6).

*   *   *   *   *

And this self-diversity of God comes out even more in the works of the re-creation. Then it is not Elohim, but Jehovah, not God in general, but the Lord, the God of the covenant, who reveals Himself and who makes Himself known in wonders of redemption and salvation. As such He redeems and leads His people, not by His word alone which

He speaks or has conveyed to them, but also by means of the Angel of the covenant (the Angel of the Lord). This Angel appears already in the history of the patriarchs: to Hagar (Gen. 16:6 ff.), to Abraham (Gen. 18 ff.), and to Jacob (Gen. 28:13 ff.). This Angel reveals His grace and power especially in the emancipation of Israel from the bondage of Egypt.[2] This Angel of the Lord does not stand on the same plane of importance as the created angels; rather, He is a special revelation and manifestation of God. On the one hand, He is clearly distinguished from God, who speaks of Him as of His Angel, and yet, on the other hand, is one in name with God Himself, and in power, in redemption and blessing, in worshipfulness and honor. He is called God in Genesis 16:13, the God of Bethel in Genesis 31:13, exchanges places with God or the Lord (Gen. 28:30, 32 and Ex. 3:4), and He bears the name of God within Him (Ex. 23:21). He redeems from all evil (Gen. 48:16), rescues Israel from the hand of the Egyptians (Ex. 3:8), cleaves the waters and dries up the sea (Ex. 14:21), preserves the people of God in the way, brings them safely into Canaan, causes them to triumph over their enemies (Ex. 3:8 and 23:20), is to be absolutely obeyed as though He were God Himself (Ex. 23:20), and always encamps around those who fear the Lord (Ps. 34:7 and 35:5).

Just as in His re-creating work, Jehovah carries out His redemptive activities through this Angel of the covenant, so He by His Spirit gives out all kinds of energies and gifts to His people. In the Old Testament the Spirit of the Lord is the source of all life, all weal, and all ability. He grants courage and strength to the judges, to Othniel (Judges 3:10), Gideon (Judges 6:34), Jephthah (Judges 11:29), and to Samson (Judges 14:6 and 15:14). He grants artistic perception to the makers of the priests' garments, the tabernacle, and the temple,[3] and He gives wisdom and understanding to the judges who bear the burden of the people alongside of Moses (Num. 11:17, 25). He gives the spirit of prophecy to the prophets,[4] and renewal and sanctification and guidance to all of God's children (Ps. 51:12-13 and 143:10).

In short: the Word, the promise, the covenant, which the Lord gave to Israel at the exodus from Egypt, have existed throughout the ages, and still stood fast even after the Captivity in the days of Zerubbabel, so that the people had no need to fear (Haggai 2:4-5). When the Lord led Israel out of Egypt He became the Savior of Israel. And this disposition of God towards His people came to expression in the fact that in all their oppression He was oppressed (He regarded the affliction of

---

2. Ex. 3:2; 13:21; 14:19; 23:20-23; 32:34; 33:2; and Num. 20:16.
3. Ex. 28:3; 31:3-5; 35:31-35; and 1 Chron. 28:12.
4. Num. 11:25,29; 24:2-3; Micah 3:8; and like passages.

His people as His own affliction), and that He therefore sent them His Angel to preserve them. He redeemed them by His love and grace and He took them up and carried them as His own throughout those days of old. He sent them the Spirit of His holiness in order to lead them in the ways of the Lord (Isa. 63:9-12). In the days of the Old Covenant, the Lord through the high priest laid His threefold blessing on the people of Israel: the blessing of vigil, the blessing of grace, and the blessing of peace (Num. 6:24-26).

Thus gradually, then, but ever more unmistakably, the threefold distinction within the Divine being comes to expression already in the history of God's leading of Israel. However, the Old Testament includes the further promises that in the future there will be a higher and richer revelation. After all, Israel repudiated the Word of the Lord and vexed His Holy Spirit (Isa. 63:10 and Ps. 106). The revelation of God in the Angel of the covenant and in the Spirit of the Lord proved to be inadequate: if God wanted to confirm His covenant and fulfill His promise, another and higher revelation would be necessary.

Such a revelation was heralded by the prophets. In the future, in the last days, then the Lord will call up out of the midst of Israel such a prophet as Moses was, and the Lord will put His words in that prophet's mouth (Deut. 18:18). This one will be a priest for ever after the order of Melchizedek (Ps. 110:4); He will be a king out of the house of David (2 Sam. 7:12-16), a rod out of the stem of Jesse (Isa. 11:1), a king, judging and seeking judgment (Isa. 16:5). A human being, a man He will be, and the son of a woman (Isa. 7:14), and He will be without form or comeliness (Isa. 53:2 ff.); but, at the same time, He will be Immanuel (Isa. 7:14), the Lord our righteousness (Jer. 23:6), the Angel of the covenant (Mal. 3:1), the Lord Himself appearing to His people (Hos. 1:7 and Mal. 3:1). And He bears the name of Wonderful, Counsellor, The mighty God, The everlasting Father, The Prince of Peace (Isa. 9:6).

This manifestation of the servant of the Lord is to be followed by a richer dispensation of the Holy Spirit. As the Spirit of wisdom and understanding, of counsel and strength, of the knowledge and fear of the Lord, this Spirit will rest upon the Messiah (Isa. 11:2; 42:1; and 61:1). He will be poured out upon all flesh, over sons and daughters, old men and young men, servants and handmaids,[5] and He will give a new heart and a new spirit, so that His people may walk in His statutes, and keep His ordinances, and do them.[6]

---

5. Joel 2:28-29; Isa. 32:15; 44:3; Ezek. 36:26-27; and Zech. 12:10.
6. Ezek. 11:19-20; 36:26; Jer. 31:31-34 and 32:38-41.

Thus the Old Testament itself points out that the full revelation of God will consist of the revelation of His triune being.

* * * * *

This promise and announcement the fulfillment of the New Testament fully satisfies. In this respect also, the unity or oneness of God is the point of departure of all revelation.[7] But out of this oneness the difference in the Divine being now, in the New Testament, comes into much clearer light. This happens first in the great redemptive events of incarnation, satisfaction, and outpouring, and next in the instruction of Jesus and His apostles. The work of salvation is one whole, a work of God from beginning to end. But there are three high moments in it, election, forgiveness, and renewal, and these three point to a threefold cause in the Divine being: that is, to the Father, the Son, and the Holy Spirit.

The very conceiving of Christ already shows us the threefold activity of God. For while the Father gives the Son to the world (John 3:16), and while the Son Himself descends from heaven (John 6:38), that Son is conceived in Mary of the Holy Spirit (Matt. 1:20 and Luke 1:35). At His baptism Jesus is anointed by the Holy Spirit, and is there publicly declared to be the beloved Son of the Father, the Son in whom He is well pleased (Matt. 3:16-17). The works which Jesus did were shown Him by the Father (John 5:19 and 8:38), and they are fulfilled by Him in the strength of the Holy Spirit (Matt. 12:28). In His dying He offers Himself to God in the eternal Spirit (Heb. 9:14). The resurrection is a raising up by the Father (Acts 2:24) and is at the same time Jesus' own act by which He is greatly proved to be the Son of the Father according to the Spirit of holiness (Rom. 1:3). And after his resurrection He, on the fortieth day, ascends in the Spirit which quickened Him on high in heaven and there He makes the angels and authorities and powers subject to Himself.

The teaching of Jesus and the apostles agrees fully with the lesson of those events themselves.

Jesus came to earth to declare the *Father* and to make His name known among men (John 1:18 and 17:6). The name of father applied to God as creator of all things was also used by the pagans. This meaning of the term is supported also by Scripture at various places.[8] Besides, the Old Testament several times uses the designation Father to refer to God's theocratic relationship to Israel because in His marvelous ability

---

7. John 17:3; 1 Cor. 8:4; and 1 Tim. 2:5.
8. Luke 3:38; Acts 17:28; Eph. 3:15; and Heb. 12:9.

He has created and maintained that relationship (Deut. 32:6 and Isa. 63:16). But in the New Testament a gloriously new light is shed upon this name of father as applied to God. Jesus always indicates an essential difference between the relationship in which He Himself stands to God and that in which others, say the Jews or the disciples, stand to Him. When, for example, He teaches the disciples, at their request, the "Our Father . . ." He says expressly "When *ye* pray, say . . . ." And when, after the resurrection, He announces His forthcoming ascension to Mary Magdalene, He says: "I ascend unto my Father, and your Father; and to my God, and your God" (John 20:17). In other words, God is His *own* Father (John 5:18). He knows the Son and loves Him in such a way and to such an extent as, reciprocally, only the Son can know and love the Father.[9] Among the apostles, accordingly, God is constantly referred to as the Father of our Lord Jesus Christ (Eph. 1:3). This relationship between the Father and the Son did not develop in time but existed from eternity (John 1:1, 14; 17:24). God is therefore Father in the first place because in a very unique sense He is the Father of the Son. This is His original, special personal characteristic.

In a derived sense God is further called the Father of all creatures because He is their creator and sustainer (1 Cor. 8:6, and elsewhere). He is called the Father of Israel because Israel is His handiwork by virtue of election and calling (Deut. 32:6 and Isa. 64:8), and the Father of the church and all believers because the love of the Father for the Son accrues to them (John 16:27 and 17:24) and because they have been accepted as His children and are born of Him through the Spirit (John 1:12 and Rom. 8:15).

The Father is therefore always the *Father*, the first person, He from whom in the being of God, in the counsel of God, and in all the works of creation and providence, redemption and sanctification, the initiative proceeds. He gave the Son to have life in Himself (John 5:26), and He sends out the Spirit (John 15:26). His is the election and the good pleasure (Matt. 11:26 and Eph. 1:4, 9, 11). From Him proceed the creation, providence, redemption, and renewal (Ps. 33:6 and John 3:16). To Him in a special sense the kingdom and the power and the glory accrue (Matt. 6:13). He particularly bears the name of *God* in distinction from the *Lord* Jesus Christ and the Holy Spirit. Indeed, Christ Himself as Mediator calls Him His Father, not only, but also His God (Matt. 27:46 and John 20:17) and Christ is Himself called the Christ of God.[10] In a word, the first person of the Divine being is the *Father* because *"of* Him are all things" (1 Cor. 8:6).

9. Matt. 11:27; Mark 12:6; and John 5:20.
10. Luke 9:20; 1 Cor. 3:23; and Rev. 12:10.

If God is the Father, the inference is that there also is a *Son* who received life from Him and who shares His love. In the Old Testament the name of son of God was used for angels,[11] for the people of Israel,[12] and particularly too for the theocratic king of that people.[13] But in the New Testament this name takes on a far profounder meaning. For Christ is the Son of God in a very peculiar sense; He is highly exalted above angels and prophets (Matt. 13:32; 21:27; and 22:2), and He Himself says that no one can know the Son except the Father, and no one can know the Father except the Son (Matt. 11:27). In distinction from angels and men, He is the Father's own Son (Rom. 8:32), the beloved Son in whom the Father is well pleased (Matt. 3:17), the only-begotten Son (John 1:18) whom the Father gave to have life in Himself (John 5:26).

This very special, this unique, relationship between Father and Son did not develop in time by way of the supernatural conception of the Holy Spirit, or of the anointing at baptism, or of the resurrection and ascension — though many have maintained this — but is a relationship which has existed from all eternity. The Son who in Christ assumed human nature was in the beginning with God as the Word (John 1:1), then already had the form of God (Phil. 2:6), was rich and clothed with glory (John 17:5, 24), was then already the brightness of God's glory and the express image of His person (Heb. 1:3), and precisely therefore He could in the fulness of time be sent out, given, and brought into the world.[14] Hence, too, the creation (John 1:3 and Col. 1:16) and providence (Heb. 1:3) and the accomplishment of the whole of salvation (1 Cor. 1:30) are ascribed to Him. He is not, as creatures are, made or created, but is, instead, the first-born of all creatures: that is, the Son who has the rank and rights of the first-born over against all creatures (Col. 1:15). Thus He is also the first-born of the dead, the first-born of many brethren, and therefore among all and in all He is the first (Rom. 8:29 and Col. 1:18). And even though, in the fulness of time, He assumed the form of a servant, He was nevertheless in the form of God. He was in all things like unto God the Father (Phil. 2:6): in life (John 5:26), in knowledge (Matt. 11:27), in strength (John 1:3 and 5:21, 26), in honor (John 5:23). He is Himself

11. Job. 38:7.
12. Deut. 1:31; 8:5; 14:1; 32:6,18 and Hosea 11:1.
13. 2 Sam. 7:11-14 and Ps. 2:7.
14. John 3:16; Gal. 4:4; and Heb. 1:6.

God, to be praised above all else into eternity.[15] Just as all things are
of the Father, so they are also all *through* the Son (1 Cor. 8:6).

*   *   *   *   *

Both, Father and Son, come together and are united in the *Holy
Spirit* and by means of the Spirit dwell in all creatures. True, God is
according to His nature a Spirit (John 4:24) and He is holy (Isa. 6:3) ;
but the Holy Spirit is clearly distinguished from God as Spirit. Just
as, in a comparative way of speaking, man is a spirit in his invisible
nature and also possesses a spirit, by means of which he is aware of
himself and is self-conscious, so God is a Spirit by nature and also
possesses a Spirit, a Spirit which searches the depths of His being
(1 Cor. 2:11). As such the latter is called the Spirit of God or the Holy
Spirit (Ps. 51:12 and Isa. 63:10-11). And this is done in distinction
from the spirit of an angel or of a human being or of any other creature.
But, although He is distinguished from God, from the Father and the
Son, He stands in the most intimate of relationships with both. He is
called the breath of the Almighty (Job 33:4), the breath of His mouth
(Ps. 33:6), is sent out by the Father and the Son (John 14:26 and
15:26), and He proceeds from both, not from the Father alone (John
15:26) but also from the Son, for He is also called the Spirit of Christ
or the Spirit of the Father (Rom. 8:9).

Although the Holy Spirit is in that way given or sent or poured out
by the Father and the Son, He often makes His appearance as a power
or a gift which qualifies men for their calling or office. Thus, for example, the Holy Spirit is spoken of at various places in the Acts of the
Apostles in connection with the gift of prophecy (8:15; 10:44; 11:15;
15:8; and 19:2). But it is not warranted to infer from that fact, as
many do, that the Holy Spirit is nothing more or other than a gift or
power of God. At other places He definitely makes His appearance as a
person, one who bears personal names, has personal characteristics, and
does personal deeds. Thus in John 15:26 and 16:13, 14 (although the
Greek of the word translated *Spirit* in our language is of neuter gender)
Christ uses the masculine referent: *He* shall testify of Me and glorify
Me. At the same place Christ calls Him Comforter, using the same
name that is used of Christ in 1 John 2:1, a name translated *advocate*
in the English version.

Besides these personal names all sorts of personal characteristics are
ascribed to the Holy Spirit: for example, selfhood (Acts 13:2), self-
consciousness (Acts 15:28), self-determination or will (1 Cor. 12:11).

---

15. John 1:1; 20:8; Rom. 9:5; and Heb. 1:8-9.

Besides He is credited with all kinds of personal activities, such as investigating (1 Cor. 2:11), listening (John 16:13), speaking (Rev. 2:17), teaching (John 14:26), praying (Rom. 8:27), and the like. And all this comes out most clearly and sublimely in the fact that He is placed on one and the same level with the Father and the Son (Matt. 28:19 and 2 Cor. 13:14).

The last point is the most important and it indicates the fact that the Holy Spirit is a person not merely but also very God. And Scriptures provide all the data which are necessary to make this confession. We have only to note that despite the distinction between God and His Spirit which was pointed out above, the two frequently exchange places in Scripture, so that it is quite the same whether God or His Spirit says or does a thing. In Acts 5:3-4 the lying to the Holy Spirit is called a lying to God. In 1 Corinthians 3:16 the believers are called God's temple, because the Spirit of God dwells in them. To these facts we must add that various Divine attributes, such as eternity (Heb. 9:14), omnipresence (Ps. 139:7), omniscience (1 Cor. 2:11), omnipotence (1 Cor. 12:4-6), and various Divine works, such as creation (Ps. 33:6), providence (Ps. 104:30), and redemption (John 3:3) are ascribed to the Holy Spirit quite as well as to the Father and the Son. Consequently He shares in the same glory with those two. He takes His place alongside of the Father and the Son as the cause of salvation (2 Cor. 13:14 and Rev. 1:4). It is in His name also that we are baptized (Matt. 28:19), and blessed (2 Cor. 13:14). Moreover, the blasphemy against the Holy Spirit is an unpardonable sin (Matt. 12:31-32). In other words, just as all things are *of* the Father and *through* the Son, they all exist and rest *in* the Holy Spirit.

All of these elements of the doctrine of the trinity, spread throughout the Scriptures, were gathered together, so to speak, by Jesus in His baptismal command and by the apostles in their benedictions. After His resurrection and before His ascension, Christ bids His apostles to go out and make all peoples His disciples and to baptize them in the one name in which, nevertheless, three different subjects are revealed. Father, Son, and Spirit are in their oneness and their distinction the fulness of the perfected revelation of God. Just so, too, according to the apostles the whole good and salvation of man is contained in the love of the Father, the grace of the Son, and the fellowship of the Holy Spirit.[16] The good pleasure, the foreknowledge, the power, the love, the kingdom, and the strength are the Father's. The Mediatorship, the reconciliation, the grace, and the redemption are the Son's. The regeneration, the renewal, the sanctification, the redemption are the Spirit's.

---

16. 1 Cor. 13:14; 1 Peter 1:2; 1 John 5:4-6; and Rev. 1:4-6.

The relationship in which Christ stands to the Father corresponds fully with the relationship in which the Spirit stands to Christ. Just as the Son speaks nothing and does nothing of Himself but receives everything from the Father (John 5:26 and 16:15), so the Holy Spirit takes everything from Christ (John 16:13-14). As the Son testifies of the Father and glorifies the Father (John 1:18 and 17:4, 6), so the Holy Spirit testifies of the Son and glorifies Him (John 15:26 and 16:14). Just as no one comes to the Father but through the Son (John 14:6), so no one can say that Jesus is the Lord except through the Holy Spirit (1 Cor. 12:3). Through the Spirit we have fellowship with the Father and the Son. It is in the Holy Spirit that God Himself through Christ dwells in our hearts. And if this all be so, then the Holy Spirit is, together with the Son and the Father, the one, true God, and is to be eternally lauded and praised as such.

* * * * *

To this instruction of the Holy Spirit the Christian church in its confession of the Trinity of God has said yea and amen. The church did not arrive at this rich and glorious confession without a hard and long struggle of the spirits. Centuries on end the profoundest experience of the spiritual life of the children of God and the doughtiest intellect of the fathers and teachers of the church went into the understanding of this point of the revelation of Scripture and to reproducing it purely in the confession of the church. No doubt the church would not have succeeded in this effort at the laying of foundations, if it had not been led into the truth by the Holy Spirit, and if in Tertullian and Irenaeus, Athanasius and the three Cappadocians, Augustine, and Hillary, and so many others besides, it had not received the men who, endowed and equipped with unusual gifts of godliness and wisdom, kept to the straight course.

Nothing less than the peculiar essence of Christianity was at stake in this battle of the spirits. From two sides the church was exposed to the danger of permitting itself to be wrested from the firm foundation on which it was built and so to be submerged by the world.

On the one hand, there was the threat of Arianism, so called after the Alexandrian presbyter Arius who died in the year 336. Arius held that the Father alone was the eternal and true God, inasmuch as He alone in the full sense of the word was ungenerated. Concerning the Son, the Logos, who in Christ had become flesh, he taught that, inasmuch as this Christ was generated, He could not be God but had to be a creature — a creature, it is true, who had been made before other creatures, but nevertheless was made as they were made through the will of God. And, in the same way, Arius held that the Holy Spirit was a creature or else a quality or attribute of God.

On the other side the party of Sabellianism was at work, so called after a certain Sabellius who lived in Rome at the beginning of the third century. Sabellius held that Father, Son, and Holy Spirit were but three names for one and the same God — a God who had made Himself known thus successively as His revelation progressed in various forms and manifestations. In the form of the Father, accordingly, God was operative as Creator and Lawgiver. Thereupon He worked as Redeemer in the form of the Son. And He now works in the form of the Holy Spirit as the Re-creator of the church.

While Arianism tries to maintain the oneness of God, by placing Son and Spirit outside the Divine being and reducing these to the level of creatures, Sabellianism tries to arrive at the same end by robbing the three persons of the Godhead of their independence. This it does by metamorphosing the persons into three successive modes of revelation of the same Divine Being. In the first tendency the Jewish, deistic, rationalistic mode of thinking comes to expression rather characteristically, and in the second the idea of Pagan pantheism and mysticism. The moment the church set about giving itself a fairly clear account of the truth which was later stated in the confession of the Trinity of God, these two other tendencies arose alongside at the right and left, and they accompany the confession of the church to this day. Always and again the church and each one of its members must be on guard against doing injustice on the one hand to the oneness of the Divine Being, and on the other to the three Persons within that Being. The oneness may not be sacrificed to the diversity, nor the diversity to the oneness. To maintain both in their inseparable connection and in their pure relationship, not only theoretically but also in practical life, is the calling of all believers.

In order to satisfy this requirement, the Christian church and Christian theology in the early period made use of various words and expressions which cannot be found literally in the Holy Scriptures. The church began to speak of the *essence* of God and of three *persons* in that essence of being. It spoke of the *triune* and the *trinitarian,* or of *essential* and *personal* characteristics, of the *eternal generation* of the Son and of the *proceeding* of the Holy Spirit from the Father and from the Son, and the like.

There is no reason at all why the church and the Christian theology should not use such terms and modes of expression. For the Holy Scripture was not given to the church by God to be thoughtlessly repeated but to be understood in all its fulness and riches, and to be restated in its own language in order that in this way it might proclaim the mighty works of God. Moreover, such terms and expressions are necessary in order to maintain the truth of Scripture over against its opponents and to secure it against misunderstanding and error. And history has taught throughout the centuries that a lighthearted disapproval and rejection of these names and modes of expression leads to various departures from the confession.

At the same time, we should, in the use of these terms, always remember that they are of human origin and therefore limited, defective, fallible. The church fathers always acknowledged this. For example, they held that the term *persons* which was used to designate the three ways of existence in the Divine Being did not do justice to the truth in the matter but served as an aid towards maintaining the truth and cutting off error. The word was chosen, not because it was accurate in every respect, but because no other and better was to be found. In this matter again the word is far behind the thought, and the thought is far behind the actuality. Although we cannot preserve the actuality in any but this inadequate form, we may never forget that it is the reality itself and not the word that counts. In the dispensation of glory other and better expressions will certainly be laid upon our lips.

*   *   *   *   *

The reality itself which is concerned in the confession of the holy trinity is of the highest importance, both for the mind and the heart.

For it is by that confession that the church maintains, in the first place, both the unity and the diversity in the being of God. The Divine Being is one: there is but one Being that is God and that may be called God. In creation and redemption, in nature and grace, in church and world, in state and society, everywhere and always we are concerned with one, same, living, and true God. The unity of the world, of mankind, of truth, of virtue, of justice, and of beauty depends upon the unity of God. The moment that unity of God is denied or understressed, the door is open to polytheism.

But this unity or oneness of God is, according to Scripture and the confession of the church, not a contentless unity, nor a solitariness, but a fulness of life and strength. It comprises difference, or distinction, or diversity. It is that diversity which comes to expression in the three persons or modes of being of God. These three persons are not merely three modes of revelation. They are modes of being. Father, Son, and Spirit share one and the same Divine nature and characteristics. They are one being. Nevertheless each has His own name, His own particular characteristic, by which He is distinguished from the others. The Father alone has fatherhood, the Son alone has generation, and the Spirit alone possesses the quality of proceeding from both.

To that order of existence in the Divine Being the order of the three persons in all Divine work corresponds. The Father is He *from* whom, the Son is He *through* whom, and the Spirit is He *in* whom all things are. All things in the creation, and in the redemption, or re-creation, come from the Father, through the Son and the Spirit. And in the Spirit and through the Son they are come back to Him. It is to the Father that we are particularly indebted, therefore, for his electing love, to the Son for His redeeming grace, and to the Spirit for his regenerative and renewing power.

In the second place, the church in maintaining this confession, takes a strong position over against the heresies of deism (belief in God without revelation) and pantheism (polytheism) and of Judaism and Paganism. Always there is that dual tendency in the human heart: the tendency to think of God as distant and removed and to think of self and world as independent of God, and the tendency to draw God down into the world, to identify Him with the world, and so to deify the self and the world. When the first tendency prevails in us we come to the point of thinking that we can do without God in nature, in our calling, in our business, in our science and art, and also in the work of redemption. And, if the second tendency prevails in us, we change the glory of God into the image of some creature or other, deify the world, the sun, the moon and the stars, art, science, or the state, and in the creature, usually conceived in our image, we worship our own greatness. In the first instance God is only afar off; in the second He is only nearby. In the first, He is outside of the world, above it, free from it; in the second, He is inside it and identical with it.

But the church confesses both: God is above the world, distinguished from it in essence, and yet He is with His whole being present in it and at no point in space or time separated from it. He is both afar off and nearby. He is both highly exalted above all creatures and at the same time deeply condescending to them all. He is our Creator who brought us into being by His will as creatures distinct from Him in kind. He is our Redeemer who saves us, not by our works but by the riches of His grace. He is our Sanctifier who dwells in us as in His temple. As the triune God He is one God and is *above* us, *for* us, and *in* us.

Finally, in the third place, this confession of the church is also of the greatest importance for the spiritual life. Quite unjustifiably it is sometimes maintained that the doctrine of the trinity is merely a philosophically abstracted dogma and that it possesses no value for religion and life.

The Reformed Confession of Faith takes an entirely different view of this. In Article XI of that Confession the church stated that God is one in essence and three in persons. This we know from the witness of Holy Scripture, and from the activities of the three persons, especially those which we sense within us. True, we do not base our faith in the trinity on feeling and experience; but when we believe it, we notice that the doctrine stands in intimate relationship with the spiritual experience of the children of God.

For the believers come to know the workings of the Father, the Creator of all things, He who gave them life, and breath, and all things. They learn to know Him as the Lawgiver who gave out His holy commandments in order that they should walk in them. They learn to know Him as the Judge who is provoked to terrible wrath by all the unrighteousness of men and who in no sense holds the guilty guiltless. And they learn to know Him, finally, as the Father who for Christ's sake is their God and Father, on whom they trust so far that they do not doubt but that He will supply for every need of body and soul, and that He will convert all evil which accrues to them in this vale of tears into good. They know that He can do this as Almighty God and that He wants to do it as a faithful Father. Hence they confess: I believe in God, the Father, the Almighty, Creator of heaven and earth.

Thus, too, they learn to know in themselves the workings of the Son, He who is the only-begotten of the Father, conceived in Mary of the Holy Spirit. They learn to know Him as their highest Prophet and Teacher, He who has perfectly revealed to them the secret counsel and will of God in the matter of their redemption. They learn to know Him as their only Highpriest, who has redeemed them by the one sacrifice of His body, and who still constantly intercedes for them with the Father. They learn to know Him as their eternal King, who rules them with His Word and Spirit and who shelters and preserves them in their achieved redemption. Hence they confess: I believe in Jesus Christ, God's only-begotten Son, our Lord.

And they also learn to recognize in themselves the workings of the Holy Spirit, He who regenerates them and leads them into all truth. They learn to know Him as the Operator of their faith, He who through that faith causes them to share in Christ and all His benefits. They learn to know Him as the Comforter, He who prays in them with unutterable longings and who testifies with their spirit that they are children of God. They learn to know Him as the pledge of their eternal inheritance, He who preserves them until the day of their redemption. And they therefore confess: I believe also in the Holy Spirit.

Thus the confession of the trinity is the sum of the Christian religion. Without it neither the creation nor the redemption nor the sanctification can be purely maintained.

Every departure from this confession leads to error in the other heads of doctrine, just as a mistaken representation of the articles of faith can be traced back to a misconception of the doctrine of the trinity. We can truly proclaim the mighty works of God only when we recognize and confess them as the one great work of Father, Son, and Spirit.

In the love of the Father, the grace of the Son, and the fellowship of the Holy Spirit is contained the whole salvation of men.

XI

Creation and Providence

The practical significance of the doctrine of the trinity for the life of the Christian is evidence enough that the Holy Scripture does not want to give us an abstract concept of deity, but rather wants to put us into contact, all of us personally, with the living and true God. Scripture breaks off our notions and concepts and leads us back to God Himself. Hence Scripture does not argue about God, but presents Him to us and shows Him in all the works of His hand. Lift up your eyes and behold, Scripture seems to say, who has made all these things. From the very beginning, His invisible things, His eternal power and Godhead are thoughtfully discerned from the creatures, the things that were made. We do not learn to know and to glorify God in independence from His work, but rather in and through His works in nature and in grace.

That is why the Holy Scripture points out to us constantly the mighty works of God. Scripture is at one and the same time a description of them and a song in praise of them. Just because it wants to cause us to know the living and the true God, it speaks on almost every page of His mighty deeds. As the living God He is at the same time the *operative* God. He cannot do otherwise than work. He works always (John 5:17). All life, and especially the fully blessed, eternal life of God is power, energy, activity. Such as the maker is, so is his work. Because God is the Maker, the Creator of all things, His works are great and wonderful (Ps. 92:5 and 139:14), true and faithful altogether (Ps. 33:4 and 111:7), and just and merciful (Ps. 145:17 and Dan. 9:14). Included in those works, certainly, are the creation and the maintenance of all things, heaven and earth, mankind and the myriad peoples, the wonders done in Israel and for Israel, and the works which He accomplishes through His servant.[1] And all those works praise Him (Ps. 145:10). He is the Rock whose work is perfect (Deut. 32:4).

Moreover, all those works of God are brought into being neither indifferently nor under compulsion, but deliberately and freely. So much is evident even from the fact that He makes and sustains and rules all things by His Word. It is by speaking, by commanding, that He calls

---

1. Gen. 2:2,3; Ex. 34:10; Job 34:19; Isa. 19:25; John 9:4; and elsewhere.

things into existence (Ps. 33:9). Without the Word which in the beginning was with God and was God, nothing was made that was made
(John 1:3). In Job 28:20 ff. and Proverbs 8:22 ff. the truth is so presented as if God, upon creating the world, first consulted wisdom, con-
templating and searching it and making all things with it (Ps. 104:24
and Jer. 10:12). Holy Scripture also expresses this matter differently.
It says that God brings everything into being according to His will or
counsel. In other words, all the works of God, both those of creation
and those of redemption, are the product not only of His thought but also
of His will. Humanly speaking, we can say that every work of God is
preceded by a deliberation of the mind and a decision of the will. In
some passages of Scripture the word used is counsel,[2] in some it is establishment or decree,[3] in some it is purpose,[4] in some ordination,[5] and
in some it is the favor or good pleasure of God.[6] St. Paul speaks of the
good pleasure and of the counsel of God's will (Eph. 1:5, 11).

Concerning that counsel of God Scripture further teaches that it is
excellent and wonderful (Isa. 28:29 and Jer. 32:19), independent
(Matt. 11:26), immutable (Heb. 6:17), indestructible (Isa. 46:10),
and that God is sovereign over all things, also over the transgression of
the unrighteous in delivering Christ up to the cross and to death (Acts
2:23 and 4:28). The fact that things and events, including the sinful
thoughts and deeds of men, have been eternally known and fixed in that
counsel of God does not rob them of their own character but rather establishes and guarantees them all, each in its own kind and nature and
in its own context and circumstances. Included in that counsel of God
are sin and punishment, but also freedom and responsibility, sense of
duty and conscience, and law and justice. In that counsel of God everything that happens is in the very same context it is in when it becomes
manifest before our eyes. The conditions are defined in it quite as well
as the consequences, the means quite as much as the ends, the ways as the
results, the prayers as the answers to prayer, the faith as the justification, sanctification, and glorification. According to the terms of that
counsel, God gave His only-begotten Son so that whoever believed on
Him should have eternal life.

Understood in this way, in the sense of the Holy Scriptures, according to the Spirit, the confession of the ever-wise counsel of God is a
source of rich comfort. Thus we come to know that it is no blind chance,
dark destiny, no unreasonable or malign will, nor any undeflectable

---

2. Ps. 33:11; Prov. 19:21; Isa. 46:10; and Acts 2:23.
3. Gen. 41:32; Ps. 2:7; Isa. 10:23 and 14:27.
4. Jer. 51:12; Rom. 8:28; 9:11; Eph. 1:11; 3:11; and 2 Tim. 1:9.
5. Acts 10:42; 13:48; 17:31; Rom. 8:29,30; and Eph. 1:5 and 11.
6. Isa. 49:8; 53:10; 60:10; 61:2; Matt. 11:26; Eph. 1:5 and 9.

natural force which governs mankind and the world, but that the governance of all things rests in the hands of an almighty God and a merciful Father. Certainly, faith is necessary to understand this. For often we fail to see this, and men walk about on the earth in riddles. But it is the faith which keeps us constant in the struggle of life, and because of it we move into the future hopefully and confidently. For the ever-wise counsel of the Lord stands forever and remains eternally in force.

The beginning of the carrying out of this counsel of the Lord was the creation of the world. Just as the Holy Scriptures alone can give us to know the counsel of God, so they alone show us the origin of all things, telling us of God's creative omnipotence. The question as to the origin of things, of man and animal and plant, and of the whole world, is an old question, but it always remains an appropriate one. Science can supply no answer to it. Science is itself a creature and a product of time. It takes its position on the basis of things as they are made and assumes the existence of the things it investigates; from the nature of the case, therefore, science cannot go back to the time when things were not yet. Science cannot penetrate to the moment when they were given reality.

Accordingly, experience, empirical investigation, can tell us nothing about the origin of things. But the reflection of philosophy, too, has throughout the ages sought in vain for an explanation of the world. Weary of thought, the philosophers often rested at last in the fact that the world had no origin, that it existed eternally and will continue to exist so. It is a conclusion which different philosophers developed in different directions. Comparatively few of them supposed that this world as we know it was eternal or that it would eternally remain so. A few did hold this, but their interpretation runs into so many difficulties that it is at present generally repudiated. Instead, the idea of evolution or development has gained ground. According to this idea nothing *is,* and everything *becomes.* What the entire universe presents therefore, is the spectacle of something which never began and which will never cease — a continuing *process,* therefore.

Evolution is, no doubt, a wonderful thing, but always it must assume that there is something which is evolving and which carries within itself the germ of development. Naturally evolution is not and cannot itself be a creative force, causing and bringing things into being; it is at best an expression of the process through which things go when once they exist. The theory of evolution, consequently, lacks the potential of explaining the origin of things. It tacitly proceeds from the idea that those things in their undeveloped state eternally existed. The theory of evolution begins with an assumption which is quite undemonstrable and, accordingly, also takes its position on faith. In this it is like the theory of creation of all things by the hand of God.

But to make this tacit assumption does not yet vindicate the theory of evolution. It can maintain that things have always existed in an undeveloped state. Even so, however, it must give itself some sort of account of the original condition in which things existed and out of which the present world has formed itself. Two answers are given to this, depending upon which of two thought currents one prefers. In the world generally we take notice of two types of phenomena or manifestations. We usually call these spirit and matter, soul and body, invisible and visible things, psychical and physical phenomena. But such a dualism is not satisfying. Nowadays people want to be monistic and try to lead everything out of one principle. So it is that theorists of evolution can choose to go in one of two directions in accounting for the original nature of things.

In the first place they can say that *matter* was primary, eternal, and having always had energy as its potential. That is the direction of materialism. It holds that matter is the eternal, the originally immutable constituent of the world, and it now seeks to explain energy in terms of matter, the soul in terms of the body, and the psychical in terms of the physical. But one can, in the second place, also take the other position, and say that *energy* was the primary thing, that it is and remains the ground of all existing things, that matter is an expression or manifestation of such energy, and that the body does not create the soul but the soul the body. That is the direction of pantheism (polytheism). It holds that energy is the eternal basic principle of all things, and it tries to derive the present world from that elemental energy. This original energy, held to be pervasive throughout the world, pantheism endows with all kinds of beautiful and resplendent names, whether of spirit, mind, soul, or other. But in using these names pantheism has something else in mind than is usually denoted by those terms. It is not thinking of a personal God who has reason and wisdom, understanding and will. It is thinking, rather, of an unconscious, non-rational and non-volitional force, a force which turns out to become consciousness, reason, and will in man only in the course of its evolutionary process. The eternal energy is not itself spirit but is called spirit because in its development it can become so.

In both of these possibilities, that of materialism and that of pantheism, a principle is assumed to be extant at the beginning of the evolution of the world, a principle which the one thinks of as predominantly matter and the other as predominantly spirit, and of which no clear idea can be formed. It is something far less positive than negative. As a matter of fact it is nothing definite; it merely has the potential of becoming everything. It is an absolute potentiality (an infinite possibility), a deified abstraction of thought. At bottom it is the imagining of something, in the absence of the one true God, in which scientific man puts his confidence in explaining the world, but which is no more deserving of such confidence than the gods of the nations.

The Holy Scripture takes a very different position. What it tells us about the origin of things is not offered to us as the result of scientific investigation nor in the interest of a philosophical explanation of the world, but in order that we through it should come to know the one, true God and put all of our trust in Him alone. It is an explanation which does not proceed from the world but from God. It holds that not the world but God is eternal. Before the mountains were brought forth or ever the earth and the world were made, even from everlasting to everlasting, He is God (Ps. 90:2). He is Jehovah, who is, and was, and shall be, who is beyond the reach of all words, a fulness of immutable *being*. In distinction from Him the world has *become* and is always *becoming*. The thing that Holy Scripture is primarily on guard against is the confusion of God with His creation. Scripture cuts off all unbelief at the root, but all false belief and superstition also. God and the world are in essence distinguished from each other. They are distinguished as Creator and creature.

Being a creature, the whole world has its origin in God. There is no such thing as eternal matter or eternal spirit existing alongside of God. Heaven and earth and all things were called into being by Him. That is the force of the word *create* in the Bible. In a more general sense, Scripture uses this word also for the works of maintenance (Ps. 104:30 and Isa. 45:7). But in a narrower sense, Scripture denotes by it that God brought all things into being out of nothing. True, the actual expression that God made all things *out of nothing* does not occur in Scripture. It occurs first in the second book of the Maccabees (7:28). Besides, this term, *out of nothing,* can lead to misunderstanding. What is nothing does not exist and cannot therefore be the principle or origin out of which things have come to be. After all, nothing can come from nothing. What Scripture to the contrary says is that the world was called into existence by the will of God (Rev. 4:11) and that the things which are seen were not made of things which do appear (Heb. 11:3). All the same, the expression *out of nothing* can be taken in a usable sense and can perform excellent service over against all kinds of heresy. For it denies that the world was made out of some stuff or matter or energy which co-existed eternally alongside of God. According to the Scripture, God is not solely He who *formed* the world but also He who *created* it. Humanly speaking, we can say that God first existed alone, and thereupon the whole world was brought into being by His counsel and will. An absolute non-being preceded the being of the world, and to this extent we can rightly say that God made the world out of nothing.

Such surely is the expressed teaching of Scripture: that God existed from eternity (Psalm 90:2) but that the world had a beginning (Gen. 1:1). Many a time we read that God did something or other — predestined, say, or loved — from before the foundation of the world (John 17:24 and Eph. 1:4). He is so powerful that He has but to speak and things are (Ps. 33:9), and to call those things which are not as though they were (Rom. 4:17). He gives the world its being solely through His will (Rev. 4:11). He has made all things, heaven and earth and all that is in them (Ex. 20:11 and Neh. 9:6). Of Him and through Him and to Him are all things (Rom. 11:36). Hence He is also the almighty Possessor of heaven and earth (Gen. 14:19, 22), who does all things that please Him, to whose power no limit is appointed, on whom all creatures are in an absolute sense dependent (Ps. 115:3 and Dan. 4:35). The Holy Scripture knows nothing of an unformed eternal matter alongside of God. He is the one, absolute cause of all this and all that happens. The visible things were not made of things that do appear, but the whole world was framed by the word of God (Heb. 11:3).

* * * * *

If God who is the eternal and all-blessed being has created the world through His will, the question naturally arises: *why* and *to what end* did He do it? In order to find an answer to this question, science and philosophy have constantly attempted to make the world a necessity and as such to deduce it from the being of God. Again, two possibilities offered themselves. Some presented the matter as though God were so full and so rich that He could not command the situation, that He lacked power over His own being, and that the world consequently flowed out of Him as a stream from its source, or as the water flows out of a vessel that is over-full. Others took the very opposite position that God in Himself was poor and empty, possessed of a hungry desirous will, and that He accordingly brought the world into existence in order to fill Himself out and to supply Him in His need. According to either of these two views, the world was a necessity for God, be it to relieve Him of His superfluity or to compensate Him for His need.

Both representations are incompatible with Scripture. Scripture takes a very different and diametrically opposed point of view. According to those two positions, the center of gravity has been shifted from

God to the world, and God exists *for* the world. God is the lesser being, and the world is the greater, for the world serves to redeem and to save God who is wretched by reason of abundance or inadequacy. Even though this thought is still held by thinkers of repute in our time, it is nevertheless a blasphemous idea. Scripture, which is the word of God, and which from beginning to end takes God's part, declares plainly and powerfully and loudly that God does not exist for the world but that the whole world and all its creatures exist for God, for His sake and for His glory.

God, surely, is in Himself the all-sufficient and the all-blessed. He does not need the world nor any creature in any way for His own perfection. Can a man be profitable unto God? Is it any gain to the Almighty that thou art righteous, or that thou makest thy ways perfect? (Job 22:2-3). The righteousness of man is no advantage to Him, nor does human transgression impoverish Him. He is not worshipped with men's hands, as though He needed any thing, seeing He giveth to all life, and breath, and all things (Acts 17:25). Hence it is that Scripture so strongly emphasizes the fact that God has caused all things to be by an act of His will. There was no such thing as force or necessity in the being of God which caused Him to bring the world into being. Creation is in its entirety a free act of God. It cannot be explained as the inevitable consequence of the righteousness of God, even though His righteousness also is manifested in it, for to whom could God possibly owe anything? Nor can the creation be deduced from His goodness or love, even though both of these, too, are manifested in the world, for the life in love of the triune God required no object of love beyond Himself. Indeed, the cause of the creation is simply and solely the free power of God, his eternal good pleasure, His absolute sovereignty (Rev. 4:11).

This is not to say, of course, that the creation of the world was an irrational act, a thing done arbitrarily. In this, as in much besides, we must rest in the sovereignty and good pleasure of God as the end of all contradiction, and we are exercised in this by a quiet confidence and childlike obedience. All the same, God had His wise and holy reasons for the act of creation.

Scripture proves this to us in the first place by presenting the creation to us as an act of the *triune* God. When God makes man, He first takes counsel with Himself, and says: Let us make man in our image, after our likeness (Gen. 1:26). So it is that all works of God rest on a Divine deliberation. Before creation He consulted with wisdom (Job 28:20 ff. and Prov. 8:22 ff.). And in time He created all things through the Word which was with God in the beginning and which was God

(John 1:1-3),[7] and He created them in the Spirit who searches out the depths of God, gives life to His creatures, and garnishes the heavens.[8] Therefore the Psalmist cries out: How manifold are Thy works! In wisdom hast Thou made them all: the earth is full of Thy riches (Ps. 104:24).

In addition, the Holy Scripture teaches us that God has created all things and that He sustains and rules them for his own honor. The purpose for which the creation was made cannot lie in that creation itself, for the establishment of the purpose precedes the means. Scripture generally teaches, therefore, that just as everything is from God, so also everything is through Him and to Him (Rom. 11:36). And the Scriptures develop this more particularly when they report that the heavens declare the glory of God (Ps. 19:1), that God glorifies Himself in Pharaoh (Ex. 14:17) and in the man blind from his birth (John 9:3), that He grants all the favors of grace for His name's sake (Isa. 43:25 and Eph. 1:6), that Christ has come in order to glorify the Father (John 17:4), and that one day every knee shall bow and every tongue confess His glory (Phil. 2:10). It is God's good pleasure to bring the excellences of His triune being into manifestation in His creatures, and so to prepare glory and honor for Himself in those creatures. For this glorification of Himself, too, God does not need the world, for it is not the creature who is independently and self-sufficiently exalting His honor; rather, it is He Himself who by means of the creature or without him glorifies His own name and revels in Himself. God, therefore, never seeks out the creature to find something there that He is lacking. No, the whole world in its length and breadth is for Him a mirror in which He sees His excellences at play. He always remains resting in Himself as the highest good, and He remains eternally blessed by His own blessedness.

* * * * *

Scripture tells us not merely that God called the world into being out of nothing, but tells us also something about the way in which that creation took place.

It begins with the report that *in the beginning* God created heaven and earth (Gen. 1:1). That beginning points out the moment from which those things which were made began to exist. God Himself has no beginning, nor can have. Nor can the Word that was with God and itself was God, for that too was from eternity. No, this beginning marks the moment when created things came into existence. Time and space,

---

7. See also Eph. 3:9; Col. 1:16; and Heb. 1:2.
8. Job 26:13; 33:4; and 1 Cor. 2:10.

too, had their beginning then. True, these two are not independent creatures, called into being by a separate mighty act of God. We read nothing of the kind in the account of the creation. Nevertheless time and space are indispensable forms of existence for created beings. God alone is eternal and omnipresent. Creatures, because they are creatures, are subject to time and space, though not all of them are this in the same way. Time makes it possible for a thing to continue existing in a succession of moments, for one thing to be *after* another. Space makes it possible for a thing to spread out to all sides, for one thing to exist *next to* another. Time and space therefore began to exist at the same time as the creatures, and as their inevitable modes of existence. They did not exist beforehand as empty forms to be filled in by the creatures; for when there is nothing there is no time nor space either. They were not made independently, alongside of the creatures, as accompaniments, so to speak, and appended from the outside. Rather they were created in and with the creatures as the forms in which those creatures must necessarily exist as limited, finite creatures. Augustine was right when he said that God did not make the world *in* time, as if it were created into a previously existing form or condition, but that He made it together *with* time and time together *with* the world.

Next, the first verse of Genesis reports that in the beginning God created the heaven and the earth. By heaven and earth, Scripture here means what it means elsewhere (Gen. 2:1, 4 and Ex. 20:11): namely, the whole world, the whole universe, which according to the will of God was from the beginning divided into two parts. Those parts were the earth with all that is on it and in it, and the heavens which comprise everything that is outside of and above the earth. To the heavens in this sense of Scripture belong the firmament and the air and the clouds (Gen. 1:8, 20), the stars constituting the hosts of heaven (Deut. 4:19 and Ps. 8:3), and also the third heaven, or the heaven of heavens, which is the dwelling place of God and of the angels.[9] And when the first verse of Genesis reports that God created heaven and earth in the beginning, we are not, on the one hand, to understand this as being simply a little caption or summing up of all that is to follow, nor, on the other hand, as indicating that the act of God described in Genesis 1:1 immediately called into being the heavens and the earth in their completed condition.

The first interpretation is refuted by the fact that the second verse begins with the conjunction *and*: *And* the earth was without form, and void. A second fact is therefore being added in a continuing series to

---

9. 1 Kings 8:27; Ps. 2:4; 115:16; Matt. 6:9, and other places.

the fact reported in verse one. And the second interpretation cannot be accepted because heaven as a firmament does not come to be until Genesis 1:8, and because heaven and earth are not denominated "finished" until Genesis 2:1.

Although we cannot speak on this point with absolute certainty, we may consider it likely that the heaven of heavens, the dwelling place of God, was brought into existence by the first creative act of God reported in Genesis 1:1 and that then the angels also came into existence. For in Job 38:4-7 the Lord answers Job from the whirlwind that no man was present when He laid the foundations of the earth and set the cornerstone of it, but that He did complete that work accompanied by the song of the morning stars and the shouting of the sons of God for joy. These sons of God are the angels. The angels therefore were present at the completion of the earth and the creation of man.

For the rest, very little is told us about the creation of the heaven of heavens and its angels. After having mentioned it briefly in the first verse, the account of Genesis proceeds in the second verse to the broader report of the finishing of the earth. Such a finishing or arrangement was necessary, for, although the earth had already been made, nevertheless it existed for a while in a wild and empty state and was covered with darkness. We do not read that the earth became wild, that is, *without form*. Some have held that it was so, and in taking this position they thought of a judgment that had accrued through the fall of the angels to the already perfected earth. But Genesis 1:2 reports merely that the earth *was* without form, that is, that it existed in a formless or shapeless state, undifferentiated into light and darkness, the several bodies of water, dry land and sea. It was only the works of God, described in Genesis 1:3-10, which put an end to that formlessness of the earth. Just so it is reported that the original earth was void. It lacked the garnishing of plant and tree, and was not yet inhabited by any living being. The works of God, summed up in Genesis 1:11 ff., put an end to this emptiness of the earth, for God did not create the earth for it to be void, but in order that men should live in it (Isa. 45:18). Clearly therefore the works of God in the arrangement or completion of the void and formless earth are divided into two groups. The first group of works or acts are introduced by the creation of light. It brings differentiation and distinction into being, form and shape, tone and color. The second group begins with the forming of the bearers of light, sun and moon and stars, and serves further to populate the earth with inhabitants — birds and fishes, and animals and man.

The whole work of creation according to the repeated testimony of the Scriptures[10] was completed in six days. There has, however, been a good deal of difference of opinion and freedom of speculation about those six days. No one less than Augustine judged that God had made everything perfect and complete at once, and that the six days were not six successive periods of time, but only so many points of vantage from which the rank and order of the creatures might be viewed. On the other hand, there are many who hold that the days of creation are to be regarded as much longer periods of time than twenty-four hour units.

Scripture speaks very definitely of days which are reckoned by the measurement of night and morning and which lie at the basis of the distribution of the days of the week in Israel and its festive calendar. Nevertheless Scripture itself contains data which oblige us to think of these days of Genesis as different from our ordinary units as determined by the revolutions of the earth.

In the first place we cannot be sure whether what is told us in Genesis 1:1-2 precedes the first day or is included within that day. In favor of the first supposition is the fact that according to verse 5 the first day begins with the creation of light and that after the evening and the night it ends on the following morning. But even though one reckons the events of Genesis 1:1 and 2 with the first day, what one gets from that assumption is a very unusual day which for a while consisted of darkness. And the duration of that darkness which preceded the creation of light is nowhere indicated.

In the second place, the first three days (Gen. 1:3-13) must have been very unlike ours. For our twenty-four hour days are effected by the revolutions of the earth on its axis, and by the correspondingly different relationship to the sun which accompanies the revolutions. But those first three days could not have been constituted in that way. It is true that the distinction between them was marked by the appearance and disappearance of light. But the Book of Genesis itself tells us that sun and moon and stars were not formed until the fourth day.

In the third place, it is certainly possible that the second series of three days were constituted in the usual way. But if we take into account that the fall of the angels and of men and that also the Flood which followed later caused all sorts of changes in the cosmos, and if, in addition, we notice that in every sphere the period of becoming differs remarkably from that of normal growth, then it seems not unlikely that the second series of three days also differed from our days in many respects.

---

10. Gen. 1:2; Ex. 20:11 and 31:17.

Finally, it deserves consideration that everything which according to Genesis 1 and 2 took place on the sixth day can hardly be crowded into the pale of such a day as we now know the length of days to be. For on that day according to Scripture there occurred the creation of the animals (Gen. 1:24-25), the creation of Adam (Gen. 1:26 and 2:7), the planting of the garden (Gen. 2:8-14), the giving of the probationary command (Gen. 2:16-17), the leading of the animals to Adam and his naming them (Gen. 2:18-20), and the sleep of Adam and the creation of Eve (Gen. 2:21-23).

However all this may have been, the six days remain the creation week within which the heaven and the earth and all their hosts were made. These days indicate the temporal order in which the creatures successively came into being, but at the same time they contain a suggestion of the relationship of rank in which these creatures stand over against each other. No scientific investigation can overthrow this relationship. The formless precedes the formed in rank and order, the inorganic precedes the organic, the plant precedes the animal, and the animal precedes man. Man is and remains the crown of creation: the making and the preparation of the earth issues in him, and converges upon him. Hence, too, Scripture tells us so little about the creation of heaven and of the angels, limiting itself primarily to the earth. In an astronomical sense the earth may be small and insignificant. In point of mass and weight it may be outdone by thousands of planets and suns and stars. But in a religious and moral sense it remains the center of the universe. The earth and the earth alone has been chosen to be the dwelling place of man. It has been chosen to be the arena of struggle in which the great battle must be fought against every evil power. It has been chosen to serve as the place for the establishment of the kingdom of heaven.

All that was created is subsumed in Scripture under the name of heaven and earth and all the host of them (Gen. 2:1) or under the term *world*. The original of the words translated simply *world* in our Bibles sometimes designates the physical globe of the earth (1 Sam. 2:8 and Prov. 8:31), and sometimes rather more the earth as the dwelling place of man and to the extent that it is inhabited by man (Matt. 24:14 and Luke 2:1). Sometimes those original words denote the world in its temporal, changing, transient nature,[11] and then again they tend to stress the world as the unification and wholeness of all creatures taken together (John 1:10 and Acts 17:24). These last two meanings especially have a rich content. In other words, one can, as it were, always look at the

11. Ps. 49:2 ("earth"); Luke 1:70; and Eph. 1:21.

world from two points of view: in its breadth and in its length.

In the first instance, the world is a unit, a coherent whole, but one which in its unity nevertheless exhibits an unmistakably rich differentiation. From the very beginning at which it was created and formed, the world comprised heaven and earth, visible and invisible things, angels and men, plants and animals, the animate and inanimate and the spiritual and non-spiritual beings. All of those creatures are again infinitely differentiated. Among the angels there are thrones and powers, dominions and principalities. Among mankind there are men and women, parents and children, rulers and subjects, peoples and nations, tongues and languages. And in a somewhat similar way plants and animals, and in a sense minerals, too, are again subdivided into classes and groups, families and species, varieties and types. Within limits all of these creatures have and retain the peculiar nature which they received from God (Gen. 1:11, 21ff.), and as such are all subject to their own laws. They exist *after* each other not only in the sense that they were created, the one after the other, and continue to exist now in their higher or lower order, but they also exist *next to* each other and it is so that they continue to be themselves up to the present day. Creation is not uniform but is pluriform in character, and both in its entirety and in its parts, the richest and most beautiful of varieties.

At the same time the world continues its existence in length, in depth of time. The fact that everything that God made was very good (Gen. 1:31), does not mean to say that everything already was what it could become and what it had to become. Just as man, although created after the image of God, nevertheless received a calling and a destination which he had to achieve in the way of works, so the world, when it was created, stood at its beginning and not at its end. It had a long history ahead of it, a century long history, in which it could ever more richly and clearly manifest the excellences of God. Creation and development do not therefore exclude each other. Creation, rather, is the starting point of all development. Because God has created a world inexhaustible in its rich differentiation and variety, in which the various kinds of creatures have their own natures, and in that nature each has received its own thought and property and law, therefore and only therefore evolution is possible. All such evolution takes its point of departure, and at the same time its direction and its purpose, from this creation. Even though sin has worked disturbance and havoc with this evolution or development, God nevertheless fulfills His counsel, sustains the world, and conducts it to its destination.

When Scripture speaks in this way about the world it tacitly proceeds from the assumption that there is but *one* world. In the theses of the philosophers this matter is often presented very differently. Not only were there many — and still are — who held that various worlds co-exist *alongside of* each other, and that not the earth alone but other planets also were inhabited by living and rational creatures, but they maintained also that various worlds succeed one another in time. The present world therefore was not the only one, but had been preceded by innumerable other worlds and would be succeeded by further ones. Some even attached to this the idea that everything which now has existence had its being perfectly in an earlier world and will enjoy such existence again in a later one. All that is, in short, exists in a continuing process; everything is subject to the eternal law of appearance and disappearance, emergence and submergence, rising and setting.

Scripture quietly passes by all these imaginations. It tells us that in the beginning God created this world, that it runs through a history centuries in duration, and that after this historical process that eternal Sabbath will enter in which remains for the people of God. It knows nothing about the habitability of other planets. True, it teaches that the world is infinite in variety, that there are men not only but angels also, and that in addition to an earth there is also a heaven. For the rest, it holds to the position that only man was created in the image of God, that the Son of God did not assume the nature of angels but the nature of mankind, and that the kingdom of heaven spreads out and is actualized on this earth.

Just so, too, Scripture tells us that the world is *finite*. That thought implies, in the first place, that the world has had a beginning and that it was created together with time. The question of how long the world has existed adds nothing to this, and subtracts nothing from it. Even though the world had existed thousands or millions of years longer than it has, that would not constitute it eternal in the sense that God is eternal. Even then the world would be temporal, limited, co-existent with time. It is important to notice this, for Scripture, which teaches that the world has a beginning, nevertheless teaches also that it has no end. It will, of course, have an end in its present form, for the form of this world passes away, but not in its substance and essence. But, even though the world and men and angels continue to exist everlastingly in the future, they remain creatures and never share the eternity which God possesses. The world exists in time and continues to exist in it, even though in another dispensation an entirely different standard of measurement is used than is employed now on this earth. And, just as it is limited to time, so the world is limited to space. True, the newer science has infinitely extended our field of vision; the world has become an awesomely bigger place than it was for our forefathers; we become giddy at hearing the number and the magnitude of the stars, each of which is a world in itself, and the distances separating them from the world go beyond conception. But for all that the world cannot be thought of as eternal in the sense that God is eternal. The difference between the eternal and the everlasting is one of kind, not of degree. We cannot conceive of a time and space beyond the world. We cannot imagine that we should somewhere be able to touch on the boundary of the universe, and be able at that point to stare into an empty void. Time and space co-extend with the world, extending so far as the world extends, and insofar as these exist they are filled with created things. But, all together — time, space, and world — is finite. For the sum of finite parts, no matter how unutterably large they are, never amounts to infinity. God alone is eternal, omnipresent and infinite.

Finally the Scriptures teach us that the world is *good*. It takes a certain amount of courage to say that in these days. The tone of the eighteenth century, it is true, was very optimistic; men in that age looked at everything from the bright side. They were taught that God had created the best of all possible worlds. But the nineteenth and this our twentieth century take a very different view of life, the world, and society. Poets and philosophers and artists teach us in our time that all is in misery in the world, that the world itself is as bad as can be, and that if it were one degree worse it could not exist. All that exists, according to the thinking of many, is deserving only of annihilation. And, although some still want to enjoy so much of the world as can still give a bit of pleasure (Let us eat and drink for tomorrow we die), others surrender themselves to discouragement and world-weariness or in visionary dreams hope for a future, a socialistic utopia, a bliss beyond the grave, a nirvana — something at least which the present cannot give.

Scripture takes a different view of this matter. It tells us first that the world was good, very good, in the form in which it left God's hand (Gen. 1:31). It adds to this in the second place that because of the sin which has entered in, the earth is cursed, man is subject to corruption and death and all creation is subject to vanity. Nowhere is the frailty and transiency of life, the insignificance and pettiness of all that exists, the depth and the pain of suffering taught us so affectingly and vividly as in the Holy Scriptures. But they do not stop at that point. They go on, in the third place, to explain that nevertheless in this fallen and guilty and vain world the good pleasure of God is being fulfilled. They teach that because of this destination to which the world is being conducted this world may again be called good; and they teach that despite sin the world is, and will become, and remains a means by which God glorifies His attributes, and an instrument which He makes serviceable to the honor of His name. And, finally, the Scriptures conclude this their instruction concerning the world by giving the glorious promise that this world, with all of its suffering and oppression, becomes good for us again when we subject our will to that honor of God and make it serviceable to His glory. All things work together for good to them that love God (Rom. 8:28). They learn to glory even in tribulation (Rom. 5:3). Their faith is the victory that overcomes the world (1 John 5:4).

*   *   *   *   *

All of these considerations naturally and directly lead from Creation to Providence. After all, from the very moment that the world in its entirety or each of its creatures was called into being by the creative act of God, they immediately come under the surveillance of God's providence. There is no gradual transition here, nor any gulf or breach. For just as the creatures, because they are creatures, cannot come up *out* of themselves, so too they cannot for a moment exist *through* themselves. Providence goes hand in hand with creation: the two are companion pieces.

Hence an intimate connection and close relationship exists between them. And it is of the highest importance to maintain, over against every deistic threat, this inseparable connection of creation and providence. By deism that tendency of thought is meant which is willing to accept an original creation but for the rest holds that God withdrew from the world and left it to its own devices. In such an instance the notion of creation serves only to give the world its independent existence, and in this sense it is an idea which was still accepted by even Kant and Darwin. But the idea was that in creating the world God had endowed it with total independence and equipped it with an adequacy of gifts and energies, so that it can in and through itself exist perfectly well and can also under all circumstances save itself. The world, according to the familiar figure, was thought of as a watch or a clock which, once it is wound up, goes its own way unattended. Naturally this was an idea which led to the further thought that the world has no need of any revelation but can come by the necessary truth in its own strength and from its own inherent resources. Deism thus brought rationalism in its wake — the movement, that is, which holds that reason can arrive at all truth in and through its own resources. In the same way, deism gives rise to Pelagianism — that is, the doctrine according to which the will of man can itself achieve his salvation. For, according to deism, the will of man quite as well as his reason, was created to be independent, and was equipped with such permanent gifts and energies as make the work of any Mediator of salvation superfluous.

It is necessary, then, in view of this deistic alternative, to cling to the relationship between creation and providence. Scripture does this. It calls the work of providence a life-giving and a preserving activity (Job 33:4 and Neh. 9:6), a renewing (Ps. 104:30), a speaking (Ps. 33:9), a willing (Rev. 4:11), a working (John 5:17), an upholding of all things by the word of His power (Heb. 1:3), a caring (1 Pet. 5:7), and, yes, even a creating (Ps. 104:30 and Isaiah 45:7). What is implied in all these expressions is that after the creation of the world God did not leave the world to itself, looking down upon it from afar. The living God is not to be pushed to one side or into the background after the creation issues from His hand. The word providence means that God supplies the world with what it needs.[12] It is an act of God's mind not only, but also of His will, a carrying out of His counsel. It is an activity by which from moment to moment He keeps the world in existence.

The maintenance, which is usually taken as the first activity of providence, is therefore not a passive supervision. The point is not that He *lets* the world exist but that He *makes* it exist. This is maintenance in the true sense of the word. Very beautifully the Heidelberg Catechism describes this providence as the almighty and everywhere present power of God, whereby, as it were by His hand, He still upholds heaven, earth, and all creatures. Virtue, strength, almighty and Divine strength, proceeds from God, goes out of Him, quite as much in causing the world to continue to exist, as at first in causing it to exist. Without receiving such strength no single creature could for a moment be. The moment God removed His hand and withheld His strength the creature would sink back into nothingness. Nothing comes into being nor remains in being except as God sends out His Word and His Spirit (Psalms 104:30 and 107:25), except God speaks and commands and wills it.

This strength of God comes not from afar but from nearby; it is an omnipresent strength. God is present with all His excellences and with His whole being in the whole world and in all of His creatures. In Him we live, and move, and have our being (Acts 17:28). He is not far from any one of us (Acts 17:27). He is a God at hand, and not a God afar off. No one can hide himself in secret places so that the Lord cannot see Him. He fills heaven and earth (Jer. 23:23-24). Who could go from His Spirit or fly from His presence? He is in heaven and in the realm of the dead, in the uttermost parts of the sea and in the deep darkness (Ps. 139:7 ff.). His maintenance, His sustaining power, ex-

12. Gen. 22:8; 1 Sam. 16:1; Ezek. 20:6; and Heb. 11:40.

tends to all creatures: to the lilies of the field (Matt. 6:28), the birds of the sky (Matt. 6:26), and to even the hairs of the head (Matt. 10:30). Every creature exists according to its nature — as it exists and so long as it exists — through the power of God. Even as it is *of* Him, so it is *through* Him (Rom. 11:36). The Son, through whom God made the world, continues thereafter to uphold all things by the word of His power (Heb. 1:2-3). All things consist by Him who was before all things (Col. 1:17), and they are created and renewed by His Spirit (Ps. 104:30).

* * * * *

Because of this close relationship between creation and providence the latter is sometimes called a continuous or progressive creation. Such a designation can be taken in a good sense, but it ought nevertheless to be secured against misunderstanding. For the same seriousness with which we insist on maintaining the connection and relationship between creation and providence should be given also to maintaining the distinction between them. If the first would involve us in deism (belief in God without benefit of revelation), the second — that is, the ignoring of the distinction between the two — would involve us in pantheism. By pantheism is meant the position according to which the difference in kind between God and the world is erased, and the two are regarded as identical with each other, or, at best, as two sides of one and the same being. God is thought of, then, as the essence of the world, and the world as the manifestation of God. The relationship is like that of the ocean and its waves, reality and the forms of reality, the visible and the invisible sides of the same universe.

Scripture avoids this heresy quite as carefully as it does that of deism. So much is evident from the fact that God is presented not merely as making a beginning with the work of creation but also as completing it and resting from the work of creation.[18] At creation something is accomplished and so is completed. True, as was indicated before, the resting of God is not a desisting from *all* work, for providence, too, is work (John 5:17). But it is a desisting from the specific work designated by creation. And if creation and providence can be thought of as standing next each other in the relationship of work and rest then there can be no doubt that, however intimately connected, they are also distinguished. Creation implies the bringing of something into being out of nothing and maintenance is a causing of that something to persist in its granted existence. Creation does not therefore constitute the world independent, for an independent creature is a contradiction in terms, but it does con-

---

13. Gen. 2:2; Ex. 20:11; and 31:17.

stitute the world an essence which is to be distinguished from the essence of God. It is not merely in name and form that God and the world are to be distinguished from each other, but in essence, in being. They differ as time differs from eternity, the infinite differs from the finite, and the Creator differs from the creature.

Even for itself alone it is of the highest importance to cling to this difference in essence between God and the world. Whoever belittles or denies this distinction falsifies religion, pulls God down to the level of the creature, and in principle becomes guilty of the same sin which Paul ascribes to the pagans when he says that they, knowing God, did not glorify Him, nor were thankful (Rom. 1:21). But there is a further consideration which makes holding to the distinction necessary.

If God were identical with the world, and also in no essential way therefore to be distinguished from mankind, then every thought and deed of men would immediately and directly have to be charged to God's responsibility. Then sin too is His responsibility — in short, there is no longer such a thing as sin. Now it is true that on the one hand Holy Scripture very forcibly states that man in all his thoughts and deeds, and also in his sins, stands under God's rule. Man is never independent of God. The Lord looks down out of heaven, and He sees all the sons of men (Ps. 33:13). He fashions the hearts of all of them and considers all their works (Ps. 33:15). He determines their dwelling places (Deut. 32:8 and Acts 17:26). He ponders all the goings of men (Prov. 5:21 and Jer. 10:23). He does according to His will in the army of heaven, and among the inhabitants of the earth (Dan. 4:35). We are in His hand as the potter's clay and as a saw in the hands of him who draws it.[14] When man becomes a sinner, he does not by that fact emancipate himself from God. His dependence on God simply takes on a different character then. It loses its reasonable and moral nature and becomes creaturely subjection. The man who becomes a slave to sin debases himself and becomes a sheer instrument in His hand. Hence it is possible for Scripture to say that God hardens the heart of man,[15] that He puts a lying spirit into the mouth of the prophets (1 Kings 22:23), that by means of Satan He spurs David on to count the people (2 Sam. 24:1 and 1 Chron. 21:1), that He commands Shimei to curse David (2 Sam. 16:10), that He gives men up to the uncleanness of their sins (Rom. 1:24), that He sends out a strong delusion so that men should believe a lie (2 Thess. 2:11), and that He sets Christ for a fall of many (Luke 2:34).

---

14. Isa. 29:16; 45:9; Jer. 18:4; and Rom. 9:20-21.
15. Ex. 4:21ff.; Deut. 2:30; Josh. 11:20; and Rom. 9:18.

Nevertheless, irrespective of the fact that God's providence is surveillant over sin also, Scripture also firmly and resolutely maintains that the cause of sin lies not in God but in men, and that it is to be reckoned, not to God's, but to man's account. The Lord is righteous and holy, and far from all iniquity (Deut. 32:4 and Job 34:10). He is a light without darkness (1 John 1:5). He tempts no man (James 1:13). He is the overflowing fountain of all that is good and pure (Ps. 36:10 and James 1:17). He forbids sin in His law (Ex. 20) and in the conscience of every man (Rom. 2:14-15), takes no delight in iniquity (Ps. 5:5), but hates it and storms in wrath against it (Rom. 1:18), and threatens it with temporal and eternal punishment (Rom. 2:8).

These two lines of Holy Scripture, according to which sin, from beginning to end, falls under God's governance and is nevertheless chargeable to man's account can be reconciled with each other only if God and the world are on the one hand not separated from each other and yet on the other are essentially distinguished from each other. Theology undertakes to do just this when in its account of providence it speaks of *cooperation* as well as maintenance. By this term theology means to do justice to the fact that God is the *first* cause of all that happens but that under Him and through Him the creatures are active as *secondary* causes, cooperating with the first. We can speak of such secondary causes even in reference to the inanimate creatures. For although it is true that God lets His sun rise over the evil and the good and sends rain on the just and the unjust (Matt. 5:45), He does make use of the sun and the clouds on such occasions. But the distinction being made here is of much more force among rational creatures. For these have received from God's hand a reason and a will and they must use these to guide and to govern themselves. It is true that in these rational creatures also all existence and all life, every talent and every strength, are derived from God, and that, irrespective of how the talent and the strength are used, they remain under the governance of the providence of God. All the same, there is a distinction to be made between the first and the secondary cause, between God and man. Just as in doing good, it is God who according to His good pleasure works and fulfills the will to do it, nevertheless man also himself wills and acts. So, and to an even greater extent, it is in the doing of evil. God grants the life and energy for this also but it is nevertheless man, and man alone, who does the sinning and who is guilty of it. We simply cannot solve the riddles presented to us by the providence of God in life. But the confession that God and the world may never be separated but must always be distinguished nevertheless points the direction in which the solution must be sought and prevents us from straying either to the left or the right in our search.

*   *   *   *   *

Understood in this way, the doctrine of creation and providence is rich in encouragement and comfort. There is so much in life that is oppressive and that robs us of the strength to live and to act. There are the adversities and disappointments which we meet on life's way. There are those terrible calamities and disasters which sometimes cause hundreds and thousands of lives to be lost in nameless anguish. But life in its ordinary course also can sometimes raise doubts in the mind about the providence of God. Is not mystery the portion of all mankind? The worm of restlessness and fear gnaws at all existence. Is it not true that God has a quarrel with His creatures and that we perish in His wrath and are terrified by His anger? No, it is not the unbelievers and the frivolous only, but the children of God also, and these the most deeply of all, who are seized upon by the awful seriousness of reality. And sometimes the question forces its way from the heart up to the lips: Can it be that God created man on the earth for nothing?

But then the despondent Christian by a faith in God's creation and providence again raises his head up high. No devil, but God, the Almighty, the Father of our Lord Jesus Christ, created the world. It is in its entirety and in its parts the work of His hands, and of His hands alone. Once He had created it, He did not let it go. By His almighty and omnipresent power He sustains it. He governs and rules all things in such a way that they all cooperate and all converge upon the purpose He has established. The providence of God includes, together with the maintenance and the cooperation, also the third aspect of *governance*. He is the King of kings and Lord of lords (1 Tim. 6:15 and Rev. 19:6) and His kingdom lasts unto all eternity (1 Tim. 1:17). No accident and no necessity, no arbitrariness and no force, no mere caprice nor iron destiny controls the world and its history and the life and lot of mankind. Behind all secondary causes there lurks and works the almighty will of an almighty God and a faithful Father.

It speaks for itself that no one can really believe this with his heart and confess it with his mouth except the person who knows himself to be a child of God. The faith in providence stands in the most intimate of relationships with the faith in redemption.

True, the providence of God belongs to those truths which to some extent are ascertainable from the general revelation in nature and history. Some of the pagans have often expressed and described it in a beautiful way. One of them said that the gods see and hear everything, that they are omnipresent and that they care for all things. And another one of them said that the order and the arrangement of the universe were maintained by God and for His sake. But none of them knew the confession of the Christian that this God who maintains and governs all things is his God and his Father for Christ His Son's sake. The faith in the providence of God was consequently shaken by doubt in the pagan world and often proved inadequate in the face of the vicissitudes of life. The eighteenth century was very optimistic and held that God had created the best of all possible worlds. But when in the year 1755 the city of Lisbon was for the most part destroyed by a terrible earthquake, many began to blaspheme the providence of God and to deny its existence. But the Christian who has experienced the love of God in the forgiveness of sins and the redemption of his soul is sure to boast with the Apostle Paul that neither tribulation, nor distress, nor persecution, nor famine, nor nakedness, nor peril, nor sword shall separate him from that love (Rom. 8:35). If God be for us, who can be against us? (Rom. 8:31). Although the fig tree shall not blossom, neither shall fruit be in the vines; the labor of the olive shall fail, and the fields shall yield no meat; the flock shall be cut off from the fold, and there shall be no herd in the stalls; yet I will rejoice in the Lord, I will joy in the God of my salvation (Habak. 3:17-18).

In such joy of heart the Christian calls on even the earth to praise the Lord: The Lord reigneth; let the earth rejoice; let the multitude of isles be glad thereof! (Ps. 97:1).

XII

The Origin, Essence, and Purpose of Man

The account of the origin of heaven and earth converges in the first chapter of Genesis upon the creation of man. The creation of the other creatures, of heaven and earth, of sun and moon and stars, of plants and animals, is reported in brief words, and there is no mention made at all of the creation of the angels. But when Scripture comes to the creation of man it lingers long over him, describes not only the fact but also the manner of his creation, and returns to the subject for further broad consideration in the second chapter.

This particular attention devoted to the origin of man serves already as evidence of the fact that man is the purpose and end, the head and crown of the whole work of creation. And there are various material details which also illuminate the superior rank and worth of man among the creatures.

In the first place, there is the special counsel of God which precedes the creation of man. At the calling into being of the other creatures, we read simply that God spoke and by His speaking brought them into existence. But when God is about to create man He first confers with Himself and rouses Himself to make men in His image and likeness. This goes to indicate that especially the creation of man rests on deliberation, on Divine wisdom and goodness and omnipotence. Nothing of course came into existence by chance. But the counsel and decision of God is far more clearly manifest in the making of man than in the creation of the other creatures.

Moreover, in this particular counsel of God, the special emphasis is placed on the fact that man is created after the image and likeness of God and therefore stands in an entirely different relationship to God than all other creatures. It is said of no other creatures, not even of the angels, that they were created in God's image and that they exhibit His image. They may possess hints and indications of one or several of God's attributes, but of man alone it is affirmed that he is created after God's image and in His likeness.

Scripture further emphasizes the fact that God created, not one man, but men, according to His likeness. At the conclusion of Genesis 1:27 they are designated as male and female. It is not man alone, nor woman exclusively, but both of them, and those two in interdependence, who are the bearers of the image of God. And, according to the blessing that is pronounced upon them in verse 28, they are such image bearers not in and for themselves alone. They are that also in their posterity, and together with their posterity. The human race in each of its parts and in its entirety is organically created in the image and likeness of God.

Finally, Scripture expressly mentions that this creation of man in God's image must come to expression particularly in his dominion over all living beings and in the subjection to Him of the whole earth. Because man is the child or offspring of God, he is king of the earth. Being children of God and heirs of the world are two things already closely related to each other, and inseparably related to each other, in the creation.

*   *   *   *   *

The account of the creation of man in the first chapter of Genesis is elaborated and amplified in the second chapter (Gen. 2:4b-25). This second chapter of Genesis is sometimes mistakenly designated the second creation story. This is erroneous because the creation of heaven and earth is assumed in this chapter, and is referred to in verse 4b in order to introduce the manner in which God formed man from the dust of the earth. The whole emphasis in this second chapter falls on the creation of man and on the way in which this took place. The big difference between the first and second chapter of Genesis comes out in these details which are told us in the second concerning the forming of man.

The first chapter tells of the creation of heaven and earth and lets these lead up to the making of man. In this chapter man is the last creature called into existence by God's omnipotence. He stands at the end of the series of creatures as the lord of nature, the king of the earth. But the second chapter, from Genesis 2:4b on, begins with man, proceeds from him as starting point, sets him at the center of things, and then relates what happened in the creation of man, how this took place for the man and for the woman, what dwelling place was appointed for him, with what vocation he was entrusted, and what purpose and destiny was his. The first chapter speaks of man as the end or purpose of the creation; the second deals with him as the beginning of history. The content of the first chapter can be comprised in the name *creation,* and that of the second chapter in the name *Paradise.*

There are three particulars which are told us in this second chapter concerning man's origin, and which serve as the elaboration of what is contained in the first chapter.

In the first place there is a fairly broad treatment of the first dwelling place of man. The first chapter simply stated in general terms that man was created after God's image and that he was appointed lord over the whole earth. But it gives no hint as to where on the face of the globe man first saw the light of life and where he first lived. This we are, however, told in the second chapter. When God had made the heaven and the earth, and when He had called the sun, moon, and stars, the plants and birds, the animals of the land and those of the water, then no specific place had yet been set aside as a dwelling for man. Hence God rests before He creates man and prepares for him a garden or Paradise in the country of Eden, east of Palestine. That garden is arranged in a particular way. God lets all kinds of trees come up out of the soil there — trees beautiful to see and serviceable for food. Two of these trees are designated by name, the tree of life planted in the middle of the garden, and also the tree of the knowledge of good and evil. The garden was laid out in such a way that a river which had its point of origin higher up in the territory of Eden flowed through it, and then forked out into four streams, the Pison, the Gihon, the Tiger, and the Euphrates.

A great deal of toil and effort has in the course of the centuries gone into trying to determine where Eden and the garden of Eden were located. Various representations have been put forward about that one river that came up in Eden and flowed through the garden, about the four rivers into which that major stream parted, about the name of the territory of Eden, and about the garden inside it. But all of these representations have remained conjectures. None has been established by solid proof. Two interpretations would, however, seem to deserve the preference. The first is the one according to which Eden lay towards the north in Armenia; the other holds that it was farther south, in Babylonia. It is hard to decide between these two. The details given in Scripture are no longer adequate to determine just where this territory lay. But when we recall that the people who sprang from Adam and Eve. though banned from Eden, nevertheless at first lingered in that general area (Gen. 4:16), and that Noah's ark after the flood came to rest on Mount Ararat (Gen. 8:4), and that the new mankind after the flood spread out from Babel over the earth (Gen. 11:8-9), then it can hardly be doubted that the cradle of humanity stood in that area bounded by Armenia on the North and Shinar in the South. In modern times scholarship has come to reinforce this teaching of Scripture. True, in the past, historical investigation made all sorts of guesses about the original home of mankind, seeking it, in turn, in all parts of the earth, but it is more and more retracing its steps. Ethnology, the history of civilization, philology all point to Asia as the continent where once the cradle of mankind stood.

A second feature to attract attention in Genesis 2 is the probationary command given to man. Originally this first man was simply called *the man* (*ha-adam*) for he was alone for a while and there was no one beside him who was like him. It is not until Gen. 4:25 that the name Adam occurs without the definite article. There the name first becomes individual. This indicates clearly that the first man, who for a while was the only human being, was the beginning and origin and head of the human race. As such he received a double task to perform: *first,* to cultivate and preserve the garden of Eden, and, *second,* to eat freely of all the trees in the garden except of the tree of the knowledge of good and evil.

The first task defines his relationship to the earth, the second his relationship to heaven. Adam had to subdue the earth and have dominion over it, and this he must do in a twofold sense: he must cultivate it, open it up, and so cause to come up out of it all the treasures which God has stored there for man's use; and he must also watch over it, safeguard it, protect it against all evil that may threaten it, must, in short, secure it against the service of corruption in which the whole of creation now groans.

But man can fulfill this calling over against the earth only if he does not break the bond of connection which unites him with heaven, only if he continues to believe God at His word and to obey His commandment. The twofold task is essentially therefore one task. Adam must have dominion over the earth, not by idleness and passivity but through the work of his head and heart and hand.

But in order to rule, he must serve; He must serve God who is his Creator and Lawgiver. Work and rest, rule and service, earthly and heavenly vocation, civilization and religion, culture and *cultus,* these pairs go together from the very beginning. They belong together and together they comprise in one vocation the great and holy and glorious purpose of man. All culture, that is, all work which man undertakes in order to subdue the earth, whether agriculture, stock breeding, commerce, industry, science, or the rest, is all the fulfillment of a single Divine calling. But if man is really to be and remain such he must proceed in dependence on and in obedience to the Word of God. Religion must be the principle which animates the whole of life and which sanctifies it into a service of God.

A third particular of this second chapter of Genesis is the gift of the woman to the man and the institution of marriage. Adam had received much. Though formed out of the dust of the earth, he was nevertheless a bearer of the image of God. He was placed in a garden which was a place of loveliness and was richly supplied with everything good to behold and to eat. He received the pleasant task of dressing the garden and subduing the earth, and in this he had to walk in accordance with the commandment of God, to eat freely of every tree except the tree of the knowledge of good and evil. But no matter how richly favored and how grateful, that first man was not satisfied, not fulfilled. The cause is indicated to him by God Himself. It lies in his solitude. It is not good for the man that he should be alone. He is not so constituted, he was not created that way. His nature inclines to the social — he wants company. He must be able to express himself, reveal himself, and give himself. He must be able to pour out his heart, to give form to his feelings. He must share his awarenesses with a being who can understand him and can feel and live along with him. Solitude is poverty, forsakenness, gradual pining and wasting away. How lonesome it is to be alone!

And He who created man thus, with this kind of need for expression and extension can in the greatness and grace of His power only choose to supply the need. He can only create for him a helpmeet who goes along with him, is related to him, and suits him as counterpart. The account tells us in verses 19 to 21 that God made all the beasts of the field and all the fowls of the air, and brought them unto Adam to see whether among all those creatures there was not a being who could serve Adam as a companion and a helper. The purpose of these verses is not to indicate the chronological order in which animals and man were made, but rather to indicate the material order, the rank, the grades of relationship in which the two sorts of creatures stand over against each other. This relationship of rank is first indicated in the fact that Adam named the animals.

Adam therefore understood all the creatures, he penetrated their natures, he could classify and subdivide them, and assign to each of them the place in the whole of things which was their due. If, accordingly, he discovered no being among all those creatures who was related to himself, this was not the consequence of ignorance nor of foolhardy arrogance or pride; rather, it stemmed from the fact that there existed a difference in *kind* between him and all other creatures, a difference not of degree merely but of essence. True, there are all kinds of correspondences between animal and man: both are physical beings, both have all kinds of need and desire for food and drink, both propagate offspring, both possess the five senses of smell, taste, feeling, sight, and hearing, and both share the lower activities of cognition, awareness, and perception. None the less, man is different from the animal. He has reason, and understanding, and will and in consequence of these he has religion, morality, language, law, science, and art. True, he was formed from the dust of the earth, but he received the breath of life from above. He is a physical, but also a spiritual, rational, and moral being. And that is why Adam could not find a single creature among them all that was related to him and could be his helper. He gave them all names, but not one of them deserved the exalted, royal name of *man*.

Then, when man could not find the thing he sought, then, quite apart from man's own witting and willing, and without contributive effort on his own part, God gave man the thing he himself could not supply. The best things come to us as *gifts;* they fall into our laps without labor and without price. We do not earn them nor achieve them: we get them for nothing. The richest and most precious gift which can be given to man on earth is woman. And this gift he gets in a deep sleep, when he is unconscious, and without any effort of will or fatigue of the hand. True, the seeking, the looking about, the inquiring, the sense of the need precedes it. So does the *prayer*. But then God grants the gift sovereignly, alone, without our help. It is as though He conducts the woman to the man by His own hand.

Thereupon the first emotion to master Adam, when he wakes up and sees the woman before him, is that of marvelling and gratitude. He does not feel a stranger to her, but recognizes her immediately as sharing his own nature with him. His recognition was literally a *re*cognition of that which he had felt he missed and needed, but which he could not himself supply. And his marvelling expresses itself in the first marriage hymn or epithalamium ever to be sounded on the face of the earth: "This is now bone of my bones, and flesh of my flesh: she shall be called Woman, because she was taken out of man." Adam therefore remains the source and head of the human race. The woman is not merely created *alongside of* him but *out of* him (1 Cor. 11:8). Just as the stuff for making Adam's body was taken from the earth, so the side of Adam is the basis of the life of Eve. But just as out of the dust of the earth the first man became a living being through the breath of life which came from above, so out of Adam's side the first woman first became a human being by the creative omnipotence of God. She is out of Adam and yet is another than Adam. She is related to him and yet is different from him. She belongs to the same kind and yet in that kind she occupies her own unique position. She is dependent and yet she is free. She is *after* Adam and *out of* Adam, but owes her existence to God alone. And so she serves to help the man, to make his vocation of subduing the earth possible. She is his helper, not as mistress and much less as slave, but as an individual, independent, and free being, who received her existence not from the man but from God, who is responsible to God, and who was added to man as a free and unearned gift.

*   *   *   *   *

Thus the Scripture reports the origin of man, of both the male and the female. Such is its thought about the institution of marriage and the beginning of the human race. But in these days a very different construction is put upon these things, and this is done in the name of science and allegedly with the authority of science. And as this new construction penetrates farther and farther until it reaches even the masses of the people, and since it is of the greatest importance for a world and life view, it is necessary to devote our attention to it for a few moments, and to subject the basis on which it rests to an appraisal.

If a person repudiates the Scriptural account of the origin of the human race, it becomes necessary of course to give some other account of it. Man exists, and no one can escape asking the question where he came from. If he does not owe his origin to the creative omnipotence of God, he owes it to something else. And then no solution remains except to say that man gradually developed himself out of the antecedent lower beings and worked himself up to his present high position in the order of being. *Evolution* is, therefore, the magic word which in our times must somehow solve all problems about the origin and essence of creatures. Naturally, since the teaching of creation is repudiated, the evolutionist must accept that something or other existed in the beginning inasmuch as nothing can come from nothing. The evolutionist, however, in view of this fact, proceeds from the wholly arbitrary and impossible assumption that matter and energy and motion existed eternally. To this he adds that before our solar system came into being, the world consisted simply of a chaotic gaseous mass. This was the starting point of the evolution which gradually resulted in our present world and all of its creatures. It is by evolution that the solar system and the earth came into existence. By evolution the layers of the earth and the minerals came into being. By evolution the animate came into being out of the inanimate through an endless series of years. By evolution plants, and animals, and men came to be. And inside the pale of the human, it was again by evolution that sexual differentiation, marriage, family, society, state, language, religion, morality, law, science, art and all the other values of civilization in a regular order came into existence. If only one may proceed from this one assumption that matter and energy and motion existed eternally, then, it is supposed, one no longer needs to postulate a God. Then the world is self-explanatory. Science, it is then believed, constitutes God entirely unnecessary.

The theory of evolution goes on to develop its idea of the origin of man in the following way. When the earth had cooled off, and thus become fit for the birth of living creatures, life arose under the circumstances then extant, very probably in such a way that at first inanimate albuminous combinations formed themselves which, affected by various influences, developed various properties, and that these albuminous entities by way of combination and mingling with each other gave rise to protoplasm, the first germ of life. Thence began the biogenetic development, the development of living beings. It was a process which may have taken a hundred million years of time.

This protoplasm formed the albuminous nucleus of the cell which is now regarded as the basic constituent of all living beings, whether plants, or animals, or men. Unicellular *protozoa* were thus the earliest organisms. According to whether these were mobile or immobile, they developed in time into plants or into animals. Among the animals the *infusoria* stand lowest in the scale, but out of these there gradually come up, by way of various intermediate and transitional stages, the higher kinds of animals, known as the vertebrate, invertebrate, molluscs and radiate animals. Thereupon the vertebrate animals are again divided into four classes: fishes, amphibians, birds, and mammals. This group, in turn, is divided into three orders: the duck-billed, the marsupials, and the placentate animals; and this last is again subdivided into the rodents, the ungulate animals, the beasts of prey, and the primates. The primates in turn are classified as semi-apes, apes, and anthropoids.

When we compare the physical organism of man with that of these various animals, we discover, according to the evolutionist, that man, in an order of increasing resemblance, is closest in kind to the vertebrates, the mammals, the placentate animals, and the primates, and that he resembles most closely of all the anthropoids, represented by the orang and the gibbon in Asia, and by the gorilla and the chimpanzee in Africa. These are therefore to be regarded as the closest relatives of man. True, they differ from man in size, shape, and the like, but they are altogether like him in their basic physical structure. All the same, man did not come from one of those kinds of apes now extant, but from an anthropoid long since extinct. Apes and men are according to this theory of evolution blood relatives, belong to the same race, though they are to be regarded rather as nephews and nieces than as brothers and sisters.

Such is the idea of the theory of evolution. Such, according to it, was the course of events. But the evolutionist also felt called upon to say something about the way in which all this took place. It was easy enough to say that plants and animals and men had formed an unbroken and rising series of beings. But the evolutionist felt that he ought to do something towards demonstrating that such a development was actually possible, that an ape, for instance, could gradually come to be a man. Charles Darwin in 1859 attempted such a demonstration. He noticed that plants and animals — roses and doves, for example — could by artificially assisted natural selection be brought to exhibit significant modifications. Thus he hit upon the idea that in nature, too, such a natural selection might have been operative, a selection not artificially controlled by human intervention, but unconscious, arbitrary, natural. With this thought a light dawned on him. For by accepting such a theory of natural selection he supposed himself in a position to explain how plants and animals gradually undergo changes, how they can overcome defects in their organization and can achieve advantages, and that in such a way they constantly equip themselves better for successful competition with others in the struggle for existence. For, according to Darwin, life is always and everywhere in the whole creation just that: a struggle for existence. Superficially observed, it may seem that there is peace in nature, but this is a deceptive appearance. Rather, there is that constant struggle for life and the necessaries for life, for the earth is too small and too meager to supply all the beings that are born into it with the requisite foods. Hence millions of organisms perish because of need; only the strongest survive. And these strongest ones, who are superior to the others because of some property they have developed, gradually transfer their acquired, advantageous characteristics to their posterity.

Hence there is progress and ever higher development. Natural selection, the struggle for existence, and the transfer of old and newly acquired characteristics explain, according to Darwin, the appearance of new species, and also the transition from animal to man.

* * * * *

In evaluating this theory of evolution it is necessary above all to make a sharp distinction between the *facts* to which it appeals and the *philosophical view* with which it looks at them. The facts come down to this: that man shares all kinds of characteristics with other living beings, more particularly with the higher animals, and among these in turn especially with the apes. Naturally, these facts were for the most part known before Darwin also, for the correspondence in physical structure, in the several organs of the body and in their activities, in the five senses, in the perceptions and awarenesses, and the like, is something which all who look may see, and simply is not susceptible to denial. But the sciences of anatomy, biology, and physiology, and also that of psychology, have in recent times investigated those corresponding characteristics much more thoroughly than was done before. The characteristics of resemblance have accordingly increased in number and importance. There were other sciences too which contributed their part to confirming and extending these similarities between man and animal. The science of embryology, for instance, indicated that a human being in its beginnings in the womb resembles a fish, an amphibian, and the lower mammals. Paleontology, which busies itself with the study of conditions and circumstances in ancient times, discovered remnants of human beings — skeletons, bones, skulls, tools, ornaments, and the like — which pointed to the fact that centuries ago some people in some parts of the earth lived in a very simple way. And ethnology taught that there were tribes and peoples who were widely separated both spiritually and physically from the civilized nations.

When these facts, brought together from various sides, became known, philosophy soon busied itself with combining them into an hypothesis, the hypothesis of the gradual evolution of all things, and specifically also of man. This hypothesis did not come up after the facts were discovered nor because of them, but existed a long time ago, was sponsored by a number of philosophers, and was now applied to the facts, some of which were newly discovered. The old hypothesis, the old theory, now came to rest, it was supposed, on the firmly founded facts. A sort of hurrah went up because of the fact that now all the riddles of the world, except that one of the eternal matter and energy, were solved and all secrets were discovered. But hardly had this proud edifice of the evolutionary philosophy been built when the attack upon it began and it started to crumble. Darwinism, says a distinguished philosopher, came up in the 1860's, staged its triumphal procession in the 1870's, was thereupon questioned by some few in the 1890's, and since the turn of the century has been strongly attacked by many.

The first and sharpest of the attacks was launched against the manner in which, according to Darwin, the several species had come into existence. The struggle for existence and natural selection did not suffice as an explanation. True, there is often a fierce struggle in the plant and animal worlds, and this struggle has a significant influence on their nature and existence. But it has by no means been proved that this struggle can cause new species to come into being. The struggle for existence can contribute to the strengthening of tendencies and abilities, of organs and potentialities, by way of exercise and effort. It can develop what is present already, but it cannot bring into being what does not exist. Besides, it is an exaggeration, as any one knows from his own experience, to say that always and everywhere nothing exists except struggle.

There is more than hatred and animosity in the world. There is also love and cooperation and help. The doctrine that there is nothing anywhere but warfare on the part of all against all is just as onesided as the idyllic view of the eighteenth century that everywhere in nature there is rest and peace. There is room for many at the big table of nature, and the earth which God gave as a dwelling place for man, is inexhaustibly rich. Consequently, there are many facts and manifestations which have nothing to do with a struggle for existence. Nobody, for instance, can point out what the colors and figures of the snail's skin, the black color of the underbelly in many vertebrate animals, the graying of the hair with increasing age, or the reddening of the leaves in the autumn have to do with the struggle for existence. Nor is it true that in this struggle the strongest types always and exclusively win the victory, and that the weakest are always defeated. A so-called coincidence, a fortunate or unfortunate circumstance, often mocks all such calculations. Sometimes a strong person is taken away in the strength of his years, and sometimes a physically weak man or woman reaches a ripe old age.

Such considerations led a Dutch scholar to substitute another theory for that of Darwin's natural selection, that of mutation, according to which the change of species did not take place regularly and gradually, but suddenly sometimes, and by leaps or jumps. But in this matter the question is whether these changes really represent new species or simply modifications in the species already extant. And the answer to that question hinges again on just what one means by species.

Not only the struggle for existence, natural selection, and the survival of the fittest have lost status in this century, but also the idea of the transfer of acquired characteristics. The transfer of natural, inherited characteristics from parents to children from the nature of the case tends rather to plead against than for Darwinism, inasmuch as it implies the constancy of species. Centuries on end men beget men and nothing else. Concerning the transfer of acquired as distinguished from inherited characteristics there is now so much difference of opinion that nothing can be said about it with certainty. This much, however, is certain, that acquired characteristics very often are not transferred by the parents to the children. Circumcision, for instance, was practised by some people for centuries, and yet left no traces in the children after all that while. Transfer by inheritance takes place only inside certain boundaries and does not effect any change of kind or species. If the modification is artificially induced, it must also be artificially maintained or else it is lost again. Darwinism, in short, cannot explain either heredity or change. Both are facts whose existence is not denied, but their connection and relationship still lie beyond the pale of our knowledge.

More and more, therefore, Darwinism proper, that is, Darwinism in the narrower sense, namely, the effort to explain change of species in terms of the struggle for existence, natural selection, and the transfer of acquired characteristics was abandoned by the men of science. The prediction of one of the first and most eminent of opponents of Darwin's theory was literally fulfilled: namely, that this theory for explaining the mysteries of life would not last till even the end of the nineteenth century. But more important is the fact that criticism has not been directed against Darwin's theory alone but against the theory of evolution itself also. Naturally, facts remain facts and may not be ignored. But theory is something else, something built upon the facts by thought. And what became more and more evident was that the theory of evolution did not fit the facts but was even in conflict with them.

Geology, for instance, revealed that the lower and higher sorts of animals do not follow each other in sequence but as a matter of fact existed alongside of each other ages ago. Paleontology did not come up with a single piece of conclusive evidence for the existence of transitional types between the several species of organic beings. Still, according to Darwin's theory of extremely gradual evolution by way of extremely small changes, these types should have been present in quantity. Even the ardently sought after and energetically pursued intermediary type between man and the ape was not discovered. Embryology, it is true, does point to a certain external similarity between the various stages in the development of the embryo of man and that of other animal bodies. But this similarity is external for the simple reason that from an animal embryo a human being is never born, nor an animal from a human embryo. In other words, man and animal go in different directions from conception on, even though the internal differences cannot then be perceived. Biology has up to this time offered so little support to the proposition that life generated itself that many now accept the impossibility of that and are returning to the idea of a special life force or energy. Physics and chemistry, in proportion to the extent to which they have pressed their investigations, have found more and more secrets and marvels in the world of the infinitely small, and have caused many to return to the thought that the basic constituents of things are not material entities but forces. And — to mention no further evidences — all the efforts that have been put forth to explain consciousness, freedom of the will, reason, conscience, language, religion, morality, and all such manifestations, as being solely the product of evolution have not been crowned with success. The origins of all these manifestations, like those of all other things, remain shrouded in darkness for science.

For it is important to note finally that when man makes his appearance in history he is already man according to body and soul, and he is already in possession, everywhere and at all times, of all those human characteristics and activities whose origins science is trying to discover. Nowhere can human beings be found who do not have reason and will, rationality and conscience, thought and language, religion and morality, the institutions of marriage and the family, and the like. Now if all of these characteristics and manifestations have gradually evolved, such an evolution must have taken place in prehistoric times, that is, in times of which we know *nothing* directly, and about which we make surmises only on the basis of a few facts perceived in later times. Any science, therefore, which wants to burrow through to that prehistoric time and to discover the origins of things there, *must* from the nature of the case take recourse to guesses, surmises, and suppositions. There is no possibility here for evidence or proof in the strict sense. The doctrine of evolution generally and that of the descent of man from the animal particularly are not supported in the least by facts supplied by historic times. Of all the elements on which such theories are built nothing remains in the end but a philosophical world-view which wants to explain all things and all manifestations in terms of the things and manifestations themselves, leaving God out of account. One of the proponents of the evolutionary view admitted it bluntly: the choice is between evolutionary descent or miracle; since miracle is absolutely impossible we are compelled to take the first position. And such an admission demonstrates that the theory of the descent of man from lower animal forms does not rest on careful scientific investigation but is rather the postulate of a materialistic or pantheistic philosophy.

* * * * *

The idea of the origin of man is very closely related to that of the *essence* of man. Many nowadays talk differently, saying that man and the world, irrespective of what was their origin and their development in the past, are what they are now and will remain such.

This position is of course entirely correct: reality remains the same, irrespective of whether we form a true or a false idea of it. But the same holds of course concerning the origin of things. Even though we imagine that the world and mankind came into being in some particular fashion — gradually, say, during the course of centuries, by all sorts of infinitesimally small changes through self-generation — such a supposition does not, of course, change the actual origin. The world came into being in the way that it did, and not in the way we wish it or suppose it. But the *idea* we have of the origin of things is inseparably connected with the *idea* we have of the essence of things.

If the first is wrong, the second cannot be right. If we think that the earth and all the realms of nature, that all creatures and particularly also human beings, came into being without God solely through the evolution of energies which are residual in the world, such an idea must necessarily have a most significant influence on our conception of the *essence* of world and man.

True, the world and man will remain themselves irrespective of our interpretation; but *for us* they become different, they increase or decrease in worth and significance according as we think of their origin and their coming into existence.

This is so evident that it requires no ampler illumination or confirmation. But because the notion that we can think what we please about the origin of things, inasmuch as what we think of their essence is unaffected by it, is a notion which comes back again and again — for example, in the doctrine of Scripture, the religion of Israel, the person of Christ, religion, morality, and the like — it may be useful now, in consideration of the essence of man, to indicate the falsity of that notion once more. It is not difficult to do so. For if man has gradually evolved himself, so to speak, without God and solely through blindly operative natural forces, then it follows naturally enough that man cannot differ essentially from the animal, and that. in his highest development also, he remains an animal. For a soul distinguished from the body, for moral freedom and personal immortality, there is then no room at all. And religion, truth, morality, and beauty then lose their proper (absolute) character.

These consequences are not something which we impose on the proponents of the theory of evolution but something rather which they themselves deduce from it. Darwin, for instance, himself says that our unmarried women, if they were educated under the same conditions as honey bees are, would think it a sacred duty to kill their brothers even as the working bees do, and mothers would try to murder their fertile daughters without anybody caring to intervene. According to Darwin, therefore, the whole of the moral law is a product of circumstances, and consequently it changes as the circumstances change. Good and evil, even as truth and falsehood, are therefore relative terms, and their meaning and worth are, like fashions, subject to the changes of time and place. So, too, according to others, religion was but a temporary aid, something of which man in his inadequacy for the struggle against nature made use, and which now too can serve as an opiate for the people, but something which on the long run will naturally die out

and disappear when man has come into his full freedom. Sin and transgression, felony and murder do not constitute man guilty but are after-
effects of the uncivilized state in which man formerly lived, and they
decrease in proportion to the extent that man develops and society im-
proves. Criminals are, accordingly, to be regarded as children, animals,
or insane types, and should be dealt with accordingly. Prisons should
give way to reformatories. In short, if man is not of Divine but of animal origin and has gradually "evolved" himself he owes everything to
himself alone, and is his own lawgiver, master, and lord. All these inferences from the (materialistic or pantheistic) theory of evolution come
to expression very clearly in contemporary science as well as in contemporary literature, art, and practical polity.

Reality, however, teaches something quite different. Man can make
himself believe, if he wants to, that he has done everything himself and
that he is bound by nothing. But in every respect he remains a dependent creature. He cannot do as he pleases. In his physical existence, he
remains bound to the laws laid down for respiration, the circulation
of the blood, digestion, and procreation. And if he runs counter to these
laws and pays no attention to them, he injures his health and undermines
his own life. The same is true of the life of his soul and spirit. Man
cannot think as he pleases, but is bound to laws which he has not himself thought out and laid down, but which are implied in the very act of
thinking and come to expression in it. If he does not hold to those laws
of thought, he snares himself in the net of error and falsehood. Nor can
man will and act as he pleases. His will is under the discipline of reason
and conscience; if he disregards this discipline and degrades his willing
and acting to the level of arbitrariness and caprice, then there is sure
to be self-reproach and self-indictment, regret and remorse, the gnaw-
ing and the compunction of the conscience.

The life of the soul, therefore, no less than the life of the body, is
built on something other than caprice or accident. It is not a condition
of lawlessness and anarchy but is from all sides and in all its activities
determined by laws. It is subject to laws of truth and goodness and
beauty and so it demonstrates that it has not generated itself. In short,
man has from the very beginning his own nature and his own essence
and these he cannot violate with impunity. And so much stronger is
nature in these matters than theory that the adherents of the doctrine
of evolution themselves keep talking of a human nature, of immutable
human attributes, of laws of thought and ethics prescribed for man, and
of an inborn religious sense. Thus the idea of the essence of man comes
into conflict with the idea of his origin.

In Scripture, however, there is perfect agreement between the two ideas. There the essence of man corresponds to his origin. Because man, although he was formed from the dust of the earth according to the body, received the breath of life from above, and was created by God Himself, he is a unique being, has his own nature. The essence of his being is this: he exhibits the *image* of God and His *likeness*.

* * * * *

This image of God distinguishes man from both the animal and the angel. He has traits in common with both, but he differs from both in having his own unique nature.

The animals, too, of course, were created by God. They did not come into being of their own accord but were called into existence by a particular word of the power of God. Besides, they were immediately created in various kinds, even as the plants were. All men are descended from one parental pair and thus constitute one generation or race. This is not true of the animals; they have, so to speak, various ancestors. Hence it is remarkable that zoology up to this time has not yet succeeded in tracing all animals back to one type. It begins by at once designating some seven or some four major groupings or basic types.

Presumably it is therefore true that most of the animal types are not distributed over the whole earth, but live in particular areas. The fishes live in the water, the birds in the air, and the land animals for the most part are limited to definite territories: the polar bear, for instance, is found only in the far north, and the duck-billed platypus only in Australia. And so in Genesis it is specifically stated that God created the plants (1:11) and also the animals after their kind — that is, according to types. Naturally, this does not mean to say that the types which were originally created by God were exactly those into which science, that of Linnaeus, say, now classifies them. For one thing our classifications are always liable to error because our zoology is still defective and inclined to regard variants as types and vice versa. The artificial, scientific concept of an animal type is very difficult to establish and is always very different from the natural concept of type for which we are always still seeking. Moreover, in the course of centuries a great many animal kinds have died out or been destroyed. From the remains, whether whole or blasted, which we have of some of them, it is evident that various kinds of animals, such as the mammoth, for instance, which no longer exists, once abounded in quantity. And in the third place it should be remembered that as a result of various influences big modifications and changes have taken place in the animal world which often make it difficult or even impossible for us to trace them back to an original type.

Further, it is remarkable that in the creation of the animals even as in that of the plants these were indeed called into being by a particular act of Divine power, but that in this act nature also performed a mediate service. Let the earth bring forth grass, we read in Genesis 1:11, the herb yielding seed, and the fruit tree yielding fruit, and it was so (verse 12). The report is the same in Gen. 1:20: Let the waters bring forth abundantly the moving creature that hath life, and fowl that may fly above the earth, and it was so (verse 21). Again in verse 24: Let the earth bring forth the living creature after his kind, cattle, and creeping thing, and beast of the earth after his kind, and it was so. Thus in each instance, nature is used by God as an instrument. It is the *earth* which, although naturally conditioned and equipped for it by God, brings forth all those creatures in their bountiful differentiation of kind.

This peculiar origin of animals sheds some light, too, on their nature. This origin demonstrates that the animals are much more closely related to the earth and to nature than man is. True, the animals are living beings, and as such they are distinguished from the inorganic, inanimate creatures. Hence, too, they are often called living souls (Gen. 1:20, 21, and 24). In the general sense of a principle of life the animals too have a soul.[1] But this *living* principle of the soul in the animal is still so closely bound to nature and to the metabolism of matter that it cannot arrive at any independence or freedom, and it cannot exist when separated from the metabolism or circulation of matter. At death, therefore, the soul of the animal dies. From this it follows that the animals, at least the higher animals, do have the same sense organs as man, and can sense things (hear, see, smell, taste, and feel). They can form images or pictures, and relate these images to each other. But animals do not have reason, cannot separate the image from the particular, individual, and concrete thing. They cannot metamorphose the images nor raise them into concepts, cannot relate the concepts and so form judgments, cannot make inferences from the judgments nor arrive at decisions, and cannot carry out the decisions by an act of the will. Animals have sensations, images, and combinations of images; they have instincts, desires, passions. But they lack the higher forms of desire and knowledge which are peculiar to man; they have no reason and they have no will. All this comes to expression in the fact that animals do not have language, religion, morality, and the sense of beauty; they have no ideas of God, of the invisible things, of the true, the good, and the beautiful.

Thus man is raised high above the animal plane. Between the two there is not a gradual transition but a great gulf. That which constitutes the very nature of man, his peculiar essence, namely his reason and his

---

1. Gen. 2:19; 9:4, 10, 12, 16; Lev. 11:10; 17:11; and elsewhere.

will, his thought and language, his religion and morality, and the like, are alien to the animal. Therefore the animal cannot understand man although man can understand the animal. Nowadays the science of psychology tries to explain the soul of man in terms of the soul of the animal, but this is to reverse the right order. The soul of man is the key for getting at the soul of the animal. The animal lacks what man has, but man has all that is peculiar to the animal.

This is not to say that now, too, man knows the nature of animals through and through. The whole world is for man a problem whose solution he seeks after and can seek after, and so too every animal is a living mystery. The significance of the animal by no means consists of the fact that the animal is useful to man, providing him with food and shelter, clothing and ornament. Much more is contained in the subduing and having dominion over the earth than that man should, in greed and egotism, freely turn everything to his advantage. The animal world has significance also for our science and art, our religion and morality. God has something, has much, to tell us in the animal. His thoughts and words speak to us out of the whole world, even out of the world of plants and animals. When botany and zoology trace out these thoughts, these sciences, as, indeed, the natural sciences in general, are glorious sciences, which no man, certainly no Christian, may despise. Moreover, how rich the animal world is in moral significance for man! The animal points to the boundary beneath, above which man must raise himself, and to the level of which he must never sink. Man can become an animal and less than an animal if he dulls the light of reason, breaks the bond with heaven, and seeks to satisfy all his desire in the earth. Animals are symbols of our virtues and our vices: the dog shows us the image of loyalty, the spider of industry, the lion of courage, the sheep of innocence, the dove of integrity, the hart of the soul thirsting for God; and, just so too, the fox is the image of cunning, the worm of misery, the tiger of cruelty, the swine of baseness, the snake of devilish guile, and the ape, who most nearly resembles the form of man, declares what an impressive physical organization amounts to without spirit, the spirit that is from above. In the ape man sees his own caricature.

*   *   *   *   *

Just as man differs by the image of God from the animals below him, he is distinguished by it also from the angels above him. The existence of such beings as angels cannot, apart from Scripture, be proved by scientific argument. Science knows nothing about them, cannot demonstrate that they exist, and cannot demonstrate that they do not exist.

But it is remarkable that a belief in the existence of beings who are above man occurs among all peoples and in all religions, and that men, when they have rejected the testimony of the Scriptures concerning the existence of angels, nevertheless, in all sort of superstitious forms, come back to a belief in the existence of supramundane beings. Our present generation abundantly proves this. Angels and devils are no longer held to exist and in their stead a belief has arisen in many circles in latent forces, mysterious natural powers, ghosts, apparitions, visitations of the deceased, animated stars, inhabited planets, Mars-men, living atoms, and the like. Interesting in connection with all these ancient and new manifestations is the position which the Holy Scripture has over against them. Irrespective of whether falsehood or truth lies at the basis of them, Scripture forbids all fortune telling,[2] sorcery,[3] astrology,[4] necromancy,[5] enchantment or the consulting of oracles,[6] all conjuring and wizardry,[7] and the like, and so makes an end of all superstition as well as of all unbelief. Christianity and superstition are sworn foes. There is no science, enlightenment, or civilization that can safeguard against superstition; only the word of God can protect us from it. Scripture makes man most profoundly dependent upon God, but precisely in so doing emancipates him from every creature. It puts man into a right relationship with nature and so makes a true natural science possible.

But the Scriptures do teach that there are angels, not the mythical creations of the human imagination, not the personifications of mysterious forces, not the deceased who have now climbed to higher levels, but spiritual beings, created by God, subject to His will, and called to His service. They are beings, therefore, of whom, in the light of Scripture, we can form a definite idea, and such as have nothing in common with the mythological figures of the Pagan religions. In knowledge they are raised high above man,[8] and in power,[9] but they were nevertheless made by the same God and the same Word (John 1:3 and Col. 1:16), and they have the same reason and the same moral nature, so that, for instance, it is said of the good angels that they obey God's voice and do His pleasure (Ps. 103: 20-21), and of the evil angels that they do not stand in the truth (John 8:44), that they lead astray (Eph. 6:11), and that they sin (2 Peter 2:4).

---

2. Lev. 19:31; 20:27; and Deut. 18:10-14.
3. Deut. 18:10; Jer. 27:10; and Rev. 21:8.
4. Lev. 19:26; Isa. 47:13; and Micah 5:11.
5. Deut. 18:11.
6. Lev. 19:26 and Deut. 18:10.
7. Deut. 18:11 and Isa. 47:9.
8. Matt. 18:10 and 24:36.
9. Ps. 103:20 and Col. 1:16.

But, in spite of this correspondence between them, there exists a big difference between angels and men. It consists, in the first place, of the fact that the angels do not have soul and body, but are pure spirits (Heb. 1:14). True, at the time of their revelation they often appeared in physical forms, but the several forms in which they appeared[10] point to the fact that these assumed forms of manifestation were temporary and that they changed in accordance with the nature of the mission. Never are the angels called souls, living souls, as the animals are and as man is. For soul and spirit differ from each other in this respect that the soul, too, is by nature spiritual, immaterial, invisible, and, even in man is a spiritually independent entity though it is always a spiritual power or spiritual entity which is oriented to a body, suits a body, and without such a body is incomplete and imperfect. The soul is a spirit designed for a physical life. Such a soul is proper to animals and particularly to man. When man loses his body in death, he continues to exist, but in an impoverished and bereft condition, so that the resurrection on the last day is a restoration of the lack. But the angels are not souls. They were never intended for a bodily life and were not given earth but heaven as a dwelling place. They are pure spirits. This gives them great advantages over man, for they stand higher in knowledge and power, stand in a much freer relationship to time and space than men do, can move about more freely, and are therefore exceptionally well adapted to carrying out God's commands on earth.

But — and this is the second distinction between men and angels — those advantages have their opposite side. Because the angels are pure spirits, they all stand in a relatively loose relationship with reference to each other. They were all originally created together and they all continue to live alongside each other. They do not form one organic whole, one race or generation. True, there is a natural order among them. According to Scripture there are a thousand times a thousand angels,[11] and these are divided into classes: cherubims (Gen. 3:24), seraphims (Isa. 6), and thrones, dominions, principalities, and powers (Eph. 1:21 and Col. 1:16; 2:10). And there is further distinction of rank within the groups: Michael and Gabriel have a special place among them.[12] Nevertheless, they do not constitute one race, are not blood relatives, did not beget each other. It is possible to speak of a mankind but not of an angelkind. When Christ assumed the human nature He was immediately related to all men, related by blood, and He was their brother according to the flesh. But the angels live next to

---

10. Gen. 18:2; Judges 18:3; and Rev. 19:14.
11. Deut. 33:2; Dan. 7:10; and Rev. 5:11.
12. Dan. 8:16; 9:21; 10:13, 21; and Luke 1:19, 26.

each other, each one accountable for himself and not for the others, so that a portion of them could fall and a portion remain faithful to God.

The third distinction between man and angel is related to the second. Because the angels are spirits and are not related to the earth, because they are not related by blood, and do not know such distinctions as father and mother, parents and children, brothers and sisters, therefore there is a whole world of relationships and connections, ideas and emotions, desires and duties of which the angels know nothing. They may be more powerful than men, but they are not so versatile. They stand in fewer relationships, and in riches and depth of the emotional life man is far superior to the angel. True, Jesus says in Matthew 22:30 that marriage will end with this dispensation, but nevertheless the sexual relationships on earth have to a significant extent increased the spiritual treasures of mankind, and in the resurrection, too, these treasures will not be lost but will be preserved into eternity.

If to all this we add the consideration that the richest revelation of God which He has given us is revealed to us in the name of the Father, and in the name of the Son—who became like unto us and is our prophet, priest, and king — and in the name of the Holy Spirit who is poured out in the church and who causes God Himself to dwell in us, then we feel that not the angel, but man, was created after the image of God. Angels experience His power, and wisdom, and goodness, but human beings share in His eternal mercies. God is their Lord, but He is not their Father; Christ is their Head, but He is not their Reconciler and Savior; the Holy Spirit is their Sender and Guide but He never testifies with their spirit that they are children and heirs of God, and joint-heirs with Christ. Hence the eyes of the angels are cast upon the earth, for there God's richest grace has appeared, there the struggle between heaven and earth is fought out, there the church is formed into the body of the Son, and there the conclusive blow will someday be struck and the final triumph of God be achieved. Hence it is that they desire to look into the mysteries of salvation being revealed on earth and to learn to know from the church the manifold wisdom of God (Eph. 3:10 and 1 Peter 1:12).

Angels, accordingly, stand in numerous relationships with us, and we in many-sided relationship with them. Belief in the existence and activity of angels is not of the same worth as the belief with which we trust in God and love, fear, and honor Him with our whole heart. We may not put our trust in any creature or in any angel; we may not worship the angels or in any way give them religious honor.[13] In fact, there is in Scripture not a single word about any guardian angel, appointed to

---

13. Deut. 6:13; Matt. 4:10; and Rev. 22:9.

serve each human being in particular, or about any intercession on the part of the angels in our behalf. But this does not mean that believing in angels is indifferent or worthless. On the contrary, at the time when revelation came into being, they played an important role. In the life of Christ they appeared at all turning points of His career, and they will one day be manifested with Him upon the clouds of heaven. And always they are ministering spirits sent out to minister for them who shall be heirs of salvation (Heb. 1:14). They rejoice in the repentance of the sinner (Luke 15:10). They watch over the faithful (Ps. 34:7 and 91:11), protect the little ones (Matt. 18:10), follow the church in its career through history (Eph. 3:10), and bear the children of God into Abraham's bosom (Luke 16:22).

Therefore we are to think of them with respect and speak of them with honor. We are to give them joy by our repentance. We are to follow their example in the service of God and in obedience to His word. We are to show them in our own hearts and lives and in the whole of the church the manifold wisdom of God. We are to remember their fellowship and together with them declare the mighty works of God. Thus there is difference between men and angels, but there is no conflict; differentiation but also unity; distinction but also fellowship. When we arrive at Mount Zion, the city of the living God, the heavenly Jerusalem, then we come also to the many thousands of angels and rebind the tie of unity and love that was broken by sin (Heb. 12:22). Both they and we have our own place in the rich creation of God and achieve our peculiar function there. Angels are the sons, the mighty heroes, the powerful hosts of God. Men were created in His image and are God's *generation*. They are His *race*.

*   *   *   *   *

If the image of God is the distinguishing earmark of man, we owe it to ourselves to get a clear idea of the content of it.

We read in Genesis 1:26 that God created man in His image and after His likeness in order that man should have dominion over all creatures, particularly over all living creatures. Three things deserve consideration in that. In the first place, the correspondence between God and man is expressed in two words: *image* and *likeness*. These two words are not, as many have supposed, materially different, different in content, but serve to amplify and support each other. Together they serve to state that man is not an unsuccessful portrait, or a somewhat similar one, but that he is a perfect and totally corresponding image of God. Such as man is in miniature, such is God in the large, the infinitely large outline, for man is such as God is. Man stands infinitely far beneath God and is nevertheless related to Him. As creature man is absolutely dependent upon God and yet as man he is a free and independent being. Limitation and freedom, dependence and independence, immeasurable distance and intimate relation over against God, these have been combined in an incomprehensible way in the human being. How a mean creature can at the same time be the image of God — that goes far beyond our grasp.

In the second place, we are told in Genesis 1:26 that God created men (the term is plural) in His image and after His likeness. From the very beginning the intention was that God would not create one man, but men, in his image. Therefore He immediately created man as *man and woman,* the two of them not in separation from each other but in relationship and fellowship with each other (verse 27). Not in the man alone, nor in the woman alone, but in both together, and in each in a special way, the image of God is expressed.

The contrary is sometimes affirmed on the ground that in 1 Corinthians 11:7 Paul says that man is the image and glory of God and that woman is the glory of man. This text is frequently abused so as to deny the image of God to the woman and to debase her far below the level of the man. But Paul is there not speaking of man and woman considered apart from each other but about their relationship in marriage. And then he says that it is the man and not the woman who is the head. And he deduces this from the fact that the man is not from the woman, but the woman from the man. The man was created first, was first made in the image of God, and to him God first revealed His glory. And if the woman shares in all this, this takes place mediately, from and through the man. She received the image of God, but after man, in dependence upon him, by way of his mediation. Hence man is the image and glory of God directly and originally; the woman is the image and glory of God in a derived way in that his is the glory of man. What we read of this matter in Genesis 2 must be added to what we read of it in Genesis 1. The way in which woman is created in Genesis 2 is the way along which she receives the image of God as well as the man (Gen. 1:27). In this is contained the further truth that the image of God rests in a number of people, with differentiation of race, talent, and powers — in short in mankind — and further that this image will achieve its full unfolding in the new humanity which is the church of Christ.

In the third place, Genesis 1:26 teaches us that God had a purpose in creating man in His image: namely, that man should have dominion over all living creatures and that he should multiply and spread out over the world, subduing it. If now we comprehend the force of this subduing under the term culture, now generally used for it, we can say that culture in the broadest sense is the purpose for which God created man after His image. So little are *cultus* and culture, religion and civilization, Christianity and humanity in conflict with each other that it would be truer to say God's image had been granted to man so that he might in his dominion over the whole earth bring it into manifestation. And this dominion of the earth includes not only the most ancient callings of men, such as hunting and fishing, agriculture and stock-raising, but also trade and commerce, finance and credit, the exploitation of mines and mountains, and science and art. Such culture does not have its end in man, but in man who is the image of God and who stamps the imprint of his spirit upon all that he does, it returns to God, who is the First and the Last.

* * * * *

The content or meaning of the image of God is unfolded further in later revelation. For instance, it is remarkable that after the Fall, too, man still continued to be called the image of God.

In Genesis 5:1-3 we are reminded once more that God created man, man and woman together, in His image, and that He blessed them, and that Adam thus begot a son in his own likeness, after his image. In Genesis 9:6 the shedding of man's blood is forbidden for the reason that man was made in the image of God. The poet of the beautiful eighth psalm sings of the glory and majesty of the Lord which reveals itself in heaven and earth, and most splendidly of all in insignificant man and his dominion over all the works of God's hands. When Paul spoke to the Athenians on Mars' Hill, he quoted one of their poets approvingly: For we are also His offspring (Acts 17:28). In James 3:9 the Apostle by way of demonstrating the evil of the tongue makes use of this contrast: that with it we bless God, even the Father, and with it we curse men who are made after the similitude of God. And Scripture not only calls fallen man the image of God, but it keeps on regarding and dealing wih him as such throughout. It constantly looks upon man as a reasonable, moral being who is responsible to God for all his thoughts and deeds and words and is bound to His service.

Alongside of this representation, however, we find the idea that through sin man has lost the image of God. True, we are not anywhere told this directly in so many words. But it is something that can clearly be deduced from the whole teaching of Scripture concerning sinful man. After all, sin — as we shall consider more specifically later — has robbed man of innocence, righteousness, and holiness, has corrupted his heart, darkened his understanding, inclined his will to evil, turned his inclinations right-about-face, and placed his body and all its members in the service of unrighteousness. Accordingly man must be changed, reborn, justified, cleansed, and sanctified. He can share in all these benefits only in the fellowship with Christ who is the Image of God (2 Cor. 4:4 and Col. 1:15) and to whose image we must be conformed (Rom. 8:29). The new man, accordingly, who is put in the fellowship with Christ through faith, is created in accordance with God's will in true righteousness and holiness (Eph. 4:24) and is constantly renewed in knowledge after the image of Him that created him (Col. 3:10). The knowledge, righteousness, and holiness, which the believer obtains through the fellowship with Christ, have their origin, and example, and final purpose in God and they cause man again to share in the Divine nature (2 Peter 1:4).

It is upon this teaching of Holy Scripture that the distinction usually made in Reformed theology between the image of God in the broader and the narrower sense is based. If, on the one hand, after his fall and disobedience, man continues to be called the image and offspring of God, and, on the other hand, those virtues by which he especially resembles God have been lost through sin and can only be restored again in the fellowship with Christ, then these two propositions are compatible with each other only if the image of God comprises something more than the virtues of knowledge, righteousness, and holiness. The Reformed theologians recognized this, and over against the Lutheran and the Roman theologians they maintained it.

The Lutherans do not make the distinction between the image of God in the broader and in the narrower sense. Or, if they do make the distinction, they do not attach much importance to it nor understand its significance. For them the image of God is nothing more or less than the original righteousness, that is, the virtues of knowledge, righteousness, and holiness. They recognize the image of God only in the narrower sense and do not appreciate the need of relating this image of God to the whole human nature. Thus the religio-moral life of man is held to be a special and isolated area. It is not related to, and it exercises no influence upon, the work to which man is called in state and society, and in art and science. Once the Lutheran Christian shares in the forgiveness of sins and the fellowship with God through faith, he has enough. He rests in that, and enjoys it, and does not concern himself to relate this spiritual life, backwards, to the counsel and election of God, and, forwards, to the whole earthly calling of man.

From this, in the other direction, it follows that man, when through sin he has lost the original righteousness, is bereft of the whole image of God. Nothing of it is left him, not even small remains: and so his rational and moral nature, which is still his, is underestimated and maligned.

The Roman Catholics, on the contrary, do make a distinction between the image of God in the broader and narrower sense, although they do not usually employ these words for it. And they, too, are concerned to find a relationship between the two. But for them this relationship is external, not internal; it is artificial, not real; mechanical, not organic. The Romans present the matter as though man is conceivable without the virtues of knowledge, righteousness, and holiness (the image of God in the narrower sense) and can in reality also exist thus. In that event, too, man still has some religious and moral life but only in such a kind and to such a degree as can come from natural religion and natural morality. It is a religion and morality which, as it were, remains limited to this earth, and it can never pave the way for him to heavenly blessedness and the immediate vision of God. Besides, although in the abstract it is possible that such a natural person can, without possessing the image of God in the narrower sense, fulfill the duties of natural religion and of natural moral law, still, as a matter of fact, this is very difficult inasmuch as man is a material, physical, and sensuous person. After all, desire is always characteristic of this sensuous nature of man. Such lust or desire may not in itself be sin but it certainly is a tempting occasion for sin. For, by nature, this sensuous character, being physical, is opposed to the spirit, and constitutes a threat to it always. The threat is that reason and will will be overcome by the power of the flesh.

For these two reasons, according to Roman Catholic thought, God in His sovereign favor has added the image of God in the narrower sense to the natural man. He could have created man without this image. But because He foresaw that man would then very easily fall prey to fleshly desire, and also because He wanted to raise man to a higher state of blessedness than is possible here on earth, that is, to the heavenly glory, and to the immediate presence of Himself, therefore God added original righteousness to the natural man and so lifted him from his natural state to a higher and supernatural vantage point. Thus a twofold purpose was achieved. In the first place, man could now, what with the help of this supernatural addition, easily control the desire which flesh is naturally heir to; and, in the second place, by fulfilling the supernatural duties prescribed for him by the original righteousness (the image of God in the narrower sense), man could now achieve a supernatural salvation corresponding to his further endowment. Thus the supernatural *addendum* of original righteousness serves two purposes for the Roman Catholic: it serves as a restraint upon the flesh, and it clears the way for merits to heaven.

The Reformed theologians take their own point of view between the Roman Catholic and Lutheran positions. According to Scripture, the image of God is larger and more inclusive than the original righteousness. For, although this original righteousness has been lost through sin, man continues to carry the name of the image and offspring of God. There remain in him some small remains of the image of God according to which he was originally created. That original righteousness could not, therefore, have been an endowment, separate and independent, and quite unrelated to human nature generally. It is not true that man at first existed, be it in thought only or in actuality also, as a purely natural being, to whom, then, original righteousness was later superadded from above. Rather, in thought and creation both, man was one with that original righteousness. The idea of man includes the idea of such righteousness. Without it man can neither be conceived of nor exist. The image of God in the narrower sense is integrally related with that image in the broader sense. It is not accurate to say that man *bears* the image of God merely: he *is* that image of God. The image of God is identical with man, is as inclusive as the humanity of man. To the extent that, even in the state of sin, man remained man, to that extent he has preserved remnants of the image of God; and to the extent that he has lost the image of God, to that extent he has ceased to be man, true and perfect man.

After all, the image of God in the narrower sense is nothing other than the spiritual wholeness or health of man. When a human being becomes sick in body and soul, even when he becomes insane in mind, he continues to be a human being. But he has then lost something that belongs to the harmony of man, and has received something in its stead which conflicts with that harmony. Just so, when through sin man has lost the original righteousness, he continues to be man, but he has lost something that is inseparable from the idea of man and has received something instead that is alien to that idea. Hence, man, who lost the image of God, did not become something other than man: he preserved his rational and moral nature. The thing that he lost was not something which really did not belong to his nature in the first place and what he received instead was something that seized upon and corrupted his whole nature. Just as the original righteousness was man's spiritual wholeness and health, so sin is his spiritual disease. Sin is moral corruption, spiritual death, death in sins and transgressions, as Scripture describes it.

Such a conception of the image of God permits the whole teaching of Holy Scripture to come into its own. It is a conception which at one and the same time maintains the relationship and the distinction between nature and grace, creation and redemption. Gratefully and eloquently this conception acknowledges the grace of God which, after the fall, too, permitted man to remain man and continued to regard him and deal with him as a rational, moral, and responsible being. And at the same time, it holds that man, bereft of the image of God, is wholly corrupted and inclined to all evil. Life and history are available to confirm this. For even in its lowest, deepest fall, human nature yet remained human nature. And, no matter what acme of achievement man may accomplish, he remains small and weak, guilty and impure. Only the image of God constitutes man true and perfect man.

*   *   *   *   *

If, now, we try briefly to survey the content of the image of God, the first thing that comes up for attention is man's spiritual nature. He is a physical, but he is also a spiritual being. He has a soul which, in essence, is a spirit. This is evident from what the Holy Scripture teaches concerning the origin, essence, and duration of the human soul. As to that origin, we read concerning Adam that he, unlike the animals, received a breath of life from above (Gen. 2:7) and in a sense this holds for all men. For it is God who gives every man his spirit (Eccles. 12:7), who forms the spirit of man within him (Zechariah 12:1), and who, therefore, in distinction from the fathers of the flesh, can be called the Father of spirits (Heb. 12:9). This special origin of the human soul determines its essence also. True, Scripture several times ascribes a soul to animals (Genesis 2:19 and 9:4, and elsewhere) but in these instances the reference, as some translations also have it, is to a principle of life in the general sense. Man has a different and a higher soul, a soul which in very essence is spiritual in kind. This is evident from the fact that Scripture does ascribe a peculiar spirit to man but never to the animal. Animals do have a spirit in the sense that as creatures they are created and sustained by the Spirit of God (Ps. 104:30) but they do not, each of them, have their own, independent spirit. Man has.[14] Because of its spiritual nature the soul of man is immortal; it does not as in the animals die when the body dies, but it returns to God who has given the spirit (Eccles. 12:7). It cannot, like the body, be killed by men (Matt. 10:28). As spirit it continues to exist (Heb. 12:9 and 1 Peter 3:19).

This spirituality of the soul raises man above the plane of the animal, and gives him a point of resemblance with the angels. True, he belongs to the sensuous world, being earthly of the earth, but by virtue of his spirit he far transcends the earth, and he walks with royal freedom in

---

14. Deut. 2:30; Judges 15:19; Ezek. 3:14; Luke 23:46; Acts 7:59; 1 Cor. 2:11 and 5:3-4.

the realm of spirits. By his spiritual nature man is related to God who is Spirit (John 4:24) and who dwells in eternity (Isa. 57:15).

In the second place, the image of God is revealed in the abilities and powers with which the spirit of man has been endowed. It is true that the higher animals can by sensation form images and relate these to each other, but they can do no more. Man, on the contrary, raises himself above the level of images and enters the realm of concepts and ideas. By means of thought, which cannot be understood as a movement of the brain but must be regarded as a spiritual activity, man deduces the general from the particular, rises from the level of the visible to that of the invisible things, forms ideas of the true, the good, and the beautiful, and he learns to know God's eternal power and Godhead from God's creatures. By means of his willing, which must also be distinguished from his sinful desire, he emancipates himself from the material world and reaches out for invisible and suprasensuous realities. His emotions even are by no means set in motion merely by useful and pleasurable things inside the material world but are roused and stimulated also by ideal, spiritual goods which are quite insusceptible to arithmetical calculation. All of these abilities and activities have their point of departure and their center in the self-consciousness by which man knows himself and by means of which man bears within himself an ineradicable sense of his own existence and of the peculiarity of his rational and moral nature. Besides, all these particular abilities express themselves outwardly in language and religion, in morality and law, in science and art, — all of them, of course, as well as many others, peculiar to man and not to be found in the animal world at all.

All these abilities and activities are characteristics of the image of God. For God, according to the revelation of nature and Scripture, is not an unconscious, blind force, but a personal, self-conscious, knowing, and willing being. Even emotions, dispositions, and passions such as wrath, jealousy, compassion, mercy, love, and the like, are without hesitancy ascribed to God in the Scriptures, not so much as emotions which He Himself passively undergoes, but as activities of His almighty, holy, and loving being. Scripture could not speak in this human way about God if in all his abilities and activities, man were not created in the image of God.

The same holds true, in the third place, of the body of man. Even the body is not excluded from the image of God. True, Scripture expressly says that God is Spirit (John 4:24), and it nowhere ascribes a body to Him. Nevertheless, God is the creator also of the body and of the whole sensuous world. All things, material things too, have their origin and their existence in the Word that was with God (John 1:3 and

Col. 1 :15), and therefore rest in thought, in spirit. Moreover, the body, although it is not the cause of all those activities of the spirit, is the instrument of them. It is not the ear which hears but the spirit of man which hears through the ear.

Hence all those activities which we accomplish by means of the body, and even the physical organs by which we accomplish them, can be ascribed to God. Scripture speaks of His hands and feet, of His eyes and ears, and of so much more, in order to indicate that all that man can achieve by way of the body is, in an original and perfect way, due to God. He that planted the ear, shall He not hear? He that formed the eye, shall He not see? (Psalm 94 :9). To the extent, therefore, that the body serves as tool and instrument of the spirit, it exhibits a certain resemblance to, and gives us some notion of, the way in which God is busy in the world.

* * * * *

All this belongs to the image of God in the broader sense. But the likeness of God and man comes out much more strongly in the original righteousness with which the first man was endowed and which is called the image of God in the narrower sense. When Scripture puts the emphasis on this original righteousness, it thereby declares that what matters most in the image of God is not that it exists but what it is. The main thing is not *that* we think and hate and love and will. The likeness of man and God gets its significance from *what* we think and will, from *what* the object of our hatred and love is. The powers of reason and will, of inclination and aversion, were given to man precisely for this purpose that he should use them in the right way — that is, according to God's will and to His glory. The devils, too, have retained the powers of thought and will, but they put these solely into the service of their hatred and enmity against God. Even the belief in God's existence, which in itself is a good thing, gives the devils nothing but trembling, and the fear of His judgment (James 2 :19). Concerning the Jews, who called themselves children of Abraham and named God their Father, Jesus once said that, if this were so, they would do the works of Abraham and would love Him whom God had sent. But because they were doing precisely the opposite and sought to kill Jesus, they betrayed that they were really of the father the devil and wanted to do his will (John 8 :39-44). The desires which the Jews fostered, and the works which they did, constituted them despite all their keen discrimination and energy like unto the devil. And so, too, the human likeness to God comes out not chiefly in the fact that man possesses reason and understanding, heart and will. It expresses itself principally in pure knowledge and perfect righteousness and holiness, which together constitute the image of God in the narrower sense, and with which man was privileged and adorned at his creation.

The knowledge which was given to the first man did not consist of the fact that he knew everything and had nothing further to learn about God, himself, and the world. Even the knowledge of the angels and of the saints is susceptible to growth. So was the knowledge of Christ on earth up to the end of His life. That original knowledge of the first man implies rather that Adam received an adequate knowledge for his circumstance and calling and that this knowledge was pure knowledge. He loved truth with his whole soul. The lie, with all of its calamitous consequences of error, doubt, unbelief, and uncertainty, had not yet found a place in his heart. He stood in the truth, and he saw and appreciated everything as it really was.

The fruit of such knowledge of the truth was righteousness and holiness. Holiness means that the first man was created free of all taint of sin. His nature was unspoiled. No evil thought, deliberation, or desire came up out of his heart. He was not innocent or simple, but he knew God, and he knew the law of God that was written in his heart, and he loved that law with his whole soul. Because he stood in the truth, he stood also in love. Righteousness means that the man who thus knew the truth in his mind, and who was holy in his will and in all his desires, thereby also corresponded wholly to God's law, wholly satisfied the demands of His justice, and stood before His face without any guilt. Truth and love bring peace in their wake, peace with God, and ourselves, and the whole world. The man who himself stands in the right place, the place where he belongs, also stands in the right relationship to God and to all creatures.

Of this state and circumstance in which the first man was created we can no longer form an idea. A head and a heart, a mind and a will, all of them altogether pure and without sin — that is something which lies far beyond the pale of all our experiences. When we stop to reflect how sin has insinuated itself into all our thinking and speaking, into all our choices and actions, then even the doubt can rise in our hearts whether such a state of truth, love, and peace is possible for man. Holy Scripture, however, wins the victory and conquers every doubt. In the first place, it shows us, not only at the beginning but also in the middle of history, the figure of a man who could with full justice put the question to his opponents: Which of you convinceth me of sin? (John 8:46). Christ was very man and therefore also perfect man. He did no sin neither was guile found in His mouth (1 Peter 2:22). In the second place, Scripture teaches that the first human couple were created after God's image in righteousness and holiness as the fruit of known truth.

Thus the Scriptures maintain that sin does not belong to the essence of human nature, and that it can therefore also be removed and separated from that human nature.

If sin cleaves to man from his earliest origin, and by virtue of the nature which is his, then from the nature of the case there is no redemption from sin possible. The redemption from sin would then be tantamount to the annihilation of human nature. But now, as it is, not only can a human being exist without sin in the abstract, but such a holy human being has actually existed. And when he fell, and became guilty and polluted, another man, the second Adam, rose up without sin, to set fallen man free from his guilt and to cleanse him of all pollution. The creation of man according to the image of God and the possibility of his fall include the possibility of his redemption and re-creation. But whoever denies the first cannot affirm the second; the denial of the fall has as its other side the comfortless preaching of human irredeemability. In order to be able to fall, man must first have stood. In order to lose the image of God he must first possess it.

*   *   *   *   *

The creation of man according to the image of God — we read in Genesis 1:26 and 28 — had as its nearest purpose that man should fill, subdue, and have dominion over the earth. Such dominion is not a constituent element of the image of God. Nor does it, as some have maintained, constitute the whole content of that image. Moreover, it absolutely is not an arbitrary and incidental addendum. On the contrary, the emphasis that is placed upon this dominion and its close relationship with the creation according to the image of God indicate conclusively that the image comes to expression in the dominion and by means of it must more and more explain and unfold itself. Further, in the description of this dominion, it is plainly stated that to a certain extent it was, indeed, immediately given to man as an endowment, but that to a very great extent it would be achieved only in the future. After all, God does not say merely that He will make "men" in His image and likeness (Gen. 1:26), but when He has made the first human couple, man and woman, He blessed them and said to them: Be fruitful, and multiply, and replenish the earth, and subdue it (Gen. 1:28), and He further gave Adam the particular task of dressing and keeping the garden (Gen. 2:15).

All this teaches very plainly that man was not created for idleness but for work. He was not allowed to rest upon his laurels, but had to go straight into the wide world in order to subdue it to the power of his word and will. He was given a big, a widely distributed, a rich task on the earth. He was given an assignment which would cost him centuries of effort to accomplish. He was pointed in a direction incalculably far away which he had to take and which he had to pursue to the end. In short, there is a big difference and a wide separation between the *condition* in which the first man was created and the *destination* to which he was called. True, this destination is closely related to his nature, just as that nature is closely related to his origin, but there is distinction all the same. The nature of man, the essence of his being — the image of God according to which he was created — had to come to a constantly richer and fuller unfolding of its content by means of its striving towards its destination. The image of God, so to speak, had to be spread to the ends of the earth and had to be impressed on all the works of men's hands. Man had to cultivate the earth so that it would more and more become a revelation of God's attributes.

The dominion of the earth was therefore the nearest but not the sole purpose to which man was called. The nature of the case points to that fact. Work which is really work cannot have its end and final purpose in itself but always has as its further objective to bring something into being. It ceases when that objective has been reached. To work, simply to work, without deliberation, plan, or purpose, is to work hopelessly and is unworthy of rational man. A development which continues indefinitely is not a development. Development implies intention, course of action, final purpose, destination. If, then, man at his creation was called to work, that implies that he himself and the people who should issue from him should enter into a rest after the work.

The institution of the seven-day week comes to confirm and reinforce this conviction. In his work of creating God rested on the seventh day from all His work. Man, made in the image of God, immediately at the time of the creation gets the right and the privilege to follow in the Divine example in this respect also. The work which is laid upon him, namely, the replenishing and subduing of the earth, is a weak imitation of the creative activity of God. Man's work, too, is a work which is entered upon after deliberation, which follows a definite course of action, and which is aimed at a specific objective. Man is not a machine which unconsciously moves on; he does not turn about in a treadmill with an unchangeable monotony. In his work too man is man, the image of God, a thinking, willing, acting being who seeks to create something, and who in the end looks back upon the work of his hands with approbation. As it does for God Himself, man's work ends in resting, enjoyment, pleasure. The six-day week crowned by the Sabbath dignifies man's work, raises him above the monotonous movement of spiritless nature, and presses the stamp of a Divine calling upon it. Whoever, therefore, on the Sabbath day enters into the rest of God in accordance with His purpose, that person rests from his works in the same glad way as God rests from His (Heb. 4:10). This holds true of the individual and it also holds true of the church and of mankind generally. The world, too, has its world's work to perform, a work which is followed and concluded by a Sabbath. There remains a rest for the people of God. Each Sabbath Day is but an example and foretaste of it and at the same time also a prophecy and a guarantee of that rest (Heb. 4:9).

That is why the Heidelberg Catechism rightly says that God created man good and according to His own image *in order that* he might rightly know God his Creator, heartily love Him, and live with Him in eternal blessedness to praise and glorify Him. The final purpose of man lay in the eternal blessedness, in the glorification of God in heaven and on earth. But in order to arrive at this end man first had to fulfill his task on earth. In order to enter into the rest of God he first had to finish God's work. The way to heaven goes through the earth and over the earth. The entrance to the Sabbath is opened by the six days of work. One comes to eternal life by way of work.

*   *   *   *   *

This teaching of the purpose of man so far rests entirely upon thoughts which are expressed in Genesis 1:26-3:3. But the rest of the second chapter has another important constituent element to add to it. When God places man in paradise, He gives him the right to eat freely of all the trees in the garden except one. That one He singles out as an exception, the tree of knowledge of good and evil. Man is told that he may not eat of that tree, and that on the day he eats of it he will die the death (Gen. 2:16-17). To all that is *commanded* is now added one thing that is *forbidden*. The commandments were known to Adam partly from a reading of his own heart, partly from God's spoken word. Adam did not invent them. God created them in him and communicated them to him. Man is not religiously and morally autonomous. He is not his own lawgiver, and he may not do as he pleases. Rather, God is his only Lawgiver and Judge (Isa. 33:22). All those commandments which Adam received now resolved themselves into this one requirement that he who was created as the image of God should in all his thinking and doing, and throughout his life and work, remain the image of God. Man had to remain such personally in his own life, but also in his marriage relationship, in his family, in his six-day working week, in his rest on the seventh day, in his replenishing and multiplying, in his subduing and having dominion over the earth, and in his dressing and keeping of the garden. Adam was not to go his own way but had to walk in the way that God appointed for him.

But all those commandments, which, so to speak, gave Adam ample freedom of movement and the whole earth as his field of operation are augmented, or, better, are limited, by one proscription. This proscription, not to eat of the tree of the knowledge of good and evil, does not belong to the image of God, is not a constituent element of it, but, quite to the contrary, fixes its boundary. If Adam transgresses this proscriptive command, he loses the image of God, places himself outside the fellowship of God, and dies the death. By this command therefore the obedience of man is tested. This command will prove whether man will follow God's way or his own way, whether he will keep to the right path or go astray, whether he will remain a son of God in the house of the Father or want to take the portion of goods that is given him and go to a distant country. Hence, too, this proscriptive command is usually given the name of the probationary command. Hence, too, it has in a certain sense an arbitrary content. Adam and Eve could find no reason why just now the eating of this one particular tree was forbidden. In other words, they had to keep the command not because they fathomed it in its reasonable content and understood it, but solely because God had said it, on the basis of His authority, prompted by sheer obedience, out of a pure regard to their duty. That is why, further, the tree whose fruit they might not eat was called the tree of the knowledge of good and evil. It was the tree which would demonstrate whether man should arbitrarily and self-sufficiently want to determine what was good and what evil, or whether he would in this matter permit himself to be wholly led by the command which God had given concerning it and keep to that.

The first man, therefore, was given something, indeed, was given much to *do;* he was also given something, though this was little, which he was *not* to do. Generally the last requirement is the more difficult of the two. There are quantities of people who are willing to do incredibly much for the sake, say, of their health, but who are willing to *give up* nothing for it, or at least very little. They regard the slightest self-denial as an unbearable burden. That which is forbidden gives off a kind of mysterious lure. It raises questions about why and what and how. It prompts doubt and excites the imagination. This temptation which emanated from the proscriptive command the first man had to resist. This was the struggle of faith which was given him to fight. But, in the image of God according to which he was created, he also received the strength by which he could have remained standing and have conquered.

Nevertheless it becomes apparent from the probationary command even more clearly than from the institution of the seven-day week that the end or destiny of man is to be distinguished from his creation. Adam was not yet at the beginning what he could be and had to become at the end. He lived in paradise, but not yet in heaven. He still had a long way to go before he arrived at his proper destination. He had to achieve eternal life by his "commission" and "omission." In short, there is a big difference between the state of innocence in which the first man was created, and the state of glory for which he was destined. The nature of this difference is further illuminated for us by the rest of revelation.

Adam was dependent upon the change of night and day, waking and sleeping, but we read of the heavenly Jerusalem that there shall be no night there (Rev. 21:25 and 22:5) and that the redeemed by the blood of the Lamb stand before the throne of God and serve Him night and day in His temple (Rev. 7:15). The first man was bound to the apportionment of the week into six work days and one day of rest, but for the people of God there remains hereafter an eternal, unintermittent rest (Heb. 4:9 and Rev. 14:13). In the state of innocence man daily required food and drink, but in the future God shall destroy both the belly and meats (1Cor. 6:13). The first human couple consisted of man and woman and was accompanied by the blessing: be fruitful and multiply. But in the resurrection men do not marry nor are given in marriage, but are as the angels of God in heaven (Matt. 22:30). The first man, Adam, was of the earth, earthy, had a natural body and so became a living soul, but the believers in the resurrection receive a spiritual body and will then bear the image of heavenly man, the image of Christ the Lord from heaven (1 Cor. 15:45-49). Adam was created in such a way that he could stray, could sin, could fall and die; but the believers even on earth are in principle raised above this possibility. They can no longer sin, for whosoever is born of God does not commit sin, for his seed remains in him: and he cannot sin, because he is born of God (1 John 3:9). They cannot fall even to the very end for they are kept through faith unto salvation ready to be revealed in the last time (1 Peter 1:5). And they cannot die, for those who believe in Christ have, already here on earth, the eternal incorruptible life; they shall not die in all eternity, and though they were dead they should yet live (John 11:25-26).

In looking at the first man, therefore, we must be on guard against two extremes. On the one hand, we must, on the basis of Holy Scripture, maintain that he was immediately created in the image of God in true knowledge, righteousness, and holiness: he was not at first a small, innocent child that had to develop into maturity; he was not a being who, mature in body, was spiritually without any content, taking a neutral position between truth and falsehood, good and evil; and still less was he originally an animal being, gradually evolved out of animal existence, who now at long last by virtue of struggle and effort had become man.

Such a representation is in irreconcilable conflict with the representation of Scripture and with sound reason.

Still, on the other hand, the state of the first man should not be exaggeratedly glorified as is so often done in Christian doctrine and preaching. No matter how high God placed man above the animal level, man had not yet achieved his highest possible level. He was able-not-to-sin, but not yet not-able-to-sin. He did not yet possess eternal life which cannot be corrupted and cannot die, but received instead a preliminary immortality whose existence and duration depended upon the fulfillment of a condition. He was immediately created as image of God, but he could still lose this image and all its glory. He lived in paradise, it is true, but this paradise was not heaven and it could with all of its beauty be forfeited by him. One thing was lacking in all the riches, both spiritual and physical, which Adam possessed: *absolute certainty*. As long as we do not have that, our rest and our pleasure is not yet perfect; in fact, the contemporary world with its many efforts to insure everything that man possesses is satisfactory evidence for this. The believers are insured for this life and the next, for Christ is their Guarantor and will not allow any of them to be plucked out of His hand and be lost (John 10:28). Perfect love banishes fear in them (1 John 4:18) and persuades them that nothing shall separate them from the love of God which is in Christ Jesus their Lord (Rom. 8:38-39). But this absolute certainty was lacking to man in paradise; he was not, together with his creation in the image of God, permanently established in the good. Irrespective of how much he had, he could lose it all, both for himself and for his posterity. His origin was Divine; his nature was related to the Divine nature; his destiny was eternal blessedness in the immediate presence of God. But whether he was to reach that appointed destination was made dependent upon his own choice and upon his own will.

XIII

Sin and Death

The third chapter of Genesis already tells us of the fall and the disobedience of man. Presumably it was not a long period after his creation before he made himself guilty of transgressing the Divine commandment. Creation and fall are not co-existent and are not to be identified with each other. They differ from each other in nature and essence, but chronologically they are close together.

Such was the circumstance for man and very likely it was so also in the world of the angels. Holy Scripture gives us no detailed account of the creation and fall of the angels; it tells us only so much of that as we need to know for a right understanding of man and his fall. It refrains from all further elaboration and makes no gesture at all towards satisfying our curiosity. But we do know that there are angels, that a large number fell away from the midst of them, and also that this fall took place at the beginning of the world. It is true that some have placed the time of their creation and fall much farther ahead, in the time preceding Genesis 1:1, but Scripture gives no ground for it.

The beginning of the whole work of creation falls in Genesis 1:1, and in Genesis 1:31 it may well be that it is said of the whole work of creation and not of the creation of the earth alone that God saw what He had made, and, behold, it was very good. If so, the rebellion and the disobedience of the angels must have taken place after the sixth day of creation.

On the other hand, it is definite, too, that the fall of the angels preceded that of man. Sin did not break out on earth in the first instance, but in heaven, in the immediate presence of God, and at the foot of His throne. The thought, the wish, the will to resist God arose first in the heart of the angels. It may be that pride is the primary sin and this was the beginning and the principle of their fall. In 1 Timothy 3:6 Paul advises the church not to choose as a bishop someone who has been a member for only a short while, lest he be lifted up with pride and fall into the condemnation of the devil. If by this judgment or condemnation of the devil is meant the judgment into which the devil fell when he exalted himself against God, then we have here an index to the fact that in the devil sin began as self-exaltation and pride.

However this may be, the fall of the angels preceded that of man. After all, man did not come to the transgression of the law of God by himself exclusively but was moved to it from outside himself. The woman, deceived by the serpent and tempted, was in the transgression (2 Cor. 11:3 and 1 Tim. 2:14). Certainly we are to think of that snake not as a symbolical manifestation but as an actual snake, for we are plainly told that this snake was subtler, wiser than any beast of the field (Gen. 3:1 and Matt. 10:16). Just as certainly, however, revelation in its further development gives us to understand that a demonic power made use of the snake to beguile man and to lead him astray. Already at several points in the Old Testament we read that Satan is an accuser and tempter of men (Job 1:1; Chron. 21:1; and Zech. 3). But the awful power of darkness is first revealed when the Divine heavenly light has first dawned over the world in Christ. Then it becomes manifest that there is yet another sinful world than the one that is here on earth. There is a spiritual realm of evil of which innumerable demons, wicked, impure spirits, the one more iniquitous than the other (Matt. 12:45) are the subject servants, and of which Satan is chief and head. This Satan is named by various names. He is not only called Satan, which is Adversary, but also the devil, which is the blasphemer (Matt. 13:39), the enemy (Matt. 13:39 and Luke 10:19), the evil one (Matt. 6:13 and 13:19), the accuser (Rev. 12:10), the tempter (Matt. 4:3), Belial, which is meanness or worthlessness (2 Cor. 6:15), Beelzebul or Beelzebub, the name by which originally the fly-god honored in Ekron was designated (2 Kings 1:2 and Matt. 10:25), the prince of the devils (Matt. 9:34), the prince of the power of the air (Eph. 2:2), the prince of this world (John 12:31), the god of this age or world (2 Cor. 4:4), and the great dragon and that old serpent (Rev. 12:9).

This realm of darkness did not exist from the beginning of creation but came into being at the fall of Satan and his angels. Peter says generally that the angels sinned and were therefore punished by God (2 Peter 2:4), but Jude in the sixth verse of his letter indicates more particularly the nature of their sin and declares that they did not maintain their own principle, that is, the estate which God had given them, and that they left their habitation in heaven. They were not satisfied with the status in which God had placed them, and desired something more. This rebellion took place at the beginning, for the devil sins from the beginning (1 John 3:8), and from the very beginning it was aimed at the corruption of man. Jesus expressly states that Satan was a murderer from the beginning, that he did not abide in the truth but is a liar (John 8:44).

From this Satan came the temptation of man. It came by way of attachment to the command God had given not to eat of the tree of the knowledge of good and evil. The apostle James testifies that God is far above temptation, and that He tempts no man. Naturally the meaning of this is not that God tries no man or puts him to the proof. Scripture frequently reports instances in which He does just this, be it in Abraham, Moses, Job, Christ Himself, or immediately in the first man, Adam. But when someone fails in the test, he is immediately inclined to charge God with the guilt of the fall and to say that God tempted him, that is, tried him with the intention of making him fall, or put him to a test in which he must necessarily fail.

We see that after the fall, Adam immediately made this charge. It is the secret inclination of every man to do so. James is at pains to counteract this tendency and he states definitively and firmly that God Himself is far above the level of temptation and that He never tempts anyone. He never tries anyone with the intention of causing him to fall, and he never puts anyone to a test which he has not the capacity to sustain (1 Cor. 10:13). The probationary command given to Adam was designed to cause his obedience to become manifest, and it by no means was beyond the range of his powers. Humanly speaking, man could easily have kept that command, for it was light, not at all comparable in weight to all that had been given and allowed him.

But just that which God always intends for the good Satan always construes for the bad. He abuses the probationary command and makes of it a temptation, a secret attack on the obedience of the first man, and by means of it he patently intends to cause man to fall. First the proscriptive command which God has given is represented as an arbitrarily added burden, as an unfounded limitation of man's freedom. Thus there is sown in Eve's soul the seed of doubt concerning the Divine origin and the justness of the command. Next that doubt is developed into unbelief by means of the thought that God has given the command lest man become like Himself, knowing good and evil even as He. This unbelief in turn serves the imagination and makes the transgression appear to be, not the way to death, but the way to everlasting life, to equality with God. The imagination then does its work on the inclination and effort of man, so that the forbidden tree begins to take on another guise. It becomes a lust to the eye and a desire to the heart. Desire, having thus conceived, banishes the will and bears the sinful deed. Eve took of the fruit thereof and did eat, and gave also to her husband with her, and he did eat (Gen. 3:1-6).

* * * * *

In this simple but profound psychological way Scripture tells the history of the fall and of the origin of sin. In this way sin continues still to come into being. It begins with the darkening of the understanding, continues with the excitement of the imagination, stimulates desire in the heart, and culminates in an act of the will. True, there is a very great difference between the genesis of the first and that of all later sins. The later sins assume a sinful nature in man and make that their point of contact. No such nature existed in Adam and Eve, for they were created in the image of God. But we do well to remember that in all their perfection they were nevertheless created in such a way that they could fall, and further that sin, by virtue of its nature, always has a quality of unreasonableness and arbitrariness about it. When someone has sinned, he always tries to excuse or justify himself, but in this he never succeeds. There is never a reasonable basis or ground for sin. Its existence is and remains always lawlessness. True, some in our time try to maintain that the misdoer is brought to his sinful act by circumstances or by his disposition, but such internal or external inevitability is in one's own conscience always subjected to overwhelming contradiction. Neither rationally nor psychologically is sin to be traced back to a disposition or action which has any reason or right to exist.

This is particularly true of the first sin that was committed, the first sin of man in paradise. Nowadays there are often modifying circumstances. These do not justify the sin, but they do limit the measure of the guilt. But in the sin of that first human couple there is not so much as a single circumstance to be pleaded for as a modifying factor in the guilt. As a matter of fact, all that can be designated as context of the event — such as the special revelation which informed them of the probationary command, the content of the probationary command being such that it demanded so little of self-denial, the seriousness of the threat of penalty attached to the transgression, the terribleness of the consequences, the holiness of their nature — all this aggravates rather than lessens the extent of the guilt.

We can shed some light on the *possibility* of the fall, but the transition to the *actuality* of it remains shrouded in darkness. Scripture makes not so much as a single effort to render this transition understandable. Therefore Scripture also lets sin stand unmodified in its properly sinful character. There *is* such a thing as sin, but it is *illegitimate*. It was and is and will eternally remain in conflict with the law of God and with the testimony of our own conscience.

By relating these two things, that is, by giving, on the one hand, a psychological account of the coming into existence of sin, something the truth of which each of us feels every moment in his own life, and by letting sin, on the other hand, starkly stand in its unreasonable and unjustifiable nature, the account of the fall in Genesis 3 raises itself immeasurably above all that human wisdom in the course of the centuries has been able to give out on the subject of the origin of sin. That there is sin and misery is something, after all, which we know not merely from Scripture; it is something that is preached to us daily and every moment by the whole of a groaning creaturedom. The whole world stands in the sign of the fall. And if the world round about us did not proclaim it to us, then we should still be reminded of it from moment to moment by the voice of conscience, which continuously accuses us, and by the poverty of the heart which testifies of nameless woe.

That is why, everywhere and at all times, the question would not down among mankind: Why the evil? Why the evil of sin and the evil of misery? That is the question which, even more than the question as to the origin of man, has preoccupied the thought of men and has pressed upon their hearts and heads hour upon hour. But now compare the solutions which human wisdom has proffered to the question with the simple answer that Scripture gives to it.

Naturally the solutions are by no means alike, the solutions of human wisdom, that is. But they nevertheless exhibit a certain relationship and it is with reference to that they can be classified. The most commonly presented solution is the one according to which sin does not live *in* man nor come *out* of him but attaches itself to him from without. By nature, this idea has it, man is good; his heart is uncorrupted. The evil lies in the circumstances, in the environment, in the society in which man is born and reared. Take these circumstances away, reform society — introduce, for example, the equal distribution of goods to all men — and man will naturally be good. There will be no more reason for him to do evil.

This thought as to the origin and essence of sin has at all times had many supporters because man is always inclined to transfer his guilt to the circumstances. But it is a view which was particularly honored when, since the eighteenth century, the eyes were opened to political and social corruption, and a radical turning upside down of state and society was praised as the sole panacea for all ills. But in this matter of the natural goodness of man, the nineteenth century brought again a certain amount of disillusionment. At present the number is by no means small of those who call the nature of man radically evil and who despair of his redemption.

Thus that other explanation came into vogue again which sought the origin of sin in the sensuous nature of man. Man has a soul but he also has a body; he is spirit but he is body too. The flesh in itself always has certain sinful tendencies and inclinations, more or less impure desires, base passions, and thus stands naturally opposed to the spirit with its images, ideas, and ideals. Inasmuch as man, when he is born, continues for years to live a sort of botanical and animal life, and remains a child living in terms of concrete images, it speaks for itself that the flesh should for years and years be the dominant element and keep the spirit in subjection. Only gradually, according to this point of view, does the spirit emancipate itself from the power of the flesh. But, be it very gradually, the development from carnality to spirituality does continue in mankind and in the individual person.

In some such way thinkers and philosophers have repeatedly spoken of the origin of sin. But in more recent times they have received strong support from the theory that man is himself descended from the animal, and in his heart really still is an animal.

Some go on to infer from this fact that man will remain an animal forever. But some nurse the hope that, inasmuch as man has already developed so gloriously far in comparison with his origins, he will go on still farther in the future, and perhaps even become an angel. However that may be, the animal descent of man seemed to provide a remarkable solution to the problem of sin. If man traces his descent from animal life, then it is perfectly natural and need be no cause for marvel that the old animal keeps operating in him and sometimes still defies the restraints of decency.

According to many, therefore, sin is nothing more than a vestigial influence and remnant of the earlier animal condition. Sensuality, theft, murder, and the like, are practices which were common among the earliest peoples even as they are among animals, and they turn up again at the present time in backward individuals, among the so-called criminals. But these people, who fall back into the ancient and original practices, are properly not to be thought of as criminals, but as backward, weak, sick, and more or less insane persons, and they are not to be punished in prisons but rather to be treated in hospitals. What the wound is to the body, that the criminal is to society. Sin is an illness which man takes with him from his animal pre-existence and which he only gradually subdues.

If one draws this line of argumentation on through to its logical conclusion and seeks the explanation of sin in sensuality, in the flesh, in animal origin, one arrives naturally at the doctrine, often taught in the past, that sin takes its point of departure in matter, or, more generally expressed, in the finite existence of all creatures. In antiquity this was a favorite view. According to it, spirit and matter are opposed to each other as are light and darkness. The opposition is eternal and the two can never come to a true and complete communion with each other. Matter, then, is not something that has been created. The God of light could not have created this dark thing. It must have existed eternally alongside of God, formless, dark, shut off from all life and light. Even when it was later cast into form and shaped by God and used for the building of this world, it still remained incapable of taking up the spiritual idea in itself and of returning to it. Dark in itself it will not admit the light of thought.

In some thinkers this dark matter is traced back to a Divine origin of its own. In that event, there come to be two Gods, who co-exist from all eternity, a God of light and a God of darkness, a good God and an evil God. Others again will try to trace the two eternal principles of good and evil back to a single Godhead, and thus make of God a dual being. There is in Him an unconscious, dark, and secret basis out of which a conscious, clear, and luminous nature comes to expression. The first is the basic origin of the darkness and evil in the world, and the second is the source of all light and life.

If, now, we take one step further, we arrive in the modern day at the doctrine taught by some philosophers that God in Himself is nothing but a dark nature, a blind force, an eternal hunger, an arbitrary will, who comes to consciousness and so becomes light only in mankind. That, certainly, is the diametrically opposite view from the one taught by the revelation of the Scripture. This Scripture tells us that God is light and that in him is no darkness at all and that in the beginning all things were made by the Word. But the philosophy of our day says that God is darkness, nature, abysm, and that light dawns for Him only in the world and in mankind. It is therefore not man who needs saving by God, but it is God who is unsaved and who must look to man for His redemption.

This ultimate conclusion is, of course, not quite so strictly drawn by everyone who dallies with the theory, nor so bluntly put, but it is all the same the end of the route followed by those who adhere to the views of the origin of sin mentioned above. However they may differ among each other, they all have this in common that they look for the origin and seat of sin, not in the will of the creature, but in the structure and nature of things, and therefore in the Creator who is the cause of that structure and nature. If sin lurks in circumstances, in society, in sensuality, in the flesh, in matter, then the responsibility for it is to be charged to Him who is the Creator and Sustainer of all things. And then man goes scot free. In that event, sin did not begin at the time of the fall but at the time of creation. Creation and fall are then identical. Then existence, then being itself, is sin. Moral imperfection is the same as finitude. And redemption is absolutely impossible or it culminates in the annihilation of the real, in nirvana.

The wisdom of God is exalted high above this human speculation. The latter charges God with the responsibility and vindicates man; the second justifies God and charges man with the guilt. Scripture is the book which from beginning to end vindicates God and implicates man. Scripture is a great and mighty theodicy, a justification of God, of all His attributes and of all His works, and in this it is joined by the testimony of the conscience of all people. True, sin is not something which goes on outside the pale of His providence; the fall did not take place outside the scope of His foreknowledge, His counsel, and His will. The whole development and history of sin is guided by Him, and it will up to its end remain bound to His direction. Sin does not constitute God planless and powerless; over against sin, too, God remains God, perfect in wisdom, goodness, and power.

In fact, He is so good and powerful that He brings good to pass out of evil, and He can compel evil against its nature to cooperate in the glorification of His name and the establishment of His kingdom. But sin nevertheless continues to keep its sinful character. If in a particular sense one can say that God willed sin inasmuch as without His will, and outside its pale, nothing can come into being or exist, still, it should then always be remembered it is as *sin* that He willed it, something which is abnormal and ought not to have been at all, something illegitimate, therefore, and in conflict with His command.

Thus vindicating God, Scripture at the same time maintains the nature of sin. If sin does not have its origin in the will of the Creator, but in the essence or being which precedes the will, it immediately loses its moral character, becomes a physical and natural thing, an evil inseparable from the existence and nature of things. Sin is then an independent reality an original principle, a sort of evil matter such as in bygone times illness was also held to be. But Scripture teaches us that sin is not of this kind and that it cannot be. For God is the Creator of all things, of matter also; and when the work of creation was completed, He regarded the things He had made and, behold, they were very good.

Sin therefore does not belong to the nature of things. It is a manifestation which is moral in character, operating in the ethical sphere, and consists of departure from the ethical norm which God by His will established for rational man. The first sin consisted of the transgression of the probationary command and thus of the whole moral law, which, together with the probationary command, has its seat in the same Divine authority. The many names which Holy Scripture uses to designate sin — transgression, disobedience, unrighteousness, ungodliness, enmity against God, and the like, all point in the same direction. Paul says plainly that by the law is the knowledge of sin (Rom. 3:20) and John declares that all sin, the smallest as well as the greatest of sins, is unrighteousness, lawlessness, transgression (1 John 3:4).

If transgression is the very character of sin then that character cannot lie in the nature or essence of things, be they matter or spirit, for things owe their essence and existence to God alone, He who is the fountain of all goods. The evil can therefore only come *after* the good, can only exist through the good and on the good, and can really consist of nothing but the corruption of the good. Even the wicked angels, although sin has corrupted their whole nature, nevertheless as creatures are and remain good. Moreover, the good, in so far as it is in the essence and being of things, is not annihilated by sin, though bent in another direction and abused. Man has not lost his being, his human nature, through sin. He still has a soul and body, reason and will, and all kinds of emotions and interests.

But all of these gifts, good in themselves and coming down from the Father of lights, are now used by men to serve as weapons against God and put in the service of unrighteousness. Sin, accordingly, is not merely a lack or want, not even merely a lack of what man originally possessed. The situation is not like that of a person who was rich and has become poor, who has suffered a loss and must now get along with a great deal less than he once had. Sin is more than that. It is a deprivation of that which man, in order to be truly human, ought to have; and it is at the same time the introduction of a defect or inadequacy which is not proper to man.

According to contemporary science, illness is not a particular substance or matter, but rather a living in changed circumstances, in such a way, in fact, that the laws of life do indeed remain the same as they are in a healthy body but the organs and functions of that life are disturbed in their normal activity. Even in the dead body the functioning does not cease, but the activity that begins then is of a destructive, disintegrating kind. In this same sense, sin is not a substance in itself, but that sort of disturbance of all the gifts and energies given to man which makes them work in another direction, not towards God but away from Him. Reason, will, interests, emotions, passions, psychological and physical abilities of one kind or another — these all were once weapons of righteousness but they have now by the mysterious operation of sin been converted into weapons of unrighteousness. The image of God which man received at his creation, was not a substance, but it was nevertheless so really proper to his nature that he, losing it, became wholly misshapen and deformed.

If anyone could see man as he is, internally and externally, he would discover traits in him which resemble Satan more than they do God (John 8:44). Spiritual sickness and death took the place of spiritual health. But the first no more than the second is a constituent element of his being. When Scripture insists on the moral nature of sin it thereby maintains also the redeemability of man.

Sin does not belong to the essence of the world, but is something, rather, which was introduced into the world by man. That is why it can again be removed from the world by the power of Divine grace which is stronger than every creature.

*   *   *   *   *

The first sin which man committed did not long stand alone. It was not the sort of action which, having done it, man could shake off or brush aside. After that sin, man could no longer go on as though nothing had happened. In the very moment in which man entertained sin in his thought and imagination, in his desire and will, at that moment a tremendous change took place in him. This is evident from the fact that immediately after the fall Adam and Eve tried to conceal themselves from God and from each other. And the eyes of them both were opened, and they knew that they were naked (Gen. 3:7). Suddenly, in an instant, they stood over against each other in a different relationship. They saw each other as they had never before seen each other. They dared not and could not freely and unreservedly look into each other's eyes. They felt themselves to be guilty and impure, and they sewed fig leaves together in order to cover themselves against each other. Nevertheless they shared the same situation with each other and felt that they were one in the common fear and necessity for hiding themselves from the face of God in the middle of the trees of the garden.

The fig leaves served to hide their shame and disgrace from each other partially, but they were inadequate for confronting God's face, and so they fled, fled into the densest depths of the foliage in the garden. Shame and fear had mastered them, for they had lost the image of God and felt themselves to be guilty and impure before His face.

That is always the consequence of sin. Over against God, ourselves, and our fellow human beings, we lose that inner, spiritual spontaneity and freedom, for these are realities which only the consciousness of guiltlessness can excite in our hearts. But the terribleness of the first sin is even more vividly exhibited in the fact that its influence spreads from the first human couple out over all mankind. The first step in the wrong direction has been taken, and all of the descendants of Adam and

Eve follow them in the same track. The universality of sin is a fact which forces itself upon the consciousness of everyone. It is a fact which is indisputably established, as well by the evidence of experience as by the teaching of Holy Scripture.

It would not be difficult at all to gather testimonials to this universality of sin from all places and times. The simplest and the most learned of people agree about this. No one, they would say, is born without sin. Everybody has his weaknesses and defects. Among the illnesses of mortal man the darkening of the understanding also has its place, and by this is meant not only the inevitability of error but also the love of error. No one is free in his conscience. The conscience makes traitors of us all. The heaviest burden that mankind has to bear is the burden of guilt. Such are the sounds that come to our ears from all sides in the history of mankind. Even they whose fundamental principle is that of the natural goodness of men are compelled at the end of their investigation to acknowledge that the seeds of all sins and misdeeds are hidden in the heart of every man. And philosophers have registered the complaint that all men are evil by nature.

*   *   *   *   *

Holy Scripture confirms this judgment which mankind has declared against itself. When in the third chapter of Genesis it has given the account of the fall, it traces out in the succeeding chapters how sin spread out and increased in the human race, and how it eventually reached such a climax that the judgment of the flood became a necessity. Concerning the generation of men antedating that flood it is said that the wickedness of men was very great on the earth, and that every imagination of man's heart was evil continually, that all flesh had corrupted its way upon the earth and was corrupt before God (Gen. 6:5, 11, 12). But the great flood brings with it no change in the heart of man. After that flood, too, God says of the new humanity which is to come forth out of Noah's family that the imagination of man's heart is evil from his youth on up (Gen. 8:21).

All the saints of the Old Testament concur in this Divine testimony. No one — such is the plaint of Job — can bring a clean thing out of an unclean one (Job 14:4). There is no man that sinneth not, Solomon confesses in his prayer at the dedication of the temple (1 Kings 8:46). We read in Psalms 14 and 53 that when the Lord looks down from heaven upon the children of men to see if there be any that understand and seek Him, He sees nothing but filth and iniquity. They are all gone aside, they are all together become filthy; there is none that doeth good, no, not one. No one can stand before the face of the Lord, for in His sight no man living is justified (Ps. 143:2). Who can say? I have made my heart clean, I am pure from my sin? (Prov. 29:9). In short, there is not a just man on earth that doeth good, and sinneth not (Eccles. 7:20).

All of these statements are so general, so universally cast, that they permit of no exception. They do not come from the lips of the wicked and ungodly, who often have no concern about their own sins or those of others, but they come up out of the heart of the pious who have learned to know themselves as sinners before the face of God. And they do not make this judgment concerning others alone in the first place, concerning those, in other words, who live in manifest sin as heathen and are cut off from the knowledge of God. In fact, they begin with themselves and their own people.

Scripture does not write up the saints for us as people who have lived on earth in the perfection of holiness. It pictures them as sinners who have sometimes made themselves guilty of very serious transgressions. It is precisely the saints who, although they remain conscious of the righteousness of their cause, feel their guilt the most deeply and who come before the face of the Lord with a humble confession.[1] Even when they rise up to testify against the people, and to convince them of their apostacy and unfaithfulness, they end by including themselves with the people as one of them and give voice to the common confession: We lie in our shame and our disgrace covers us. We have sinned with our fathers, we have committed iniquity, from our youth on up to the present day.[2]

The New Testament, also, does not permit the least doubt about this sinful state of the whole human race. The whole preaching of the gospel is built on this assumption. When John preaches the nearness of the kingdom of heaven, he requires that men repent and let themselves be baptized, for circumcision, sacrifices, and the keeping of the law have not been able to grant righteousness to the people of Israel though they need this to enter into the kingdom of God. Thus there went out to him Jerusalem and all Judaea, and were baptized of him in Jordan, confessing their sins (Matt. 3:5, 6). Christ made His appearance with this same preaching of the kingdom of God, and He, too, testifies that only regeneration, faith, and repentance can open up access to the kingdom.[3]

It is true that in Matthew 9:12 and 13 Jesus says that they who are whole have no need of the physician, and that He has not come to call the righteous but sinners to repentance. But the context indicates that Jesus is thinking of the Pharisees in speaking of the whole and their righteous-

---

1. Ps. 6; 25; 32; 38; 51; 130; and 143.
2. Jer. 3:15; Isa. 6:5; 53:4-6; 64:6; Dan. 9:5 ff.; and Ps. 106:6.
3. Mark 1:15; 6:12; and Job 3:3.

ness, they who frowned on His sitting down with publicans and sinners, exalted themselves high above these, and who in their vaunted righteousness felt no need for the pursuing love of Jesus.

In verse 13 Jesus expressly states that if the Pharisees understood that God did not in His law want external sacrifices but inner spiritual mercy, they would have come to the conviction that they as well as the publicans and sinners were guilty and impure and that they needed repentance in His name. He Himself limits His labor for the time being to the lost sheep of the house of Israel (Matt. 15:24), but after His resurrection He gives His disciples the mandate to go out into the whole world and to preach the Gospel to all creatures, for salvation is for all men bound to belief in His name (Mark 16:15-16).

In agreement with this, the apostle Paul begins his letter to the Romans with a comprehensive argument that the whole world is guilty before God and that therefore no flesh shall be justified by the deeds of the law (Rom. 3:19-20). Not only the heathen who have not known and glorified God (Rom. 1:18-32) but also the Jews who pride themselves in their advantages but at bottom make themselves guilty of the same sins (Rom. 2:1-3:20) — all are together concluded in sin (Rom. 3:9; 11:32; and Gal. 3:22). And this is to be in order that every mouth should be stopped and the mercy of God alone should be glorified in their salvation.

Indeed, this universal sinfulness is so fundamentally the basis of the preaching of the Gospel in the New Testament that the word *world* takes on a very unfavorable connotation because of it. Taken by itself the world is, of course, and all that is in it, created by God,[4] but through sin it has become so corrupted that it now stands over against God as an antagonistic force. It does not know the Word to which it owes its existence (John 1:10). The whole of it lies in wickedness (1 John 5:19), stands under Satan as its prince (John 14:30 and 16:11), and it passes away in all its lust and desirability (1 John 2:16). Whoever loves the world proves that the love of the Father is not in him (1 John 2:15), and whoever wants to be a friend of the world will become an enemy of God (James 4:4).

*　*　*　*　*

This terrible state in which humanity and world exist naturally raises the question as to what is the origin and cause of it. Whence the first sin not only, but whence the universal sinfulness, whence the guilt and corruption of the whole human race to which everybody is subjected

---

4. John 1:3; Col. 1:16; and Heb. 1:2.

from his birth on — everyone except Christ? Is there a connection between the first sin committed in Paradise and the flood of iniquities which thereupon has inundated the world? And, if so, what is the nature of this connection?

There are those who, together with Pelagius, totally deny such a connection. According to them every sinful deed is an action which stands by itself, which introduces no change into human nature, and which can therefore in the next moment be succeeded by an exceptionally good deed. After Adam had transgressed the commandment of God, he remained, in his inner nature, his disposition, and his will, altogether the same. So too all the children to spring from this first human couple are born in quite the same guiltless and indifferent nature as Adam originally had.

There is — so this argument goes — no such thing as sinful nature, or sinful disposition or habit, for all nature is created by God and remains good. There are only sinful deeds and these do not form an unintermittent continuous series, but they are such as can constantly be interchanged with good deeds and are related to the person himself in no other way than by a perfectly free choice of the will. The only influence which passes over from the sinful deeds or actions to the person himself or to others in his neighborhood is that of bad example. Once we have done a sinful deed, we are likely to do it again, and others are likely to follow our example. The universal sinfulness of the human race must be explained in this way; that is, in terms of imitation. There is no such thing as inherited sin at all. Everybody is born in innocence, but the bad example which people generally give has a bad influence on contemporaries and descendants alike. Prompted by custom and habit, all follow out the same sinful course, even though it is not impossible and not improbable that here and there some individual has asserted himself against the force of custom, has gone his own way, and has lived holily on earth.

This effort to explain the universal sinfulness of mankind is, however, not only in conflict with Holy Scripture at every point, but it is also so superficial and inadequate that it is rarely, at least in theory, totally supported by anyone. It is refuted by facts from our own experience and our own lives. We all know from experience that a sinful action is not external to us, like a dirty garment which can be taken off and laid aside; rather, it is intimately connected with our inner nature and leaves ineradicable traces upon it. After each sinful act we are no longer what we were before. Sin makes us guilty and it makes us unclean; it robs us of peace of mind and heart, is followed by regret and remorse, confirms us in the inclination, the listing, towards evil, and gets us into a condition in which, finally, we can no longer offer resistance to the power of sin but succumb to even the slightest temptation.

Moreover, it also goes straight against experience to hold that sin takes hold of a person only from without. True, bad example can exercise a tremendous influence. We see that in the children who are born to bad parents and grow up in a godless and normless moral environment. And, on the contrary, being born from pious parents and being reared in a religious and morally wholesome community is a blessing which cannot be appreciated enough. But all that is but one side of the matter. That bad environment could not have such an evil influence on a child if the child himself did not have a disposition to evil in his heart; and, accordingly, a good environment would not often fail to influence a child if that child had in his birth received a pure heart susceptible to all good.

We know better: the environment is simply the occasion on which sin comes to development in us. The root of sin lies deeper and lurks in our hearts. Out of the heart of men, Jesus said, proceed evil thoughts, adulteries, fornications, murders, theft, and all kinds of other unrighteousnesses (Mark 7:21). It is a statement which is confirmed by the experience of everyone. Almost without our willing and knowing it, impure thoughts and images come up in our consciousness. On some occasions, when we meet with adversity or opposition, the wickedness that lay deeply concealed breaks out into the open. Sometimes we are startled by it ourselves and would like to escape from ourselves. The heart is deceitful above all things, and desperately wicked: who can know it? (Jer. 17:9).

Finally, if imitation of bad example were the only origin of sin in humanity, its absolute universality would not be explainable. Accordingly, Pelagius taught that here and there people had presumably lived sinlessly. But those exceptions only shed a more glaring light on the untenability of the Pelagian position. For, apart from Christ Himself, there has never been a person on earth who was free from sin.

It is not necessary that we have known everybody, person for person, to make this judgment. Scripture speaks most unambiguously in this spirit. The whole history of mankind goes to prove it. And our own heart is the key to an understanding of the heart that is living in other people. We are all of like passions and together we constitute not only a natural but also a moral unity. There is one human nature that is common to all men, and this nature is guilty and impure. The evil tree does not come from the bad fruits, but the bad fruits come from the bad tree, and are to be accounted for in terms of it.

Others have acknowledged the justness of these considerations and accordingly introduced certain modifications into the teaching of Pelagius. These admit that the absolute universality of sin cannot be the result merely of following a bad example, and that moral evil does not come to man simply from the outside, and they see themselves compelled to the confession that sin dwells inside man from the time of his conception and birth on, and that he takes his corrupted nature from his parents. But they maintain that this moral corruption, which is in man by nature is not sin proper, does not have the quality of guilt, and therefore also is undeserving of punishment. The innate moral corruption becomes sin, guilt, and culpability only when man as he develops into maturity freely acquiesces in it, accepts responsibility for it, so to speak, and by his free will converts it into sinful deeds.

*   *   *   *   *

This semi-Pelagian view may make a significant concession, but it proves upon reflection to be very inadequate, nevertheless. For sin consists always of unlawfulness, illegitimacy, in the transgression and departure from the law which God laid down for His rational and moral creatures. Such departure from the law can take place in the deeds of men, but it can also come to expression in his dispositions and inclinations, that is, in his nature as he brings it with him from his conception and birth. Semi-Pelagianism acknowledges this and speaks of a moral corruption which is antecedent to the choices and actions of a man. But if one takes this seriously one cannot escape the conclusion that the moral corruption which is now innate in human nature also is sin and guilt, and that it is therefore punishable. There are only the two possibilities. Human nature is in harmony with the law of God and is what it ought to be. In that event it is not morally corrupt. Otherwise human nature is morally corrupt, does not correspond to the law of God, is therefore unlawful and unjustifiable, and consequently renders man guilty and culpable.

There is little that can be said against such argumentation, but nevertheless there are many who try to escape from its inevitability by describing the moral corruption which man brings with him from his birth by the ambiguous term *lust*. Naturally the use of this word is not wrong in itself. Scripture also uses it often. But under the influence of the ascetic tendency, which gradually arose in the Christian church, theology has often used this word in a very limited sense. It tended to think of it solely as referring to the procreative passion, which is proper to man, and so arrived at the idea that this passion, although given to man at creation, and therefore not sinful in itself, nevertheless constituted a very likely occasion for sinning.

It was Calvin who took issue with this notion of lust. He did not object to calling the moral corruption with which man is born by the name of lust. But he wanted the word to be understood properly. One distinction which he thought necessary was the distinction between desire and lust. Desires are not sinful in themselves. Each of them was given man at the creation. Because as man he is a limited, finite, dependent creature, he has innumerable needs and consequently also innumerable desires. When he is hungry, he desires food; when he is thirsty, he desires water; and when he is tired, he desires rest. The same holds true of the spiritual in him. The mind of man was created in such a way that it desired the truth, and the will of man, thanks to its nature as created by God, desires the good. The desire of the righteous is only good, we read in Proverbs 11:28. When Solomon desired not riches but wisdom, this thing was good in the sight of the Lord (1 Kings 3:5-14). And when the poet of Psalm 42 panted for God as the hart pants after the water brooks, that too was a good and a precious desire.

Desires are not therefore sinful in themselves, but they, like the mind and the will, have been corrupted by sin and so have come into conflict with the law of the Lord. Not the strictly natural desires but the desires spoiled by sin, and therefore unregulated and overdone, are sinful desires.

And to this, in the second place, must be added the fact that sins are by no means limited to the sensuous and physical nature of man. They are characteristic of his sinful spiritual nature too. The sexual passion is not the only natural desire; it is but one among many. This passion is not sinful in itself either, for it was given man at his creation. And it is not the only passion which was corrupted by sin, for all desires, natural and spiritual, have become wild and undisciplined because of sin. The good desires of man have been metamorphosed into bad desires.

If the moral corruption of man is in this sense called desire or lust, its sinful character and its guilt are of course certain. It is this lust which in a particular commandment of the Lord is expressly forbidden (Ex. 20:17). And Paul says in so many words that he would not have known sin if the law had not said, Thou shalt not covet (Rom. 7:7). When Paul came to know himself, and measured not only his deeds but also his inclinations and desires against the touchstone of the law of God, it became apparent to him that these, too, were corrupted and impure and that they reached out towards the forbidden. For Paul the law of God is the only source of the knowledge of sin and its only measurement. One cannot get at what sin is by wishing or by imagination, but only by the law of God, which determines how and what man ought to be before the face of God in his external and internal life, in body and spirit, in word and deed, in thought and inclination. Measured by the yardstick of that law, there can be no doubt that the nature of man is corrupt and that his lust is sinful. It is not only that man thinks and acts sinfully: he *is* sinful from the time of his conception.

After all, it would be an untenable position psychologically, also, to hold that desire in itself is not sinful, but only becomes so through the will. To take such a position would be to embrace the unreasonable thought that the will of man stands neutral and external to desire, is itself as yet uncorrupted by sin, and can therefore freely decide whether or not it will go along with the desire. It is true that according to experience it is certainly possible that in many instances a person, on the basis of all sorts of considerations, such as fashion, community respectability, and the like, can counter his sinful desire by means of his reason and will, and prevent it from taking the form of sinful deeds. In natural man, too, there is still a struggle between impulse and duty, desire and conscience, lust and reason.

But this struggle is different in principle from the struggle which goes on in the regenerate man between body and spirit, between the old man and the new. It is a struggle conducted from the outside against the outbursting of lust. But it does not invade the inner fortress of the heart, nor attack the evil at its roots. Accordingly, it is a conflict which can serve to restrain the evil lust and to limit it, but it cannot cleanse it internally nor renew it. The sinful character of the lust is not changed by it. Nor is that all. Even though reason and will can sometimes suppress desire and lust, these are in their turn often subdued and put into the service of lust. They do not stand opposed to it in principle but by nature themselves delight in it: they feed and foster it, and they justify and vindicate it. Not seldom they let themselves be carried along by lust to such an extent that man is robbed of all independence and becomes a slave of his passions. The evil thoughts and the evil desires come up out of the heart and then proceed to darken understanding and pollute the will. The heart is so subtle that it can even deceive the understanding head.

* * * * *

Both of the efforts to explain the universal sinfulness of man come down to this: that they seek the cause of it in each man's fall individually. According to Pelagianism each man falls in independence of all others. This he does by freely choosing to follow the bad example of others. According to semi-Pelagianism each man falls by himself alone because quite by his own choice he takes the inherited but not sinful desire up into his will and converts it into a sinful deed. Both do injustice to the moral realities which are certain to the consciences of everybody, and both leave unexplained how the absolutely universal sinfulness of the human race can stem from a million times a million decisions of the human will.

Nevertheless these efforts have in recent times, be it in a new and different form, found numerous adherents. Formerly, too, there had been those who believed in a pre-existence of man. But Buddhistic influences have in late years given considerable impetus to this belief. The supposition is that men have lived eternally, or at least centuries before their appearance on earth; or otherwise — and this is a more philosophical form of the theory — it holds that the sensuous life of man on earth must be distinguished from that form of his existence which is quite conceivable even though it cannot be visualized.

To this the further idea is then added that people in this actual or imagined pre-existence all fell, each of them individually, and that in punishment for it they must live here upon the earth in these gross, material bodies and so prepare themselves for another life hereafter in which they will again receive rewards according to their works. There is, thus, only one law which governs the whole of human life before, during, and after the life on this earth, and that is the law of requital: Everybody received, receives, and will receive what he has earned by his works. Everybody reaps what he has sowed.

This Indian philosophical idea is remarkable for this reason: it tacitly proceeds from the assumption that in this earthly life the fall of each individual by himself is inconceivable. But for the rest it no more gives an explanation of the universality of sinfulness than does the Pelagian theory. It merely pushes the difficulty back a while, from this life on earth to a pre-existent life, a life, incidentally, of which no one has any recollection, for which no single ground exists, and which is in fact pure fantasy. Moreover, the teaching that everyone will be rewarded according to performance is a hard doctrine for the poor and the sick, the miserable and the destitute. There is no compassion in it. It stands in dark contrast to the rays of Divine grace of which the Scripture speaks.

But — and this is to be noted especially in the present connection — this Indian philosophy is in full agreement with the Pelagian doctrine on this score: that it seeks the origin of universal sinfulness in the separate fall of each individual person. Both views agree that mankind consists of an arbitrary aggregate of souls who have lived eternally or at least for centuries next to each other, who have no relationship to each other in point of origin or essence, and each of whom must look after his own fortunes. Each of them fell for himself alone, receives his own deserved wages, and tries as well as he is able to save himself. The thing that brings people together really is the misery in which they all together exist, and pity or sympathy is therefore the highest of the virtues. But the theory has this further obvious implication: namely, that those who live a fortunate life on earth can appeal to the law of requital and thereupon glory in their virtues, and look down with disdain upon the unfortunate who, after all, have also according to that law received what was coming to them.

*   *   *   *   *

We must get a clear view of these things if we are to appreciate Scripture and the light it sheds on the problem of the universal sinfulness of mankind. Scripture does not rest content with fantasy or imagination, but acknowledges and reveres the facts established by the conscience. Scripture projects no fantasy of a pre-existence of souls before their entrance into the life on earth, and knows nothing of a fall that has taken place, be it before or during the life on earth, in each individual person. In place of the individualistic and atomistic representations of Buddhism and Pelagianism Scripture postulates an organic view of the human race.

Mankind does not consist of an aggregate of individual souls who have accidentally come together from all sides at a given place, and who, for better or for worse, must now somehow, because of their many contacts, get along with each other as best they may. Mankind is a unity, rather, one body with many members, one tree with many branches, one kingdom with many citizens. Nor is mankind to become such a unity only in the future by way of some external combination. It was that from the beginning, and it still is that in spite of separation and schism, for it has one origin and one nature. Physically mankind is one because it has come from one blood. Juridically and ethically mankind is one because, on the very basis of the natural unity, it has been placed under one and the same Divine law, the law of the covenant of works.

From this Holy Scripture deduces that mankind remains one also in its fall. It is so that Scripture views mankind from its first to its last page. If there is any distinction among men, in rank, status, office, honor, talents, and the like, or if Israel in contradistinction from the other nations is chosen as the Lord's inheritance, then this is owing solely to the grace of God. It is this grace alone which does the discriminating (1 Cor. 4:17). But in themselves all men are alike before God, for they are all sinners, sharing in common guilt, tainted by the same impurity, subject to the same death, and requiring the same redemption. God has included them all under the same disobedience in order that He should be merciful to them all (Rom. 11:32). No one has the right to be arrogant, and no one has the right to give himself up to despair.

That this is the continuous view of Scripture concerning the human race needs no further contention; it is evident enough from what was said above about the universal sinfulness of man. But this organic oneness of the human race in point of law and morality gets a special and profound treatment from the apostle Paul.

When in his letter to the Romans he has first set forth the fact that the whole world is damnable in the sight of God (Rom. 1:18-3:20), and when he thereupon has explained how all righteousness and forgiveness of sins, all reconciliation and all life have been accomplished by Christ and are available in Him for the believer (Rom. 3:21-5:11), he concludes in chapter 5, verses 12-21 (before he proceeds to describe in the sixth chapter the moral fruits of the righteousness of faith), by once more summarizing the whole content of the salvation which we owe to Christ, and he contrasts this in a context of world history to all the guilt and misery which have accrued to us in Adam.

By one man, he says, sin came into the world, and together with death accrued to all men. For that sin, which the first man committed, was quite different in character from other sins. It is called transgression, different in kind from the sins which men committed in the time between Adam and Moses (Rom. 5:14), and an offense (Rom. 5:15 ff.), a disobedience (Rom. 5:19), and as such it forms the sharpest of contrasts with the absolute, death-tested obedience of Christ (Rom. 5:19).

Therefore the sin which Adam committed did not remain limited to his person alone. It continued to operate in and through the whole human race. For, what we read is not that by one man sin came into one person but into the world (Rom. 5:12), and also death which carried on in all men, and justifiably so, because all men had sinned in that one man.

That such is Paul's thought can be proved from the fact that he derives from the transgression of Adam the death of the people who lived from Adam to Moses, and who could not have sinned with a transgression like to that of Adam (inasmuch as at that time there was no positive law, that is, no law of the covenant to which a specific condition and threat was attached). But if Romans 5:12 ff. should still leave any doubt about this, it would be removed by what Paul says in 1 Corinthians 15:22.

For there we read that all men die, not in themselves, not in their parents or grandparents, but in Adam. That is to say that men are not subject to death first of all because they or their ancestors have personally become guilty, but they have all already died in Adam. It was determined already in the sin and death of Adam that these all should die. The point is not that in him they have all become mortal, but that really they have in an objective sense already died in him. Already *then* the sentence of death was pronounced, even though its execution, so to speak, followed later. Now Paul recognizes no other death than a death which is the result of sin (Rom. 6:23). If all men have died in Adam then they have also all sinned in him. By the transgression of Adam sin and death could come into the world and accrue to all men because that transgression had a peculiar character. It was the transgression of a particular law, and it was transgressed not by Adam alone but by Adam as head of the human race.

Only if Paul's thought in Romans 5:12-14 is understood in this way can full justice be done to what is said in the following verses about the consequences of Adam's transgression. It is all the development of a single basic idea. By the transgression of one man (Adam) many (descendants) have died (verse 15). The guilt (that is, the judgment or sentence which God as Judge pronounces) by this one who sinned became a judgment which comprehended the whole human race (verse 16). By the offense of that one man death reigned in the world over all men (verse 17). By the offense of one, judgment came upon all men to condemnation (verse 18). And, in final epitome, by the disobedience of the one, the many (all the descendants of Adam) were constituted sinners. By that disobedience they all immediately came to stand before the face of God as sinful men (verse 19).

The seal is placed upon this interpretation of Paul's thought by the comparison which he introduces between Adam and Christ. In the connection of Romans 5 Paul does not treat the origin of Adam's sin, but the fulness of the salvation achieved by Christ. In order to exhibit this salvation in all its glory, he compares and contrasts it with the sin and death which have spread out over the human race from Adam. In other words Adam is serving in this context as example and type of the One that should come (verse 14).

In the one Adam and through his transgression the human race was condemned, and in the one man Jesus Christ that race has by a judicial verdict of God been declared free and justified. By one man sin came into the world as a force or power which ruled over all men; just so one man accomplished the governance of Divine grace in mankind. By one man death came into the world as evidence of the rule of sin; by one man also, namely, Christ Jesus our Lord, grace began to rule by way of a righteousness that leads to eternal life. The comparison of Adam and Christ holds in all applications. There is only this one difference: sin is mighty and powerful, but Grace is far superior in riches and abundance.

Christian theology has comprised these thoughts of Holy Scripture in the doctrine of original sin. One can argue against this doctrine, or deny it, or mock it. But that is not to stop the testimony of the Scriptures nor to abolish the *facts* on which this teaching is based. The whole history of the world is proof of the fact that mankind, both in its entirety and in its individual membership, is *guilty* before the face of God, has a *morally corrupted* nature, and is at all times subject to *decay* and *death*. Original sin, accordingly, includes first of all the fact of *original guilt*. In the first man the many who stem from him have, through his disobedience, by a righteous judgment of God been constituted sinners (Rom. 5:18).

In the second place, original sin includes *original pollution*. All men are conceived in sin and born in unrighteousness (Ps. 51:7) and are evil from youth on up (Gen. 6:5 and Ps. 25:7), for no one can bring a clean thing from an unclean one (Job 14:4 and John 3:6). This taint or pollution not only spreads itself out over all men but it also saturates the whole of the individual being. It attacks the heart, which is deceitful above all things, sick unto death, and never to be fathomed in its guile (Jer. 17:9), and which as the source of the issues of life (Prov. 4:23) is the source also of all unrighteousnesses (Mark 7:21-22). Proceeding from the heart as center, this pollution darkens the understanding (Rom. 1:21), inclines the will to evil and makes it powerless to do the truly good (John 8:34 and Rom. 8:7), taints or defiles the conscience (Titus 1:15), and makes of the body with all of its members, its eyes and ears, its hands and feet, its mouth and tongue, a weapon of unrighteousness (Rom. 3:13-17 and 6:13). This sin is such that everybody, not by his own "sins of commission" first of all, but from the time of his conception is subject to death and corruption (Rom. 5:14). All men have already died in Adam (1 Cor. 15:22).

Hard as this original sin may now seem to be, it rests on a law which governs the whole of human life, whose existence no one can successfully deny, and against which no one registers any objection so long as it is working in his favor.

When parents have collected property in one form or another for the benefit of the children, those children never object to appropriating the property thus left them by their parents' death. They do not object to obtaining the inheritance even though they have not earned it, in fact, even though by their scandalous conduct they have sometimes proved themselves unworthy of it and go through it unrighteously, in extravagant wantonness of living. If there are no children, the most remote relatives, the grand nephews and second cousins, put in their appearance, in order without any qualm of conscience to share in the inheritance which unknown and neglected members of the family have unexpectedly left behind. All of that holds of material things. But there are also spiritual goods, the values of rank and status, of honor and good name, of science and art, which children inherit from their parents, which they have in no way earned, and which they nevertheless appropriate without protest, as indeed they gratefully may. It can be said, therefore, that such a law of inheritance is generally operative, in families, generations, peoples, in state and society, in science and art, and in all mankind. The next generation lives on the goods which the preceding generation has collected; posterity takes up in all spheres of life the work which the ancestors were doing. And there is no one who, if it is profitable to him, registers a protest against this gracious arrangement of God.

All that changes, however, when this same law of inheritance works to somebody's disadvantage. When children are appealed to for support of their poor parents, they immediately cut off all relationship with those parents and point the way to the church relief or the public poor funds. When blood relatives feel themselves injured because some member of the family has in their estimation married below the proper rank, or has done some disreputable thing, they immediately leave him in the lurch and show him their disfavor. To some extent, greater or less, the tendency is present in everyone to enjoy the advantages of community and interrelationship but to reject the corresponding obligations. That tendency is in itself, however, a powerful proof of the fact that among people there is such a community of privileges and of duties. There is a oneness, a solidarity, a community whose existence and operation no one can deny.

True, we do not know just how this solidarity operates and has its influence. The laws of inheritance, for instance, according to which the material and spiritual goods of the parents are deeded to the children, are still unknown to us. We do not understand the mystery: how an individual person, born from the community and reared by it, grows up to a status of independence and freedom, and then takes up in the community his own and sometimes powerful and influential position. We cannot point to the boundary where community or solidarity ceases and the personal independence and individual responsibility begin. But all this does not take away from the fact that such a solidarity exists, and that people, be it in small or in large communities of interrelationship, are united to each other in real solidarity. There are individuals, but there is also an invisible bond which binds whole families, generations, peoples into a powerful unit. There is an individual soul, but there is also, be it in a metaphorical sense, a popular or national "soul." There are personal characteristics, but there are also social characteristics peculiar to a given circle of people. There are particular, individual sins, but there are also general, social sins. And thus too there is individual guilt, but also common social guilt.

This solidarity which expresses itself in a thousand ways in the relationships between people carries with it again and again, and naturally enough, the idea of the representation of the many by the few. We cannot be present at everything ourselves nor do everything personally. People are spread over the whole earth and they live at great distances from each other. They do not all live at the same time but follow upon each other in successive generations. Moreover, they are not all equally able and wise. They differ infinitely in talents and abilities. Hence at every moment some few are called to think and to speak, to decide and to act in the name and in the place of the many. As a matter of fact no real community is possible without inequality of gifts and calling, without representation and substitution. No body is possible unless there are numerous differentiated members, and if all of those members are not governed by a head which thinks for them all and makes its decisions in the name of them all. The father has this same kind of role for the family, the manager for his organization, the board of directors for their society, the general for his army, the congress or parliament for its electorate, and the king for his realm. And the subordinates share in the consequences which follow in the wake of their representatives' actions.

All that, however, concerns only a small and limited circle of mankind. In such a circle one man can to some extent, too, be a blessing or a curse to many, but the influence is nevertheless limited to a fairly restricted sphere. Even such a man of power as Napoleon, though his jurisdiction and influence were never so large, takes but a small place in the history of the world, and a transient one at that. But Scripture tells us of two people who occupied an entirely peculiar position, who both of them stood at the head of nothing less than mankind itself, whose power and influence extends not merely to a nation or family of nations, not merely to a country or continent, not merely to a century or combination of centuries, but to the whole of humanity, to the ends of the earth, and to all eternity. Those two persons are Adam and Christ. The one stands at the beginning, the other at the center of history. The first is the head of the old mankind and the second is the head of the new. The one is the origin of sin and death in the world and the other the fountainhead and spring of righteousness and life.

By virtue of the absolutely unique positions which these two occupy at the head of mankind, they are comparable with each other. There are analogies or correspondences of place, significance, and influence between them in all the forms of solidarity which are manifested among men in family, tribe, nation, and the like. And all of these analogies or correspondences can and may serve as illuminating exposition of the influence which went out from Adam and Christ to the whole human race. They can to a certain extent reconcile us to the law of inheritance operating even in our highest life, that is, in our religious and moral life, inasmuch as this law does not stand alone but is generally relevant and is part and parcel of the organic existence of mankind. All the same, Adam and Christ occupy a wholly unique place. They have a significance for the human race such as no one, no world conqueror or genius of the first rank, could ever achieve. The legacy by which Adam involved us all in his transgression alone makes it possible for us to be fully reconciled to God in Christ.

It is, after all, the same law which condemns us in the first man and acquits us in the second. If, without our knowing it, we had not been able to share in the condemnation of Adam, it would not have been possible either for us in the same way to be received again in grace in Christ. If we have no objection to taking advantages which we have not earned but which come to us as a gift or an inheritance, we have no right either to quarrel with that legacy when it brings us evil. Shall we receive good at the hand of God, and shall we not receive evil? (Job 2:10). Let us not then charge Adam with guilt but rather thank Christ who has loved us so exceedingly. Let us not look back to Paradise but forward to the cross. Behind that cross lies the crown which can never fade away.

*   *   *   *   *

The original sin in which man is conceived and born is not a dormant, passive quality, but a root, rather, from which all kinds of sin come up, an unholy fountain from which sin continuously wells up, a force which is always impelling the heart of man in the wrong direction — away from God and from communion with Him and towards corruption and decay. From this original sin, therefore, those sins are to be distinguished which used to be called *actual* sins and included all those transgressions of Divine law which the individual personally commits, be it more or less wittingly, and with a more or less deliberate will. All such sins have a common origin: they stem from the heart of man (Mark 7:23). The human heart is the same for all people, in all places, and at all times — so long, that is, as it is not changed by regeneration and renewal. One human nature is common to all the descendants of Adam, and it is, for all men, guilty and polluted. There is, accordingly, no reason at all for anybody to separate himself from others and to say: Depart from me; I am holier than thou. The pride of the self-righteous, the pride of the noble, the self-exaltation of the wise, is, with a view to the human nature which all share alike, absolutely without justification. Of the thousands of sins that exist there is not one of which anybody could say that he is a total stranger to it and has nothing to do with it. The seeds of all iniquities, even of the most heinous, lie in the very heart which we all carry in our bosoms. The transgressors and criminals are not a peculiar race, but come up out of the society of which we are all members. They merely exhibit what is going on in continuous agitation and turbulence in the secret center of every man.

Inasmuch as they come up out of a single root, all the sins in the life of each person individually, and thus also in the life of a family, generation, race, people, society, and the whole of mankind, are organically related to each other. The sins are innumerable in quantity, so that some have tried for a grouping or classification of them. They have spoken of seven cardinal or primary sins (pride, avarice, intemperance, unchastity or immorality, sloth, envy, and wrath). Or, again, they were classified according to the instrument with which they were committed, such as sins of thought, word, and deed, or as venial or spiritual sins. Sometimes they were grouped according to the commandments of which they constituted violations, such as sins against the first and the second table, that is, against God and against the neighbor and ourselves. Or they were classified according to the form in which they were expressed, such as the sins of omission and of commission. And there were distinctions of degree, such as secret and public sins, human and diabolical sins, and the like.

But, however they may differ from each other, they never stand by themselves as sheer arbitrary entities, each in discrete isolation; they are always at bottom interrelated, the one influencing and leaving its mark on the other. Just as in illness the law of sound living continues to operate but is now active in disturbed form, so the organic character of the life of man and of mankind comes to expression in sin. The expression it takes is such that life now develops in a direction diametrically opposed to that which was originally intended.

Sin is a slippery plane, and we cannot go along with it a way and then turn around at some arbitrarily selected spot and reverse our course. A distinguished poet spoke profoundly and beautifully of the curse of the wicked deed by saying of it that it continuously gives birth to evil. Scripture sheds full light upon this matter for us. In James 1:14-15 it explains how the sinful deed in man arises in an organic way. When someone is tempted to evil the cause of it does not lie in God, but in his own lust. This lust is the mother of sin. This lust is not in itself, however, enough to bring forth sin (that is, the sinful deed, whether of thought, word, or deed). It must first conceive and become pregnant. That happens when the reason and the will are united with the lust. It is then, when lust is impregnated by the will, that it brings forth the sinful deed. And when this sin in turn grows up, develops, and reaches its maturity, it bears death.

So it is for each particular sin, but so it is also that the various sins are mutually related. The same apostle points to this fact when, in chapter 2:10, he says that whoever keeps the whole law and falters in one point of it has become guilty of all. For the same Lawgiver who has prescribed that particular commandment has prescribed them all. In the one particular commandment the transgressor attacks the Giver of them all, and he thus undermines all authority and all power. By virtue both of its origin and of its nature or essence, the law is one law. It is an organic body, which, violated in one of its members, becomes wholly deformed. It is a chain, which, when one of its links is broken, comes apart. The person who transgresses one of the commandments in principle sets all the commandments aside, and thus goes from bad to worse. He becomes, as Jesus said, a servant, or a slave, of sin (John 8:34), or, as Paul put it, he is sold under the dominion of sin, so that he is no more independent of sin than a slave is of the master who has bought him (Rom. 7:14).

This organic view is applicable also to the sins which manifest themselves in particular areas of human life. There are personal and individual sins, but there are also common, social sins, the sins of particular families, nations, and the like. Every class and status in society, every vocation and business, every office and profession brings with it its own peculiar dangers and its own peculiar sins. The sins of urbanites differ from those of village people, those of farmers from the sins of merchants, those of the learned from those of the untutored, those of the rich from those of the poor, and those of the children from those of adults. But this precisely goes to show that all those sins in each sphere are interdependent with each other. Statistics confirm this when they indicate that particular misdeeds occur in particular age groups, seasons, generations, classes, and circles, and occur with a rhythmical regularity. As it happens we take notice of only a very small portion of the sins of our limited group, and of that only superficially. But if we could penetrate through to the essence of appearances, and trace out the root of sins in the hearts of people, we should very probably come to the conclusion that in sin, too, there is oneness, idea, plan, pattern — in a word, that in sin too there is *system*.

Scripture raises a corner of the veil when it relates sin, both in point of its origin and of its development and fulfillment, to the kingdom of Satan. Since Satan has tempted man and brought him to his fall (John 8:44), he has in the moral sense become the prince of the world and the god of this age (John 16:11 and 2 Cor. 4:4). Although condemned by Christ and cast out (John 12:31 and 16:11), and thus operative mainly in the heathen world (Acts 26:18 and Eph. 2:2), he nevertheless continues to attack the church from without. That church, therefore, must with its whole armor engage in battle with him (Eph. 6:11). And he organizes his total resources in order at the end of days once more to launch a final and decisive attack upon Christ and His kingdom (Rev. 12ff.). It is not when we fix our attention upon a single sin, or upon the sins of a particular person or people, but when instead we fasten it upon the whole realm of sin in mankind, taking advantage of the light shed upon it by Scripture, then we for the first time understand what the real nature and intention of sin is. In principle and essence it is nothing less than enmity against God, and in the world it aims at nothing less than sovereign dominion. And every sin, also the smallest, being as it is a transgression of the Divine law, serves this final objective in connection with the whole system. The history of the world is not a blindly operating evolutionary process, but an awful drama, a spiritual struggle, centuries-long in duration, a warfare between the Spirit from above and the spirit from below, between Christ and anti-Christ, between God and Satan.

* * * * *

However, although this view of sin must be the dominant consideration, it must not be allowed to tempt us into one-sidedness, nor to obliterate the distinction which separates the various sins. It is true that the sins, like the virtues, are one and indivisible, and that whoever has committed one of them has committed them all in principle (James 2:10). But this is not to say that all sins are equal in kind and degree. There is a difference between sins of error or ignorance, and sins of presumption (Num. 15:27 and 30), between the sins against the first and those against the second table (Matt. 22:37-38), between sensuous and spiritual sins, human and diabolical sins, and so on. Because the commandments of the one law differ among each other, and because the transgression of these commandments can take place in very different circumstances and with more or less approbation of the will, therefore not all sins are equally grave nor deserving of the same punishment. The sins committed against the moral law are graver than those committed against the ceremonial laws, for obedience is better than sacrifice (1

Sam. 15:22). The person who steals prompted by hunger is less culpable than the person prompted by greed (Prov. 6:30). There are gradations of wrath (Matt. 5:22). And, even though desiring a married woman in one's heart is already to commit adultery, the person who does not fight against that desire but succumbs to it goes on to commit adultery in deed also.

If we were to do injustice to this distinction between sins, we should be getting into conflict with both Scripture and reality. It is true that in a moral sense people are born equal. At their beginning they all bear the same guilt and are all defiled by the same taint. But as they grow up they differ from each other nonetheless, and they differ widely. Believers sometimes fall into grave sins, must be constantly fighting against the old man in their nature, and can on this earth achieve but a small beginning of the perfect obedience. And among those who have not known the name of Christ or have not believed in Him there are those who yield themselves to every upsurge of ungodliness and who imbibe sin like water. But there are also many among them who differentiate themselves by a civically respectable and highly ethical life, and who can serve as models of virtue even to Christians. True, the seeds of evil lie embedded in every human heart; and the more we increase in self-knowledge the more we recognize the truth of the confession that by nature we are prone to hate God and our neighbor, are incapable of any good, and inclined to all evil. But this evil tendency does not in all people to the same extent go on to the point of evil deeds. Not all who walk the broad way walk equally fast or make the same progress.

The cause of this difference does not lie in man but in the restraining grace of God. The heart is the same in all people. Always and everywhere in all people the same evil imaginations and desires come up. The imaginations of the heart are only evil from youth on. If God were to abandon mankind and give them up to the desires of their hearts, then earth would become a hell and no human society or human history would be possible. But just as the fire in the earth is kept under control by the hard crust of the earth, and only now and then, and only in certain places, bursts out in awful volcanic explosions, so the evil thoughts and lusts of the human heart are suppressed and restrained from all sides by the life of society. God has not given man free rein, but puts the wild animal that is in him under harness, in order that He may maintain His counsel for the human race and execute it. He keeps operative in man a natural love, a craving for company, a sense of religion and of morality, conscience and a notion of law, reason and will. And He puts man in a family, a community, a state, all of which, what with their public opinion, notions of decency, feeling for work, discipline, punishment, and the like, restrain him, and oblige and educate him to a civically respectable life.

Through all these many and powerful influences sinful man is enabled still to achieve much good. When the Heidelberg Catechism says that man is wholly incapable of doing any good, and inclined to all evil, then by this *good,* as the *Articles against the Remonstrants* clearly state, we are to understand *saving* good.

Of such saving good man is by nature wholly incapable. He can do no good which is internal, spiritual good, which is perfectly pure in the eyes of God who searches the heart, which is in total agreement, both in a spiritual and in a literal sense, with the demands of the law, and which therefore according to the promise of that law should be able to earn eternal life and heavenly blessedness. But this is absolutely not to say that man should not by the common grace of God be in position to bring much good to pass. In his personal life he can by his reason and will restrain his evil imaginations and lusts and apply himself to virtue. In his community and social life he can honestly and faithfully fulfill his obligations and assist in the promotion of welfare and culture, science and art. In one word, by means of all the forces with which God surrounds the natural sinful man, he enables him still to live a human life here on earth.

But all these powers are not enough to renew the man within, and often prove inadequate even to keep unrighteousness within bounds. We do not even have to think in this connection of the criminal world which is to be found in every society and which has its own life. But it is also in conquests, colonizations, religious and race wars, popular revolutions, national revolts, and the like, that the terrible range of the unrighteousness in the human heart comes to expression. The refinement of culture does not rule it out, but rather fosters a shamelessness in executing the unrighteousness. The apparently most noble of deeds prove, upon closer examination, not seldom motivated by all sorts of sinful considerations of selfishness and ambition. Whoever understands something of the wickedness and subtlety of the human heart is not at all surprised that there is so much evil in the world. Rather, he marvels that so much good can still be found in the world, and he worships the wisdom of God who with such a human race still knows how to accomplish so much. It is of the Lord's mercies that we are not consumed, because His compassions fail not (Lam. 3:22). There is continuous struggle between the sin of people which tries to break out and the grace of God which binds it and renders human thought and action serviceable to His counsel and plan.

*   *   *   *   *

This grace of God can humble a man, even if only in the sense of Ahab (1 Kings 21:29) or of the inhabitants of Nineveh (Jon. 3:5 ff). But a man can also on the long run set himself against such grace. In that case the awful manifestation which in the Scripture is called *hardening* of the heart sets in. Pharaoh is the typical example of it. It is reported also of others in Scripture, but the nature and progress of hardening are nevertheless most lucidly exhibited in Pharaoh. He was a powerful prince, standing at the head of a great kingdom, proud at heart and unwilling to bow before the signs of God's power. Those signs followed upon one another in regular order, and they increased in miraculous power and destructive force. But according to the same crescendo, Pharaoh grew evil and obstinate. His promptings to yield and to bow before this miraculous power lost more and more of the character of integrity. Finally, with his eyes wide open to the facts, he strode straight to his doom.

It is a tremendous soul struggle which we see before us in this drama of Pharaoh, and one which can be seen from God's side as well as from man's side. Now it is said that the Lord hardens Pharaoh's heart,[5] at another time that Pharaoh himself hardens his heart,[6] or that his heart was hardened.[7] There is in this phenomenon of hardening a Divine and a human operation; there is in it an operation of Divine grace which constantly becomes more and more of judgment, and an operation of human resistance which more and more takes on the character of a conscious and determined enmity against God. And Scripture describes this hardening in the same way at other places. In Deuteronomy 2:30, Joshua 11:20, and Isaiah 63:17 the Lord hardens; and in other places[8] it is the people who harden themselves. There is interaction here, a struggle, a wrestling between the two which is not to be separated from the revelation of Divine grace. Such an interaction is related to general revelation, but it is particularly special grace which has the characteristic of bringing about a judgment, and a schism and separation, between people (John 1:5; 3:19; and 9:39). Christ is set for a fall and a rising again (Luke 2:34). He is a rock of salvation and a rock of stumbling and offense (Matt. 21:44 and Rom. 9:32). The Gospel is unto death or unto life (2 Cor. 2:16). It is hidden from the wise and prudent and revealed to the babes (Matt. 11:25). And in all this the counsel and good pleasure of God and at the same time the law of the religious and moral life become evident.

---

5. Ex. 4:21; 7:3; 9:12; 10:20 and 27.
6. Ex. 7:14; 9:7; and 9:35.
7. Ex. 8:15, 19, 32 and 9:34.
8. 1 Sam. 6:6; 2 Chron. 36:13; Ps. 95:8; Matt. 13:15; Acts 19:9; and Rom. 11:7, 25.

The sin of hardening reaches its ultimate culmination in the blasphemy against the Holy Spirit. Jesus speaks of that on the occasion of a serious difference from the Pharisees. When He had healed a man who was blind and dumb and possessed of a devil, the multitudes marvelled so greatly that they called out: Is this not the Son of David, the Messiah, promised of God to the fathers?

But this homage given to Christ aroused only hatred and enmity among the Pharisees, and they declared, to the contrary, that Jesus had cast out the devil through none other than through Beelzebub, the prince of the devils. Thus they took the diametrically opposed position. Instead of acknowledging Christ as the Son of God, the Messiah, who cast out devils by the Spirit of God and established God's kingdom on earth, they say that Jesus is an accomplice of Satan and that His work is diabolical. Over against this terrible blasphemy Jesus preserves His dignity; He refutes the charge and points out how unreasonable it is, but at the end of the rebuttal He adds this grave admonishment to what He has said: All manner of sin and blasphemy shall be forgiven unto men: but the blasphemy against the Holy Ghost shall not be forgiven unto men, neither in this world, neither in the world to come (Matt. 12:31-32).

The words themselves and the context in which they appear clearly indicate that the blasphemy against the Holy Spirit does not take place at the beginning or in the middle of the way of sin but at the end. It does not consist of doubt or unbelief concerning the truth which God has revealed, nor of a resistance to and a grieving of the Holy Spirit, for these are sins which can be committed also by believers, and indeed often are. But the blasphemy against the Holy Spirit can take place only when there has been in the consciousness such a rich revelation of God and such a powerful illumination of the Holy Spirit that man is fully convinced in his heart and conscience of the truth of the Divine revelation.[9]

The sin consists of this, rather, that such a person, regardless of all objective revelation and subjective enlightenment, despite the fact that he has known and tasted of the truth as truth, nevertheless in full awareness and with deliberate intent calls that truth a lie and castigates Christ as a tool of Satan. In this sin the human becomes the diabolical. No, it does not consist of doubt and unbelief, but cuts off the possibility of these as it does of remorse and prayer (I John 5:16). It has gone way beyond the moment of doubt and unbelief, remorse and prayer. Notwithstanding the fact that the Holy Spirit is acknowledged as being the Spirit of the Father and of the Son, He is nevertheless, in diabolical

---

9. Heb. 6:4-8; 10:25-29; and 12:15-17.

wickedness, blasphemed. In its culmination sin becomes so godlessly brazen that it shakes off every vestige of shame, throws off all covering and stands stark naked, despises all apparent reasons, and, out of sheer delight in evil, takes its stand against God's truth and grace. It is therefore a grave admonishment which Jesus holds up to us in this teaching concerning the blasphemy against the Holy Spirit. But we must not forget the comfort which is contained in the teaching. For if this sin is the one unforgivable sin, then all other sins, even the greatest and most severe, can be forgiven. They can be forgiven not by way of human penitential exercises but through the riches of the Divine grace.

* * * * *

If sin can be forgiven and washed away only through grace, the implication is that in itself it deserves punishment. Scripture proceeds from this assumption when it threatens sin with the punishment of death even before sin has come into the world (Gen. 2:17). Moreover, it constantly proclaims the judgment of God against sin, irrespective of whether that judgment be effected already in this life (Ex. 20:5) or on the great day of judgment (Rom. 2:5-10). For God is the Just One and the Holy One, who hates all wickedness,[10] who by no means holds the guilty innocent,[11] but who visits upon all unrighteousness His anger (Rom. 1:18), His curse (Deut. 27:26 and Gal. 3:10), and His wrath (Nahum 1:2 and 1 Thess. 4:6), and who will reward every man according to his works.[12] Conscience testifies of this in everybody when it judges him because of his evil thoughts, words, and deeds, and when it often pursues him with a sense of guilt and of remorse, and of cringing and fear because of the judgment. Among all people the administration of justice is based on this idea of the culpability of sin.

But the human heart ever and again comes into conflict with this severe judgment because it feels itself condemned by it. And science and philosophy have often entered into the service of the heart and have tried to assign the most attractive of reasons for separating the work and the reward, the evil and the punishment. Just as art must be practised for its own sake, so, according to this representation, good must be done for its own sake, and not for the hope of reward; and just so, evil should be avoided because it is what it is and not because penalty is attached to it. There is no such thing as reward for virtue or punishment for sin. The only penalty attached to sin is the result which its own

---

10. Job 34:10; Ps. 5:5; and Ps. 45:7.
11. Ex. 34:7; and Num. 14:18.
12. Ps. 62:12; Job 34:11; Prov. 24:12; Jer. 32:19; Ezek. 33:20; Matt. 16:27; Rom. 2:6; 2 Cor. 5:10; 1 Peter 1:17; and Rev. 22:12.

nature by virtue of natural law inevitably brings with it. Just as the virtuous man has peace of heart so the sinner by his consciousness of guilt, anxiety, and fear is tormented, or, if his sins be those of drunkenness or sensuality, he is visited by ill health.

In modern times this philosophy of the sinful and erring heart has appealed for support to the doctrine of evolution, according to which man is descended from the animal, and in the core of his being really always remains an animal, and that he must inevitably, deterministically, do and be what he does and is. Man is not a free, rational-moral being; he is not responsible for his actions; his deeds cannot be held against him as being guilty; he simply is what he has to be. Just as there are flowers which give off a pleasant fragrance and flowers which give off an unpleasant odor, and just as there are gentle and slaughterous beasts, so there are people who are useful to society and people who are detrimental to it. True, society, in the interests of self-preservation, has the right to segregate those harmful individuals and to lock them up, but this is not punishment. No one man has the right to pass judgment upon another man and to condemn him. Criminals are not so much wicked as they are insane. They suffer from an inherited weakness or from a defect fostered and nurtured by society itself. Such people, accordingly, do not belong in a jail-block but in a hospital or sanitarium, and can lay claim to humane, medical, or educational treatment.

In fairness to the facts, it must be said that this new criminal theory is in part a reaction to another extreme to which people went in the past. If nowadays criminals are regarded as mentally ill, formerly the mentally ill and all kinds of other unfortunates were often regarded as criminals, and people whetted their wits on conceiving devices which would cause the most terrible pains in persons who were regarded as guilty and deserving of punishment. But, even though this goes some way towards motivating the new theory, it does not excuse it or make it right. The new is just as one-sided as the old. It does injustice to the gravity of sin, robs man of his moral freedom, degrading him to the level of the machine, boldly defies the moral nature of man with its conscience and sense of guilt, and in principle undermines the whole basis of authority, government, and the administration of law.

Irrespective of the efforts which science can put to work to prove the inevitability of sin, any person in whom the conscience has not yet been seared into insensitivity feels himself obliged to do the good and responsible for doing wrong. Certainly the hope of reward is not the sole and most important motive for doing good, and certainly the fear of punishment may not be the only thing that prompts men to refrain from evil. But whoever, prompted by these same subordinate motives, does the good and refrains from evil, be it merely in an external sense, is nevertheless still in a better situation than the one who, despising such motivations, goes on now to live according to impulse. Besides, virtue and fortune, and also sin and punishment, are inseparably connected with each other not merely in consequence of an external reckoning, but they are present also in the moral consciousness from the very beginning. The true and real love of the good, that is, the full fellowship with God, means that man is taken up in his entirety, both internally and externally, into that fellowship. And sin, with an equal comprehensiveness, implies at its culmination the corruption of man in soul and body.

* * * * *

The punishment which God appointed for sin is death (Gen. 2:7), but this temporal bodily death by no means stands alone. It is preceded and followed by many other penalties.

As soon as man had sinned, his eyes were opened: he was ashamed of his nakedness, and hid himself in fear from the face of God (Gen. 3:7-8). In man, shame and fear are inseparable from sin because he immediately feels himself guilty and defiled by his sin.

Guilt, which is relationship to punishment, and pollution or defilement, which is moral corruption, are the consequences which set in immediately after the fall. But to these natural penalties God adds further definite punishments. The woman is punished as woman, and also as mother: she shall bear children in pain, and nevertheless her desire shall always be for the man (Gen. 3:16). And man is punished in the calling which was specifically entrusted to him, in the cultivation of the earth, in the work of his hands (Gen. 3:17-19). True, death does not take place immediately after the transgression; it is even postponed for hundreds of years, for God does not abandon His intents with the human race. But the life that is now granted man becomes a life of suffering, full of struggle and grief, a preparation for death, a continuous death. Man did not because of sin merely become mortal: he began to die. He dies constantly from the cradle to the grave. His life is nothing other than a short and vain battle with death.

This fact comes to expression in the many plaints which are raised in Scripture concerning the frailty, transience, and vanity of human life. Man was dust, even before the fall. According to the body he was made of the dust of the earth, and thus, earthy of the earth, he was a living soul (1 Cor. 15:45, 47). But that life of the first man was intended to be spiritualized and glorified, governed by the spirit in the way of keeping the Divine law. Now, however, as a result of the transgression, the law goes into operation: dust thou art and unto dust shalt thou return (Gen. 3:19).

Instead of becoming spirit, man became flesh through sin. Now his life is a shadow, a dream, a watch in the night, a span, a step, a wave of the ocean which comes up, breaks, and disappears, a ray of light that shines and is gone, a flower which blooms and wilts away. It really is not worth the full and glorious name of life. It is constant death in sin (John 8:21 and 24), a death in sins and trespasses (Eph. 2:1).

Such is life, looked at from the inside, as it is internally corrupted, wasted, and dissolved by sin. And from without, too, it is constantly threatened from every side. Immediately after the transgression, man was driven from Paradise. He may not return to it in his own right, for he has forfeited the right to life, and such a place of rest and peace is no longer suitable for fallen man. He must go into the wide world to earn his bread in the sweat of his brow and so to fulfill his calling. Unfallen man is at home in a Paradise, and the blessed live in heaven, but sinful, though redeemable, man gets the earth as his sojourning place — an earth which shares in his fall, which for his sake is accursed, and which, together with him, is made subject to vanity (Rom. 8:20).

Thus the internal and the external agree again : there is harmony between man and his environment. The earth on which we live is not a heaven but it is not a hell either. It stands between the two and has something of the quality of each. We cannot point out in particular the relationships between the sins of men and the calamities of life. Jesus Himself warns against doing this. He says that the Galileans, whose blood Pilate had mingled with their sacrifices, were not sinners above others (Luke 13:1-3), and the son who was born blind was not punished because of his own sins or the sins of his parents, but was thus afflicted in order that the works of God should be revealed (John 9:3). We are therefore not to infer from the fact that afflictions and calamities accrue to someone, that his personal guilt brought them on. The friends of Job argued so and were mistaken.

There is no doubt, however, that according to the teaching of all Scripture a connection exists between the fallen human race on the one hand, and the fallen earth on the other. They were created in harmony with each other, were both together subjected to vanity, are both in principle redeemed by Christ, and will sometime together be raised and glorified. The present world is neither the best nor the worst possible, but it is a good world for fallen man. Because of itself it brings forth only thorns and thistles, it compels man to work, preserves him from decay, and in the bottom of his heart nurses the inextinguishable hope that there will yet be a durable good and an eternal happiness. This hope makes him live, even though it be but a life of short duration and full of restlessness.

For all life which is still man's by nature is subject to the decay of death. If a person is strong he keeps up the struggle seventy or eighty years, but life is usually cut off much sooner, in the strength of the years, in the flower of youth, soon after or even before birth. Scripture says that this death is a judgment of God, a payment in punishment of sin, and this truth is felt in the heart of all mankind and of each individual person. Even the so-called primitive peoples proceed from the idea that in essence man is mortal, and that it is not immortality which must be proved but death which must be explained. Nevertheless, there are many who in ancient or more recent times have held that death, not as an external thing coming violently from without but internally as a process of dissolution, is an altogether natural and inevitable phenomenon. In itself, according to this view, death is not terrible; it merely seems so to man because the instinct of life fights against it. When in its progress science has made further conquests, it will more and more hem in an untimely death and will raise the natural death owing to failure of energies to a higher level. And then men will die just as peacefully and calmly as plants do that wilt away or as animals that are exhausted.

But even though there are some few who speak in that way, there are others who sound quite a different note indeed. The men of science are by no means in agreement about the causes and nature of death. Over against those who see in death a natural and necessary end of life there are many who find death an even greater riddle than life, and who roundly declare that there is not a single reason why living beings should from some inner necessity have to die. They even say that the universe was originally an immeasurable living being, that death put in its appearance later, and that there still are some undying animals. And such language is eagerly absorbed at the present time by those who believe in a pre-existence of souls and who regard death as a change of form which man undergoes in order to rise to a higher life — like the caterpillar who becomes a butterfly.

This difference of views is in itself evidence for the fact that science cannot penetrate to the deepest and final causes of things, and can no more explain death than it can explain life. Both remain a mystery to science. The moment it tries to put forth an explanation it runs the danger of doing injustice either to the reality of death or to that of life. Science says that life was originally eternal, but then it must answer the question as to where death came from; it speaks of it as an appearance merely, a change of form. Otherwise it tries to understand death as altogether natural. In that event it does not know what to make of life ard finds itself compelled to deny immortality. In both cases it erases the boundary line between death and life, and between sin and holiness.

The confession that death is a payment for sin, although it is not proved by science, is not disproved by it either. It simply lies outside the pale of scientific investigation and beyond its reach. Moreover this confession does not need the evidence of science. It is based on the Divine testimony and is confirmed hour by hour in the fear of death by which men throughout their lives are subject to bondage (Heb. 2:15). Whatever, therefore, may be said in evidence of its necessity or in defense of its legitimacy, death remains unnatural. It is unnatural with a view to the essence and destiny of man, in connection with his creation after the image of God, for the fellowship with God is incompatible with death. God is not a God of the dead, but of the living (Matt. 22:32). On the contrary, death is altogether natural for fallen man, for sin, when it is finished, brings forth death (James 1:15). After all, in Holy Scripture, death is not to be equated with annihilation, any more than life includes nothing more than naked existence. Life is enjoyment, blessedness, superabundance, and death is misery, poverty, hunger, the want of peace and blessedness. Death is dissolution, separation, of what belongs together. Man, created in God's image, is at home in communion with God. There he lives, fully, eternally, blessedly. But when he severs that fellowship he dies in that same moment and continues always to die further. His life is deprived of joy, peace, and blessedness, and has become a dying in sin. And this spiritual death, this separation between God and man, continues in the body and culminates in eternal death. For, at the separation of body and soul, man's lot is determined, but his existence is not yet over. For it is appointed unto men once to die, and after that the judgment (Heb. 9:27).

And who can stand in that judgment?

XIV

The Covenant of Grace

To that question all mankind has at all times and in all places given the answer that men, such as they are, may not appear before the face of God nor dwell in His presence. There is no one who can say or dares to say: I have made my heart clean, I am pure from my sin (Prov. 20:9). Everybody feels himself to be guilty and defiled, and everybody acknowledges, if not to others, at least internally to himself, that he is not what he should be. The hardened sinner has moments in which restlessness and turmoil master him; and the self-righteous in the last instance always continue hoping that God will blink at what is lacking and accept the intent for the deed.

True, there are many who try to banish these serious thoughts from their minds and plunge into life as though there were no God and no commandment. They deceive themselves with the hope that there is no God (Ps. 14:1), that He does not bother about the sins of men, so that whoever does evil is good in His sight (Mal. 2:17), that He does not remember evil nor see it (Ps. 10:11 and 94:7), or else that, as perfect Love, He may not seek out and punish the wrong (Ps. 10:14). And whoever holds to the demand of the moral law and lets the ethical ideal stand in its loftiness, can only agree that God must punish the wrong. God is love, indeed, but this glorious confession comes into its own only when love in the Divine being is understood as being a holy love in perfect harmony with justice. There is room for the grace of God only if the justice of God is first fully established.

After all, the whole history of the world gives an irrefutable testimony to this justice of God. We cannot speculate out of the world the special revelation in Christ which tells us of the love of God; if we were to do that the general revelation with its benefits and blessings would be lost to us. But if we were, but for a moment, in our thoughts to leave the revelation in Christ to one side, there would remain very little ground for belief in a God of love. For if the history of the world clearly teaches us anything, it is this: that God has a quarrel with His creature. There is disagreement, separation, conflict between God and His world. God does not agree with man, and man does not agree with God. Each goes his own way, and each has his own idea and will about things. The thoughts of God are not our thoughts, and His ways are not our ways (Isa. 55:8).

Therefore the history of the world is also a judgment of the world. No, it is not as one poet has said, *the* judgment of the world, for that will come at the end of days, and it is not judgment alone for the earth is still full of the riches of God (Ps. 104:24). All the same, the history of the world is a judgment, a history full of judgments, full of struggle and war, of blood and tears, calamities and afflictions. Above it are written the words which Moses once spoke when he saw the race of the Israelites dying away before his eyes: We are consumed by thine anger, and by thy wrath are we troubled (Ps. 90:7).

This testimony of history to the justice of God is confirmed by the fact that mankind has always looked for, and still looks for, a lost Paradise, for a lasting bliss, and for a redemption from all evil that oppresses it. There is in all men a need for, and a seeking after, redemption. It is just this which specifically comes to expression in religion. True, one can take the word *redemption* in so large a sense that it includes all the labor which men do on the earth. For when man by the work of his hands tries to supply the needs of his life, when he tries to defend himself against all kinds of antagonistic forces in nature and among men, and when in science and art he strives to subdue the whole earth, all that has also the purpose of being liberated from evil and ushered into the good.

Nevertheless the concept of redemption is never applied to this kind of human labor. No matter how much such effort makes the life of man a pleasanter and richer thing, there lives in mankind a sense that all such progress and civilization does not satisfy for the deepest human needs nor rescue them from their worst distress. Redemption is a religious concept and is at home only in the sphere of religion. Religion preceded all culture and civilization, and right up to the present day religion continues to occupy its own position alongside of science, art, and technology. It cannot be supplanted or compensated for even by the magnificent results of human effort. Religion supplies a unique need in man, and its tendency after the fall is always to rescue him from a particular distress.

Hence the idea of redemption comes up in all religions.

It is true that sometimes religions are classified as natural, ethical, and redemptive religions. When that is done the redemptive kind is distinguished from the other two as a special kind. But such a classification is rightly disputed. In a general sense, the notion of redemption is proper to all religions. All the religions of the peoples want to be redemptive religions. There is difference about the nature of the evil from which redemption is wanted, about the way in which it can be obtained, and about the highest good that men should strive for. But all religions aim at the redemption from evil and at obtaining of the highest good. In religion the big question is always: What shall I do to be saved? Precisely that which cannot be obtained by culture or civilization, by a subduing and having dominion over the earth, precisely that is the thing sought for in religion: lasting happiness, eternal peace, perfect blessedness. In religion man is always concerned with God. True, in his sinful condition, man represents God to himself mistakenly, different from what He is, seeks Him with a wrong motivation and in the wrong way and the wrong place, but he does seek God, if haply he may feel after Him, and find Him (Acts 17:27).

This need for redemption, which is common to all humanity, and which seeks satisfaction in the many self-willed religions of the peoples, is in itself, and is for Christianity, of very great importance. For this need is continually aroused in the hearts of people and kept alive there by God Himself. It illustrates that God has not yet entirely left the human race to its own ways. It is an ineradicable hope, and it enables men on their long and fearful journey through the world to keep on living and working. And it serves as a guarantee and a prophecy of the fact that there is such a redemption, and that, whereas men seek it in vain, it is out of sheer mercy freely given of God.

*   *   *   *   *

In order to understand aright and to appreciate the better this great redemption which God's grace has prepared in Christ, it will be useful to pause a moment or two before the efforts which have been put forth by men, outside the pale of special revelation, to be delivered of evil and to come into possession of the highest good. The moment we do that we are struck by the great difference, and at the same time by the great uniformity, which characterizes all of these efforts.

The great difference comes out already in the large number of religions which have existed through the centuries, and which still exist, among men. Indeed, the number is greater than that of the nations and languages. Just as thorns and thistles come up out of the earth, the false religions grow up out of human nature. They grow up rank. They are so numerous and so different, that they can hardly be surveyed and are not susceptible to any satisfying classification. Inasmuch as religion occupies a central position, it takes on a different character according to how it views the relationship of God and the world, of nature and spirit, of freedom and necessity, destiny and guilt, history and culture. According to whether evil is regarded as positive or negative, as a permanent identity or a passing moment in the development of civilization, as being natural or moral, sensuous or spiritual in character, the idea of redemption changes, as does the way in which men seek to obtain it.

Still, when we try to peer into the essence of all these religions, they all seem to have all kinds of traits of similarity and relationship. In the first place every religion tries to comprehend a whole of ideas about God and the world, about spirits and men, about soul and body, and about the origin, essence, and purpose of things. Every religion brings with it a doctrine, a world and life view, a dogma. In the second place, no single religion is satisfied with a merely rational apprehension of these ideas, but urges men by means of those ideas and with their assistance to penetrate through to the supernatural world of God and spirits and to become united with them. Religion is never dogma and doctrine alone. It involves also the affection of the feelings, the attitude of the heart, and the enjoyment of the Divine favor. But men at all times and in all places know that this favor of the Godhead is not naturally theirs. On the one hand, men have a sense of the fact that they must have that favor if they are to obtain eternal happiness and the salvation of their souls; and, on the other hand, they feel just as profoundly that they lack this favor, and that because of their sins they do not have the fellowship with God. Hence, in every religion, a third constituent enters in, namely the effort in some way or other to obtain this favor and fellowship and to assure its continuance in the future. Every religion comes with a cluster of related ideas, tries to foster particular affections and feelings, and prescribes a series of practices.

These religious practices, in turn, are divided into two kinds. To the first class belong all those practices which can be subsumed under the term *worship* and which consist principally of religious assemblies, sacrifices, prayers, and songs. But religion never remains limited to these directly religious practices. Because religion occupies a central place in life, it saturates the whole of that life, and tries to bring it into line with itself. Every religion raises some ethical ideal aloft and proclaims a moral law according to which a person, in his personal, domestic, civic, and social life, too, must conduct himself. There are in every religion, ideas, feelings, and actions which are in part relevant to worship and in part to the moral life, and which may therefore be called both cultic and ethical.

There is not a single religion in which any of these constituent elements are missing. But there is a great deal of difference about the content that is contained in each of these elements, about the relationship in which they stand to each other, and about the worth which each of them has. Paul says that the essence of the heathendom of the Gentiles consists of this, that men have changed the glory of the uncorruptible God into an image made like to corruptible man, and to birds, and four-footed beasts, and creeping things. According to the extent that the Godhead is identified with the universe, with nature, with men or animals, the religious concepts change, and thence also the religious emotions and actions.

Three chief types can be distinguished. When the Divine is identified with the mysterious forces of nature, religion becomes denatured into gross superstition and fearful magic. Then soothsayers and magicians serve to provide men with power over the arbitrariness of invisible Divine beings. If the Divine is thought of as being like the human, the religion takes on a more humane character but all the same it falls easily into a ritualistic worship of forms or else into sheer moralism. And when the Divine is conceived of as the idea, the soul, or the substance of the world, the religion retreats from the appearance of things into the mysticism of the heart, and seeks fellowship with God by way of asceticism (withdrawal, abstinence) and ecstasy (spiritual transport). In the various religions, one or another of these chief forms comes to expression, but never to the point of mutually excluding the other. Redemption is always sought in the way of understanding and knowledge, of will and action, and of heart and emotions.

Philosophy enters into support of this. Philosophy, too, occupies itself with the idea of redemption and seeks for a world view which satisfies both the mind and the feelings. Philosophy came up out of religion, periodically takes elements from religion into its own system, and for many serves as a kind of religion. Despite all of its speculation and reflection, however, it does not come out at a point beyond the basic ideas of religion. The moment philosophy deduces a principle for the conduct of life from its world view, it tries to open up a way to redemption in the knowledge of the mind, the moral deeds of the will, and the experiences of the heart. Without special revelation the religion of men and the philosophy of thinkers do not have a right knowledge of God, and hence no right knowledge of man and the world, and of sin and redemption. Both do indeed seek after God, if, haply, they might seek and find Him, but find Him they do not.

*   *   *   *   *

Hence special revelation is added to the general revelation. In it God, on His own part, comes out into the open from His secret place, makes Himself known to man, and prepares Himself a dwelling place in man.

Between the self-conceived and self-willed religions, on the one hand, and the religion based on the special revelation to Israel and on Christ there is, consequently, a difference in principle. In the first it is always man who tries to find God, but who constantly shapes a false idea of Him and therefore never gets a true insight into the nature of sin and the way of redemption; but in the second, in the religion of the Holy Scriptures, it is always God who seeks man, who discloses man to himself in his guilt and impurity, but who also makes Himself known as He is in his grace and compassion. From the depths of the human heart there rises the plaint: Would that God would rend the heavens and come down. In Christianity the heavens do open, and God descends to the earth. In the other religions it is man whom we always see at work, trying by the achievement of knowledge, by keeping all kinds of rules, or by withdrawal from the world into the secrecy of his own inner life, to obtain redemption from evil and communion with God. In the Christian religion the work of men is nothing, and it is God Himself who acts, intervenes in history, opens the way of redemption in Christ and by the power of His grace brings man into that redemption and causes him to walk in it. Special revelation is the answer which God Himself gives in word and deed to the questions which through His own guidance arise in the human heart.

Immediately after the fall God already comes to man. Man has sinned and is seized upon by shame and fear. He flees his Creator and hides himself in the dense foliage of the garden. But God does not forget him. He does not let go of him, but condescends, seeks him out, talks with him, and leads him back to fellowship with Himself (Gen. 3:7-15).

And this thing that happened thus immediately after the fall, continues in history from generation to generation. We see the same thing happening again and again. In the whole work of redemption it is God and God alone who manifests Himself as the seeking and calling One, and as the speaking and acting One. The whole of redemption begins and ends in Him. It is He who puts Seth in the place of Abel (Gen. 4:25), who causes Noah to share in His favor (Gen. 6:8) and preserves him in the judgment of the flood (Gen. 6:12 ff.), who calls Abram and takes him up in His covenant (Gen. 12:1 and 17:1), who, out of grace alone, chooses the people of Israel as His inheritance (Deut. 4:20 and 7:6-8), who in the fulness of time sends His only-begotten Son into the world (Gal. 4:4), and who now in this dispensation out of the whole human race gathers a church which He has elected to eternal life, and who preserves them for the heavenly inheritance unto the end (Eph. 1:10 and 1 Peter 1:5). Just as in the work of creation and providence, so in the work of the redemption, the re-creation, God is also the alpha and the

omega, the first and the last, the beginning and the end (Isa. 44:6 and
Rev. 22:13). He can be no other and no less, for He is God: Of Him,
and through Him, and to Him are all things (Rom. 11:36).

That God is the first in the work of salvation is evident not only from
the fact that special revelation proceeds wholly from Him, but also is
clearly manifested in the fact that the whole of that redemptive work
depends upon an eternal counsel. We indicated previously that the
whole creation and providence of God comes up out of such a counsel.
But in Scripture we are told in (if possible) even clearer language and
in even stronger phrasing that such an eternal and immutable counsel
also lies at the basis of the whole work of redemption, of re-creation.

There is mention made at various points of Scripture of a counsel
which precedes things (Isa. 46:10), which works all things (Eph. 1:11),
and which has as its content especially the work of redemption (Luke
7:30 and Acts 20:27). This counsel is not a counsel of His mind only
but also of His almighty will (Eph. 1:5, 11), is unbreakable (Isa. 14:27
and 26:10), immutable (Heb. 6:17), and will stand forever (Ps. 33:11
and Prov. 19:21). Other names are also used, and shed further light on
the matter; besides *counsel,* we read of a *good pleasure* which God has
manifested to men in Christ (Luke 2:14), and which delights in their
being brought in and accepted as children of God (Eph. 1:5 and 9). We
read of a *purpose* which goes about the work of election (Rom. 9:11 and
Eph. 1:9), which is purposed in Christ Jesus (Eph. 3:11), and which
realizes itself in the calling of those who love God (Rom. 8:28). We
read, further, of an *election* and *foreknowledge* which has its source in
grace (Rom. 11:5) and which has Christ as its center (Eph. 1:4), particular persons as its object (Rom. 8:29), and their salvation as its purpose (Eph. 1:4). And, finally, we read of an *ordination* or *foreordina-
tion* which by means of the proclaiming of the wisdom of God (1 Cor.
2:7) culminates in the adoption of children by Jesus Christ to Himself
and in eternal life.[1]

When we gather all these data of Holy Scripture together it becomes
apparent that the counsel of God has especially three matters as its content.

The first is election, by which is meant that gracious purpose of God
according to which He ordained those whom He had before known in
love to be conformed to the image of Christ (Rom. 8:29). It is possible
also to speak of an election of peoples or nations, for in the days of the
Old Testament Israel alone among all the nations was chosen to be the
inheritance of the Lord; and in the New Testament dispensation one
people is acquainted with the Gospel much earlier than another. But

---

1. Acts 13:48; Rom. 8:29; and Eph. 1:5.

this acceptance of nations is not the whole scope of the Biblical election. As, within mankind, it extends to the nations, so, within the nations, it extends to individuals. An Esau is rejected and a Jacob is accepted (Rom. 9:13). And those whom God foreknew, those He also in time called, justified, and glorified (Rom. 8:30).

But, even though election has particular persons as its object, those persons are not the ground or basis of it. That basis is solely the grace of God. The Lord has mercy on whom He will have mercy, and compassion on whom He will have compassion; so then it is not of him who wills nor of him who runs, but of God who shows mercy (Rom. 9:15 and 16). Faith too does not avail here, for faith cannot be the condition or ground of election, inasmuch as it is rather the result or fruit of it. After all, that faith is a gift of God (Eph. 2:8). The believers are precisely elected in Christ from before the foundations of the world in order that in time they should arrive at the faith, and by faith should be holy and without blame before the face of God (Eph. 1:4). Consequently there are always so many who believe as are ordained unto eternal life by God (Acts 13:48). The will of God is for us the final ground of all that is and all that happens, and so, too, His good pleasure is the deepest cause to which the distinction in the eternal destiny of men can be traced.

In the second place, there is contained in the counsel of redemption the achievement of that whole salvation which God wants to grant to His elect. In the plan of redemption, not only the persons who are to inherit eternal salvation are indicated, but the Mediator who will prepare this salvation for them is also pointed out. To this extent Christ Himself can be called the object of God's election. Naturally He can be called this not in the sense that He, like the members of His church, was elected to come up out of a condition of sin and misery into a state of redemption and salvation. But He can be called that in this other meaning that He who was the Mediator of the creation would also be the Mediator of the re-creation, and would bring it about entirely by His passion and death. That is why He is called the servant of the Lord, the elect of God (Isa. 42 ff. and Matt. 12:18). As Mediator He is subordinate to the Father and obedient to Him.[2] He has a command and a work to fulfill which the Father has assigned to Him.[3] And as the reward for His finished work He receives His own glory, the salvation of His people, and the highest might in heaven and on earth.[4]

The counsel of redemption, therefore, goes on without the Son no more than does that of creation and redemption. We read in so many

---

2. Matt. 26:42; John 4:34; Phil. 2:8; and Heb. 5:8.
3. Isa. 53:10; John 6:38-40; 10:18; 12:49; and 17:4.
4. Ps. 2:8; Isa. 53:10; John 17:4, 24; and Phil. 2:9.

words that the eternal purpose was purposed in Christ Jesus (Eph. 3:11), and that those who arrive at faith in time are chosen in Christ before the foundation of the world (Eph. 1:4). That does not mean to say that Christ is the cause or foundation of the election, for He is Himself the object of the Father's electing in the sense delimited above, and cannot any more serve as the ground and cause of salvation than He can serve as these for creation and providence. But just as creation and providence, both as counsel and as reality, proceed from the Father through the Son and so come into being, so the plan of salvation is also made through the Father in and with the Son. Together with the Father He designates Himself as the Mediator of redemption and as the Head of His church. And from this we may infer that the election, even though it has particular persons as its object, rules out all possibility of accident or arbitrary choice. For the purpose of that election is not to pick up a few people at random, to bring them to salvation, and to let them stand loosely alongside of each other as single individuals. In His election God aims at nothing less than placing Christ the Mediator at the Head of His church, and to conform the church to the body of Christ.[5] In an organic sense it is mankind that is saved in the church, and in the new heaven and earth the world is restored.

Hence, in the third place, the working out and the application of the salvation wrought by Christ is also included in the counsel of God. The plan of redemption is established through the Father in the Son but it is established also in the fellowship of the Spirit. Certainly, just as creation and providence come into being from the Father through the Son and in the Spirit, so the redemption or re-creation takes place only through the applicatory activity of the Holy Spirit. It is the Spirit who is earned, promised, and sent by Christ (John 16:7 and Acts 2:4, 17), who testifies of Christ and receives everything from Christ (John 15:26 and 16:13, 14), and who now works regeneration in the church (John 3:3), faith (1 Cor. 12:3), the adoption (Rom. 8:15), the renewing (Titus 3:5), and the sealing unto the day of redemption (Eph. 1:13 and 4:30). And all this the Holy Spirit can work out and bring into being because, together with the Father and the Son, He is the one true God who lives and reigns eternally. The love of the Father, the grace of the Son, and the fellowship of the Holy Spirit are well founded for the people of the Lord in the eternal and immutable counsel of God.

* * * * *

This counsel of God, consequently, is also inexpressibly rich in comfort. It is often presented quite differently — that is, as a cause of dis-

---

5. 1 Cor. 12:12, 27; Eph. 1:22-23; and 4:16.

couragement and despair. It is said against this counsel that if everything is determined from eternity, man is a mere toy in the hands of Divine caprice. What good is it for a person to exert himself and to lead a virtuous life? If he is reprobate, rejected, he will be lost anyway. And — so the argument continues — what harm is it for a person to live in sin and to surrender to the most gruesome godlessness and immorality? If a person is elected, he will be saved anyway! Such a counsel of God leaves no room whatsoever for any freedom and responsibility of man. May he live then according to the dictates of his heart, and may he sin in order that grace may abound the more!

That the confession of the counsel of God has often been abused in this way is most certainly true. Nor has it been since Augustine and Calvin alone that this abuse has been practiced. It happened already in the days of Jesus and the apostles. For it is said of the Pharisees and scribes that they rejected the counsel of God against themselves which became apparent to them in the baptism of John, so that what should have served them as a means of conversion became in their hands an instrument for their doom (Luke 7:30). The apostle Paul calls it blasphemy when he is charged with lauding the doing of evil in order that good might come out of it (Rom. 3:8), and he puts a restraining hand on the mouth of puny man who dares find fault with God (Rom. 9:19-20). To do this Paul has the fullest right. For the counsel of God not only determines the results, but it also governs the means. It includes not merely the consequences, but also the causes. And it establishes just such relationships as are seen to exist in life itself. The counsel of God does not therefore annihilate the rational and moral nature of man, but creates it, rather, and guarantees it, and always to the same extent as history causes us to know it.

The abuse that is made of this confession is the more serious because the counsel of God is revealed and proclaimed in Holy Scripture, not so that we should deny the reality of it, and harden ourselves against it, but, on the contrary, so that we, sensing our guilt and helplessness, should depend upon that counsel of God with a childlike faith, and should in all distress and need put the full confidence of our whole heart into it. For if salvation to a greater or lesser extent depended upon man, upon his faith and his good works, then salvation would be eternally lost to him. But the counsel of God teaches us that the work of redemption is from beginning to end the work of God, that it is most uniquely the divine work. Redemption, quite as much as creation and providence, is solely the work of God. No man was His counsellor or gave to Him, so that it must be recompensed to him again (Rom. 11:34-35). Father, Son, and Holy Spirit together have thought out the whole work of redemption and have determined it, and they are the ones also who will carry it out and will complete it. Man does nothing in it. All things are of God, through Him, and unto Him. Hence our soul can rest in it with unperturbed certainty. It is God's will, his eternal, independent, and immutable will, that in the church mankind be restored and saved.

We are convinced of this comfort of election even more when we remember that the counsel of God is a work of His mind not merely, but also of His will, is not a thought merely which belongs to the realm of eternity but also an almighty power which realizes itself in time. So it is with all God's excellences and perfections : they are not passive, silent attributes, but are almighty powers, full of life and action. Every attribute is His being. When God is called the Righteous and the Holy, this implies that He reveals Himself as such also, and that He bears His justice in upon this world and the consciences of men and maintains it there. When He is called Love the implication is not merely that in Christ He looks upon us with approbation, but also that He manifests that love and pours it into our hearts through the Holy Spirit. When He calls Himself our Father, this carries with it also the implication that He regenerates us, adopts us as children, and by His Spirit testifies with our spirit that we are His children. When He makes Himself known as the Gracious and Merciful One, He does not merely say it, but demonstrates it also by in very fact forgiving our sins and comforting us in all afflictions. Just so, too, when Scripture speaks to us of the counsel of God, it thereby proclaims to us that God Himself executes that counsel and fully actualizes it. The counsel of redemption itself is a work of God in eternity, but as such it is also the principle, the motivating power, and the guarantee of the work of redemption in time. Therefore, regardless of what may happen with the world, with mankind, or with ourselves, the ever-wise counsel of God will forever stand and forever remain active. Nothing can ever deflect His high decision : it will remain from generation to generation. There is no ground whatsoever for discouragement or despair. Everything certainly shall be as God in His wisdom and love determined it. His almighty and gracious will is the guarantee of the redemption of mankind and the rescue of the world. In the great afflictions our hearts therefore remain at peace in the Lord.

*   *   *   *   *

As soon as man has fallen, therefore, the counsel of redemption begins to work. Quite on His own initiative God comes down, seeks man out, and calls him back to Himself. True, an investigation and a hearing takes place then, and a declaration of guilt and announcement of penalty. But the punishment pronounced upon the snake, the woman, and the man is at the same time a blessing and a means of preservation. After all, in the mother-promise (Gen. 3:14-15) the fact is not only that the snake was debased, and the evil power whose instrument it was stood condemned. It was also declared that from then on there would be enmity between the seed of the serpent and the seed of the woman, and that it is God Himself who calls this enmity into being and who will establish it. The culmination of this enmity and strife will be that the seed of the serpent will bruise the heel of the seed of the woman indeed, but nevertheless that the seed of the woman will bruise the head of the seed of the serpent.

In this mother-promise is contained nothing less than the announcement and institution of the covenant of grace. True, the word covenant is not named in this context. It is a word which can be used only later, in connection with Noah, Abraham, and others, when men have in their various struggles against nature, and against animals, and by the practical experience of life, come to know the necessity and usefulness of contracts and covenants. Nevertheless in principle and essence there is present in the mother-promise all that constitutes the meaning of the covenant of grace. By his transgression — such is that meaning — man has departed from obedience to God, has left His fellowship, and has sought out the friendship of Satan and entered into contract with him. And now God comes in His grace to break up this covenantal relationship between men and Satan, and to put enmity there instead of the friendship that has been concluded between them. By an almighty deed of His gracious will, God brings the seed of the woman, which the woman had surrendered to Satan, back to His own side. He adds to this the promise that the seed of the woman, despite many kinds of adversity and oppression, will nevertheless sometime gain the total victory over the seed of the serpent. There is nothing conditional and uncertain about this. God Himself comes to man, He Himself plants the enmity, He initiates the warfare, and He promises the victory. Man has no part in this except to listen to it and to accept it in childlike faith. Promise and faith are the content of the covenant of grace which is now set up for man, which disclose the way to the Father's house to this fallen and straying creature, and which gives access to the eternal salvation.

There is a big difference, therefore, between the way in which man before the fall was to share in the eternal life, and the way in which alone he can obtain it after the fall. Then the rule held: Do this and thou shalt live. By way of perfect obedience to God's command he was to set about inheriting eternal life. In itself that was a good way, which, had man but remained on it to the end, would with absolute certainty have led him to the heavenly salvation. And God has not, on His part, broken that rule. He still holds to it. If there were a man who could perfectly keep God's law, he would still receive eternal life as his reward.[6]

Man, however, made that way of salvation impossible for himself. He can no longer keep the law because he has broken the fellowship with God and no longer loves, but hates, His law (Rom. 8:7). And now the covenant of grace opens up for him a different and safer way. According to it man need no longer work to enter into life. According to it, man immediately at the beginning receives the eternal life, accepts it in childlike faith, and out of that faith proceeds to bring forth good works. The order is reversed. Before the fall the rule was: through works to eternal life. Now, after the fall, in the covenant of grace, the eternal life comes first, and out of that life the good works follow as fruits of faith. Before, man had to mount up to God, to full fellowship with Him; now, after the fall, God comes down to man and seeks a dwelling place in his heart. Then the working days preceded the Sabbath; now the Sabbath begins the week and hallows all its days.

Now that there is such a way to the heavenly sanctuary for fallen man, a fresh and newly laid way, an absolutely certain and rewarding way (Heb. 10:20), it is owing altogether to God's grace and to the counsel of redemption. The counsel of redemption, fixed in eternity, and the covenant of grace with which man is acquainted immediately after the fall, and which is then set up, stand in the closest of relationships with each other. They are so closely related that the one stands or falls with the other. There are many, it is true, who are committed to a different idea. These take their vantage point in the covenant of grace and from that position deny and attack the counsel of redemption. In the name of the purity of the Gospel they reject the confession of election. Actually they thus destroy the covenant of grace and convert the Gospel once more into a new law.

After all, when the covenant of grace is separated from election, it ceases to be a covenant of grace and becomes again a covenant of works. Election implies that God grants man freely and out of grace the salvation which man has forfeited and which he can never again achieve in his own strength. But if this salvation is not the sheer gift of grace but in some way depends upon the conduct of men, then the covenant of grace is converted into a covenant of works. Man must then satisfy some condition in order to inherit eternal life. In this, grace and works stand at opposite poles from each other and are mutually exclusive. If salvation is by grace it is no longer by works, or otherwise grace is no longer grace. And if it is by works, it is not by grace, or otherwise works are not works (Rom. 11:6). The Christian religion has this unique

---

6. Lev. 18:5; Ezek. 20:11, 13; Matt. 19:16 ff.; Rom. 10:5; and Gal. 3:12.

characteristic, that is *the* religion of redemption, sheer grace, pure religion. But it can be recognized and maintained as such only if it is a free gift coming up out of the counsel of God alone. So far from election and the covenant of grace forming a contrast of opposites, the election is the basis and guarantee, the heart and core, of the covenant of grace. And it is so indispensably important to cling to this close relationship because the least weakening of it not merely robs one of the true insight into the achieving and application of salvation, but also robs the believers of their only and sure comfort in the practice of their spiritual life.

A richer light is shed upon this relationship when the covenant of grace is seen in the context not exclusively of election but also of the whole counsel of redemption. Election is not the whole counsel of redemption, but is a part, the first and principal part, of it. Included and established in that counsel is also the way in which the election is to be actualized—in short, the whole accomplishment and application of redemption. We know that the election was purposed in Christ, and that the counsel of God is not merely a work of the Father but also a work of the Son and of the Holy Spirit. It is a Divine work of the Holy Trinity. In other words the counsel of redemption is itself a covenant — a covenant in which each of the three Persons, so to speak, receives His own work and achieves His own task. The covenant of grace which is raised up in time and is continued from generation to generation is nothing other than the working out and the impression or imprint of the covenant that is fixed in the Eternal Being. As in the counsel of God, so in history each of the Persons appears. The Father is the source, the Son is the Achiever, and the Holy Spirit is the one who applies our salvation. Hence everybody immediately and to the same extent does injustice to the work of the Father, the Son, or the Spirit, when he removes the foundation of eternity from time by loosening history from its anchorage in the gracious, almighty Divine Will.

* * * * *

All the same, though time cannot do without eternity, and although history stands in the closest relationship with God's thought, the two are not in every way the same. There is this big difference between them that in the history of time the eternal idea of God comes to be revealed and actualized. The counsel of redemption and the covenant of grace cannot and may not be separated, but they differ from each other in this respect, that the second is the actualization of the first. The plan of redemption is not enough in itself. It needs to be carried out. As a decision, it carries its implementation and actualization within itself, and itself brings these about. It would even lose its character as counsel and decision if it did not in time achieve realization and manifestation. And so it happens. Immediately after the fall, the covenant of grace is made known to man and is concluded with him, and thereupon it continues itself in history from generation to generation. The thing that is one thing in the decision unfolds itself in the breadth of the world and develops itself in the course of the centuries.

When we give our attention to this historical development of the covenant of grace, we detect a trio of remarkable characteristics in it.

In the first place, the covenant of grace is everywhere and at all times one in essence, but always manifests itself in new forms and goes through differing dispensations. Essentially and materially it remains one, whether before, or under, or after the law. It is always a covenant of grace. It is called this because it issues from the grace of God, has grace as its content, and has its final purpose in the glorification of God's grace.

Just as it was in its very first announcement, which fixed the enmity, began the struggle, and promised the victory, so God remains the first and the last in all the dispensations of the covenant of grace, whether of Noah, Abraham, Israel, or the New Testament church. Promise, gift, grace are and remain the content of it. In the course of time what is included in it is much more plainly unfolded, and it becomes more apparent how rich the content of the covenant is. But in principle it is all already contained in the mother-promise. The one, great, all-inclusive promise of the covenant of grace is: I will be thy God, and the God of thy people. That is comprehensive and includes everything, the whole accomplishment and application of salvation, Christ and his benefits, the Holy Spirit and all His gifts. A single straight line runs from the mother-promise of Genesis 3:15 to the apostolic blessing of 2 Corinthians 13:13. In the love of the Father, the grace of the Son, and the fellowship of the Holy Spirit is contained the whole of salvation for the sinner.

We have to note particularly therefore that this promise is not conditional, but is as positive and certain as anything can be. God does not say that He will be our God if we do this or that thing. But He says that He will *put* enmity, that He *will* be our God, and that in Christ He *will* grant us all things. The covenant of grace can throughout the centuries remain the same because it depends entirely upon God and because God is the Immutable One and the Faithful One. The covenant of works which was concluded with man before the fall was violable and it was violated, for it depended upon changeable man. But the covenant of grace is fixed and established solely in the compassion of God. People can become unfaithful, but God does not forget His promise. He cannot and may not break His covenant; He has committed Himself to maintaining it with a freely given and precious oath: His name,

His honor, and His reputation depends on it. It is for His own sake that He obliterates the transgressions of His people and remembers their sins no more.[7] Therefore the mountains may depart and the hills be removed, but His kindness will not depart from us, nor shall the covenant of His peace be removed, says the Lord who has mercy on us (Isa. 54:10).

However unchangeable the covenant of grace is in its essence, it changes in its forms, and takes several shapes in the several dispensations. In the period before the great flood a separation had also taken place between the Sethites and the Canaanites, but the promise all the same had not yet been confined to one person and race. It spread itself out over all men. A formal separation had not yet taken place; general and special revelation still flowed in the same river-bed. But when in that circumstance the promise threatened to be lost, the flood became necessary, and Noah took the promise with him in the ark. Even then the promise continued for a long time to be general. But when, after the flood, a new danger arises for the progress of the covenant of grace, then God no longer extirpates men, but lets the people go their own ways, and segregates Abraham to be the bearer of the promise. The covenant of grace finds its realization then in the families of the patriarchs. These families are separated from the other nations by circumcision as a seal of righteousness, and by faith as a sign of the circumcision of the heart.

At Sinai the covenant of grace is established with Israel as the seed of Abraham. But, since Israel is a nation or people, and must live before the face of God as a holy people, the covenant of grace now assumes a national form and character. It makes use now of the law, not merely of the moral law, but also of all kinds of civic and ceremonial laws, in order thus, as a schoolmaster or disciplinarian, to lead the people to Christ. The promise was older than the law, and the law did not come in the stead of the promise, but was added to the promise, precisely in order to bring it further development and to prepare it for its fulfillment in the fulness of time. In Christ the promise gets its fulfillment, the shadow its body, the letter the spirit, and servitude its freedom. As such the promise makes itself free of all external, national boundaries, and, as at the beginning, it spreads itself out again over the whole of mankind.

Irrespective, however, of the forms in which the covenant of grace manifests itself, it always has the same essential content. It is always the same Gospel (Rom. 1:2 and Gal. 3:8), the same Christ (John 14:6

7. Isa. 43:25; 48:9; and Jer. 14:7, 21.

and Acts 4:12), the same faith (Acts 15:11 and Rom. 4:11), and always confers the same benefits of forgiveness and eternal life (Acts 10:43 and Rom. 4:3). The light by which the believers travel differs, but their route is always the same.

The second peculiarity or remarkable characteristic of the covenant of grace is that in all of its dispensations it has an organic character.

Election fixes the attention on particular, individual persons, who have been known of God beforehand and therefore are in time called, justified, and glorified, but it does not yet in itself indicate the relationship between these persons. But Scripture tells us further that election took place in Christ (Eph. 1:4 and 3:11), and therefore went into operation in such a way that Christ could appear as Head of His church, and the church could form the body of Christ. The elect, accordingly, do not stand loosely alongside of each other, but are one in Christ. Just as in the days of the Old Testament the people of Israel were a holy people of God, so the church of the New Testament is a chosen generation, a royal priesthood, a holy nation, a peculiar people (1 Peter 2:9). Christ is the Bridegroom, and the church is His bride; He is the vine, and they are the branches; He is the Cornerstone, and they are the living stones of God's building; He is the King, and they are the subjects. So intimate is the unity between Christ and His church that Paul comprises both of them in the name of Christ: For as the body is one, and has many members, and all the members of that one body, being many, are one body: so also is Christ (1 Cor. 12:12). It is one communion or fellowship, endeavoring to keep the unity of the Spirit in the bond of peace. There is one body and one spirit, even as they are called in one hope of their calling: One Lord, one faith, one baptism, one God and Father of all, who is above all, and through all, and in them all (Eph. 4:3-6).

Thus the election cannot have been an arbitrary or accidental deed. If it was governed by the purpose of constituting Christ a Head and the church His body, then it has an organic character and already includes the idea of a covenant.

But in the testimony that the election was purposed or done in Christ something further is indicated. After all, the organic unity of the human race under one head becomes apparent first of all not in Christ, but in Adam. Paul expressly calls Adam an example of those who should come (Rom. 5:14) and he calls Christ the last Adam (1 Cor. 15:45). In this the covenant of grace seems to have the basic ideas and lines of the covenant of works; it is not the discarding but the fulfillment, rather, of that covenant, just as faith does not make the law of no effect but rather confirms it (Rom. 3:21). On the one hand, as was indicated above, the covenant of works and that of grace are very sharply to be distinguished from each other; on the other, they are very intimately related. The big difference consists of this: that Adam has forfeited his place at the head of the human race, and lost it, and that he has been supplanted by Christ. Christ, however, takes upon Himself the fulfillment not only of what the first man has done amiss but also of what he should have done and did not do; He satisfies for us the demands made by the moral law; and He now gathers together into one unit His whole church in the form of a renewed humanity under Himself as Head. In the dispensation of the fulness of times, God gathers everything in one again in Christ — all things in heaven and on earth (Eph. 1:10).

Such a gathering can take place only in an organic way. If the covenant of grace itself is thought of as organic in Christ then it must also be organically set up and continued. Hence we observe that in history the covenant is never concluded with one discrete individual, but always with a man and His family or generation, with Adam, Noah, Abraham, Israel, and with the church and its seed. The promise never concerns a single believer alone, but in him his house or family also. God does not actualize His covenant of grace by picking a few people out of humanity at random, and by gathering these together into some sort of assemblage alongside of the world. Rather He bears His covenant into mankind, makes it part and parcel of the world, and sees to it that in the world it is preserved from evil. As the Redeemer or Re-Creator, God follows the line which He drew as Creator, Sustainer, and Ruler of all things. Grace is something other and higher than nature, but it nevertheless joins up with nature, does not destroy it but restores it rather. Grace is not a legacy which is transferred by natural birth, but it does flow on in the river-bed which has been dug out in the natural relationships of the human race. The covenant of grace does not ramble about at random, but perpetuates itself, historically and organically, in families, generations, nations.

A third and final characteristic of the covenant of grace goes paired with the second, namely, that it realizes itself in a way which fully honors man's rational and moral nature. It is based on the counsel of God, yes, and nothing may be subtracted from that fact. Behind the covenant of grace lies the sovereign and omnipotent will of God, which is penetrated by Divine energy, and which therefore guarantees the triumph of the kingdom of God over the whole power of sin.

But that will is not a necessity, a destiny, which imposes itself on man from without, but is, rather, the will of the Creator of heaven and earth, One who cannot repudiate His own work in creation or providence, and who cannot treat the human being He has created as though it were a stock or stone. Further, that will is the will of a merciful and kind Father, who never forces things with brute violence, but successfully counters all our resistance by the spiritual might of love. The will of God is not a blind, irrational force: it is *will,* wise, gracious, loving, and at the same time free and omnipotent *will.* Therefore God works indeed in conflict with our darkened understanding and our sinful will, so that Paul can say of the Gospel that it is *not after man,* not in correspondence with the foolish insights and errant desires of fallen man (Gal. 1:11). But it is so that the will of God must act, precisely because He wants to deliver us from all the error of sin and to restore our rational and moral nature in its wholeness and soundness.

This accounts for the fact that the covenant of grace, which really makes no demands and lays down no conditions, nevertheless comes to us in the form of a commandment, admonishing us to faith and repentance (Mark 1:15). Taken by itself the covenant of grace is pure grace, and nothing else, and excludes all works. It gives what it demands, and fulfills what it prescribes. The Gospel is sheer good tidings, not demand but promise, not duty but gift. But, in order that as promise and gift it may be realized in us, it takes on the character of moral admonishment in accordance with our nature. It does not want to force us, but it wants nothing other than that we freely and willingly accept in faith what God wants to give us. The will of God realizes itself in no other way than through our reason and our will. That is why it is rightly said that a person, by the grace He receives, himself believes and himself turns from sin to God.

Inasmuch as the covenant of grace enters into the human race in this historical and organic manner, it cannot here on earth appear in a form which fully answers to its essence. Not only does there remain much in the true believers which is diametrically opposed to a life in harmony with the demand of the covenant: Walk before My face, and be upright; be holy for I am holy. But there can also be persons who are taken up into the covenant of grace as it manifests itself to our eyes and who nevertheless on account of their unbelieving and unrepentant heart are devoid of all the spiritual benefits of the covenant. That is the case now not only, but has been so throughout all ages. In the days of the Old Testament by no means all were Israel which were of Israel (Rom. 9:6), for it is not the children of the flesh but the children of the promise that are counted for the seed (Rom. 9:8 and 2:29). And in the New Testament church there is chaff in the grain, evil branches on the vine, and earthen as well as golden vessels.[8] There are people who display a form

8. Matt. 3:12; 13:29; John 15:2; and 2 Tim. 2:20.

of godliness, but who deny the power thereof (2 Tim. 3:5).

On the basis of this conflict between essence and appearance, some have tried to make a distinction and a separation between an internal covenant, which was made exclusively with the true believers, and an external covenant, comprehending the external confessors. But such a separation and difference cannot stand in the light of the Scriptural teaching. What God has joined together, no man may put asunder. No one may take away from the demand that being and appearance answer to each other and from the demand that confessing with the mouth and believing with the heart shall correspond (Rom. 10:9). But, even though there are no two covenants standing loosely alongside of each other, it can be said that there are two sides to the one covenant of grace. One of these is visible to us; the other also is perfectly visible to God, and to Him alone. We have to keep to the rule that we cannot judge of the heart, but only of the external conduct, and even of that defectively. Those who, as the human eye sees them, are walking in the way of the covenant must according to the judgment of love be regarded and treated as our fellows in grace. But in the final analysis it is not our judgment, but God's, that determines. He is the Knower of hearts and the Trier of the reins. With Him there is no respecting of persons. Man looks on the outward appearance but God looks on the heart (1 Sam. 16:7).

Let everyone, therefore, examine himself, whether he be in the faith, whether Jesus Christ be in him (2 Cor. 13:5).

XV

The Mediator of the Covenant

The counsel of redemption is not a human enterprise whose carrying out depends upon all kinds of unforeseen circumstances and is therefore highly uncertain. It is a counsel which is carried out with absolute certainty, because it is the decision of God's gracious and almighty will. As it was fixed in eternity, so it will be carried out in time. All that the doctrine of faith has still to treat, therefore, is the way in which the immutable counsel of the Lord concerning the salvation of His humankind is implemented and applied. And since that counsel was concerned mainly with three big issues, namely, the Mediator by whom the salvation had to be earned, the Holy Spirit by whom it had to be applied, and the people to whom it had to be given, this instruction in the Christian faith must in what follows also address itself to those three matters.

It must deal first with the person of Christ who by His passion and death is to achieve salvation. Next, it must point out the way in which the Holy Spirit causes the elect to share in the person of Christ and in all His benefits. And in the third place it must give some attention to the people who come to share in the salvation wrought by Christ, and must treat of the church as the body of Christ.

Finally, the instruction will naturally culminate in the fulfillment of the salvation which hereafter awaits the believers. The whole treatment will show that the counsel of redemption in all its parts is well ordained and secured. The unspeakable grace, the manifold wisdom, and the almighty power of God are made manifest in it.

In the person of Christ all of these excellences or attributes immediately become plain. It is true that belief in a mediator is not peculiar to Christendom. All men and all nations live with a sense not only of the fact that they do not share in salvation, but they all also have the conviction in their heart that this salvation must be pointed out and given to them in some way or other by specific persons. The thought is generally widespread that man as he is cannot approach God nor dwell in His presence; he requires a go-between to disclose the way to Deity for him. In all religions, therefore, mediators are found who, on the one hand, make

Divine revelations known to men, and, on the other, convey the prayers and the gifts of men to the Deity.

Sometimes lower gods or spirits serve as such mediators, but often, too, they are men gifted with supernatural knowledge and power and standing in a particular aura of holiness. In the religious life of the nations they take an important place, and on all important occasions in private and public life, such as calamities, wars, illnesses, enterprises, and the like, they are consulted. Be it as soothsayers or magicians, as saints or priests, they point out the way which, as they suppose, men must take to share in the favor of the Deity, but they are not themselves that way. The religions of the nations are independent of the persons of the mediators. This holds true even of the religions founded by particular persons. Buddha and Confucius, Zarathustra and Mohammed are indeed the first confessors of the religion founded by each of them, but they are not themselves the content of such religion. Their connection with it is in a sense accidental and external. Their religion could remain the same even though their name should be forgotten or their persons be supplanted by others.

In Christianity, however, all this is very different. True, the idea has sometimes been expressed that Christ, too, never wanted to be the sole Mediator, and that He would gladly acquiesce in the neglect of His name, if only His principle and Spirit lived on in the church. But others, who have themselves cut off all connection with Christianity, have in an impartial way attacked this idea and have refuted it. Christianity stands in a very different relationship to the person of Christ than the other religions do to the persons who founded them. Jesus was not the first confessor of the religion named after His name. He was not the first and the most important Christian. He occupies a wholly unique place in Christianity. He is not in the usual sense of it the founder of Christianity, but He is the Christ, the One who was sent by the Father, and who founded His Kingdom on earth and now extends and preserves it to the end of the ages. Christ is Himself Christianity. He stands, not outside, but inside of it. Without His name, person, and work there is no such thing as Christianity. In one word, Christ is not the one who points the way to Christianity, but the way itself. He is the only, true, and perfect Mediator between God and men. That which the various religions in their belief in a mediator have surmised and hoped, that is actually and perfectly fulfilled in Christ.

*   *   *   *   *

In order to appreciate fully this unique significance of Christ, we must proceed from the idea of the Scriptures that Christ began to exist, unlike us, at His conception and birth, but centuries before — in fact, that from eternity He was the only-begotten and beloved Son of the Father. In the Old Testament already the Messiah is designated as the Father of eternity who is an eternal Father for His people (Isa. 9:6), and as one whose goings forth (origin and source) have been from of old, from everlasting (Micah 5:2). The New Testament carries on that idea, but gives even clearer expression to the eternity of Christ. It is implied in all those passages in which the whole earthly work of Christ is presented as the fulfillment of a work which was laid upon Him by God. True, it is said of John the Baptist also that He had to come and did come as a second Elijah (Mark 9:11-13 and John 1:7). But the emphasis put upon the fact that Christ came into the world to fulfill His work, and the number of times this is said, point to the truth that this expression is used in a special sense.

We do not read in a general sense only that He went out from the Father in order to preach (Mark 1:38), that He came in order to call sinners to repentance and to give His soul as a ransom for many (Mark 2:17 and 10:45). Something else is added. It is expressly said also that He is sent out for the preaching of the Gospel (Luke 4:43), that it is the Father who has sent Him (Matt. 10:40 and John 5:24 ff.), that He has proceeded from the Father and has come in His name (John 5:43; 8:42, and elsewhere), that He came down from heaven and came into the world.[1] Thus Jesus knows Himself to be the only Son who was beloved of the Father and was sent out into the vineyard after all the other servants (Mark 12:6). He who was the Son of David was already David's Lord (Mark 12:37), was before Abraham (John 8:58), and had glory with the Father before the world was (John 17:5 and 24).

This self-awareness of Jesus concerning His eternal existence is more specifically unfolded in the apostolic witness. In Christ that eternal Word which at the beginning was with God and itself was God became flesh (John 1:1 and 14). He was the brightness of His glory, and the express image of His person, who stands higher than all the angels not only but can lay claim to their worship also, who is an eternal God and an eternal King, who always remains the same and whose years shall not fail (Heb. 1:3-13). He was rich (2 Cor. 8:9), found Himself in the form of God so that He was like the Father not only in essence, but also in form, status, and glory. He regarded this equality with God not as something which He should keep and use for Himself (Phil. 2:6), but instead He laid it aside to put on the form of a man and a servant (Phil. 2:7 and 8), and in that way was exalted to the Lord who was from heaven and as such was a contrast to Adam, the man of the earth

---

1. John 3:13; 6:38; 12:46; and 18:37.

(1 Cor. 15:47). In one word, Christ, just as the Father, is the Alpha and the Omega, the first and the last, the beginning and the end (Rev. 1:11, 17; and 22: 13).

Hence the activity of this incarnate Son of God did not begin only at His appearance upon the earth, but goes back to the creation. By the Word were all things without exception made (John 1:3 and Heb. 1:2 and 10). He is the firstborn, the head, the beginning of every creature (Col. 1:15 and Rev. 3:14). He *is* before all things (Col. 1:17). Creatures are made through him not only, but they consist by Him also (Col. 1:17) and are from moment to moment upheld by the word of His power (Heb. 1:3). And they are also created *for* Him (Col. 1:16), for God appointed Him, who was the Son, as the heir of all things (Heb. 1:2 and Rom. 8:17). Hence from the very beginning there is a close relationship between the Son and the world and an even closer one between the Son and men. For in Him was life, the full, rich, inexhaustible life, the source of all life in the world, but that light was for men who were created after the image of God, and were in possession of a rational, moral nature, a source of Divine truth which men had to know and regard (John 1:14). It is true that man by sin then became darkness, but the light of the Word nevertheless shone in that darkness (John 1:5), it lightened every man that came into the world (John 1:9), for the Word was and remained in the world, and continued working in the world, although it was not known by that world (John 1:10).

The Christ who appears on earth in the fulness of time is therefore, according to the account which Holy Scripture gives of Him, not a man as other men are, not a founder of a religion and a preacher of a new moral law. His position is unique. He was from eternity as the only-begotten of the Father. He was the Creator, Sustainer, and Governor of all things. In Him was the life and the light of men. When He appears in the world, He comes to it not as a stranger, but as its Lord, as one who is related to it. The redemption or re-creation is related to the creation, grace to nature, the work of the Son to the work of the Father. Redemption is built on foundations laid in creation.

* * * * *

The significance of Christ becomes even plainer to us if we study its relationship to Israel. There was a certain indwelling and inworking of the Word (the Logos) in the whole world and in all men. But even though the Light shone in the darkness, the darkness did not comprehend it, and although the Word was in the world, the world did not know it (John 1:5 and 10). But the Word stood in a far closer relationship to Israel, for of all nations Israel was the nation accepted as His inheritance, and therefore it can in John 1:11 be called the property of the Word, which was with God in the beginning and which itself was God. Israel was "His own," and He was among Israel not as among other men. He *came* to Israel deliberately and after centuries of preparation. According to the flesh Christ is from the fathers (Rom. 9:5). And it is true that He was rejected of "His own" — of the world we read that it did not know Him, but of the Jews the statement is much stronger, namely, that they did not receive Him, that they despised, and rejected Him — but His coming was not therefore in vain, for as many as received Him obtained power to become the sons of God (John 1:12).

When in John 1:11 we read of the Word that He came to His own, the reference is without doubt to the incarnation, to the coming of Christ in the flesh. But the statement implies all the same that the relationship of ownership existing between the Word and Israel came into existence not first of all through and after the incarnation but had already obtained long before. Israel was His own and therefore He came to His own in the fulness of time. In the same moment in which Jehovah accepted Israel as His own that people stood in a particular relationship also to the Word (the Logos). He is after all Himself the Lord whom Israel sought, the Angel of the covenant who was suddenly to come to His temple (Mal. 3:1), and who had lived and worked in Israel from of old. In many places in the Old Testament we read of that Angel of the Covenant or Angel of the Lord. As was pointed out in connection with the doctrine of the Trinity, it is by that Angel that the Lord reveals Himself to His people in a special way. Although He is distinguished from the Lord, this Angel is nevertheless so much one with Him, that the same names, characteristics, works, and honor can be given Him as are given God Himself. This Angel is the God of Bethel (Gen. 31:13), the God of the fathers (Ex. 3:2 and 6) who promised Hagar the multiplying of her seed (Gen. 16:10 and 21:18), who led and delivered the patriarchs (Gen. 48:15 and 16), who rescued the people of Israel from Egypt and safely conducted them to Canaan.[2] The Angel of the covenant gives Israel the assurance that the Lord Himself is in her midst as a God of redemption and salvation (Isa. 63:9). His appearing was a preparation and heralding of that perfect self-revelation of God which was to take place in the fulness of time in the incarnation. The whole Old Testament dispensation was an always closer approximation of God to His people. It ends in Christ's living eternally in their midst (Ex. 29:43-46).

This teaching of the nature and activity of the Word, before it appeared in Christ in the flesh, is of the highest importance for a right interpreta-

---

2. Ex. 3:8; 14:21; 23:20; and 33:14.

tion of the history of mankind and for a true view of the people and the religion of Israel. For thus it is possible to acknowledge all the true, and the good, and the beautiful which can still be encountered in the pagan world, and at the same time to maintain the special revelation which was given the people of Israel. While the Word and the wisdom of God was operative in the whole world, it manifested itself in Israel as the Angel of the Covenant, as the manifestation of the name of the Lord. In the Old and New Testament the covenant of grace is one. The believers of the Old Testament are saved in no other way than we are, nor are we saved in any other way than they. It is the same belief of the promise, the same reliance on the grace of God which grants the access to salvation then and now. And the same benefits of forgiveness and regeneration, of renewal and eternal life were then given to the believers and are now given them. They all walk on the same way, be it that the light which falls upon the believers of the Old and New Testaments differs in brightness.

Another important detail goes coupled with this, however. Paul says of the Ephesians that formerly, when they still lived as heathen, they were without Christ, aliens from the covenants of the promise, having no hope and without God in the world (Eph. 2:11-12). In other words, they lived in a very different condition from that of the Jews before the coming of Christ. For they had no promise of God to which they could cling. They lived without hope in the world, and they had no God for their heart whom they could know and serve. Naturally, the apostle does not mean to say by this that the heathen did not believe in any gods, for he says elsewhere, of the Athenians for instance, that they were religious in all things, and he speaks of a revelation which God permitted to come in part to them also (Acts 17:24 ff. and Rom. 1:19 ff.). But, though they knew God, they did not glorify Him as God, neither were thankful; they became vain in their imagination and served gods which by nature are not gods (Rom. 1:21 ff. and Gal. 4:8). And just so Paul does not deny that the heathen entertain all kinds of expectations concerning the future both on this and on the other side of the grave, but he gives expression to the thought that all those expectations, as well as the gods that were being served, are vain for the reason that no firm, indubitable promise of God in Christ lies at the basis of them.

This was different in Israel. To this people God entrusted His words (Rom. 3:2). He adopted them as children, lived with His glory in their midst, gave them successive dispensations of the Covenant in the form of the law, of worship, and particularly in those promises which looked to the coming of the Messiah and pointed to Him as issuing from Israel according to the flesh (Rom. 9:4-5). But even though Christ, so far as the flesh is concerned, is from the fathers, He is more than man. He is God, to be praised forever above all things (Rom. 9:5), and He existed and worked also in the days of the Old Testament. The Christians in Ephesus, so long as they were pagans, lived without Christ, but the Israelites of old, on the other hand, were related to Christ, that is, to the promised Christ, who as Mediator existed then too and was active. He was active in the dispensation of His benefits, but active in this, too, that He by word and prophecy and history prepared for His own coming in the flesh and threw over the whole people of Israel His heralding shadow. It was the shadow of the body of those spiritual goods which He Himself should in the fulness of time achieve and present.

The apostle Peter speaks plainly and clearly in this same way in the first chapter of his first letter. When he treats there the subject of the great salvation which in principle the believers share even now, and which for the rest they may fully expect in the future, he demonstrates the glory of that salvation by particularly remarking that the prophets of the Old Testament made it the object of their study and reflection. After all, all prophets had this in common that they prophesied of the grace which now in the days of the New Testament is being granted the believers. They received knowledge of this by revelation, but this revelation did not make them passive. Rather it put them, so to speak, to work themselves. The revelation stimulated them and aroused them to study and investigate industriously themselves, not after the manner of the philosophers, who by their own reason tried to understand the mysteries of creation, but as holy men of God, who made the special revelation, the future salvation in Christ, the object of their research. In such study they were guided not by their own thoughts but permitted themselves to be led by the Spirit of God. The matter which they investigated and on which they did their research was at what time and what kind of time the Spirit of Christ who was in them would by His preliminary testimony acquaint them with the suffering which Christ must undergo, and the glory which would await Him later (1 Peter 1:10-11). It was Christ Himself who in the Old Testament gave His Spirit to the prophets, and so heralded and foreshadowed through that Spirit His own coming and work. The testimony of Jesus in the hearts of His own concerning Himself is evidence of the fact that they possess the Spirit of prophecy (Rev. 19:10).

By the testimony of this Spirit Israel arrived at those rich and glorious hopes which are summed up under the name of Messianic expectations.

*   *   *   *   *

These Messianic hopes or expectations are usually classified into two groups. To the first group belong those expectations which in general have a bearing upon the future of the Kingdom of God. These, too, are of great importance, and stand in the closest possible relationship to the covenant of grace. Certainly that promise implies that God will be the God of His people and of their seed. It is relevant therefore not only to the past and present but also to the future. It is true that this people repeatedly makes itself guilty of disloyalty, falling away, and a breach of the covenant over against the Lord. But precisely because it is a covenant of *grace,* the disloyalty, the unfaithfulness, of the people can do nothing to invalidate the faithfulness of God. The covenant of grace is from the nature of the case an eternal covenant which reproduces itself from generation to generation. When, therefore, the people do not walk in the way of the covenant, God can for a while abandon it, subject it to chastisement, judgment, or captivity, but He cannot violate His covenant, for it is a covenant of grace which does not depend on the conduct of men, but rests solely in God's compassion. He cannot destroy the covenant, for His own name, and glory, and honor would be involved. After the demonstration of wrath, consequently, His kindness invariably shines through, and after the judgment comes the mercy, after the suffering the glory.

In all this Israel in the course of the centuries was instructed by prophecy. Through prophecy it obtained an insight into the essence and purpose of history such as we encounter among no other people. The Old Testament makes it clear to us that the coming into its own, the realization, of the will of God, that the kingdom of God, is the content and course and end of history. It is His counsel, His counsel of favor and redemption, which exists in eternity and which will conquer all resistance. Beyond the suffering lies the glory, and beyond the cross the crown. God will sometime triumph over all His enemies and will cause His people to share in the fulfillment of all His promises. A kingdom of righteousness and peace is coming, of spiritual and material well-being. And Israel will share in the glory of that kingdom, but also the other nations. For the unity of God carries with it the unity of mankind and the unity of history. Then the earth will be full of the knowledge of the Lord and then the promise of the covenant reaches the perfect fulfillment: I will be a God unto thee, and ye shall be my sons and daughters.

The prophecies and psalms are full of these hopes. Nor is that all. They go on to tell of the *way* in which the kingdom of God will in the future be established and fulfilled. Then these hopes become the Messianic expectations in the narrower sense, and they tell us how the rule of God on earth will in the future be determined by one specific person,

by the Messiah, and will by Him be effected. It is true that some in
our time have tried to separate all these Messianic expectations from the
original religion of Israel, and to transfer them to the time of the captivity. But this is a position which is vigorously attacked and satisfactorily refuted by others. The Messianic hopes all move around two ideas :
the day of the Lord, which will be a day of judgment for the peoples
and for Israel ; and the Messiah who thereupon will bring the redemption to pass. And both of these ideas are not ideas first entertained by
the prophets of the eighth century, but existed long before this time and
were, rather, more specifically worked out by the prophets whose books
are preserved to us.

Scripture itself tells us as much by tracing the expectations of the
future back to the oldest times. Naturally they then still have a general
character but that fact serves precisely as proof of their age, and the
gradual development which thereupon can be distinguished in these expectations serves as powerful reinforcing evidence. In the mother-
promise of Genesis 3:15 enmity is put between the seed of the woman
and the seed of the serpent, and there the promise is made that the first
will bruise the head of the other. By the seed of the woman we are to
think, along with Calvin, first of all of the human race, which, returned
to God's side by the covenant of grace, must engage in attack upon all
power antagonistic to God, and which in Christ receives its Head and
Lord. History demonstrates that this human race which is conducting
warfare against the seed of the snake by no means comprises all peoples,
but is more and more becoming delimited and confined. The promise
maintains itself only in the line of Seth.

When the first mankind has been destroyed by the flood, a separation
soon enters into the family between Ham and Japheth on the one hand
and Shem on the other. And the promise is now particularized in such a
way that Jehovah becomes the God of Shem, that Japheth is enlarged
greatly and later comes to live in the tents of Shem, and Canaan is their
servant (Gen. 9:26-27). Later when the pure knowledge and worship
of God again threatens to become lost, Abraham is chosen out of the
generation of Shem, and he is given the promise that he, blessed of the
Lord, will be a blessing to many, in fact, that all the generations of the
earth will greatly desire and seek the blessing which God grants to
Abraham and his seed, and thus they all will be blessed in Him, that is,
in Abraham's seed (Gen. 12:2-3). Among the sons of Jacob and the
tribes of Israel Judah is later designated as the one who will enjoy
status above that of all his brothers. In accordance with his name he
became the praised one (Gen. 29:35) and mighty one among his brethren (1 Chron. 5:2). They laud and praise him and his enemies subject

themselves to him; and this rule of Judah will last until one comes whom the peoples will obey (Gen. 49:8-10). The name Shiloh in verse 10 of Genesis 49 is hard to understand and is variously interpreted, but the idea of a blessing being spoken over Judah is very plain nevertheless. Judah has first place among all the tribes of Israel; he has lordship over his brothers, and out of him comes the future ruler of nations.

This promise was fulfilled incipiently in David, and in him passes over into a new phase of development. For when David had received rest from all his enemies, the plan arose in his mind to build the Lord a house. But instead of David building the Lord a house, the Lord has him informed by the mouth of Nathan that He will make David a house by making the royal line hereditary in his generation. The Lord will make David's name great as that of the mighty on earth. After David's death, the Lord will put his son Solomon on the throne and be a Father to him, and he will finally establish his house and his kingdom forever. He will make David's throne endure into eternity (2 Sam. 7:9-16 and Ps. 89:19-38). From this time on the hope of Israel's saints is fixed on David's house, and sometimes prophecy simply stops at that point, with the prophecy thus generally taken.[3]

*   *   *   *   *

But history taught that not a single king of the house of David satisfied the expectation. And in connection with this history, prophecy pointed ever more clearly to the future in which the true son of David should appear and should sit on His Father's throne forever. Gradually this future son of David began to be designated by the given name of Messiah. Messiah at first and for a long time remained a general name and it designated everyone who in Israel was chosen and anointed to some office or other. The anointing with oil was among Oriental people a practice in general use, and served to soften the skin burnt by the sun, and to restore the body to freshness and suppleness (Ps. 104:15 and Matt. 6:17). It was a sign of joy (Prov. 27:9), and was not indulged in bereavement (2 Sam. 14:2 and Dan. 10:3); it served as a token of hospitality and friendliness,[4] was applied as a remedy for illness,[5] and was a token of respect for the dead.[6] This anointing was also taken up in worship and so received a religious significance. Jacob lifted the stone on which he had rested his head as a pillow at Beersheba to serve as a monument, and poured oil over it as a sign of dedication

3. Amos 9:11; Hos. 3:5; Jer. 17:25 and 22:4.
4. Ps. 23:5; 2 Chron. 28:15 and Luke 7:46.
5. Mark 6:13; Luke 10:34; and James 5:14.
6. Mark 16:1; Luke 23:56; and John 19:40.

to the Lord who had appeared to him.[7] Later, in accordance with the law given to Moses, the tabernacle, its equipment, and its altar were anointed in order to hallow them and set them apart for the service of the Lord. And the same anointing took place for persons who were called to a special service.

A few times we read of the anointing of prophets. Elijah anointed Elisha (1 Kings 19:16) and in Psalm 105:15 the word *anointed* is used synonymously with the word *prophets*. Besides, the priests, including the high priest especially, were anointed (Lev. 8:12, 30 and Ps. 133:2). Thus the high priest can be called the anointed priest (Lev. 4:3, 5 and 6:22). And particularly we read of the anointing of kings: of Saul (1 Sam. 10:1), of David (1 Sam. 16:13 and 2 Sam. 2:4), of Solomon (1 Kings 1:34), and of others. Hence the kings are called the anointed of the Lord (1 Sam. 26:11 and Ps. 2:2). From this point on the use of anointing spreads out to other purposes. Several times in Scripture the term *anointed* is used of those persons whom God chooses and equips for His service, even though in a literal sense no anointing with oil has taken place. In Psalm 105:15 the patriarchs are designated by the words *anointed* and *prophets*. In other places the people of Israel, or otherwise perhaps their king, are called anointed.[8] In Isaiah 45:1 the term is applied to Cyrus. After all, the anointing with oil is but a sign which, on the one hand, indicates the dedication to the service of God, and, on the other, the election, calling, and preparation for that service by God Himself. When David was anointed by Samuel the Spirit of the Lord came upon him from that day forward (1 Sam. 16:13).

In this sense the name of Messiah, that is, anointed, became particularly appropriate for the future King of David's house. He, after all, is uniquely the Anointed, for He has been appointed by God Himself and has been anointed not merely with the token of oil but without limit by the Holy Spirit Himself (Ps. 2:2, 6 and Isa. 61:1). Just when the name of Messiah (Anointed) began to be used as a given name without the article cannot be said with certainty. But in Dan. 9:25 the name seems already to appear in this form, and by the time of Jesus' sojourn on earth the name in this sense was in common use. In John 4:25 the Samaritan woman says to Jesus, I know that Messias cometh. There the article is missing. Although the term *anointed* therefore at first had a general meaning and could be used to designate various persons, it gradually became a given name and was applied solely to the future king

---

7. Ex. 29:36; 30:23; and 40:10.
8. Ps. 84:10; 89:39; Habak. 3:13.

who was to come from the house of David. He is uniquely the Messiah, the Anointed One. He alone is Messiah.

*   *   *   *   *

The image of that Messiah is now developed and worked out in the prophecy of the Old Testament in all kinds of ways. In the foreground there is always the idea of His kingship. He is called the Anointed, because He has been anointed as king (Ps. 2:2, 6). On the basis of the promise given him, David himself expects that out of his house will come forth a ruler of men who will rule in righteousness. God has made an eternal covenant with him, ordered in all things and sure (2 Sam. 23:3-5). And such is the expectation of all the prophets and psalmists. The salvation of Israel in the future is inseparably bound up with the royal house of David, and the future king of that house is at the same time the King of the Kingdom of God. The kingdom of God is not a poetic figure or philosophical concept but is a reality, a component part of history. It comes from above, is spiritual, ideal, and nevertheless comes into being in time under a king of David's house. It is a kingdom of God and yet is a thoroughly human, earthly, and historical kingdom. Hence the future kingdom of God is painted for us in prophecy in tints and colors taken from the circumstances then extant, which are not to be taken in a literal sense, but nevertheless give a deep impression of the reality of that kingdom. It is not the image of a dream. It is actualized here on earth, in history, under a King of David's house.

But, even though this kingdom of Messiah is second to none on earth in tangible reality, it nevertheless differs greatly from it. In spite of the fact that it always comes into being in battle against and conquest of all enemies,[9] it is a kingdom of perfect righteousness and peace,[10] whose righteousness consists especially of this that the needy will be rescued and the poor be helped (Ps. 72:12-14). But for the rest it spreads itself out over all enemies up to the ends of the earth, and remains standing into all eternity.

At the head of the Kingdom there is a prince who is indeed a man but who nevertheless transcends all men in worth and honor. He is a man, is born from the line of David, is a son of David, and is called a son of man.[11] But all the same He is more than man. He sits in the place of honor at God's right hand (Ps. 110:1), is David's Lord (Ps. 110:1), and is the Son of God in a particular sense (Ps. 2:7). He is

---

9. Ps. 2:1 ff.; 72:9 ff.; and 110:2.
10. Ps. 2:8; 45:7; 72:5, 8, 17; and 110:2, 4.
11. 2 Sam. 7:12 ff.; Isa. 7:14; 9:5; Micah 5:2; and Dan. 7:13.

Immanuel, God with us (Isa. 7:14), the Lord our righteousness (Jer. 23:6 and 33:16), in whom the Lord Himself in grace comes to His people and dwells among them. For prophecy it is the same whether the Lord or Messiah rules over His people. Sometimes it is said that the Lord and then again that His anointed king will appear to judge the nations and to redeem Israel. Thus, for example, in Isaiah 40:10 and 11, we read: The Lord will come with strong hand, and His arm will rule for Him ... He shall feed His flock like a shepherd. And in Ezekiel 34:23 we read that the Lord will set up one Shepherd, namely, His servant David, who will feed His people and be their Shepherd. Of the new Jerusalem the prophet Ezekiel says that its name shall be: The Lord is there (Ezek. 48:35), and Isaiah presents the same fact by saying that in the Messiah God is with us (Isa. 7:14). Ezekiel combines both thoughts when he says, I the Lord will be their God, and my servant David a prince among them (Ezek. 34:24), even as Micah also says that Messiah will feed the people of Israel in the strength of the Lord, in the majesty of the name of the Lord His God (Micah 5:4). This is the reason why in the New Testament both series of texts can be interpreted in a Messianic way. In Messiah God Himself comes to His people; He is more than man, He is the perfect revelation and indwelling of God, and therefore also bears Divine names. He is called Wonderful, Counsellor, The mighty God, Eternal Father, Prince of Peace (Isa. 9:5).

*   *   *   *   *

Irrespective of how great the worth and power of this Messiah may be, however, prophecy adds a trait which is very remarkable. He is to be born, it is reported, in a very perilous time and in very humble circumstances. It may be that this thought is already implied in the statement of Isaiah that a virgin, a young woman, shall conceive and bear a son, and that this son will share in the passion of His people, for He shall eat only butter and honey, these being the chief products of a country that has been devastated and is not being rebuilt (Isa. 7:14-15). But in any case this is clearly expressed in Isaiah 11:1 (Compare Isaiah 53:2). There the prophet says that a rod will come up out of the stem of Jesse, and that a branch will burgeon up out of its roots. In other words, in the time in which Messiah is born the royal house of David will still exist, but it will be without a throne, and therefore like a trunk which has been broken off, but which can nevertheless still give off a shoot. Micah gives expression to the same thought in different words when he says that the house of Ephratah, that is the royal house of David, so-called because Ephratah was the area in which Bethlehem, the birthplace of David, lay, though it was the smallest among the thou-

sands of Judah, should nevertheless give rise to a Ruler who should be
great even to the ends of the earth (Micah 5:2). Hence, in Jeremiah
23:5 and 33:15, and in Zechariah 3:8 and 6:12, the Messiah is also
designated by the term *branch*. When Israel is destroyed and Judah is
steeped in calamity, when virtually all hope is gone and all expectation
is extinguished, then the Lord will raise up a Branch out of the royal
House of David who will build the temple of the Lord and establish His
kingdom on earth. However much the Messiah therefore may appear
in might and glory, He will also appear in lowliness, riding not upon a
warhorse but seated, as a sign of peace, on an ass, upon a colt the foal
of an ass (Zech. 9:9). He will be King but also Priest. Both offices
will be combined in Him as in Melchizedek, and He will hold them both
into eternity (Ps. 110:4 and Zech. 6:13).

This idea of the lowliness of the Messiah serves as a transitional idea
to that other one according to which Isaiah presents the coming One as
the suffering servant of the Lord. The people of Israel had to be a
priestly kingdom (Ex. 19:6). It had to serve God as a priest and then
rule the earth royally, just as man originally was created in the image
of God and therefore was given the Lordship over the whole earth. In
the picture for the future, therefore, now the one destiny and then the
other is placed in the foreground. Again and again in the prophecies
and psalms we read that God will do right by His people and grant them
victory over all their enemies. Sometimes this victory is described in
very strong terms: God will arise, His enemies will be destroyed, and
those who hate Him will flee from His face; He will drive them away
as smoke is driven; as wax melts in the fire the ungodly will disappear
from before the face of God; He will wound the head of His enemies
and the scalp of such as go on in trespasses; He will bring His people
again from the depths of the sea, so that they may dip their foot in the
blood of His enemies, and the tongue of their dogs may be painted red
in it.[12] All of these curses are not an expression of personal vengeance
but are descriptions in the language of the Old Testament of the wrath
of God over His people's enemies. But that same God who in that way
punishes the wicked will give righteousness, peace, and joy to all His
people, and that people will serve Him in total unanimity. Through
oppression and suffering His people will come to a state of glory and
salvation in which the Lord will make a new covenant, will write His
law within them, and grant them a new heart and a new spirit, so that

12. Ps. 68:2-3, 21-24; compare Ps. 28:4; 31:18; 55:9; 69:23-29; 109:6-20;
137:8-9; and others.

they will walk in His statutes, and will keep His judgments to do them
(Ezek. 36:25 and elsewhere).

These two characteristics of the picture of the future Israel are also
to be found in the Messiah. He will be a King who will break His enemies to pieces with a rod of iron and will dash them like potters' vessels (Ps. 2:9 and 110:5 and 6). Nowhere is there a more realistic presentation of this victory over God's enemies than in Isaiah 63:1-6. There
we read how the Lord comes with dyed garments, glorious in His apparel and travelling in the greatness of His strength, speaking righteousness and mighty to save. And in answer to the prophet's question,
Why art Thou red in thine apparel, and Thy garments like those of one
who treadeth the winefat?, the Lord gives the answer, I have trodden
the wine press alone; and of the people there was none with Me; I will
tread them in Mine anger, and trample them in My fury; and their blood
shall be sprinkled upon My garments, and I will stain all My raiment.
For the day of vengeance is in Mine heart, and the year of My redeemer
is come. In Revelation 9:13-15 certain traits of this description are
applied to Christ, when in the last days He shall return and overthrow
all His enemies. And this is quite as it should be, for He is a Savior
and a Judge, a Lamb and a Lion at one and the same time.

Indeed He is also a Redeemer and a Savior. Just as the Lord is righteous and merciful, just as His day is a day of wrath and a day of
redemption, just as Israel will rule in royal authority over its enemies
and will serve God as a priest, so the Messiah is simultaneously the
anointed King of God and the suffering servant of the Lord. In Isaiah
especially He manifests Himself in this latter form. In that connection
the prophet thinks first of the people of Israel, which is living in a state
of captivity, and which precisely by that way of suffering has a calling to
fulfill over against the heathen. But as this prophecy develops in Isaiah,
this suffering figure takes on more and more of the character of a specific
person, who as a priest by his suffering propitiates for the sins of his
people, who as a prophet proclaims this salvation to the ends of the
earth, and who as a king gets his share among the great and divides the
spoil with the strong (Isa. 52:13-53:12).

In the anointed King the Lord reveals His glory, His strength, the
majesty and highness of His name (Micah 5:3); in the suffering
servant of the Lord He reveals His grace and the riches of His mercy
(Isa. 53:11). Prophecy among Israel ends in these two figures, and that
prophecy is rooted in history. Israel is itself as a people the son of God
(Hos. 11:1), a priestly kingdom (Ex. 19:6), clothed with the glory of
the Lord (Ezek. 16:14), but is at the same time also God's servant
(Isa. 41:8-9), sharing in the reproach with which the enemies reproach

the Lord (Ps. 89:51-52), and for His sake being killed all the day long, and being counted as sheep for the slaughter (Ps. 44:22). Both the glory and the suffering of Israel, of Israel as a people generally and of its servants such as David, Job, and others in particular, have a prophetic character. Both point to Christ. The whole of the Old Testament with its laws and institutions, its offices and ministrations, its facts and promises, is a foreshadowing of the suffering that should come upon Christ, and of the glory which should follow upon it (1 Peter 1:11). Just as the church in the days of the New Testament became one plant with Christ in being dead unto sin and alive unto God (Rom. 6:11), and just as with its body it fills up that which is behind of the afflictions of Christ (Col. 1:24) and also in the image of Christ is changed from glory to glory (2 Cor. 3:18), so the church of the Old Testament in all of its suffering and glory was a preparation and shadowing of the humiliation and exaltation of that Priest-King who in His time would found the Kingdom of God on earth.

There can be no doubt that the New Testament looks upon itself in this light and in this way conceives of its relationship to the Old Testament. Jesus says that the Scriptures testify of Him (John 5:39 and Luke 24:27), and this is a thought which lies at the basis of the whole of the New Testament and is often also plainly stated. The first disciples of Jesus acknowledged Him as the Christ because they found in Him that One of whom Moses and the prophets had spoken (John 1:45). Paul testifies that Christ died, was buried, and was raised according to the Scriptures (1 Cor. 15:3-4). Peter writes that the Spirit of Christ in the prophets testified beforehand of the sufferings of Christ and the glory that should come (1 Peter 1:11). And all the books of the New Testament indicate either directly or indirectly by implication that the whole Old Testament has come to its fulfillment in Christ. The law with its ethical, ceremonial, and civic prescriptions, with its temple and altar, with its priestship and sacrifices, and just so prophecy with its promise of the anointed King of David's house but also of the suffering servant of the Lord — these point to the Christ as fulfillment. The whole Kingdom of God, foreshadowed in Israel's people and history, delineated beforehand in national forms in the law, and proclaimed in Old Testament language in the prophets, drew near in Christ and in Him and His church came down from heaven upon earth.

This intimate relationship between Old and New Testament is of the highest importance for the validity and genuineness of the Christian faith. For the confession that Jesus is the Christ, the Messiah promised to Israel, forms the heart of the Christian religion, and distinguishes it from all other religions. It is therefore seriously attacked by Jews,

Mohammedans, and all other pagan peoples, and in our time also by many who bear the name of Christians. These try to contend that Jesus never thought of Himself as the Messiah nor presented Himself as such, or, at most, that He couched His inner religious consciousness and His high moral calling in that temporary form, and that this form of it has no significance for us now. But the testimonies of the New Testament are too numerous and too strong to permit of holding to such an attitude very long. And therefore in most recent times others go much farther. They cannot deny that Jesus took Himself to be the Messiah and that He arrogated to Himself all kinds of supernatural characteristics and abilities. But instead of bowing to this fact, and of accepting Jesus as He Himself said He was, they infer that Jesus was a human being who was subject to illusions, enthusiasms, and all kinds of aberrances. In fact, the attack goes so far that some ascribe all sorts of illnesses of soul and body to Jesus and so explain the exalted conception which He entertained of Himself. This struggle concerning the person of Jesus, which in late years has again taken on such a serious character, proves again that the question, What think ye of the Christ?, as it did in previous periods of history, now again occupies and divides the minds of men. Just as the Jews entertained various ideas of Jesus, and some held Him to be John the Baptist, others Elijah, and others Jeremiah or one of the prophets (Matt. 16:13-14), and just as then also some thought Him beside Himself and possessed of devils (Mark 3:21-22), so it continued through the centuries, and so it is still. Even if we leave to one side those who claim that Christ is an illusionist and enthusiast, there are still thousands who, while recognizing that He is a prophet, do not confess Him as the Christ of God.

And yet Christ lays full claim to this designation and is satisfied with no other confession. He is a man, and is described as such on all pages of the New Testament. He is, although the eternal Word, born into time (John 1:14 and Phil. 2:7). He shares our flesh and blood and is like unto the brethren in all things (Heb. 2:14 and 17). He is from the fathers according to the flesh (Rom. 9:5). He is Abraham's seed (Gal. 3:16), He sprang out of Judah (Heb. 7:14 and Rev. 5:5), He is descended from David (Rom. 1:3), and He is born of a woman (Gal. 4:4). He is a human being in the full, true sense, having a body (Matt. 26:26), a soul (Matt. 26:38) and a spirit (Luke 23:46), a human mind (Luke 2:52), a human will (Luke 22:42), the human feelings of joy and sadness, wrath and mercy (Luke 10:21 and Mark 3:5), and the human needs of rest and relaxation, food and drink (John 4:6-7 and elsewhere). Everywhere and always Jesus manifests Himself in the New Testament as a human being to whom nothing human is strange. He was in fact, as we are, tempted in all things, but He was without sin (Heb. 4:15). In the days of His flesh He offered up prayers and supplications with strong crying and tears, and He learned obedience by the things which He suffered (Heb. 5:7-8).

His contemporaries, accordingly, did not for a moment doubt His real human nature. Usually He is designated in the Gospels by the ordinary simple name of *Jesus*. True, this name was given Him at the expressed burden of the angel, and it has the significance that He is the Savior of His people (Matt. 1:21). But in itself this name was known in Israel from of old and was borne by many persons. The name Jesus is the Greek form of the Hebrew name Jehoshua or Joshua, and is derived from a verb which means to rescue or to save. The successor to Moses was first called Oshea but later was called Jehoshua or Joshua by Moses (Num. 13:16) and is referred to in Acts 7:45 and Hebrews 4:8 by the name Jesus. And thus in the New Testament we read of still other persons who bore the name (Luke 3:29 and Col. 4:11). The name alone, therefore, could not have led the Jews to think that the son of Mary was the Christ.

Usually, therefore, they speak of Him as the man named Jesus (John 9:11), the son of Joseph, the carpenter, whose sisters and brethren we know (Matt. 13:55 and John 6:42), the son of Joseph of Nazareth (John 1:45), Jesus the Nazarene,[13] Jesus the Galilean (Matt. 26:69), and the prophet of Nazareth in Galilee (Matt. 21:11). And the usual title by which Jesus is addressed is that of Rabbi or Rabboni, meaning teacher, master, or my master (John 1:38 and 20:16), the name by which in that time the scribes and Pharisees were usually addressed (Matt. 23:8), and He not only appropriates this title but also lays unique claim to it (Matt. 23:8-10). These designations and titles do not yet imply, of course, that people acknowledged Him as Christ. This is not even necessarily the case when they address Him by the general term Lord (Mark 7:28), by the phrase Son of David (Mark 10:47) or when they call Him a prophet (Mark 6:15 and 8:28).

* * * * *

But, though He is very and true man, Jesus is aware from the beginning that He is more than man and He is acknowledged and confessed as such in an ever growing sense by all His disciples. And this is not the case merely, as is so often alleged, in the Gospel of John and in the Letters of the apostles, but can be plainly read also in the Gospels of Matthew, Mark, and Luke. After all, the contrast which men are try-

---

13. Matt. 2:23; Mark 10:47; John 18:5, 7; 19:19; and Acts 22:8.

ing to make in modern times between the historical Jesus and the Christ of the church is totally untenable. They put it this way, that Jesus was no more and wanted to be no more than a pious Israelite, a religious genius, an exalted teacher of the youth, and a prophet such as formerly so many had appeared in Israel. And all that is further confessed by the church concerning that historical Jesus — His supernatural conception, His Messianic office, His atoning death, His resurrection, His ascent into heaven, and the like — is held to be the product of imagination and to have been added to the original picture of the Master by the disciples.

But against this whole conception there are so many and such serious objections that it can satisfy no one. After all, if those many facts named above are unreal, but were fancied and taken up into the legend of Jesus, one must provide some sort of explanation of how the disciples came to such dramatizations and whence they derived the material for these artfully designed fables. The impression made by Jesus' unusual personality does not lend itself to such fantasy at all. Such an impression, be it of an highly exalted person, would not have a single component element of the Christ whom the church confesses. And those component elements, therefore, one must seek — and they are sought — among the Jewish sects of the time, or among the Greek, Persian, Indian, Egyptian, or Babylonian religions, and so Christianity is robbed of its independence and uniqueness and is scraped together out of heathen and Jewish heresies.

But, besides, those three Gospels were written by men who themselves had the firm conviction that Jesus was the Christ. They were written in a time when the church had already existed for some time, when the preaching of the apostles had already extended to all sides of the then known world, and when Paul had already written numerous letters. Nevertheless those Gospels were generally accepted and acknowledged. Nothing is known in the first period of the churches about a conflict between the apostles and their fellow-workers concerning the person of Christ. They all stand in the belief that Jesus is the Christ, that God has made this Jesus, whom the Jews have crucified, a Lord and Christ, and in His name grants repentance and the forgiveness of sins (Acts 2:22-38).

This faith was from the beginning the foundation of the Christian church. Paul contends in the fifteenth chapter of his first letter to Corinth that the Christ of the Scriptures, the Christ who died, was buried, and was raised, was the content of the apostolic preaching and the object of the Christian faith, and that without those two facts the preaching and the faith would be vain and the salvation of those who fell asleep in Christ would be a mirage. There is no choice but between these two:

the apostles are false witnesses of God, or they have testified to and proclaimed that which was from the beginning, that which they had seen with their eyes, which they had looked upon, which their hands had handled of the Word of life. Just so, too, Jesus was a false prophet or He was the faithful witness, the first born of the dead, and the prince of the kings of the earth, who loved us and washed away our sins in His blood, and made us kings and priests unto God and His Father (Rev. 1:5 and 6). There is no conflict between the historical Jesus and the Christ of the church. The testimony of the prophets is the unfolding and interpretation, given under the guidance of the Holy Spirit, of the self-witness of Christ. The structure of the church rests on the foundation of the apostles and prophets, of whom Christ is the chief cornerstone (Eph. 2:20). And no one can lay another foundation than that which is laid by them (1 Cor. 3:10).

*   *   *   *   *

However attractive the task otherwise would be, there is no opportunity now at this point to give a full account of the content of that witness which Christ gave of Himself and which the apostles gave of their Master and Lord. Nevertheless the attention should for a few moments go to certain of the particulars.

Just as did John the Baptist, so also Jesus came with the preaching that the kingdom of God was near and that citizenship in that kingdom was obtainable only in the way of faith and repentance (Mark 1:15). But He puts Himself into a very different relationship to that kingdom than John or one of the other prophets. These all have prophesied of it (Matt. 11:11-13), but Jesus is the owner and possessor of it. True, He received it from the Father, who ordained it for Him in the eternal counsel (Luke 22:29). But therefore precisely it is *His* kingdom, over which with sovereign sway He governs things in favor of His disciples. It is the Father who prepared a wedding festival for His Son (Matt. 22:2), but it is nevertheless the Son who is the bridegroom (Mark 2:19 and John 3:29), and who in the future union with His own will celebrate His own marriage (Matt. 25:1). The Father is the owner of the vineyard, but the Son is nevertheless the heir (Matt. 21:33 and 38). Thus Jesus calls the kingdom of God *His* kingdom also, and He speaks of *His* church as grounded on the rock of confession of Him (Matt. 16:18). He is greater than Jonah or Solomon (Matt. 12:39, 42). For His sake everything, father, mother, sisters, brothers, houses, fields, one's life itself, must be forsaken and denied. He who loves father or mother more

than Him is not worthy of Him. He who denies or confesses Him before men will correspondingly be confessed or denied of Him before His
Father who is in heaven.

To this high place which Jesus ascribes to Himself in the kingdom
of heaven all His words and works conform. They correspond perfectly
to the will of His Father. Jesus is the absolutely sinless one. He is
aware of not a single transgression of the will of God and never confesses a single error or sin. True, He permits Himself to be baptized of
John but absolutely not in order thereby, like the others, to receive the
forgiveness of sins (Matt. 3:6). For John precisely, inasmuch as His
baptism was a baptism of repentance and the forgiveness of sins, entered
a protest against baptizing Jesus. And Jesus acknowledges the objection,
but removes it by saying that He is not letting Himself be baptized to
personally receive the forgiveness of sins, but to fulfill all righteousness
(Matt. 3:14-15). Moreover, He declines the address of the rich young
man: good master (Mark 10:18), but this He does not at all to deny
moral perfection. The rich young man came to Jesus as in those days
one came to the Scribes and Pharisees with all sorts of salutations and
tokens of esteem (Matt. 23:7). He wanted to flatter Jesus, and ingra-
tiate himself with Him, by calling Him good master. Jesus is not served
by such flattery. He does not want to be greeted and honored in the
way that the Scribes were. Good, in the absolute sense that He is the
source of all blessings and benefits, is God alone. Jesus accordingly by
no means here denies His moral perfection, but enters His protest rather
to the thoughtless flattery of the rich young man. So also in Gethsemane. His human nature sees the suffering that awaits Him looming
up big, and proves its reality by praying that this cup be allowed to pass,
but in that same moment He demonstrates His perfect subjection and
obedience by the addition: Not My will, but Thine, O Father, be done
(Matt. 26:39)!

But even in that moment, whether in Gethsemane or upon Golgotha,
not a single confession of sin comes from His lips. On the contrary,
all that He is, and says, and does, is in perfect accord with God's holy
will. All things which He reveals in His words and deeds concerning
God and His kingdom are given Him of the Father (Matt. 11:27).

He taught, not as the scribes. scholastically cavilling, but as one hav-
ing authority, as one who had received full prophetic authority from
God Himself (Matt. 7:29), and that same authority became manifest in
His deeds. He casts out the devils by the Spirit of God (Matt. 12:28),
and with the finger of God (Luke 11:20), has power to forgive sins
(Matt. 9:6), and power also to lay His own life down and to take it up

again (John 10:18). All this power He received of the Father. Jesus traces all His words and works back to the command of His Father.[14] To do the Father's will is His meat (John 4:34), so that at the end of His life He can say that He has glorified the Father, manifested His name, and finished His work (John 17:4, 6). This relationship in which Jesus places Himself in His person, His words, and His works, to the kingdom, comes to expression in His Messianic character. There now is, and there long has been a good deal of investigation of whether or not Jesus regarded Himself as the promised Messiah, and if so how He came to this awareness.

Concerning the first there can be no doubt at all in the mind of anyone who with an unprejudiced mind reads the Gospels — not that of John only, but those of Matthew, Mark, and Luke also. Just to mention a few things: In the synagogue at Nazareth Christ declared that the prophecy of Isaiah was that day being fulfilled (Luke 4:17 ff.). To the question of John the Baptist as to whether or not He was the Messiah, He answers affirmatively by pointing to his works (Matt. 11:4 ff.). The confession of Peter: Thou art the Christ, the Son of the living God, He appropriates, and He sees in it a revelation of His Father (Matt. 16:16-17). The prayer of the mother of Zebedee's children comes up out of the belief that Jesus is the Messiah, and it is thus that Jesus takes it up and interprets it (Matt. 20:20). His explanation of the 110th Psalm (Matt. 22:42), His entry into Jerusalem (Matt. 21:2 ff.), His appearance in the temple (Matt. 21:12 ff.), His institution of the Holy Supper (Matt. 26:26 ff.) — these all rest on the assumption that He is the Messiah, David's Son and Lord, and that He can supplant the old covenant with a new one. And what is absolutely conclusive is the fact that it was for nothing else than the confession that He was the Christ, the Son of God, that He was condemned and put to death (Mark 14:62). The superscription of the cross, Jesus the Nazarene, the King of the Jews, puts the seal of validity upon this.

How and in what way Jesus came to this consciousness is another question. But the general idea of it, now so very commonly accepted, is that Jesus at first knew nothing about this, and that the thought came to Him late, after His baptism, or even later after and by way of the confession of Peter. The supposition then is that He accepted it under pressure, or as a less appropriate but unavoidable form of His religious-moral calling. All such surmises, however, lie outside reality and are diametrically opposed to the testimony of Scripture and with the essence of Jesus' personality. Now there was without doubt a development of

---

14. John 5:19, 20, 30; 8:26, 28, 38; 12:50; and 17:8.

the human consciousness of Christ, for we read in so many words that He increased in wisdom and stature, and in favor with God and man (Luke 2:52). His human insight into His own person, into the work that the Father had given Him to do, into the nature of the Kingdom which He came to found, was gradually illuminated and deepened in the quiet family at Nazareth under the guidance of the mother, with the help of the Old Testament Scriptures.

However, already as a boy in the temple He knew that He must be about His Father's business (Luke 2:49). And before He let Himself be baptized of John He knew that He did not need that baptism for the forgiveness of sins but that He was to have it in order in all things to be obedient to the will of God. That baptism accordingly was for Jesus not a break with a sinful past, for this He did not have. Rather, it was on His part a total surrender and dedication to the work that the Father had given Him to do, and, on God's part, it was a total equipping and fitting out for that work. John recognizes Him immediately as Messiah, and, the day after, the disciples whom He has chosen acknowledge Him as such also (John 1:29-52).

* * * * *

But this confession was, so to speak, a preliminary one. It was by no means what it should be and what it was to become. It went paired with all kinds of error concerning the nature of the Messiahship. The disciples in spite of themselves thought that Jesus would be a Messiah such as the Jews of that time generally pictured him: a king who engaged the heathen nations in battle and put Israel in glory at the head of those nations. When, after His public appearance, Jesus did not respond to this expectation, even a John the Baptist fell prey to doubt (Matt. 11:2 ff.). And the disciples had to be constantly corrected by Jesus and better instructed on this point. The Jewish Messiah expectation was so deeply ingrained in the soul that even after the resurrection they ask Jesus whether He will at this time restore the kingdom to Israel (Acts 1:6).

These mistaken conceptions which were being generally entertained, also in the circle of the disciples, made it necessary for Jesus in His preaching to follow a specific, pedagogical line of interpretation. It is well known that Jesus in the first period of His ministry never says in so many words that He is the Christ. The content of His preaching is the kingdom of heaven, and He explains the nature, origin, process, and fulfillment of that kingdom at length, especially by means of parables. And His works are works of mercy: healing all sorts of illnesses and sicknesses among the people. Those works testify of him, and from them His disciples, also John the Baptist, must make up their minds as to who He is and what the character of the Messiahship is. It can be put even more strongly: it seems as if His Messiahship is a secret which may not be made public. More than once His works put those about Him onto the thought that He was the Christ, but then He commanded sharply that they should tell no man.[15] In fact, even when, towards the end of His life, His disciples have come to know Him better, and nevertheless, by the mouth of Peter, on the way to Caesarea Philippi, confess Him as the Christ, the Son of the living God — even then He commands them straitly that they shall tell no one (Matt. 16:20 and Mark 8:30). Jesus was the Christ but He was that in a different sense than the Jews at that time represented it to be. He did not want to be the Messiah and He could not permit Himself to be it according to their expectations. When that threatened He slipped away in order not to be taken by force and exalted as a king (John 6:14-15). He was Messiah and He wanted to be Messiah but in harmony, not with the will and the favor of the people; He wanted to be Messiah in harmony with the will and the counsel of the Father, with the prophecy of the Old Testament.

That is why He chooses, as a name to designate Himself, the peculiar name of Son of man. It comes from His lips repeatedly in the Gospels. No doubt the name is derived from Daniel 7:13 where the kingdoms of the world are presented in the guise of animals but the dominion of God comes in the form of the Son of man. The passage in some Jewish circles also was construed in a Messianic sense, and the name was therefore, at least to some, known as a designation of the Messiah (John 12:34). All the same the term seems not to have been a common name, and seems not to have had a fixed significance. No such fleshly expectations could be connected with this name as with the name, Son of David, King of Israel. Hence this name was most suitable for Jesus, for it gave expression, on the one hand, to the idea that He was the Messiah promised in prophecy, and, on the other, to the idea that He was not this according to the prevailing idea of the Jewish people.

This can be proved by the use which Jesus makes of the name. He uses this title in reference to Himself in two series of places, namely in such texts as those in which He speaks of His poverty, suffering, and humiliation, and in those in which He speaks of His might, majesty, and exaltation. Thus, for example, He says in the first kind: The Son of man came not to be ministered unto, but to minister, and to give His

---

15. Matt. 8:4; 9:30; 12:16; Mark 1:34-44; 3:12; 5:43; 7:36; 8:26; and Luke 5:13.

life a ransom for many (Matt. 20:28). In the other kind, He declares before the high court that He is in very fact the Messiah, and He adds to this the statement: Hereafter shall ye see the Son of man sitting on the right hand of power, and coming in the clouds of heaven (Matt. 26:64). The same kind of thoughts come to us when we compare such passages as Matthew 8:20, 11:19, 12:40, 17:12, 18:11, 20:18, and others like them, with such passages as Matthew 9:6, 10:23, 12:8, 13:41, 16:27, 17:9, 19:28, 24:27, 25:13, and the like. Jesus characterizes Himself by this name in His full Messianic character, in His humiliation, in His exaltation, in His grace and in His might, as Savior and as Judge.

And in that name He comprises the whole Old Testament prophecy concerning the Messiah. As we indicated earlier, this expectation developed in two directions, in that of the anointed King of David's house and in that of the suffering servant of the Lord. By and large these two lines run parallel to each other throughout the Old Testament but in Daniel they meet. The Kingdom of God will in the true, full sense be a dominion, but that dominion will be a human dominion, the dominion of the Son of man. And thus Jesus now also says that He most certainly is a King, the King of Israel, the King promised and anointed of God. But He is that nevertheless in a sense different from the one the Jews entertain. He is a King who rides on a colt, the foal of an ass, a King of righteousness and peace, a King who is also Priest, a King who is also Savior. Might and love, righteousness and grace, exaltation and humility, God and man are conjoined in Him.

He is the perfect fulfillment of the whole Old Testament law and prophecy, of all the suffering and all the glory which were preparatory and foreshadowed in Israel, the counterpart of the kings and priests in Israel, the counterpart of the people of Israel itself, which had to be a priestly kingdom, and a royal priesthood. He is King-Priest and Priest-King, Immanuel, God with us. Hence the Kingdom which He came to preach and establish is at the same time internal and external, invisible and visible, spiritual and physical, present and future, particular and universal, from above and from below, coming down from heaven and yet existing on the earth. And Jesus will return. He came to preserve the world, to save it; He will return to judge it.

* * * * *

One further feature must be added to this picture of Jesus as the Gospels hold it up to us. It is this: that He is conscious of being the Son of God in a very special sense.

In the Old Testament, this name, Son of God, was also used for angels (Job 38:7), for the people of Israel,[16] for the judges among that people (Ps. 82:6), and for the kings.[17] In the New Testament Adam is called the son of God (Luke 3:38), the children of God are designated by it (2 Cor. 6:18), and there the name is especially given to Christ. From various sides and by various persons He is named by that name: by John the Baptist and by Nathaniel (John 1:34 and 49), by Satan and the possessed,[18] by the high priest, the multitude of the Jews, and the centurion (Matt. 26:63 and 27:40, 54), by the disciples (Matt. 14:33 and 16:16), and by the evangelists (Mark 1:1 and John 20:31). It is true that Jesus does not usually call Himself by that name, but He nevertheless accepted this confession of His Divine Sonship without protest, and on some occasions He roundly states that He is the Son of God.[19]

There can be no doubt, of course, that the various persons who thus addressed Him did not all use the name in the same profound sense. This name did not have one and the same significance on the lips of the centurion (Matt. 27:54), of the High Priest (Matt. 26:63), and of Peter (Matt. 16:16). The centurion was a heathen and he did not call Jesus the Son of God but rather a son of God. The High Priest in this connection was thinking especially of the Messianic identity for he was questioning Jesus whether He was the Christ, the Son of God. But when Peter, who had long gone about with Jesus, emphatically confesses Him as the Christ, the Son of the living God, who has the words of eternal life, there no doubt is a profounder meaning in his statement than in the others, a meaning which the disciples later, after the resurrection, came gradually to understand more fully and more richly.

It is true that in an Old Testament, Theocratic sense Jesus can also be designated by the name, Son of God. As the King anointed of God He can and may be called God's Son. He is the Son of the Most High, to whom the Lord God will give the throne of His father David (Luke 1:32). He is the holy seed which was born of Mary (Luke 1:35), the Holy One of God, as the possessed man called Him (Mark 1:24). He is the Son of the Blessed, as the High Priest used this expression by way of more specifically delimiting the Messiah (Mark 14:61). But this Theocratic Sonship has in Jesus a profounder meaning than those others sensed, and in Him it comes up out of a different relationship to the Father. He has become God's Son not merely by being supernaturally conceived in Mary (Luke 1:35), nor because at baptism He received

16. Ex. 4:22; Deut. 14:1; Isa. 63:8; and Hos. 11:1.
17. 2 Sam. 11:14; Ps. 2:7; and Ps. 89:27, 28.
18. Matt. 4:3; 8:29; and Mark 3:11.
19. Matt. 16:16-17; 26:63-64; and 27:40, 43.

the Holy Spirit without measure (Matt. 3:16). He has become that still less because He in virtue of the resurrection has been made Lord and Christ by God (Acts 2:36). True, on those occasions He was recognized and greeted by the Father as being the Son, but His Messianic worthiness did not then have its first beginning. That goes back much farther. And Scripture teaches us that Jesus really is not called the Son of God because He is the anointed King of Israel, the Messiah, but, quite the reverse, that He has been made King by God because in an entirely unique sense He was God's Son.

It is beyond all doubt that elsewhere in the Scripture the matter is presented in just this way. As early as Micah 5:2 we read that the goings forth of the Ruler of Israel have been from of old, from everlasting. In Hebrews 1:5 and 5:5, the seventh verse of the second Psalm, This day have I begotten Thee, is explained by reference to the eternity in which Christ as the Son, as the brightness of His glory, and the express image of His person, has been begotten of the Father. And in Romans 1:4 the apostle declares that Christ is powerfully *proved* to be the Son of God by the resurrection from the dead. He was in a special sense the Son of God from eternity,[20] but in His supernatural conception, His baptism, and His resurrection this became more and more fully apparent.

This same teaching we find also in the Gospels according to Matthew, Mark, and Luke. Jesus is aware of standing in a relationship to the Father which is essentially different from that of all other persons. Already as a lad He knew that He had to be about His Father's business (Luke 2:49). At His baptism, and later again, after the transfiguration on the mount, God declares openly, by means of a voice from heaven, that this is His beloved, only Son, in whom He is well pleased (Matt. 3:17 and 17:5).

He speaks of Himself as the Son who is exalted far above the angels (Matt. 24:36 and Mark 13:32). Other men sent out from God are but servants, but He is the only Son, the Son beloved of the Father and His heir (Mark 12:6-7). The kingdom in which He reigns was appointed to Him by the Father (Luke 22:29). He sends to His disciples the promise of His Father (Luke 24:49). And He will one day come in the glory of His Father (Mark 8:38). He never speaks of our Father, but always of His Father, and, accordingly, puts the prayer, Our Father, upon the lips of His disciples (Matt. 6:9). In one word, He is *the* Son (Mark 13:32), while all of His disciples are children of their Father (Matt. 5:45). All things were delivered to Him by the Father, for no man knows the Son, but the Father, and neither does any man know

20. Rom. 8:32; Gal. 4:4; and Phil. 2:6.

the Father but the Son, and he to whom the Son will reveal Him (Matt.
11:27). And after the resurrection He gives the disciples the mandate
to teach all nations, baptizing them in the name of the Father, and of the
Son, and of the Holy Spirit, teaching them to observe all that He has
commanded them (Matt. 28:19).

The Gospel of John, in which it is not only the evangelist but the
apostle also who is speaking, adds nothing essentially new to this, but
works it all out more deeply and widely. In this Gospel, too, the name,
Son of God, sometimes still has a Theocratic sense,[21] but generally it
has a deeper significance. Not only is Jesus frequently called the Son
of God by others (1:34, 50 and 6:69) but He calls himself   this
also.[22] And in even more instances He speaks of Himself as the Son
without adding any further qualification. As such He ascribes to Himself
the power to do wonders (9:35 and 11:4), to raise the dead, spiritually
and physically, and to make them alive (5:20 ff.), and, as the Jews also
understood, He made Himself equal with God (5:18 and 10:33 ff.).
Accordingly He spoke of the Father, and of Himself as the Son, in such
an intimate way that these speeches are appropriate only if God is in a
very special sense His Father, only if He is His own Father (5:18).
All that He ascribes to the Father He ascribes also to Himself. The
Father gave Him power over all flesh (17:2) so that the destiny of all
men depends on the relationship in which they place themselves to Him
(John 3:17 and 6:40). Like the Father, He makes alive or quickens
whom He will (5:21), executes judgment over all (5:27), does all that
the Father does (5:19), and received from the Father the power to have
life in Himself (5:26). He and the Father are one (10:30). He is in
the Father and the Father is in Him (10:38), and to see the Father is
to see Him (14:9). True, the Father is greater than He (14:28), for
the Father has sent Him, as Jesus repeatedly declares (5:24, 30, and
37). But this does not take away from the fact that He was in the glory of God from before the incarnation and that He will return to it
presently (17:5). His Sonship is not based on His mission, but His
mission is based on His Sonship.[23] Therefore He is *the* Son, the only-
begotten Son,[24] the only-begotten of the Father (1:14), the Word which
in the beginning was with God, and was God (1:1), the Savior of the
world (4:42) whom Thomas addresses and confesses as his Lord and
his God (20:28).

---

21. John 1:34, 50; 11:27; and 20:31.
22. John 5:25; 9:35; 10:36; and 11:4.
23. John 3:16, 17, 35; 5:20; and 17:24.
24. John 1:18; 3:16; and 1 John 4:9.

XVI

The Divine and Human Nature of Christ

The testimony which, according to Scripture, Christ has given of Himself is developed and confirmed by the preaching of the apostles. The confession that a man, named Jesus, is the Christ, the Only-Begotten of the Father, is in such direct conflict with our experience and with all of our thinking, and especially with all the inclinations of our heart, that no one can honestly and with his whole soul appropriate it without the persuasive activity of the Holy Spirit. By nature everybody stands in enmity to this confession, for it is not a confession natural to man. No one can confess that Jesus is the Lord except through the Holy Spirit, but neither can anyone speaking by the Holy Spirit call Jesus accursed; he must recognize Him as his Savior and King (1 Cor. 12:3).

Hence when Christ appears on earth and Himself confesses that He is the Son of God, He did not leave it at that, but He also had a care, and He continues to have a care, that this confession finds entrance into the world, and is believed by the church. He called His apostles, and He instructed them, and made them witnesses to His words and deeds, to His death and resurrection. He gave them the Holy Spirit who brought them personally to the confession that Jesus was the Christ, the Son of the living God (Matt. 16:16), and who later caused them, from the day of Pentecost on, to minister as preachers of those things which their eyes had seen, and they beheld, and their hands had handled of the Word of life (1 John 1:1). The apostles were really not the real witnesses. The Spirit of truth, proceeding from the Father, is the original, infallible, and almighty witness to Christ, and the apostles are that only in Him and through Him (John 15:26 and Acts 5:32). And it is that same Spirit of truth who by means of the testimony of the apostles brings the church of all ages to the confession and preserves them in it: Lord, to whom shall we go? Thou hast the words of eternal life. And we believe and are sure that Thou art the Christ, the Son of the living God (John 6:68-69).

When the four Evangelists in regular order report the events of the life of Jesus, they usually refer to Him simply by the name of Jesus without any more particular qualification or addendum. They tell us that Jesus was born in Bethlehem, that Jesus was led into the wilderness, that Jesus saw the multitude and went up the mountain, and so on. Jesus, the historical person who lived and died in Palestine, is the object of their chronicle. And so we find a few times in the letters of the apostles, too, that Jesus is designated simply by His historical name. Paul says, for instance, that no one can say that *Jesus* is the Lord except by the Holy Spirit (1 Cor. 12:3). John testifies that whoever believes that *Jesus* is the Christ is born of God (1 John 1:5; compare 2:22 and 4:20). And in the book of Revelation we read of the faith of Jesus, and of the witnesses and witness of *Jesus*.

Still, in the letters of the apostles the use of this name without qualification is rare. Usually the name occurs in connection with: the Lord, Christ, the Son of God, and like designations, and the full name usually reads: Our Lord Jesus Christ. But, irrespective of whether the name Jesus is used alone or in connection with other names, the connection with the historical person who was born in Bethlehem and who died on the cross always comes to expression in it.

The whole New Testament, that of the epistles or letters as well as that of the gospels, rests on the foundation of historical events. The Christ-figure is not an idea nor an ideal of the human mind, as many in past ages maintained, and as some in our time also assert, but is a real figure who manifested Himself in a particular period and in a particular person in the man Jesus.

True, the various events in the life of Jesus recede into the background in the letters. Those letters have a different purpose than the gospels have. They do not chronicle the history of the life of Jesus but point out the significance which that life has for the redemption of mankind. But all of the apostles are familiar with the person and life of Jesus, are acquainted with His words and deeds, and they proceed to show us that this Jesus is the Christ, exalted by God to His own right hand, in order to grant repentance and the forgiveness of sins (Acts 2:36 and 5:31).

Often, therefore, in the letters of the apostles mention is made of events in the life of Jesus. They picture Him before the eyes of their auditors and readers (Gal. 3:1). They stress the fact that John the Baptist was His herald and precursor (Acts 13:25 and 19:4), that He comes from the family of Judah and the stem of David (Rom. 1:3; Rev. 5:5 and 22:16), that He was born of a woman (Gal. 4:4), was circumcised on the eighth day (Rom. 15:8), that He was brought up in Nazareth (Acts 2:22 and 3:6), and that He also had brothers (1 Cor. 9:5 and Gal. 1:19). They tell us that He was perfectly holy and sinless,[1] that He presented Himself to us as an example (1 Cor. 11:1 and 1 Peter 2:21), and that He spoke words that have authority for us (Acts 20:35 and 1 Cor. 7:10-12). But it is especially His dying that is significant for us. The cross stands at the central point in the apostolic preaching. Betrayed by one of the twelve apostles whom He chose (1 Cor. 11:23 and 1 Cor. 15:5), and not recognized by the princes of this world as the Lord of glory (1 Cor. 2:8), He was put to death by the Jews (Acts 4:10; 5:30; and 1 Thess. 2:15), dying on the accursed wood of the cross.[2] But, even though He suffered greatly in Gethsemane and upon Golgotha,[3] He has by the pouring out of His blood achieved the reconciliation and an eternal righteousness.[4] And therefore God raised Him up, exalted Him to His right hand, and appointed Him Lord and Christ, Prince and Savior for all nations.[5]

*   *   *   *   *

From these few data it is adequately evident that the apostles did not deny, ignore, or neglect the facts of Christianity but that they fully honored them and penetrated their spiritual significance. No trace is to be found in them of any separation or conflict between the redemptive event and the redemptive word, however much some in the past have tried to postulate such a conflict. The redemptive event is the actualization of the redemptive word; in the second the first takes on its real and concrete form and is at the same time therefore its illumination and interpretation.

If any doubt about this remains at all, it is entirely removed by the battle which the apostles already in their day had to conduct. It was not merely in the second, third, and following centuries but also in the apostolic period that certain men appeared who regarded the facts of Christianity of subordinate and transient importance, or else ignored them altogether, and who held that the idea was the main thing or in itself quite enough. What difference does it make, they argued, whether or not Christ bodily rose from the grave? If only He lives on in the spirit, our salvation is sufficiently assured! But the apostle Paul thought very differently about that and in 1 Corinthians 15 he placed the reality and the significance of the resurrection in the clearest possible light. He preaches Christ *according to the Scriptures,* that Christ who,

1. 2 Cor. 5:21; Heb. 7:26; 1 Peter 1:11; 2:22; and 1 John 3:5.
2. Gal. 3:13; Col. 2:14.
3. Phil. 2:6; Heb. 5:7-8; 12:2 and 13:12.
4. Rom. 3:25; 5:9; and Col. 1:20.
5. Acts 2:32, 33, 36; 5:30, 31; Rom. 8:34; 1 Cor. 15:20; Phil. 2:9; and other passages.

according to the counsel of the Father, died, was buried, and was raised again, who after His resurrection was seen of many disciples, and whose resurrection is the foundation and surety of our salvation. And, if possible, John puts even more emphasis on the fact that he is a declarer of what he has seen with his eyes and handled with his hands of the Word of life (1 John 1:1-3). The principle of the antichrist is this that he denies the incarnation of the Word; and the Christian confession, to the contrary, consists of the belief that the Word has become flesh, that the Son of God has come by water and by blood (John 1:14 and 1 John 3:2-3 and 5:6). The whole apostolic preaching of the letters and of the gospels, hence of the whole New Testament, comes down to the claim that *Jesus,* born of Mary and crucified, is — witness the evidence of His exaltation — the *Christ,* the Son of God.[6]

Now it deserves notice that, in connection with the content and purpose of the apostolic preaching, the use of the single name *Jesus,* without further qualification, is rare in the letters. Usually the apostles speak of Jesus Christ, or of Christ Jesus, or, even more fully, of *the* or *our* Lord Jesus Christ. Even the Evangelists who in their chronicle for the most part speak of Jesus make use, either at the beginning or at an important turning point of their gospel, of the full name Jesus Christ.[7] This they do by way of indicating who the person is concerning whom they are writing their evangel. In the Acts and in the letters this usage becomes the regular practice. The apostles speak not of a human being whose name was Jesus, but, by adding the terms Christ and Lord, and the like, they give expression to their appreciation of who that man is. They are preachers of the gospel that in the man Jesus the Christ of God has appeared on the earth.

Thus they had gradually, during their going about with Him, learned to know Him. And especially after that important hour in Caesarea Philippi a light had dawned for them upon His person, and they had all confessed with Peter that He was the Christ, the Son of the living God (Matt. 16:16). Thus Jesus had revealed Himself to them, at first more or less concealed under the name *Son of man,* but gradually more clearly and plainly as the end of His life approached. In the highpriestly prayer He designates Himself by the name Jesus Christ whom the Father has sent (John 17:3). Precisely because He gave Himself out to be the Christ, the Son of God, He was charged by the Jewish court with blasphemy and was condemned to die (Matt. 26:63). And the superscription above His cross read: Jesus of Nazareth the King of the Jews (Matt. 27:37 and John 19:19).

---

6. John 20:31; 1 John 2:22; 4:15; 5:5.
7. Matt. 1:1, 18; 16:20; Mark 1:1; John 1:17; and 17:3.

It is true that the disciples could not reconcile these Messianic claims of Jesus with His approaching passion and death (Matt. 16:22). But through the resurrection, and after it, they learned to know also the necessity and the meaning of the cross. Now they recognized that God had by the resurrection made this Jesus, whom the Jews had destroyed, to be Lord and Christ and had exalted Him to be a Prince and Savior (Acts 2:36 and 5:31). This does not mean to say that before His resurrection Jesus was not yet Christ and Lord, and that He became this only after the resurrection, for Christ had proclaimed Himself as the Christ beforehand and He was then also acknowledged and confessed as such by the disciples (Matt. 16:16). But before the resurrection He was Messiah in the form of a servant, in a form and shape which concealed His dignity as Son of God from the eyes of men. In the resurrection and after it He laid aside that form of a servant, He re-assumed the glory which He had with the Father before the world was (John 17:5), and was therefore appointed as Son of God in power, according to the spirit of holiness that dwelt in Him (Rom. 1:3).

It is therefore that Paul can say that He now, after it has pleased God to reveal His Son to him, no longer knows Christ according to the flesh (2 Cor. 5:16). Before His repentance He knew Christ only according to the flesh, judged Him solely by His external appearance, according to the form of a servant in which He walked about on the earth. Then he could not believe that this Jesus, who was without any glory and was even hanged on the cross and put to death, was the Christ. But by his conversion all that has changed. Now he knows and judges Christ not according to appearance, not according to external, temporal, servant forms, but according to the spirit, according to what was in Christ, according to what He really was internally and in His resurrection externally proved to be.

And the same can in a sense be said of all the apostles. It is true that they had before the passion and death of Christ been brought to a believing confession of His Messianic reality. But in their mind there remained an irreconcilability of this reality with the passion and death. The resurrection, however, reconciled this conflict for them. He was to them now the same Christ who has descended into the lower parts of the earth and is ascended up far above all heavens, in order that He might fulfill all things (Eph. 4:9). Speaking of Christ, the apostles think in one and the same breath of the deceased and of the raised Christ, of the crucified and of the glorified Christ. They connect their gospel with the historical Jesus not only, who lived a few years back in Palestine and died there, but also to that same Jesus as He is, exalted, and seated at the right hand of God's power. They stand, so to speak, at the point of bisection of the horizontal line, which is tied to the past, to history, and the vertical line, which connects them with the living Lord in heaven. Christianity is therefore an historical religion, but at the same time a religion which lives in the present out of eternity. The disciples of Jesus are not, according to His historical name, Jesuites, but, according to the name of His office, Christians.

* * * * *

This peculiar position which the apostles took in their preaching after the resurrection is the reason why they no longer referred to Jesus by His historical name merely, but virtually always spoke of Him as Jesus Christ, Christ Jesus, our Lord Jesus Christ, and so on. As a matter of fact the name Christ soon lost its official significance in the circle of the disciples and began to take on that of a given name. The conviction that Jesus was the Christ was so strong that He could simply be called Christ, even without the article preceding it. This occurs a few times even in the gospels.[8] But with the apostles, particularly with Paul, this becomes the rule. Moreover, the two names, Jesus Christ, were more than once reversed, especially by Paul, with a view to accentuating even more the Messianic reality of Christ, and then the name became Christ Jesus. This designation, Jesus Christ or Christ Jesus, was the pre-eminent name for the early churches. The use and significance of the name in the Old Testament is carried over to Christ in the New. The Name of the Lord, or the Name alone, was in the Old Testament the denomination of the revealed glory of God. In the days of the New Testament that glory has appeared in the person of Jesus Christ; and thus the strength of the church now stands in His name. In that name the apostles baptize (Acts 2:38), speak and teach (Acts 4:18), heal the cripple (Acts 3:6), and forgive sin (Acts 10:43). This name is resisted and it is attacked (Acts 26:9). The confession of it brings on suffering (Acts 5:41). It is appealed to (Acts 22:8) and is magnified (Acts 19:17). In this sense the name of Jesus Christ was a sort of compendium of the confession of the church, the strength of its faith, and the anchor of its hope. Just as Israel in ancient times gloried in the name of Jehovah, so the church of the New Testament finds its strength in the name of Jesus Christ. In this name the name of Jehovah has come into its full revelation.

The name of *Lord,* which in the New Testament is constantly connected with that of Jesus Christ, points in the same direction. In the gospels Jesus is addressed by the name Lord a number of times by persons who were not of the disciples, but nevertheless call on Him for help.

---

8. Matt. 8:2, 6, 21; 15:22; 17:15; and other passages.

In such instances the name usually carries no more force than that of Rabbi or Master. But we also find this name often spoken by the disciples.[9] Further, in the gospel accounts the name of Jesus is sometimes interchanged by Luke and John with that of Lord.[10] And, finally, Jesus Himself also makes use of that name, designating Himself as the Lord.[11]

In the mouth of Jesus Himself and of the disciples this name of the Lord takes on a much profounder significance than is contained in the appellation *Rabbi* or *Master*. Just what everybody who came to Jesus for help and addressed Him with the name Lord meant by it cannot be said with certainty. But Jesus was in His own consciousness the teacher, the master, the Lord pre-eminently, and He ascribed an authority to Himself which went far beyond that of the scribes. So much is evident already in such passages as Matthew 23:1-11 and Mark 1:22 and 27 where Jesus exalts Himself as the only Master above all other. But it is much more resolutely expressed, and is put beyond all possibility of doubt, when He calls Himself a Lord of the Sabbath (Matt. 12:8) and elsewhere calls Himself David's Son and David's Lord (Matt. 22:43-45). In these claims nothing less is involved than that He is the Messiah, who is seated at the right hand of God, shares His power, and judges of the living and the dead.[12]

This deep significance which attaches itself to the name of Lord is owing in part also, presumably, to the fact that the names of Jehovah and Adonai of the Old Testament were translated by the Greek *kurios*, Lord, in the New, that is, by the same word which was also applied to the Christ. As Christ more and more clearly explained Himself, who He was, and as the disciples understood better and better which revelation of God had come to them in Christ, the name of Lord took on a richer and richer significance. Texts of the Old Testament in which God was spoken of were applied to the Christ in the New without hesitation. Thus in Mark 1:3 the text from Isaiah, Prepare ye the way of the Lord, make His paths straight, is referred to and applied to the preparation by John the Baptist as its fulfillment. In Christ, God Himself, the Lord, has come to His people. And the disciples, by confessing Jesus as Lord, have thus more and more clearly expressed that God Himself had revealed and given Himself to them in the person of Christ. It is Thomas who mounts to the very climax of this confession during Jesus' sojourn

---

9. Matt. 14:28, 30; 26:22; 11:3; 21:15, 16, 17, and 21.
10. Luke 1:43; 2:11, 38; 7:13, 31; 10:1; 11:39; 17:6; and John 4:1; 6:23; 11:2; 20:2, 13, 18, 25, and 28; and so on.
11. Matt. 7:21; 12:8; 21:3; 22:43-45; Mark 5:19; and John 13:14.
12. Matt. 21:4, 5; 13:35; 24:42ff.; and 25:34ff.

on earth when he falls at the feet of the resurrected Christ and addresses Him with the words: My Lord and my God (John 20:28).

After the resurrection the name of Lord becomes the name commonly used for Jesus in the circle of His disciples. We find it continually in the Acts and in the letters, especially the letters of Paul. Sometimes the name Lord is used alone, but usually it goes combined with other designations: the Lord Jesus, or the Lord Jesus Christ, or our Lord Jesus Christ, or our Lord and Savior Jesus Christ, and so on. By using this name of Lord the believers express that Jesus Christ who was humiliated to the point of death and the cross, has by reason of His perfect obedience been raised to Lord and Prince (Acts 2:35 and 5:31), who is seated at God's right hand (Acts 2:34), who is Lord of all (Acts 10:36): first of all the church which He has purchased with His blood (Acts 20:28), and further of all creation which He will sometime judge as the Judge of living and dead (Acts 10:42 and 17:31).

Whoever, therefore, shall call upon the name of Jesus as Christ and Lord, shall be saved (Acts 2:21 and 1 Cor. 1:2). To be Christian is to confess with the mouth and to believe with the heart that God has raised Him up from the dead.[13] The content of the preaching is: Christ Jesus, the Lord (2 Cor. 4:5). So completely is the essence of Christianity epitomized in this confession that in the writings of Paul the name of Lord almost comes to be used as a given name applied to Christ in His distinction from the Father and the Spirit. As Christians we have one God, the Father, of whom are all things, and we in Him, and one Lord Jesus Christ, by whom are all things, and we by Him, and one and the selfsame Spirit, dividing to every man severally as He will (1 Cor. 8:6 and 12:11). Just as the name of God in the writings of Paul becomes the domestic name of the Father, so the name of Lord becomes the domestic name of Christ.

The apostolic blessing, accordingly, prays that the church may have the grace of the Lord Jesus Christ, the love of God, and the fellowship of the Holy Spirit (2 Cor. 13:13). The one name of God interprets itself in the three persons of Father, Son, and Spirit (Matt. 28:19).

* * * * *

If Christ, according to the testimony of the apostles, occupies so high a place, it is no wonder that all kinds of Divine attributes and works are ascribed to Him, and that even the Divine nature is recognized in Him.

---

13. Rom. 10:9; 1 Cor. 12:3; and Phil. 2:11.

The figure we encounter in the person of Christ on the pages of Scripture is a unique figure. On the one hand, He is very man. He became flesh and came into the flesh (John 1:14 and 1 John 4:2-3). He bore the likeness of sinful flesh (Rom. 8:3). He came of the fathers, according to the flesh (Rom. 9:5), of Abraham's seed (Gal. 3:16), of Judah's line (Heb. 7:14), and of David's generation (Rom 1:3). He was born of a woman (Gal. 4:4), partook of our flesh and blood (Heb. 2:14), possessed a spirit (Matt. 27:50), a soul (Matt. 26:38), and a body (1 Peter 2:24), and was human in the full, true sense. As a child He grew, and waxed strong in spirit, and increased in wisdom and stature, and in favor with God and man (Luke 2:40 and 52). He was hungry and thirsty, sorrowful and joyful, was moved by emotion and stirred to anger.[14] He placed Himself under the law and was obedient to it until death.[15] He suffered, died on the cross, and was buried in a garden. He was without form or comeliness. When we looked upon Him there was no beauty that we should desire Him. He was despised, and unworthy of esteem, a man of sorrows and acquainted with grief (Isa. 53:2-3).

Nevertheless this same man was distinguished from all men and raised high above them. Not only was He according to His human nature conceived by the Holy Spirit; not only was He throughout His life, despite all temptation, free from sin; and not only was He after His death raised up again and taken into heaven; but the same subject, the same person, the same *I* who humiliated Himself so deeply that He assumed the form of a servant and became obedient unto the death of the cross, already existed in a different form of existence long before His incarnation and humiliation. He existed then in the form of God and thought it no robbery to be equal with God (Phil. 2:6). At His resurrection and ascension He simply received again the glory which He had with the Father before the world was (John 17:5). He is eternal as God Himself, having been with Him already in the beginning (John 1:1 and 1 John 1:1). He is the Alpha and the Omega, the first and the last, the beginning and the end (Rev. 22:13); He is omnipresent, so that, though walking about on the face of the earth, He is simultaneously in the bosom of the Father in heaven (John 1:18 and 3:13); and after His glorification He remains with His church and fulfills all in all;[16] He is unchangeable and faithful and is the same yesterday, and today, and forever (Heb. 13:8); He is omniscient, so that He hears prayers;[17] He is the One who knows all men's hearts (Acts 1:24; unless the reference here is to the Father); He is omnipotent so that all things are subjected

---

14. Matt. 4:2; John 11:35; and 19:28; and elsewhere.
15. Gal. 4:4; Phil. 2:8; Heb. 5:8; and 10:7, 9.
16. Matt. 28:20; Eph. 1:23; and 4:10.
17. Acts 1:24; 7:59; 16:13; Rom. 10:13 and elsewhere.

unto Him and all power is given to Him in heaven and on earth, and is the chief of all kings.[18]

While in possession of all these Divine attributes, He also shares in the Divine works. Together with the Father and the Spirit He is the creator of all things (John 1:3 and Col. 1:5). He is the firstborn, the beginning, and the Head of all creatures (Col. 1:15 and Rev. 3:14). He upholds all things by the word of His might, so that they are not only of Him but also continuously in Him and through Him (Heb. 1:3 and Col. 1:17). And, above all, He preserves, reconciles, and restores all things and gathers them into one under Himself as Head. As such He bears especially the name of the Savior of the world. In the Old Testament the name of Savior or Redeemer was given to God,[19] but in the New Testament the Son as well as the Father bears this name. In some places this name is given to God,[20] and in some places it is given to Christ.[21] Sometimes it is not clear whether the name refers to God or to Christ (Tit. 2:13 and 2 Peter 1:1). But it is Christ in whom and through whom the saving work of God is wholly effected.

All this points to a unity between Father and Son, between God and Christ, such as nowhere else exists between the Creator and His creature. Even though Christ has assumed a human nature which is finite and limited and which began to exist in time, as person, as Self, Christ does not in Scripture stand on the side of the creature but on the side of God. He partakes of God's virtues and of His works; He possesses the same Divine nature. This last point comes into particularly clear expression in the three names which are given Christ: that of the Image, the Word, and the Son of God.

Christ is the Image of God, the brightness of God's glory, and the express image of His person.[22] In Christ the invisible God has become visible. Whoever sees Him sees the Father (John 14:9). Whoever wants to know who God is and what He is must behold the Christ. As Christ is, such is the Father. Further, Christ is the Word of God (John 1:1 and Rev. 19:13). In Him the Father has perfectly expressed Himself: His wisdom, His will, His excellences, His whole being. He has given Christ to have life in Himself (John 5:26). Whoever wants to learn to know God's thought, God's counsel, and God's will for mankind and the world, let him listen to Christ, and hear Him (Matt. 17:5). Finally, Christ is the Son of God, *the Son,* as John describes Him, often without any further qualification (1 John 2:22 ff. and Heb. 1:1, 8), the

18. Matt. 28:18; 1 Cor. 15:27; Eph. 1:22; Rev. 1:4; and 19:16.
19. Isa. 43:3, 11; 45:15; Jer. 14:8; and Hos. 13:4.
20. 1 Tim. 1:11; 2:3; Titus 1:3; and 2:10.
21. 2 Tim. 1:10; Tit. 1:4; 2:13; 3:6; 2 Peter 1:11; 2:20; and 3:18.
22. 2 Cor. 4:4; Col. 1:15; and Heb. 1:3.

one and only-begotten, the own and beloved Son, in whom the Father is well pleased.[23] Whoever would be a child of God, let him accept Christ, for all who accept Him receive the right and the power to be called the children of God (John 1:12).

Scripture finally places its crown upon this testimony of Scripture by also allowing Him the Divine name. Thomas confessed Him already before the ascension as his Lord and his God (John 20:28). John testifies of Him that as the Word He was with God at the beginning and Himself was God. Paul declares that He is from the fathers according to the flesh but that according to His essence He is God above all, to be blessed forever (Rom. 9:5). The letter to the Hebrews states that He is exalted high above the angels and is by God Himself addressed by the name of God (Heb. 1:8-9). Peter speaks of Him as our God and Savior Jesus Christ (2 Peter 1:1). In the baptismal mandate of Jesus as reported in Matthew 28:19, and in the benedictions of the apostles,[24] Christ stands on one line with the Father and the Spirit. The name and essence, the attributes and works of the Godhead are recognized in the Son (and the Spirit) as well as in the Father.

Jesus the Christ, the Son of the living God — upon this stone is the church built. From the very beginning the wholly unique significance of Christ was clear to all believers. He was confessed by them all as the Lord who by His teaching and life had accomplished salvation, the forgiveness of sins, and immortality, who was thereupon raised by the Father to His right hand, and who would soon return as Judge to judge the living and the dead. The same names that are given Him in the letters of the apostles are given Him also in the earliest Christian writings. By those names He is addressed in the early prayers and songs. All were convinced that there is one God, that they were His children, one Lord who had made sure and granted to them the love of God, and one Spirit, who caused them all to walk in newness of life. The baptismal mandate of Matthew 28:19, which came into general use at the end of the apostolic period, is the evidence of this unanimity of conviction.

But the moment Christians began to reflect on the content of this confession, all kinds of difference of opinion became apparent. The members of the church, who were previously educated in Jewry or heathendom and for the most part were among the untutored of the country, were not in position immediately to appropriate the apostolic teaching in their own minds. They lived in a society in which all kinds of ideas and currents of thought were criss-crossing, and thus they continuously were subject to much temptation and error. Even during the life of the

23. Matt. 3:17; 17:5; John 1:14; Rom. 8:32; Eph. 1:6; and Col. 1:13.
24. 2 Cor. 13:13; 1 Peter 1:2; and Rev. 1:4-6.

apostles we notice that various heretical teachers had forced their way into the church and tried to wrench it from the fixity of its belief. At Colosse, for instance, there were members who did injustice to the person and work of Christ and changed the gospel into a new law (Col. 2:3 ff. and 16 ff.). At Corinth certain libertines stood up, who, abusing Christian liberty, wanted to be bound to no rule (1 Cor. 6:12 and 8:1). The apostle John in his first letter conducts an argument against certain so-called prophets who denied the coming of Christ into the flesh and thus did violence to the genuineness of His human nature (1 John 2:18 ff.; 4:1 ff.; 5:5 ff.).

And so it remained in the post-apostolic period. In fact, the errors and heresies grew in variety, force, and distribution from the second century on. There were those who believed in the real human nature of Christ, in His supernatural birth, His resurrection and ascension, but who recognized the Divine in Him in nothing more than an unusual measure of the gifts and powers of the Spirit. These were thought of as having been given Him at His baptism in order to equip Him for His religious-moral task. The followers of this movement lived under the influence of the deistic, Jewish idea of the relationship of God and the world. They simply could not conceive of a more intimate relationship between God and man than one which consisted of a sharing of gifts and abilities. Jesus, accordingly, was indeed a richly endowed person, a religious genius, but He was and He remained a man.

But others, brought up formerly in heathendom, found themselves attracted rather to the polytheistic idea. They thought that they could very well understand that Christ, according to His inner nature, should be one of the many, or even perhaps the highest, of all Divine beings. But they could not believe that such a Divine, pure being could have assumed a material and fleshly nature. And so they sacrificed the real humanity of Christ and said that it was only temporarily, and in appearance merely, that He had gone about on earth, much as the Angels according to Old Testament report had often done. Both thought-currents, both movements, continue up to the present day. At one time the Divinity of Christ is sacrificed to the humanity; at another it is the humanity that is sacrificed to the Divinity. There are always extremes which sacrifice the idea to the fact, or the fact to the idea. They do not comprehend the unity and harmony of the two.

* * * * *

But the Christian church from the very beginning stood on a different basis and in the person of Christ confessed the most intimate, the profoundest, and therefore the altogether unique, communion of God and man. Its representatives in the earliest period sometimes expressed themselves in an awkward way. They had to struggle, first to form a somewhat clear notion of the reality, and then to give expression to this idea in clear language. But, all the same, the church did not for that reason let itself be pushed off its base. Rather, the church avoided the one and the other extreme and clung to the teaching of the apostles concerning the person of Christ.

However, when one and the same person shares in the Divine nature and also is very man, it follows that an effort at definition must be made, and at a sharp delineation of how that person is related both to the Deity and to the world. And when this effort was made, a path of error and heresy defined itself again to the right and to the left.

When, in other words, the unity of God — which is a fundamental truth of Christianity — was understood in such a way that the being of God was perfectly coterminus and coincident with the person of the Father, then there remained no room in the Godhead for the Christ. Christ then was pushed outside the pale of deity, and placed alongside of man, for between the Creator and the creature there is no gradual transition. One could then go on to say with Arius that in time and status He transcended the whole world, that He was the first among created creatures, and that He was superior to them all in position and in honor. But Christ thus remains a creature. There was a time when He did not exist, and it is in time that He, like every other creature, was called into existence by God.

In the attempt, however, to hold to the unity of God and at the same time to grant the person of Christ the place of honor proper to Him, it is easy to fall into another error, the error named after its foremost proponent, Sabellius. While Arius, so to speak, identified the being of the Godhead with the person of the Father, Sabellius sacrificed all three of the persons to the being of the Godhead. According to His teaching, the three persons, Father, Son, and Spirit, are not eternal realities, contained in the being of the Godhead, but they are forms and manifestations in which the one Divine Being manifests Himself successively in the course of the centuries: namely, in the Old Testament, in the earthly sojourn of Christ, and after Pentecost. Both heresies have throughout the centuries found their adherents. The so-called Groningen Theologie, for instance, renewed essentially the doctrine of Arius, and Modern Theology at first walked in the way of Sabellius.

It required much prayer and much struggle for the church to take the right way through all these heresies, the more so because each of them was modified and mingled with all sorts of departures and variations. But under the leadership of great men, eminent by reason of their piety as well as their power of thought, and therefore justly called fathers of the church, that church remained faithful to the teaching of the apostles. At the Synod of Nicea in 325 the church confessed its faith in the one God, the Father, the Almighty, creator of all things visible and invisible, and in one Lord Jesus Christ, the Son of God, who was begotten by the Father as the only-begotten, that is, out of the being of God, God of God, Light of Light, very God of very God, begotten, not made, being of one substance with the Father, by whom all things in heaven and earth were made, and in the Holy Spirit.

Very significant as this Nicean result was it by no means put a stop to the doctrinal disputes. On the contrary, the confession of Nicea gave opportunity for new questions and different answers. For, although the relationship of Christ to the being of God and to the world of men was now determined in the sense that in His person He shared in both, and that He was in His own person both God and man, the question would not down as to the nature of that relationship between those two natures in one person. In the answer to that question, too, various ways were taken.

Nestorius concluded that if there were two natures in Christ, there also had to be two persons, two selves, which could only be made one by some moral tie such as that which obtains in the marriage of a man and a woman. And Eutyches, proceeding from a like identification of person and nature, came to the conclusion that if in Christ there was but one person, one self, present, then the two natures had to be so mingled and welded together that only one nature, a Divine-human one, would emerge from the blending. In Nestorius the distinction of the natures was maintained at the cost of the unity of the person; in Eutyches the unity of the person was maintained at the cost of the duality of the natures.

After a long and vehement struggle, however, the church got beyond these disputes. At the Council of Chalcedon in 451 it stated that the one person of Christ consisted of two natures, unchanged and unmingled (against Eutyches), and not separated nor divided (against Nestorius), and that these natures existed alongside of each other, having their unity in the one person. With this decision which, later, at the Synod of Constantinople in 680 was amplified and completed on one specific point, the century-long struggle about the person of Christ came to an end. In these disputes the church had preserved the essence of Christianity, the absolute character of the Christian religion, and thus also its own independence.

* * * * *

It is of course self-evident that this confession of Nicea and Chalcedon may not lay claim to infallibility. The terms of which the church and its theology make use, such as person, nature, unity of substance, and the like, are not found in Scripture, but are the product of reflection which Christianity gradually had to devote to this mystery of salvation. The church was compelled to do this reflecting by the heresies which loomed up on all sides, both within the church and outside of it. All those expressions and statements which are employed in the confession of the church and in the language of theology are not designed to explain the mystery which in this matter confronts it, but rather to maintain it pure and unviolated over against those who would weaken or deny it. The incarnation of the Word is not a problem which we must solve, or can solve, but a wonderful fact, rather, which we gratefully confess in such a way as God Himself presents it to us in His Word.

But, understood in this way, the confession which the church fixed at Nicea and Chalcedon is of great value. There have been many, and there still are many, who look down upon the doctrine of the two natures from a lofty vantage point, and try to supplant it by other words and phrases. What difference does it really make, they begin by saying, whether we agree with this doctrine or not? What matters is that we ourselves possess the person of Christ, He who stands high and exalted above this awkward confession. But before long these same persons begin introducing words and terms themselves in order to describe the person of Christ whom they accept. Nobody can escape from this situation, for what we do not know we cannot claim to possess. If we believe that we have the Christ, that we have communion with Him, that we are His own, then such belief must be confessed with the mouth and be spoken in words, terms, expressions, and descriptions of some kind or other. And then history has taught that the terms of the attackers of the Doctrine of Two Natures are far poorer in worth and force, and that they often, indeed, involve doing injustice to the incarnation as Scripture explains it to us.

In modern times, for instance, there are many who think of the Doctrine of Two Natures as the acme of unreasonableness and who in their minds form an entirely different picture of the person of Christ. They cannot deny that there is something in Christ which differentiates Him from all men and raises Him above them all. But this Divine element which they recognize in Christ they regard not as a partaking of the Divine nature itself, but as a Divine endowment or strength granted to Christ in a particularly high degree. They tend to say, accordingly, that there are two sides to Christ, a Divine and a human side; or that He can be looked at from two points of view; or that He lived in two successive states, that of humiliation and that of exaltation; or that He, although human, by His preaching of the Word of God and the founding of His kingdom, nevertheless was the extraordinary and perfect vehicle of God's revelation and so has obtained for us the value of God. But any unprejudiced reader will feel that these representations are simply so many modifications in the language of the church not merely, but also that they make something of the person of Christ other than that which the church at all times on the basis of the testimony of the apostles has confessed.

After all, Divine gifts and powers are in a certain sense given to everyone, for all good and perfect gifts come down from the Father of lights. And even the unusual gifts, such as were the portion of the prophets, for example, do not raise these prophets above the plane of human beings. Prophets and apostles were men of like passions as we have. If Christ therefore received no more than extraordinary gifts and powers, He was no more than a human being, and then there can be no such thing as an incarnation of the Word in Him. But then He cannot, as others nevertheless maintain, by virtue of His resurrection and ascension be raised to the being of God, or have obtained the value or worth of God for us. The separation between God and man is not a gradual difference but a deep gulf. The relationship is that of Creator and creature, and the creature from the nature of his being can never become Creator, nor have the significance and worth for us human beings of the Creator, on whom we are absolutely dependent.

It is remarkable, therefore, that some in modern times, after having compared all these newer representations concerning the person of Christ with the teaching of the church and of Scripture, have come to the honest conclusion that in the last analysis the doctrine of the church does most justice to the doctrine of Scripture. The teaching that Christ was God and man in one person is not a product of heathen philosophy but is based on the apostolic witness.

This certainly is the mystery of salvation that He who was Himself with God in the beginning and was God (John 1:1), who was in the form of God and did not think it robbery to be equal with God (Phil. 2:6), who was the brightness of God's glory and the express image of His person (Heb. 1:3), in the fulness of time became flesh (John 1:14), was born of a woman (Gal. 4:4), humbled Himself, having taken on the form of a servant, and was made in the likeness of men (Phil. 2:7).

* * * * *

Christ was God, and is God, and will forever remain God. He was not the Father, nor the Spirit, but the Son, the own, only-begotten, beloved Son of the Father. And it was not the Divine being, neither the Father nor the Spirit, but the person of the Son who became man in the fulness of time. And when He became man and as man went about on earth, even when He agonized in Gethsemane and hung on the cross, He remained God's own Son in whom the Father was well pleased (had all His pleasure). It is true, of course, as the apostle says, that Christ, being in the form of God, did not think it robbery to be equal with God, yet made Himself of no reputation and emptied Himself (Phil. 2:6-7). But it is a mistake to take this to mean, as some do, that Christ, in His incarnation, in the state of humiliation, completely or partly divested Himself of His Divinity, laid aside His Divine attributes, and thereupon in the state of exaltation gradually assumed them again. For how could this be, since God cannot deny Himself (2 Tim. 2:13), and as the Immutable One in Himself far transcends all becoming and change? No, even when He became what He was not, He remained what He was, the Only-Begotten of the Father. But it is true that the Apostle says that in this sense Christ made Himself of no reputation: being in the form of God, He assumed the form of a man and a servant. One can express it humanly and simply in this way: before His incarnation Christ was equal with the Father not alone in essence and attributes, but He had also the form of God. He looked like God, He was the brightness of His glory, and the expressed image of His person. Had anyone been able to see Him, he would immediately have recognized God. But this changed at His incarnation. Then He took on the form of a human being, the form of a servant. Whoever looked at Him now could no longer recognize in Him the Only-Begotten Son of the Father, except by the eye of faith. He had laid aside His Divine form and brightness. He hid His Divine nature behind the form of a servant. On earth He was and He looked like one of us.

The incarnation therefore also implies in the second place that He who remained what He was also became what He was not. He became this at a point in time, at a particular moment in history, at that hour when the Holy Spirit came over Mary and the power of the Most High overshadowed her (Luke 1:35). But all the same this incarnation was prepared for during the centuries.

If we are to understand the incarnation aright, we can say that the generation of the Son and the creation of the world were preparatory to the incarnation of the Word. This is not at all to say that the generation and the creation already contain the incarnation. For Scripture always relates the incarnation of the Son to the redemption from sin and the accomplishment of salvation.[25] But the generation and creation, especially also the creation of man in the image of God, both teach that God is sharable, in an absolute sense within, and in a relative sense out-

---

25. Matt. 1:21; John 3:16; Rom. 8:3; and Gal. 4:4, 5.

side of, the Divine being. If this were not the case, there would not be any possibility of an incarnation of God. Whoever thinks the incarnation of God impossible in principle also denies the creation of the world and the generation of the Son. And whoever acknowledges the creation and generation can have no objection in principle to the incarnation of God in human nature.

More directly the incarnation of the Word was prepared for in the revelation which began immediately after the fall, continued in Israel's history, and reached its climax in the blessing of Mary. The Old Testament is a constantly closer approximation of God to man with a view, in the fulness of time, to making perpetual dwelling in him.

Since the Son of God, who took on human nature in Mary, had existed before that time, and from eternity, as the person of the Son, His conception in Mary's womb did not take place through the will of the flesh nor the will of the man, but by the overshadowing of the Holy Spirit. It is true that the incarnation is linked with the preceding revelation and completes it, but it is not itself a product of nature or of humanity. It is a work of God, a revelation, the highest revelation. Just as it was the Father who sent His Son into the world, and the Holy Spirit who overshadowed Mary, so it was the Son Himself who took of our flesh and blood (Heb. 2:14). The incarnation was His own work; He was not passive in regard to it. He became flesh by His own will and His own deed. Therefore He sets aside the will of the flesh and the will of the man, and prepares a human nature for Himself in Mary's womb through the overshadowing of the Holy Spirit.

That human nature did not exist beforehand. It was not brought down with Christ from heaven and borne into Mary from the outside and, so to speak, conducted through her body. The Anabaptists teach this in order to hold to the sinlessness of the human nature in Christ. But in taking this stand, they are following in the example of the ancient gnosticism, and proceed from the idea that flesh and matter are in themselves sinful. But in the incarnation, also, Scripture holds to the goodness of creation and to the Divine origin of matter.

Christ took His human nature *from* Mary.[26] So far as the flesh is concerned, He is from David and the fathers.[27] Therefore this nature in Him is a true and perfect human nature, like ours in all things, sin excepted.[28] Nothing human was strange to Christ. The denial of the coming of Christ in the flesh is the beginning of the antichrist (1 John 2:22).

---

26. Matt. 1:20; Luke 2:7; and Gal. 4:4.
27. Acts 2:30; Rom. 1:3; and 9:5.
28. Heb. 2:14, 17; and 4:15.

Just as the human nature of Christ did not exist before the conception in Mary, so it did not exist for sometime before, nor for some time after, in a state of separation from Christ. The seed conceived in Mary, and the child that was born of her, did not first grow up independently into a man, into a person, a self, in order then to be assumed by the Christ and united with Himself. This heresy, too, had its supporters in earlier and later times, but Scripture knows nothing of it. That holy thing which was conceived in Mary's womb was from the beginning the Son of God and from the beginning He bore that name (Luke 1:35). The Word did not later take a human being unto Himself, but *became* flesh (John 1:14). And therefore the Christian church in its confession said that the person of the Son did not assume a human person but a human nature, rather. Only in that way can the duality of the natures and the unity of the person be maintained.

For — and this is the third point which requires our attention in this matter — even though Scripture states as plainly as possible that Christ was the Word and that He became flesh, that according to the flesh He was from the fathers but that according to His essence He is God over all, blessed forever, still in that Christ it always presents *one* person to us. It is always the same Self that speaks and acts in Christ. The child which is born bears the name of the mighty God, the everlasting Father (Isa. 9:6). David's Son is at the same time David's Lord. The same one who came down is the one who ascended up far above all heavens (Eph. 4:10). He who according to the flesh is from the fathers is according to His essence God over all, blessed forever (Rom.9:5). Though going about on earth He was and He remained in heaven, in the bosom of the Father (John 1:18 and 3:13). Born in time and living in time He nevertheless is before Abraham (John 8:58). The fulness of the Godhead dwells bodily in Him (Col. 2:9).

In short, to one and the same subject, one and the same person, Divine and human attributes and works, eternity and time, omnipresence and limitation, creative omnipotence and creaturely weakness are ascribed. This being so, the union of the two natures in Christ cannot have been that of two persons. Two persons can through love be intimately united with each other, it is true, but they can never become one person, one self. In fact, love implies two persons and effects only a mystical and ethical unity. If the union of the Son of God with human nature were of this character it could at best be distinguished in degree but not in kind from that which unites God with His creatures, specifically with His children. But Christ occupies a unique position. He did not unite Himself in a moral way with man, and did not take an existing human being up into His fellowship, but He prepared a human nature for Himself in Mary's womb and *became* a human being and a servant. Just as a human being can go from one state of life to another, and can live at the same time or in succession in two spheres of life, so, by way of analogy, Christ, who was in the form of God, went about on earth in the form of a servant. The union which in His incarnation came to be effected was not a moral union between two persons, but a union of two natures in the same person. Man and woman, no matter how intimately united in love, remain two persons. God and man, although united by the most intimate love, remain different in essence. But in Christ man is the same subject as the Word which in the beginning was with God and Himself was God. This is a unique, incomparable, and unfathomable union of God and man. And the beginning and end of all wisdom is this: And the Word was made flesh, and dwelt among us, and we beheld His glory, the glory as of the only-begotten of the Father, full of grace and truth (John 1:14).

In this union Christ in the unity of His person commands all the attributes and powers which are proper to both natures. Some have tried to effect a still stronger and closer union of the two natures by teaching that the two natures, immediately at the incarnation, were welded into one Divine-human nature, or that the Divine nature divested itself of its characteristics and condescended to the limitation of human nature, or that the human nature lost its properties and received those of the Divine nature (be it all of them, or just some of them such as omnipresence, omnipotence, omniscience, and quickening power.) But the Reformed confession has always repudiated and attacked such a welding of two natures into one and such a communication of the properties of the one nature to the other. It was a view of the two natures which resulted in a mingling and confusion of them and so in a pantheistic denial of the difference in essence between God and man, Creator and creature.

True, there is an intimate relationship between the two natures and their properties and powers. But it is a relationship which comes into being in the unity of the person. A stronger, deeper, more intimate union is inconceivable. Just as — to make a comparison and not an equating of the two — soul and body are united in one person and nevertheless remain distinguished from each other in essence and properties, so in Christ the same person is the subject of both natures. The difference between soul and body is the assumption and condition of the inner union of the two in one and the same human being, and so too the difference between the Divine and the human nature is the condition and basis of their union in Christ. The welding of the two natures into one and the communication of the properties from one to another make for no more intimate relationship, but make for a mingling or fusion, and, in point of fact, impoverish the fulness which is in Christ. They subtract either from the Divine, or from the human, nature, or from both natures, and weaken the word of the Scripture that in Him, that is, in Christ, the *fulness* of the Godhead bodily dwells (Col. 2:9 and 1:19). That fulness is maintained only if both natures are distinguished from each other, communicating their properties and attributes not to each other, but placing them, rather, in the service of the one person. So it is always the same rich Christ who in His humiliation and exaltation commands the properties and powers of both natures and who precisely by that means can bring those works to pass, which, as the works of the Mediator, are distinguished on the one hand from the works of God and on the other hand from the works of man, and which take a unique place in the history of the world.

By this Doctrine of the Two Natures one has the advantage that everything which Scripture says of the person of Christ and everything it ascribes to Him comes into its own. On the one hand He then is and remains the one and eternal Son of God, who with the Father and the Spirit has made all things, sustains and governs them,[29] and who therefore may remain the object of our worship. He was such an object already in the days of the apostles,[30] even as He was then, and now yet is, the object of the faith and confidence of all His disciples.[31] But He cannot and He may not be both of these things unless He is true God, for it is written: Thou shalt worship the Lord Thy God and Him only shalt thou serve (Matt. 4:10). The basis for the religious worship of Christ can be only His Divine nature, so that whoever denies this and yet maintains the worship becomes guilty of deifying the creature and of idolatry. The Divinity of Christ is not an abstract doctrine but something which is of the highest importance for the life of the church.

On the other hand, the Christ became very man and perfect man, like us in all things, sin excepted. He was infant, child, youth, and man, and He grew in wisdom and in favor with God and man (Luke 2:40 and 52). All this is not appearance and illusion merely, as those must say who hold that the Divine properties belong to the human nature, but it is the full truth. There was in Christ a gradual development, a progressive growth in body, in the powers of the soul, in favor with God and man. The gifts of the Spirit were not given to Him all at once, but successively in ever greater measure. There were things which He had to

---

29. John 1:3; Col. 1:15, 16; and Heb. 1:2.
30. John 14:13; Acts 7:59; 9:13; 22:16; Rom. 10:12-13; Phil. 2:9; and Heb. 1:6.
31. John 14:1; 17:3; Rom. 14:9; 2 Cor. 5:15; Eph. 3:12; 5:23; Col. 1:27; and other passages.

learn, and which at first He did not know (Mark 13:32 and Acts 1:7). Even though He was in possession of the not-able-to-sin state of being, there was in Him, because of His weak human nature, the possibility of being tempted and of suffering and dying. So long as He was on the earth He was not according to His human nature in heaven, and hence He too did not live by sight but by faith. He fought and He suffered, and in all this He clung fixedly to the word and the promise of God. Thus He learned obedience from the things which He suffered, continually established Himself in obedience, and so sanctified Himself.[32] And in this at the same time He left us an example, and became the author of eternal salvation unto all them that obey Him (Heb. 5:9).

32. John 17:19 and Heb. 5:8 and 9.

XVII

The Work of Christ in His Humiliation

The incarnation is the beginning and introduction to the work of Christ on earth, it is true, but it is not the whole meaning, nor the most important meaning of that work. It is good to try to get a true understanding and a right idea about this, for there are those who think that the assumption of the human nature itself completes the full reconciliation and union of God and man. Proceeding from the idea that religion is the kind of fellowship between God and man in which both need and complete each other, they argue that this fellowship, disturbed by sin, or not available to man on the lower, sensuous level, was first expressed and actualized in history by Christ. The uniqueness of Christianity then consists of the fact that the idea of religion which is planted as instinct and nucleus in human nature achieves its fulfillment in the person of Christ.

Now it is no doubt a high honor for mankind that the only-begotten Son, who was in the form of God and in the bosom of the Father, assumed the form of man. For by this assumption Christ is related to all men. He partook of flesh and blood with them, and they have soul and body, head and heart, mind and will, ideas and feelings in common with each other. Christ is in this natural sense the brother of us all, flesh of our flesh, and bone of our bone. But this natural, physical likeness, however important it is, may not be confused or identified with the spiritual and moral communion. Among people too, we must remember, it is possible that members of the same family and blood relatives are in a spiritual sense separated from each other a long way, or even diametrically opposed to each other. Jesus Himself says that He came upon the earth to set a son at variance against his father, and the daughter against her mother, and the daughter-in-law against her mother-in-law, and that a man's foes shall be they of his own household (Matt. 10:35, 36). Natural descent therefore says nothing about spiritual relationship. The commonness of blood and the fellowship of the spirit often are poles apart.

If Jesus had done no more, consequently, than assume the human nature and so give expression to the unity of God and man, it would be entirely beyond comprehension how we could enter into fellowship with

Him and be reconciled with God. Rather He would, by assuming a sin-less human nature and by living in an unperturbed fellowship with God, have introduced further division among us, have plunged us deep under the sense of our helplessness, inasmuch as we, weak, sinful creatures, could never follow in His high example anyhow. The incarnation of the Son of God, therefore, without anything further, cannot be the reconcil-ing and redeeming deed. It is the beginning of it, the preparation for it, and the introduction to it, but it is not that deed itself.

For, if the incarnation had itself effected the reconciliation and union of God and man, there would have been no place for a living, and espe-cially not for a dying, of the Lord Jesus. It would have sufficed then for Him, be it by way of conception and birth or by some other way, to have assumed a human nature, to have gone about on earth for some while, and then to have returned to heaven. There would have been no need for the whole, deep humiliation of Christ.

But Scripture teaches us something very different. It tells us that the Son of God not merely became man, became like us in all things, sin ex-cepted, but also that He took the form of a servant, humiliated Himself, and became obedient to death, even to the death of the cross (Phil. 2:7-8). It became Him to fulfill all righteousness (Matt. 3:15), and to be Himself sanctified by suffering (Heb. 2:10). This was appro-priate and becoming not only but also had to be so. It was written that the Christ should suffer and on the third day arise from the dead (Luke 24:46 and 1 Cor. 15:3-5). The Father sent Him in order to fulfill His work on earth (John 4:34), and even gave Him a commandment to lay down His life and to take it up again (John 10:18). All that Christ experienced therefore was the carrying out of what God's hand and counsel had before determined to be done (Acts 2:23 and 4:28). On the cross for the first time Christ could say that everything was finished and that He had done all that the Father had given Him to do (John 17:4 and 19:30). Although in the gospels the life of Jesus is compara-tively briefly depicted, His last passion and dying is comprehensively told. Just so the apostolic preaching rather rarely goes back to the con-ception and birth of Jesus, but puts all emphasis upon the cross, the death, and the blood of Christ. It is not by the birth but by the death of His Son that we are reconciled to God (Rom. 5:10).

By way of this view of Scripture the whole life of Christ takes on a unique significance for us and a surpassing value. It is a perfect work which the Father has given Him to do. It can be regarded from various points of view and approached from various sides, and it is so that we must view and approach it if we are to survey its content and its scope. But we must never forget that it is *one* work. It comprehends and fills

Christ's whole life from the conception up to the death on the cross. Just as the person of Christ is one in the differentiation of His natures, so His work too is one work. It is pre-eminently *the* work of God on earth. It is a work which, looking backward, is related to the counsel and foreknowledge of God with its revelation in Israel and its guidance of the nations, and which, looking forward, continues itself in modified form in the work which Christ even now still does in His state of exaltation. It is a work which has its central point in time on this earth, but which comes up out of eternity, roots in eternity, and extends into eternity.

* * * * *

Since ancient times this one work of Christ has been comprised in the doctrine of the three offices, and it is especially due to Calvin that this scheme of treating Christ's work has found general entrance into the doctrine of salvation. Nevertheless, objection has been raised to it again and again, and especially this consideration has been pushed to the fore that the three offices in the life of Jesus are not to be distinguished and that their activities flow into each other. It is a consideration, however, which can be raised against a misconception of the three offices, but not against the classification itself.

If the idea were that Jesus executed the three offices of prophet, priest, and king as though they stood discretely alongside of each other, or each of them successively in time, then such a classification and division of the work of Christ would indeed be mistaken. For, though it is true that now one office of Christ comes into the foreground, and then another, so that, for instance, His public ministry reminds of His prophetic, His last passion and death of His priestly, and His exaltation to the Father's right hand of His kingly office, still, essentially Jesus was at all times and places busy in all three offices simultaneously. When He spoke, He proclaimed the word of God as a prophet, but in this He at the same time exhibited His priestly mercy, and His royal might, for by His word He healed the sick, forgave sins, and subdued the storm. He was the King of truth. His miracles were signs of His Divine mission and of the truth of His word, but they were at the same time a revelation of His compassion upon all sorts of afflicted ones, of His dominion over disease and death, and the power of Satan. His death was a putting the seal to His life, but also a sacrifice of perfect obedience, and a willing act of power in the laying down of life. In short, His whole manifestation, word, and work has simultaneously a prophetic, priestly, and kingly character.

But having seen this truth in the foreground, we must go on to look at the person and work of Christ from the viewpoint of the three offices.

There are advantages attaching to such a method which would be lost if we pursued some other.

In the first place such a treatment stresses the truth that the coming, and, indeed, the whole life of Christ on earth, is the exercise and carrying out of an office given Him by the Father. In connection with Jesus we cannot speak of a business, a trade, or even of a moral calling which He Himself has chosen. According to Holy Scripture He was assigned to an office. That is the difference between an office and a profession or trade: one cannot choose it, but only receive it by appointment from a power which stands above us. It is true that He is distinguished from Moses in this regard that He, unlike a servant, but as the Son of His own house, has been faithful to the Father in all things (Heb. 3:5-6). But all the same He was faithful to Him that appointed Him an Apostle and High Priest of our profession (Heb. 3:2). He did not Himself take the honor of being High Priest. He was thus glorified by God Himself who said to Him: Thou art my beloved Son: this day have I begotten Thee (Heb. 5:5). Accordingly, Jesus constantly puts the whole emphasis on the fact that the Father has sent Him; that it is His meat to do the will of the Father; that He has received from the Father a commandment as to what He shall do and say; that He has finished the work of the Father on earth, and the like.[1]

This appointment to office obviously took place before the time at which Christ became man. For Scripture teaches not only that Christ was with God in the beginning and Himself was God, but it further expressly states in Hebrews 10:5-7 that He, coming into the world, said: Sacrifice and offering Thou wouldest not, but a body hast Thou prepared for Me (in order in this body, by yielding it to death, to carry out God's will) ; in burnt offerings and sacrifices for sin Thou hast had no pleasure. But then, when Thou hadst prepared Me a body, then said I, Lo, I come to do Thy will, O God! The coming into the world, the incarnation, therefore, already belonged to the carrying out of the work which the Father laid upon Him to do. The commissioning preceded the incarnation, did not take place in time but from eternity.

Hence it is elsewhere said that Christ was foreordained from before the foundation of the world (1 Peter 1:20), that the election was made and grace was given us in Christ before the world began (Eph. 1:4 and 2 Tim. 1:9), and that the book of life which lies open before God's face from before the foundation of the world is the property of the Lamb that was slain (Rev. 13:8 and 17:8). To conceive of the work of Christ as the exercise of an office is to relate that work to the eternal counsel. He bears the name of Messiah, Christ, the Anointed, because He has

---

1. John 4:34; 5:20, 30; 6:38; 7:16; 8:28; 10:18; 12:49, 50; 14:10, 24; and 17:4.

been ordained of the Father from eternity and has in time been anointed by Him with the Holy Spirit.

In the second place, the three offices with which Christ was commissioned are a reference to the original calling and purpose of man. It is by no means accidental or arbitrary that Christ was appointed precisely to the three offices of prophet, priest, and king, and not to other offices or to more of them. Rather, this is based on the purpose of God for the human race and thus on human nature. Adam was created in the image of God, in true knowledge, righteousness, and holiness, in order that as prophet he should proclaim the words of God, as king he should righteously rule over created things, and as priest dedicate himself and all his own to God as a well pleasing sacrifice. He received a mind in order to know, a hand in order to rule, and a heart to comprehend everything in love. In the unfolding of the image of God, in the harmonious development of all his gifts and powers, in his exercise of the three offices of prophet, priest, and king lay the purpose and destiny of man. But man violated this high calling. And that is why Christ came to earth: to again exhibit the true image of man and to bring his destiny to perfect fulfillment. The doctrine of the three offices lays a firm connection between nature and grace, creation and redemption, Adam and Christ. The first Adam is type, herald, and prophecy of the last Adam, and the Last is the counterpart and fulfillment of the first.

In the third place, the doctrine of the three offices ties in directly with the revelation of the Old Testament. When mankind, fallen in Adam, became more and more corrupt, God chose a particular people as His own. In connection with that calling Israel also received again, as a people, a prophetic, priestly, and kingly task. It had to be a kingdom of priests and a holy nation to the Lord (Ex. 19:6). But in a special sense that task was assigned to the men who were called of God to serve in Israel as prophets, priests, and kings. Even though in its entirety as a nation Israel could be called the Anointed of the Lord, this name nevertheless was especially appropriate to the prophets, priests, and kings. But all of these men were sinners and they could not, therefore, fulfill their offices truly. Like the people as a whole they pointed away from themselves and towards another who should be prophet, priest, and king at one and the same time, and who was to be called the Anointed of the Lord in a unique sense (Isa. 61:1). Christ is the fulfillment of the whole Old Testament revelation. He is the counterpart of all Israel and of all its prophets, priests, and kings. In fact, it is He who in them and through them testifies of Himself and prepares for His coming (1 Peter 1:11).

Finally, it is only if we deal with the work of Christ in terms of the three offices that it comes into its own. There have always been one-sided tendencies in the Christian church which saw in Him only the prophet, like the rationalists, or which occupied itself solely with His priestly passion, like the mystics, or which would hear of Him only as a king, like the Chiliasts. But we need a Christ who is all three at once. We need a prophet who proclaims God to us, a priest who reconciles us with God, and a king who in the name of God rules and protects us. The whole image of God must be restored in man — knowledge, yes, but also holiness and righteousness. The whole man must be saved, according to soul and body, according to head and heart and hand. We need a Savior who redeems us perfectly and entirely and who fully realizes in us our original purpose. Christ does this. Because He Himself is prophet, priest, and king, He in turn makes us prophets, priests, and kings unto God and His Father (Rev. 1:6).

*   *   *   *   *

Although anointed from eternity, and although already active in a preparatory way in the days of the Old Testament as Mediator of the Covenant of Grace, Christ first fully and actually took on himself the offices of prophet, priest, and king, when He came into the world, and said: Lo, I am come to do Thy will, O God. It was then that He first assumed that human nature which equipped him for doing the work of the Mediator. He had to be man in order to reveal God's name to men, in order to be able to suffer and die on the cross, and in order as king of the truth to witness to the truth.

His being conceived by the Holy Spirit was therefore at the same time already a preliminary preparation of the human nature of Christ for the work to which He should later be called. All kinds of objections have been brought up in modern times against the confession that Christ was conceived by the Holy Spirit and born of the Virgin Mary, and many efforts have been put forth to explain this account of Matthew and Luke as a Jewish or pagan interpolation in the original gospel. But the result has been rather that the truth of this history has been confirmed and better established than before. It cannot be derived from the Jews or the Pagans. It is a story, and a history, which rests, as is evident also from the language in which it is reported, on the testimony of Joseph and Mary themselves. Naturally there was a considerable period in which this miraculous conception was known only to Joseph and Mary and perhaps a few further confidants. From the nature of the case, it did not lend itself to public communication.

Only later, when the works and words, and particularly also the resurrection of Christ made it clear who and what He was, only then did Mary take the step of revealing to the small circle of the disciples this secret of Jesus' conception. But even after that time this conception by the Spirit never occupied the foreground in the preaching of the apostles. It is probably assumed in a number of places,[2] but except in Matthew and Luke it is nowhere expressly stated. All the same it is an essential component of the gospel and it corresponds totally with the whole doctrine of the person of Christ which Scripture teaches. He was, we remember, the Only-Begotten Son who, as the Word, was with God and was God from the beginning, who Himself was active at the conception, and through the activity of the Holy Spirit prepared Himself a human nature in Mary's womb (Phil. 2:6-7). The prophecy of Isaiah 7:14 (and 9:6; and compare Matt. 1:25) was fulfilled in Him that a virgin (a young, unmarried woman) should conceive and bear a son, and should call his name Immanuel, who should bear also the names of Wonderful, Counsellor, The mighty God, The everlasting Father, The Prince of Peace.

By this conception through the Holy Spirit this human nature of Christ was from its beginning free from all human sin. Since the Son of God as a person existed already beforehand, and since that person did not unite itself with an existing human being, but, through the activity of the Holy Spirit, prepared itself a human nature in Mary's womb, He was not included in the covenant of works, had no original guilt to bear, and could not become contaminated by any pollution of sin. The teaching of Rome that Mary herself was untainted and pure in her conception, and that she lived holily, is unnecessary, unfounded, and even in conflict with what Scripture says about Mary.[3] Mary enjoyed a high honor, an honor greater than the prophets and apostles ever had. She is the blessed, the favored, among women, and the mother of the Lord (Luke 1:42-43). But she herself was like all flesh, like all men; and that holy thing which was born of her (Luke 1:35) was not owing to the purity of her nature, but to the creative and the sanctifying activity of the Holy Spirit in her womb.

Even though the human nature which Christ took from Mary was holy, it was nevertheless a weak human nature. This is expressed in Scripture by the statement that He became man not only but also flesh (John 1:14), that He was sent in the likeness of sinful flesh (Rom. 8:3), that He took upon Himself the form of a servant (Phil. 2:7), and that He became like us in all things, sin excepted (Heb. 2:17 and 4:15). Christ had to assume such a weak human nature in order to be tempted, in order to learn obedience from suffering, in order to be able to struggle and in the struggle to sanctify Himself, in order to sympathize with us

---

2. Mark 6:3; John 1:13; 7:41, 42; Rom. 1:3, 4; 9:5; Phil. 2:7; and Gal. 4:4.
3. John 2:4; Mark 3:31; and Luke 11:28.

in our weaknesses and to be a compassionate and faithful high priest: in short, in order to be able to suffer and die. Although He was like Adam before the fall in this respect that He was without sin, He was in other ways very different from Adam. For Adam was created adult at once, but Christ was conceived in Mary's womb and was born as a helpless babe. When Adam came, everything stood ready for him, but when Christ came to earth no one had counted on His coming and there was even no place for Him in the inn. Adam came to rule, and to subject the whole earth to his dominion. Christ came not to be served, but to serve, and to give His life a ransom for many.

The incarnation of the Son of God was not only therefore a deed of condescending goodness, such as it still remains in the state of exaltation; but it was simultaneously also a deed of deep humiliation. The humiliation began with the conception itself, and continued through His life up to His death and the grave. Christ was not a human hero whose motto is Excelsior, who overcomes every obstacle, and finally achieves the pinnacle of his fame. On the contrary He descended always lower and deeper and more intimately into our fellowship. The way down into these depths was marked by tiers or steps: conception, birth, the lowly life in Nazareth, baptism and temptation, opposition, disparagement, and persecution, agony in Gethsemane, condemnation before Caiaphas and Pilate, crucifixion, death, and burial. The way led ever farther down from His home with the Father, and it led ever nearer to us in the fellowship of our sin and our death, until finally in the deepest depth of His suffering He gave utterance to the anxious plaint about being forsaken of God. And then He could also give utterance to the cry of victory: It is finished!

To this humiliation belong, in addition to the conception and birth themselves, the simple circumstances in which Jesus was born in a stable in Bethlehem, the persecution to which He was exposed by Herod, the flight to Egypt which was forced upon Him and His parents, and also the quiet, inner life which Jesus led during His childhood years in Nazareth. Very little is reported of this in the gospels, for the gospels were not at all intended, in the new-fashioned sense, to be a "life of Jesus," but rather to cause us to know Christ as the Son of God, the Savior of the world, and the Only-Begotten of the Father. In connection with that purpose, the little that is told us about Jesus' childhood and youth is sufficient.

Matthew tells us that Jesus, after His return from Egypt, went to live with His parents in Nazareth of Galilee (Matt. 2:23). There his mother had lived earlier (Luke 1:26), and there Jesus spent His days until His public ministry in Israel (Luke 2:39, 51; and Mark 1:9). Only after

He had stood up in their synagogue and was rejected by His townsmen, did He come to reside in Capernaum (Luke 4:28ff. and Matt. 4:13). But He always kept the name of Nazarene. In this, Matthew saw a fulfillment of the Old Testament prophecy (Matt. 2:23), not of a particular statement, for Nazareth and Nazarene are mentioned nowhere in the Old Testament, but of prophecy as a whole, such as it is to be found in all of the prophets, namely, that Christ should have a humble, modest origin (Isa. 11:1), and that the light should dawn upon the darkness of the Galilee of the nations (Isa. 8:22 and 9.1).

We know that Jesus in the retired life which He lived for years in Nazareth was a child who was obedient to His parents (Luke 2:51). As a child He grew up physically and waxed strong in spirit, and increased in favor with God and man (Luke 2:40 and 52). When He was twelve years old He went with His parents, whether for the first time or for another time, to Jerusalem to celebrate the Passover (Luke 2:41 ff.), and there He exhibited by His questions and answers His wisdom in the midst of the Jewish scribes not only, but He also revealed to His parents the consciousness of His calling: that as the Son He must be busy in the things (or the house) of His Father (Luke 2:49). On the Sabbath Day, He went, as was His custom, to the synagogue (Luke 4:16), and during the week days He presumably assisted His father at his trade. At least He is Himself later called the Carpenter (Mark 6:3). His later life casts this much further light on these young years: that we know He could read and write, was thoroughly familiar with the Old Testament, saw through the party of the Pharisees and Sadducees, knew the moral need of the people, was well abreast of the civic and political life of the time, and that He loved nature and frequently withdrew into solitude for communion with God. Meager as these data are, they all point to the fact that Jesus in those withdrawn years of His life was preparing Himself for the task which awaited Him in public life later. It became more and more clear to Him as man what He was and what He had to do. His Sonship and His Messiahship, with all that was connected with these and issued from them, came to loom always clearer before His mind's eye. And finally, at the age of thirty, the time arrived in which He should be made manifest to Israel (John 1:31).

The occasion for this public manifestation was the preaching which John the Baptist had begun in the south, in the wilderness of Judaea. Sent by God to tell Israel that in spite of its descent from Abraham, its circumcision, and its self-righteousness, it was guilty and polluted and therefore needed the baptism of repentance unto the forgiveness of sins, this messenger of God by his plea for penitence caused a big movement among the Jewish people and prepared the way for the coming Messiah.

Many went out to him, from Jerusalem and Judaea and the whole country round about the Jordan, to be baptized of him, confessing their sins. Although he protested against baptizing Jesus, because he saw in Jesus the Messiah, He who alone could in truth baptize with the Holy Spirit and with fire, and who personally had no need for baptism, still, Jesus insisted on it and said that He had to undergo baptism because it became Him to fulfill all righteousness (Matt. 3:15).

Accordingly, Jesus does not say that He had to be baptized because He needed repentance and forgiveness. He did not, like the others at the Jordan, make a confession of sin. But He saw in John a prophet, yes, and much more than a prophet, His own herald and pathfinder (Matt. 11:7-14) and He saw in His baptism not an arbitrary ceremony, conceived by John himself, but a burden, a task, which he had received from heaven (Mark 11:30). The baptism of John therefore rested on the will of God and was a part of the righteousness which Jesus had to fulfill. When Jesus undergoes that baptism He subjects Himself, on the one hand, to the will of the Father, and, on the other, puts Himself into the most intimate of relationships with the people who in that baptism receive repentance and the forgiveness of sins. The baptism of John is for Jesus the stately surrender to the whole will of God, the public entrance into communion with all His people, the royal entrance to the Messianic arena.

Hence baptism had a meaning for Him which differed from its meaning for others. He did not Himself personally receive the sign and seal of His repentance and forgiveness, but He was baptized with the Holy Spirit and with fire, as He alone can give such baptism. At a later time some sects thought that at the moment of His baptism for the first time the Divine nature or power of Christ united itself with the man Jesus. This idea is heresy, for it does violence to the incarnation of the Word in the conception. But so much is certain: the baptism of Jesus was His full preparation for His office. For when He came up out of the water the heavens were opened, and the Spirit of God descended upon Him, and a voice was heard from heaven, saying, This is My Son, My Beloved, in whom I am well pleased (Matt. 3:16-17). Although it was understood by few, the day of Jesus' baptism was the day of His revelation to Israel and the beginning of His public work as Messiah.

Still, before He begins that work, He withdraws for a few days into the solitude of the desert. He met not a single human being, was surrounded solely by restful nature and the wild animals, and yielded Himself up to fasting, meditation, and prayer. What the nature of this meditation was becomes somewhat apparent to us from the account of the temptation. The temptation by Satan, which took place at the end of the forty days, and of which a detailed account is given by Matthew, formed a climax in the struggle through which Jesus went, but it was by no means the only one. Luke states in so many words that throughout those forty days He was tempted of the devil (4:2), and that the devil, after having ended all the temptation, departed from Him for a season (4:13). Jesus after all was in all points tempted like as we are, yet without sin (Heb. 4:15).

But the temptation in the desert concerned the plan of His public work. After the baptism, He was full of the Holy Spirit (Luke 4:1), and it was the Spirit who led Him up to the desert to be tempted of the devil (Matt. 4:1). Jesus was now fully and very clearly aware of the fact that He was the Son of God, the Messiah, and that He was in command of Divine powers. But what kind of use was He now going to make of them? Would He apply them in order selfishly to supply His own need, or by means of bowing the knee to an earthly power obtain an earthly kingdom, or again, by way of dramatic signs and wonders, win the people? The tempter tries him on all three of the points. But Jesus remains firm on all counts. He clings fixedly to the Word of God and by means of that Word He wards off all the temptations. He subjects Himself to the will and the way of the Father, establishes Himself in His obedience, and sanctifies Himself as a sacrifice unto God. Hence He knows from His own experience not only what it is to be tempted, and can pity us in our weaknesses, but because He did not, like Adam, succumb to temptation, He can also help those who are tempted (Heb. 2:18 and 4:15).

* * * * *

In this way Jesus was prepared for the public ministry of His offices and was introduced into assuming those offices. Of these three, the prophetic office in that first period is the one that is most emphasized. In fact, soon after He began His public work He was recognized by the people not only as a teacher (that is, as master, rabbi), but He was also welcomed as a prophet. After He had raised the young man at Nain, the multitude cried out: A great prophet is risen up among us, and God has visited His people (Luke 7:16). And so it remained up to the end of His life. Because of His words and His works many held Him to be a prophet, even when they had no notion at all of His priestly and kingly offices or even were averse to these. Indeed, as a prophet, as a person, that is, who can teach us concerning God and Divine things better than others can, He is honored up to the present day by all who attach any value whatsoever to religion. But these same people attack the idea that Christ is a priest and a king as an outdated

Jewish notion. It is as a prophet that He is held high: even Mohammed in the Koran grants Him this dignity.

But Jesus Himself wanted to be prophet in another and different sense from that by which the Jews recognized Him as such. When He, after having been baptized by John and tempted in the desert, returned to Galilee, He soon thereafter put in His appearance at the synagogue of Nazareth, and there he applied the prophecy of Isaiah 11:1 to Himself. The Spirit of the Lord was upon Him to preach the gospel to the poor and to heal the broken-hearted (Luke 4:16 ff.). He did not represent Himself as a prophet alongside of others, but rather as being high above them. The earlier prophets had been servants, but He is the Son (Matt. 21:37). He is the only Master (Matt. 23:8, 10 and John 13:13-14). It is true that He has in common with all prophets the gifts of calling and anointing, of revelation and preaching of the Word of God, of prediction and miraculous power. Yet He far transcends them all and is exalted high above them. His calling and anointing date from eternity; His separation and preparation began as early as the conception by the Holy Spirit; at His baptism He receives the Spirit without measure and a voice from heaven hails Him as the Beloved Son in whom the Father is well pleased; the fact is not that He receives occasional revelations from time to time, but, rather, that He is the revelation, the full revelation of God, the Word that was with God, was God, and became flesh; He was and He continually remained in the bosom of the Father, and in His whole life He spoke and did nothing except He had received a command to do it; what He gave, consequently, was not a part of revelation which would have to be amplified later by others, but He is at once the perfect revelation of God and the one which fulfills and concludes every previous prophecy. Theretofore God had at sundry times and in divers ways spoken to the fathers by the prophets, but in these last days He spoke through the Son (Heb. 1:1). Indeed, the prophecy which in the Old Dispensation had come from the fathers is owing to Him; it was the Spirit of Christ who testified in the prophets (1 Peter 1:11) and Christ was the content of that testimony (Rev. 19:10).

The preaching of Christ was therefore in the profoundest sense self-revelation. It was a proclaiming of His own person and work. When He manifested Himself publicly, He made John the Baptist and the Old Testament prophets His point of departure: The Kingdom of God is at hand; repent and believe the gospel (Matt. 3:2 and 4:17). But the earlier prophets and John the Baptist were heralds, and they saw the Kingdom of God in the future (Matt. 11:10-11). Now however the time is fulfilled and in the person of Christ the Kingdom of God has come down to the earth. True, God is the King and the Father of it

(Matt. 5:16, 35, 45). But the Father has ordained it unto Him in order that He should according to the Father's good pleasure grant it to His disciples.[4]

In His preaching Christ unfolds the origin and the nature of that kingdom, the way that leads to it, the benefits it comprehends, its gradual development, and its final fulfillment. This He does not in philosophical argumentation or theological discourses, but in proverb and parable. He borrows His figures of speech from natural phenomena, or from the events of daily, practical life, and He speaks to the multitude always in such a living and vivid way that they can hear it and understand it (Mark 4:33). However, when many nevertheless did not understand His words or took exception to them, that was an evidence of the hardness of their hearts and also of the good pleasure of the Father who has hidden the things of the kingdom from the wise and the understanding and has revealed it to babes (Matt. 11:25 and 13:13-15). But in themselves His words were always simple and comprehensible, even though they dealt with the deepest mysteries of the kingdom of God. For, in the person of the Son and heir, He is Himself the commander and distributor, yes the revealer and interpreter of them. In His appearing, in His word and His work, Jesus has declared the Father to us (John 1:18). Whoever has seen Him has seen the Father (John 14:9).

The word which Christ preached was therefore essentially no other than that which had been declared in the days of the Old Testament. It included both law and gospel, but Jesus was not a new lawgiver, amplifying and improving the law of God in the Old Testament. And the gospel preached by Christ was no other than that which God had revealed ever since paradise. Jesus did not come to earth to destroy the law or the prophets, but to fulfill them (Matt. 5:17). And He has fulfilled them by purging them of false interpretations and human additions, and by bringing them to their full actualization in His own person and work. Hence Christ stands in a different relationship to the law than Moses stood in, and in a different relationship to the gospel than the prophets. For it is true that the law is given by Moses and that the gospel is proclaimed by the prophets, but grace and truth have come by Jesus Christ (John 1:17). Moses carried the law in his hands on two stone tables, and in this work He could easily have been supplanted by some other. Just so, too, the prophets were indeed preachers of the gospel, but they were not themselves the gospel. But Christ bore the law within His inmost self and perfectly fulfilled the will of God without any defect; and He was a proclaimer of the gospel not only, but its

---

4. Matt. 11:27; Luke 12:32; and 22:29.

content also, the greatest gift that God has given the world. Grace and truth have come by Him and are inseparable from His person.

* * * * *

The words of Jesus are accompanied and confirmed by His works. These too belong to His office, to the fulfillment of the Father's will (John 4:34). He did not do them of His own accord, but the Father gave all things into His hands (Matt. 11:27 and John 3:35), and the Son did nothing except what He had seen the Father doing (John 5:19). It was the Father Himself, remaining in the Son, who fulfilled these works (John 14:10). And just as they were Divine in origin, so they all also bore a Divine character, not merely because they were miracles and departed from the ordinary course of nature, but also because they were unusual and were not done by others. For while others always followed their own will, Jesus never sought His own interest or His own pleasure (Rom. 15:3). Instead, denying Himself, He fulfilled the will of the Father. Nevertheless, among all those works the miracles occupy an important place. On the one hand they are signs and evidences of God's Divine mission and power,[5] and on the other hand they are such deeds as are intended for human physical and spiritual need. The miracles of Jesus are all miracles of redemption and healing, and as such belong to the exercise of His priestly office.

This is evident from the limits which Jesus Himself imposes in the doing of miracles. In the desert He had resisted the temptation of Satan to apply His Divine power to the benefit of His own person. And throughout His whole life He held off this temptation. The thing that He says in the garden of Gethsemane, namely, that He could pray to the Father and the Father would send Him more than twelve legions (Matt. 26:53) is applicable to the whole of His public activity. Again and again He refuses to perform signs in order to satisfy the curiosity of the people,[6] and it is not seldom that He sees the revelation limited by the unbelief which He encounters (Matt. 13:58). Again and again, too, the people whom He heals in a miraculous way receive the command to say nothing about it (Mark 1:34, 44; and 3:12). Jesus did not want to feed the mistaken ideas concerning the Messiah that might be fostered by His works.

Further, the works which Jesus did belong to the priestly office for this reason also that they are manifestations of His inner compassion.

5. John 2:11; 3:2; 4:54; 7:31; 9:16; 10:37; 11:4; and other passages.
6. Matt. 12:38; 16:1; and John 4:48.

We read of it again and again,[7] and the evangelist Matthew sees in these healings a fulfillment of the prophecy of Isaiah that He took our infirmities upon Him and carried our sicknesses (Matt. 8:17). Elsewhere this prophecy is applied to the death of Christ, by which He atoned for our sins (John 1:29 and 1 Peter 2:24). But sin and disease go together. As the compassionate High Priest, Christ removed our sin not only, but in doing so also the cause of all our misery. And in the various miracles which He performs, in the driving out of demons, in the healing of the blind and deaf, the crippled and the maimed, in resurrecting the dead and in commanding the force of nature, He gives conclusive evidence of the fact that He can perfectly redeem us from all our misery. There is no guilt so great, nor any sin, and there is no misery so deep, but He can remove it by His priestly compassion and His kingly power.

Naturally, His priestly activity comes to expression especially in His last passion and dying, but the giving of His soul as a ransom for many is a fulfillment of the service which He came to do on earth, and which He has accomplished throughout His life (Matt. 20:28). As the Lamb of God He bore the sin of the world constantly. His humiliation began at His incarnation, was a continuous life of obedience by suffering, and was finished in the death on the cross (Phil. 2:8 and Heb. 5:8). It was by the Father that Christ was ordained to be priest as well as prophet. And just as He did His prophetic office, so also He fulfilled His priestly office throughout His life.

Nevertheless, it is remarkable that in the New Testament Christ nowhere bears the name of priest except in the letter to the Hebrews. It is true that His life and death are repeatedly presented as a sacrifice, but the name itself is used only in the Hebrews. There is sound reason for that. Certainly Christ is priest, but He is that in a very different sense from the priests of the Old Testament under the law of Moses. For those came from the line of Aaron and the tribe of Levi. They were only priests and not at the same time prophets and kings. They lived and they served for a short while and then had to be supplanted by others. They brought sacrifices of steers and goats which could not take away the sins. But this is not so for the Christ. He Himself came from the tribe of Judah and could not therefore lay claim to the priesthood (Heb. 7:14).

According to the letter to the Hebrews, consequently, Christ was not a priest after the order of Aaron, but after that of Melchizedek. This had already been foretold in Psalm 110: The Messiah was to be a priest who was going to combine royal dignity with the office and eternally remain priest. The letter to the Hebrews develops this thought further and

---

7. Matt. 9:36; 14:14; 15:32; and further passages.

argues fully that Christ is a priest not after the order of Aaron but after that of Melchizedek, because He is at the same time a king, because He is perfectly righteous and sinless — a king of righteousness, because He remains priest permanently and is never supplanted, because He brings an offer of His own body and blood and not of bullocks and goats, because by this sacrifice He achieves a perfect salvation for His people, and, finally, because He thus brings an eternal peace into being and is a king of peace (Heb. 7:10). The practical admonishment deduced from all this for the Jewish Christians — who were exposed to the threat of apostacy — is that they do not have a single reason for going back but rather are called to go forward (6:1). That which the Old Testament priests, their sacrifices and intercessory prayers, served as types and symbols to represent, namely, to give the people access to the presence of God, that is perfectly and eternally fulfilled in Christ. He opened up a new and living way to eternal life, and by it Christians may boldly and in the full assurance of faith come to the throne of grace (4:16 and 10:19 ff.).

*   *   *   *   *

Just as the priestly office is related to the prophetic, so it is related also to the kingly office of Christ in the most intimate way. One of the peculiarities of the priestly office in Christ is its connection with the kingship (Ps. 110:4 and Heb. 7:17). After all, it was Israel's calling to be a priestly kingdom to the Lord (Ex. 19:6). And, even though the offices were distinguished in Israel, prophecy foretold that the Messiah, the branch that should come up out of his own place, and should build the temple of the Lord, was to bear the glory (the royal majesty) and to sit and rule upon His throne. The Messiah, uniting the royal and priestly functions within Himself, would by that union bring the perfect peace to pass which His people needed (Zech. 6:12-13).

This connection with the office of the priest gives the kingship of Christ a peculiar character. He is to come from David's house, yes (2 Sam. 7:16), but at a time when the house of David will have fallen into decay (Micah 5:1). He will be a righteous king and fitted out with the salvation of God, but He will also be humble, and, in token of His humility, will ride upon an ass — in fact, upon a colt the foal of an ass (Zech. 9:9). And just as the Messiah in His appearing will not display an earthly glory and power, so His kingdom, too, will not be established by violence and weapons. In fact, in that day He will cut off the chariot from Ephraim and the horses from Jerusalem, and the battle bow will He cut off, and the Messiah will speak peace to the heathen, and His dominion will be from sea to sea, and from the river even to the ends of the earth (Zech. 9:10; compare Ps. 72).

This prophecy concerning the coming Messiah was perfectly fulfilled in Christ. The New Testament constantly and emphatically states that He is of the house of David and that by virtue of the laws of the kingdom of Israel, too, He has a claim on His throne. The two genealogical tables (Matt. 1 and Luke 3) designate Him as the Son of David. The Angel announces to Mary that the Lord will give to her Son, who should be called the Son of the Most High, the throne of His father David, and will appoint Him king over the house of Jacob into eternity (Luke 1:32-33). He is generally acknowledged as the Son of David.[8] To this descent from David the thought is connected that He is a king and has a claim on a kingdom (Luke 23:42).

He is, however, a king in a different sense from that in which the Jews of that time expected their Messiah. He never brings to bear His legal claims to the throne of His father David, not before the rulers of the Jewish people, nor before King Herod, nor before the Roman Caesar. He resists the temptation by worldly powers to achieve dominion over the world (Matt. 4:8-10). When the multitude, after the miraculous feeding, want to seize on Him violently and make Him king, He eludes them and seeks out the solitude of prayer on the mount (John 6:15 and Matt. 14:23). True, He constantly exhibited His royal power, but He exhibited it not in a show of dominion as the rulers of the nations did, but in serving and in giving His soul as a ransom for many (Matt. 20:25-28). His being a king came to expression in the force with which He spoke, with which He proclaimed His laws for the kingdom of heaven, subjected the forces of nature to Himself, commanded sickness and death to desist, Himself on the cross laid aside His life in order thereafter to take it up again, and one time as king and judge will judge the living and the dead.

But this spiritual significance which Christ, in harmony with the prophecy of the Old Testament, gives to His kingship, must not tempt us to think that He is not really a king and that it is only in a figurative sense that He should bear that name. Because He is priest according to the order of Melchizedek and not Aaron, and for that reason is better priest than the priests of the Old Testament, so, too, because He is a different king than the rulers of the nations are, He is the more and a better king. He is the very, the true, king, and the kings of the earth are kings only in image and likeness. He is the King of kings, the prince of the kings of the earth, the king who rules, internally and externally,

---

8. Matt. 9:27; 12:23; 15:22; 20:30; 21:9; and Rom. 1:3.

spiritually and physically, in heaven and on earth, unto the ends of the earth and into all eternity.

He never, not for God nor for man, drops any part of any one of His legitimate claims to this perfect and eternal kingship. During His sojourn on earth, too, He never yielded any of His Divine or of His human rights. He did not try to get His rights by violence, but wanted to arrive at them solely by way of a perfect obedience to God. But by so doing He strengthened His claims. He proved in His humiliation to be the Son of God and thus He must also be the heir of all things.

In order to demonstrate that He is really a king, He stages His triumphal entry into Jerusalem on the Sunday which opens the week of the passion. There was now no longer any danger that the nature of His kingship should be misconceived. For a life of ministering obedience, in which by word and deed He had warded off all earthly power from Himself, now lay behind Him. The enmity between Him and the people had now mounted to its highest peak; and in the course of this same week they would be laying violent hands on Him and offering Him up the prey of death. Although, before, He had evaded the effort to make Him king, He now takes the initiative of His royal entry into Jerusalem (Matt. 22:1). Before He dies He must therefore, once more, openly and before all the people make Himself known as the Messiah, sent of God, born of David. And this revelation He makes in harmony with the prophecy of a future king who should be humble and riding upon a colt the foal of an ass. It was because He was the Messiah, the Divine Son, the King of David's house that He was condemned by the Sanhedrin and by Pilate. He was a King (Matt. 27:11). The superscription above the cross, quite against the wishes of the Jews, testified to this fact once more (John 19:19-22).

* * * * *

This whole life of Christ, in its prophetic, its priestly, and its kingly activities, issued at last in death. The death is the fulfillment of the life. Jesus came to die. He Himself was clearly conscious of that. Already at His first, public appearance in the synagogue of Nazareth, He applied the prophecy concerning the suffering servant of the Lord to Himself (Luke 4:16ff.), and was therefore perfectly aware of the fact that He would be led as a lamb to the slaughter. He was the Lamb that takes away the sin of the world (John 1:29). The temple of His body was to be broken but after three days it would also be raised again (John 2:19). As Moses raised the serpent in the desert, so, according to the counsel of God, the Son of man must be raised on the cross (John 3:14; compare 12:32, 33). He was the grain of wheat which had to fall into the ground and die in order to bring forth fruit. (John 12:24).

Thus Jesus from the very beginning of His public ministry designates, by way of images and parables, that death is to be the end of His life. As that end approached, He gave clearer and more direct expression to this fact. Especially after Peter, in the name of all the apostles, in that decisive moment at Caesarea Philippi, had confessed Jesus as the Christ, the Son of the living God, He began to show them that He had to go to Jerusalem, and suffer many things of the elders and chief priests and scribes, and be killed, and be raised again the third day (Matt. 16:21). The disciples did not understand this and they did not want to face it. Peter went so far as to take Him confidentially aside, and to begin scolding Him, saying, Be it far from Thee, Lord; this shall not be unto Thee! But Jesus saw a temptation in these words, and He roundly replied: Get thee behind me, Satan. Thou art an offense unto me, for thou savorest not the things that be of God, but those of men (Matt. 16:22-23). This firmness of Christ in surrendering Himself unto death gets the Divine approbation a few days later on the mount of transfiguration. His going to Jerusalem is in harmony with the meaning of the law and the prophets (Moses and Elijah) and with the will of the Father. He remains the beloved Son in whom the Father has pleasure. And the disciples are not, like Peter, to rebuke Him but obediently to submit to Him and to hear (Matt. 17:1-8).

Still that death was not a thing which Jesus sought out. He did not challenge the Pharisees and Scribes to lay hands on Him. Even though He knows that His hour has come (John 12:23 and 17:1), it is Judas who voluntarily sells and betrays Him, and the servants of the chief priests and Pharisees who take Him captive, and the members of the sanhedrin and the governor Pontius Pilate who condemn Him and bring Him to death. The counsel of God does not exclude the historical circumstances nor obliterate the guilt of man. On the contrary, through the determined counsel and foreknowledge of God was He yielded up, but in such a way that the Jews took Him and with the hands of the unjust nailed Him to the cross and put Him to death (Acts 2:23 and 4:28).

This death of Christ stands at the midpoint of the apostolic preaching, not later on only but from the very beginning,[9] and not in Paul's witness only but in that of all the apostles. It was only after the resurrection of Christ that, under the instruction of the Holy Spirit, the necessity and significance of Jesus' suffering and death were understood. It was acknowledged then that the passion and death were also a fulfillment of His prophetic activity, a proof of the truth of His teaching, and a sealing of His whole life. Under Pontius Pilate He made the good confession (1 Tim. 6:13) and in His guiltless and patient suffering left us an

---

9. Acts 2:23 ff.; 3:14 ff.; and 4:10 ff.

example, so that we should follow in his steps (1 Peter 2:21). He is the faithful Witness (Rev. 1:5 and 3:14) who as apostle and high priest is the achiever and content of our profession (Heb. 3:1) and who creates and finishes the faith in us (Heb. 12:2). And just so the death of Christ is a revelation of His kingly power, for His death was not a fate He had to undergo, but a deed which He Himself willingly and voluntarily achieved (John 10:17-18). His dying on the cross was a being exalted above the earth and a victory over His enemies,[10] for it was the most perfect obedience to the commandment of the Father (John 14:31).

Nevertheless, according to the apostolic teaching, we are not to rest at this death of Christ. In His dying, Jesus was not only a witness and a guide, a martyr and a hero, a prophet and a king. He was above all active in it as a priest. It is His high-priestly function which in His death comes out into the foreground the most. His dying was, according to the teaching of the whole Scripture, a *sacrifice* freely given the Father by Him.

When the New Testament presents the death of Christ under this name, it ties in directly with the Old Testament. Sacrifices existed from the oldest of times. We read of them in connection with Cain and Abel, with Noah and the patriarchs, and we find them among all nations and in all religions. Generally it can be said that their purpose is by offering a material gift, consisting of living or inanimate goods which are destroyed in a dignified way according to a definite ceremony, to make sure of the favor and fellowship of Deity or of newly acquiring them. For His people of Israel, too, the Lord included these sacrifices in His law. But in Israel they were given a different role and took on a different meaning.

In the first place, the sacrifices were limited in Israel to the offering of animals (cattle, sheep, lambs, goats, bullocks, doves) and the products of the land (flour, oil, wine, frankincense) and could be brought only to Jehovah the God of Israel. The offering of human beings, the drinking of blood, and the mutilation of the body was forbidden.[11] Moreover all offerings to idols, to the dead, and to "holy" animals were violations of the will of God.[12] In the second place, the sacrifices in Israel were of far less importance than the moral laws. Obedience is better than sacrifice and to hearken than the fat of rams. The Lord desires mercy, and not sacrifice, and the knowledge of God more than burnt offerings.[13] In the

---

10. John 3:14; 8:28; 12:32 and 34.
11. Gen. 22:11; Deut. 12:23; 14:1; 18:10; and other passages.
12. Ex. 32:4 ff.; Num. 25:2 ff.; Hos. 11:2; Jer. 11:12; Ezek. 8:10; and Ps. 106:28.
13. 1 Sam. 15:22; Hos. 6:6; 14.2; Mic. 6:6; Ps. 40:7; 50:7-14; 51:18, 19; and Prov. 21:3.

third place, the sacrifices in Israel, even as the priesthood, the temple, the altar, and the whole ceremonial dispensation, stood in the service of the promise. They did not effect the covenant of grace, for that covenant rests solely upon God's gracious election; they served only to keep the covenant in force in Israel and to establish it.

Just as the whole people of Israel, by virtue of God's calling and election, was a kingdom of priests (Ex. 19:6), and the priesthood was but a subordinate and temporary institution, so the sacrifices (specifically the burnt offerings, sin offerings, and guilt offerings) were but a ceremonial pointing of the way along which the sins which the Israelites committed within the pale of the covenant (committed, that is, not with raised hand but unwittingly, unawares) could be reconciled.[14] For the grave, deliberate sins, those which broke the covenant and aroused God's wrath, although they were often civically punished, there was only an appeal to the mercy of God, who thereupon forgave them, though sometimes after the intervention of persons such as Abraham (Gen. 18:23-33), Moses,[15] Phinehas (Num. 25:11), or Amos (Amos 7:4-6; compare Jer. 15:1).[16]

By this whole ceremonial service, God instructed His people, in the first place, in the sense that the covenant of grace, with all of its goods and benefits, was due to mercy alone. It has its origin and basis in unmerited compassion: I will be gracious to whom I will be gracious, and will show mercy on whom I will show mercy (Ex. 33:19). Further, by these ceremonial institutions, the Lord caused Israel to understand that He could grant the benefit of forgiveness of sins only along the way of atonement. Sin, in other words, is always such as to arouse the wrath of God, and to make man guilty and polluted. In general, therefore, a sacrifice is necessary, to subdue the wrath of God, to deliver man from his guilt and impurity, and to cause him to share again in the favor and fellowship of God. There were of course sins for which the law specified no particular sacrifice as the means of atonement. The atonement was, so to speak, left to God Himself. It is He Himself who in those instances atones for sins and thus forgives them. Forgiveness assumes atonement and includes it.[17] But even for the sins committed unawares, and for which a specific sacrifice was designated in the law, it was in the last analysis God who by means of the offer, the priest, the altar, covered

---

14. Lev. 4:22, 27; 5:15, 18; Num. 15:25ff.; 35:11; Josh. 20:3, and 9.
15. Ex. 32:11-14 and Num. 14:15-20.
16. Ex. 33:19; 34:6; Ps. 78:38; 79:8, 9; Isa. 43:25; Micah 7:18; and other passages.
17. Ps. 65:4; 78:38; 79:9; Prov. 16:6; Isa. 27:9; Jer. 18:23; and Ezek. 16:63.

the sins and removed them (Lev. 17:11 and Num. 8:19). The whole service of atonement proceeds from Him and was ordained by Him.

The real means of atonement or reconciliation was the blood of the animal sacrificed. The blood is the seat of the soul, the seat of the animal principle of life, and therefore the Lord gave it upon the altar as the element that makes atonement for the soul (Lev. 17:11). But in order to serve as expiatory agent that blood by the slaying of the animal — which the person who had sinned brought to the temple and on which he laid his hand — had to be poured out in death and afterwards sprinkled about on the altar by the priest (Ex. 29:15 ff.). The laying on of hands, the slaying, and the sprinkling of the altar pointed out the way along which the blood as the seat of the soul became the element of atonement. And when in that way the blood had atoned for the sins, covered them, and removed them, then the guilt was forgiven, the pollution was purged, and the fellowship of the covenant with God was restored. Priesthood and people, temple and altar, and all the utensils of the service were by the blood given to the Lord; they were all sanctified in order that the Lord might dwell in the midst of the children of Israel and be a God to them (Ex. 29:43-46).

But this entire sacrificial service was preliminary and possessed only a shadow of coming benefits (Heb. 10:1). The tabernacle in the wilderness was but an image of the true sanctuary (Heb. 8:5). The priests were sinners themselves, and had to make atonement not only for the people, but also for themselves (Heb. 7:27 and 9:7), and they were also prevented by death from always remaining (Heb. 7:23). The blood of bulls and goats could not take the sins away, nor purge the conscience (Heb. 9:9, 13; and 10:4). Hence these animals had to be brought again and again (Heb. 10:1). In one word, it was all external, weak, unprofitable, and not faultless (Heb. 7:18 and 8:7), and it pointed to a better future. Pious Israel learned to know this better in the course of the centuries; it yearned for the days in which the Lord would set up a new covenant, Himself bring on the true atonement, and cause His people to share in the benefits of forgiveness and renewal.[18] In Isaiah particularly this expectation gets its most beautiful expression. His book of comfort begins with the announcement to Jerusalem that her warfare is accomplished, that her iniquity is pardoned, that she has received of the Lord's hand double for all her sins (Isa. 40:2). Thereupon it unfolds the prophecy of the servant of the Lord who takes upon Himself

---

18. Jer. 31:33 ff.; 33:8; Ezek. 11:20; and 36:25 ff.

our illnesses and griefs, our transgressions and punishment, and so brings us healing and peace (Isa. 53:2 ff.).

* * * * *

Quite in agreement with the Old Testament the New Testament sees in the death of Christ a sacrifice which is brought for our sins. Jesus did not say merely that He was come to fulfill the law and the prophets and all righteousness (Matt. 3:15 and 5:17), but He also applied to Himself the prophecy of Isaiah and regarded Himself as the servant of the Lord, who was anointed by the Spirit of the Lord, and who had to preach the gospel to the poor (Luke 4:17 ff.). He came so that, in harmony with the commandment of the Father, He should lay down His life and take it up again, should give His life for His sheep, and by His death should prepare His flesh and His blood as a food and drink which remains unto eternal life.[19] His death is the true sacrifice and perfect fulfillment of all sacrifices which in the days of the Old Testament were offered according to the prescriptions of the law.

After all, the death of Christ is the most perfect of surrenders to the will of the Father, an evidence that He did not come to be served but to serve. As such it is a ransom paid for the liberation of many from the power of sin in which they lay bound (Matt. 20:28). It is the fulfillment of the covenantal offer made in the preamble to the Old Covenant (Ex. 24:7), and it lays the basis for the New Covenant (Matt. 26:28 and Heb. 9:15-22). It is called a sacrifice and an offering (Eph. 5:2 and Heb. 9:14, 26), and it actualizes the idea of the Passover sacrifice,[20] of the sin offerings and guilt offerings,[21] and of the sacrifice made on the great day of atonement.[22]

Not only are the sacrifices of the Old Testament fulfilled in Christ but also all the requirements which these had to meet and the actions which accompanied them. The priest who did the offering had to be a man without any blemish (Lev. 21:17 ff.), and such an high priest is Christ, holy, harmless, undefiled, and separate from sinners (Heb. 7:26). The animal which was sacrificed had to be whole and unblemished (Lev. 22:20 ff.) and Christ is accordingly without blemish and without spot (1 Peter 1:19). Just as the animal of the sacrifice had to be slain by the hand of the priest (Ex. 29:11), so Christ was slain as a lamb and purchased us for God by His blood (Rev. 5:6-9). No bone of the Passover lamb might be broken (Ex. 12:46), and therefore also Christ died

---

19. John 2:19; 3:14; 6:51; 10:11, 15, 18; 12:24; and 15:13.
20. John 1:29; 1 Cor. 5:7; 1 Peter 1:19; Rev. 5:6; and other passages.
21. Rom. 8:3; 2 Cor. 5:21; Heb. 13:11; and 1 Peter 3:18.
22. Heb. 2:17 and 9:12ff.

without any bone being broken (John 19:36). After the slaying the priest took the blood of the animal and sprinkled it, if it was a sin offering, in the holy place (Lev. 16:15 and Num. 19:4), or, if it was a covenant offering, on the people (Ex. 24:8); and just so Christ once also by His own blood entered into the holy place (Heb. 9:12), and He sprinkles that blood upon His people (1 Peter 1:2 and Heb. 12:24). When the sin offering was made the blood of the animal was brought into the holy place, but the body was burned with fire without the camp (Lev. 16:27). In the same way Christ, in order that He might sanctify the people with His own blood, suffered without the gate (Heb. 13:12). Just as in the Old Testament cult the blood, as the seat of life, by its being poured out in death and sprinkled on the altar became the element proper of the atonement, so also in the New Covenant the blood of Christ is the effective cause of the atonement, forgiveness, and purging of our sins.[23]

When therefore the New Testament speaks in this sense of Christ's suffering and dying as a sacrifice, it makes use of a figure of speech, it is true, and borrows its terms from those of the sacrificial cult of the Old Covenant. But we are not to infer from this fact that such a representation is accidental and unreal, and one which we can safely, with impunity, disregard. On the contrary, Scripture proceeds precisely from the idea that the sacrifices in the days of the Old Testament were the image and the shadow and that they received their fulfillment in the sacrifice of Christ. Just as Christ was truly prophet, priest, and king, and not such only by way of figure or comparison, so too His surrender in death was not a sacrifice in a figurative sense but in the most essential and true significance of that word. We cannot therefore do without calling the death of Christ a sacrifice. To lose the word is immediately to lose the reality also. And that reality is the most important of all realities for us: it is the source of salvation.

After all, when the death of Christ is called a sacrifice, the implication is that He has given Himself up to be an offering and a sacrifice to God for a sweet smelling savor (Eph. 5:2). True, Christ was a gift and an evidence of the love of God (John 3:16). God commended His love toward us in that, while we were yet sinners, Christ died for us (Rom. 5:8). He spared not His own Son but delivered Him up for us all (Rom. 8:32). The birth, the life, and also the suffering and the death of Christ demonstrate and assure us of the love of God. But this love of God does not put His justice to one side. Rather, properly seen,

---

23. Matt. 26:28; Acts 20:28; Rom. 3:25; 5:9; 1 Cor. 11:25; Eph. 1:7; Col. 1:20; Heb. 9:12, 14; 12:24; 1 Peter 1:2, 19; 1 John 1:7; 5:6; Rev. 1:5; 5:9; and other passages.

it includes that justice within itself. It is a love which does not rob sin of its character of sin, but which in the atonement finds out a way of forgiveness. It was according to the commandment of the Father that Christ had to die,[24] and that He by His death satisfied the justice of God.[25] In the death of Christ God, in forgiving the sins which before had been committed under His longsuffering, perfectly maintained His justice, and at the same time Himself opened up the way by which, while preserving His justice, He justified all those who in faith belong to Jesus.

In the second place, the sacrifice of Christ is a demonstration both of His "passive" and "active" obedience. In former times, the passive obedience was put into the foreground so far that the active obedience virtually disappeared behind it. But lately so much emphasis is put upon the active obedience that the first does not get its just due. According to Scripture, however, both go together, and they are to be viewed as the two sides of one and the same matter. Christ has at all times, from His conception and birth on, been obedient to the Father. His whole life is to be viewed as a fulfilling of God's justice, His law, and His commandment. Coming into the world, He said: Lo, I come to do Thy will, O God (Heb. 10:5-9). But that obedience first perfectly demonstrated itself in His death, and more specifically in the death of the cross (Phil. 2:8). The New Testament is full of it: that through the suffering and death of Christ for the first time sin is atoned for, forgiven, and removed. Not only the fulfilling of the law, but also the bearing of the guilt belonged to the will of the Father which Christ had to effect.

Hence, and in the third place, the sacrifice of Christ is related to our sins. Already in the Old Testament we read that Abraham offered a burnt offering in the place of his son (Gen. 22:13), that by the laying on of hands the Israelite caused a sacrificial animal to take his place (Lev. 16:1), and that the servant of the Lord was wounded for our transgressions and bruised for our iniquities (Isa. 53:5). In the same way the New Testament establishes a very close connection between the sacrifice of Christ and our sins. The Son of man came into the world to give His life a ransom for many (Matt. 20:27 and 1 Tim. 2:6). He was delivered up for, or for the sake of, our sins (Rom. 4:25), He died in relationship to our sins,[26] or, as it is usually put, on behalf of our sins.[27]

---

24. Matt. 26:54; Luke 24:25; Acts 2:23; and 4:28.
25. Matt. 3:15; 5:17; John 10:17, 18; Rom. 3:25, 26.
26. Rom. 8:3; Heb. 10:6, 18; 1 Peter 3:18; 1 John 2:2; and 4:10.
27. Luke 22:19-20; John 10:15; Rom. 5:8; 8:32; 1 Cor. 15:3; 2 Cor. 5:14, 15, 21; Gal. 3:13; 1 Thess. 5:10; Heb. 2:9; 1 Peter 2:21; and others.

The communion into which Christ, according to the Scriptures, has entered with us is so intimate and deep that we cannot form an idea or picture of it. The term *substitutionary suffering* expresses in only a weak and defective way what it means. The whole reality far transcends our imagination and our thought. A few analogies can be drawn of this communion, it is true, which can convince us of its possibility. We know of parents who suffer in and with their children, of heroes who give themselves up for their country, of noble men and women who sow what others after them will reap. Everywhere we see the law in operation that a few work, struggle, and fight in order that others get the fruit of their labor and enjoy its benefits. The death of one man is another man's livelihood. The kernel of grain must die if it is to bear fruit. In pain the mother gives birth to her child. But all of these are but so many comparisons, and they cannot be equated with the fellowship into which Christ entered with us. For scarcely for a righteous man will one die, though one might conceivably die for a good man. But God commends His love towards us in that, while we were yet sinners, Christ died for us (Rom. 5:7 and 8).

There really was no fellowship between us and Christ, but only separation and opposition. For He was the only-begotten and beloved Son of the Father, and we were all like the lost son. He was just and holy and without any sin, and we were sinners, guilty before the face of God, and unclean from head to foot. Nevertheless, Christ put Himself into fellowship with us, not merely in a physical (natural) sense, by putting on our nature, our flesh and blood, but also in a juridical (legal) sense, and in an ethical (moral) sense, by entering into the fellowship with our sin and death. He stands in our place; He puts Himself into that relationship to the law of God in which we stood; He takes our guilt, our sickness, our grief, our punishment upon Himself; He who knew no sin was made sin for us that we might be made the righteousness of God in Him (2 Cor. 5:21). He becomes a curse for us in order that He should redeem us from the curse of the law (Gal. 3:13). He died for all in order that they who live should not henceforth live unto themselves, but unto Him which died for them, and rose again (2 Cor. 5:15).

This is the mystery of salvation, the mystery of the Divine love. We do not understand the substitutionary suffering of Christ, because we, being haters of God and of each other, cannot come anywhere near calculating what love enables one to do, and what eternal, infinite, Divine love can achieve. But we do not have to understand this mystery either. We need only believe it gratefully, rest in it, and glory and rejoice in it. He was wounded for our transgressions, and bruised for our iniquities. The chastisement of our peace was upon Him; and with His stripes we are healed. All we like sheep had gone astray; we have turned everyone to his own way. And the Lord has laid on Him the iniquity of us all (Isa. 53:5 and 6).

What shall we say of these things? If God be for us, who can be against us? He spared not His own Son but delivered Him up for us all. How shall He not with Him also freely give us all things? Who shall lay anything to the charge of God's elect? It is God that justifies. Who is he that condemns? It is Christ that died, yes, rather, that is risen again, who is even at the right hand of God and who also makes intercession for us (Rom. 8:31-34).

XVIII

The Work of Christ in His Exaltation

The benefits which Christ has achieved for us by His great love are so rich that they simply cannot be calculated or estimated at their just value. They comprehend no less than a whole and perfect salvation. They consist of redemption from the greatest of evils, namely, sin with all its consequences of misery and death, and of the granting of the highest good, namely, the fellowship with God and all its blessings. Later there will be opportunity to discuss those benefits in detail. But they must be mentioned in passing here if we are to understand the work of Christ in its deep significance.

Among all the benefits which we owe to Christ's profound humiliation, atonement is the principal one. It is expressed in the New Testament by two words of the original which are variously translated in the English as propitiation, reconciliation, or atonement. The first word — or, strictly speaking, several words, but of the same root — is found in Romans 3:25, Hebrews 2:17, 1 John 2:2 and 4:10, and it is a word which originally means *to cover* and so designates the atonement effected by the sacrifice. The thought is that the sacrifice, or rather the blood of the sacrifice — for the blood is the seat of life, and when it is poured out and sprinkled it is the atoning element proper — covers the sin (guilt, pollution) of the person making the offer from the face of God, and thus, in consequence of its effect, removes the provocation of God's wrath. Because of the pouring out and sprinkling of the blood, in which the life, the soul, of an innocent and unblemished animal is spent, God lays aside His wrath, changes His disposition towards the sinner, forgives his transgression, and admits him again to His presence and fellowship. And the forgiveness which takes place after the atonement is then so perfect that it can be called a blotting out (Isa. 43:25 and 44:22), a casting behind one's back (Isa. 38:17), or a casting of the sins into the depths of the sea (Micah 7:19). The atonement obliterates the sins so completely that it is as if they never were committed. It banishes wrath and causes God's face to shine upon His people in Fatherly favor and good will.

In the Old Testament all this pointed to the sacrifice of Christ in the future. He is the high priest who by His sacrificial blood covers our sins from God's face, averts His wrath, and makes us share in His grace and favor. He is the means of propitiation (Rom. 3:25), He *is* the propitiation (1 John 2:2 and 4:10). As the high priest He is active on our behalf with God, atoning for the sins of the people (Heb. 2:17). There are many, it is true, who reject such an objective reconciliation of God and ourselves through Christ. These say that God is love, that He requires no reconciliation, and that such an atonement is proper only to a primitive, legalistic, Old Testament idea of God — precisely such an idea as is set aside and condemned in the New Testament. But these forget that sin because of its guilty and unholy character arouses God's wrath and deserves punishment not only under the Mosaic law but outside of it also, and above it, and in the New Testament.[1] They forget that Christ and His sacrifice are not only the gift and revelation of the love of God but also of His justice (Acts 4:28 and Rom. 3:25), and that the forgiving love of God does not exclude atonement but rather assumes it and confirms it. For forgiveness is always a perfectly voluntary and gracious deed of God. It assumes the condition that God has the right to punish, and it consists, then, of the sort of acquittal which is compatible with the maintenance of justice. If, now, one begins by denying God the right to punish, one not only does injustice to the guilty and unholy character of sin, but one also refuses to let the gracious, forgiving love of God come into its own. Atonement then ceases to be a personal, voluntary, gracious act and is changed into a natural process. Scripture teaches, however, that Zion is redeemed by justice, and that Christ by His sacrifice has satisfied that justice, and averted His wrath because of our sin.[2]

It is from this objective atonement or reconciliation which Christ has achieved for us with God that the other kind, for which a different word is used in the New Testament, is distinguished. This word is used in Romans 5:10, 11, and in 2 Corinthians 5:18, 19, and 20, and has the original meaning of exchanging, recalculating, balancing (as in an account). It points to the new disposition of grace which God has taken towards the world on the basis of the sacrifice brought by Christ. Because Christ by His death has covered our sin and averted God's wrath, God changes His attitude towards the world into one of reconciliation, and He tells us this in His gospel, which is therefore called the word of reconciliation.

This reconciliation, too, is something objective. It is not something which comes into being for the first time in virtue of our faith and repentance, but which rests on the atonement (satisfaction) which Christ

---

1. Gen. 2:17; 3:14 ff.; Rom. 1:18; 5:12; 6:23; Gal. 3:10; and Eph. 2:3.
2. Isa. 1:27; Rom. 5:9, 10; 2 Cor. 5:18; and Gal. 3:13.

has made, and it consists of the reconciling, gracious relationship of God to us, and we receive it and accept it in faith (Rom. 5:11). Because God has laid aside His hostile disposition towards us on the basis of the death of Christ, we are admonished on our part also to put aside our hostility, to let ourselves be reconciled with God, and to enter into the new, reconciling relationship in which God has placed Himself towards us. Everything is finished. There is nothing left for us to do. We can with our whole soul and for all time rest in the perfect work of redemption which Christ has achieved. We may accept in faith the fact that God has laid aside His wrath and that in Christ He is a reconciled God and Father for guilty and unholy sinners.

Whoever sincerely believes this gospel of reconciliation in principle receives immediately all other benefits which were achieved by Christ. For in the attitude of peace which God takes towards the world in Christ all of the other benefits of the covenant of grace are included. Christ is one and cannot be divided nor be accepted in part. The chain of salvation cannot be broken. Those whom God beforehand predestinated, those He also called, and those He called He also justified, and those He justified, He also glorified (Rom. 8:30). All therefore who are reconciled with God through the death of His Son receive the forgiveness of sins, the adoption as children, the peace with God, the right to eternal life and the heavenly inheritance.[3] They stand in a status of fellowship with Christ, are crucified, buried, and raised with Him, and set in heaven, and are made more and more conformable to His image.[4] They receive the Holy Spirit who renews them, leads them into the truth, testifies of their adoption as children, and accompanies them to the day of the redemption.[5] In this fellowship of the Father, the Son, and the Holy Spirit, the believers are free from the law,[6] and are raised above all power of world and death, of hell and Satan.[7] God is for them; who can be against them (Rom. 8:31).

* * * * *

The perfect sacrifice which Christ accomplished on the cross is of infinite power and worth, abundantly adequate for the reconciliation of the sins of the whole world. Holy Scripture always relates that whole world to the redemption and re-creation. The world was the object of God's love (John 3:16). Christ came into the world not to condemn the world

---

3. Rom. 5:1; 8:17; Gal. 4:5.
4. Rom. 6:3ff.; 8:29; Gal. 2:20; and Eph. 4:22-24.
5. John 3:6; 16:3; Rom. 8:15; and Eph. 4:30.
6. Rom. 7:1 ff.; Gal. 2:19; 3:13; 4:5; and 5:1.
7. John 16:33; Rom. 8:38; 1 Cor. 15:55; 1 John 3:8; and Rev. 12:10.

but to save it.[8] In Him God reconciled the world, all things in heaven and on earth, to Himself. Christ, accordingly, was a propitiation not only for the sins of those who at a given time believe in Him, but also for the whole world (1 John 2:2). Just as the world was created by the Son, so also it is destined to belong to Him as the Son and heir (John 1:29; 2 Cor. 5:9; and Col. 1:20). It is the Father's good pleasure in the dispensation of the fulness of times again to gather all together in *one* with Christ as head, all, that is, in heaven and on earth (Eph. 1:10). There are times coming of the restitution of all things; according to the promise of God we look for a new heaven and a new earth in which righteousness dwells (Acts 3:21 and Rev. 21:1).

Because of this abundant adequacy of Christ's sacrifice for the whole world, the gospel of reconciliation must also be preached to all creatures. The promise of the gospel is that whoever believes in the crucified Christ shall not perish but have eternal life, and this gospel must be proclaimed and presented without distinction to all nations and people to whom God according to His good pleasure sends the gospel. It must be accompanied by the imperative of repentance and belief. Scripture does not leave the least doubt about this. In the Old Testament already it is said that the Lord has no pleasure in the death of the wicked but in his repentance and life (Ezek. 18:23 and 33:11). There it is further said that all the nations shall sometime share in the blessings of Israel.[9] The missionary idea is already contained in the promise of the Old Testament covenant of grace. But it is expressed with crystal clarity when Christ Himself appears on earth and has accomplished His work. He is the light of the world, the Savior who gives life to the world,[10] who has other sheep besides Israel which He must also bring (John 10:16); and He therefore predicts and commands that the gospel will be preached in the whole world.[11]

When, after the day of Pentecost, the apostles bring this gospel to the Jews and Gentiles, and establish churches everywhere, it can almost be said that their sound is gone out over the whole world, and their words to the ends of the world (Rom. 10:18), and that the saving grace of God has appeared to all men (Titus 2:11). In fact, intercession for all men, and particularly for kings and all those who are in positions of authority, is good and pleasing to the Lord, since He wants all men to be saved and to come to the knowledge of the truth (1 Tim. 2:4). And the delay of the return of Christ is the evidence of God's long-suffering,

---

8. John 3:17; 4:42; 6:33, 51; and 12:47.
9. Gen. 9:27; 12:3; Deut. 32:21; Isa. 42:1, 6; and elsewhere.
10. John 3:19; 4:42; 6:33; 8:12.
11. Matt. 24:14; 26:13; 28:19; and Mark 16:15.

since He wills that none be lost but that all come to repentance (2 Peter 3:9).

This universality of the preaching of the gospel has its advantages for the world in its entirety and for those who will never believe in Christ as their Savior. In His incarnation Christ honored the whole human race, and became a brother of all men according to the flesh. The light shines in the darkness and by His coming into the world enlightens every man. The world was made by Him, and the fact remains so, though it did not know Him (John 1:3-5). By the call to faith and repentance which Christ gives out to all who live under the gospel He gives many external blessings in home and society, in church and state, and those, too, enjoy these who do not in their own hearts hear that gospel. They lie within the domain of the Word, are protected from terrible sins, and, in distinction from the pagan nations, share in many external privileges. Moreover, we may not forget that Christ by His passion and death achieved the emancipation of the creature from the bondage of corruption, the renewal of heaven and earth, the restitution and mutual reconciliation of all things, also of angels and of men. In Christ the organism of the human race, the world as the creation of God, is preserved and restored (Eph. 1:10 and Col. 1:20).

However much we must hold to this absolute universality of the preaching of the gospel and of the offer of grace, we are not to infer from it that therefore the benefits of Christ were achieved and destined for every individual person. This is conclusively denied already by the fact that in the days of the Old Testament God let the heathen go in their own ways and chose only the people of Israel as His own. It is denied also by the fact that in the fulness of time, notwithstanding the universality in principle of the gospel preaching, He limited the promises of His grace throughout the centuries to a small portion of mankind.

The general statements which are found here and there in Scripture, cannot be taken in an absolute sense by anyone but must be taken in a relative sense by all. They were all written under the deep impression of the distinction between the dispensation of the Old and of the New Testaments. We can hardly imagine it any longer, but the apostles who grew up in the particularism of Judaism, felt profoundly the tremendous change which Christ introduced into the relationship of nations. They speak of it constantly as of a great mystery which has remained mysterious throughout the centuries, but has now been revealed to His holy apostles and prophets through the Spirit. They held it a mystery that the heathen should be fellow-heirs of the same body and that they should share in the promise of Christ. The middle wall of partition is broken. The blood of the cross has made peace. In Christ there is neither Jew nor Greek, neither barbarian nor Scythian. All limitation of nation and tongue, of descent and color, of age and family, of time and place has fallen away. All that matters in Christ is a new creature. The church is gathered out of every race and tongue and nation and people.[12]

But the moment Scripture enters into the question for whom Christ achieved His benefits, to whom He grants them and applies them, and who as a matter of fact therefore share in them, it always relates His work to the church. Just as in the Old Testament there was a special people whom God chose to be His heir, so this thought of a special people of God continues to live on in the New Testament. True, the New Testament people are no longer limited to the fleshly descendants of Abraham. Now, on the contrary, it is made up of Jews and Gentiles, and out of all nations and groups of people. But this church of the New Testament is now properly the gathering of the people of God (Matt. 16:18 and 18:20), it is the New Testament Israel (2 Cor. 6:16 and Gal. 6:16), the true seed of Abraham (Rom. 9:8 and Gal. 4:29). For this people Christ poured out His blood and achieved salvation. He came to save His people (Matt. 1:21), to give His life for His sheep (John 10:11), to gather all the children of God into one (John 11:52), to grant life to all those given Him by the Father and raise them at the last day (John 6:39 and 17:2), to purchase the church of God by His blood, and to sanctify and cleanse it with the washing of water by the word (Acts 20:28 and Eph. 5:25-26). As high priest Christ prays not for the world, but for those whom the Father has given Him and who by the word of the apostles will believe on Him (John 17:9 and 20).

There is, consequently, the most perfect agreement between the work of the Father, the Son, and the Holy Spirit. As many as are chosen of the Father are purchased by the Son, and through the Spirit they are re-born and renewed. The Holy Scriptures tell us plainly, very plainly, that these are many, very many.[13] Scripture teaches us this not in order that we should with our defective insight and arbitrary norm limit and curtail this number, but in order that, in the midst of struggle and apostasy we should firmly be assured that from beginning to end salvation is the work of God, and that therefore this work will be continued despite all opposition. The pleasure of the Lord shall prosper in the hand of His servant (Isa. 53:10).

Since the work of salvation is God's work and His alone, the benefits of Christ would never reach us if He had not been raised from the

---

12. Rom. 16:25, 26; Eph. 1:10; 3:3-9; Col. 1:26, 27; 2 Tim. 1:10, 11; Rev. 5:9; and elsewhere.
13. Isa. 53:11, 12; Matt. 20:28; 26:28; Rom. 5:15, 19; Heb. 2:10; and 9:28.

dead and seated in exaltation at the right hand of God. A Jesus who had died would be enough for us if Christianity were nothing more, and needed to be nothing more, than a doctrine for us to grasp with our mind, or a moral prescription and example which we had to follow. But the Christian religion is something very different and much more than that. It is the perfect redemption of the whole man, of the whole organism of mankind, and of the whole world. And Christ came to earth in order in this full sense to save the world. He did not come to achieve the possibility of salvation for us all, and then to leave to our free will the question of whether or not we would take advantage of the possibility. Instead, He humiliated Himself and became obedient even to the death on the cross in order really, perfectly, and eternally to save us.

Hence His work is not done at the point of His death and burial. True, in His highpriestly prayer He said that He had finished the work that the Father had given Him to do (John 17:4), and He cried out on the cross, It is finished (John 19:30). But these statements had reference to the work that Christ had to do on earth. They referred to His work of humiliation, the accomplishment of our salvation. And that work is done; it is complete and perfect. By His life and death salvation is so perfectly accomplished that no creature need ever add to it, nor is able to. But the achievement of salvation must be distinguished from the application and distribution of it. These are quite as necessary as the first. What good would a treasure of valuables do us if it remained always beyond our reach and was never put into our possession? What good would a Christ do us, who had died, indeed, for our sins, but who had never been raised for our justification? What would be the advantage of a Lord who had died and who had not been exalted to the Father's right hand?

As Christians, however, we confess and rejoice in a crucified Lord who is at the same time a risen Lord, in a humiliated but also in a glorified Savior, in a King who is the first but also the last, who was dead but now lives in all eternity, and who has the keys of hell and of death (Rev. 1:18). After His death Christ arose and became alive again in order that He might rule over both the living and the dead (Rom. 14:9). In His exaltation He completes the building for which in His death He laid the foundation. He is raised far above all principality, and power, and might, and was given to be the Head of the church, so that He might fulfill all in all (Eph. 1:20-23). In virtue of the resurrection He was made a Lord and Christ, a Prince and Savior, in order that He might give Israel repentance and the forgiveness of sins, and put all enemies under His feet.[14] God highly exalted Him and

---

14. Acts 2:36; 5:31; and 1 Cor. 15:25.

gave Him a name above every name, so that at the name of Jesus every knee should bow, of things in heaven, and things in earth, and things under the earth, and that every tongue should confess that Jesus Christ is Lord, to the glory of God the Father (Phil. 2:9-11).

The exaltation of Christ, therefore, is not an accidental appendage or arbitrary addendum to the humiliation which in the days of His flesh He suffered. But, even as the humiliation, it is an indispensable component of the work of redemption which Christ has to complete. In the exaltation the humiliation gets its seal and crown. The same Christ who descended into the lower parts of the earth also ascended up far above all heavens, that He might fulfill all things (Eph. 4:9-10). Just as the work of humiliation was assigned Him, so was that of exaltation. He must do it; it is *His* work; no one else can do it. The Father has highly exalted Him precisely because Christ has so deeply humiliated Himself (Phil. 1:9). The Father has committed all judgment to the Son because He was willing to become the Son of man (John 5:22). And the Son was exalted, and in the state of exaltation He continues His work in order to prove that He is the perfect, true, and almighty Savior. And He will not rest until He has delivered up the Kingdom, perfect and complete, to the Father, and can present His bride, the church, to the Father without spot or wrinkle (1 Cor. 15:24 and Eph. 5:25). The honor of Christ itself depends upon the completion of this work of salvation, His name is involved, His fame hinges on it. He exalts His own and He brings them where He Himself is, in order that they may behold His glory (John 17:24); and at the end of the ages He will Himself return to be glorified in His saints, and to be admired in all them that believe (2 Thess. 1:10).

*   *   *   *   *

According to the Reformed confession, the exaltation began with His resurrection, but according to many other confessions it began earlier — namely, with the descent into hell. This descent is very differently interpreted. The Greek church takes it to mean that Christ with His Divine nature and His human soul went into the underworld in order to liberate the souls of the saintly forefathers, and to bring these, together with the soul of the murderer on the cross, to paradise.

According to the Roman Catholic church Christ actually with His soul descended into the underworld, and remained there so long as His body rested in the grave, in order to emancipate the souls of the saints, which were remaining there without suffering until salvation had been achieved, from the state of death, to bring them to heaven, and to cause them to share in the blessed contemplation of God. The Lutheran church makes a distinction between the actual quickening of Christ and His resurrection or physical manifestation after the grave, and teaches that in the short interval between these two Christ in both soul and body descended into hell in order there to announce His victory to the devils and the condemned. And many theologians, especially in modern times, hold that Christ before His resurrection, whether in soul alone or in body also, went to the underworld to preach the gospel to those who died in their sins, and to give them opportunity to repent and believe.

The wide difference of opinion in this matter proves that the original meaning of the words *descended into hell* has been lost. We do not know the source of this clause in the creed, nor what it was really intended to say. Scripture says nothing about any literal, actual, spatial descent into hell. In Acts 2:27 Peter applies the words of Psalm 16 to Christ: Thou wilt not leave my soul in hell nor suffer thine Holy One to see corruption. But it is evident that in this instance the word *hell* must be taken to mean *grave*. Although in His soul Christ was in paradise, in His body He lay in the grave, and thus in the interim between His death and His resurrection, He was in the state of death. In Ephesians 4:9 Paul says that the same one who has ascended also descended into the lower parts of the earth. But this is not a reference to the descent into hell; it is a reference, rather, to the incarnation in which Christ came down to the earth or to His death in which He descended into the grave. And in 1 Peter 3:19-21 Peter in any event is not speaking of what Christ did between His death and resurrection; he is speaking, rather, of what Christ did through His Spirit before the incarnation in the days of Noah, or of what He did after His resurrection when He was already made alive in the Spirit. There is in Scripture not the slightest ground for teaching a *spatial* descent into hell.

The Reformed church accordingly has abandoned this interpretation of the credal article and has interpreted it to refer either to the hellish pains and agonies which Christ suffered before His death, both in Gethsemane and on Golgotha, or has related it also to the state of death in which Christ was while His body lay in the grave. Both interpretations get their unity from the Scriptural idea that the hour of Christ's surrender in death was the hour of His enemies and that of the power of darkness (Luke 22:53). Christ knew that this hour was coming, and He voluntarily delivered Himself up to it.[15] In that hour in which He displayed the highest spiritual might of His love and obedience (John 10:17-18) He appeared to be entirely helpless. The enemies were doing with Him as they pleased. Darkness triumphed over Him. In very fact, not now in a spatial, but in a spiritual sense, He descended into hell.

---

15. John 8:20; 12:23, 27; 13:1; and 17:1.

But the power of darkness was not its own. It was given by the Father (John 19:11). The enemies of Jesus did not understand that they were merely agents and instruments, and that without their knowledge or will they were carrying out what God's hand and counsel had before determined should be done (Acts 2:23 and 4:28). In His humiliation, too, Christ was the mighty one who Himself freely laid His life aside and gave His soul a ransom for many. The hour of the might of darkness was His own hour (John 7:30 and 8:20). In His death He conquered death by the power of His love, by His perfect self-denial, by His absolute obedience to the will of the Father. Therefore it was impossible that He, the Holy One, should be contained or ruled by death, or be forsaken of God and yielded up the prey to corruption (Acts 2:25-27). On the contrary, the Father raised Him,[16] and Christ Himself arose in His own right and in His own strength.[17] The pangs of death were, so to speak, the labor pains of a new life (Acts 2:24). Christ is the first*born* of the dead (Col. 1:18).

This resurrection consisted of the quickening of His dead body and of His arising from the grave. The opponents of the resurrection get into serious difficulty because of this fact. Formerly they tried to account for the record of this event by saying that Jesus had died in appearance only, or that His body was stolen by the disciples, or that the disciples had suffered from delusion and merely imagined that they had seen Him. But all these explanations were abandoned, the one after the other. More recently many take flight into spiritism and see a welcome explanation of Jesus' resurrection in that. They say, accordingly, that something objective took place indeed. The disciples saw something. There had been a manifestation to them of the Christ who had died in the body but was continuing alive in the spirit. The spirit of Christ appeared to them and revealed itself to them. Some even add a pious touch to all this and say that it was God Himself who had the spirit of Christ appear to them in order to assuage their sorrow, and to assure them of the victory over death and the indestructibility of life. The appearances of Christ in other words were so many "telegrams from heaven" bearing a Divine message of the spiritual might of Christ.

But this whole spiritistic, or spiritualistic, account is unworthy of the Bible and is diametrically opposed to its testimony. According to all the gospel writers, the grave was found empty on the third day, and the first manifestation took place on that day.[18] Without following a regular order and without giving complete summaries, the evangelists and Paul

---

16. Acts 2:24; 3:26; 5:30; 13:37; Rom. 4:25; 1 Cor. 15:14; and elsewhere.
17. John 11:25; Acts 2:31; Rom. 1:4; 14:9; 1 Cor. 15:21; 1 Thess. 4:14.
18. Matt. 28:6; Mark 16:6; Luke 24:3; John 20:2; and 1 Cor. 15:4-5.

tell us that Jesus appeared to the women, particularly to Mary Magdalene, to Peter, to the disciples without Thomas and to the disciples with Thomas, and to many others, even to five hundred brethren at once. At first these manifestations took place near and in Jerusalem, and later in Galilee, where He, as Mark expressly says, went before them (Mark 16:7). And all agree that Christ appeared in the same body in which He was laid into the grave. It was a body of flesh and bone such as a spirit does not have (Luke 24:39). It could be handled (John 20:27), and could benefit from food (Luke 24:41 and John 21:10).

Nevertheless, Christ left a very different impression upon people after His resurrection than He did before. Those who saw Him were startled and afraid, and threw themselves down before Him, and worshipped Him (Matt. 28:9, 10 and Luke 24:37). He appeared in another form than that which He had before manifested (Mark 16:12), and sometimes He was not immediately recognized (Luke 24:16, 31). There is a big difference between the resurrection of Lazarus and that of Jesus. The first returns from death to His former, earthly sphere of life, but Jesus does not go back. He goes ahead to the way which leads to the ascension. When Mary thinks that she has received her Master and Lord back from death, and is going to enjoy the former companionship with Him, Jesus deflects her and says, Touch me not, for I am not yet ascended to my Father, but go to my brethren and say unto them, I ascend unto my Father, and your Father, and to my God, and your God (John 20:17). After the resurrection Christ belongs to the earth no longer, but to heaven. And that is why His form is changed, even though He has assumed the same body that He laid in the grave. Paul puts it this way: that in dying a natural body is sown but that at the resurrection (of Christ as well as of the believers) a spiritual body is raised (1 Cor. 15:44). In both instances it is one body, for the spiritual is not here opposed to the physical, but to the natural. But in the physical body which the first man received there is a large part of life that lies beyond the pale of spirit and exists more or less independently. And in the spiritual body, "meats and the belly" will be destroyed (1 Cor. 6:13) and whatever is material will be subjected and made serviceable to the spirit.

* * * * *

The physical resurrection of Christ is not an isolated historical fact. It is inexhaustibly rich in meaning for Christ Himself, for the church, and for the whole world. In general it means the victory in principle over death. By a *man* death came into the world. The transgression of the law of God opened up the way of death to mankind, for death is the wages of sin.[19] Therefore the conquest of death could take place only by a *man*. A *man* had to effect the resurrection from the dead. Even though an angel, even though the own Son of God had descended into the realm of the dead, and thereupon returned to heaven, it would have profited us nothing. But Christ was the Only-Begotten of the Father not only but also true and perfect man. He was God and the Son of man. As man He suffered, died, and was buried, and as man He arose and returned from the realm of the dead. In the resurrection of Christ it was proved that there was a man who could not be contained by death, could not be ruled by Satan, by the power of corruption, who was stronger than the grave and death and hell. In principle, therefore, Satan has as a matter of fact no longer the dominion over death. Christ by His death has overcome death (Heb. 2:14). Even though Christ alone had arisen, and even though no one else should ever arise from the grave, there is in any event a man who is stronger than he. The gates of the realm of death which had closed upon Him had to open again at His command. The prince of this world has nothing in Him (John 14:30).

If this be so, it is self-evident that what matters at the resurrection of Christ is precisely the *physical* resurrection. A spiritual resurrection would not be enough, and would be only half of a victory — that is, no victory at all, but a defeat rather. Then the whole of man, then man as man, as he is in soul and body, would not have been removed from the pale of death's dominion. Then Satan would have remained the conqueror in a large area. Anyhow, a spiritual resurrection, that is, regeneration and renewal, could take place in Christ, for He is holy, free of all guilt, and taint, and sin. If He was to prove His strength over sin He could do so only by bodily returning from the realm of the dead, and so exhibit His spiritual power in the world of matter. By His physical resurrection it was first proved that He, by His obedience even unto the cross and the grave, had perfectly conquered sin and all its consequences, including death, had, so to speak, thrown it back out of the human world, and had ushered in a new life of incorruptibility. Death may therefore have come into the world by a *man;* but the resurrection from the dead came also by a *man* (1 Cor. 15:21). Christ is Himself the resurrection and the life (John 11:25).

That suffices to demonstrate the significance of the resurrection of Christ, but it can also be established in greater detail — and, first of all, its significance for Christ Himself. If the death on the cross had been the end of Jesus' life, and had not been followed by a resurrection, the Jews would have been vindicated in their condemnation. In Deuter-

---

19. Rom. 5:12; 6:23; and 1 Cor. 15:21.

onomy 21:23 we read that a hanged person is accursed of God. The argument at that place is that the body of a criminal, after death, is not to remain on the wood overnight on which it was hanged, but be removed the same day and be buried. If it remained on the cross it would defile the land which the Lord had given His people. The Mosaic Law does not have in it the phenomenon of crucifixion. But when Jesus was delivered up to the Gentiles (Matt. 20:19) and by wicked hands was crucified (Acts 2:23), then He was, not after His death only, but before it and in it, an example of the forbidding severity of the law, and of being accursed before God. For the Jews who knew the law, the death on the cross was not only a painful and disgraceful punishment, but also an evidence that the crucified one was laden with God's wrath and curse. Jesus, hanged on the cross, was in the eyes of the Jews an offense and a curse (1 Cor. 1:23 and 12:3).

But now comes the resurrection and reverses the whole judgment. He who made God to be sin for us is the one who personally knew no sin. He who became accursed for our sake is the blessed of the Father. He who on the cross was the forsaken of God is the Son in whom the Father is well pleased. The rejected of the earth is the crowned one of heaven. The resurrection is therefore the evidence of Christ's Sonship. He who was from the seed of David according to the flesh is declared by the resurrection to be the Son of God with power, according to the spirit of holiness which was in Him (Rom. 1:3-4). Christ spoke the truth and made the good confession before Caiaphas and Pontius Pilate when He testified to being the Son of God. It is not the Jews and the Romans who in their judgment and sentence were proved right, but Christ. He is the just one who was nailed to the cross with wicked hands and put to death. The resurrection is the Divine reversal of the sentence which the world passed on Jesus.

This evidence manifested in the resurrection of the Sonship and Messiahship of Christ does not exhaust its significance for Christ, however. It was for Him also the entrance to an entirely new state of life, the beginning of an ever progressive exaltation. Not only in eternity (Heb. 1:5), nor only upon His appointment as high priest (Heb. 5:5), but also in His resurrection (Acts 13:33) God said to Him, Thou art My Son, this day have I begotten Thee. The resurrection is the day of Christ's crowning. He was Son and Messiah already before His incarnation. He was that also in His humiliation. But then His inner being was hidden under the form of a servant. Now, however, God openly cries out and declares Him to be Lord and Christ, Prince and Savior.[20] Now Christ takes up again that glory which He had before with the

20. Acts 2:36; 5:31; and Phil. 2:9.

Father (John 17:5). After this He takes on "another form," another figure, a different form of existence. He who was dead has become alive, and lives in all eternity, and He has the keys of heaven and of hell (Rev. 1:18). He is the Prince of life, the source of salvation, and the one appointed by God to be the Judge of the living and the dead.[21]

Further, the resurrection of Christ is a fountain of good for His church and for the whole world. It is the Amen of the Father upon the Finished of the Son. Christ was delivered up for our sins and raised for our justification (Rom. 4:25). Just as our sins and Christ's death are closely related, so there is an intimate relationship between Christ's resurrection and our justification. He did not achieve our justification by His resurrection but by His death (Rom. 5:9, 19), for that death was a sacrifice which fully atoned for the sins, and which brought in an eternal righteousness. But because He had achieved the perfect reconciliation and forgiveness for all our sins by His passion and death, He arose and had to arise. In the resurrection He Himself and we with Him were justified. His arising was the public declaration of our acquittal. And that is not all. Christ was raised for our justification in this other sense also that He could appropriate to us personally the acquittal implied in His resurrection. But for His being raised again the reconciliation wrought by His death could not have been worked out and applied. It would have been comparable to a piece of dead capital. But now Christ is raised by His resurrection to the position of Lord, Prince, and Savior and He can by way of faith cause us to share in the accomplished reconciliation. His resurrection is at one and the same time the evidence and the source of our justification.

But when Christ arose to the end of arrogating to us personally the achieved reconciliation and forgiveness, His work implies a further benefit. Just as there is no forgiveness without a preceding reconciliation, so too there is no forgiveness without a succeeding sanctification and glorification. The objective ground for this inseparable connection between justification and sanctification lies in Christ Himself. He not only died, but was also raised up. And what He died, He died unto sin (that is, towards the propitiation for sin and its extirpation), so that what He lives, He lives unto God (Rom. 6:10). His life now belongs, now that after His death He has perfectly loosed the bonds of sin, solely to God. Hence when Christ now arrogates to a person by way of faith the fruits of His death — namely, repentance and forgiveness of sin — He at the same time also gives that person a new life. He cannot divide Himself, nor separate His death and resurrection. In fact, He can distribute and apply the fruits of His death because He Himself has been

21. Acts 3:15; 4:12; 10:42.

raised. As the Prince of life He alone commands the benefits of His death. Just as He himself therefore once died unto sin, thereafter to live solely unto God, so He died for all in His death so that those who live (in virtue of having died and been raised with Christ) should no longer live unto themselves, but unto Him who died and was raised for them (2 Cor. 5:15 and Gal. 2:20).

In the same way there is an inseparable bond of connection between the forgiveness of sins and the renewing of life regarded, now, from the subjective side. For, whoever accepts the forgiveness of sins with a believing heart has at that moment, even as Christ did in His death, broken off all relationship to sin. He has said farewell to sin, for sin which is forgiven and the forgiveness of which is accepted in faith with great joy, can only be hated. Such a person has, as Paul puts it, died unto sin (Rom. 6:2) and therefore can no longer live in it. By faith, and by baptism as the sign and seal of it, he has entered into the communion of Christ, is crucified, dead, and buried with Him, in order that henceforth he should walk in newness of life (Rom. 6:3 ff.).

To this sanctification the glorification is also connected. By the resurrection the believers are born again to a lively hope (1 Peter 1:3). By it they have obtained the imperturbable conviction that the work of salvation has been not only begun and continued, but also will be carried out to the end. In heaven the incorruptible, undefilable, and unfading legacy is preserved for them, and on earth they are by God's might preserved in the faith for the salvation which in the last time will be revealed to them. How, indeed, could it be otherwise? God has manifested His love toward us in this respect that Christ died for us while we were yet sinners. Much more, then, we, being justified by the blood of Christ, will be preserved by God from His wrath, especially from the wrath which will be manifested in the last judgment.

For those who are in Christ there is no wrath and no condemnation, but only peace with God and the hope of His glory. Formerly, while they were still enemies, and subjected to His wrath, God reconciled Himself with them through the death of His Son. Now that God has put aside His wrath towards them, and has given them peace and love, He will preserve them through the life that Christ now has in virtue of the resurrection, and in which as their intercessor He is busy with the Father (Rom. 6:8-10). The resurrection of Christ thus goes on into all eternity. In its time it brings with it the resurrection of the believers, their regeneration, and the victory over heaven and earth.[22]

Only when we understand this rich, eternal significance of the resurrection of Christ can we appreciate why the apostles, and Paul in

---

22. Acts 4:2; Rom. 6:5; 8:11; and 1 Cor. 15:12ff.

particular, put so much emphasis upon its historical character. All of the apostles are witnesses to the resurrection (Acts 1:21 and 2:32). And Paul maintains that without the resurrection the preaching of the apostles is vain and false. The forgiveness of sins, resting on the reconciliation, and accepted in faith, would not then have taken place, He says, and the hope of a blessed resurrection would be without foundation. The Divine Sonship and the Messianic identity of Christ would then be gone, and He would be no more than a teacher of virtue. But if the resurrection has taken place then in it the Father has declared and has crowned Christ the Reconciler of sins and the Prince of life and the Savior of the world.

*   *   *   *   *

The resurrection is the beginning of Jesus' exaltation, and it is followed after forty days by the ascension. The event is reported very briefly.[23] But it was predicted by Christ.[24] It is a component of the apostolic preaching.[25] Everywhere the apostles proceed from the idea that Christ according to His human nature, in body and in soul, is in heaven. After all, the forty days which Christ spent on earth after His resurrection were a preparation for His ascension and a transition to it. Everything went to show that He no longer belonged to the earth. His form was another than He had before His death. He appeared and disappeared in a mysterious way. The disciples felt that the relationship in which they now stood to Him was very different from the former companionship. His life no longer belonged to the earth, but to heaven.

In the ascension He becomes invisible not by a process of spiritualization or translation into deity. What happens is an exchange of place. He was on earth and He went to heaven. He went up from a specific place, the Mount of Olives, less than a mile from Jerusalem in the direction of Bethany (Luke 24:50 and Acts 1:12). Before He separated from His disciples He blessed them. In an attitude of blessing He leaves the earth and goes up to heaven. Thus He had come, thus He had lived, and thus He now returned. He is Himself the content of all the blessings of God, the achiever, the possessor, and the distributer of them all (Eph. 1:3).

The ascension was also His own deed. He had the right to it and the power to do it. He went up in His own strength.[26] His ascension is a

---

23. Mark 16:19; Luke 24:51; and Acts 1:1-12.
24. Matt. 26:64; John 6:62; 13:3, 33; 14:28; 16:5, 10, 17, and 28.
25. Acts 2:23; 3:21; 5:31; 7:55; Eph. 4:10; Phil. 2:9; 3:20; 1 Thess. 1:10; 4:14-16; 1 Tim. 3:16; 1 Peter 3:22; Heb. 4:14; 6:20; 9:24; Rev. 1:13; and elsewhere.
26. John 3:13; 20:17; Eph. 4:8-10; and 1 Peter 3:22.

triumph in an even stronger sense than the resurrection. In it He triumphs over the whole earth, over all the laws of nature, over the gravity of matter. What is more, His ascension is a triumph over all the hostile diabolical and human forces which were robbed by God of their armor in the cross of Christ, were exhibited in their helplessness, and bound to Christ's chariot of victory (Col. 2:15). They are led away now as captives by Christ Himself (Eph. 4:8). The same thought is put by Peter in a different way. He says that Christ after having been quickened by the spirit went up into heaven (for the words "went" and "is gone" of 1 Peter 3:19 and 22 the Greek has the same word, so that the addition in verse 22 of "into heaven" simply designates where He went), and that at His ascension He preached to the spirits in prison His victory, and took His place at the right hand of God, angels and authorities and powers being made subject to Him.

The ascension which is Christ's own deed, is also a being taken up into heaven by God.[27] Because Christ has perfectly finished the Father's work, He is not only raised by the Father but also admitted to His immediate presence. The heavens are opened for Him, the angels go out to meet Him, and they conduct Him in (Acts 1:10). He even went beyond heaven, ascending up far above all heavens (Heb. 4:14 and Eph. 4:10) in order to take His seat at God's right hand on the throne of His majesty. The chief place beside God is Christ's. Just as the resurrection is a preparation for the ascension, so the ascension is this for the seating at the right hand of God. In the Old Testament this place had already been promised the Messiah (Ps. 110:1). Jesus said more than once that He would presently be seated on the throne of His majesty,[28] and after His ascension He took possession of that seat (Mark 16:19). And in the apostolic preaching this being seated at the right hand of God is often mentioned and its significance is set forth.[29]

In the expressions which Scripture uses to report this step of the exaltation a certain variation can be detected. Sometimes it is said that Christ *sat down* or *is set* (Heb. 1:3 and 8:1). Then again we read that the Father said to Him, Sit Thou on My right hand (Acts 2:34 and Heb. 1:13), or that the Father *set Him* there (Eph. 1:20). Sometimes the emphasis falls on the act of taking the seat (Mark 16:19), sometimes on the condition or state of being seated (Matt. 26:64 and Col. 3:1). The place where Christ is seated is designated by the words: on the right hand of power (Matt. 26:64), on the right hand of the power of God (Luke 22:69), on the right hand of the Majesty on high (Heb.

---

27. Mark 16:19; Luke 24:51; Acts 1:2, 9, 11, 22; and 1 Tim. 3:16.
28. Matt. 19.28; 25:31; and 26:64.
29. Acts 2:34; Rom. 8:34; 2 Cor. 5:10; Eph. 1:20; Col. 3:1; Heb. 1:3; 8:1; 10:12; 1 Peter 3:22; Rev. 3:21; and other passages.

1:3), on the right hand of the throne of the Majesty in the heavens (Heb. 8:1), or on the right hand of the throne of God (Heb. 12:2). Generally the phrasing is that Christ is seated there, but sometimes the expression is that He *is* there (Rom. 8:34), or *stands* there (Acts 7:55-56), or walks in the midst of the seven golden candlesticks (Rev. 2:1 and other places). But always the thought is the same: After His resurrection and ascension Christ has the highest place beside God in the whole universe.

This thought is expressed in the form of a figure derived from earthly relationships. We can speak of heavenly things only in a human way, by means of comparisons. Just as Solomon did honor to his mother Bathsheba by placing her in a chair at his right hand,[30] so the Father glorifies the Son by sharing His throne with Him (Rev. 3:21). The meaning is that Christ on the basis of His perfect obedience has been exalted to the highest sovereignty, majesty, dignity, honor, and glory. He received not only His glory once more, which according to His Divine nature He had had with the Father before the world began (John 17:5), but was now also crowned with honor and glory according to His human nature (Heb. 2:9 and Phil. 2:9-11). All things have been subjected to Him, except Him who did put all things under Christ (1 Cor. 15:27). And even though we do not now see that all things are subjected to Him, we know that He will reign as King until He has put all His enemies under His feet (Heb. 2:8 and 1 Cor. 15:25). That will take place at His return when He comes to judge the living and the dead. His being seated at the right hand of God and the whole of His exaltation ends and reaches its pinnacle in the return for judgment (Matt. 25:31-32).

*　*　*　*　*

In this state of exaltation Christ continues the work which He began on earth. True, there is a great difference between the work which Christ achieved in His humiliation and that which He accomplishes in His exaltation. Just as His person appears in another form, so His work takes on a different shape and form. After His resurrection He is no longer a servant, but a Lord and Prince; and so His work now is no longer a sacrifice of obedience, such as He perfectly brought in His death on the cross. But the Mediatorial work nevertheless goes on in another form. He did not at His ascension enter upon an unproductive rest — the Son works always as does the Father (John 5:17) — but instead now applies the fulness of His achieved salvation to His church. Just as Christ by His passion and death was in the resurrection and as-

---

30. 1 Kings 2:19; compare Ps. 45:9; and Matt. 20:21.

cension raised to the Head of the church, so that church must now be conformed to the body of Christ and be fulfilled to the fulness of God. The work of the Mediator is a great, mighty, Divine work which began in eternity and which continues in eternity. But at the moment of the resurrection it was divided into two parts. Until then the humiliation of Christ took place; after that time His exaltation began. And both are equally indispensable to the work of salvation.

Accordingly, Christ remained active in the state of exaltation as prophet, priest, and king. He had been anointed as such from eternity. He had exercised these official activities in the state of humiliation. And, be it in a different way, He continues these activities in heaven now.

That He remained active as a prophet after the resurrection becomes apparent from His preaching. He continued preaching to His disciples up to the time of His ascension. The forty days which Jesus spent on earth after His resurrection constitute an important part of His life and teaching. We usually do not pay enough attention to this. But the moment we attentively survey what Jesus said and did during those forty days, we detect that these shed an entirely new light on His person and His work. Naturally we do not have as profound a sense of this as the apostles had, for we live after them and have had the benefit of their instruction, but the disciples who had gone about with Jesus and had lost all hope at the time of His death became very different people in those forty days, and learned to understand Jesus' person and work as they had been unable to understand it before.

The resurrection itself cast a surprising light on the death of Christ and on His whole previous life. But this redemptive event, too, did not remain an isolated entity; just as it had been preceded, so it was now followed by a redemptive word. The angels at the grave immediately announced to the women who were looking for Jesus, that He was not there *as He had said* (Matt. 28:5-6). And Jesus Himself explained to the travellers to Emmaus that Christ had to suffer and so enter upon His glory, and He showed them this from everything that had been written concerning Him in the Scriptures (Luke 24:26-27; compare 44-47).

The disciples now learn to know Him in a different form from that in which He formerly went about with them. He is no longer the humble Son of man who has come to minister and not to be ministered to, and to give His soul a ransom for many. He has laid aside the form of a servant and shows Himself in the form of glory. He now belongs to another world. He is going on to His Father, while the disciples remain behind because they have a calling to fulfill on earth. The former confidential fellowship does not return. It is true that there will later be a different and even more intimate relationship between Jesus and His disciples so that they will then understand that it was to their advantage that Jesus went. But that will be a fellowship in the spirit, differing greatly from that which they had enjoyed. And now, after the resurrection, Jesus reveals Himself in such glory and wisdom to His disciples that Thomas comes to make the confession which none of them had ever made: namely, that Jesus was his Lord and his God (John 20:28).

During those forty days Jesus sheds more and more light on His own person and work. But He also gives a more particular explanation of what the disciples' calling and task is now to be. When Jesus had been buried and everything seemed to be over and gone, the plan may well have secretly been formed by the disciples to return to Galilee, and to take up the former work. But on the third day they heard of manifestations which had taken place, to Mary Magdalene, and to the other Mary (Matthew 28:1, 9 and John 20:14 ff.), to Peter (Luke 24:34 and 1 Cor. 15:5), and to the travellers to Emmaus (Luke 24:13 ff.), and thereupon they remain for a while in Jerusalem. On the evening of that same day the disciples, except for Thomas, were honored with an appearance, and eight days later they received another, this time in the company also of Thomas. Then they followed Jesus, who had preceded them into Galilee (Matt. 28:10), and a number of further appearances then took place (Luke 24:44 ff. and John 21). At the same time He gave them the assignment of returning to Jerusalem to be witnesses of His ascension.

At each of these appearances He explained to the disciples what their future calling was to be. They were not to return to their former work, but as His witnesses they had to preach repentance and the forgiveness of sins to all nations, beginning at Jerusalem.[31] The apostles get all kinds of instructions (Acts 1:2). They are taught concerning the things of the kingdom of God (Acts 1:3). Their power is defined (John 20:21-23 and 21:15-17), and the preaching of the gospel to all creatures is bound upon their hearts. Now they know what they are to do. For the time being they are to remain in Jerusalem until they are girded on with power from on high (Luke 24:49 and Acts 1:4, 5, and 8), and thereafter they are to be His witnesses, in Jerusalem, in Judaea and Samaria, and to the uttermost parts of the earth (Acts 1:8).

The whole content of His teaching during the forty days is epitomized in the final words which Jesus spoke to His disciples (Matt. 28:18-20). There He says first that all power is given Him in heaven and on earth. True, He had earlier also received that power (Matt. 11:27), but He now takes possession of it on the basis of His merits, and proceeds to use it for the purpose of granting the benefits which He achieved to the

31. Matt. 28:19; Mark 16:15; Luke 24:47, 48; and Acts 1:8.

church which He has purchased with His blood. In the name of this perfection of power, so to speak, He gives His disciples the mandate to make disciples of all nations by baptizing them in the name of the Father, the Son, and the Holy Spirit, and to teach them to observe all things which He has commanded them. Because He has been given all power in heaven and on earth, Jesus lays claim to the discipleship of all nations. And He acknowledges such as His disciples as are taken up by baptism into fellowship with that God who has made Himself known in His perfected revelation as Father, Son, and Holy Spirit, and who now continue to walk in His commandments. And by way of encouragement He finally adds that He will be with them always, even unto the end of the world. Bodily He leaves them, spiritually He stays with them, so that it is not they but He who gathers His church and who rules and protects it.

After His ascension, too, Christ remains active as prophet. The preaching of the apostles, whether orally or in the writing of their letters, ties in with the instruction of Jesus, not with that which they received from Him before His death alone, but also with that which they received from Him during the forty days between His resurrection and ascension.

We must not overlook this last named fact. It is only that which explains why the apostles stood in the conviction from the very beginning that Christ had not only died, but had been raised and was seated on the right hand of God as Lord and Christ, Prince and Savior, and the sinner's whole salvation was contained in the love of the Father, the grace of the Son, and the fellowship of the Holy Spirit.

The preaching of the apostles ties in with Jesus' instruction not only: it is also the explanation and elaboration of that instruction. Jesus by His Spirit Himself continued the work of prophecy in the hearts of His disciples. By the Spirit of truth He lead them into all truth, for that Spirit did not testify of Itself, but testified of Christ, caused them to remember and reflect upon what He had said, and proclaimed coming things to them (John 14:26; 15:26; and 16:13). Thus the apostles were equipped to bring that Holy Scripture of the New Testament into being which, taken together with the books of the Old Testament, is a lamp upon the path of the church, and a light before its feet. It is Christ Himself who gave this Word to His church and who by means of it progressively carries out His office. He preserves and distributes it, explains and interprets it. It is the instrument by which He makes the nations His disciples, by which He incorporates them into the fellowship of the Triune God, and makes them to walk in His commandments.

By His Word and His Spirit Christ is always with us still, unto the end of the world.

*   *   *   *   *

What holds for the prophetic office of Christ is applicable also to His priestly office. It is not an office which He received for a time only. He exercises it into all eternity. In the Old Testament this eternal character of the priesthood was foreshadowed in the separation of the house of Aaron, and the tribe of Levi for the service of the temple. It is true that the individual persons who ministered in that service all died in turn, but they were immediately replaced by others. The priesthood remained. The coming Messiah, however, was not to be merely an ordinary priest, serving for a time and thereupon giving way to a successor, but was to be priest into eternity according to the order of Melchizedek (Ps. 110:4). In distinction from the descendants of Aaron and Levi who were hindered by death from remaining always priests (Heb. 7:24), Melchizedek in his mysterious figure gives us an image of the everlasting duration of Christ's highpriestship. He is a king of righteousness and peace at one and the same time, and is unique in the whole history of revelation, in that no mention is made of his generation, his birth, or his death. In a typical sense he was thus like the Son of God and remained a priest into eternity (Heb. 7:3).

But what Melchizedek was only in point of example, Christ is in reality. Christ could in the full sense be an eternal high priest because He was the Son of God who existed from eternity (Heb. 1:2-3). He sacrificed Himself on earth and in time, but He came from above, in His essence belonged to eternity, and could therefore also offer Himself up in time through the Holy Spirit (Heb. 9:14). In so far as Christ as the Son of God was prepared from eternity to come into the world and to fulfill God's will (Heb. 10:5-9) He was also already a priest from eternity. With a view to the fulfillment of that will of God in the days of His flesh, one can say that the priestship of Jesus began on earth.[32] And this priestship on earth was again a means for Christ by His resurrection and ascension to become high priest in the heavenly kingdom and to remain such into eternity. It is an interesting idea in the letter to the Hebrews that the life and work of Christ on earth is not to be regarded as final but as a preparation for His eternal priestly service in heaven.

Some have inferred from this that according to this letter to the Hebrews Christ was by no means a priest while He was on earth, and that He first assumed the office when He ascended into heaven and went into

----

32. Heb. 2:17; 5:10; 6:20; 7:26-28.

the holy of holies. They base this idea especially on the fact that the priests on earth came from the tribe of Levi, and had to be such in order to sacrifice according to the law, and that Jesus did not stem from Levi but from Judah, and that He never as a priest made offerings in the temple at Jerusalem (Heb. 7:14 and 8:4). If, then, Christ was nevertheless a priest, He could be that only in heaven, and would require something there to sacrifice (Heb. 8:3). And so it was maintained that what He offered there was His own blood with which He entered in the heavenly holy of holies (Heb. 9:11-12).

But this conclusion is certainly inaccurate. For just as all other apostolic writings do, so this letter to the Hebrews also puts the strongest emphasis on the fact that Christ *once,* that is, on the cross, offered Himself up and thus brought about an eternal salvation.[33] The forgiveness of sins — that great benefit of the New Testament — was fully achieved by that one sacrifice, and the New Testament, which was established in His blood, put an end to the Old.[34] Sin, death, and the devil have been destroyed by His sacrifice,[35] and by His blood He has sanctified and perfected all those who were obedient to Him (Heb. 10:10, 14 and 13:12). Precisely because Christ brought this one perfect sacrifice on the cross, He can as High Priest take His place at the right hand of God (Heb. 8:1). He no longer suffers and dies, but as conqueror He sits upon the throne.[36] And the important thing in the plea of the apostle is precisely that we have such a high priest as is seated on the right hand of the throne of majesty in the heavens (Heb. 8:1). Of any sacrificing such as Christ did on earth there can be no possibility now in heaven.

And yet Christ is and remains high priest in heaven. As such He has been set at the right hand of God. Yes, in a certain sense it can be said along with the letter to the Hebrews that there He first became high priest according to the order of Melchizedek, and there first assumed His eternal priestship.[37] The whole life on earth was a preparation, so that now in heaven as eternal high priest He could be busy on our behalf. He was the Son, and He had to be that in order to be able to become our high priest,[38] but that was not enough. Even though He was the Son He had to learn obedience from suffering (Heb. 5:8). The obedience which He possessed as Son (Heb. 10:5-7) He had to exhibit as a human being in His suffering, in order thus to become our high priest.[39] All the

---

33. Heb. 7:27; 9:12, 26, 28; 10:10-14.
34. Heb. 4:16; 8:6-13; 9:14-22.
35. Heb. 2:14; 7:27; 9:26; and 28.
36. Heb. 1:3, 13; 2:8, 9; 10:12.
37. Heb. 2:17; 5:10; and 6:20.
38. Heb. 1:3; 3:6; and 5:5.
39. Heb. 2:10ff.; 4:15; 5:7-10; and 7:28.

suffering which overcame Christ, all the temptations to which He was exposed, the death to which He was subjected — all these served as means in the hand of God to sanctify and perfect Christ for the priestly service which He must now fulfill in heaven before the face of God. Naturally this sanctification and perfecting of Christ is not to be taken in a moral sense, as though He became obedient only gradually through struggle. The apostle is thinking, rather, of a sanctification in a positive and official sense. Christ had to maintain His obedience as Son over against all temptation and so fully equip Himself for being high priest in eternity.

By way of obedience Christ perfectly obtained this office of high priest at God's right hand on the throne of majesty. On the basis of His suffering and death, on the basis of His one perfect sacrifice, He is now seated on the right hand of the majesty in the highest heavens. It is *by* His own blood, not *with* it, that He entered once into the holy of holies (Heb. 9:12), and He is there now, in the true tabernacle, built by God Himself. He is busy there as minister (Heb. 8:2). Now for the first time He is fully, eternally, priest after the order of Melchizedek (Heb. 5:10 and 6:20). Just as in the Old Testament, the high priest once a year, on the great day of atonement, went into the holy of holies with the blood of the goat slain for himself, and with that of the goat slain for the people, in order to sprinkle it on and around the mercy-seat, so Christ, by the blood of His sacrifice on the cross opened up the way to the true sanctuary in heaven (Heb. 9:12). He does not take the blood which He poured out upon Golgotha with Him into heaven in a literal sense, nor does He offer or sprinkle it there in the real sense, but by His own blood He goes into the true tabernacle. He returns to heaven now as a Christ who has *died* and been raised, who has been dead but is now living into all eternity (Rev. 1:18). He stands in the midst of the throne as the Lamb that was *slain* (Rev. 5:6). In His person He is the means of propitiation: He *is* the propitiation for our sins and for the sins of the whole world (1 John 2:2).

Accordingly His highpriestly service in heaven consists of His appearing before the face of God on our behalf (Heb. 9:12). There, in doing all that is to be done with God for the propitiation of the sins of His people, He proves Himself to be a merciful and faithful high priest (Heb. 2:17). He comes to the aid of those who are tempted (Heb. 2:18 and 4:15), and brings many sons to glory (Heb. 2:10). In the way of obedience He has Himself become a Captain for all those who go to God through Him. He is their Captain, their Guide, in faith, for He Himself exercised faith and can therefore bring others to the faith and preserve them in it up to the end (Heb. 12:2). He is the Captain of their life (Acts 3:15) — in the Greek the word used in the Acts at this place is the same as the one translated Captain in the Hebrews — because He has first earned that life by His death, and can therefore now give it to others. He is the Captain of their salvation (Heb. 2:10) because He has Himself opened up the way to salvation and walked upon it, and can therefore guide others on it and bring them into the sanctuary (Heb. 10:20).

Always and in all things, therefore, Christ is our intercessor with the Father. Just as on earth He prayed for His disciples, and also for His enemies (Luke 23:34), and in the highpriestly prayer He commended the whole church to the Father (John 17), so in heaven He continues this intercession for His own. True, we are not to understand this as though Christ were lying prostrated before the Father, beseeching and imploring Him to show mercy. For the Father Himself loves us and gave us His Son as evidence of this love. But the intercession of Christ does imply that this love of the Father is never granted us except in the Son who has become obedient unto the death of the cross. The intercession of Christ is not therefore a beseeching for grace, but the expression of a powerful will (John 17:24), the request of the Son that the heathen be given Him as His inheritance and the ends of the earth as His possession (Ps. 2:8). It is the crucified and glorified Christ, it is the own Son of the Father, who was obedient but who was also exalted on the throne of majesty. It is the merciful and faithful high priest who sanctified and perfected this service in heaven, and through whom the intercession of the Father is presented.

Over against all the charges which the law, Satan, and our own hearts bring against us, He takes upon Himself our defense (Heb. 7:25 and 1 John 2:2). He comes to our aid in all our temptations. He has pity for all our weaknesses. He purifies our consciences. He perfectly sanctifies and saves all those who pass through Him to God. He prepares a place for them in the Father's house where there are many mansions and where there is room for many (John 14:2, 3), and He preserves for them the heavenly inheritance (1 Peter 1:4). Therefore the believers have nothing to fear. They may boldly go to the throne of grace (Heb. 4:16; 10:22) and have themselves received from Christ in heaven the Spirit of adoption as children, by whom they cry, Abba, Father, and by whom the love of God is shed abroad in their hearts (Rom. 5:5 and 8:15). Just as Christ is their intercessor with the Father in heaven, so the Holy Spirit is the Father's intercessor in their hearts.[40] An important tenet of our Christian confession is this, therefore: that we have such a high priest who is set at the right hand of the throne of the Majesty in the

40. John 14:16, 26; 15:26; and 16:7.

heavens (Heb. 8:1). Hence we do not need a priest, a sacrifice, an altar, or a temple here on earth any longer.

* * * * *

Christ continues to exercise the kingly office also after His resurrection in heaven. Concerning this fact there can be less difference of opinion for the reason that by His resurrection and ascension Christ was exalted by the Father to be Lord and Christ, Prince (Captain) and Savior, and was set at the right hand of the throne, and received a name above every name.[41] The kingship of Christ is more clearly apparent in His exaltation than in his humiliation.

Within the pale of this one kingship Holy Scripture makes a distinction. There is a kingship of Christ over Zion, over His people, over the Church,[42] and there is also a kingship which He exercises over His enemies.[43] The first is a kingship of grace, and the other is a kingship of power.

In relationship to the church the name of King is often used interchangeably in the New Testament with the name of Head. Christ stands in so intimate a relationship with the church which He bought with His blood that a single name is not enough to give an idea of its content. Thus it is that Scripture presents all kinds of figures of speech in order to make clear something of what Christ means for His church. He is what the bridegroom is for the bride (John 3:29 and Rev. 21:2), the man for the woman (Eph. 5:25 and Rev. 21:9), the firstborn for his brethren (Rom. 8:29 and Heb. 2:11), the cornerstone for the building (Matt. 21:42, Acts 4:11, and 1 Peter 2:4-8), the vine for the branches (John 15:1-2), and the head for the body. All that and much more Christ is for His church.

Especially that last figure occurs again and again. Jesus Himself says in Matthew 21:42 that the statement of Psalm 118:22 has been fulfilled in Him: The stone which the builders refused is become the head stone of the corner. Just as the cornerstone serves to bind the walls of a building together and to establish it, so Christ, although rejected of the Jews, was chosen by God to serve as a cornerstone in order that the theocracy, the reign of God over His people, should achieve its realization in Him. The apostle Peter recalls this idea in Acts 4:11 and works it out more specifically in his first letter. There he refers it to Psalm 118:22 not only, but also to Isaiah 28:16. He presents Christ as the living stone laid

---

41. Acts 2:36; 5:31; Phil. 2:9-11; and Heb. 1:3-4.
42. Ps. 2:6; 72:2-7; Isa. 9:6; 11:1-5; Luke 1:33; and John 18:33.
43. Ps. 2:8, 9; 72:8; 110:1, 2; Matt. 28:18; 1 Cor. 15:25-27; Rev. 1:5; and 17:14.

by God in Zion to which the believers as living stones are added (1 Peter 2:4-6). And Paul develops the image in this sense that the church is built on the foundation laid by the apostles and prophets in their preaching of the gospel, and that Christ now is Himself the cornerstone of the building of the church which has been laid on that foundation (Eph. 2:20). Elsewhere Christ is Himself called the foundation of the church (1 Cor. 3:10). But here, in Ephesians 2:20, He is called the cornerstone. Just as the building has its principle of firmness in the cornerstone, so the church has its existence solely in the living Christ.

But the figure of a building, although it presents Christ as the head of the corner, was not yet adequate for designating the intimacy of the relationship between Christ and His church. The connection between a cornerstone and a building is, after all, an artificial relationship, but the unity of Christ and His church is a living bond of unity. Jesus spoke of Himself, accordingly, not merely as a stone which was raised by God to be the head of the corner, but also as the vine which brings forth the branches and feeds them with its sap. (John 15:1-2). Peter used his figure boldly and spoke of living stones, and Paul mentions not only of a building which grows and of a body which is built (Eph. 2:21 and 4:12) but also repeatedly represents Christ as the head of the body of the church. Every local church is a body of Christ, and the members of the church.

Every local church is a body of Christ, and the members of the church are related to each other as members of the same body, needing and serving each other (Rom. 12:4-5 and 1 Cor. 12:12-27). But also the whole church of Christ in its entirety is His body. By virtue of His resurrection and ascension He has been raised to be the head of it.[44] As such He is the principle of life of the church. He grants the church its life at the beginning, but He also feeds it, cares for it, and preserves and protects it. He causes the church to thrive and prosper, causes each of its members to achieve his full maturity, and He also unifies them all and makes each work to the other's benefit. In a word He fulfills it to the fulness of God.

In the days of the apostle Paul there were heretical teachers who said that out of the depths of the Divine being all sorts of spiritual beings emanated in a descending series, and that these together constitute His fulness or pleroma. Over against this Paul presents the fact that the whole fulness of God exclusively dwells in Christ and that it dwells in Him bodily,[45] and that Christ causes this fulness in turn to dwell in His church which is His body and the fulness (that is, the body filled full

---

44. Eph. 1:22-23; 4:15, 16; 5:23; Col. 1:18; and 2:19.
45. Col. 1:19; 2:9; compare John 1:14 and 16.

by Christ) of Him that filleth all in all (Eph. 1:23). In the church there is nothing, no gift, no power, no office, no ministry, no faith, no hope, no love, no salvation except as it comes from Christ. And Christ goes on with this fulfillment (completion: Col. 2:10) until the church as a whole and in its parts will be filled with the fulness of God.[46] Then the church will have been formed and God will be all in all (1 Cor. 15:28).

But Christ is also called by the name Head in another sense. In 1 Cor. inthians 11:3 Paul says that Christ is the head of every man. In Colossians 2:10 Paul calls Him the head of all principality and power, that is, of all angels, because He is the firstborn of every creature (Col. 1:15). And in Ephesians 1:10 He speaks of God's purpose in the fulness of time to gather together in one all things in Christ (the Greek word means to summarize or recapitulate all things under one head), all things both which are in heaven and which are on earth. It is clear, however, that the name of head has a different significance in these contexts than it has when Christ is called the head of His church. In the second instance Paul is thinking especially of the organic relationship, the unifying principle of life, of Christ and His church. But when Christ is called the head of the man, or of angels, or of the world, the figure of a sovereign and king is being stressed. All creatures without exception are subordinate to Christ, even as He Himself as Mediator is subordinated to the Father (1 Cor. 11:3). While He exercises a sovereignty of grace over the church and therefore is frequently called the head of the church, He is vested with a sovereignty of power over all creatures. And in that relationship He is seldom called a head but often a King and Lord. He is the King of kings and the Lord of lords, the Prince or Chief of the kings of the earth, and as king He will reign until His enemies have been put under His feet.[47]

This kingship of power may not be identified with the absolute sovereignty which Christ, according to His Divine nature, has in common with the Father and the Spirit. The omnipotence which is the Son's from eternity is to be distinguished from the power of which Christ speaks in Matthew 28:18 and which is given Him specifically as Mediator in both of His natures. As Mediator Christ has His church to gather, to rule, and to protect, and in order to do that He must already be mightier than all His enemies and all the enemies of the church. But that certainly is not the only reason why the kingship of power has been granted Christ. There is the further reason that as Mediator He must also *triumph* over all His enemies. He does not meet them in the field

---

46. John 1:16; Eph. 3:19; and 4:13.
47. 1 Cor. 15:25; 1 Tim. 6:15; Rev. 1:5; 17:14; 19:16.

and defeat them in battle by means of His Divine omnipotence, but He shows them the power which He has earned by His suffering and death. The conflict between God and His creature is a conflict of justice and righteousness. Just as the church is redeemed in the way of justice, so the enemies of Christ will some day be condemned in the way of justice. Over against them God will not, as He certainly will be able to do, make use of His omnipotence, but He will triumph over them through the cross (Col. 2:15). If God were to pursue His enemies with His omnipotence, they would not for a moment be able to exist. But He lets them be born and He lets them live, generation after generation, century after century. He showers His benefits upon them, and grants them all those gifts which they possess in soul and body, but which they on their part abuse by employing them against Him. God can do this and He does do it, because Christ is Mediator. Even though now not all things are yet subjected to Him, He is nevertheless crowned with honor and glory, and He will reign as King until His enemies will feignedly have subjected themselves to Him. Finally, at the end of times, when the whole history of the world, and that of each individual person, will have ended, everyone will in His own conscience have to agree with Christ on seeing all that God, for the sake of the Mediator has given in the way of spiritual and material gifts. Willingly or unwillingly every knee will sometime bow to Him, and every tongue confess, that Christ is Lord, to the glory of God the Father (Phil. 2:10-11). And one day, as the Son of man, Christ will pronounce the final judgment over every creature. And He shall condemn none save those who in their own conscience, convicted by the Holy Spirit, are condemned already (John 3:18 and 16:8-11).

XIX

The Gift of the Holy Spirit

The first work which Christ does after His exaltation to the right hand of the Father is to send out the Holy Spirit. At His exaltation He Himself accepted from the Father the Holy Spirit promised in the Old Testament, and therefore He can now, as He promised His disciples He would, share it with His disciples (Acts 2:33). The Spirit He gives proceeds from the Father, is given Him by the Father, and is thereupon given to the church (Luke 24:49 and John 14:26).

This sending of the Holy Spirit which took place on the day of Pentecost is a unique event in the history of the church of Christ. Just as the creation and the incarnation, it took place but once. It was not preceded by any granting of the Spirit equal to it in importance, and none has ever followed it. Just as Christ in His conception assumed the human nature, never again to lay it aside, so the Holy Spirit on the day of Pentecost chose the church as His dwelling place and temple, never again to be separated from it. Scripture clearly indicates the unique significance of this event on Pentecost by speaking of it as an *outpouring* or a *shedding* of the Holy Spirit.

This is not, of course, to say that there is no mention made of various kinds of activity and granting of the Holy Spirit before the day of Pentecost. We have previously observed that the Spirit together with the Father and the Son is the Creator of all things, and that in the sphere of redemption He is the Implementer of all life and salvation, of all talent and ability. But there is a difference between the activity and the granting of the Holy Spirit in the days of the Old Testament and in those of the New. The difference is remarkable and essential. This is apparent first of all from the fact that the Old Dispensation always looked forward still to the appearing of the Servant of the Lord upon whom the Spirit of the Lord was to rest in all its fulness as the Spirit of wisdom and understanding, the Spirit of counsel and might, the Spirit of knowledge and of fear of the Lord (Isa. 11:2). And, in the next place, the Old Testament itself predicts that even though there was then already a certain granting and activity of the Holy Spirit, that Spirit would not be poured out over all flesh, over sons and daughters, old and young, menservants and maidservants, until the last days.[1]

Both promises were fulfilled in the New Testament. Jesus is the Christ, the Anointed of God, pre-eminently. He was not only conceived by the Holy Spirit in Mary's womb, and was not only anointed at His baptism without measure by that Spirit, but He also continuously lived and worked through that Spirit. By that Spirit He was led into the desert (Luke 4:1), and by Him He returned to Galilee (Luke 4:14), preached the gospel, healed the sick, cast out devils,[2] delivered Himself up to death (Heb. 9:14), was raised, and as the Son of God was revealed in power (Rom. 1:4). In the forty days which elapsed between His resurrection and His ascension, He gave His disciples charges through the Holy Spirit.[3] And at His ascension by which He subjected all enemies to Himself and subordinated all angels, principalities, and powers to Himself (Eph. 4:8 and 1 Peter 3:22), He fully received the Holy Spirit and all His powers. Ascending on high, He took captivity captive, gave gifts to men, and was exalted above all heavens, in order that He should fulfill all things (Eph. 4:8-10).

This taking possession of the Holy Spirit by Christ is so absolute an appropriation that the apostle Paul can say of it in 2 Corinthians 3:17 that the Lord (that is, Christ as the exalted Lord) is the Spirit. Naturally Paul does not by that statement mean to obliterate the distinction between the two, for in the following verse He immediately speaks again of the Spirit of the Lord (or, as another translation has it, of the Lord of the Spirit). But the Holy Spirit has become entirely the property of Christ, and was, so to speak, absorbed into Christ or assimilated by Him. By His resurrection and ascension Christ has become the quickening Spirit (1 Cor. 15:45). He is now in possession of the seven Spirits (that is, the Spirit in His fulness), even as He is in possession of the seven stars (Rev. 3:1). The Spirit of God the Father has become the Spirit of the Son, the Spirit of Christ, the Spirit who, not only in the Divine being, but in harmony with it, also in the dispensation of salvation, proceeds from the Father and the Son, and is sent by the Son quite as much as by the Father (John 14:26; 15:26; and 16:7).

On the basis of His perfect obedience Christ obtained the full and free command over the Holy Spirit and over all the gifts and powers of that Spirit. He can now share it with whom He will and in the measure that He will, not in conflict, naturally, but quite in accordance with the will of the Father and of the Spirit both, for the Son sends the Spirit

1. Isa. 44:3; Ezek. 39:29; and Joel 2:28 ff.
2. Matt. 12:28; Luke 4:18 and 19.
3. Acts 1:2; compare John 20:21-22.

of the Father (John 15:26). And the Father sends the Spirit in the name of the Son (John 14:26). And the Spirit will not speak of Himself, but will speak that which He hears: just as Christ Himself on earth always glorified the Father, so the Spirit in His turn will glorify Christ, receive everything from Christ, and show it to Christ's disciples (John 16:13-14). The Holy Spirit, accordingly, freely puts Himself in the service of Christ. And in the Spirit and through the Spirit Christ gives of Himself and His benefits to the church.

It is not by might or violence, therefore, that Christ rules in the kingdom given Him by the Father. He did not do this in His humiliation, and He does not do it in His exaltation. His entire prophetic, priestly, and kingly activity He continues to carry on in a spiritual way from His place in heaven. He fights only with spiritual weapons. He is a king of grace and a king of might, but in both kinds He leads His regiment out through the Holy Spirit, who, in turn, makes use of the Word as a means of grace. By that Spirit He instructs, comforts, and leads His church, and dwells in it. And by the same Spirit He convicts the world of sin, righteousness, and judgment (John 16:8-11). The eventual victory which Christ will gain over all His enemies will be a triumph of the Holy Spirit.

* * * * *

After Christ has been raised to the right hand of God, the second promise of the Old Testament can be realized. It speaks of a pouring out of the Holy Spirit over all flesh. Christ must first have earned and appropriated that Spirit fully for Himself before He can give it to His church. Before that time, that is before the ascension, the Holy Spirit was not yet, because Christ was not yet glorified (John 7:39). Naturally, this does not mean to say that before the glorification of Christ the Holy Spirit did not yet exist, for not only is reference made to the Holy Spirit again and again in the Old Testament but the gospels also report that John the Baptist was filled with the Holy Spirit (Luke 1:15), that Simeon was led to the temple by the Holy Spirit (Luke 2:26-27), that Jesus was conceived by Him and anointed by Him, and so on. Moreover, the meaning cannot be that the disciples did not know before the day of Pentecost that a Holy Spirit existed. For they had been taught otherwise by the Old Testament and by Jesus Himself. Even the disciples of John who said to Paul at Ephesus that they had not received the Holy Spirit and that they had not heard whether there was a Holy Spirit (Acts 19:2) could not have meant to indicate their ignorance of whether or not the Holy Spirit existed. What they meant to say is that they had not noticed any unusual operation of the Holy

Spirit, that is, the event of Pentecost. For they knew that John was a prophet sent by God and qualified by the Spirit. But they had remained disciples of John, had not joined Jesus and His group, and so lived outside the pale of the church which on the day of Pentecost received the Holy Spirit. On that day there was such an outpouring of the Holy Spirit as there had never been before.

The Old Testament had already given expression to this promise, and Jesus, too, took it up and repeatedly returned to it in His teaching. John the Baptist had already said of the Messiah, who was to come after him, that He would not, like Himself, baptize with water, but with the Holy Spirit and with fire (that is, with the purging and consuming fire of the Holy Spirit).[4] And in harmony with this statement, Jesus promised His disciples that after His exaltation He would send them the Holy Spirit from the Father who would lead them into all truth. In saying this, He was plainly making a distinction between two kinds of activity of the Holy Spirit. By the one kind the Holy Spirit, having been poured out into the hearts of the disciples, comforts them, leads them into truth, and remains with them eternally.[5] But this Spirit of comfort and guidance is given only to the disciples of Jesus. The world cannot receive this Spirit, for the world does not see Him nor know Him (John 14:17). On the contrary, in the world the Holy Spirit carries out a very different activity: living in the church and thence exercising His influence upon the world, the Spirit convicts it of sin, righteousness, and judgment, and condemns it on all three counts (John 16:8-11).

Jesus fulfills His promise to the disciples in the narrower sense, that is, to the apostles, even before His ascension. When, on the evening of the day of His resurrection, He appeared to His disciples for the first time again, He introduced them in a dignified way into their apostolic mission, He breathed on them, saying, Receive ye the Holy Spirit; those whose sins ye remit, they are remitted unto them, and those whose sins ye retain, they are retained (John 20:22-23). For the apostolic office which they must exercise presently they require the particular gift and strength of the Spirit. And this Christ Himself gives them before His ascension. It is distinct from that which on the day of Pentecost He will give the disciples in fellowship with all believers.

The outpouring proper took place forty days later. The Jews were then celebrating their feast of Pentecost in celebration of the harvest and of the law-giving on Sinai. The disciples were in Jerusalem awaiting the fulfillment of Jesus' promise, and were constantly in the temple, praising and blessing God (Luke 24:49, 53). But they were now not

---

4. Matt. 3:11; and John 3:11.
5. John 14:16; 15:26; and 16:7.

alone. They continued with one accord in prayer and supplication, with
the women, and Mary the mother of Jesus, and with His brethren, and
with many others, the number of names together being about a hundred
and twenty (Acts 1:14, 15; and 2:1). And as they were thus gathered
there came suddenly and unexpectedly a sound from heaven, resembling
a rushing mighty wind, and it filled the place not only where the disciples
were gathered but the whole house also. At the same time tongues appeared which looked like little flames of fire, which divided above the
heads of those gathered there, and remained seated upon them. Accompanied by these signs, which signified the purging and illuminating
activity of the Holy Spirit, the outpouring took place. They were all
filled with the Holy Spirit (Acts 2:4).

The same expression occurs earlier also (Ex. 31:3; Micah 3:8; and
Luke 1:41). But the difference lies on the surface. Heretofore the Holy
Spirit had come down to a few, independent persons, and only temporarily for a specific purpose. Now it descended upon the whole church
and upon all its members, and it remains dwelling and working there
permanently. Just as the Son of God appeared more than once in the
days of the Old Testament but chose human nature as a permanent dwelling only at the conception in the womb of Mary, so formerly, too, there
was all kinds of activity and gift of the Holy Spirit, but only on the day
of Pentecost does He make the church His temple which He continually
sanctifies, builds up, and which He will never forsake. The indwelling
of the Holy Spirit gives the church of Christ an independent existence.
That church is no longer contained by the nation of Israel nor the boundaries of Palestine, but lives now independently through the Spirit that
dwells in it, and it spreads itself out over the whole earth. Out of the
temple on Zion God proceeds to dwell in the body of the church of Christ,
and so on that day this church is born as mission church and world
church. The ascension of Christ has its necessary consequence and the
proof of its reality in the descent of the Holy Spirit. Just as this Spirit
first sanctified Christ through suffering, perfected Him, and led Him
to the highest pinnacle, so He is now committed in the same way to
forming the body of Christ until it achieves its full maturity and constitutes the fulfillment, the pleroma, of Him who fulfills all in all.

*   *   *   *   *

This outpouring of the Holy Spirit was accompanied in the early period for the disciples of Christ by all kinds of extraordinary powers and
operations. As soon as on the day of Pentecost they were filled with
the Holy Spirit, they began to speak in other tongues, as the Spirit gave
them utterance (Acts 2:4). According to the description of Luke we

are to regard this wonder as a miracle of speech or language and not as a miracle of hearing. Luke was a friend and fellow-worker of Paul and knew the phenomenon of speaking with tongues as it took place, for instance, at Corinth, very well. He speaks of it himself in Acts 10:46-47 and 19:6. No doubt the phenomenon of Pentecost was related to the speaking with tongues. Otherwise Peter could not have said that Cornelius and those with him had received the Holy Spirit just as Peter and the other apostles had (Acts 10:47; compare 11:17 and 15:8). Nevertheless there was a difference. For, in 1 Corinthians 14, as in Acts 10:46 and 19:6, the speaking with tongues is not modified by the adjective *strange*. But Acts 2:4 expressly mentions the word *other* tongues. When the members of the church at Corinth speak in tongues, they are not understood unless an interpretation follows later on (1 Cor. 14:2 ff.). But in Jerusalem the disciples were already speaking in other tongues before the multitude came up and heard them. A miracle of hearing is therefore out of the question (Acts 2:4). And when the multitude of people heard it, they understood what was said, for everybody heard the disciples in his own language in which he was reared (Acts 2:6, 8). The other languages of which verse 4 speaks are doubtlessly the languages which verse 6 calls the languages of the auditors, and which in verse 8 are still more specifically designated as the ones in which those who heard were born. They were not therefore incomprehensible sounds in which the disciples spoke, but other tongues, *new* tongues, as Mark says in Chapter 16:17 of his letter, and such as they had not expected from untutored Galileans (Acts 2:7). In all those languages they proclaim the wonderful works of God, and particularly those which in the most recent time He had done in the raising and exaltation of Christ (Acts 2:4 and 14ff.).

We are not to take Luke's account of this as though it meant to say that the disciples of Jesus at that moment knew and could speak all the possible languages of the earth. Nor does the account mean to say that all of the disciples spoke all of the other tongues. The purpose of this miracle of languages was not even that the disciples should preach the gospel to the strangers in their own tongues for the reason that they could not otherwise understand it. For the fifteen names listed in verses 9-11 do not represent as many different languages. They are designations of the countries from which the strangers had come to Jerusalem on the occasion of Pentecost. And all of the strangers named there understood Aramaic or Greek, so that in this respect no qualifying of the apostles for speaking new languages was needed. Later in the New Testament, too, we do not again find any mention made of this gift of strange languages. Paul, the apostle to the Gentiles, who would then certainly have received the gift rather than others, never speaks of it. He could get on very well with the Aramaic and the Greek in the world of His time.

The speaking in strange tongues on the day of Pentecost was therefore a unique event. It was related, it is true, to the speaking of tongues generally known and referred to elsewhere, but it was a speaking of a particular sort and a higher form. Paul ranked that general and common kind lower in importance than prophecy. But the thing that took place at Jerusalem was a combination of the speaking with tongues and prophecy. The operation of the Holy Spirit, then first poured out in its fulness, was so powerful that it dominated the whole consciousness and expressed itself in the speaking of articulated sounds which were recognized by the auditors as being their own languages. The purpose of this miracle was not, therefore, to equip the disciples with the knowledge of strange languages, but rather, in an unusual way, to leave a powerful impression of the great event that had now taken place. And how could this be done better than by having the small, newly established world church proclaim in many tongues the mighty deeds of God? At the creation the morning stars sang together and all the children of God rejoiced. At the birth of Christ the multitude of heavenly hosts raised the jubilee of God's good will. On the birthday of the church that church itself sings the wonderful works of God in myriad tones.

* * * * *

Even though the speaking with tongues has an important place among the signs of Pentecost, we must remember that the pouring out of the Spirit in that first period became manifest in many unusual powers and operations. The gift of the Spirit was generally given after someone had come to the faith, sometimes at baptism (Acts 2:28), or at the laying on of hands before baptism (Acts 9:17), or at the laying on of hands after baptism (Acts 8:17 and 19:6). But usually it consisted of the granting of a particular power. Thus we read that by the Spirit the disciples were given boldness to speak the word (Acts 4:8 and 31), a particular strength of faith (Acts 6:5 and 11:24), comfort and joy (Acts 9:31 and 13:52), wisdom (Acts 6:3 and 10), speaking with tongues (Acts 10:46; 15:8; and 19:6), prophecy (Acts 11:28; 20:23; and 21:11), manifestations and revelations,[6] miraculous healings,[7] and the like. Just as did the works which Jesus performed, so these unusual

---

6. Acts 7:55; 8:39; 10:19; 13:2; 15:28; 16:6; and 20:22.
7. Acts 3:6; 5:5, 12, 15, 16; 8:7, 13; and elsewhere.

powers which were made manifest in the church caused great fear and perturbation.[8] On the one hand they did provoke opposition, driving the heart of the enemies to hatred and persecution; but, on the other hand, they also prepared the soil for receiving the seed of the gospel. They were necessary in that first period to provide entrance for the Christian confession in the world.

Throughout the whole apostolic period these unusual operations of the Spirit continued. We know this especially from the witness of the apostle Paul. He was Himself, in his own person, abundantly endowed with these special gifts of the Spirit. In an unusual way, that is, by a revelation of Jesus Christ Himself, He was brought to repentance on the way to Damascus, and called to be an apostle (Acts 9:3 ff.), and later, too, revelations came to Him periodically.[9] He knows himself to be in possession of the gift of knowledge, of prophecy, of doctrine, of speaking with tongues (1 Cor. 14:6 and 18). He performs signs, wonders, and works which are evidences of his apostleship (2 Cor. 12:12). He preaches in demonstration of the Spirit and power (1 Cor. 2:4). Christ Himself wrought by him to make the Gentiles obedient, by word and deed, through mighty signs and wonders, by the power of the Spirit of God (Rom. 15:18-19).

But, although Paul is fully conscious of his apostolic office and its dignity and always maintains it as absolutely as possible, he knew that the gifts of the Spirit were not given to him alone but also to all the believers. In 1 Corinthians 12:8-10 (compare Rom. 6:8) Paul cites a number of these gifts, and he says of them that they are distributed by the Spirit in differing proportions and to each according to the will of the Spirit. The apostle values all of those gifts very highly. They are not owing to the believers themselves for these have nothing which they have not received, and therefore have no basis at all for exalting themselves and despising others (1 Cor. 4:6-7). But all of those gifts and powers are achieved by one and the same Spirit. They are a fulfillment of the prophecy made in the Old Testament (Gal. 3:14) and are to be regarded as first fruits which herald a great harvest and as an earnest of our future, heavenly inheritance.[10]

Nevertheless, Paul gives out an appraisal of all these unusual gifts which differs significantly from that of many members of the church. There were persons at Corinth who exalted themselves on the basis of the gifts given them by the revelation of the Spirit, and who looked down with disdain on those who had received lesser gifts or no gifts at

---

8. Acts 2:7, 37, 43; 3:10; 4:13; 5:5, 11, 13, and 24.
9. Acts 16:6, 7, 9; 2 Cor. 12:1-7; and Gal. 2:2.
10. Rom. 8:23; 2 Cor. 1:22; 5:5; Eph. 1:14; and 4:30.

all. These persons did not apply their gifts to the benefit of others, but flaunted them. And they attached a particular importance to the mysterious and incomprehensible speaking with tongues. But Paul points out their mistake (1 Cor. 12-14). In the first place, he points to the norm by which all of these gifts must be measured. That norm is the confession of Jesus as Lord. Whoever speaks through the Spirit of God can not call Jesus accursed. Only those who confess Jesus as Lord demonstrate that they speak through the Holy Spirit. The earmark of the Spirit and of all His gifts and operations is His being bound to the confession of Jesus as Lord (1 Cor. 12:3).

Next, Paul points out that the gifts of the Spirit, although all answering to one norm, are nevertheless greatly differentiated, and that they are given to everyone not according to his merit or worth, but according to the sovereign will of the Spirit (1 Cor. 12:4-11). They are not therefore to be the occasion or basis for self-exaltation and the despising or disdaining of others. Rather, they must all be heartily and willingly applied to the benefit of the neighbor, for all believers are members of one body and need each other (1 Cor. 12:12-30). But if the gifts are used to that end, if they are devoted to that which is profitable (1 Cor. 12:7), that is, beneficial to others, to the edifying of the church, as it is called (1 Cor. 14:12), then gradations become evident among the gifts themselves, for the one is more beneficial to the edifying of the church than the other, and so one can speak of good gifts, better gifts, and best gifts. Therefore the Apostle advises the believers in 1 Corinthians 12:31 that they may certainly covet the *best* gifts.

In that energetic aspiration to the best gifts, love is the pre-eminent way. Without it, the greatest gifts are without value (1 Cor. 13:1-3). Love far transcends all others in virtue (1 Cor. 13:4-7). Love transcends all the gifts in duration, for all gifts will sometime cease, but love is eternal. Among the three virtues, faith, hope, and love, love is again of highest worth (1 Cor. 13:8-13). Therefore it is to be pursued above all things, even though the following after spiritual gifts is in itself commendable (1 Cor. 14:1). But in this pursuit the attention must be directed to such gifts as serve to edify the church and thus most exercise love. Viewed from this point of view, prophecy stands much higher than speaking with tongues. For they who speak with tongues are not understood, speak mysteries which are incomprehensible to the auditors, speak into the air, leave mind and judgment out of account, do not bring the unbelieving to the faith, but leave the impression of being mentally ill. If there are members of the church who possess this power, they are to make use of it with restraint, and are preferably to accompany it with an interpretation. If no interpretation can be given, let them keep still in the church! On the contrary, those who prophesy, those who through the revelation of the Spirit proclaim the word of God, speak edification, admonishment, and comfort to men. They build up the church, and they win the unbelieving. Irrespective therefore of what gift a person may have received, it has its norm of genuineness in the confession of Jesus as Lord and its purpose in the edifying of the church. God is not a God of confusion but of peace.

This beautiful treatment of spiritual gifts bore its fruit not only for the church at Corinth, but keeps its significance for the church of all ages. For always and again there are persons and parties who attach more importance to unusual manifestations, to revelations and miracles, than to the operation of the Spirit in regeneration, conversion, and the renewing of life. The abnormal and unusual always attracts attention, and the normal and usual goes unnoticed. People take to revelations, appearances, transports of the soul, and theatrical extravagances, and have closed eyes for the gradual and steady maturing of the kingdom of God. Paul was of a different mind. Much as he esteems the unusual gifts of the spirit, he admonishes the brethren in Corinth: Be not children in understanding, but be children in malice, and in understanding be men (1 Cor. 14:20).

Thus the apostle shifts the center of gravity from the temporal and transient revelations of the Spirit to the regular religious and moral work which He continuously accomplishes in the church. Such an idea of the work of the Spirit was prepared for already in the days of the Old Testament. Then, too, all kinds of extraordinary gifts and powers were ascribed to the Holy Spirit, but, as the prophets and the psalmists were led more deeply into the apostacy of the people of Israel and into the subtlety and wickedness of the human heart, they declared more clearly and strongly that only a renewal by the Holy Spirit could make the people of Israel a people of God in the real sense. The Ethiopian cannot change his skin, nor the leopard his spots. So they also can do no good that are accustomed to do evil (Jer. 13:23). God by His Spirit must change the hearts of the people, if they are to walk in His ways, and keep His ordinances and statutes. The Spirit of the Lord alone works the true, spiritual, and moral life.[11]

The preaching of Jesus in the gospel according to John confirms all this. In His conversation with Nicodemus Jesus explains that there is no access to the kingdom of God, nor any sharing in it, except through regeneration, and that this rebirth can take place only through the Holy Spirit (John 3:3-5). And in His farewell addresses (John 14-16) He develops in detail the idea that the Spirit whom He will send from the

---

11. Ps. 51:12 and 13; Isa. 32:15; and Ezek. 36:27.

Father after His glorification is to take His place among the disciples. It is therefore beneficial to them that Jesus Himself go. Otherwise the Comforter could not come to them. But when He Himself goes to the Father He can and He will send the Spirit. For Christ's going to the Father will be the evidence that He has perfectly finished the work on earth that He was to do. In heaven He can and He may then take His seat at the Father's right hand, may function as high priest and intercessor for the church on earth, and may desire everything from the Father which that church needs. In other words, He can then pray the Father for the Holy Spirit in all His fulness and send the Spirit to His disciples. And this Spirit will then take His place among them. In the future the Spirit will be their comforter, their guide, their intercessor, and their advocate.

In this the disciples will suffer no loss. For when Jesus went about on earth, He went in and out with His disciples, it is true, but there were all kinds of aloofness and misunderstanding among them. But the Spirit who is to come will not remain standing outside of them or alongside of them, but will dwell with*in* them. Christ's stay on earth was temporary, but the Spirit whom He will send will never leave them, but will remain with them into eternity. Indeed, Christ Himself will come to them again in that Spirit. He does not leave them as orphans, but He returns to them and joins Himself with them in the Spirit in a way which had before been impossible. Then they will see Him again. They will live, as He lives. They will acknowledge that Christ is in the Father, and they in Him, and He in them. And in Christ the Father comes to them. Through the Spirit both come. Father and Son both come to the disciples and make their dwelling in them in the Spirit. That, then, is the thing that the Holy Spirit will, in the first place, accomplish: a communion between the Father and the Son, on the one hand, and between the disciples, on the other. It is a fellowship such as has never existed before.

And when the disciples share this fellowship and live by it, when they are joined with Christ as the branch is with the vine, when they are not servants but friends, then that same Spirit who has caused them to share in this fellowship will also in the future as the Spirit of truth lead them into all truth. He will not only give them to reflect on what Christ personally told and taught them, but He will constantly be witnessing to them of the Christ. He will say what He has heard from Christ and has received from Him, and He will even declare future things to them. The disciples will not only have the fellowship with Christ and the Father, but they will also be conscious of having it. The Holy Spirit will enlighten them concerning Christ, concerning His oneness with the

Father, and concerning their relationship to both the Father and the Son. The final purpose is that all believers be one even as — so Christ puts it in His own words — Thou, Father, art in Me, and I in Thee, that they may also be one in us, that the world may believe that Thou hast sent Me (John 17:21 ff.).

When on the day of Pentecost the outpouring of the Holy Spirit took place, the extraordinary manifestations by which this rich shedding of the Spirit revealed itself, naturally enough, in that first period, attracted the attention. But we may not for that reason close our eyes to the other and really much more significant fact that the disciples by the gift of the Spirit were united in the most intimate way into one, independent, holy church. Christ was the Lord and Savior of that church, and all the believers mutually continued steadfastly in the apostles' doctrine and fellowship, and in breaking of bread, and in prayers (Acts 2:42). The unity of which Christ had spoken was for a time realized in the church at Jerusalem. When the enthusiasm of the first love later gave way to a calmer attitude of heart and mind, when churches were added in other places and among other peoples, when, later still, all kinds of schism and separation came up in the Christian church, then the unity which binds all the believers took on a different form, became less vital and profound, sometimes even very weak or such as not to be felt at all. But we are not to forget in the midst of all difference and strife that in essence the unity of the church has remained until this day. In the future it will become even more gloriously manifest than it was for that brief period in Jerusalem.

* * * * *

It is the apostle Paul who of all the apostles most holds this ideal of the unity of the church up before our view and who himself holds to it in spite of all division of which he, in his day too, was already a witness. The church is one body, and all its members need each other and must serve each other (Rom. 12:4 and 1 Cor. 12:12ff.). But it is such a unity because it is the body of Christ.[12] The unity of the church roots in the fellowship with Christ and comes up out of it. Christ is the head of every believer, of every local congregation, and also of the church as a whole. All believers are new creatures whom God has created in Christ unto good works in order that they should walk in them (2 Cor. 5:17 and Eph. 2:10). Christ lives and dwells in them, and they live, move, and have their being in Christ: Christ is their life.[13] The combination *in Christ* (in the Lord, in Him) occurs more than a hundred and fifty

---

12. Rom. 12:5; Eph. 1:23; and Col. 1:24.
13 Rom. 6:11; 8:1 and 10; 2 Cor. 13:5; Gal. 2:20; Phil. 1:21; and Col. 3:4.

times in the New Testament. It indicates that Christ is the constant source not only of the spiritual life, but that as such He also immediately and directly dwells in the believer. The unity is as close as that between a cornerstone and a temple, a man and a woman, the head and the body, the vine and the branch. The believers are in Christ as all things by virtue of creation and providence are in God. They live in Him as the fish lives in water, the bird in the air, the man in his vocation, the scholar in his study. Together with Him they are crucified, dead, and buried, are raised again, seated at the right hand of God, and glorified.[14] They have put Him on, have assumed His form, and they show in their body both the suffering and the life of Christ, and are perfected (fulfilled) in Him. In short, Christ is all and in all.[15]

This close relationship is made possible by the fact that Christ shares Himself with the believer through the Spirit. Because by His passion and death Christ has so perfectly earned the Spirit and all His gifts and powers that He, Christ Himself, can be called the Spirit (2 Cor. 3:17), He has also earned the right to give that Spirit to whom He will. The Spirit of God has become the Spirit of Christ, the Spirit of the Son, the Spirit of the Lord.[16] To have received that Spirit is to say that one has received Christ, for whoever has not the Spirit of Christ does not belong to Christ, is not His own (Rom. 8:9-10). Just as God gives Him to the world, so Christ gives Himself to the church through His Spirit. The believers are one Spirit with Him (1 Cor. 6:17). They are temples of the Holy Spirit through whom God Himself dwells in them (1 Cor. 3:16, 17 and 6:19). They are, they confess, they walk, they pray, and they rejoice in the Spirit.[17] They are spiritual beings, understanding and judging the things of the Spirit (Rom. 8:2 and 1 Cor. 2:14). They are continuously led by the Spirit and are accompanied by Him up to the day of the redemption.[18] By that Spirit they all have access to the Father and are built up together on the foundation of the apostles and prophets for a habitation to God (Eph. 2:18 and 22).

In terms such as these the Holy Scriptures account for that wonderful unity which exists between Christ and His church, and which later came to be designated by the term *mystical union*. As a matter of fact we cannot understand this unity in its depth and intimacy. It far transcends our thought. It is certainly to be distinguished in nature and kind from the unity which exists among the three persons of the Godhead, for all three of those persons share in one and the same Divine being, and it is

---

14. Rom. 6:4 ff.; Gal. 2:20; 6:14; Eph. 2:6; Col. 2:12, 20; and 3:3.
15. Rom. 13:14; 2 Cor. 4:11; Gal. 4:19; Col. 1:24; 2:10; and 3:11.
16. Rom. 8:9; 1 Cor. 2:16; 2 Cor. 3:18; Gal. 4:6; and Phil. 1:19.
17. Rom. 8:4, 9, 15; 14:17; and 1 Cor. 12:3.
18. Rom. 8:15-16; 2 Cor. 1:22; Eph. 1:13; and 4:30.

precisely in essence that Christ and the believers remain distinct from each other. True, the unity of Christ and the church is more than once compared with that between Christ and the Father.[19] But at those times Christ is not speaking of Himself as the Son, the Only-Begotten, but of Himself as the Mediator, who will be raised to the right hand of God, and through whom the Father will carry out His good pleasure. Just as the Father has chosen His own in Christ from before the foundation of the world (Eph. 1:4) to the glory of His grace in which He has made them accepted in the Beloved (Eph. 1:6-7 and Acts 20:28), so He also gathers them all in Christ in one (Eph. 1:10). The Father dwells in Christ as the Mediator and so gives Himself and His blessings to the church.

Close and inseparable as the relationship between the Father and the Mediator is, that between Christ and the believers is equally so. In inner power it surpasses every union that can be found among creatures and even that which exists between God and His world. Distinguished on the one hand from all pantheistic admixture, it is on the other hand far superior to all deistic juxtaposition and all contractual relationship. Scripture teaches us something about its nature by comparing it with the relationship between a vine and its branches, the head of a body and its members, a man and a woman. It is a relationship which fully and eternally unites the whole Christ with His church and with its members in the depth of their being and in the essence of their personality. It is a relationship which began in eternity when the Son of God declared Himself to be ready for the Mediatorship. It obtained its objective existence in the fulness of time when Christ put on the human nature, entered into the fellowship of His people, and delivered Himself up in death for His own. And it is personally actualized in each individual when the Holy Spirit comes into him, incorporates him into Christ, and when he, on his part, acknowledges and exercises this unity with Christ.

This fellowship with the person of Christ brings with it the sharing in all His blessings and benefits. There is no sharing in the benefits of Christ unless we share in His person, for the benefits are not to be separated from the person. That would to a certain extent be conceivable if the benefits which Christ conferred were material goods. A man can give us his money and property without giving us himself. But the benefits which Christ gives are spiritual in kind. They consist above all of His favor, His mercy, His love, and these are gifts which are thoroughly personal in kind and are not to be separated from the person of Christ. The treasury of benefits has not been deposited somewhere on earth, in the hands, say, of pope or priest, or in church or sacrament.

---

19. John 10:38; 14:11, 20; and 17:21-23.

It is to be found exclusively in Christ Himself. He is that treasury. In Him the Father turns His friendly, gracious face to us, and that is all our salvation.

And, conversely, there is no fellowship with the person of Christ without a sharing in His treasures and benefits. The relationship between the Father and Christ is in this respect again the basis and the example of the relationship between Christ and His church. The Father gave Himself to the Son, specifically also to the Son as the Mediator of God and men. The Father has retained nothing for Himself but has given all to Christ. All things were delivered to Him by the Father (Matt. 11:27 and John 3:35). All that the Father has is His (John 16:15 and 17:10). The Father and Christ are one; the Father is in Him, and He is in the Father (John 10:38 and 17:21-23). And so, in His turn, Christ gives Himself and all His benefits to the church through the Holy Spirit (John 16:13-15). He keeps nothing for Himself. Just as the fulness of the Godhead dwells in Him bodily (Col. 1:19 and 2:9), so He also perfects the church unto the measure of the stature of His fulness until it is filled to the fulness of God.[20] He is all in all (Col. 3:11).

It is a fulness which we receive in Christ, a Divine fulness, a fulness of grace and truth, a fulness which is never exhausted, and which grants grace for grace (John 1:14 and 16). This fulness dwells in Christ Himself, in His person, in His Divine and in His human nature, during the state of His humiliation and that of His exaltation. There is a fulness of grace in His incarnation: For ye know the grace of our Lord Jesus Christ, that, though He was rich, yet, for your sakes, He became poor, that ye through His poverty might be rich (2 Cor. 8:9). There is a fulness of grace in His living and dying, for in the days of His flesh He learned obedience from the things which He suffered, and being made perfect, He became the author of eternal salvation to all them that obey Him (Heb. 5:7-9). There is a fulness of grace in His resurrection, for by it He was shown to be the Son of God in power and has begotten us again unto a lively hope (Rom. 1:4 and 1 Peter 1:3). There is a fulness of grace in His ascension for by it He took captivity captive, and gave gifts unto men (Eph. 4:8). There is a fulness of grace in His intercession for by it He can perfectly save all those that come to God by Him (Heb. 7:25). There is a fulness of grace in Him unto forgiveness, regeneration, renewal, comfort, preservation, leading, sanctification, and glorification. It is a long, broad, deep stream of grace, and it bears the believers along from beginning to end, into eternity. It is a fulness which gives grace for grace, grace instead

---

20. Eph. 1:23; 3:19; 4:13 and 16.

of grace, which immediately supplants the one grace by another, exchanging it for the former one, interchanging them. There is no desisting in this, no interim. It is all grace and nothing but grace which comes to the church in Christ.

* * * * *

The benefits which Christ gives in His fellowship can therefore very well be comprehended under the one term *grace*. But that one name then comprises a fulness, a riches of blessing, which cannot be surveyed. At the beginning of the last preceding chapter, mention was made of the reconciliation which Christ had accomplished with the Father by His satisfying sacrifice. In Christ God has laid His wrath aside and placed Himself in an attitude of grace towards the world (2 Cor. 5:19). And for the person who accepts this reconciliation with a believing heart, a series of benefits flow — indeed, salvation itself. Scripture mentions many of them — calling, regeneration, faith, justification, forgiveness of sins, adoption as children, freedom from the law, spiritual liberty, hope, love, peace, joy, gladness, comfort, sanctification, preservation, perseverance, glorification, and others besides. A total summing up is really impossible, for they include everything which the church as a whole and each individual believer in particular, throughout all ages and in all circumstances, in prosperity and adversity, in life and death, on this side the grave and hereafter into all eternity, has received and will receive of the fulness of Christ.

Because of this quantity and richness of benefits, it is impossible to develop them all fully. It is highly difficult to get a good survey of them all. And there is some risk too in treating them in a regular order and in assigning to each benefit its place in the context of the whole. The classification, accordingly, differs greatly among theologians. But in the main three major groups of benefits can be defined. In the first place, there is the group of benefits which prepares man for the covenant of grace, introduces him into it, and gives him the ability, on his own part, with a willing heart to receive the blessings of that covenant, and to accept them. These are the benefits of calling, regeneration (in the narrower sense), faith, and repentance. A second group comprises those blessings which change the status of man in God's sight, free him from guilt, and so renew his mind. These are particularly the benefits of justification, forgiveness of sins, adoption as children, the testimony of the Holy Spirit with our Spirit, freedom from the law, spiritual liberty, peace and joy. And, in the next place, there is a third group of benefits, and these introduce a change into the condition of man, redeem him from the taint of sin, and renew him according to the image of God. To this group belong especially regeneration (in the broader sense), the dying and being raised with Christ, the continuous conversion, the walking in the Spirit, and the perseverance up to the end. All of these benefits are perfected and completed in the heavenly glory and salvation which God prepares hereafter for His own. A separate chapter will be devoted to that at the end of this instruction in the Christian religion.

Before giving more specific attention to each of these groups of benefits, we ought to observe that all of them, even as the person of Christ itself, can be granted only through the Holy Spirit. We noticed above that the Father is in Christ, that only in Christ He turns His gracious face to us, and that only in Him the Father comes to make His dwelling with us. But just so, too, Christ is in the Holy Spirit, and He can come to us and wants to come to us only through that Spirit. By the Spirit Christ gives Himself to us and gives His benefits to us. The Spirit is called the Holy Spirit precisely because He stands in a particular relationship to the Father and to Christ, and accordingly puts us into a particular relationship with both the Father and the Son. We must not suppose, therefore, that we can ever in any way come into fellowship with the Father and with Christ except through the Holy Spirit. Let every one that names the name of Christ depart from iniquity (2 Tim. 2:19).

According to the Scriptures the Holy Spirit is the Factor and Implementer of regeneration and of faith (John 3:5 and 1 Cor. 12:4). He justifies us in our consciousness and testifies of our adoption as children.[21] He pours out the love of God into our hearts, gives us peace and joy, and delivers us from the law, the flesh, and from sin and death.[22] He is the Comforter and Advocate who defends our cause, protects and supports us, and who does not, as Christ does in His human nature, leave us, but remains with us always, comforting us and praying for us.[23] Not only is the spiritual life quickened by Him, but it is also continuously maintained and led by Him: He is the law and the rule of it (Rom. 8:2, 14 and Gal. 5:18). He renews and sanctifies that life, causes it to bear fruit, and makes it pleasing to God.[24] The whole life of the Christian is a walking in the Spirit (Rom. 8:4 ff. and Gal. 5:16 and 25). He binds all the believers into one body and builds them up

---

21. Rom. 8:15; 1 Cor. 6:11; and Gal. 4:6.
22. Rom. 5:5; 8:2; and 14:17.
23. John 14:16; Acts 9:31; and Rom. 8:26.
24. Rom. 15:13, 16; Gal. 5:23; 2 Thess. 2:13; Titus 3:5; and 1 Peter 1:2.

into one temple, a dwelling place of God (Eph. 2:18-22 and 4:3-4). He guarantees the heavenly inheritance,[25] and will one day effect their resurrection and glorification (Rom. 8:11 and 1 Cor. 15:44).

In short, Christ and all His benefits, the love of the Father, and the grace of the Son, become our portion only in the fellowship of the Holy Spirit.

---

25. 2 Cor. 1:22; 5:5; Eph. 1:13; and 4:30.

XX

The Christian Calling

In order to include us in the fellowship of His person and His benefits, Christ makes use not only of the Spirit whom He has poured out in the church, but also of the Word which He has given it for its instruction and direction. And He has laid down that kind of connection between the two which makes them both together serviceable to the exercise of His prophetic, priestly, and kingly office. But it is not an easy task to get a sound idea of this relationship or to define it clearly. There have always been very different views of the relationship of Word and Spirit, and these different representations continue alongside of each other up to the present time.

On the one hand there are those who regard the preaching of the Word as adequate in itself and who do injustice to the operation of the Spirit. These are the followers of Pelagius who in remote and more recent times pursued this heresy. They look upon Christianity as being exclusively a doctrine, see in Jesus nothing but a lofty example, and make of the gospel merely a new law. They hold that sin has indeed weakened man but not that he is spiritually dead. They maintain that he has retained the freedom of the will, and that the preaching of the gospel is in itself enough, if man is so inclined, to bring him into line with the example of Jesus' work and ways. No need is felt for the regenerating influence of the Holy Spirit. The personality and Divinity of the Spirit are denied and attacked. At best the Holy Spirit is thought of as a force which proceeds from God or, more specifically, from the person of Jesus, and which fosters a sort of moral disposition and ideal purpose in the church.

There are others who follow a very different course of thought. They are called zealots, antinomians, enthusiasts, or mystics, and they talk much of the Spirit, and they underestimate the role of the Word in the conversion of men. As they see it the Word, the Holy Scripture, the preaching of the gospel, is not the spiritual reality itself, but is only a token and symbol of it. In itself the Word is but a dead letter which cannot penetrate to the heart of man nor implant there the principle of the new life. At best the Word can have only an enlightening influence on the mind. But it gives off no power or force which can change and convert the heart. That can take place only and does take place only through the Holy Spirit, who penetrates immediately and directly from God into the inmost being of man and makes him share in the reality of which the Word is but the sign. The spiritual man is therefore directly born of God and taught of God. He alone understands the Scripture, gets behind the letter to the core and essence of it. This spiritual man does for a time make use of Scripture as a norm and guiding principle, but it is not the source of his religious knowledge, for he is subjectively taught by the Spirit of God and gradually grows beyond the Scriptures.

As the influence of the Spirit gradually emancipates the heart of man more and more completely from the Scriptures, the heart of man also comes to stand more independent of the person of Christ and the whole of historic Christianity. In its further development, then, mysticism turns into rationalism. For when the internal operation of the Spirit is separated from the word of Scripture, it loses its special character and can no longer be distinguished from the common operation of the Spirit of God in the reason and conscience of man. God by nature dwells with His Spirit in every man, according to this view, and from his birth, man has the internal word written on his heart. To this Christ only gave a certain inflection. Something is true not because it is written in the Bible but because it is true. Christianity is the original natural religion. It is as old as the world and in its essence it lies at the basis of all historical religions. Mysticism is always and again going over into rationalism, and rationalism periodically falls back into mysticism. The extremes touch each other and shake hands.

The Christian church has always tried to avoid these heresies and to keep Word and Spirit in relationship with each other. But in doing this it has in its several confessions nevertheless followed several courses. The Roman church, for instance, sees in the Holy Scripture and in the ecclesiastical tradition not a real means of grace but only a source of truth. The rational apprehension of this truth is called faith. But because this faith is purely an approbation, it is inadequate for salvation, and consequently has only a preparatory use to that end. The real saving grace is extended for the first time in the sacrament, and thus Rome recognizes the work of the Holy Spirit above all things in the founding and maintaining of the church in its offices of teaching, shepherding, and ministering at the altar, and next in the supernatural grace, virtues, and gifts given to the faithful by means of the sacrament.

Against this attempt to separate the saving operation of the Spirit from the word, and to attach it only to the sacrament, the Reformation took up the cudgels. It restored Scripture not only as the one, clear, and adequate source of truth, including tradition, but honored it also as a means of grace and restored to the word its primary place in relation to the sacrament. Accordingly the Reformation felt itself compelled to reflect more deeply on the relationship of Word and Spirit. It was compelled to do this the more because on all sides the old heresies were revived and were finding powerful defenders. While the Socinians returned to the teachings of Arius and Pelagius, regarded the gospel as a new law, and felt no need for a particular operation of the Holy Spirit, the Anabaptists again took the way of mysticism, glorified the internal word, and spoke of Holy Scripture as a dead letter and an empty symbol.

It required a great deal of effort to find the right path again. The Lutheran and the Reformed churches took different ways. The Lutherans united Word and Spirit so completely as to run the risk of identifying them, and to lose the distinction between them altogether. They even came to the point of enclosing the saving grace of the Spirit in the word and to permit Him entrance to man only through the word. Since Holy Scripture came into being by the Holy Spirit, that Spirit had made His power of converting residual in the word, depositing it there, so to speak, as in a vessel. Just as bread has a natural, internal, nutritive power, so Scripture received from the Spirit who brought it into being an inner spiritual power to save man. Scripture is therefore not merely to be credited with a power to enlighten the mind and morally influence the will, but by the indwelling influence of the Holy Spirit it has also an inner, heart-renewing, and saving power. And the Holy Spirit never works in any way except through the word.

The Reformed churches simply could not take this view, for in this matter, too, their principle was relevant that the finite can never absorb and comprehend the infinite. Word and Spirit consequently might be very intimately related, but they also remain distinct. The Spirit can work and sometimes does work without the word. When the Spirit joins Himself with the Word, He does so because of His free choice. In accordance with His good pleasure He usually does work in connection with the word, and in the place where the word is present and is preached, namely, in the sphere of the covenant of grace, in the communion of the church. But even then He lives, not as the Lutherans represented it, in Holy Scripture or the preached word, but in the church as the living body of Christ. Nor does the Spirit work through the word as through a vehicle of His power. While combining His operation with that of the word, He Himself personally penetrates to the heart of man and renews it to eternal life.

* * * * *

If we are to get a right understanding of the relationship of Word and Spirit, we must proceed from the fact that, not only in the offer of Christ and all His benefits, but also in all of His works with the world, God makes use of the word as a means. In Holy Scripture the word is never an empty sound or a meaningless sign, but always a thing of power and of life. It has in itself something of the personality, of the soul, of the speaker and therefore never returns void, always effects something.

When God speaks, it is done (Ps. 33:9). His word does not return to Him void, but accomplishes that which He pleases, and prospers in the thing for which it is sent (Isa. 55:11). By His word He brought everything into being from nothing at the beginning (Gen. 1:3 ff. and Ps. 33:6), and by the word of His power He upholds all things (Heb. 1:3). This word has such a creative and sustaining power because God Speaks in the Son (John 1:3 and Col. 1:15), and through the Spirit (Ps. 33:6 and Ps. 104:30), and in both these, as it were, gives Himself to His creatures. There is a voice of God in all creatures; they all rest on thoughts which He has spoken. They all owe it to the word of God that they exist and that they are such as they are.

But these thoughts, embodied by God in the world, are not understood by all creatures, but only by rational creatures, only by man. Because he is created in God's image, man himself can also think and speak, can take up into His awareness the thoughts of God laid down in His creation, can make these his spiritual property, and also thereupon give them back in his own speech. When he first came perfect from the hand of the Creator, He could understand the speech of God, which came to him internally in the moral law written on his heart, and which came to him from without in the probationary command which was added to the moral law. At that time God went about with man as He did with no other creature. God entered into covenant with him, took him up into His fellowship, and required of him that he consciously and willingly walk in His ways. The moral law was the content and the proclamation, the rule and the norm, of the original covenantal relationship which God established with the newly created man.

Now man by his deliberate disobedience has broken that covenant and has robbed himself of the spiritual power to keep the law of God and so to achieve eternal life. But God, on His part, has not withdrawn Himself from the creation nor altogether abandoned mankind. Although it can be said of the heathen, the Gentiles, that God left them, in distinction from Israel, to their own ways, He continues to reveal Himself to them in His power and Godhead, does not leave Himself without witness among them, and determines their times and the bounds of their habitation, in order that they should seek the Lord, if haply they might feel after Him and find Him.

There is, therefore, a speech of God which continues to go out to every one. The confessors of the Reformed faith have always acknowledged this by speaking of a "material call" which can be encountered outside the pale of the Christian world also, and which is the privilege of all men and all nations. The Gentiles do not share in the calling through the word of the Gospel, but that does not mean that they receive no calling at all. God speaks to them also, in nature (Rom. 1:20), in history (Acts 17:26), in the reason (John 1:9), and through the conscience (Rom. 2:14-15). True, this calling is inadequate for salvation, for it does not know of Christ, who is the only way to the Father, and the only name given under heaven unto salvation (John 14:6 and Acts 4:12), but it is nevertheless of great value and may not be underestimated in its significance.

After all, this calling which God issues to all men in His common grace may not be a proclamation of the gospel, but it is certainly a preaching of the law. Although man because of the darkness of his understanding often construes it amiss, and interprets and applies it mistakenly, it has nonetheless the same moral law as its content, materially and essentially, as the one which God originally gave man and wrote upon his heart. That calling, therefore, no matter how corrupted and denatured, nevertheless still lays down the requirement that man must love God above all things and his neighbor as himself. True, the Gentiles do not have the law in that perfect form in which God later gave it to Israel, but they nevertheless do the things of the law. In all their thoughts and deeds they let themselves be guided by moral rules and thus prove that these things of the law are written in their hearts, and that they feel themselves bound to them in their consciences (Rom. 2:14-15).

The bond between God and man has not, therefore, despite sin, been entirely severed. God does not leave man to himself, and man can not get away from God. Instead, he remains lying within the pale of God's revelation, and under the bonds of His law. God continues to speak to man, in nature and history, in reason and conscience, in blessings and judgments, in the leadings of life and the experiences of the soul. By means of this rich and powerful speech God maintains in man the consciousness of his responsibility. He causes him to strive for a religious, moral life and has him charged and condemned by his own conscience after his transgression. It is not an external duress but an internal moral obligation which unites man to God and His revelation. It is a witness of the Spirit of God which in fallen man also still lets itself be heard in an admonishment to good. For, to the extent that there is a general voice of God and a general enlightenment by the Word (Logos) in man, there exists also an operation of the Spirit of God. By that Spirit God dwells in every creature, and by Him we live, and move, and have our being (Acts 17:28). The general "material" call is not only external and objective in that by nature and history, reason and conscience it proclaims God's revelation and specifically His law to man, but it also has an internal and subjective side in that it morally obligates each individual person to that revelation, and in his own conviction makes him duty bound to maintain God's law.

It is true, of course, that God does not renew and save man by this proclamation of the law, for this the law cannot do in that it is weak through the flesh (Rom. 8:3). But God does by this means curb sin, hold down the passions, and restrain the stream of iniquities. A human society and a civic righteousness is made possible by it, and these in turn open up the way for a higher civilization, a richer culture, and a flowering of arts and sciences. In very fact the earth is still full of the good things of God. The Lord is good to all, and His mercies are over all His works. He causes His sun to rise over the evil and the good and His rains to fall on the just and the unjust. He does not leave Himself without witness, but does good, and gives us rain from heaven, and fruitful seasons, filling our hearts with food and gladness.[1]

* * * * *

From this general testimony or speech of God which comes to us in nature and conscience, that special calling is to be distinguished which is contained in the word of the gospel and which is directed to all who live within the boundaries of Christendom. The general calling is not, however, abandoned in this special calling, and is not obliterated by it, but rather is absorbed in it and strengthened. This is proved by the fact that Holy Scripture which is the word of special revelation acknowledges the general revelation in nature and history, confirms it, and purges it of all false admixtures. That the heavens declare God's glory, and the firmament shows His handiwork (Ps. 19:1), that the invisible things of God from the creation of the world are clearly seen, being understood by the things that are made (Rom. 1:20), and that the work of the law is

---

1. Ps. 104:24; 145:7; Matt. 5:45; Acts 14:7.

written in the hearts of men (Rom. 2:15) — all that is something which is understood far better by the Christian, taught by Scripture, than it is by the person who must live solely by the light of reason.

Even stronger evidence of the continuing relevancy of the general revelation is the fact that the moral law, which was known to the Gentiles only imperfectly and impurely, was purely and perfectly proclaimed by God on Sinai and was held up to His people Israel as a rule of life. When Christ came to earth, He did not discard this law, but He fulfilled it (Matt 5:17), first of all in His person and life, but further also in the life of all who follow in His footsteps and walk in the Spirit.[2] According to this example the Christian church in its confession, preaching, and teaching gave a place to the law quite as well as to the gospel.

Law and gospel are the two component parts of the Word of God. The two are distinguished from each other but they are never separated. They accompany each other throughout Scripture, from the beginning to the end of revelation. The discrimination of law and gospel is therefore a very different distinction from that between the Old and New Testament. It is so confused and identified by all who see in the law an imperfect gospel and in the gospel a perfected law. But the two distinctions differ mutually from each other and are therefore to be carefully kept from being identified. Old and New Testament are the names of two successive dispensations of the same covenant of grace and therefore of the two groups of books of the Bible corresponding to these two dispensations. But the distinction between law and gospel puts us on a very different plane. These terms designate, not two dispensations of one and the same covenant, but two entirely different covenants. The law really belongs to the so-called covenant of works which was concluded with the first man and which promised him eternal life in the way of perfect obedience. But the gospel is the proclamation of the covenant of grace which was made known for the first time after the fall of man, and which gives him eternal life by grace, through faith in Christ.

The covenant of grace is, however, not the discarding or annihilating, but rather the fulfilling, of the covenant of works. The difference between the two is mainly that in our stead Christ fulfills the requirements which God by reason of the covenant of works can bring to bear on us. Hence it is that the covenant of grace, although in itself it is pure grace, can from the very beginning put the law of the covenant of works into its service, unite itself with that law, and by the Spirit of Christ bring it to fulfillment in the believers. The law keeps its place in the covenant of grace, not in order that we by keeping it should try to earn eternal life, for the law cannot do this because of the weakness of the flesh, but, in

---

2. Rom. 3:31; 8:3; 11:8-10; and Gal. 5:14.

the first place, in order that through it we should come to know our sin, our guilt, our misery, and our helplessness, and, struck down and stripped by the consciousness of guilt, should take refuge in the grace of God in Christ (Rom. 7:7 and Gal. 3:24), and, in the second place, in order that we, having died and been raised with Christ, should walk in newness of life and so fulfill the righteousness of the law (Rom. 6:4 and 8:4).

Thus there is no room in Christianity for antinomianism, for despising or violating the law. Law and gospel should go together, as in the Scriptures, so also in preaching and teaching, in doctrine and in life. They are both indispensable and real constituent parts of the one complete word of God. All the same, identifying the two is as bad as separating them. Nomism, which makes of the gospel a new law, is in error no less than antinomianism. Law and gospel differ from each other not in degree but in kind. They differ as demand and gift differ, as commandment and promise, and as question and offer differ. It is true that the law as well as the gospel comprises the will of God, and that it is holy, wise, good, and spiritual,[3] but it has become impotent by reason of sin, does not justify but rather aggravates sin, and provokes wrath, doom, and death.[4] And over against this stands the gospel which has Christ as its content (Rom. 1:3 and Eph. 3:6), and which brings nothing but grace, reconciliation, forgiveness, righteousness, peace, and eternal life.[5] What the law demands of us is given us in the gospel for nothing.

* * * * *

If law and gospel are distinguished, in this way, it follows that the general calling, too, which in nature and conscience comes to all men, and the special calling which reaches everyone who lives in Christendom, do not differ in degree but in essence and kind. The difference does not consist of the fact that Christianity offers us a better, more perfect law than is known to the Gentiles, but of this, rather, that it proclaims something new, brings us the gospel, and in that gospel acquaints us with the person of Christ. Not in the law alone but especially in the gospel of the grace of God lies the distinction between heathendom and Christianity, between general and special revelation, between the calling which comes to all men and that in which Christians share alone. The general calling which is directed to all men is not embodied in a literal, clear, and unmistakable word of God, but is in complicated form contained in

---

3. Rom. 2:18, 20; 7:12, 14; 12:10.
4. Rom. 3:20; 4:15; 5:20; 7:5; 8:9, 13; 2 Cor. 3:6ff.; and Gal. 3:10, 13, 19.
5. Acts 2:38; 20:34; Rom. 3:21-26; 4:3-8; 5:1-2; and elsewhere.

the revelation which God gives also to the Gentiles in the works of their hands and in their own reason and conscience, and it is something which must be deduced from these by investigation and reflection. But the moment the Gentiles tried so to investigate and reflect, they fell into error both on the score of religion and on that of morality. Outside the pale of special revelation, men, although knowing God, have not glorified or been grateful to Him, but have become vain in their imaginings, and their foolish heart was darkened, and they fell into all kinds of idolatry and immorality (Rom. 1:21 ff.).

The revelation in nature and the calling in the reason and the conscience accordingly proved to be inadequate. In special revelation, therefore, God no longer speaks through the nature of creatures, but makes use of the unique, literal word which man himself uses as the highest and best expression of his thoughts. This making use of the word in special revelation was necessary also for a further reason. Nature, outside as well as inside of man, remains always the same. The heavens now still tell of God's glory in the same way that they did a thousand or several thousands of years ago. And, despite all his development and civilization, man is still in his essence and nature, in his heart and his conscience, exactly what his most ancient predecessors were.

But special revelation is not included in the order of nature. It came into being along the historical way, in a century-long history, and it has its mid-point in the historical person of Christ. Nature cannot save us; only a person can. But we can, according to God's plan, never come to know anything concerning historical events and persons, which, as we know, are not always with us as natural things are, but come and go, appear and disappear, except by means of the word, be it the spoken or the written word, and be it recorded in letters or in other signs. From the character of particular, historical revelation it accordingly follows that it must make use of the word in order to make itself known from generation to generation and from place to place. The general calling comes by way of nature, and the special calling comes by way of the word. The first has especially the law as its content, and the second has especially the gospel.

The gospel began its course already in Paradise. God first revealed it there, then had it proclaimed by the patriarchs and the prophets and had it represented by the sacrifices and other ceremonies of the law, and finally fulfilled it through his only-begotten Son. Nor was that all. He also had the word of the gospel recorded scripturally in the books of the Old and New Testaments, and further entrusted it for preservation, proclamation, interpretation, defense, and dissemination to the church, so that it would become known to all creatures.

On the same day on which the church of Christ received this task and began carrying it out, the outpouring of the Holy Spirit took place. And, conversely, at the same moment in which the Holy Spirit made the church His dwelling place, the church as an independent community of believers, and as the bearer of the word of the gospel, and as the pillar and firmness of the truth, had its beginning. Although in a preparatory way they were united earlier, Word and Spirit on the day of Pentecost were fully and definitively united. They work together in the service of Christ who is the King of the church and the Lord of the Spirit, and who is depicted for us in the Word, and is given us as our portion through the Spirit. Truth and grace go together because Christ is full of both (John 1:14).

* * * * *

The calling by means of the word far transcends the calling by means of nature. For while the latter permits man to hear only the voice of the law and holds up before him the requirement, Do that and thou shalt live, the calling by means of the word proceeds from Christ, has the grace of God as its content, and offers man the most desirable of benefits freely: namely, the forgiveness of sins and eternal life by way of faith and repentance. If one pays attention solely to the content of this calling, one could for a moment foster the hope that, upon hearing it, all men would immediately receive it with joy and with gladness of heart. For what can a human being who is a sinner and who is headed for corruption possibly have to object to the gospel which assures him of the grace of God, and which wants to give him perfect salvation, without any effort on his own part except that of receiving this good tiding with a childlike faith?

Nevertheless, reality tells us something very different. Throughout the centuries there has been a separation between those who serve the Lord and those who do not serve Him. In the family of Adam, Abel and Cain each went a different way. The human race before the flood was divided into the line of Seth and that of Cain. And after the flood, this division continued in the generation of Shem and in that of his brothers. The families of the patriarchs saw the division manifest itself in Isaac and Ishmael, in Jacob and Esau, and later in Israel and the other nations. Even the people of the covenant were not all Israel who were physically descended from Abraham, but the children of the promise were counted for the seed (Rom. 9:6-8). And in the days of the New Testament we are confronted by the same fact. Many are called, but few are chosen (Matt. 22:14). Not only is there a sharp contrast between church and world, but in the church itself there are thousands who are indeed hearers of the word but are not doers of it (James 1:22). Even though one were to repudiate Christianity altogether, one would not get rid of this contrast. For there are and there remain everywhere the good and the evil, the just and the unjust. There is a difference in rank and status, in gift and strength, in riches and honor, but there exists among them an even deeper difference, one that is religious and moral in character.

This fact of inequality is so manifest and has such a serious character that everybody must reckon with it. But there have always been many who have tried to explain this moral inequality, just as they have tried to explain other differences among men, on the basis of the free will which has been given them. They hold that the will of man, despite sin, remained free, and that it retained the ability to do good. Or otherwise they hold that the human will, though more or less weakened by sin, nevertheless, through the general enlightenment of the Word (the Logos; John 1:9), or through the grace of the Holy Spirit, granted before baptism or in baptism, has been strengthened, and has received sufficient strength to receive the call of the gospel.

This explanation is absolutely unacceptable, even in itself, apart from the teaching of Holy Scripture. According to this account it is not God who makes distinctions among people, but the people themselves who do it. But if God is God, His counsel governs all things, He is the Creator of heaven and earth, and by His providence He sustains and rules all creatures. It is unreasonable to suppose that He should govern the whole of nature and every little detail of all things, and that He should yet have excluded from His counsel the great all-comprehending event, working itself out even into eternity, of the spiritual difference or inequality among men, and have left this to human decision. Whoever entertains this thought is in principle destroying the idea of God's counsel and providential rule, withdraws the whole of world history from the reach of God's hand and makes its future an unpredictable thing by robbing it of its end and purpose, and ascribes to God a passive and awaiting attitude which conflicts with His being and His works.

This spiritual distinction among men, although it is the most important is not the only distinction among them. There are all kinds of difference and variety among creatures, and especially among those who are gifted with reason. Men differ in rank and status, in sex and age, in gifts of the mind and in powers of the body. They differ in this respect, too, that they are born within the pale of Christendom or outside it, and can or cannot hear the calling voice of the gospel. All of these differences cannot be explained or accounted for by the decisions or attitudes of men, for they precede such decisions and dispositions and more or less strongly influence and affect them. If, however, one does not wish to rest content with the good pleasure of God as determinative of this, and if one keeps looking for the solution in the differing attitudes of men, one must take refuge in untenable assumptions. The Lutherans, for example, did not want to recognize the sovereign disposition of God in the fact that one person is born under the light of the gospel, and another is not, and maintained that the calling of the word came to all men at the time of Adam, Noah, and the apostles (their appeal was especially to Rom. 10:18 and Col. 1:23), and that it was lost again only because of their own fault. Of this same kind is the thought which occurs in Origen, and is again being shared by many in modern times, that originally human souls were created alike and at the same time, but that these, in accordance with their varying conduct in their pre-existence, received different bodies as their portion on earth.

All of these assumptions add to the difficulties of the problem and contribute nothing to its solution. In this respect, too, there is no rest for man until he rests in the Father-heart of God and acknowledges the deepest ground of the inequality of creatures as being His sovereign and unfathomable counsel. The differing dispensations of the general and particular callings do not have their basis in the superiority of one people to another, or in a better use of the light of nature, but in the sovereign good pleasure and unmerited love of God (Canons of Dort, III, iv, 7). And the same holds for the spiritual inequality which obtains between those who hear the voice of the gospel with a believing heart, and those who despise it and choose to go in their own way. It is not man, but God, who makes the distinction here. The calling itself is different by which He comes to the one and to the other. And in this calling by the word, Scripture makes the further distinction between an external and an internal calling.

* * * * *

But before demonstrating the adequate grounds for making this distinction, we must emphasize the fact that it is by no means intended in some way or other to rob the so-called external calling of its power and worth.

For, in the first place, it must be declared that this calling on God's part remains serious and well meant. As many as are called by the gospel, are earnestly called. For God seriously and sincerely says in His word what gives Him pleasure — namely, that the called should come to him. And He earnestly and seriously promises all who come

to him a rest for their souls and eternal life (Canons of Dort, III, iv,
8). Those who accept the distinction between the external and internal
calling continue to ascribe to the first the same power and significance
which, according to the opponents of this distinction, accrue to the whole
calling. They do not by their distinction put mankind into a less favorable condition than that in which, according to the opponents, mankind
does exist. For the word of the gospel by which the external calling
comes to them is not a dead letter, but a power of God unto salvation
to everyone that believes (Rom. 1:16), quick, and powerful, and sharper
than any two-edged sword (Heb. 4:12), and the means of regeneration
(1 Peter 1:23). It is the same word of which God makes use in the
internal calling, and is itself not barred from every influence of the Holy
Spirit. For the Holy Spirit testifies not only in the hearts of the believers that they are children of God (Rom. 8:16), but He also penetrates to the consciences of those whom He convicts of sin, righteousness, and judgment. And Calvin was therefore not mistaken when he
spoke of a lower operation of the Spirit which goes paired with the
external calling.

In consequence the rejection of the external calling never takes place
with impunity. Those who despise the gospel cannot appeal to their
helplessness, for they do not reject it because they are helpless. If that
were so they would appeal to the grace of God which offers them the
salvation. But they reject the gospel, rather, because they feel strongly
that they can save themselves, and because they mean to be saved without the grace of God. That many, called by the gospel, do not come and
do not repent, is not the fault of the gospel, nor of the Christ offered
them in the gospel, nor of God who calls them by the gospel, and who
Himself also grants many gifts to those whom He calls. The fault,
rather, lies in those who are called, of whom some, being indifferent, do
not accept the word of life. Others accept it but not into the inmost
recesses of their hearts and therefore after the brief joy of a temporary
faith fall back again. Others suffocate the word by the thistles of the
cares and pleasures of the world and bring forth no fruit. Such is the
teaching of the Savior in the parable of the sower and the seed (Canons
of Dort, III, iv, 9).

And, in the third place, this external calling is not without results. In
general it can be said of it that God achieves His purpose by means of it.
For of the word of this external calling, too, it can be said that it does
not return void, but accomplishes the thing He pleases, and prospers in
the thing for which He sends it (Isa. 55:11). By means of it He maintains His claim upon the creature and achieves the honor of His name.
And, further, it is by no means neither here nor there how men react

to this external calling. Among the heathen there is great difference between the ways in which they react to the calling of nature. Socrates and Plato are not to be named in one breath with Caligula and Nero. And so it is by no means the same thing whether the gospel is mocked and blasphemed, on the one hand, or accepted with an historical or temporary belief, on the other. True, between these two kinds of faith and a saving faith of the heart there is an essential difference. But that is not to equate them with total unbelief. On the contrary, they are fruits of God's common grace and they carry with them many temporal blessings. They lay men under obligation to the truth, restrain them from many terrible sins, cause them to live a modest, respectable life, and richly contribute to the formation of that Christian society which for the life of humanity and the influence of the church is of the greatest significance.

Besides, it deserves to be noticed that this external calling of God often serves in God's hand as a means of preparing the work of grace in the hearts of His own. There is indeed no prevenient grace in the sense that the external calling graduates to the internal calling without a change or that the natural man gradually grows up into a child of God. No more than in nature is there in grace a gradual transition from death to life or from darkness to light. But there is such a thing as a prevenient or preparatory grace if that is taken to mean that God, who is the Implementer of all grace, is also the creator of nature, and fixes a bond of connection between them which He thereafter always maintains. In carrying out the counsel of redemption He follows the line which He Himself in the work of creation and providence has drawn. Just as in a Zaccheus He effected the desire to see Jesus (Luke 19:3) and just as He brought about responsiveness in the multitude who heard Peter (Acts 2:37), so He cares and governs His own in such a way that they are prepared for the hour in which He glorifies His grace in them, and He Himself conducts them by His almighty hand to that time.

* * * * *

Irrespective, however, of the real power and worth of this external calling, it is not in itself sufficient to change the heart of man and effectually to move him to a believing acceptance of the gospel. This insufficiency of the external calling must, however, be understood properly. The gospel, which it proclaims, is not as gospel inadequate, for it comprehends the whole counsel of redemption, displays Christ before our eyes in all His benefits, and requires no amplification of content. Nor is this gospel a dead letter which must be quickened by the Spirit, nor any empty sound or vain symbol which stands in no real relationship to the reality it points to. For, although Paul says of the servant that he is nothing (1 Cor. 3:7), because he can be supplanted by another, or be ignored altogether, he does not say this of the gospel. On the contrary, the gospel is a power of God unto salvation (Rom. 1:16 and 1 Cor. 15:2), is not the word of men but the word of God, quick and powerful,[6] and in a certain sense always doing its work, for if it is not a savor of life unto life it is a savor of death unto death (2 Cor. 2:16). Christ who is the content of the gospel leaves no one in a neutral state: He brings a crisis, a judgment, a division into the world (John 3:19 and 9:39), and by His word, which penetrates to the inmost being of man, He reveals the inclinations and thoughts of the heart (Luke 2:35 and Heb. 4:12). He becomes a rock of offense to those who despise Him as a rock of refuge, and is foolishness to those who reject Him as wisdom, and spells the fall of those for whom He is not the resurrection.[7]

But this dual operation of the word of the gospel proves precisely that the difference in result for those who accept it and those who reject it cannot be accounted for in terms of that word alone, and therefore not in terms of the external calling. True, the word of the gospel, irrespective of by whom and to whom it is brought, is always a **word of God**, living and powerful. But the expression, *word of God,* by no means always has the same meaning in the Scriptures. Sometimes it means the power of God by which He creates and sustains the world.[8] At another time it is the name of special revelation, by means of which God makes something known to the prophets (Jer. 1:2, 4 and 2:1, and other places). It is used several times to designate the content or meaning of revelation, irrespective of whether this consist of the law or of the gospel (Ex. 20:1 and Luke 5:1, and elsewhere). In the last instance the word remains a word of God, it is true, so far as its meaning goes, but it is not directly and immediately spoken by God as is the word which obtains in creation and providence. Rather, it is garbed in the form of the human word, can be spoken and written down by human beings, and has therefore, as it were, obtained an independent existence. In this sense, too, of course, it remains in terms of its content a living and powerful word, but it also shares in the characteristics of human words and as such can exercise only a moral influence. This moral influence is not to be lightly esteemed. It is much stronger than a merely rational instruction, for the word of the gospel is not only a source of our knowledge of God and of Divine matters, but it is also a means of grace.

---

6. John 6:63; Heb. 5:12; and 1 Peter 1:25.
7. Luke 2:34; 1 Cor. 1:18 and 1 Peter 2:7.
8. Gen. 1:3; Ps. 33:6; Matt. 4:4; and Heb. 1:3.

But such a rational and religious-moral operation of the gospel is not enough. It would be enough if man had not fallen or if through the fall he had not lost his spiritual freedom. But Scripture testifies and life confirms every day that the mind of man is darkened (Eph. 4:18 and 5:8), that in his will he is bound as the slave of sin (John 8:34 and Rom. 6:20), and that he is dead in sins and trespasses (Eph. 2:1-2). Therefore he cannot see the kingdom of God (John 3:3), cannot comprehend or receive the things of the Spirit of God (1 Cor. 2:14), cannot subject himself to the law of God (Rom. 8:7), and in and of himself can conceive or do no good (John 15:5 and 2 Cor. 3:5). The gospel is most certainly intended for man, but it is not designed *according to* him, that is, in accordance with his wishes and thoughts (Gal. 1:11). And that is why man, when he is left to his own ways, rejects and opposes it.

But in this the riches of the grace of God consist, that He, in spite of all this, adds the operation of the Spirit to the calling of the word for all those whom He has chosen unto eternal life. In the Old Testament already the Holy Spirit was the implementer and the guide of the spiritual life (Ps. 51:12 and 143:10). But He is there especially promised as the One who in the days of the New Testament will teach all men, who will grant a new heart, and write the law of the Lord upon it.[9] To that end He was also poured out on the day of Pentecost. Together with the apostles and through them He was to testify of Christ and further dwell in the church in order to regenerate it (John 3:5), to bring it to the confession of Jesus as its Lord (1 Cor. 12:3), to comfort and to lead it, and eternally to remain with it.[10] And, operating out of the church, the Spirit was to penetrate the world and to convict it of sin, righteousness, and judgment (John 16:8-11).

Not objectively only, but subjectively also, the work of redemption is God's work, and His alone. It is not of him who wills nor of him who runs but of God who shows mercy (Rom. 9:16). There is an external calling which comes to many (Matt. 22:14), but there is also an internal effectual calling which is the consequence of election (Rom. 8:28-30). God gives the gospel not only but He also has it preached in power and in the Holy Spirit (1 Cor. 2:4 and 1 Thess. 1:5 and 6), and He Himself gives the increase (1 Cor. 3:6-9). He opens the heart (Acts 16:14), enlightens the mind (Eph. 1:18 and Col. 1:9-11), bows the will (Acts 9:6), and works both the willing and the doing of His good pleasure (Phil. 2:13).

---

9. Isa. 32:15; Jer. 31:33; 32:39; Ezek. 11:19; 36:26; and Joel 2:8.
10. John 14:16; Rom. 8:14; and Eph. 4:30.

The fact that those who are thus called also come to Christ and are converted must not be ascribed to human merit, as though a man should be able by his free will to distinguish himself from others. It must be ascribed to God who, even as He elected His own in Christ from eternity, also in time powerfully and effectually calls them, gives them faith and repentance, and, having delivered them from the power of darkness, transfers them to the kingdom of His Son, in order that they should declare the virtues of Him who has called them out of darkness into His marvelous light, and in order that they should boast not in themselves but in the Lord, as the apostolic writings constantly testify (Canons of Dordt, III, iv, 10).

* * * * *

The nature of this internal calling is indicated to us in various ways in the Holy Scriptures. It is true that this term itself is not found there, but the reality designated by it is referred to again and again. Even nature gives a clue to what is happening in the sphere of grace. Creation sheds light on redemption, even as the redemption sheds light in turn on creation. Jesus explained the nature, the characteristics, and the laws of the kingdom of heaven in parables based on nature and the daily life. Especially in the parable of the sower He demonstrated the different effects of the word of the gospel in the hearts of men.

In the natural sphere the law is operative that in order to have awareness or knowledge of a thing a definite relationship is necessary between man and the object he wants to see or know. If a person is to see anything there must be an object, yes, but also an opened eye, and besides a light which ministers to both. If a person is to hear, there must be more than air waves and sounds. There must be the open ear to receive the sound. And if a person is to understand the objects which he perceives with his organs of sense, he requires also a heart to know. We must be related to the thing we see in order to absorb it and to appropriate it as our spiritual property. The blind cannot see and the deaf cannot hear, but neither can the indifferent understand. A musically insensitive person does not grasp the world of tones, and the aesthetically insensitive person cannot delight in a poem or a painting. A relationship has to be present, a bond of harmony between man and the world has to be established, if there is to be any awareness or knowledge.

In the natural sphere that relationship has, generally speaking, remained in force. True, sin has also left its mark in this area, so that the blind, the deaf, the insane, and many other unfortunates, have none of it, and all people find it more or less weakened or disturbed. But in general it can be said that in the natural sphere God has permitted that relationship to continue. Man can still see and hear, perceive and think, learn and know.

But in the spiritual sphere this relationship has been completely broken by sin. The imaginations of the human heart are wicked from youth on (Gen. 8:21). An ox knows his owner and an ass his master's crib, but Israel does not know and the people of the Lord do not consider (Isa. 1:3). The generation of men is like children, sitting in the markets and calling to their fellows, and saying, We have piped unto you, and you have not danced, and we have mourned unto you and you have not lamented (Matt. 11:16-17). This people have no eyes to see, no ears to hear, nor any heart to understand (Isa. 6:9 and Matt. 13:14-15). Even when God revealed Himself to them in nature, they did not know Him and were not thankful (Rom. 1:21), and when He reveals Himself to them in the gospel, they do not understand the things of the Spirit of God, are offended by the foolishness of the cross, and kick against the pricks.[11] By nature man is dead to God, to His revelation, to all spiritual and heavenly things. He is indifferent to them, is not interested in them, thinks only of the things that are below, and has no delight in a knowledge of the ways of the Lord. The relationship between God and man has been broken. There is no spiritual fellowship or unity between them any longer.

Hence the internal calling in general consists of the fact that it restores the bond of relationship again, and again relates man to God spiritually, so that he will listen to God's word and understand it. Scripture designates this influence of the Holy Spirit in the internal calling by the name of revelation. When Simon Peter in the parts of Caesarea Philippi confesses Jesus as the Christ the Son of the living God, the Savior tells him: Blessed art thou, Simon Barjona, for flesh and blood has not revealed it to you, but my Father which is in heaven (Matt. 16:17). And just so the apostle Paul testifies that at his conversion it pleased God to reveal His Son in him (Gal. 1:16). This revelation does not refer to the objective appearance of Christ. For when Peter confessed Him as Christ, the Savior had lived and worked on earth for years, and had also more than once declared Himself to be the Messiah (for example, Matt. 11:5ff.) and been acknowledged as being such by others (Matt. 8:29 and 14:33). But Jesus was never before so clearly and resolutely confessed to be the Messiah and the Son of God, and therefore He says that a subjective revelation in the heart and mind of Peter was the only thing that could bring him to such a valiant and clear confession. God Himself illumined the apostle internally in such a way that he now saw in Christ what he had never before so plainly seen in Him.

---

11. Acts 9:5; 1 Cor. 1:23; and 2:14.

The revelation referred to in these contexts consists, in other words, of an internal illumination. In the natural sphere our eye is given light by the sun, and it in turn then lightens the whole body, as a candle lightens a house (Matt. 6:23). Mind and reason are enlightened in man by the word that was with God, that made all things, that was the light of men, and that still lightens every man that comes into the world (John 1:1-9). And because of this illumination of the mind, man can be aware of the world, investigate it, and know it. So it is that a man's wisdom makes his face to shine (Prov. 8:1). So too there is illumination in the spiritual sphere. The poet prayed for it already in the Old Testament day when he said: Open Thou mine eyes, that I may behold wondrous things out of Thy law (Ps. 119:18). And in the New Testament Paul speaks of a revelation (Gal. 1:16) and elsewhere of an illumination in which he has shared. God, who is the Creator of light, has also shined in his heart, in order that as an apostle in the preaching of it he should cause the glory of God to shine for others, and so should lead them to the knowledge of it (2 Cor. 4:6; compare Eph. 3:9).

Elsewhere this activity of the Holy Spirit in the internal calling is described as an opening of the heart by the Lord Christ (Acts 16:14) or of the understanding (Luke 24:45), so that the word of God may be understood and received in its proper sense. Again this activity is represented as an increase or growth which God gives to the word preached by the apostles (1 Cor. 3:5-9). For the apostles are but servants, co-laborers with God, instruments in His hand, so that it is not really they who labor, but the grace of God that is with them (1 Cor. 15:10). Indeed, they really are nothing, but God is all, for He gives the increase to the seed of the word, and the church is accordingly altogether His culture and His building. Certainly, such a power as is necessary to quicken a dead sinner lies beyond the ability of every creature, of every angel and apostle. Nothing less than the Divine, omnipotent power is necessary for this, the same power that raised up Christ from the dead.

We know that for the believers at Ephesus the apostle Paul prays that God may in the future give them the Spirit of wisdom and of revelation, in order that they may know Him and so that He may enlighten them, so far as the eyes of their understanding (their heart) is concerned. Thus they may come to know, first, what a marvelous hope and expectation God grants those whom He has called; second, what riches of the glory of the inheritance await them in the future; and, third, what is the measure of the surpassing greatness of His power which He displays before the believers from the beginning of their calling, throughout their life, and up to the final glory. They can form some idea of the greatness of this power by measuring it against that which God achieved in Christ when He raised Him up from the dead, and set Him far above all principality and power at His right hand in heaven. In the calling, regeneration, preservation, and glorification of the believers the same power of God is manifested as was exhibited at the resurrection, ascension, and exaltation of Christ.

Quite in accordance with the Holy Scriptures, therefore, the Reformed church confesses that when God carries out His good pleasure in the elect and works the true repentance in them, He not only has the gospel externally preached to them, and not only powerfully enlightens the mind through the Holy Spirit, in order that they may rightly understand and discriminate the things that are of the Spirit of God, but He also penetrates to the inner man with the powerful operation of that same regenerating Spirit. And this operation, in the words of that same confession, is an entirely supernatural one, a very powerful and at the same time a very sweet, wonderful, mysterious, and unspeakable operation, which, according to the testimony of the Scriptures (given, we must remember, by the author of this same working or influence), is not less in power than the power exhibited at the creation or at the resurrection of the dead (Canons of Dordt, III, iv, 12).

* * * * *

The change which is brought about in man by this operation of the Holy Spirit goes by the name of regeneration. The word does not occur in Scripture only, nor does it occur there first, but was from ancient times employed in the religion of the Indians to indicate the change which the soul undergoes at death. According to the Indian religion, we recall, the soul after death does not live in a condition of separation, but immediately goes into another body, whether that of a person, an animal, or a plant, depending upon its conduct in the previous embodiment. Every birth leads to death, but every death also leads to another birth; every human being is subjected to a centuries-long continuing series of "regenerations" that is, to ever new embodiments of the same soul. And there is redemption from this terrible law and from all the suffering of the world, according to Buddhism, only when man in himself knows how to quiet the yearning for being and only when by all kinds of works of abstinence and withdrawal he labors at his own annihilation, or at least at the neutralization of his consciousness. This doctrine of "rebirths" came into Europe in antiquity, and also again in the last century. And even now there are some who see in this teaching the sum of all wisdom.

But Scripture speaks of the regeneration of men in an entirely different sense. It uses this noun in two places: once in Matthew 19:28 where

Jesus is thinking of the renewal of the world which will precede the
kingdom of glory; and again in Titus 3:5 where Paul says that God has
saved us not by works of righteousness which we have done, but according to His mercy by the washing of regeneration and renewing of the
Holy Spirit. It is difficult to make out whether Paul is thinking at this
point of baptism, as a sign and seal of regeneration, or whether he is
comparing the benefits of regeneration and the renewal of the Holy
Spirit with a bath into which the believers have stepped down. Be that
as it may, the addendum, *renewal of the Holy Spirit,* proves that in thinking of regeneration we are to think of a spiritual and moral change which
has taken place in the believers upon their conversion. The context confirms this conception, for it tells us that theretofore the believers also
were sometimes foolish, disobedient, deceived, serving divers lusts and
pleasures, living in malice and envy, and the like (Titus 3:3), but that
they have now been saved, reborn, and renewed, and made heirs according to the hope of eternal life (verses 4-7). And they are accordingly admonished to maintain good works (verse 8), for precisely by
the regeneration and renewal they have obtained the ability and desire
to do this again.

However, even though the noun regeneration occurs only twice in
Scripture, the reality itself is often referred to in different words and
images. Even the Old Testament warns the people of Israel that they
are not to glory in the external sign of circumcision, but that they must
circumcise the foreskin of their hearts and be no more stiffnecked
(Deut. 10:16). And the Old Testament also promises that the Lord
their God will Himself circumcise their hearts and that of their seed in
order that they may love the Lord their God with all their hearts and
with all their souls (Deut. 30:6). This promise came into its fulfillment
for the saints in the history of Israel (Ps. 51:12), but it is to receive a
much richer fulfillment in their future, when God will make a new covenant with His people, will pour out His Spirit over all, will give them
a heart of flesh instead of a heart of stone, and will write His law upon
their hearts.[12]

When that future is at hand and the kingdom of heaven has come
near, John the Baptist makes his appearance, preaching repentance as
the condition of entrance into the kingdom. After all, the people of
Israel, in spite of its external privileges, is corrupt through and through.
In spite of its circumcision it requires baptism, the baptism of repentance
unto the forgiveness of sins, a baptism in which a man is entirely submerged in order as a new man to come up to a new life (Matt. 3:2 ff.).
And Jesus takes that same preaching of repentance and faith upon His

---

12. Jer. 24:7; 31:31-34; 32:39; Ezek. 11:19; 36:26-28; Joel 2:28; and elsewhere.

lips, Himself submits to baptism, and ministers it to all who want to be His disciples (Mark 1:14-15 and John 4:1, 2). Whoever would enter the kingdom must break with his whole former life, must lose his soul (Matt. 10:39), must forsake everything (Luke 14:33), must take up his cross and follow after Him (Matt. 10:38), must become a child (Matt. 18:3), must return to the Father with a confession of sin (Luke 15:18), and must enter into eternal life through the strait gate and the narrow way (Matt. 7:14). Whoever does that is fitted for it by God Himself, for men are evil (Matt. 7:11). Out of their hearts nothing but unrighteousness comes forth (Matt. 15:19). They cannot bring forth good fruit out of a corrupt tree (Matt. 7:17). If there is to be any good fruit, therefore, the tree must first be made good, and God alone can do that (Matt. 19:26). Those who, as a plant, are planted by the heavenly Father are children of God and citizens of the kingdom of heaven (Matt. 15:13), and are they whom the Son has revealed to the Father, and the Father to the Son (Matt. 11:27 and 16:17). Although they formerly were spiritually dead, they have now a share in the true life and await eternal life (Matt. 8:22 and Luke 15:24; 18:30).

In all this teaching of Christ as the first three gospel accounts present it to us, the word regeneration does not occur, but the reality itself is clearly represented. Thus, when Jesus in his interview with Nicodemus says that no one can see and enter into the kingdom of God except he be born again (from above) of water and of the Spirit (John 3:3-8), His testimony does not conflict with that of the other gospels; rather, over against this teaching of Nicodemus He briefly and sharply epitomizes what He elsewhere more elaborately and popularly had set forth. We know that Nicodemus was a prominent person, a teacher of Israel, a member of the Sanhedrin. He had heard of Jesus' miracles and therefore regarded Him as a teacher sent of God. But he was not yet sure in his own mind; he remained in doubt. And so he went by night — by night lest he should excite the suspicion and enmity of the Jews — to Jesus in order to find out by way of a confidential interview whether He was indeed the Messiah. Accordingly, Nicodemus begins the conversation with the acknowledgment that he takes Jesus to be a teacher who has come from God and who has been qualified by God to do the works which He does. And to this he apparently wants to attach the question as to what a man must do to enter into the kingdom of heaven. But Jesus does not give him time to put the question, and immediately replies: Verily, verily, I say unto you, Except a man be born again from above, he cannot see the kingdom of God. And so in one gesture He cuts off in Nicodemus all consideration of human merit and of Pharisaical keeping of the law as a means to the kingdom.

Hence Jesus does not speak literally of a being born *again* (a second time, anew), but of a being born from above. The emphasis does not fall on the fact that for entrance into the kingdom a second birth is necessary, although regeneration, naturally enough, can be so designated. But over against Nicodemus Jesus wants especially to stress the fact that only a being born *from above* (verse 3), of water and the Spirit (verse 5), of the Spirit (verse 8) opens up the kingdom to a man. This birth is in contrast to that of the flesh, for what is born of the flesh is flesh (verse 6). It is a birth not of the blood, nor of the will of the flesh, nor of the will of man, but of God (John 1:13). Hence it is just as incomprehensible in its origin and bearing as is the wind, but it is possible nonetheless for it is a birth of the Spirit (verse 8). After Jesus has first said generally that it is a birth of water and of the Spirit (in the original both terms lack the article) (verse 5), He specifically speaks in verses 7 and 8 of *the* Spirit (this time with the article) in order to indicate that this Spirit, as the Spirit of God, can bring this great work of rebirth into being. In speaking of water (verse 5) Jesus is not in the first place thinking of baptism, but is rather describing the nature of being born from above. It is a birth which has the quality of renewal and purging. Water is the image of this (Ezek. 36:25; compare the image of Spirit and fire in Matt. 3:11). And it is a birth which gives being to a new spiritual life. This the being born from above can accomplish because it is a birth of *the* Spirit, of God Himself (verse 6-8).

Other passages of the New Testament elaborate upon this basic teaching of Christ. Regeneration is a work of God. It is He out of whom the believers are born (John 1:13 and 1 John 3:9; 5:18. He effectually calls them (Rom. 8:30). He quickens them (Eph. 2:1), and begets them (James 1:18), and regenerates them (1 Peter 1:2). But He does not grant this benefit except in the communion with Christ to whom He has given His own (John 6:37, 39), to whom He draws them (John 6:44), and in whom He incorporates them (Rom. 6:4; Eph. 2:1; and Gal. 2:20). This He does through the gift of the Holy Spirit who penetrates into the heart of man and who is the principle of the new life.[13] In virtue of their birth of God the believers are His workmanship, created in Christ (Eph. 2:10), His husbandry and His building (1 Cor. 3:9), a new creature (2 Cor. 5:17). Regeneration is not a work of human strength, is not a product of a long, gradual development of natural life, but is rather a break with the old mode of existence and the creative beginning of a new spiritual life. It is the dying of the old and the rising of the new man (Rom. 6:3 ff.).

---

13. John 3:3, 5, 8; 6:63; Rom. 8:9; 1 Cor. 12:3; and 1 Peter 1:2.

Still, on the other hand, regeneration is not a second creation, quite out of nothing as at the first, but a *re*-creation of man who has by his birth from his parents received his first life. In regeneration he remains essentially the same person, the same self, the same personality. Paul says of himself that he has been crucified with Christ and thus himself no longer lives, but that Christ lives in him. But then he goes on to say: The life which I now live in the flesh I live by the faith of the Son of God (Gal. 2:20). His self has died and been buried with Christ, but it has also immediately risen with Christ. It has not been annihilated and supplanted by another, but has been reborn and renewed. Thus also he says of certain believers in Corinth that they were once fornicators, idolaters, adulterers, and the like, but that they have been washed, and sanctified, and justified in the name of the Lord Jesus, and by the Spirit of our God (1 Cor. 6:9-11). The continuity, unity, and solidarity of the human being are not broken by regeneration. Rather, a tremendously important change is brought about in them.

This change is spiritual in character. Whatever is born of the spirit is spirit (John 3:6). It lives out of the Spirit and walks according to the Spirit. Regeneration injects a principle of new life into man, a principle which the Holy Spirit creatively brings into being in connection with the resurrection of Christ from whom He receives everything (1 Peter 1:3). He plants a seed in the heart (1 Peter 1:23) out of which an entirely new person comes up. In a very mysterious and secret way regeneration has its beginning and its mid-point in the core of the human personality, in his selfhood, so to speak (Gal. 2:20), but from there it spreads out to all the abilities of the person: to his mind (Rom. 12:2; 1 Cor. 2:12; and Eph. 4:23); to his heart (Heb. 8:10 and 10:16; 1 Peter 3:4), to his will (Rom. 7:15-21), to his desires and inclinations (Rom. 7:22), and to his spirit and soul and body (1 Thess. 5:23 and Rom. 6:19). A perfect man is born who, although not yet mature, and having to struggle still against all kinds of sins of the flesh (Gal. 5:17), nevertheless desires to live in newness of the Spirit (Rom. 6:4 and 7:8).

According to that new man, the believers are *re*-created in the image of Christ in true righteousness and holiness.[14] They no longer bear the image of the first man, of the first Adam, but exhibit the image of the second man, the Lord out of heaven (1 Cor. 15:48-49). They have been crucified to the world, and no longer live themselves but live in Him who died and was raised for them (2 Cor. 5:15; Gal. 2:20; and 6:14). They have received a different center for all of their thinking and doing, for they live, move, and have their being in Christ, have in their baptism put Him on as a garment, exhibit His form and are always transformed

---

14. Rom. 8:29; Eph. 4:24; and Col. 3:10.

more and more according to His image, from glory to glory, as of the Spirit of the Lord.[15] And in that fellowship with Christ they are children of the heavenly Father, who love God and the brethren, and who will some day be like God because they shall see Him as He is (1 John 3:2; 5:2; and elsewhere). Thus richly and gloriously the Holy Scripture speaks of regeneration, and this it does not in the first place so that we should discriminate rightly this doctrine as such, but so that we should personally share in this great benefit of the grace of God and should learn to live as children of God in this evil world. What a power would be coming out of the church if it not only wrote the image of Christ into its confession but also exhibited it in the practical life of all who are in and around it!

*   *   *   *   *

So much is certain: by the fruits the tree is known. A good tree brings forth good fruits, and the good man brings forth good things out of the good treasure of his heart (Matt. 7:17 and 12:33, 35). If the regeneration pours a new principle of life into the heart, that must and will become evident in the works which proceed from that spiritual life. These are in the main two: faith, on the side of the mind; and repentance, on the side of the will.

Very generally stated, faith, also as we speak of it in our daily life, is the acceptance of a testimony. We believe something when we have not ourselves seen something or become aware of it, but are assured of it nevertheless because some other reliable person has either orally or in written form, either in the past or in the present, told us of it. This basic meaning the word retains also when it is transferred to the religious sphere, and it has to preserve that meaning, since we know nothing of the whole content of the gospel, of the person and work of Christ, other than we have received by the testimony of the apostles. Only through their word can we believe in Christ (John 17:20). Through fellowship with the apostles we come to the fellowship with the Father and with His Son Jesus Christ (1 John 1:3).

Nevertheless, the word *faith,* when it is used in the religious sphere and is specifically designated in the Holy Scriptures as the way to the kingdom of heaven, is very significantly modified in meaning by this special use. One can also accept the gospel as one accepts a testimony concerning some historical person or event, but that is not to receive the gospel as the gospel, and in that case the faith by which one accepts it is not the true faith. The experience of all prophets, preachers,

---

15. 2 Cor. 3:18; Gal. 3:27; and 4:19.

apostles, and servants of the word in the church and in the pagan world
—yes, and the experience of Jesus Himself — has always been that the
word found no acceptance with many and had no effect. Who has
believed our report, and to whom is the arm of the Lord revealed? The
people who hear the gospel carry very different attitudes of mind to it
and take very different positions over against it.

Jesus described these various attitudes and positions in His parable
of the sower. For some the seed of faith falls by the wayside at the
boundary of the field, and the birds come and eat it. Those are the
indifferent ones, the insensitive, the imperturbable ones who hear the
word but listen to it as to an affair which is none of theirs. They have
not the slightest interest in it personally, and they suppose that it is not
intended for them. The word does not fall into the field of their heart,
but alongside of it, on the hard and packed pathway. Often, indeed,
they do not even recall it in memory. It goes in at one ear and out at
the other. After a few moments, it is as though they had not heard it
at all. The birds, all kinds of ideas of contradiction, belittlement, unbelief, and blasphemy, used as means by the Evil One, drive the word out
of their minds. They have heard it but they do not know what it means
(Matt. 13:4, 19).

For others the seed of the word falls in stony places where it has not
much depth of soil. It grows up fast, precisely because it has no depth
of earth, but when the sun has gone up, it is scorched, because it has no
rootage. Those are the superficial, shallow, flighty persons. They not
only hear the word, but also immediately accept it with joy. The gospel
appeals to them because of its beauty, its loftiness, its simplicity or loveliness, and it also makes a certain impression upon them. They are
moved and stirred by it, perceive a kind of power in it, and form all
sorts of fine resolutions in consequence. But they do not let the truth
make a deep impression upon them and shoot roots deeply into their
hearts. They give it a place in their memory, in their imagination, in
their reason and understanding, but they do not open up the depths of
their being to it. There is a thin layer of soil on the surface where the
word falls, but underneath everything is cold, inert, and hard as a rock.
Hence they cannot bear the oppression and temptation that comes,
nor the persecution and the trials. When those come, they are offended
and fall away. Their faith is temporary (Matt. 13:5, 6, 20 and 21).

Then there are those for whom the seed falls between the thorns, and
the thorns grow up along with the seed (Luke 8:7), and they choke it,
so that it cannot bear fruit. Those are the worldly-minded hearers of
the word, whose hearts are full of thorns, full of the cares of the world
and of the temptations of riches, those who are entirely taken in by

the cares or temptations of the world. They listen to the word, and they accept it too. Sometimes it penetrates through all those worldly troubles and pleasures and reaches their hearts. The thought sometimes comes up in them that it might be better to break with the world and to seek the kingdom of God. Sometimes the fear of the judgment masters them. But just when the seed of the word is at the point of germination, the thorns come, the worldly cares and lusts, and they choke the birth of the new life. These persons never reach the point of forsaking everything, to take up their cross, and to follow Jesus. The might of the world is too much for them (Matt. 13:7 and 22).

There is, accordingly, an approbation and an acceptance of the gospel which is nevertheless not the true faith. True, there are the haughtily indifferent ones, such as Pilate, who with a belittling smile turn aside from the gospel (John 18:38). There are also those who, like the proud Pharisees and the wise Greeks, find the cross an offense and a foolishness, and who burst out against it in wild enmity and hatred.[16] But there are others who believe and do not come to the point of confession, and who love the praise of men more than the praise of God (John 12:42-43). Throughout their lives, right on up to their death, they remain hearers of the word without becoming doers of it.[17] Like Simon of Samaria, they accept the gospel for the signs and great miracles which take place by means of it (Acts 8:13 ff.). Like an Agrippa they are moved at a given point in their lives to become Christians (Acts 26:27-28). Like a Demas they serve the gospel for years and then again love this present world (2 Tim. 4:10). There are all kinds of faith: temporal faith, historical faith, "miraculous" faith, that is, a faith prompted by signs and wonders. They all bear the name of faith, but they are not the reality of it. They exhibit a form of godliness but deny the power thereof (2 Tim. 3:5).

The true, the saving, faith is distinguished from those other kinds in three respects. In the first place, it has a different origin. Historical faith, temporal faith, and miraculous faith are not in themselves wrong. They are better than total unbelief and bitter enmity. They also have a temporary usefulness. But they are the gifts only of God's common grace and were given also to natural men. But saving faith is a gift of God, even as all salvation is (Eph. 2:8). It is a gift of God's special grace (Phil. 1:29), a consequence of election (Acts 13:48; Rom. 8:30; and Eph. 1:5). It is a work of the Holy Spirit (1 Cor. 12:3) and a fruit of repentance (John 1:12-13).

16. Matt. 12:24; John 8:22; and 1 Cor. 1:23.
17. John 1:11; 3:3; 3:19-20; 6:44; 8:47; 1 Cor. 2:14; and others.

Those who share in only the natural birth belong to the world, are from below, love the darkness better than the light, and do not understand the word. But regeneration tells why some follow the calling of the gospel and accept Christ (John 1:12-13). They are born of God, they are of the truth, they are led to Christ by the Father, they hear His voice, they understand His words, and they follow Him.[18] And the Holy Spirit out of whom they are born testifies with their spirit that they are children of God (Rom. 8:16) and puts the confession upon their lips that Christ is their Lord (1 Cor. 12:3).

By virtue of this origin the true, saving faith is, in the second place, also to be distinguished from the other kinds in essence. Beyond doubt there is an element of knowledge in it, for it is concerned with a testimony about invisible, eternal things which we ourselves have not seen and cannot see. It cannot build up the truth out of the regenerated life, nor out of subjective religious experience and feeling. For, although the believers have received the unction or anointing of the Spirit from the Holy One, namely, Christ, and know all things (1 John 2:20), they owe that Spirit precisely to Christ, and remain bound to the word of truth which they have heard from the beginning (1 John 2:21-24). And, together with the whole church, they are built on the foundation of the apostles and prophets (Eph. 2:20).

But the knowledge which is peculiar to saving faith is of a special kind. It is not purely a theoretical knowledge, taken up solely in the mind and the memory, which for the rest leaves man cold and indifferent. It does not stand on one and the same level with the knowledge which is obtained in science by investigation and reflection, and it is not to be equated with the acceptance of an historical report of something that has happened in the past. The knowledge of faith is a practical knowledge, a knowledge of the heart rather than of the head, a knowledge with a personal, profound, soul-absorbing concern, for it pertains to something in which the self in its inmost essence is concerned, something in which my existence, my life, my soul, my salvation is involved. Faith is an approbation and an acceptance, therefore, and a knowledge of a testimony coming to a person; but it is an acceptance of that testimony in its application to oneself, a receiving of the word of the preaching of God, not as a human word, but as the word of God (1 Thess. 2:13). It is an appropriation by the self of the gospel as a message which God sends to me personally.

Connected with this, in the third place, is the fact that the saving faith differs from the others in its object. Historical faith stops at the external report and does not penetrate further. Temporal faith sees a certain

18. John 3:3, 5; 6:44; 8:47; and 10:5 and 27.

beauty in the report, and delights in it, but really refuses acknowledgement to its real content and meaning. And the miraculous faith attaches itself to the signs and wonders, but is essentially indifferent to the One who works them. However, when we accept the gospel with a true heart as a word which God is giving to us personally, such saving faith cannot leave us empty and fruitless. Just as little as someone who notices, while travelling, that his family is in great danger will quietly pursue his journey, so little will someone who really believes the gospel in its application to himself, and who therefore knows that he is guilty and lost, and that there is redemption only in Christ Jesus, will remain cold and indifferent to it all. On the contrary, true belief immediately begins to operate in those who have received it. It gives them no rest, but drives them on to the Christ. Such faith does not rest content with the external report but reaches through to the person of whom that report speaks.

It was thus already in the Old Testament. The saints who appear before us there are always busy and active with God Himself. A few times this is called believing,[19] but this believing is not simply a being rationally convinced that God exists, but a depending with the whole soul upon God and a living out of His word. Hence the word *belief* or *believing* or *faith* often gives place to other terms. It is constantly said of the saints that they trust in God, take refuge in Him, hope for Him, fear Him, expect all things from Him, await Him, lean upon Him, seek Him, and the like. Thus it is also in the New Testament. The apostles, who have described it for us, are not historical writers in the usual sense of the word but witnesses, rather, of what they have seen, and heard, and handled of the word of life. They live in the communion of Christ and speak out of it. To believe is to accept Christ, not simply the testimony concerning Him set down by the apostles. It is an acceptance of Christ Himself (John 1:12). It involves a putting on of Christ as one puts on a garment (Gal. 3:27). It involves, further, a dying with Christ and being raised with Him (Rom. 6:4), a living in His fellowship (Gal. 2:20), a remaining in Him as the true vine, and the like. And in and through Christ, God is the Father of the saints, and they are His sons and daughters (2 Cor. 6:18).

In short, saving faith is not only a certain knowledge, a firm assurance, an undoubted certainty concerning the prophetic and apostolic testimony as the word of God, but is at the same time a sure confidence, as of one person in another, in Christ Himself as the fulness of grace and truth revealed in Him by God. The one stands in inseparable connection with the other. Without knowledge no confidence or trust is possible. For how should we trust anyone whom we do not know? But,

---

19. Gen. 15:6; Ex. 14:31; 2 Chron. 20:20; Isa. 28:16; and Habak. 2:4.

conversely, too, if the knowledge does not lead to confidence and trust, it was not the right kind of knowledge. They that know the name of the Lord put their trust in Him (Ps. 9:10). But those who do not trust Him have not yet learned to know Him from His word as He really is. Whoever seeks the Christ outside the pale of His word through the Spirit alone loses the norm for testing the spirits and eventually comes to the point of identifying his own spirit with the Spirit of Christ; and whoever studies the word without the Spirit of Christ is studying the portrait while ignoring the person of whom it is a representation.

That is why Christ gave both: His word and His Spirit. And it is the Spirit of Christ who makes the same testimony in the word of Scripture and in the hearts of the believers. In regeneration the Spirit plants the word in our hearts (James 1:18, 21 and 1 Peter 1:23, 25), and He conducts the spiritual life of the believers, in accordance with His nature, always back to the word in order so to feed and to strengthen it. Here on earth we never graduate beyond the need for the Scripture, for this Scripture is the only means to bring us into fellowship with the actual Christ, who was crucified, but now is seated at the right hand of God. Christianity is an historical religion but also a religion of the present. It has a word which draws for us the portrait of Christ, but it also has a Spirit by whom the living Christ Himself dwells in our hearts. That is why faith is knowledge and trust both. It is an acceptance of Christ Himself in the garment of Holy Scripture.

* * * * *

Just as faith is the fruit of regeneration on the side of the mind, so repentance is the expression of the new life on the side of the will. Repeatedly we are told of this already in the Old Testament. After its emancipation Israel was led of the Lord to Sinai and there taken up into His covenant. As the people of God, Israel had to keep that covenant and had to obey His voice; it had to become a priestly kingdom and a holy nation (Ex. 19:5-6). But already in the wilderness it became guilty of unfaithfulness and disobedience. In Canaan this apostacy even increased, for there Israel lived among pagan peoples. When the first generation had died and another generation had come up which did not known the Lord nor the work that He had done for Israel, then the children of Israel did that which was evil in the sight of the Lord, and served Baal (Judges 2:10-11).

Hence the preaching of repentance became necessary in Israel. At first the Lord raised up judges who delivered the people out of the hands of their enemies and led Israel back to the service of the Lord. Later, from Samuel on, the prophets came to warn Israel to repent from its evil ways and to keep the commandments and statutes of God in accordance with the law which He had given to the fathers (2 Kings 17:13). Samuel made a beginning with this (1 Sam. 7:3) and all the prophets repeated this preaching: they are all preachers of penitence and conversion, but they are also proclaimers of the forgiveness of sins and of perfect redemption.[20] And then a certain repentance was sometimes perceptible among the people. When they were enslaved by their enemies and oppressed, they began to call unto the Lord (Judges 3:9, 15 and 4:3, and elsewhere). The pious kings, Asa, Jehoshaphat, Josiah, and Hezekiah, brought a greater or a lesser reformation into being.[21] Jonah even went to Nineveh, and in response to his preaching the people of Nineveh believed in God, called for a fasting, put on sackcloth, and repented of their evil way (Jonah 3:5 and 10). Of Ahab it is said that after Elijah's warning of judgment he humbled himself before the face of the Lord (1 Kings 21:27 and 29), and it is reported of Manasseh that at the end of his life he sought the face of the Lord and acknowledged that the Lord is God (2 Chron. 33:12).

Even though in some this repentance presumably was earnestly intended and sincere, it was for the mass of the people little more than an external change. As Jeremiah reports, they did not repent with their whole heart, but feignedly (Jer. 3:10). Therefore the prophets continued their preaching of repentance. They kept holding up the requirement and duty of repentance. They continually stressed the fact that not the people in its entirety only but also each person individually must repent, depart from his evil way, and turn to the Lord (Ezek. 18:23, 32 and 33:11). And when the people continue to ignore these admonishments, the thought ripens among the prophets that their preaching will have the effect of a judgment upon the people (Isa. 6:10), that Israel is a wild branch of the vine (Jer. 2:25), that it can no more repent than an Ethiopian can change his color or a leopard his spots (Jer. 13:23), and that it is God who must grant the repentance and give the new heart.[22] And they look forward eagerly to the day in which God will make a new covenant, and will circumcise the hearts of the people, and write His law upon them.[23]

That day dawns, according to the preaching of John the Baptist and Jesus, when the kingdom of heaven is come nigh. And both of them preach that no efforts to keep the law and no Pharisaical self-righteousness, but only repentance and faith can open up the way to the kingdom

---

20. Jer. 3:12, 14; 18:11; 25:5; Ezek. 14:6; 18:30-32; 33:11; Hos. 12:6; 14:3; Joel 2:12-13; and other passages.
21. 1 Kings 15:11ff.; 22:47; 2 Kings 23:15; and 2 Chron. 33:12.
22. Ps. 51:12; Jer. 31:18; Lam. 5:21.
23. Deut. 30:2, 6; Ps 22:28; Hos. 3:5; Jer. 24:7; 32:33.

and all its benefits (Mark 1:4, 15). To indicate this repentance the New Testament uses two words in the original. The first of these is a noun or a verb[24] and means an internal spiritual change, a change in moral disposition. The other term[25] refers rather more to the external conversion, the change in direction of life, something which is the revelation and consequence of the internal change. In Acts 3:19 and 26:20 the two words are combined: Repent and be converted, that is, change your disposition and your conduct, come to your senses and turn about face.

When in the days of the apostles the gospel was preached to the Jews and the Gentiles and was accepted by them, it required also an external change visible to others. The Jews had to break off their keeping of the Mosaic law, especially the circumcision and the whole sacrificial service, and the Gentiles had to bid farewell to their idolatry, image worship, and religious practices. It required a good deal of self-denial and courage to go over to Christianity. The person who did it usually did it in virtue of conviction of heart, sincerely, and truly, for no honor or profit could be obtained by it. The two matters expressed in the two Greek words for repentance and conversion were therefore usually very closely related. The internal and the external change went together.

This radical turn-about, both internal and external, obtained its seal in holy baptism (Acts 2:38): whoever submitted himself to baptism broke with his whole past, left his kin, was crucified to the world, died with Christ, and together with Him was buried in baptism; but he at the same time arose with Christ to a new life, put on Christ as a garment, as a new and different dress in which he exhibited himself to the world, became a disciple, follower, servant, and soldier of Christ, a member of His body, and a temple of the Holy Spirit.[26] So long as the Christian church had to spread out into the world of Jews and Gentiles, the repentance was not merely an internal change but also an external conversion, a leaving behind of the service of the dumb idols (1 Cor. 12:2 and 1 Thess. 1:9), of the poor and weak principles and rudiments of religion (Gal. 4:3 and Col. 2:8, 20), of dead works (Heb. 9:14 and 1 Thess. 1:9), of public sins and transgressions,[27] in order from this time on to serve the living and true God (Heb. 9:14 and 1 Thess. 1:9), and to embrace the Lord (1 Cor. 6:15-20).

But when this mission period was past and the church perpetuated itself in the generations, then conversion did not change in its essen-

24. Matt. 3:2, 8, 11; 9:13; 11:20; Acts 2:38; 2 Cor. 7:9, 10.
25. Matt. 13:15, Luke 1:16, 17; 22:32; Acts 9:35; 11:21; 14:15; 15:19; 26:18. 20; and other passages.
26. Rom. 6:3 ff.; Gal. 3:27; and Col. 2:11 and 12.
27. 1 Cor. 6:10; Eph. 2:2-3; Col. 3:5, 7; and Titus 3:3.

tial nature, it is true, but from the nature of the circumstance it did lay aside that particular external form in which it formerly expressed itself. Children were taken up into the covenant from their birth, they received holy baptism as the sign and seal of this, and were thus, even before their personal consciousness and approbation could take place, incorporated into the church of Christ. Naturally it often happened that members of the church who were baptized at a later age or as children would later fall into lesser or graver sins. There were sects, such as those of the Montanists and the Novatians, who held that the graver sins ought not and could not be forgiven by the church; but the church itself took a different position and admitted back into its communion those who had strayed or fallen if they returned sorrowfully, made confession of their sins, and subjected themselves to the ecclesiastical penalties.

Gradually the sacrament of penance grew out of this. In this the believers who had become guilty of lesser or greater sins confessed these in the confessional for the priest, exhibited a perfect or an imperfect sorrow or remorse (perfect when one is sorry for his sins because one has sinned against God, imperfect when one fears the consequences, or the like), and finally carried out the prayers and good works which the father of the confessional prescribed for the penitent. Thus the repentance in the Roman Church came to be entirely externalized. The heart of the matter was transferred from the internal change of disposition to the confession and the satisfaction, for an imperfect sorrow was enough to procure the forgiveness of sins. And one could get around the prescribed temporal penalties by means of an indulgence.

It was at this point in particular that the Reformation by Luther had its point of departure. By his reading of the New Testament he came to the discovery that conversion in the sense of Scripture was something very different from the penance that Rome made of it. But Luther still separated repentance and faith too far from each other. He had in his own conscience felt the curse of the law and found his comfort in the justification of the sinner through faith alone. As he thought of it, conversion in the sense of remorse, penance, regret came about by way of the law, and faith by way of the gospel. Calvin later saw into the nature of this relationship better, and gave out a somewhat different account of it. As do the Scriptures, so he made a distinction between a false and a true conversion (Jer. 3:10), between a sorrow of the world, and a godly sorrow (2 Cor. 7:10). between regret, sorrow for a sinful deed, and a hearty remorse because we have provoked God's wrath because of our sin. Sorrow for a sinful deed can also take place in the children of the world. When sin has a very different consequence from the expected, when it leads to loss and shame, the world too senses regret. A Cain

(Gen. 4:13), an Esau (Heb. 12:17), and a Judas (Matt. 27:3) are evidence of it. Such a sorrow does not lead to true repentance, but leads to death and brings with it despair, bitterness, and hardness of the heart.

But the true conversion and repentance does not consist of such a sorrow which regrets the consequences of sins, but consists rather of an inner breaking of the heart (Ps. 51:19 and Acts 2:37), or a grief because of sin itself, because it is in conflict with God's will and provokes His wrath, and of a sincere remorse and a hating and fleeing of sin. Such repentance does not come up out of the old but out of the new man. It assumes a saving faith and is the fruit of such faith. It is a grief which God wills and which God works and its bearings are towards God, and it brings about a repentance to salvation not to be repented of (2 Cor. 7:10). When the lost son has come to his senses, and concludes to return home, he says: I will arise, and go to my *Father,* and I will say to him, Father, I have sinned against heaven and before thee (Luke 15:18). He takes the name of Father upon his lips even though he is still far from Him. He *dares* to go to the Father and to confess his sins before His face because in the depths of his heart he believes that the Father is his Father. We should not dare to turn around towards God if we did not trust inwardly in our souls through the Holy Spirit that as a Father He will accept our confession of sins and forgive us. The true repentance stands in inseparable connection with the true, saving faith.

Hence the full treatment of man's conversion does not belong to the doctrine of misery and redemption but to that of gratitude (Heidelberg Catechism: Sunday 33). Sometimes the word conversion is taken in a larger sense and then it comprehends the whole change which must take place in a person to become a child of God and a citizen of the kingdom. Just as Jesus in John 3 speaks only of regeneration, and elsewhere, as, for example, in Mark 16:16, only of faith as the way that leads to salvation, so in Matthew 4:17 He mentions only repentance. After all, one cannot possess the one benefit without the other. Faith and repentance are in principle contained in the new life of regeneration, and they inevitably come out of it into expression in time. But, although these cannot be separated from each other, they can be distinguished, and then repentance is a fruit of regeneration which at the same time presupposes faith. Even then it is and remains a gift and a work of God, not only at its beginning but also in its continuance.[28] But it is, by virtue of the new life that was poured out, a deed of man[29] which is not limited to a moment but which continues throughout life.

28. Jer. 31:18; Lam. 5:21; Acts 5:31 and 11:18.
29. Acts 2:38; 11:21; Rev. 2:5, 16 ff.

Repentance is, despite its oneness in essence, different in form according to the persons in whom it takes place and the circumstances in which it takes place. The way upon which the children of God walk is one way but they are varyingly led upon that way, and have varying experiences. What a difference there is in the leading which God gives the several patriarchs; what a difference there is in the conversion of Manasseh, Paul, and Timothy! How unlike are the experiences of a David and a Solomon, a John and a James! And that same difference we encounter also outside of Scripture in the life of the church fathers, of the reformers, and of all of the saints. The moment we have eyes to see the richness of the spiritual life, we do away with the practice of judging others according to our puny measure. There are people who know of only one method, and who regard no one as having repented unless he can speak of the same spiritual experiences which they have had or claim to have had. But Scripture is much richer and broader than the narrowness of such confines. In this respect also the word applies: There are diversities of gifts but the same Spirit; and there are differences of administrations but the same Lord. And there are diversities of operations, but it is the same God which worketh all in all (1 Cor. 12:4-6). The true repentance does not consist of what men make of it, but of what God says of it. In the diversity of providences and experiences it consists and must consist of the dying of the old and the rising of the new man.

What is the dying of the old man? It is a hearty sorrow that we have by our sins provoked God's wrath and in which we more and more hate those sins and flee from them.

And what is the rising of the new man? It is hearty joy in God through Christ, and a desire and love for living in all good works for God's sake.

XXI

Justification

Regeneration, manifesting itself in the fruits of faith and repentance, opens the way to the kingdom of God. Whoever is a citizen of this kingdom presently comes to share in all the benefits which are the content of that kingdom. They can be summarized in the trio: righteousness, holiness, and blessedness. It is the first of these that is now to be considered.

Righteousness is usually defined as that steadfast and constant will of a rational being which gives to each his own. It includes in the first place a spiritual disposition or attitude on the part of the person to whom it is credited, and in the second place a policy and a conduct over against others, which issues from the basic disposition or attitude, and which recognizes the rights which are theirs. Although Scripture, as we shall see, introduces a unique modification into this usual idea of justice or righteousness, it nevertheless proceeds from the same basic thought. Righteousness is the justness which a person himself possesses and the just action which he does in relation to others.

In this sense the Old Testament already ascribes justice or righteousness to God. He is the Rock whose work is perfect, for all His ways are judgment: a God of truth and without iniquity, just and right is He (Deut. 32:4). This righteousness is not deduced in Scripture from a reflection of the Divine being, but is ascribed to God on the basis of His revelation. Thus He made Himself known to His people from the beginning. He has not spoken in secret, in a dark place of the earth, nor said to the seed of Jacob, Seek me in vain. He is the Lord who speaks righteousness, who declares things that are right. While the heathen worship a god who cannot save them, He has made Himself known to Israel as Jehovah, beside whom there is no God, and He is a just God and a Savior (Isa. 45:19-21). As the just Lord He lives in the midst of Israel. He does no iniquity. Every morning He brings His judgment to light (Zeph. 3:5).

That righteousness of God came to expression first of all in the laws which He gave the people. For us righteousness consists of the fact that in our being and in our conduct we correspond to a law. But we cannot speak of the righteousness of God in any such sense. For there is no law above Him to which He must correspond. His righteousness consists of the fact that He harmonizes perfectly with Himself. All rights and laws have their origin in Him; and all these laws are righteous because He gave them in harmony with His own being and will. What nation, Moses once asked, is there that has statutes and judgments so righteous as all this law which I set before you this day? (Deut. 4:8). And the saints answer: The statutes of the Lord are right, rejoicing the heart; the commandment of the Lord is pure, enlightening the eyes. The fear of the Lord is clean, enduring forever: the judgments of the Lord are true and righteous altogether. More to be desired are they than gold, yea, than much fine gold: sweeter also than honey and the honeycomb (Ps. 19:8-11; 119).

But the righteousness of God is manifested further in this, that He maintains these laws in force and requires that His people live according to them. He laid His commandment already upon the first man (Gen. 2:16). And after the fall, too, He waives none of His requirements. His judgments, such as the great flood and the confusion of tongues are evidence of this. He holds all the Gentiles bound in their conscience to His law (Rom. 1:20, 32 and 2:15). In particular, however, He lays His claim upon His people of Israel, whom in sovereign love He accepted as His own, and who therefore must keep His covenant, obey His voice, and walk in His ways (Ex. 19:5). In this the Lord requires nothing unwarranted from His people for He has on His own part expended all upon His vineyard, and He expects that it bring forth good grapes (Isa. 5:4). The Lord had made known to them what was good, and what more does He require of them now but that they do justly, love mercy, and walk humbly with their God?[1]

Finally, His righteousness manifests itself in the fact that He judges and will judge all peoples, His own people of Israel also, strictly according to justice. God is lawgiver and king, but He is also judge (Isa. 33:22). Sometimes, it is true, over against the complaining people who say that God condemns in order Himself to be righteous (Job 40:2), the absolute sovereignty of His doing is emphasized, and the accent falls on the fact that the inhabitants of the earth are reputed as nothing, and that God does according to His will with the army of heaven and the inhabitants of the earth, and that none can stay His hand or say to Him, What doest Thou? (Dan. 4:35). He is the Maker of all things, with whom no creature can quarrel or contend (Isa. 45:9). He is the potter in whose hand Israel is as clay (Jer. 18:6 and Isa. 10:15). But these statements do not by any means serve to represent God as a tyrant who

---

1. Micah 6:8; Amos 5:14-15; and Isa. 1:16-17.

operates arbitrarily. Rather, they call on man to humble himself and to bow to the majesty of God's thoughts and the incomprehensibility of His ways (Isa. 55:8-9). He is a terrible majesty and mighty in strength; but He does not disdain. Rather, He pays attention to man and deals with him according to right (Job 36:5 and 37:23).

And this He can do because He is omniscient and absolutely righteous. In the case of earthly rulers this is often quite otherwise, and that is why they are admonished again and again in the Old Testament not to have respect of persons in judgment,[2] not to accept a gift,[3] not to oppress the poor and the stranger, the orphan and the widow,[4] to pronounce the righteous righteous, the unjust unjust, and to judge the people with a righteous judgment.[5] For he that justifies the wicked, and he that condemns the just, even they both are an abomination to the Lord.[6] The righteous Lord, however, loves righteousness; His countenance beholds the upright.[7] His right hand is full of righteousness; justice and judgment are the habitation of His throne.[8] He is impartial, is not a respecter of persons, takes no gifts,[9] and the rich and the poor are alike the work of His hands.[10] He is not one to look only upon the outward appearance, for He looks upon the heart;[11] indeed, He tries the hearts and the reins.[12] One day He will judge the world in righteousness, and minister judgment to the people in uprightness.[13] He will be exalted in judgment and sanctified in righteousness.[14]

* * * * *

If, however, the righteousness of God consists of this that He deals strictly according to justice and judges all men by the standard of His holy law, how then can any son of man ever be declared free of guilt by God and receive from Him the right to eternal life?

Certainly there can be no doubt about the fact that all men without exception are guilty of transgressing the law of God, and are deserving of the punishment which He has appointed for such transgression. Since the disobedience of Adam a stream of unrighteousnesses has had

2. Deut. 1:17; Lev. 19:15; and Prov. 24:23.
3. Deut. 16:19; Ex. 23:8; and Isa. 5:23.
4. Ex. 23:6, 9; Ps. 82:2-4; and Isa. 1:12.
5. Deut. 16:19 and 25:1.
6. Prov. 17:15, 26; 18:5; and 24:24.
7. Ps. 11:7; 33:5; 99:4; and Jer. 9:23.
8. Ps. 48:11; 89:14; and 97:2.
9. Deut. 10:17 and 2 Chron. 19:7.
10. Job 34:19.
11. 1 Sam. 16:6; and 1 Chron. 28:8.
12. Ps. 7:10; Jer. 11:20; and 20:12.
13. Ps. 9:8; 96:13; and 98:9.
14. Isa. 5:16.

unbroken sway over the human race. The imagination of the thoughts of the human heart are evil continually, from youth on up (Gen. 6:5 and 8:21). All are born unclean; they are all gone aside, and there is none that does good, no, not one.[15] There is no man that does not sin, and none that can say, I have made my heart clean: I am pure from my sin.[16] If God were to mark iniquities, who could stand?[17] If, now, this is the human situation, how can there be such a thing as his justification before God and by God?

Nevertheless that same Old Testament which so plainly proclaims the sinfulness and unrighteousness of the whole human race again and again makes mention of the righteous and of the upright in heart, and of these as living in a world full of rancor. Thus Noah is called a just man and perfect in his generations (Gen. 6:9 and 7:1) and Job receives from God Himself the testimony that there is none like him on the earth, a perfect and an upright man, one who fears God and eschews evil.[18] In the Psalms, too, constant reference is made to a small group of righteous ones who stand in contrast to the wicked and suffer much at their hands.[19] The Proverbs are continually concerned with that same contrast among men.[20] Just so, too, the prophets make a distinction between a small nucleus of the people which remains true to the Lord and the great masses who give themselves up to idolatry and iniquity.[21] Ezekiel especially makes a very sharp distinction between the righteous and the wicked, and in doing so he is thinking not of groups among the people but of individual persons.[22]

But this is not the only thing which strikes us in the Old Testament. Still more surprising is the fact that these just ones (the upright of heart, or however they may be called) are not at all afraid of the righteousness of God and never once entertain the fear that they will be obliterated by His judgment. Indeed, for the godless that righteousness will prove terrible.[23] But the saints make this very righteousness the basis of their appeal and call upon it; they pray for answer to their plea and for deliverance because God is the God of righteousness (Ps. 4:1 and 143:1), and they expect that He, precisely because He is the righteous God who tries the hearts and reins, will establish them (Ps. 7:9), deliver them (Ps. 31:2), redeem them (Ps. 34:22), see that justice accrues to them

---

15. Job 14:4; 25:4-6; Ps. 51:7; and Ps. 14:3.
16. 1 Kings 8:46; Prov. 20:9; and Eccles. 7:20.
17. Ps. 130:3 and 143:2.
18. Job 1:1, 7; and 2:3.
19. Ps. 1:5; 14:5; 32:11; 33:1; 34:16 and elsewhere.
20. Prov. 2:20-22; 3:33; 4:18; 10:3 and elsewhere.
21. 1 Kings 19:18; Isa. 1:8-9; 4:3; and 6:5.
22. Ezek. 3:18 ff.; 18:5 ff.; and 33:8 ff.
23. Isa. 59:16-18; Jer. 11:20; 20:12; Ps. 7:12; 9:5-6; 28:4; and 129:4.

(Ps. 35:23 ff.), forgive them (Ps. 51:16), answer them and quicken them (Ps. 119:40 and 143:1), and bring their souls out of trouble (Ps. 143:11).

This appeal of the righteous to the righteousness of God sometimes goes a step farther and takes the form, at first so incredible to us, of asking God to deliver them according to *their* righteousness. Job cannot admit that he is guilty, and is conscious of his pure and upright conduct (Job 29:12 ff. and 31:1 ff.), and in the end the Lord confirms his righteousness over against Job's friends (Job 42:7). In the Psalms we frequently hear this note sounded: Judge me, Lord, according to my righteousness and according to my integrity.[24] To Isaiah the plaint of the people is this one: My way is hid from the Lord, and my *judgment* is passed over from my God. But the prophet has been sent to them precisely to proclaim to them in the name of the Lord that this is not the situation. After the chastisement, the discipline, will follow the redemption, the deliverance. The warfare is accomplished, the iniquity is pardoned (Isa. 40:2), and the Lord brings His righteousness near and His salvation will not tarry (Isa. 46:13). Just as in His redemptive way He repeatedly intervenes in the lives of His saints, causes their sentence to come forth from His Presence (Ps. 17:2), executing justice for the needy and oppressed,[25] so in the end He will plead the cause of His people.[26] He will lay bare His holy arm in the eyes of all the nations, will cause a word of righteousness to proceed from His mouth, and through righteousness He will establish His people.[27] He is a just God and a Savior (Isa. 45:21). In Him are righteousness and strength; from Him is all their righteousness; and in the Lord will all the seed of Israel be justified and in Him be all their glory.[28]

It is very evident from the Old Testament, therefore, that not only are there righteous persons in Israel but also that these look for their welfare and salvation precisely to the righteousness of God. This is likely to strike us as being a little strange for we are inclined to oppose the justice of God to His mercy. The way we tend to think of it then is that we are condemned by the justice of God and saved by His mercy. But the saints of the Old Testament do not make such a contrast. They intimately relate the justice of God to His grace and mercy, His goodness and truth, His favor and faithfulness.[29] They say that the Lord is

---

24. Ps. 7:9; 17:1; 18:20-25; 24:4-6; 26:1; 37:18 and elsewhere.
25. Ps. 103:6; 140:13; and 146:7.
26. Isa. 49:25; 51:22; Jer. 50:34; 51:36; and Micah 7:9.
27. Isa. 45:23; 51:5; 52:10; and 54:15.
28. Isa. 45:24-25 and 54:17.
29. Ps. 33:5; 40:11; 51:16; 89:15; 103:17; 143:11; Jer. 9:24 and Hos. 2:18.

gracious and righteous (Ps. 112:4 and 116:5) and that His deliverances are evidences of His righteousness.[30] And that is why this righteousness, no less than the mercy of God, is for the saints the subject of continuous laud and praise.[31]

* * * * *

But how is all this possible? How can people all of whom are sinners ever stand in the holy presence of God as justified and righteous people. How can they ever have justice on their side, and how can they according to the justice of God be acquitted of their sins and guilt and be taken up into His blessed fellowship?

Can this be because Israel in the days of the Old Testament was the people of God, had the temple in their midst, and zealously brought their sacrifices of steers and bullocks? There were many in Israel who put their confidence in this and who concluded that therefore evil would not come near them. But the prophets who arose in the name of the Lord instructed the people very differently. When Israel prided itself in its external privileges the prophets all unanimously declare that these are untrustworthy reeds, penetrating the hand that leans on them. Are ye not, says the prophet Amos (9:7), as the children of the Ethiopians unto me, O children of Israel? Have I not brought up Israel out of the land of Egypt? And the Philistines from Caphtor, and the Syrians from Kir? And, over against the false persons who trusted in lying words, saying, The Temple of the Lord, The Temple of the Lord, The Temple of the Lord, Jeremiah pronounces judgment (7:14), saying, The Lord will do to that house which is called in His name even as He has done to Shiloh. So far, further, as the sacrifices and offerings were concerned, the saints in Israel knew very well that these in themselves could not be pleasing to the Lord (Ps. 40:9 and 51:6). Through the mouths of the prophets the Lord Himself: I am full of the burnt offerings of rams, and the fat of fed beasts; and I delight not in the blood of bullocks, or of lambs, or of he goats.[32]

Is the ground of the hope of salvation among the saints of the Old Testament perhaps their own righteousness? Is that why they have such good hope for the future? Do they think that their good works can stand in the judgment of God? This thought might for a moment come up in our minds when we observe, as in the person of Job, how strongly they are convinced of their innocence (Job 29:12 ff. and

---

30. Judges 5:11; 1 Sam. 12:7; and Micah 6:5.
31. Ps. 7:17; 22:31; 35:28; 40:10; 51:16; 71:15 and elsewhere.
32. Isa. 1:11; 66:2-3; Jer. 6:20; Hos. 6:6; Amos 5:21; Mich 6:6-8; Prov. 15:8; 21:27 and elsewhere.

31:1 ff.), how often they appeal to their integrity, faithfulness, and righteousness,[33] how they constantly speak of their *right* or *sentence*,[34] and, finally, how the Lord Himself reckons them as being righteous.[35] But when we come to penetrate this thought more deeply we realize that this ground also falls away.

After all, this appeal of theirs to their righteousness on the part of the saints of the Old Testament is accompanied or interchangeably supplanted by the humblest confession of sins. Job speaks not only of the sins of his youth but also in the end abhors himself and repents in dust and ashes (Job 13:26 and 42:6). In Psalm 7:9 David speaks of his integrity but elsewhere he casts off all his righteousness, confesses his transgressions before the Lord, and glories solely in the forgiveness of sins (Ps. 32:11). Daniel makes his appeal not on the basis of his righteousness but on that of the tender mercies of the Lord, which are great (Dan. 9:18). In Isaiah a saintly Israel confesses that all its righteousnesses are as filthy rags, that all have gone astray like sheep that have no shepherd, everyone turning to his own way, but that the Lord has converged all of their unrighteousness upon His Servant. In Psalm 130:3-4 the poet says that if the Lord should mark iniquities, none could stand in His presence, but that there is forgiveness with Him, that He may be feared. And all of those Old Testament saints acknowledge without distinction that God is just in His punishment of Israel; they and their fathers have sinned and were rebellious against Him.[36]

When the saints in Israel make mention of their righteousness, it is true that they certainly also think of their upright conduct and integrity before the face of the Lord, and they even pray that the Lord, who tries the hearts, will search them and see whether there be any wicked way in them.[37] But this righteousness and integrity of theirs is not intended as a moral perfection such as that of which the Pharisees of later days spoke; rather, they are thinking of a moral integrity which has its ground and source in a religious integrity, in other words, in a righteousness of faith. This becomes apparent from the fact that the righteous are also frequently represented as being the poor, the needy, the oppressed, the faithful, the humble, and the meek, they who fear the Lord and have no other hope but Him. They are the same people whom Jesus later called the poor in spirit, those who mourn, who hunger and

---

33. Ps. 7:9; 18:21; 26:1; 102:2 and elsewhere.
34. Job 27:2; Ps. 17:2; 26:1; 35:24; 43:1; Isa. 40:27 and elsewhere.
35. Isa. 53:4-6; 59:12; and 64:6.
36. Amos 3:2; Lam. 1:18; Ezra 9:6; Neh. 9:33; Dan 9:14 and elsewhere.
37. Ps. 7:9-10; 17:3; and 18:21-25.

thirst after righteousness, the weary and heavy laden, and the little children (Matt. 5:3ff. and 11:25 and 28).

And the earmark of these people is not that they are free of sin, but rather that in the midst of oppression and persecution to which they are exposed on every hand in the world, they put their trust in the Lord and seek their salvation and blessedness in Him alone. Nowhere is there any deliverance for them, neither in themselves, nor in any creature, but in the Lord their God alone. And that God, consequently, is also their God, their sun and shield, their refuge and their high tower, their buckler, their rock and strength, their deliverer and redeemer, their glory and their one and all (Ps. 18:3 and 73:25 ff.). They are His people, the sheep of His pasture, His servants and His beneficiaries.[38] They look for His salvation, cling to His word, delight in His law, and expect all things only from Him. They are not a people like the later Pharisees who in opposition to God insist on their rights and privileges, but a people rather who are on God's side and who in alliance with Him take position against His and their own enemies.

When such a people in its prayer and beseeching makes an appeal to its own and the Lord's righteousness, it means to say that the Lord is by virtue of His covenant obligated to deal justly with it over against its enemies, for it is named after Him and walks in the fear of His name. He has chosen His people not for their size or number, nor for their righteousness or integrity, but because the Lord voluntarily loved them and because of the oath which He had sworn to their fathers (Deut. 7:7 ff. and 9:5-6). The covenant with this people is based solely upon His good pleasure, upon His favor. But by virtue of that covenant it cannot be denied that He is bound to that people and has, so to speak, taken upon Himself the obligation to maintain that people, preserve it, and to grant it the whole salvation which He promised when He said to Abraham: I will establish my covenant between me and thee and thy seed after thee in their generations for an everlasting covenant, to be a God unto thee, and to thy seed after thee (Gen. 17:7).

The righteousness of God, consequently, to which a saintly Israel constantly appeals in its oppression is an appeal to that attribute according to which, by virtue of His covenant, the Lord is obligated to deliver His people from all of their enemies. It is not so much an obligation which rests upon God because of His people, but it is an obligation which rests upon Him because of Himself. He is no longer free; He freely related Himself to His people, and so He owes it to Himself, to His own covenant and His own oath, to His own word and promise, to remain the God of His people despite all their unrighteousnesses. Hence

---

38. Ps. 33:12; 95:7; and 100:3.

we so frequently read that it is for the sake of God's name, of His covenant, of His glory, of His honor, that He gives His people the benefits which He has promised them.[39] Even though the people may become unfaithful and apostate, He remembers His covenant and keeps it in force forever.[40] The righteousness of God to which a pious Israel appeals does not form a contrast to His goodness and salvation but is related to it and stands in close connection with His truth and faithfulness. It confines God to His own word and promise and obliges Him, out of sheer grace, to save His people from all their oppression.

And it was just so also that God conducted Himself in the past when He again and again rescued Israel from all of its enemies.[41] But He will do so much more richly in the future — such is their view of it — when He will set up His kingdom among His people. By virtue of His own righteousness, because He is a God of righteousness, faithfulness and truth, He will make a new covenant with them, will forgive their sins, pour out His Spirit over them, and cause them to walk in His ways (Jer. 31:31-34 and elsewhere). But He does not do this for their sake; He does it for His own sake, for His great Name's sake. I, even I, am He that blotteth out thy transgressions for mine own sake, and will not remember thy sins (Isa. 43:25). He Himself confers the righteousness which Israel requires.[42] He creates new heavens and a new earth, in which the former things shall not be remembered, nor come to mind (Isa. 65:17). In those days Judah shall be saved, and Israel shall dwell safely; and this is His name whereby He shall be called, The Lord our righteousness![43]

* * * * *

The thought that God Himself grants His people righteousness and so justifies them comes to a much richer development in the New Testament when Christ appears upon the earth and by His life and death fulfills all righteousness for His church.

Jesus Himself came with the preaching that the time was fulfilled and that the kingdom of God was at hand (Mark 1:15). By this He meant not only that before long the kingdom would come, but also that in principle in His person and work it had come already. For He is the Messiah in whom the Old Testament prophecy concerning the Servant of the Lord has obtained its fulfillment (Luke 4:17-21), and who now sets

---

39. Ps.25:11; 31:3; 79:9; 106:8; 109:21; 143:11; Isa. 49:9, 11; Jer. 14:7, 21; Ezek. 20:9, 14, 22, 44; Dan. 9:19 and elsewhere.
40. Ps. 105:8; 111:5; and Isa. 54:10.
41. Ex. 2:24; Judges 2:1; and Isa. 37:20.
42. Isa. 45:24, 25; 46:13; and 54:17.
43. Isa. 62:2; Jer. 23:6; and 33:16.

about proving this by His works. For when He heals the sick, raises the dead, casts out devils, preaches the gospel to the poor, forgives sins, that is indisputable evidence that He is the One whom prophecy promised and that the kingdom of God has come to the earth.[44] In the benefits which Christ gives, in spiritual and physical redemption, the treasures of the kingdom of heaven are made plain.

Among the treasures of that kingdom, Jesus specifically mentions righteousness. In Matthew 6:33 this righteousness is most intimately related to the kingdom of God and His righteousness. Or, as another reading has it, seek first His kingdom and righteousness, namely, that of the heavenly Father mentioned in verse 32. Just as is His kingdom, so also the righteousness in that kingdom is the property and the gift of God which He distributes through Christ. Whoever seeks and finds the kingdom of God receives at the same time the righteousness which is necessary for citizenship in that kingdom.

That is why Jesus can say elsewhere that the possession of that righteousness is a condition for entering the kingdom of God. Except your righteousness, we read, exceed the righteousness of the scribes and Pharisees, ye shall in no case enter into the kingdom of heaven.[45] This righteousness which Jesus requires of His disciples is a very different righteousness, a much deeper and more intimate righteousness, than the external fulfillment of the law with which the Jews are content; it is a spiritual and perfect righteousness, a righteousness like that of the Father (Matt. 5:20, 48). But when Jesus regards such a righteousness as being necessary for entering the kingdom of God He does not mean that a person is in his own strength to accomplish it. Were that necessary He would not have been a Messiah and His gospel would not have been a glad tiding. His purpose, rather, is to shed light upon the nature, the spiritual character, the perfection of God's kingdom: no one can enter it unless he is in perfect harmony with the law of God and shares in the perfect righteousness.

But this righteousness, which, on the one hand, is the condition and requirement for entering the kingdom, is, on the other hand, the gift of that kingdom. It is Christ Himself who confers all the benefits of that kingdom, also the righteousness of it. It is a kingdom of God and the righteousness of it is a righteousness of God (Matt. 6:33), but just as the Father appointed the kingdom to Him so He appoints it to His disciples (Luke 22:29 and 12:32). For the Father loves the Son and has delivered all things into His hand.[46] But the Father has given Him all

---

44. Matt. 9:2; 10:7, 8; 11:5; and 12:28.
45. Matt. 5:20. Compare Matt. 7:21; 1 Cor. 6:10; Gal. 3:18, 21; Eph. 5:5; and Rev. 22:14.
46. Matt. 11:27; John 3:35; 13:3; and 16:15.

this because He is the Son of man (John 5:27), that is, in order that precisely by way of obedience unto death He should achieve it for Himself. He did not come to be served, but to serve, and to give His soul a ransom for many (Matt. 20:28). In the death on the cross He permitted His body to be broken and His blood to be poured out, in order that the New Testament might be established and all the sins of His people be forgiven (Matt. 26:26-28).

On the basis of His appointment by the Father and of His own sacrifice He distributed, both before and after His death, all the benefits of the kingdom to His disciples. He healed the sick not only but also forgave sins and conferred eternal life. These benefits he conferred not upon the self-righteous Pharisees, but upon the publicans and sinners, the weary and heavily laden, the poor in spirit, and those who hungered and thirsted after righteousness. He did not come to call the righteous but sinners to repentance (Matt. 9:13) and to seek and to save that which was lost (Luke 19:10). Not self-righteousness but rebirth, faith, repentance gives access to the kingdom and all of its benefits. And that rebirth or regeneration is itself a gift and a work of the Holy Spirit (John 3:5).

* * * * *

As soon as the Holy Spirit was poured out on Pentecost, the apostles, accordingly, immediately began to preach the crucified Christ as the Prince and Savior exalted by God in order to give Israel repentance and the forgiveness of sins (Acts 2:36, 38 and 5:30-31). After the event of redemption had taken place in the death of Christ the significance of it could, in the light of the resurrection and through the leading of the Spirit, be fully explained and unfolded by the apostles. And none of these apostles did this more richly and more clearly than Paul, who was circumcised on the eighth day, of the stock of Israel, of the tribe of Benjamin, an Hebrew of the Hebrews, as touching the law a Pharisee, concerning zeal persecuting the church, and touching the righteousness which is in the law, blameless, but who counted those things which were gain to him loss for Christ (Phil. 3:5-7).

According to his own testimony Paul had struggled for years and with great zeal for the righteousness which is of the law. And he had gone a long way in it. As touching the righteousness which is in the law (Phil. 3:6) and which is obtained from the law (Phil. 3:9 and Rom. 10:5; 9:32), he was, humanly estimated, blameless. Nobody could say anything against him. On the contrary, everybody praised him. He got esteem and prestige out of it, and he would have opened up a famous career for himself among his people, if he had continued in this way.

He had gained much from it (verse 7). But when it pleased God to reveal His Son in him, then for the sake of the excellency of the knowledge of Jesus Christ His Lord, he reckoned all this old righteousness as loss, casting it off as something to be repudiated and as something useless, in order that he might win Christ, be found in Him, not having the righteousness which is in the law, but that, rather, which is by faith in Christ and which comes from God to faith.

Why the righteousness which is of the works of the law is inadequate the apostle explains elsewhere more than once. The law is indeed holy, just, spiritual, and good, but man, being carnal, was sold under sin (Rom. 7:12, 14) : it cannot quicken and it cannot by its judgment obliterate sin for it is weak through the flesh (Rom. 8:3 and Gal. 3:21). It makes demands indeed, but it grants nothing, confers no benefits. It says only that the man who does these things will live by them (Rom. 10:5 and Gal. 3:10, 12). It cannot, however, itself grant this life because the flesh does not subject itself to the law of God and cannot so subject itself (Rom. 8:7). Instead of justifying and giving life the law is now precisely the strength of sin (1 Cor. 15:56). If there were no law there would be no sin and no transgression (Rom. 4:15 and 7:8). But in the sinful condition in which man finds himself the law rouses sin, prompts desire, and causes man to long after the forbidden thing; or, rather, the sin which lives in man takes occasion through the commandment to excite all kinds of desire in the heart and to sin exceedingly.[47] What the law can do, consequently, is to give the knowledge of sin (Rom. 3:20 and 7:7), to work wrath (Rom. 4:15), and to place people under the curse (Gal. 3:10) ; but by the works of the law no man can ever be justified.[48] Judged by the law the whole world stands guilty before the face of God and is subject to its penalty (Rom. 3:19). For the wrath of God is revealed against all ungodliness and unrighteousness of men.[49]

But, if such is the righteous judgment which according to the law God pronounces upon men, who then can be saved? Even as Jesus did in Matthew 19:26, so Paul has this answer to that : With men this is impossible, but with God all things are possible. With Him this impossibility, too, is possible that he justifies the wicked and nevertheless Himself remains perfectly righteous (Rom. 3:26 and 4:5). What God most strictly condemns in His holy law, namely, the justification of the wicked,[50] what He says of Himself He will never do (Ex. 23:7), that He nevertheless does, but He does it without jeopardizing His righteousness. This is the wonder of the Gospel.

---

47. Rom. 5:20; 7:8; Gal. 3:19.
48. Acts 13:39; Rom. 3:20, 28; 8:3, 8; Gal. 2:16; and 3:11.
49. Rom. 1:18; Eph. 5:6; and Col. 3:6.
50. Deut. 25:1; Ps. 82:2; Prov. 17:15; and Isa. 5:23.

For God has proclaimed His righteousness not only in the law but in the gospel also. In the gospel His righteousness is revealed without the law, without its contribution, quite apart from it, and apparently in opposition to it (Rom. 1:17 and 3:20). This gospel existed long before; it had its beginning in Paradise. The righteousness of God which was revealed in the gospel has the witness of the law and the prophets and of the whole of the Old Testament Scripture (Rom. 3:21). Abraham was justified by it when he was still in the uncircumcision (Rom. 4:1 ff.). David also describes the blessedness of the man to whom God imputes righteousness without works (Rom. 4:6), and Habakkuk makes it a general statement: The just shall live by faith (Rom. 1:17 and Gal. 3:11). But now, in the present time (Rom. 3:21 and 26) that righteousness of God has become much more obviously manifest, for Christ has appeared and has been made righteousness unto us (1 Cor. 1:30).

The law which was given to Israel was itself of service to that full revelation of the righteousness of God in the gospel. For by exciting sin and causing the knowledge of sin, by exciting wrath and placing people under the curse, the law has been a schoolmaster and governor leading us to Christ, in order that those who were under its tutelage should in the fulness of time graduate to Christ and be justified by faith (Gal. 3:22-25). Thus the people were prepared by the discipline of the law for the appearance of the gospel. But from God's side, too, the law served the fulfillment of the promise. For in the times before Christ God in His long-suffering permitted the nations to walk in their own ways, and He overlooked and permitted the sins of His people in this sense that He did not punish them according to desert (Rom. 3:25). That is why it became necessary for Him to manifest His righteousness in the other way of the Gospel, quite apart from the law (Rom. 3:25-26). Through the law He concluded all things under sin in order that the promise of the inheritance should be given to the believers, not out of the works of the law, but out of faith in Jesus Christ.[51]

The righteousness which God reveals in the gospel consequently has its own peculiar character. It takes place without the law and yet must harmonize with the law (Rom. 3:21). It must condemn and at the same time preserve. It is a manifestation of God's justice but also of His grace (Rom. 3:23-24). It must be such that God can justify the wicked by it and in doing it nevertheless remain perfectly righteous (Rom. 3:26 and 4:5). This takes place objectively by presenting Christ as a reconciliation in His blood and subjectively by counting faith in that Christ as righteousness (Rom. 4:4-5 and Gal. 3:6). In short, the righteousness which God reveals in the gospel consists of a granting of

---

51. Gal. 3:22; Rom. 3:9; 11:32.

a righteousness of faith which as such stands in diametrical opposition to the righteousness of the works of the law, to the self-righteousness of man.[52] It is a righteousness from God through faith in Christ (Phil. 3:9).

* * * * *

In the teaching of Scripture on the justification of sinners, therefore, the whole emphasis falls on the fact that this justification, on the basis of which we are acquitted of guilt and punishment, is the gift of God. If we were justified by the works of the law, by keeping the commandments of the law, then we could come before God's judgment with our own and self-achieved judgment, and then we would, in a certain sense, have cause to glory in ourselves (Rom. 4:2). But Scripture teaches something different. Abraham had nothing whereof to glory before God because it was not by works that he was justified but by his faith that was counted to him for righteousness, and his reward was given him not according to guilt but according to grace (Rom. 4:4-5).

The righteousness which God gives us in Christ and with which alone we can stand in His presence is, accordingly, in no sense the fruit of our labor, but is in an absolute sense a gift of God, a gift of His grace. We are justified freely through the redemption that is in Christ Jesus (Rom. 3:24). The grace of God is the deepest ground and final cause of our justification. But this grace is not to be regarded as a contrast to the righteousness of God but as something inter-related with it. After all, Paul says again and again that in the gospel the righteousness of God has become manifest,[53] and just so John in his first letter (1 John 1:9) writes that God is faithful and just to forgive us our sins, if we confess them, and to cleanse us from all unrighteousness. And Peter in his second letter (2 Peter 1:1) says that we have obtained the faith through the righteousness of God and our Savior Jesus Christ.

In this the idea is contained that God, the God of justice, has in the gospel created another order of justice than that which obtained under the law. This old order, too, reveals the righteousness of God but in such a way that He gives His law to men, binds men to obedience to this law, and in the end punishes men or rewards them according to His judgment of their conduct. Inasmuch, however, as that law has become of no effect because of sin, God has in the gospel set up another order of justice. To it men must also subject themselves (Rom. 10:3) but this order in itself by way of faith grants that righteousness which they require in order to stand before the throne of God. The gospel is, ac-

---

52. Rom. 3:21; 4:2-6; 9:32; 10:3; and Phil. 3:9.
53. Rom. 1:17; 3:5, 21, 22, 25, 26; and 10:3.

cordingly, at one and the same time an order of justice and an order of grace. The grace consists of this that God who could hold us to the terms of the law and condemn us by it, opened up another way of righteousness and life in Christ. And the justice consists of this that God does not lead us into His kingdom without righteousness and sanctification, but instead has a perfect righteousness accomplished in the sacrifice of Christ and in grace gives it to us and counts it to our credit. Christ is a gift of God's love (John 3:16 and Rom. 5:8). And He is at the same time a manifestation of God's righteousness (Rom. 3:25). In the cross on Golgotha righteousness and grace were joined together. Justification is both a judicial and a gracious deed of God.

We have to thank Christ and all His benefits for this oneness of justice and grace. To Him we owe also the benefit of righteousness which we need in order to stand in the judgment of God. This righteousness which is given us in faith, is however to be carefully distinguished from the righteousness which is an attribute of God's being, and from that of the divine and human natures of Christ. For if the righteousness which is the attribute of God's or Christ's being were the ground of our justification, not only would the whole passion and death of Christ lose its value but the boundary line between the Creator and the creature would be erased and the natures of these two would be intermingled in pantheistic fashion. The righteousness which becomes ours through faith and which justifies us before God has, however, been achieved by the passion and death of Christ. God has set forth Christ to be a propitiation through faith in His blood, that is, to be a means of reconciliation effecting the remission of sins through the power of the poured out blood and by means of faith (Rom. 3:25). He was made sin for us that we might be made the righteousness of God in him (2 Cor. 5:3 and Gal. 3:13). An exchange takes place between Christ and His own; Christ takes upon Himself their sin and curse and gives them His righteousness instead. He has of God been made wisdom, and righteousness, and sanctification, and redemption unto them (1 Cor. 1:30).

This righteousness of Christ is so perfect and adequate that it requires no completion or supplementation of our own. As a matter of fact it can in no way be increased or amplified by us, for it is an organic whole. Just as the law is a whole, so that whoever would keep it entirely but should stumble on one commandment would become guilty of all (James 2:10), so too the righteousness which satisfies the demands of the law is a perfect whole and unity like the seamless robe of Jesus, woven from the top throughout (John 19:23). This righteousness has not been put together from piece or fragments. You either have all of it or none of it. We cannot get a part of it and fill in the rest ourselves. And, anyhow, what have we to give that would serve to fill out such righteousness? Certainly not the good works done before the faith. The Scriptures say most unequivocally that the imagination of the thoughts of men's hearts is evil from youth on, that what is born of the flesh is flesh, that the thought of the flesh is enmity against God and cannot submit itself to His law and that all of its righteousnesses are as filthy rags.

If good works had to amplify and fill out the righteousness which Christ has achieved, the only works that could be considered as qualifying at all would be the works which regenerate man does out of faith. For it is altogether true that the believers can do good works; just as a good tree brings forth good fruits, so a good man out of the good treasure of his heart brings forth good things (Matt. 12:35). Renewed by the Spirit of God the believer delights in the law of God after the inward man (Rom. 7:22). Nevertheless, all these works which come up out of faith are nevertheless still very imperfect and are tainted with sin; when the believer wants to do the good he finds constantly that evil is present with him (Rom. 7:21). Moreover, all of these good works already assume the righteousness granted by Christ and accepted by faith. The believer simply walks in the good works which God has before ordained and to which, as God's creation, he has been made in Christ Jesus (Eph. 2:10).

Our comfort in this matter of justification therefore is that the whole righteousness which we require comes from outside ourselves in Christ Jesus. We are not the ones who must bring it into being. But in this God reveals His righteousness in the gospel that He Himself provides a righteousness through the sacrifice of Christ. The righteousness which justifies us is a righteousness of God through faith in Christ; neither in whole nor in part is it dependent upon our works but is in its entirety perfect and adequate, a gift of God, the free gift of grace.[54] And if it be by grace then it is no more of works, otherwise grace is no more grace (Rom. 11:6). In short, Christ Himself is the righteousness with which alone we can stand before His face (1 Cor. 1:30). Through His passion and death He earned the right for Himself and His own to enter into eternal life, free from all guilt and punishment, and to take a place at the right hand of God.

The righteousness which justifies us, therefore, is not to be separated from the person of Christ. It does not consist of a material or spiritual gift which Christ can grant us apart from Himself or which we can accept and receive apart from the person of Christ. There is no possibility of sharing in the benefits of Christ without being in fellowship with the person of Christ, and the latter invariably brings the benefits

---

54. Phil. 3:9; 2 Tim. 1:9; and Tit. 3:5.

with it. In order to stand before the judgment of God, to be acquitted of all guilt and punishment, and to share in the glory of God and eternal life, we must have Christ, not something of Him, but Christ Himself. We must possess Him in the fulness of His grace and truth, according to His divine and human nature, in His humiliation and exaltation. The crucified and glorified Christ is the righteousness which God grants us through grace in the justification. And when God grants us this Christ together with all His benefits out of free grace, without any merit on our part, by way of faith, then He at the same time justifies us. He pronounces us free of all guilt and punishment, and gives us the right to eternal life, to the heavenly glory, to His own blessed, never-ending fellowship. And then we can stand before His presence as though we had never had sin, or done sin, indeed, as though we had ourselves achieved the obedience which Christ has achieved for us.

* * * * *

There are, however, two ways in which one thing or another can be given us. We can get possession of it by judicial decision, and we can, on the basis of such a court ruling, sooner or later take possession of it. Whoever in a legal testament or will is designated an heir thereby gets a right to the transferred goods in the future, but it is possible that only years later will he actually come into possession of those goods. And even when the legal right and the actual possession coincide there nevertheless remains a big difference between the two. Property is the legal, possession the actual, command of a thing. This is a distinction which does not obtain among animals, at least not in this form. An animal takes what it can get. But for man this is different. Created in the image of God, he must have a right to something in order to possess it and use it. His honor and privilege is that he does not live by predatory action. By the work of his hands he eats his own bread.

This has its application in the spiritual sphere. For we stand in all kinds of relationship to God. He is our Creator, and we are His creatures. He is the Potter and we are the clay in His fingers. He is the Builder and Architect and we are His temple. He is the Husbandman and we are the branches of His vine. He is our Father and we are His children. All of the relationships which exist in the world between bridegroom and bride, man and woman, parents and children, rulers and subjects, and the like, are called upon in Scripture to teach us the rich, many-sided relationship in which people in general, and particularly the believers, stand to Him. And none of these relationships can be neglected without our doing violence of some kind to the intimacy of that relationship. Thus, for instance, we also have the relation of a child to

God. The lost son even in his straying still bears the name of son, but
he is a lost son and a dead son, and he is found and becomes alive again
only when he returns to the Father with a confession of guilt.

But at the same time we have a relationship to God which is a legal
relationship. He is our Creator, and thus He is also our Lawgiver, King,
and Judge. Scripture tells us this repeatedly.[55] And our own hearts
tell us so. The sense of law is deeply seated in our soul. In fact, the
sense of law is everywhere and at all times the same. There may be a
difference in the content, about the particular laws and rules, but the
notion or sense of law itself has no history, any more than the notions
of time, place, movement, life, good, evil and the like have a history.
The sense of law is one of the ideas planted in human nature and one
which gradually becomes consciously articulated. There is no people so
barbarous or uncivilized but in some instances feels itself to be offended,
seizes its weapons, and defends its rights. And the relationship to God
is also included in this sense of law in the broadest sense. Every man
feels himself to be duty bound in his conscience to serve God and to
live according to His laws. And every man has the awareness that if
he does not do this he is guilty and deserving of punishment. The law
of the broken covenant of works is still operative in the heart of every
man. And the moral law proclaimed by God from Sinai simply sharpened the content of its commandments and so the duty to keep them.

This relationship of law is not obliterated by the gospel, as so many
tend to say, but is, rather, restored and fulfilled. The difference between
law and gospel is not that in the law God manifests Himself solely as
Judge and in the gospel solely as Father. And even less can the difference between the law and the gospel be equated with the difference between the Old and the New Testament. For in the Old Testament, too,
God revealed the gospel of His grace and mercy to His people Israel;
the law stood in the service of the covenant of grace, it followed upon
and it was subordinate to the promise, and was to this extent also a gift
of His Fatherly favor and of His educational wisdom. And even though
it is true that in the person of Christ the depths of God's mercies are
manifested far more plainly than was possible in the Old Testament,
still, on the one hand, the gospel of grace was not unknown in Israel,
and, on the other hand, the fulness of the gospel which appeared in
Christ was not an annihilation but a fulfillment of the law and the prophets (Matt. 5:17 and Rom. 3:31).

Hence, too, Paul states very forcefully that in the gospel the righteousness of God is revealed (Rom. 1:17 and 3:21-26). The oneness
and the correspondence of the law and the gospel come out in the fact

---

55. Gen. 18:25; Ps. 47:3, 8; Isa. 33:22; Heb. 4:12; James 4:12.

that the righteousness of God is revealed in both. And the difference comes out in the fact that in the law that righteousness is manifested according to the rule, The man who does these things shall live, whereas in the gospel that righteousness is revealed without the law and according to the rule, He who, not by works, but by faith in Him who justifies the wicked, believes, he shall have his faith counted to him for righteousness (Rom. 4:5). In the law one's own, perfect, adequate righteousness is required; in the gospel a perfect and adequate righteousness is granted by God through grace in Christ. Inasmuch as man could not and did not want to maintain the justice of God as embodied in His law, God Himself by the gift of righteousness in Christ restored and confirmed His justice. He puts His love and mercy in the service of His righteousness. By giving Himself He fulfills His own law. And in grace He counts the righteousness of Christ as ours, so that we should fulfill to the full the justice of His law, should receive complete remission of all our sins, and obtain a confident entry into His heavenly kingdom.

* * * * *

The justification, then, is certainly a gracious, but it is also a juridical, deed of God, a declaration by which He, as Judge, acquits us of guilt and punishment and gives us the right to eternal life. For Roman Catholicism and all those who seek the ground of our justification either in part or in its entirety in man himself (in his faith, in his good works, in the Christ in us, in the new principle of life, or whatever) this objection is always opposed to such a juridical declaration of righteousness, namely, that it is unreal and that it is unworthy of God. They argue that if the basis of our justification lies entirely in Christ and outside of ourselves, and if faith or good works or whatever they may be called are not credited by God as part of our righteousness, then the person who is justified is not really righteous, and then God passes an unreal and untrue judgment upon him, for man *is* not then what he is *proclaimed* to be.

Against this objection the observation should suffice that by justification Scripture always has in mind a juridical deed. It speaks repeatedly of the justification of the sinner before God, and in doing so employs a word that is borrowed from the courtroom and that always has a judicial meaning. To the judges of Israel God gave the commandment that they should declare the righteous righteous, and that they should condemn the unjust.[56] And He Himself shows His righteousness in this: He does not justify the wicked nor slay the righteous.[57] If this word

---

56. Deut. 25:1; Ps. 82:2-3; Prov. 17:15; 24:24; and Isa. 5:23.
57. Gen. 18:25; Ex. 23:7; and 2 Chron. 6:23.

of God is applied to the spiritual sphere, it retains its juridical significance. So, for instance, Jesus says that the wisdom which has appeared in Him was justified, that is, acknowledged as wisdom, of her children (Matt.11:19). And in Luke 7:29 Jesus says that the people who heard John and the publicans who were baptized with his baptism, thereby justified God, that is, acknowledged God as being righteous. The moral significance of *justifying* is in these passages excluded.

The same is true when the word is used for the saving of sinners. For Paul not only says that in the gospel the righteousness of God has been revealed (Rom. 1:19 and 3:20 ff.) but he declares also that God justifies those who are in the faith, and that in doing so He Himself remains just (Rom. 3:26), and that to the person who does not work but believes on Him that justifies the ungodly, his faith is counted for righteousness (Rom. 4:5). He sets the righteous over against the guilty and the condemned, and then exclaims: Who shall lay anything to the charge of God's elect? It is God who justifies: Who is he that condemns (Rom. 8:33-34)? Paul further uses the terms *justifying* and *imputing righteousness* interchangeably (Rom. 4:3,6, and 11) and also the term *making righteous* (Rom. 5:19), and in Romans 5:18 he says: As by the offense of one, judgment came upon all men to condemnation, so by the righteousness of one the free gift came upon all men unto justification of life. Throughout, therefore, the justifying is regarded as a juridical, a legal, action, a verdict of acquittal pronounced by the heavenly Judge upon the sinner who according to the norm of the law is wicked but who has in faith accepted the righteousness given by God Himself in Christ. Judged by that he is righteous.

Besides the fact that Holy Scriptures very plainly speak of the justification as a legal or forensic act, this further fact must be pointed out to the opponents of the doctrine of justification: They have a mistaken notion of what justification is. They say that such an acquittal of man on the basis of a righteousness outside of himself is unworthy of man, and that it leaves him quite unchanged. But this charge comes back upon the heads of those who make it, for if they justify a person on the basis of a righteousness which is in him, they must themselves certainly admit that this righteousness in man here on earth is very frail and imperfect, and must therefore conclude that God justifies a person on the basis of a very inadequate righteousness and thus makes Himself guilty of a false judgment. On the other hand, an acquittal based on the righteousness which is in Christ is a perfectly just one for it was presented perfectly by God Himself in the Son of His love. Moreover, although this justification of the sinner, this acquittal, is based solely on the righteousness which is in Christ, it does in time through faith become operative in the consciousness of man and effects important change there. Even the person who has been accused of a serious crime and is acquitted by an earthly judge is not the same. His whole relationship to the law is changed about. So too the justification of God works on in the consciousness of man and liberates him from all sense of guilt.

In a sense the justification of the sinner has already taken place in the counsel of election. It is objectively pronounced in the resurrection of Christ who was delivered up for our sins and raised for our justification (Rom. 4:25), and in the gospel which proclaims the glad tidings that in the death of Christ God stands in a relationship of reconciliation and peace to the world (2 Cor. 5:19). And subjectively this justification comes to man in the internal calling and is on his own part, accepted in faith. Justification is but one link in the chain of salvation. It is related on the one hand to the foreknowledge and calling, and on the other to the sanctification and glorification (Rom. 8:30). The justification in the tribunal of God, accordingly, comes to expression in time through faith in the consciousness of man. And the righteousness which Christ has achieved is not so much dead capital lying outside of Christ, but is rather included in His person. And Christ was raised precisely to this end that in His own time He should through the Holy Spirit share all of His benefits with His own. Once the eye of faith in man is open to this reality, his whole relationship to the law changes immediately. He who was poor then suddenly becomes rich through the riches which are in Christ Jesus; he who was guilty of transgressing all the commandments of God suddenly sees himself acquitted of all guilt and punishment; he who had merited eternal punishment sees himself credited with the right to eternal life! Together with Paul such an one glories: Who shall lay anything to the charge of the elect of God? It is God who justifies; who is it that condemns? It is Christ who has died, who has been raised, who is seated at the right hand of God, it is He who prays for us!

Finally this: justification and sanctification are not the same, and ought to be sharply differentiated from each other. For whoever neglects or erases this distinction again sets up a self-righteousness in man, does injustice to the completeness and adequacy of the righteousness of God which has been manifested in Christ, changes the gospel into a new law, robs the soul of man of its only comfort, and makes salvation dependent upon human merits. In justification, faith has only the role of a receiving agency, like that of the hand which accepts something; by it the soul places its dependence solely in Christ and His righteousness. True, Holy Scripture more than once makes use of the expression that faith is counted or reckoned to someone for righteousness,[58] and the force of this expression presumably is that faith takes the place of the righteousness which the law demands but which the sinner does not possess. But in this connection the question nevertheless arises: Why does, and why can, this faith take the place of the righteousness demanded by the law? Is this to be credited to the fact that the faith has exceptional moral value and is a good and virtuous thing which suffices for this?

There are many who hold to this view and who maintain that faith itself, quite apart from its content and its object, justifies solely and alone through its intrinsic character. But this certainly is not the teaching of Scripture. For if faith did its justifying by virtue of its moral worth, it would again take its place alongside of works and merits rather than stand opposed to them. And we know that Paul puts it as bluntly as possible that the justification which now takes place in the gospel through faith is diametrically opposed to all justification by the works of the law.[59] Moreover, this presentation of the matter is interchanged sometimes with that other, according to which justification through faith is regarded as a justification through grace, and accordingly something which excludes all glorying and merit (Rom. 3:24; 4:4ff.; and Tit. 3:5). In Romans 4:16 the apostle expressly states that the inheritance comes by faith precisely in order that it should come from grace; and this could not be said in this way if the faith justified man by reason of its own intrinsic worth and power. Finally, if faith thus interpreted could perform this service, Christ would lose all significance in the work of justification. Then the only thing that mattered would be *that* a person believed; *what* he believed would be neither here nor there. Faith would then do the justifying irrespective of whether it were faith in an idol, a demonic power, or a false prophet. And this has been held, as, for instance, when unbelieving physicians recommend to their patients a visit to Lourdes or an equivalent shrine because "faith" has "healing power."

The witness of the Scriptures is diametrically opposed to such a view. What matters there is precisely the *content* of the faith and the *object* of the faith. Faith can take the place of the righteousness demanded by the law and can be counted as righteousness, because it is faith in Christ Jesus, He who has been presented by God as a propitiation through the power of His blood (Rom. 3:25), who has borne the curse for us (Gal. 3:13), who was made sin for us (2 Cor. 5:21), who died, was raised, and is seated at the right hand of God as our intercessor

---

58. Gen. 15:6; Rom. 4:3, 5, 9, 22; and Gal. 3:6.
59. Rom. 3:20-28; 4:4ff.; Gal. 2:16; and 3:11.

(Rom. 8:34), who is made righteousness unto us (1 Cor. 1:30), and in whom we are made the righteousness of God (2 Cor. 5:21). In short, faith justifies because in Christ it comes to share in a righteousness which is just as perfect and adequate as that which is demanded by the law but which God through grace by way of the gospel now grants in Christ (Phil. 3:9). It justifies not by its own intrinsic moral worth but by its content, namely, the righteousness of Christ.

All the same, though it is of the greatest importance to see clearly the distinction between justification and sanctification and to maintain it purely, these two benefits are never, of course, separated from each other, not even for a moment. In the counsel of God they are not separated, for justification is but one link in the chain of salvation. Whom God foreknew, He also predestinated to be conformed to the image of His Son; and whom He predestinated, them He also called; and whom He called, them He also justified; and whom He justified, them He also glorified (Rom. 8:29-30). They are not separated either in the person and the work of Christ; for righteousness is not something that lies outside of Christ and can be accepted apart from His person. Christ Himself is our righteousness, and He is at the same time our wisdom, sanctification, and redemption (1 Cor. 1:30). One cannot accept the one benefit of Christ without the other, for they all together lie contained in His person. Whoever accepts Christ as his righteousness by faith, at the same time receives Him as his sanctification. Christ cannot be accepted in parts. Whoever possesses Christ possesses Him in His entirety, and he who lacks His benefits lacks His person also. Finally, in faith also the justification and sanctification are inseparably bound up with each other. True, so far as the justification goes, this faith comes into consideration solely and exclusively in its religious character as a confidence in the grace of God, as an acceptance of Christ and of the righteousness granted in Him by God; but if faith actually is and does this, then it is a living and saving faith, such as is pre-eminently the work of God (John 6:29), and such as manifests its reality and power in good works (Gal. 5:6 and James 2:20ff.). To justify is not the same thing as it is to make alive; but just as sin and death are intimately bound up with each other, so are righteousness and life. The just shall live by faith (Rom. 1:17). As by the offense of one man judgment came upon all men to condemnation, even so by the righteousness of one the free gift came upon all men unto justification of life (Rom. 5:18).

* * * * *

Hence it is that the justification includes two benefits: the forgiveness of sins and the right to eternal life. These two are related to each other and maintain the same relations to each other as do the passive and the active obedience in the work of Christ. Christ restored not only what Adam in his one transgression had spoiled, but He also achieved what Adam by his keeping of the law ought to have achieved, namely, eternal life. Whoever believes in Christ by virtue of that faith receives the forgiveness of sins,[60] and in that same moment also receives eternal life (John 3:16 and 36).

It happens that most people think very lightly of the forgiveness of sins. They present it as something altogether natural that God forgives sins and that he blinks at human inadequacies; they present the whole matter as though God must forgive sins or else prove Himself to be something other than a God of love. But the experience of life should have been equal to teaching such people something else. To forgive, sincerely to forgive, to forgive in such a way that nothing at all remains of the experienced offense — that requires a lot of doing on our part and implies a victory over ourselves which it is hard to win. True, the feeling of having been offended is often unwarranted in us; we are affected by things which ought not to affect us, and let other things pass which ought to grieve us sorely. True, our sense of right and honor has not been obliterated, but it has been spoiled and bent in a wrong direction. All the same, it can happen that we have been deeply offended by some thing or other, and that we feel violated in our honor, character, and name. It is then that it costs a lot of struggling to banish every last vestige of wrath from our hearts, and sincerely to forgive our enemy so entirely that we forget the offense and never again call it to mind. Forgiveness always presupposes the violation of a right and consists of the lifting or acquittal of the merited penalty.

All this holds true even for men. But sin and forgiveness both take on weightier content when they are, respectively, committed against God and forgiven by Him. God also lays claim to a right, the right, namely, at all times, everywhere, and in all things to be recognized as God by men, and to be served and honored as such. This right is the principle and foundation of all right, of all law; whoever touches this right touches the whole order of law, the whole moral structure of the world as it has its origin and steadfastness in Him. Whoever comes to know sin in this way, whoever regards it in the light of Holy Scripture, whoever regards it to some extent as God regards it, he will begin to think differently about the importance of the forgiveness of sins. Such an one really can hardly believe the forgiveness of sins, for it goes straight against the nature of things. There is in the first place his own heart which condemns and declares him guilty before the face of God.

---

60. Matt. 9:2; Rom. 4:7; and Eph. 4:32.

Next, there is the law, which pronounces the curse upon him and reckons him deserving of death. Then there is Satan who accuses him, and in accusing him does so in appeal to judgment and law. And there are the people who let him stand alone in his need and read out his sins to him at large. And in and behind these all he hears the voice of the righteousness of God, seeking him out, pursuing him, grasping him, and delivering him up to judgment. Who, reflecting on all this and experiencing it, can believe in the complete forgiveness of all of his sins?

But the church of Christ dares to believe it, and can and may believe it. In humility and excitement of heart it confesses: *I believe the forgiveness of sins.* I believe it, even though I do not see it. I believe it, even though my conscience accuses me of having sinned grievously against all the commandments of God, of having kept none of them, and of being prone to all evil still. And the church stands on solid ground in making this confession of belief. Whoever seeks the forgiveness of sins outside of Christ can wish for it and hope for it, but he cannot sincerely and convincingly believe it. He equates it with a kind of blinking at sin and so does violence to the seriousness, the gravity, of sin. But the gospel informs us that God forgives sins, that He can forgive them and that He does forgive them, because His right has been fully vindicated by Christ. The necessity for satisfaction of the holiness of God does not make forgiveness impossible, but paves the way for it, guarantees it, and makes us believe in it, and causes us to believe in it with unwavering confidence. So perfect therefore is the forgiveness of all our sins that in Scripture it is spoken of as a remembering no more, a casting behind one's back.[61] The Lord does not behold the iniquity of Jacob, nor see the perverseness in Israel (Num. 23:21).

This forgiveness is already contained in the counsel of God and is publicly proclaimed over the whole church in the resurrection of Christ (Rom. 4:25). It is generally announced in the gospel (Acts 5:31), and is distributed to each in particular, that is, to each believer. But even though the believer shares in the forgiveness of all of his sins, he must continuously, from day to day, keep appropriating it by faith in order to enjoy the assurance and comfort of it. It would be easy if we could, with a kind of "Once converted, always converted" attitude, go on in life according to the wishes of our own hearts; and it is true that there are many who continue to live on the basis of a bygone experience, and are content with that. But such is not the Christian life. Neither the righteousness which is in Christ Jesus, nor the faith which the Holy

---

61. Isa. 38:17; 43:25; and Heb. 8:12.

Spirit plants within us is a piece of dead capital. In the long run we become participants in the forgiveness of sins, and the assurance and certainty of this, only by exercising fellowship with Christ Himself, in the exercise of a saving faith. Hence Jesus put the prayer for the forgiveness of sins upon the lips of His disciples (Matt. 6:12). A humble confession of our sins is the way along which God proves his faithfulness and righteousness, forgives our sins and cleanses us from all unrighteousness (1 John 1:9). And in order to cause us always and continuously to sense profoundly the benefit granted us in the forgiveness of sins, Christ adds to those words petitioning for the forgiveness of sins the further words: *as we forgive our debtors.* This additional clause does not constitute the ground on the basis of which we dare to ask God or may ask God to deliver us from our sins; it is not the norm according to which we are asking God to measure, but it describes rather the disposition which must be present in the one who prays in order to enjoy and appreciate the benefit of forgiveness. It is only then that we realize to some extent what, humanly speaking, it has cost God to grant us the forgiveness of sins in Christ; it is only when we ourselves have rooted every enmity out of our own hearts and have forgiven all our debtors sincerely for all their offenses that we appreciate what God has done for us. Hence we can pray for this great, invaluable benefit with a full earnestness of soul only when we are at heart disposed towards forgiveness over against our neighbor. True, the forgiveness of sins took place at once and perfectly in God, but it is given to us and appropriated by us throughout our lives in the way of faith and repentance. The Holy Supper, too, is evidence of this also, for in it we again and again remember that Christ broke His body and poured out His blood unto the forgiveness of sins (Matt. 26:28).

The other side of this benefit of the forgiveness of sins is the right to eternal life. When John speaks of this, he is thinking particularly of the new life which is born of God and planted in us by the Holy Spirit (John 1:13 and 3:5). This *being children of God,* of which he speaks, comes up out of regeneration and consists especially of being conformed to God (John 1:13 and 1 John 1:1-3). But Paul usually speaks of this being children of God in another sense. He takes it to mean that God on the basis of the righteousness in Christ accepts us as His children and heirs.

Among the Romans the families were sharply distinguished from each other. Every family had its own privileges and rights and especially, too, its religious practices. Hence a child could go from the one family to another only by way of a formal, legal transaction, in terms of which the natural father, so to speak, sold his child to the other father who wanted to accept it as his child. In the event that the natural father had already died the transition could take place only through a formal declaration of the people in a public gathering. Only in this way could a child be liberated from his duties in the one family and subjected to those in the other.

The apostle Paul presumably derives his concept of the adoption unto children from this circumstance, and so makes clear the new relationship in which the believer stands over against God. In the Old Testament such adoption had already been the privilege of Israel (Rom. 9:4), and Israel was accordingly frequently called the son of God.[62] But such adoption is nevertheless a blessing of the new covenant, for the believers of the Old Testament were still wards under the law (Gal. 3:23 and 4:1-3). But now Christ has come in the fulness of time, has placed Himself under the law and borne its curse in order that those who were under the law should be redeemed and in order that we should receive the adoption as children (Gal. 4:4-5). Christ has purchased our freedom from bondage to the law and to sin by His death, so that we now belong to another, namely, to Him who is raised from the dead (Rom. 7:1-4), and have been accepted by God as His children and heirs (Gal. 4:7). As such we have also received the Spirit of the Son, the Spirit of adoption as children, the Spirit such as belongs to this inheritance. By means of this Spirit we are made aware of our adoption, receive the boldness to speak to God as our father, and are continually guided (Rom. 8:14-16 and Gal. 4:6). Indeed, just as this adoption as children is rooted in the eternal plan of God (Eph. 1:5) so it also extends out far into the future. For even though the believers are already children and already have the privileges of heirs (Rom. 8:17 and Gal. 4:7), they nevertheless together with every creature wait for the manifestation of the sons of God, namely, the redemption of their body (Rom. 8:18-23). It is only in the resurrection from the dead, when the body also will be perfectly redeemed, that the adoption as children is completed.

* * * * *

The benefit of justification through faith alone has in it a rich comfort for the Christian. The forgiveness of his sins, the hope for the future, the certainty concerning eternal salvation, do not depend upon the degree of holiness which he has achieved in life, but are firmly rooted in the grace of God and in the redemption which is in Christ Jesus. If these benefits had to derive their certainty from the good works of the Christian they would always, even unto death, remain

---

62. Ex. 4:22-23; Deut. 8:5; Hos. 11:1; and elsewhere.

unsure, for even the holiest of men have only a small beginning of perfect obedience. Accordingly, the believers would be constantly torn between fear and anxiety, they could never stand in the freedom with which Christ has set them free, and, nevertheless being unable to live without certainty, they would have to take recourse to church and priest, to altar and sacrament, to religious rites and practices. Such is indeed the condition of thousands of Christians both inside and outside of the Roman church. They do not understand the glory and the comfort of free justification.

But the believer whose eye has been opened to the riches of this benefit, sees the matter differently. He has come to the humble acknowledgement that good works, whether these consist of emotional excitements, of soul experiences, or of external deeds, can never be the foundation but only the fruit of faith. His salvation is fixed outside of himself in Christ Jesus and His righteousness, and therefore can never again waver. His house is built upon the rock, and therefore it can stand the vehemence of the rain, the floods, and the winds. Of course this confession, like every other article of faith, can be abused. If the faith which accepts Christ and His righteousness is taken to be a rational approbation of an historical truth, then the human being can still stand alongside of it, cold, indifferent, and dead. And then he brings no good works into manifestation out of that faith, and in fact does not accept the person of Christ along with it. But the true faith that drives the human being, stunned and defeated by the sense of guilt, drives to Christ himself, that faith will attach itself solely to the grace of God, will glory in the free forgiveness of sins, and in that moment already brings good works into being.

Indeed, this faith that rests solely upon God's grace in Christ and is accordingly conscious of the forgiveness of sins is the only faith that is equal to truly good works. For so long as we permit the forgiveness of sins to depend entirely or in part upon the emotional excitements which we enjoy, and upon the good works which we do, we continue to live more or less in dread and fear. Then we are not yet children who do things prompted by love, but are still slaves and servants who do it for reward. Then we do not do the good solely because it is good, that is, for God's sake, but do it more or less still for personal gain, in order to achieve favor by means of it and to make ourselves attractive in the eyes of God. But all this changes when by faith we understand that our salvation rests exclusively in God's grace and in the righteousness of Christ. Then we leave off building up a self-righteousness and no longer trouble ourselves with working out our own salvation, for these things are fixed already in Christ Jesus. Sure of this salvation in Christ we can put all our attention to doing good works in order so to glorify our Father. We achieve them then not for ourselves, but for the sake of the Lord. We belong to Christ who was raised from the dead in order that we should bring forth fruits unto God (Rom. 7:4). We have through the law died to the law in order that we should live unto God (Gal. 2:19). Those are for the first time truly good works which proceed from faith, are done according to God's will, and are directed to His honor.

The freedom of the Christian, accordingly, which he comes to share in justification, consists of this that he is delivered from the demand and the curse of the law. The believer is not liberated from the law in the sense that he can live according to the desires of his heart, that he, as it is nowadays put, can live out his life according to the bent and direction of his sinful nature. On the contrary, the believer is much more firmly bound to the law than was the case before, for the faith does not make the law of no effect, but establishes it (Rom. 3:31). The demand of the law is fulfilled in those who do not walk according to the flesh but according to the Spirit (Rom. 8:4). How should those who are dead to sin live in it any longer (Rom. 6:2)? But the relationship in which the believer comes to stand over against the law is very different from that in which he stood before. He is bound to it by the law of gratitude; he is however free from its demand and its curse.

In this respect the believers of the New Testament had in fact a considerable advantage over those of the Old. In the Old Testament religion continues to be described for the most part as the *fear of the Lord* and the believers are very frequently designated *servants of the Lord*. They were children, it is true, but children who were minors, and therefore like servants who are placed under guardians and wards until the time determined by the Father (Gal. 4:1-2; 3:23-24). But when the fulness of time came God sent His Son, born of a woman, born under the law (Gal. 4:4). By Himself in our stead fulfilling all righteousness (Matt. 4:15), by becoming a curse for us (Gal. 3:13), and by letting Himself be made sin for us (2 Cor. 5:21) Christ liberated us from the curse of the law and from its demand, and did this perfectly. We are no longer servants to the law, by the law we have died to the law, and we are now servants of Christ, living unto God (Rom. 7:1-4 and Gal. 2:19). We are no longer under the law but under grace (Rom. 6:15); we stand in the freedom with which Christ has made us free (Gal. 5:1). No longer does the rule hold for us: Do this and thou shalt live. The order is completely reversed. We live out of faith and we act according to the law because we enjoy it according to the inward man. Thus the law has become without effect over against the believers. It can no longer accuse them, for its guilt has been borne by Christ and its demand satisfied by Him. The law can no longer condemn them, for Christ has taken its curse upon Himself and has borne all its penalties. Even Satan can no longer have recourse to the law to accuse the brethren, for who can lay charges against the elect of God if it is God Himself who justifies them, and if it is the Christ who died and is glorified who prays for them in heaven?

At the same time that the change takes place which justification has brought about in the relationship of the believers to the law, to its demand and to its curse, a change also takes place in their relationship to all things and to the whole world. When we are reconciled to God we are reconciled to all things. When we stand in a right relationship to God we also come to stand in a right relationship over against the world. The redemption in Christ is a redemption from the guilt and punishment of sin, but it is a redemption also from the world which can so confine and oppress us. We know that the Father loved the world, and that Christ gained the victory over the world. The world can therefore still oppress us, but it cannot rob us of our good courage (John 16:33). As children of the Heavenly Father, the believers are not anxious about what they shall eat, and what they shall drink, and with what they shall be clothed, for He knows that they have need of all these things (Matt. 6:25 ff.). They do not gather treasures upon earth, but have their treasure in Heaven where neither moth nor rust corrupts, and where thieves do not break through nor steal (Matt. 6:19-20). As unknown they are nevertheless known; as dying they live; as chastened they are not killed; as sorrowful yet always rejoicing; as having nothing, and yet possessing all things (2 Cor. 6:9-10). They do not torment themselves with the "Taste not, touch not" attitude, but regard every creature of God as good and accept it with gratitude (Col. 2:20 and 1 Tim. 4:4). They remain and they work in the same calling in which they are called and are not bondservants of men but of Christ alone (1 Cor. 7:20-24). They see in the trials which fall to them not a punishment but a chastisement and a token of God's love (Heb. 12:5-8). They are free over against all creatures because nothing can separate them from the love of God which is in Christ Jesus their Lord (Rom. 8:35 and 39). Indeed, all things are theirs because they are Christ's (1 Cor. 3:21-23), and all things must work together for good to those who love God and are called according to His purpose (Rom. 8:28).

The believer who is justified in Christ is the freest creature in the world. At least, so it ought to be.

XXII

Sanctification

Inasmuch as the image of God consisted not only of knowledge and righteousness, but also of holiness, the restoration of man must restore him to a right relationship with God not only, but must also renew him internally according to the demand of His holy law. Sin is guilt, but it is also pollution. Justification delivers man from his guilt; sanctification delivers him from the pollution of sin. By the former his consciousness is changed, and by the latter his being is changed. By means of the first, man comes to stand in a right relationship again; by means of the second, man becomes good again and able to do good.

The word *holy* occurs on virtually every page of the Holy Scriptures. Just what the original, natural meaning of the Hebrew word translated *holy* in our version meant is not to be made out with certainty; in Scripture the word is never used in that original, natural sense, but always has a religious significance. Nevertheless the word as used in Scripture very probably came from a root which meant *to be cut off,* or *to be separated.* Nor is it possible to say definitely in what sense the word was first introduced into religious discussion. According to some, persons and things were first called holy because they were set apart from other persons and things, and were, so to speak, removed from common use. The opposite of the word *holy* is, accordingly, unholy, unconsecrated, mean, and profane.[1] According to others the word first meant, in reference to religious things, that persons and objects stood in a particular relationship to God, and were in that sense different from others. So much can be said for this view, namely, that people and things are never by nature themselves holy, but can become this only through a definite action which accrues to them. Nor can they sanctify themselves, for all holiness and sanctification proceeds from God. Jehovah is holy, and therefore He wants a holy people, a holy priesthood, a holy temple.[2] It is He who designates those who are his own and who are holy (Num. 16:5).

---

1. Lev. 10:10; 1 Sam. 21:5; and Ezek. 22:6.
2. Ex. 19:6; 29:43; Lev. 11:45ff.; and 19:2.

Again and again, accordingly, God is in the Old Testament called the Holy One. It is only in Daniel 4:8, 9, 18, and 5:11 that Nebuchadnezzar too speaks of his holy gods. This word *holy* when used in reference to the Divine Being does not intend to designate a particular attribute which He possesses alongside of others, but is used, rather, to give expression to His Divine greatness, sublimity, majesty, and unapproachableness. There is none holy as the Lord, for there is none beside Thee: neither is there any rock like our God (1 Sam. 2:2). He is God, and not man (Hos. 11:9). No one is able to stand before this holy God (1 Sam. 6:20). He is exalted high above the gods, glorious in holiness, fearful in praises, doing wonders (Ex. 15:11). He is terrible out of His holy places (Ps. 68:35); His name is great and terrible (Ps. 99:2, 3); to swear by His holiness is to swear by Himself (Amos 4:2 and 6:8). In short, holiness points to God in His distinction from and elevation above all creatures. He is the Holy One because He is God. Isaiah especially likes to make use of this word for God.[3]

The holiness of God manifests itself in all the relationships in which He has placed Himself over against His people. The whole of the lawgiving in Israel has its first principle in the holiness of Jehovah and has its end in the sanctification of the people. He is holy in all His revelation, in all that proceeds from Him: His name is holy (Lev. 20:3); His arm is holy (Ps. 98:1); His covenant is holy (Dan. 11:28); His word is holy (Ps. 105:42); and His Spirit is holy (Ps. 51:11 and Isa. 63:10 and 17). Hence He wants His people to be holy also.[4] And among that people He particularly wants the priests and Levites, who minister in the holy things and who are consecrated by particular ceremonies for their office, to be holy (Ex. 29). In fact, everything that stands in some relationship to the service of God, whether places, times, offerings, the garments of the priests, or the temple, and the like, must be dedicated to the Lord and be holy. The whole meaning of the giving of the law is that Israel must be a priestly nation and a holy people unto the Lord (Ex. 19:6). And the people of Israel actually is holy if in everything it answers to the law which the Lord has given it.

We must remember that this law in Israel comprised not merely moral, but also many civic and ceremonial, commandments. Holiness, therefore, consisted of perfection, in total correspondence to the law, but this perfection was not merely of a moral but also of a civic and ceremonial nature. The people, however, frequently fell into one-sidedness and sought the essence of religion in external, Levitical purity. The

---

3. Isa. 5:16; 6:3; 29:23; 30:11-12; compare Ezek. 37:28; 39:7; Habak. 1:12; and 3:3.
4. Ex. 19:6; 29:43-46; Lev. 11:44; and 19:2.

prophets, consequently, had to protest against this and had to proclaim that obedience was better than sacrifice and to hearken than the fat of rams (1 Sam. 15:22) ; and they had to say that God desired mercy and not sacrifice, and the knowledge of God more than burnt offerings (Hos. 6:6). The prophets had to preach that the Lord required nothing of them but to do justly, and to love mercy, and to walk humbly with God (Micah 6:8). They pointed out that the holiness of God consisted especially in His moral perfection, in His exaltedness above and His contrast to the sinfulness of the creature (Isa. 6:3-7). When people profane His name and His covenant, then God sanctifies Himself in righteousness (Isa. 5:16 and Ezek. 28:22). As the Holy One He most certainly punishes the enemy in order that they may know that He is the Lord (Jer. 50:29; Ezek. 36:23; and 39:7), but He will deliver His people by purging it of all unrighteousness, establishing a new covenant with it, and causing it to walk in His ways with a new heart (Jer. 31:31-34; Ezek. 36:25-29). And He will do this not for Israel's sake, but for the sake of His own great name (Isa. 43:35, and Ezek. 36:22).

*   *   *   *   *

In the same way in which God in the New Testament has in Christ given His people righteousness so in the Son of His love He has given them holiness. Christ is our holiness, our sanctification, in the same way and in the same sense as He is our wisdom, our redemption. We must know that He was first of all one who shared in a personal holiness, for otherwise He could not have achieved a holiness for us. That which was conceived in Mary by the Holy Spirit and was born of her was the Holy Thing and was given the name of the Son of God (Luke 1:35). Later, at His baptism, He received the Holy Spirit without measure and was full of the Holy Spirit (Luke 3:22 and 4:1). Those who were possessed of devils acknowledged Him as the Holy One of God (Mark 1:24 and Luke 4:34), and the disciples by the mouth of Peter made the confession: Lord, to whom shall we go? Thou hast the words of eternal life, and we have believed and known that Thou art the Holy One of God (John 6:68). In Acts 4:27 (compare 3:14), the same apostle speaks of Him as the Holy Child of God (or the holy servant of God), and in Revelation 3:7 He calls Himself the Holy and the True One. Just as Christ was conscious of His sinlessness,[5] so also all His apostles testify that He has done no wrong and that there was no deceit in His mouth.[6]

---

5. Matt. 12:50; John 4:34; and 8:46.
6. 2 Cor. 5:21; Heb. 4:15; 7:26; 1 Peter 1:19; 2:22; 3:18; 1 John 2:1; and 3:5.

We must, however, make a distinction in Christ between the holiness which He possessed by nature and that which He accomplished by His perfect obedience. His being conceived and born holy had this benefit, first of all, that He could be our Mediator (Heidelberg Catechism, Answer 16), but it also had the further benefit that He, being our Mediator from the very moment of His conception, covers the sin in which we are conceived and born with His innocence and perfect holiness before the face of God (Heidelberg Catechism, Answer 36). The holiness in which He was born He immediately made a part of the holiness which He throughout His life, even up to His death, had to achieve for His church. We know, for example, that the Father already sanctified Him before His incarnation, consecrating Him to the office of Mediator, and precisely to that end sent Him into the world (John 10:36). And Christ sanctified Himself and gave Himself up to the will of His Father before He was conceived in Mary and born of her; His incarnation was already a fulfillment of the Father's will, a deed of sanctification (Heb. 10:5-9). It was not enough that Christ was holy: He had to sanctify Himself from the moment of His conception up to the hour of His death.

As Mediator, after all, He was subjected to the severest trials and temptations, especially after He had received baptism, had been anointed by the Holy Spirit, and had begun to carry out His public ministry. The temptation of which we read in the Gospels, was the beginning of a life full of struggle; when this temptation was finished, the devil departed from Him for only a period (Luke 4:13). We cannot picture to ourselves what these temptations were, but we are expressly told that He became like the brethren *in all things,* and that He was in all points tempted like as we are, yet without sin (Heb. 2:17 and 4:15); we have no weakness but He knows of it, and no temptation but He can help us. But whereas we succumb every moment, He remains faithful to the end; He was tempted in all things, but without sin; He was obedient unto death, even the death of the cross (Phil. 2:8). He did not pray that He be spared death, but He did offer up prayers and supplications with strong crying and tears to Him that was able to save Him from death, that He might remain steadfast in His suffering and might by His death accomplish life. And He was answered in this prayer (Heb. 5:7).

But, although He was the Son, He nevertheless had to learn obedience by the things which He suffered (Heb. 5:8). He was obedient from the beginning and He *wanted to be* obedient: His meat was to do the Father's will (John 4:34). But in His passion He received the opportunity to prove that obedience; in and through His suffering He had to translate into deed and action His disposition and will to obey. Thus

He was sanctified by the things which He suffered (Heb. 2:11 and 5:9), sanctified, that is, not in the moral sense but finished, brought to the conclusion He had envisioned all along and so, by reason of the passion of His death, crowned with glory and honor (Heb. 2:9 and 12:2). Thus He was made the Captain of the salvation of the children of God and the Finisher of their faith (Heb. 2:10 and 12:2). By bearing the cross and despising the shame with a view to the joy that would await Him after His humiliation, He became the initiator, the pioneer, and the workman of the salvation of His own, and, at the same time, the One who begins that faith in them and finishes it. By perfecting Himself in the way of obedience, by seeking the glory at the right hand of the Father in no other way than through the deepest humiliation, He became the author of the eternal salvation of all those who obey Him (Heb. 5:9). He sanctified Himself, gave Himself up as a sacrifice unto death, in order that His disciples might be sanctified in truth (John 17:19). And so He was given us of God unto our sanctification (1 Cor. 1:30).

*   *   *   *   *

In order to understand the sanctification of the believers properly, one must see clearly that Christ is our sanctification in the same sense that He is our righteousness. He is a perfect and adequate Savior; He does not accomplish His work in part only, but actually and perfectly saves us; and He does not leave off His work until He has caused us to share fully in eternal life and the heavenly blessedness. By His righteousness, therefore, He not only restores us to the state of the righteous, of those who stand free in the judgment of God, in order for the rest to leave the matter in our own hands, so that, so to speak, we ourselves now proceed to earn eternal life by doing good works and conforming ourselves to the image of God; no, Christ also finishes all this work for us. He bore the guilt and penalty of sin for us, and He also kept the law for us and earned eternal life. His obedience was both *passive* and *active,* and it was both at the same time.

His resurrection was the evidence of this. By it we know that God did not leave His soul in hell (thought of in this connection, of course, not as the place of the damned, for the soul of Christ after His death was in Paradise, but as the grave, the realm of the dead, to which Christ also belonged so long as He remained in the state of death) and did not suffer His Holy One to see corruption, but made known to Him the ways of life, and filled Him full of joy with His countenance (Acts 2:27-28 and 13:35-37). In accordance with the Spirit of holiness which dwelt in Him, He was after the resurrection from the dead designated and appointed by God as His Son with power (Rom. 1:4), to be a Prince and a Savior, in order to give repentance to Israel, and forgiveness of sins (Acts 5:31), to be a Prince of life who has achieved eternal life and now gives it to His own (Acts 3:15).

But this sanctification which Christ has achieved for His church is not something which remains outside of us but something, rather, which is really shared with us. In justification we are declared free of guilt and punishment on the basis of a righteousness which is outside of us in Christ Jesus, and which through God's grace is reckoned to us and on our own part is received in faith. In sanctification, however, the holiness of Christ is most certainly poured out in us through the Holy Spirit. When Roman Catholicism therefore speaks of a grace which is poured into us, we have no objection to that in itself; we object only to the fact that this grace is regarded as a part of the righteousness on the basis of which we are declared free before God. For, if that were so, then justification and sanctification, the deliverance from guilt and the removal of the pollution, would be confused with each other; and then Christ would be robbed of the perfection of His achieved righteousness and the believing soul of its comfort and assurance. But there is actually such a thing as a grace that is poured in; there is such a thing as a Christ in us as well as a Christ for us; there is such a thing as a renewal after the image of God as well as a transmission to the state of the righteous; there is such a thing as a change in our moral condition as well as in our status before God.

As a matter of fact this sanctification must be maintained with no less resoluteness and power than justification. There have always been those who have regarded the forgiveness of sins as the one great benefit of Christ, and who denied the inner renewal of men after the image of God or, at least, neglected it and left it unexplored. These hold that if a person is justified and is conscious of this in faith, nothing further needs to happen to him. They maintain that the consciousness of the forgiveness of sins already makes him a different person. In short, for such observers, justification and regeneration are two names for one and the same thing.

Now it is altogether true that the Christian who with a true faith believes that all his sins, out of pure grace, and solely because of the merits of Christ, have been forgiven does most certainly by his awareness become a different person. He feels himself acquitted of all guilt; he has, being justified by faith, found peace with God; he stands in the freedom with which Christ has made him free; and, together with David, he can rejoice and say: Blessed is he whose trespass has been forgiven, whose sin is wholly covered; blessed is the man to whom the

Lord has not reckoned his unrighteousness! Such a change can even in a certain sense be called a regeneration, a renewal of consciousness.

But if one goes on to infer from this that justification and regeneration are altogether the same thing, he is in error and is going absolutely counter to the testimony of Holy Scripture. After all, the true, saving faith which accepts the righteousness of Christ and becomes aware of the forgiveness of sins does not come up out of the natural man but is a fruit of regeneration, and therefore already assumes a spiritual change which has taken place through the Holy Spirit. And the hearty joy and peace which the believer enjoys by reason of the assurance of the forgiveness of his sins are attributes of the spiritual man who in communion with Christ has been raised from death in sin.

Moreover, a distinction must be made between the status in which a person stands and the condition in which he finds himself. These two are so far apart that an innocent person is sometimes accused and condemned and a guilty person is sometimes acquitted by the judge. A person's status, therefore, does not yet change his condition, nor vice versa. This holds true in the natural but also in the spiritual sphere. Sin is not merely guilt, but also pollution; we are delivered from the first by justification, from the second by sanctification. Perfect salvation consists not alone of knowledge and righteousness, but also of sanctification and redemption. And therefore Christ gave out both of them: the forgiveness of sins and eternal life.

And, what is conclusive in this regard, Scripture distinguishes justification and regeneration very clearly. The promise of the Old Testament contained the idea that in the new covenant the Lord would forgive the unrighteousness of his people, but it contained the idea also that He would give a new heart upon which He would write His law.[7] He would put His Spirit in them, and cause them to walk in His statutes, and to keep His judgments, to do them (Ezek. 36:27). In order to fulfill that promise Christ not only gave His soul as a ransom for many, but after His exaltation to the right hand of the Father He also sent the Holy Spirit, in order that this Spirit should dwell and work in the church. What His Spirit accomplishes in the church we have previously noted: in and through the Spirit Christ shares Himself and all His benefits with His people.

Accordingly, after Paul in his letter to the Romans has first dealt with the subject of justification he proceeds in Chapter 6 to the subject of sanctification. Just as there were later on, so there were in the days of the apostles certain people who thought that the doctrine of free justification would affect the moral life unfavorably. They feared that

---

7. Jer. 31:33-34; and Ezek. 36:25-26.

people, prompted by such a confession, would proceed to sin in order that good might issue from it and grace be made to abound (Rom. 3:8 and 6:1). Paul refutes this charge and says that it is impossible for those who have died to sin to live in it any longer (Rom. 6:2).

He proves this by pointing out that the believers who by their faith have received the forgiveness of sins and peace with God have also by witness of their baptism been buried with Christ in His death and been raised with Him to a new life (Rom. 6:3-11). For Paul believers are always persons who have not only accepted the righteousness of God in Christ unto the forgiveness of their sins, but also have personally died and been raised in the communion with Christ, and therefore are dead to sin and alive in God.[8] In other words, the death of Christ has justifying power not only but also sanctifying power (2 Cor. 5:13). And the faith which has the true stamp upon it accepts Christ not only as a justification but also as a sanctification: in fact, the one is impossible without the other. For Christ is not to be divided and His benefits are inseparable from His person. He is at the same time our wisdom and our righteousness, our sanctification and our redemption (1 Cor. 1:30). Such He became for us of God and as such He was given us by God.

The sanctification which we must share, therefore, lies perfectly achieved in Christ. There are many Christians who, at least in their practical life, think very differently about this. They acknowledge that they are justified through the righteousness which Christ has accomplished, but they maintain or at least act as though they hold that they must be sanctified by a holiness that they must themselves achieve. If this were true, then we, in flat contradiction of the apostolic testimony,[9] would not be living under grace in freedom but under the bondage of the law. However, the evangelical sanctification is distinguished just as well from the legal one as the righteousness of God revealed in the gospel is distinguished, not in its content but in the mode of sharing it, from that which was demanded by the law. It consists of this: that in Christ God gives us the perfect sanctification along with the justification, and that He gives us this as an internal possession through the regenerating and renewing operation of the Holy Spirit.

Sanctification is therefore God's work, a work of His righteousness and of His grace at the same time. First He reckons Christ and all His benefits to our account, and thereupon He shares Him with us in all the fulness that is in Him. For it is He who circumcises the hearts (Deut. 31:6), who takes away the heart of stone and supplants it with

---

8. Gal. 2:20; 3:27; Col. 2:12.
9. Rom. 6:14; Gal. 4:31; 5:1 and 13.

a heart of flesh (Ezek. 12:19), who pours out His Spirit upon them (Joel 2:28), who creates a new spirit within them (Ezek. 11:19 and 36:26), who writes His law in their hearts, causes them to walk in His ways and makes them His people.[10] The matter is, if possible, put even more strongly in the New Testament where we read that the believers are God's workmanship, created in Christ Jesus (Eph. 2:10), a new creature (2 Cor. 5:17 and Gal. 6:15), and the work of God (Rom. 14:20). There the believers are also called God's husbandry and God's building,[11] and there we are told that all things are of God (2 Cor. 5:18). When they were buried with Christ and raised with Him, they were also washed and sanctified;[12] and they continue to be sanctified in the future,[13] until they have been wholly conformed to the image of the Son.[14] The chain of salvation cannot be broken because from beginning to end it is the work of God. He whom He has known, called, and justified, him He has also glorified (Rom. 8:30).

* * * * *

On the basis of this work of sanctification which God brings about through the Spirit of Christ in the church the believers are frequently designated *saints* in Holy Scripture. Israel was already so called in the old day (Ex. 19:6). Israel was separated from the nations in order to be the Lord's (Lev. 20:26), and in order that it should walk in His ways (Ex. 19:5). And in the future, when God should establish His new covenant, He should with even more right and with a profounder sense call His holy people the redeemed of the Lord.[15] When in the days of the New Testament the High Priest has sanctified Himself for His people, in order that they too should be sanctified in truth (John 17:19), the believers also immediately receive the name of holy ones or saints.[16] This name does not imply that in a moral sense they are free of all sin and above all sin, but rather that the New Testament church has now supplanted the ancient Israel and become the property of the Lord,[17] inasmuch as it has been sanctified in Christ and become a temple of the Holy Spirit.[18]

---

10. Jer. 31:33; 32:38; Ezek. 36:27 and 28.
11. 1 Cor. 3:9; Eph. 2:20; Col. 2:7; 1 Peter 2:5.
12. 1 Cor. 1:2; 6:11; Titus 3:5.
13. John 17:17; 2 Cor. 3:18; 1 Thess. 5:23; Eph. 5:26; Titus 2:14; and Heb. 13:20-21.
14. Rom. 8:28; 1 Cor. 15:49; and Phil. 3:21.
15. Isa. 62:12; Joel 3:17; Obad. 17; Zech. 8:3; and 14:20.
16. Acts 9:13, 32, 41; 26:10; Rom. 1:7; 1 Cor. 1:2 and elsewhere.
17. 2 Cor. 6:16; Gal. 6:16; 1 Peter 2:5.
18. John 17:19; 1 Cor. 1:30; 3:16; 6:11 and 19.

But this sanctification which Christ has given the church and which at the first was given it by the Holy Spirit places a heavy obligation upon the believers. Sanctification is a work of God, but it is intended to be a work in which the believers themselves are also active in the power of God. In the Old Testament we read at one time that the Lord Himself sanctifies His people,[19] and at another time that the people must sanctify themselves.[20] Sometimes we read that the Lord circumcises the heart (Deut. 30:6), and another time that Israel is called upon to circumcise the foreskin of their hearts (Deut. 10:16 and Jer. 4:4). At one point regeneration is called the work of God (Jer. 31:18 and Lam. 5:21), and at another time it is called the responsibility of the person himself (Jer. 3:12-13 and elsewhere). Just so in the New Testament sanctification is also presented as a gift of God in Christ and as a work of the Holy Spirit by which the believers are sanctified.[21] And yet these believers are repeatedly admonished to be perfect even as their Father in Heaven is perfect (Matt. 5:48), to do good works which glorify the Father who is in Heaven (Matt. 5:16 and John 15:8), to yield their members as servants to righteousness unto holiness (Rom. 6:19), to be holy in all their walk and conduct (1 Peter 1:15 and 2 Peter 3:11), to pursue sanctification and to fulfill it in the fear of God,[22] and to do this because without holiness no man shall see the Lord (Heb. 12:14).

The first is by no means incompatible with the second. It were truer to say that the effort of the believers in working towards their own sanctification is made possible only by the fact that it is a work of God which He fulfills in them. Certainly, grace, so far from obliterating nature, restores it. Inasmuch as man because of sin lacked the desire and the ability to walk in the ways of the Lord, he by virtue of the re-creation is again inclined and equipped, at least in principle, to live uprightly not merely in some but in all the commandments of God. When God penetrates the inward parts of the human being with the powerful operation of the regenerating Spirit, He opens the heart that is closed, mellows what is hard, and circumcises what is uncircumcised. He implants new potentialities in the will, and causes the will that was dead to become alive again, the will that was evil to become good, and the will that did not want to obey to choose His ways, and the will that was rebellious to be obedient. He moves and strengthens that will in such a way that as a good tree brings forth good fruits so it can also bring forth good works.

---

19. Ex. 31:13; Lev. 20:8; and 21:8.
20. Lev. 11:44; 20:7; and Num. 11:18.
21. John 17:17-19; 1 Cor. 1:2; and 1 Thess. 5:23.
22. 2 Cor. 7:1; 1 Thess. 3:13; and 4:3.

Consequently, when the Reformed Churches express themselves in this way in their confession (Canons of Dort) they thereby place themselves on the basis of Holy Scripture, and find definite support in the profound statement of the apostle Paul: Work out your own salvation with fear and trembling, *for* it is God who works in you both to will and to do of His good pleasure (Phil. 2:12-13). Just as in the justification the forgiveness of sins, completely prepared in Christ, can on our part only be received and enjoyed through a living and active faith, so God effects the sanctification in us only by means of us ourselves. He does not annihilate our personality, but lifts it up; He does not kill our reason and our will and our desires, but rather quickens them inasmuch as they were dead, and puts them to work. He makes us His allies and co-laborers.

But this sanctification of the believers must then be properly understood. It must not become a legal sanctification, but is and must remain an evangelical sanctification. It does not consist of the fact that the believers proceed to sanctify themselves by means of a holiness which they themselves newly and for the first time bring into being, or of one which exists already but which they by means of their exertion and good works must appropriate. The holiness revealed by God in the gospel is not only completely prepared by Christ but by His Spirit is also applied to our hearts and worked out there. Paul says it so beautifully in Ephesians 2:10: We are His workmanship, created in Christ Jesus unto good works, which God has before ordained that we should walk in them. Just as the first creation was brought into being by the Word, so the re-creation gets its being in the communion with Christ. The believers are crucified, die, are buried, and they are also raised and reborn to a new life in the fellowship with Christ.

And that re-creation has a specific purpose. It has its end in the good works which the believers do. God does not care about the tree but about the fruits, and in those fruits about His own glorification. But those good works are not independently and newly brought into being by the believers themselves. They lie completely prepared for them all and for each one of them individually in the decision of God's counsel; they were fulfilled and were earned for them by Christ who in their stead fulfilled all righteousness and the whole law; and they are worked out in them by the Holy Spirit who takes everything from Christ and distributes it to each and all according to Christ's will. So we can say of sanctification in its entirety and of all the good works of the church, that is, of all the believers together and of each one individually, that they do not come into existence first of all through the believers, but that they exist long before in the good pleasure of the Father, in the work of the Son, and in the application of the Holy Spirit.

Hence all glorying on man's part is also ruled out in this matter of sanctification. We must know that God in no way becomes indebted to us, and that He therefore never has to be grateful to us, when we do good works; on the contrary, we are beholden to God for them, and have to be grateful to Him for the good works that we do.

* * * * *

From this there follows also the significance of faith in the work of sanctification. It is by no means in justification only, but quite as much in sanctification, that by faith exclusively we are saved. For we on our part can accept Christ and His benefits and make them our own only through faith. If righteousness and holiness were products of the law we should have to bring both of them about by the doing of good works. But in the gospel they are a gift of God granted us in the person of Christ; in Him there is a fulness of grace and truth (John 1:17), of wisdom and knowledge (Col. 2:3), of righteousness and holiness (1 Cor. 1:30). In Him all spiritual blessings are contained (Eph. 1:3), and the fulness of the godhead dwells bodily (Col. 2:9). This Christ gives Himself to us through the Holy Spirit, and joins Himself with us so intimately as does the vine with the branches (John 15:2ff.), as the head with the body (Eph. 1:22-23), as the husband with the wife (Eph. 5:32), and as He Himself as Mediator is conjoined with the Father (John 14:20 and 17:21-23). The believers are one spirit with Him (1 Cor. 6:17), and one flesh (Eph. 5:30-31). Christ lives in them and they in Christ (Gal. 2:20). Christ is all in them all (Col. 3:11).

If Christ is in this way the workman of our sanctification, then on our own part the work of sanctification can be fulfilled only by faith. For sanctification is, like all the other benefits of Christ, so inseparably related to the person of Christ that we cannot receive it except in communion with Christ Himself; and this is, viewed from our side, only to be obtained and enjoyed through a true faith. After all, it is only through faith that Christ dwells in our hearts (Eph. 3:17), and that we live in Christ (Gal. 2:20). It is only through faith that we become children of God (Gal. 3:27), that we receive the promise of the Spirit (Gal. 3:14), that we receive the forgiveness of sins (Rom. 4:6) and eternal life (John 3:16). To live by faith: that is simply the opposite side of saying that Christ dwells in us (2 Cor. 13:5 and Gal. 2:20). The whole life of Christ is thus a life of faith just as the Bible saints are presented to us in Hebrews 11 as the heroes of faith, so we too are admonished to live by faith (2 Cor. 5:7), to let faith work by love (Gal. 5:6), with the shield of faith to quench the fiery darts of the wicked (Eph. 6:16), and to overcome the world (1 John 5:4). And all these admonishments correspond fully with those others which make it obligatory for the believers not to walk according to the flesh but according to the Spirit (Rom. 8:4ff.), to put aside the old man and to put on the new man,[23] to accept the Lord Jesus Christ and to walk in Him (Col. 2:6 and 1 Peter 3:16), to put on the Lord Jesus Christ and to fulfill all things in His name (Rom. 13:14 and Col. 3:17), to become mighty in the Lord and in the strength of His might (Eph. 6:10 and 2 Tim. 2:1), and to grow in the grace and knowledge of our Lord and Savior (2 Peter 3:18). In short, the sanctification in an evangelical sense is a continuous activity and exercise of faith.

Many people have objections to this teaching of Scripture. They regard it as one-sided and as being dangerous for the moral life. Sometimes they are willing to concede that in justification the law is out of the question and faith alone is determinative. But when they discuss sanctification, they maintain that faith alone is adequate, and that the law with all that it commands and all that it forbids, with all its rewards and penalties, must also come into play if a holy walk is to be fruitfully pursued and if there is to be an incentive to good works. And even though it is altogether true that the law remains the rule of life for the Christian, still the gospel never derives the exhortations to a holy war from the terrors of the law, but derives them rather from the high calling to which the believers in Christ are called. Be perfect even as your Father in Heaven is perfect (Matt. 5:48). Jesus is the vine, the disciples are His branches; they who remain in Him bear much fruit, for without Him they can do nothing (John 15:5). Together with Christ the believers have died to sin, but in Him they have become alive unto God (Rom. 6:11). They are not under the law, but under grace, and therefore sin may not reign over them (Rom. 6:14). They have through the law died to the law and belong to Christ, in order that they may live unto God (Rom. 7:4 and Gal. 2:19). They are not in the flesh but in the Spirit, and must therefore walk after the Spirit (Rom. 8:5). The night has passed by, the day has come; the works of darkness must therefore be cast off and the armor of light must be put on (Rom. 13:12). The bodies of the believers are members of Christ and temples of the Holy Spirit; hence they must flee the sin of adultery (1 Cor. 6:15ff.). They are bought with a price, and therefore they must glorify God in their body and in their spirit, for these are God's (1 Cor. 6:20). They stand in freedom, the freedom with which Christ has made them free, and in that Christ nothing avails anything but faith working by love (Gal. 5:1, 6). From that Christ they have heard and from Him they have learned that

---

23. Eph. 4:22-24; Col. 3:10; and Rom. 6:4ff.

they must cast off the old man and put on the new man created after God in true righteousness and holiness (Eph. 4:21ff.). As dear children they must be followers of God (Eph. 5:6). They must walk in love even as Christ has loved them (Eph. 5:2). They are light in the Lord, and accordingly must walk as the children of light (Eph. 5:8).

In short, we should have to record all the moral exhortations in the New Testament if we were fully to summarize all the imperatives set forth to encourage the believers to a holy walk. But the passages cited are sufficient to indicate that they are all derived from the gospel and not from the law. Irrespective of whether the apostles are addressing themselves to men or to women, to parents or to children, to masters or to servants, to women or to maids, to rulers or to subjects, they exhort them all *in the Lord*.[24] The sure foundation of God stands firm and bears this seal: Let every one who names the name of Christ depart from iniquity (2 Tim. 2:19).

*   *   *   *   *

Faith, then, is the one great work which the Christian must fulfill in his sanctification according to the principles of the gospel (John 6:29). Although this faith presents itself in a different way and is viewed from a different vantage point in the sanctification than it is in the justification, it is in both of these benefits the only and sufficient means by which we come to share in them. The gospel demands nothing other from us than faith, than the reliance of the heart upon God's grace in Christ. That faith justifies us not only, but also sanctifies and saves us. And the sanctifying power of the faith comes into fine clarity in the following considerations.

In the first place, it must be remarked that the true, unfeigned faith breaks off our false self-confidence, knocks our pride off its pedestal, and makes an end of all self-righteousness. If we leave those out of consideration who do not trouble themselves about God or His commandments, and who consume sin as they do water, and if we leave out of consideration also all those who do the good only externally out of fear of punishment, of loss, or of shame, there still remain those who earnestly strive to fulfill the demands of the moral law in their own strength. But in doing this they can never find the right vantage point to take over against that moral law, nor the genuine principle by which they are to fulfill it. They take position either above or below the law and make themselves serviceable to it or it serviceable to them. In the first instance they say that the good must be done for the benefit and profit that

---

24. Eph. 5:22ff.; 6:1ff.; Col. 3:18ff.; 1 Peter 2:13ff.; 3:1ff.

accrues to the individual or to the group because of it. In the second instance they put the moral law high above man consequently, and so make its fulfillment, inasmuch as it is regarded the more seriously, so much more impossible. Thus the natural man vacillates between Sadduceeism and Pharisaism, between freedom and authority. He cannot find the balance between the demand of the moral law and the will of man.

But faith puts an end to this vacillation. It enables us to see that the moral law stands high above us and that it demands unconditional obedience, and that it nevertheless cannot actually be fulfilled and cannot give us eternal life. And in this apparently irreconcilable opposition it surrenders itself to the grace of God, trusts His mercy, and glories in the righteousness which He Himself has brought. The true believer gives up all pretension of being able to do according to the demands of the moral law. He lets that moral ideal stand in all its sublime requirement, but at the same time gives up the hope that he can ever by his own exertion do justice to it. And thus he fixes his hope on God who in the law, but afterwards also in the gospel, has revealed His righteousness. Such a faith is, consequently, immediately the mother of many virtues: it fosters humility in man, and it fosters dependence and trust, attributes, all of them, of the greatest significance for the moral life. And thus the doing of the good gets from religion a sure foundation and an unconquerable strength.

Still other virtues go combined with these. According to the order which God Himself has appointed in the church, the promises of the gospel precede the commandments of the law. First He assures us of His favor, of the forgiveness of our sins and of our inheritance with the saints, and thereupon He leads us in the way of His testimonies and ordinances. The good tree comes before the good fruits. We do not live through good works but for them; we fulfill the law not for eternal life but out of it, for this life has been planted in our hearts through faith. It is according to this order alone that a true moral life is possible. Whoever wants to change this order about, and wants to draw his comfort, certainty, and salvation from his works, will never achieve his purpose, will be constantly torn by doubts, and will live in fear all the days of his life. God takes another way. In the gospel He gives us everything for nothing: the forgiveness of sins; the reconciliation; the annihilation of punishment; the salvation and the blessedness. He tells us that through faith in His grace we can altogether lean upon Him, and He gives us the certainty of this through the testimony of the Holy Spirit. Faith, accordingly, by virtue of its own nature, brings us comfort, peace, joy, and happiness, and these are in turn of invaluable worth for the moral life. They are all together principles and motives of a holy conduct. The purging of the conscience of all dead works has as its end and goal the services of the living God (Heb. 9:14). Those who are comforted of God are thereupon strengthened by Him in every good word and work (2 Thess. 2:17). The joy of the Lord is the strength of His people (Neh. 8:10).

In the next place, it should be pointed out that a severing as well as an appropriating activity, a destructive as well as a constructive effort is common to the saving faith which leans entirely upon God's grace in Christ. It causes the prodigal son to return from his sinful life to the father's house. It puts us into the fellowship of Christ's death and of His resurrection; it crucifies us and raises us up to a new life. Whoever truly believes in Christ dies to sin; he feels heartily sorry for it, because he has drawn down the wrath of God by it, and therefore he begins to hate and to flee it. He brings about a separation between it and himself so that he can say uprightly: I want to do the good although I do not do it and I do not want to do the evil, although I do do it (Rom. 7:19). And on the other hand faith appropriates Christ and His righteousness; it causes Christ Himself to dwell in the heart and constantly lives more fully in His communion. It causes Christ to take form in us and transforms us more and more according to His image. In short, the believer can repeat Paul's statement: I can do all things through Christ who strengthens me (Phil. 4:13).

Finally, to mention nothing further, faith is often compared, and properly so, with a hand. But a hand is not only the organ with which to take something and to make it our own: it is also the instrument by which we objectify our thought and our will. Thus faith is not only a receiving organ, but also an active force. The faith which justifies and saves is not a dead faith, but a living one. In its own nature it brings forth fruits of good works; it works by love (Gal. 5:6). Man is not justified by love, but the faith which justifies him proves his living active power in love. Without love faith is not the true saving faith (1 Cor. 13:1); and the work of love is always associated with the true faith (1 Thess. 1:3), for the end of the law (that is, of the whole apostolical preaching) is love, out of a pure heart and of a good conscience, and of faith unfeigned (1 Tim. 1:5). And this love, as the fruit of faith, is a perfect love which casts out fear (1 John 4:18), and it is at the same time the perfect fulfillment of the law.[25]

Accordingly, the gospel does not make the law of no effect, but restores and establishes it. It is true that an end has been made of the demand and curse of the law, because Christ has placed Himself under the law, satisfied its demand, and borne its curse.[26] Hence we are no

---

25. Matt. 22:37-40; Rom. 13:8-10; Gal. 5:14; and James 2:8.
26. Matt. 3:15; Gal. 3:13; and 4:4.

longer a servant but walk in liberty and in the spirit.[27] And where the Spirit of the Lord is, there is freedom (2 Cor. 3:17 and Gal. 5:18). But this freedom of faith does not remove the law, but rather brings it to fulfillment; the righteousness of the law, that which the law asks in its commandments, is fulfilled precisely in those who do not walk according to the flesh but according to the Spirit (Rom. 8:4). While the flesh makes the law of no effect because it does not want to and cannot subject itself to the law (Rom. 8:3, 7), it is precisely the Spirit of Christ which gives men life (2 Cor. 3:6), and it is the Spirit which gives light in order to prove what is the good and acceptable will of God.[28]

And for Jesus and for the apostles that will of God, despite the fact that the law has in the sense designated above been discarded, continues to be known from the Old Testament. Jesus did not come to destroy the law and the prophets, but to fulfill them (Matt. 5:17). He never so much as mentions the abandonment of the law except in so far as He prophecies the fall of the city and the temple, and the whole of the civic regime and the public worship (Matt. 24 and John 4:21-24), but He does purge it of the human doctrines which have been added to it by the Jewish schools (Matt. 5:20ff.). In His conception of the law He returns from the Pharisees back to the prophets, penetrates through to the inner character of that law, and places the internal high above the external characteristics (Mark 7:15), mercy above sacrifice (Matt. 9 and 12:7), and joins prophets and law together in love over against God and the neighbor.[29] The moral laws retain their force.

All the apostles take the same attitude towards the law and the prophets. The Old Testament retains for them the divine authority. It has been given by God (2 Tim. 3:15), has been written by holy men under the leading of the Spirit of God (2 Peter 1:21), and has been given for our instruction and comfort.[30] Hence again and again that Old Testament is quoted in order to cause the Christian church to know the will of God: Paul, for example, appeals in 1 Corinthians 14:34, to indicate the subordination of the wife to the husband, to Genesis 3:16; in 2 Corinthians 9:9, in order to urge liberality to the poor, to Psalm 112:9; and in 1 Corinthians 1:31, for the admonition to glory only in the Lord, to Isaiah 9:23. In other words, the moral law is, so far as its content is concerned, quite the same in the Old and the New Testament. It is contained in the one law of love.[31] True,

---

27. Rom. 7:1-6; Gal. 4:5, 26ff.; and 5:1.
28. Rom. 12:2; Eph. 5:10; and Phil. 1:10.
29. Mark 12:28-34; compare Matt. 7:12.
30. Rom. 15:4; 1 Cor. 10:11; 2 Tim. 3:15; 1 Peter 1:12.
31. Rom. 13:8-10; Gal. 5:14; and James 2:8.

Christ speaks of the love which the disciples must exercise among one another as of a new commandment.[32] But by this He does not mean that the commandment to love one another as believers was quite unknown before, for Leviticus 19:18 plainly teaches the opposite and Psalm 133 speaks of the loveliness of the living together in community of the brethren.

But this love which must bind the believers mutually together took on a new character in the New Testament. Because in the days of the Old Testament the church and the nation coincided, the difference between the love of the brethren and the love of the neighbor could not yet clearly be distinguished. But in the New Testament this changed: the church was severed from the national history of Israel and became an independent community. In the Holy Spirit it received its own principle of life. Now a distinction began to be made between the love of the brother and the love of all.[33] To this extent brotherly love can be called a new commandment; it binds the believers together in their difference from the world. But, for the rest, there is a single religion and a single moral law in the Old and in the New Testament. There is some clarification, it is true, and there is also a different development and application, but no external addition or mechanical amplification takes place. Christ was not a new law-giver alongside of and above Moses, but He Himself in His own life and death fulfilled the law and by His spirit He brings it to fulfillment in all those who are His disciples.

* * * * *

Although Christ and His apostles regularly relate the moral law of the Old Testament to the love of God and the neighbor, there gradually grew up in the Christian moral teaching the habit of explaining the virtues and the duties of man in explication of the Ten Commandments. This way of doing was especially a favorite with the Reformers, because they saw one of the earmarks of good works to be this, namely, that they take place according to the will of God. In so doing they took position against the Roman Catholic Church which reckoned among the good works also those actions which are based on human ordinances and laws (compare the Heidelberg Catechism, Answer 91).

Rome makes a distinction between commandments and advices, and holds that these advices were added to the law of Moses by Christ as a new and higher law-giver. In its earliest period the Christian

---

32. John 3:34; compare 15:12; 1 Thess. 4:9; 1 Peter 4:8; 1 John 3:23; 4:21; 2 John 5.
33. Gal. 6:10; 1 Thess. 3:12; and 2 Peter 1:7.

Church did not yet know this distinction; but when the period of persecution passed for the church and all kinds of people joined themselves to her, people who joined the church solely for prestige and distinction, then the moral level fell off and many seriously disposed persons withdrew into solitude. The monasticism which thus put in its appearance tried to cling to the moral idea, but it did this in a way which could not be followed by the ordinary Christians, living as they were in family and vocation. Thus there gradually came to be a distinction between the religious or clerical and the lay people, and so a higher and a lower morality came to be discriminated, a difference between commandments and advices. In other words, the commandments, contained in the ten statements were binding for all Christians, but the advices were left to the optional choice of people. Among these additions there were soon reckoned the so-called chastity, or the celibate state, on the basis of Matthew 19:11-12 and 1 Corinthians 7:7 ff.; poverty, or the disposition of all earthly possessions, in appeal to Matthew 19:21 and 1 Cor. inthians 9:14; and the absolute obedience to the superior under whose directions one places himself, in reference to Matthew 16:24 and Luke 14:26-27. But in the monastic orders these are often supplemented by all kinds of abstinences, mortifications, chastisements, all in appeal to Matthew 5:29, 39, and 42. It is true that in doing this, Rome wants to maintain that the ideal of moral perfection is the same for all believers and must be pursued by them all in the way of obedience to the commandments. But whoever adds the advices to the commandments follows a faster and a safer way to the achievement of the purpose, and also attains a greater worth and a richer reward. While the ordinary believer, who fulfills the law, remains an unprofitable servant, who has done only what was demanded of him (Luke 17:10), the other Christian, who has also followed up the advices, hears himself addressed as the good and faithful servant who has been faithful over little and is being appointed ruler over many things (Matt. 25:21).

It is natural enough that the Reformation could not endorse this distinction. Deeply convinced of the depravity of human nature, it taught that the regenerate too could not keep the law perfectly, that their best works were still tainted with sin, and that even the most saintly could achieve nothing more than a small beginning of the perfect obedience (Heidelberg Catechism, Answers 62 and 114). The believer, in other words, could never arrive at the point of achieving the advices, simply because he had more than enough to do in fulfilling the commandments themselves. Anyhow, God requires in the moral law that we love Him with all our mind, and with all our strength, and our neighbor as ourselves (Matt. 22:37 and Luke 10:27). How, then, can anything further be added to such a commandment? If God demands us in our entirety in all times and in all places for His service, then nothing remains which represents an option that we can either take or ignore, and which we can according to our free choice either give Him or withhold.

There is consequently no basis for the claim that Christ added anything as a sort of law of freedom to the required commandments of the Mosaic law. For although there are instances in which a person must refrain from marrying, must dispose of his property, must withdraw from his ordinary environment and vocation, no special option comes to him which he can follow up or neglect. Rather, the one and the same law demands in terms of the nature of the circumstances a particular application and constitutes this application a duty. The rich young man did not receive an option from Christ which he could reject as well as accept, but he received, as a touchstone of the integrity and resoluteness of his heart, the commandment to sell all that he had and to give it to the poor. From this it would be manifest whether or not he was totally committed to Christ and His kingdom. We must distinguish therefore between law and duty: the law is one and the same for all, but duty is the particular way in which the general moral law must be applied by each individual in accordance with his nature and circumstances.

The Reformers accordingly rejected all works which depended upon the determinations of men or upon the prescriptions of the church, and returned to the will of God as the norm of good works. That will, they found briefly and substantially expressed in the ten commandments. But the law of the ten commandments does not stand loosely and independently by itself; it finds itself, rather, in the middle of a rich environment. In its material content it originally was written on the heart of man created as he was by God Himself. It is partially still preserved there inasmuch as people continue to do naturally the things of the law, and so prove that the works of the law are written in their hearts (Rom. 2:14-15). Every human being has the awareness that in his existence and in his conduct he is bound to certain definite moral laws, and he feels that when he transgresses these his conscience accuses him. In Israel that law was restored by way of a particular revelation to its original purity, was made serviceable to the covenant of grace which, according to its introductory words, God had set up with His people, and was taken up in a body of rights and ordinances which had to govern the whole life of the people. Besides, this law was explained, developed, and applied throughout the history of Israel by the psalmists, proverb writers, and prophets, so that Jesus could say that the whole law and the prophets hung on the two commandments of love towards God and the neighbor (Matt. 22:40).

Accordingly, when Christ brings on the fulfillment of the Old Testament promises of salvation, He does not discard the law, but fulfills all its righteousness; by His perfect obedience He paves the way and in the Holy Spirit grants the power by which His disciples can and will walk, in principle, according to the commandments of the law. In fact, we can say that the whole bearing of the gospel is that the righteousness of the law is fulfilled in those who do not walk according to the flesh but according to the Spirit. The spiritual life of regeneration is made serviceable to the restoration of the moral life. The long series of admonishments with which the apostles as a general rule conclude their epistles are an amplification and application of the holy law of the Lord, and they are intended to help the believers to live in all their relationships and circumstances according to the will of God and the glorification of His name. The law of the ten commandments may not be separated from this rich context of affairs. Indeed, the decalogue must be viewed and explained in the light of the whole revelation of God in nature and in Scripture.

Understood in this way, the Ten Commandments are a brief summary of the Christian ethic and an unsurpassed rule for our life. There are also many other laws to which we are bound. God also laid down the laws for our thinking, for our appreciation of the beautiful, for our social life, for our study and use of nature. He laid down laws for all His creatures, for heaven and earth, for sun and moon and stars, for day and night, for summer and winter, for seed time and harvest.[34] But the moral law far outrivals these ordinances, for in distinction from them all, the moral law directs itself to the will of man, or rather to man himself as a willing being, and thus to the innermost essence of his existence, to the core of his personality. And the moral law lays down the demand that it be kept not merely in words and deeds but quite as well in thoughts and desires; the law is spiritual (Rom. 7:14); we must be perfect even as our Father who is in heaven is perfect (Matt. 5:48); and in the tenth commandment the law burrows through to the root of sin, to covetousness or desire, and constitutes this also guilty and impure before the face of God.

Besides, this law governs all the relationships in which man finds himself, whether to God, whether to his fellow man, to himself, or to the whole of nature. It governs his relationship to his fellow human beings in their various ranks and gradations, in their life, their vocations, and their property. It governs his relationship to the truth of his reason and to the integrity of his heart. And in all this it governs his relationship to the whole nature which is his environment, to his office and

---

34. Gen. 8:22; Jer. 31:35; and 33:25.

his calling, to his work and recreation, to the whole of animate and inanimate nature. And in this innermost core of his being as well as in
these rich relationships the moral law requires of man that in everything he does he shall do it to the glory of God (1 Cor. 10:31 and Col.
3:17).

When we first sense the law in this deep, spiritual sense, we are
appalled and despair of fulfilling it. If we knew of no other righteousness than that which the law requires of us, we should not be in a position to fulfill it and would not even have the desire to do so. We should
then be trying always to rob the law of its spiritual content, to external-
ize it, to suit it to our fallen condition, and would deceive ourselves
into believing that we could by a respectable civic life satisfy its high
demands. The natural man is offended by the spiritual significance of
the law, that is, by its perfection; internally he resists the absolute righteousness and holiness which it demands. But the moment we have
learned to know that other righteousness and holiness which God has
given in Christ and which through faith He makes our own, our attitude towards the law and our sense of its significance changes entirely.
True, we may still complain as Paul does that we are still carnally sold
under sin, but even so we let the law stand in its exalted sublimity, and
make no effort to pull it down off its high pedestal. We continue to
honor it as holy and righteous and good, for it is the law of God. We
love it precisely because it is so spiritual in character. We delight in
it according to the inner man. And we thank God not for the gospel
only but also for His law, for His holy, righteous, perfect law. That
law too becomes to us a revelation and a gift of His grace. How love I
Thy law; it is my meditation all the day!

* * * * *

Although the believers receive immediately in regeneration an inner
desire and love, and thus want to live according to the will of God in
all good works, they are not immediately perfect and, as a matter of
fact, do not achieve this perfection in this life. Sanctification is to be
distinguished from justification. Justification consists of a divine
acquittal which is at once completed. True, it is repeatedly applied to
the conscience, but it is not developed and increased. But the life of
sanctification is, like all the life of the creature, bound to the law of
development. It has its point of origin in regeneration, it requires
nourishment in order to grow strong, and it reaches its apex only when
it will be fully revealed with Christ.

In the Old Testament it was already said of the Messiah that He
would feed His flock like a shepherd; He would gather the lambs with

His arm and carry them in His bosom, and would gently lead those
that were with young (Isa. 41:11). And elsewhere we are told even
more fully concerning Him that the Lord has anointed Him to preach
good tidings to the meek, to bind up the brokenhearted, to proclaim
liberty to the captives, to comfort those that mourn in Zion, to give
them the garment of praise for the spirit of heaviness, beauty for ashes,
in order that they be called trees of righteousness, the planting of the
Lord, in order that He may be glorified (Isa. 61:1-3; compare Ezek.
34:16).

Hence Christ during the period of His ministry on earth does not
direct Himself only to the mature in Israel, but He comes also to the
children and ascribes the kingdom of heaven to them (Matt. 18:1-6
and 19:13-14). He calls not only the inhabitants of Chorazin and
Bethsaida, of Capernaum and Jerusalem, to repentance but also the
publicans and sinners, and He invites all those who labor and are heavy
laden in order to give them rest. He calls the heirs of the kingdom by
various names, speaking of them as those who are poor and those who
mourn, as those who hunger and those who thirst, as those who are
meek and those who are peaceful (Matt. 5:3-9), and He distinguishes
between those who are lesser and those who are greater, those who are
first and those who are last in the kingdom (Matt. 11:11; and 20:16).
He often complains about the smallness of the faith, the timidity and the
obtuseness of His disciples.[35] He rejoices when He finds great faith in
some (Matt. 8:10 and 15:28). And over against all He proves Himself
to be the good Shepherd who gathers all His sheep together into one
flock, who gives them all life and abundance, who preserves them all and
sees to it that none of them is lost (John 10:1-30).

Similar distinctions are made among the believers of the apostolic
churches. The believers of the Old Testament were still minors who
were placed under wards and guardians and to this extent did not yet
differ from servants (Gal. 4:1-2). Compared with these, the believers
of the New Testament are free sons and daughters, accepted by God
as His children and heirs, and standing in the freedom with which
Christ has made them free (Gal. 4:4-7). Nevertheless all kinds of differences still distinguish them. True, the faith which is given to the
members of the church is the same in all, but it is nevertheless given to
each in accordance with his nature and in a particular measure (Rom.
12:3); the gifts which the Holy Spirit distributes in the church are
differing gifts (Rom. 12:6-8 and 1 Cor. 12:4-11); the place which each
member of the church occupies is as different from that of other members as is true of the members of the body (Rom. 12:4-5 and 1 Cor.

35. Matt. 6:30; 8:26; 14:31; 16:8; and Luke 24:25.

12:12ff.). But, quite apart from this difference of gift and function, there is among the believers also a difference between the strong and the weak,[36] between children who still require milk (1 Cor. 3:2 and 5:12) and the perfect, the mature, who can tolerate meat and who by the exercise of discrimination have the ability to distinguish between good and evil.[37] Further, there is a difference among the believers between the young men, who have indeed overcome the wicked one but must nevertheless be careful lest they lose this victory, and the fathers who have had long experience in the struggle and have received a deeper insight into the knowledge of Him, namely, Christ, who was from the beginning (1 John 2:12-14). In addition to this, a distinction was made in the apostolic period between churches or believers who were steadfast in the faith, abundant in love, patient in suffering, and those others who allowed themselves to be misled by all kinds of error and succumbed to all kinds of sins. The letters of the apostles and particularly that of Christ to the seven churches in Asia Minor (Rev. 1-3) give us detailed descriptions of these varying circumstances.

All this teaches that man is in his spiritual as well as his natural life born as a small and weak and needy creature, and that he must gradually grow in the grace and knowledge of our Lord and Savior Jesus Christ (2 Peter 3:18). If the spiritual life develops healthily and normally, if it feeds on spiritual nourishment and drinks of the spiritual drink which is Christ (John 6:48 ff. and 1 Cor. 10:3-4), a continuous growing in grace, an establishment in it, and a progressive renewal according to the image of Christ takes place.[38] But all kinds of obstacles interpose themselves on the way of this normal development. The life of the Christian is not a quiet growth, but a continuous struggle, a struggle against enemies without, and no less a struggle against the enemy who dwells within our own bosoms.

In order to understand the nature of this struggle properly, we ought first to note that in the unregenerate also there is often a struggle present. But this is not a spiritual struggle. It is a rational struggle, a conflict between the human reason and conscience, on the one hand, and his will and desire on the other. By his reason and conscience man still remains bound to the moral law, to the world of invisible and eternal things. In his heart he still hears the imperative: Thou shalt. The moment he wants to do the evil, his better judgment offers resistance, warns him and tries to impede him. There is not a single human being who has strayed off so far or sunk so deep that he does not know something of the duality of this tension in his being. And

36. Rom. 14:1ff.; 15:1; 1 Cor. 8:7ff.; 9:22; and 10:25.
37. 1 Cor. 2:6; 3:2; 14:20; Phil. 3:15; Heb. 5:14.
38. Rom. 12:2; 2 Cor. 3:18; 4:16; Eph. 3:16; and 1 Peter 5:10.

man can under favorable circumstances sometimes be the victor in this struggle. He can counter his appetites and desires by his reason, can suppress them, and silence them; if he does, he becomes a brave, virtuous human being and he lives an honorable life. But that is not yet the true morality; it is not the Christian sanctification. For the struggle in the natural man is constantly the struggle between reason and passion, duty and desire, conscience and appetite. The battle is not waged against all of the sins, but only against some of them, and for the most part only against certain external and publicly offensive sins. The struggle is not waged against sin as sin because it elicits the wrath of God, but against certain particular sins which stand high in the world's estimate of evils, and which go accompanied by loss or shame. And the human being may on a favorable occasion restrain the evil inclination and harness it, but he cannot root it out and he can bring no internal change to pass inside his heart.

The spiritual struggle which the believers must conduct inside their souls has a very different character. It is not a struggle between reason and passion, but between the flesh and the spirit, between the old and the new man, between the sin which continues to dwell in the believers and the spiritual principle of life which has been planted in their hearts.[39] These two forces are not spatially separated, as though one part of him — the reason, for example — were regenerated, and another part of him — the heart, for example — were not. Rather, these two forces spread themselves out over the whole man and over all his powers and abilities, so that either one of them can be called a man — the one the old, and the other the new one.

It is thus that Paul usually gives expression to the distinction, but in Romans 7 he makes use of other names. There he designates the new, spiritual man as the will that loves the good and wants to do it, as the inward man who delights in the law of God. And he calls the old man the flesh, the sin that dwells in him, the law in his members which wars against the law of his spirit and takes him captive under the law of sin which is in his members. This constitutes a difference in statement, but it is the same matter. In Paul the flesh is often the name used to designate the sinful which continues in the believer and which very certainly continues to dwell in the inner man, in his soul and heart and spirit. The works of the flesh, after all, are not only adultery, fornication, and the like, but also idolatry, hatred, variance, wrath, and the like (Gal. 5:19-20). And when he thinks of the inward man, the apostle thinks not of something which lies deep inside the human being only, which continues hidden there and which never in any

---

39. Rom. 6:6; 7:14-26; 8:4-9; Gal. 5:17-26; Eph. 4:22-24; and Col. 3:9-10.

way comes to external expression, for he plainly states that the believers walk after the spirit and constitute their members weapons of righteousness. But he calls the new man the inward man in this connection because in the fearful struggle against the flesh this man so often lies deeply imbedded and so rarely reveals himself.

The struggle between the two forces consists of this, that the spirit of Christ who dwells in the believers tries to arouse all kinds of good thoughts, deliberations, inclinations and drives (such as love, joy, peace, and the like: Gal. 5:22) in their mind, heart, and will, and that the flesh on the contrary thereupon raises its voice and tries to defile the whole man with its evil lusts and desires (Gal. 5:19-20). And in this struggle the flesh appears so mighty again and again that the believers do not do, in the way and in the measure they intended, the thing they wanted to do (Gal. 5:17). When they want to do the good, evil is present with them (Rom. 7:21). The spirit, indeed, is willing, but the flesh is weak (Matt. 26:41).

The conflict, in other words, is not between reason and will, between duty and desire, but is quite differently between willing and doing, between the inner disposition and the sinful act which interposes itself and stands in its way, between the inward man of the heart recreated to God in true righteousness and holiness, and the old man who, though having lost the position of centrality, nevertheless wants to maintain himself, and who fights the harder in proportion to the extent that he loses more and more ground. This is not a battle between two faculties or two parts of man as it would be if it were conducted by the head against the heart, the reason against the passions, or the soul against the body. Rather, these two forces stand, armed and militant, over against each other battling for the whole of the human person. In one and the same reason of one and the same person there is a battle going on between faith and unbelief, between truth and falsehood; in one and the same heart there is an opposition between pure drives and desires and impure ones; in one and the same will an evil lust opposes a good one and an evil disposition takes issue with a pure one. The struggle is in very fact a struggle between two beings in one and the same being.

Psychologically this can be explained in such a way that in the field of consciousness two groups of ideas have taken position over against each other, and in the field of the heart and desires two series of passions oppose each other. True, we speak of an old and a new man in the believer, and so we give expression to the fact that in the new life the whole man has in principle been changed, and that nevertheless the power of sin continues to dwell in all his faculties and members. But actually what it is is that there are two groups of interests, ideas, inclinations, and the like, which do battle against each other and of which neither the one nor the other has been able to gain the full control of any single human faculty. If the truth of God had completely taken over and conquered the consciousness of the believer, there would naturally be no room left for error and falsehood; and if the love of God had wholly filled the heart, there would be no room for hatred, envy, wrath and the like. But that, as every one knows from his experience, is not the case; and Scripture testifies that we cannot look forward to such a perfect condition in this life. The struggle will remain until the end because the faith, the hope, the love, and all the Christian virtues will never be perfected in this life and therefore room remains in our soul for unbelief, doubt, discouragement, fear, and the like.

In every deliberation and deed of the believer, consequently, the good and the evil lie, as it were, mingled through each other. The measure and the degree to which both are present in any particular thought or deed differ greatly, of course, but nevertheless there is something of the old and something of the new man in all our actions and thoughts. All our ideas, words, and deeds are consequently tainted by sin; they require reconciliation and purging. All the same, they may be called good works to the extent that they are mingled with the faith. For all these reasons we must be on guard against Antinomianism, for this heresy separates the old from the new man and sets them over against each other in spatial distinction in a way somewhat like that which distinguishes the spirit from matter, and the soul from the body.

The result of this kind of erroneous thinking is the harmful doctrine that the sinful thoughts and deeds are to be reckoned to the account of the old man and have nothing to do with the new man. Scripture and experience both, on the contrary, teach that the believer is not an external combination of two beings, but that he remains one being, a single self, a single consciousness, heart, and will, and that no two independent beings but rather two groups of desires and dispositions are conflicting inside one and the same person.

* * * * *

The seriousness of this struggle already intimates that it will be a long time before the new man achieves the victory. Nevertheless many Christians have the idea that believers achieve perfection already upon the earth, and can here and now subdue every sinful deed and inclination. The Pelagians had taught this long ago. In the Council of Trent, Rome took a similar position, and many a Protestant group assumes it also. People tend to appeal to the fact that Holy Scriptures frequently use such glorious words to describe the Christian's condition, for example, 1 Peter 2:9-10 and 2 Peter 1:4 and 1 John 2:20. They point out that Paul, after his conversion, is fully assured of his salvation, and that he remembers the sinful past only as a memory and nothing else, and that the admonishments to the saints to be blameless in their conduct are absolute in their demands (Matt. 5:48), that these admonishments assume the possibility of achieving perfection,[40] and that the grace of God which can be obtained by prayer can avail all things.[41] Accordingly, these people argue that it were doing injustice to the riches of God's love if one regarded the moral perfection of the believer in this life unattainable, and one would at the same time be removing from the believers a strong incentive by the exertion of all their power to strive after such perfection.

Now there is in very fact no doubt about it that the Holy Scriptures speak of the privilege and the status of the people of God in the most arresting way. They refer to the Israel of the Old Testament as a priestly kingdom which God has chosen out of all the nations of the earth as His own, as an object of His love, as His portion and His honor, His son and His servant, His bride whom He adorned and perfected by the glory which He laid upon her.[42] And the believers in the New Testament are called the salt of the earth (Matt. 5:13), the light of the world (Matt. 5:14), the children of God who are born of God and accepted by Him (John 1:13 and Gal. 4:5), elect, called, holy, and sanctified (1 Cor. 1:2), a chosen generation and royal priesthood (1 Peter 2:9-10), partakers of the Divine nature (2 Peter 1:4), anointed with the Holy Spirit (1 John 2:20), made to be kings and priests by Christ Himself (Rev. 1:5), and heirs of God and joint heirs with Christ (Rom. 8:17). That which eye hath not seen, nor ear heard, neither have entered into the heart of man, the things which God hath prepared for them that love Him, *that* God has prepared for His own now in the days of the New Testament (1 Cor. 2:9). Whoever rejects the teaching of Scripture concerning sin and grace can only see gross exaggeration in all this. A radical change, such as takes place in justification and regeneration, is then neither necessary nor possible. But for Scripture, the change which the human being undergoes in faith and conversion is a change from darkness to light, from death to life, from bondage to liberty, from falsehood to truth, from sin to righteousness, from the expectation of the wrath of God to the hope of glory. And the believers who loom up before us in the Old and New Testament, and who are aware of this enormous change, can only glory in

40. Phil. 2:5; 1 Thess. 2:10; and 3:13.
41. John 14:13-14; Eph. 3:20; 2 Cor. 12:10; and Phil. 13.
42. Ex. 19:5-6; 29:43; Deut. 7:6ff.; 32:6ff.; Isa. 41:8ff.; and Ezek. 16:14.

the God of their salvation, and rejoice in His fellowship. How far we stand behind them in the joy of this faith!

Further, Scripture holds up the highest of moral ideals before the believers. The tendency is to ride rough-shod over this fact. It is said that the moral life which Christendom wants is one-sided, over-spiritual, exclusively directed to the life in heaven, quite averse to the embrace of earthly concerns, antagonistic to culture, the sort of thing which throws the poor and the oppressed the sop of eternal life hereafter but is altogether indifferent to the improvement of their condition here on earth, something which may be perhaps rich in passive virtues and full of prescriptions about subjection, long-suffering, and patience, but poor in the active virtues which can lead to a conquest and reform of the world. Hence there were many who aspired to a different, better, and higher morality, to an ethical teaching which laid down a dedication to the service of humanity as the highest duty, and which limited its point of view to that of the life on earth.

A concern for earthly interests is in itself, however, in such little conflict with Christian morality that it can in fact be said to be based and founded on the creation of man according to God's image. Man was and in a certain sense still is the image bearer of God, and he is therefore called to subdue the earth and to have dominion over the fish of the sea, the fowl of the air, and all the animals that creep upon the earth (Gen. 1:26-28 and Psalm 8). There is no book that does so much justice to the whole of nature as the Holy Scripture. Paganism is always vacillating between an arrogant abuse of the world and a slavish, superstitious fear of its mysterious power. But Moses and the prophets, Christ and the apostles, stand perfectly free over against the world, because they are raised above it by the fellowship with God. And, although it is true that Scripture enjoins it upon us to seek the kingdom of heaven first, and although it is further true that the Christians of that early period, tiny group as they were, had to withdraw from numerous circles of life and had to abstain from many things because in the world of that time virtually everything was permeated by the pagan spirit, Christianity in principle included within itself all of the elements which not only gave the freedom to subdue the world and have dominion over the earth but also made these accomplishments the duty and the calling of man.

After all, the Christian ethic is none other than the one briefly and pointedly comprised in the ten commandments and which, for the rest, is illuminated and interpreted throughout the whole of Scriptures. In those commandments the love of God stands in the foreground, but the love of the neighbor is the second law, like unto the first. In this love of the neighbor there lies contained, provided it be properly understood, not in a Buddhistic, passive sense but in its Christian, active character, the duty of mission, of reformation, and of culture. By missions the religious and moral possessions of Christianity accrue to all peoples and nations; by reformation, which is not limited to one period in the church of Christ, nor to one moment in the life of the Christian but must always go on, there takes place the progressive renewal of heart and life, of family and society according to the demand of the Lord's will; and by culture the subduing of the earth to the control of man, the dominion of matter by spirit, and of nature by the reason, takes place.

The kingdom of heaven, which must be sought first, brings all the other things in its wake (Matt. 6:33). Godliness is profitable to all things having promise of the life that now is, and of that which is to come (1 Tim. 4:8). Nothing is unclean of itself, for every creature of God is good, and nothing is to be refused if it is received with thanksgiving, for it is sanctified through the word of God and through prayer (Rom. 14:14 and 1 Tim. 4:4). Christianity, which finds the basis of all culture in the creation of man according to the image of God and its restoration in the resurrection of Christ, calls its faithful confessors to the deliberation of whatsoever things are true, honest, just, pure, lovely, of good report, and if there be any other virtue or other praise, of that also (Phil. 4:8).

No higher morality, nor any higher religion is thinkable than the one which is preached to us in the gospel. True, one can go in pursuit of another, but if he does he soon strays off into by-paths. The time in which we are living offers us the strongest of evidence for this. The morality of the Scriptures is rejected, but the thing that takes its place is continually coming into conflict with the simplest laws of the ethical life.

The first thing that happens is that all the commandments which are related to the love of God are taken out of the moral teaching. There is then no longer any concern for the love of God, of His name, His truth, and His service; indeed, how should people be able to love God when as a matter of fact they doubt or deny that He can be known, that He reveals Himself, or even that He exists. But in doing this, those who deny the relevancy of the first law undermine the commandments of the second table, for if there is no God who makes it obligatory for man to love his neighbor, what ground for such love can there exist? Consequently, the proponents of a moral teaching independent of religion are hopelessly divided on the question of what principle lies behind the love of man for his fellow man. Some try to base this love on self interest, some on the happiness it brings about, a third group on the virtue of pity, of compassion, a fourth group on the conscience, but they all together prove that without divine authority for the duty which binds the conscience there can be no such imperative.

As a consequence the proponents of such a morality get into difficulty with each of the particular commandments in which the love of the neighbor is more specifically worked out and circumscribed. It is generally said that people, although they differ greatly in religion, nevertheless remain close together in the sphere of morality. There may be some truth in this, for nature fortunately is stronger than theory, and because the work of the law stands written on the heart of every man, but for the rest reality teaches us something very different. There is not a single commandment of the second table of the law which remains unchallenged in our time. The authority of father and mother and of all those appointed over us is openly attacked and rejected. Murder is being taken less seriously as time goes on: in the case of suicide it is often smoothed over, and in the case of abortion it is not seldom defended. Marriage is regarded as a contract which is assumed for an arbitrary length of time, and adultery has its defenders and supporters. Property is in the estimate of many another name for theft. Truth is made serviceable to utility, is made dependent upon evolutional development, and is distinguished from falsehood only in time and place, or in form and degree. And as for covetousness, it celebrates its triumph in the mammonistic spirit of our age.

Over against all these bastardizations of morality Scripture maintains the moral ideal in uncurtailed and unadulterated form. It never does violence to the holiness of God and the sanctity of His law, but again and again places these in all their majesty sharply before the consciences of men. The thing that Jesus said to His disciples, Be ye perfect even as your Father in Heaven is perfect, is repeated in different words by all the apostles in their admonishments to the believers. Sin has no right at all to existence, least of all in those who are named by the name of Christ. Nothing may ever be subtracted from the demand of the moral law, least of all by those who have died with Christ and with Him been raised to a new life. And if then, in the providence of God, the old man only gradually dies out in the believer, and the new man only gradually grows up and only hereafter accomplishes perfection, all this points to the the great long-suffering and forbearance of God. This is a forbearance which He can exercise because Christ covers the sin of the church with His righteousness and holiness and guarantees the perfecting of His people.

Although the moral law, which is the rule of life for the believers, can be satisfied with nothing other than a perfect love of God and of the neighbor, it is nevertheless quite as evident that according to Scripture no single believer has ever reached such perfection or ever can reach it in this life. The saints of the Bible were all people who often faltered or stumbled, and some of them, such as a David or a Peter, fell into grave sins, although they also in the deepest remorse made confession of it afterwards. No matter whom we may choose to overhear, we never hear the affirmation which can sometimes be spoken by Christians: I do and I have no more sin. On the contrary, Abraham (Gen. 12:12), Isaac (Gen. 26:5), Jacob (Gen. 26:35), Moses (Num. 20:7-12 and Ps. 106:33), David (Ps. 51), Solomon (1 Kings 8:46), Isaiah (Isa. 6:5), Daniel (Dan. 9:4), these, and others like them, all confess to transgression and acknowledge their sins and errors.

The same holds true of the apostle Paul. He was crucified with Christ and he then walked in newness of the Spirit. He stands justified before God and is fully assured of his salvation. He gets glory, humanly speaking, for his apostolic work and is conscious of the faithfulness with which he has fulfilled his calling.[43] But besides ascribing all this to the grace of God,[44] he confesses that no good dwells in his flesh (Rom. 7:18), that the flesh lusts against the Spirit (Gal. 5:17), that to will and to do are in continual conflict in him (Rom. 7:7-25), and that he follows after perfection, but has not yet attained it (Phil. 3:12).

Moses and the prophets make a similar testimony concerning the people of Israel, Christ makes it of His disciples, the apostles of the churches entrusted to their care. Jesus calls His disciples to perfection (Matt. 5:48), and nevertheless teaches them to pray for the forgiveness of their guilt (Matt. 6:12). The Christians in Rome have been raised with Christ to dwell in newness of life (Rom. 6:3ff.), and are nevertheless admonished to make their members serviceable to righteousness unto holiness (Rom. 6:19). The Corinthians were washed, sanctified, justified in the name of the Lord Jesus, and by the Spirit of God (1 Cor. 6:11), and were nevertheless carnal (1 Cor. 3:1-4). The Galatians had received the Spirit by the preaching of the faith (Gal. 3:2), and nevertheless permitted themselves to be tempted into disobedience to the truth (Gal. 3:1). The good work was begun in the Philippians, but it was not completed (Phil. 1:6). In all the churches there are conditions, errors, and defections which are not in harmony with the Christian life. And the apostles are themselves all convinced that sin will continue to cling to the believers so long as they live. We all offend in many things (James 3:2). If we say that we have no sin, we deceive ourselves, and the truth is not in us (1 John 1:8).

Still, although perfection is not attainable in this life, the admonishments and appeals nevertheless continue useful and serious. Those who

---

43. Rom. 15:17ff.; 1 Cor. 4:3; 9:15; 15:31; 2 Cor. 1:12; 6:3ff.; 11:5ff.; Phil. 2:16ff.; 3:4ff.; and 1 Thess. 2:10ff.
44. 1 Cor. 15:10; 2 Cor. 12:9; and Phil. 4:3.

hold to the perfectibility of the believers in this life do, of course, raise this objection, and say that admonishments which cannot or at least cannot *fully* be carried out must necessarily lose their force and in time sap the energy of the believers. This is however a false piece of argumentation. From the fact that a person must do something it does not follow that he can do it. A man may have to pay a sum of money and yet not be able to pay it; in that event he nevertheless remains obligated to pay. And in this same way the moral law can never stop laying down its demand, even though human beings because of sin cannot satisfy it. And, on the contrary, it can be argued with more justice that the person who teaches the perfectibility of the believers always comes out at a lowering of the moral ideal and at a less serious sense of sin.

Certainly, whoever in thinking of sin does not think merely of external, sinful deeds, but also includes within it sinful thoughts and inclinations, can hardly seriously maintain that in this life the believers can be wholly delivered from it. One can only hold to the perfectibility of the saints if one does not take seriously the sinful nature of man, if one does not regard his sinful thoughts and inclinations as sin, and if one does violence to the absolute holiness of the law. In the form for the administration of the Holy Supper in the Reformed churches it is said that we rest assured that no sin or infirmity which still remains in us *against our will* can hinder us from being received of God in grace. There has been much dispute about whether or not the regenerate can still fall into such sins as do not take place from infirmity but are deliberate in character and must therefore be called sins of evil aforethought. Two things however are certain: the one is that in those who are really born again not only the conscience but also the new life, the disposition and the will, in a lesser or greater degree comes into opposition against those sins; and the other is that even the sins of infirmity which we do against our will are sins and are in conflict with the holiness of the law.

Moreover, the admonishments to a holy walk, so far from being useless and unbeneficial, are precisely the means by which Christ applies the righteousness and holiness given to the believers in Christ and works them out. Christ in His highpriestly prayer prays that the Father may sanctify His disciples in the truth, that is, by means of His word, which is truth (John 17:17; compare 15:3). The word which God gave us is in very fact the chief means for our sanctification; the blessing which has accrued, not only to the public preaching, but also to the reading, study, and meditation of that word in the solitude of the family circle, has simply been immeasurable for the nurture of a Christian life. To this word as the means of sanctification there is added the prayer in

Jesus' name (John 14:13-14 and 16:23-24) which gives us access to the divine majesty and fills us with confidence, since there is no one in heaven nor on earth who loves us more than Jesus Christ. To these are added further the singing of psalms and hymns and spiritual songs (Eph. 5:19 and Col. 3:16), for these exercise a deep influence on the attitude of the heart and the readiness of the will. And finally there are the watchings and fastings,[45] practices which have unjustly fallen into virtually complete disuse. All these means of sanctification prove that in this work also He does not despise the use of means.

Naturally, God is the Almighty One, and He could, had He wanted to, have perfectly sanctified all His children in the moment of regeneration. But that apparently was not His will; in the recreation He does not deny Himself as Creator. All the life of the creature is born, grows up, and only gradually reaches its maturity. Because the spiritual life is actually life it comes to be and it develops in this same way. God does not inject the righteousness and holiness of Christ into us mechanically, or pour it out as one does water into a vessel, but He works it out in us in an organic way. Hence the one detail does not conflict with the other when the Scripture constantly presents the matter as though the believers must *become* that which they *are*. The kingdom of heaven is a gift of God (Luke 12:32) and yet it is a treasure of great worth which must be sought after (Matt. 6:33 and 13:46). The believers are the branches of the vine, and they can, accordingly, do nothing without Christ, and yet they are told in His word to remain in Him, in His word, and in His love (John 15). They were elected in Christ from before the foundation of the world, and yet they must be diligent to make their calling and their election sure (Eph. 1:4 and 2 Peter 1:10). They have been sanctified by the one sacrifice of Christ, and must nevertheless follow after sanctification, without which no man shall see the Lord (Heb. 10:10 and 12:14). They are complete, and nevertheless require constant perfecting and establishment (Col. 2:10 and 1 Peter 5:10). They have put on the new man, and must nevertheless constantly put him on (Eph. 4:24 and Col. 3:10). They have crucified the flesh with the affections and lusts, and must nevertheless still mortify their members which are upon the earth (Gal. 5:24 and Col. 3:5). It is God who works in them both to will and to do according to His good pleasure, and yet they must work out their salvation with fear and trembling (Phil. 2:12-13).

These data do not conflict with each other. The one is simply the ground and guarantee of the other. Because sanctification, like the whole of salvation, is the work of God, we are admonished, obliged,

---

45. Matt. 17:21; 26:41; and Eph. 6:18.

to a new obedience, and we are also qualified for it. He grants abundant grace not that we should instantly or suddenly be holy and continue to rest in this holiness, but that we should persevere in the struggle and remain standing. He hears our prayers but does it in accordance with the law and order which He has fixed for the spiritual life. Hence we are always of good courage, for He who has begun a good work in us will finish it until the day of Jesus Christ. The believers can and they will *become* holy because in Christ they *are* holy.

* * * * *

Or is that being too boldly said? May the believers really confess that they not only are living members of the church of Christ but that they will also eternally remain that? There are many who challenge this. As a general rule the proponents of the perfectibility of the saints in this life are at the same time proponents of the possibility of their defection or apostasy. The one position stands in close relationship with the other; both products come up out of the same root; at the bottom of both ideas there lies the notion that the sanctification of man is man's own work and that it must come into being by his will. The thought is that if the believer, with the assistance of grace, makes good use of his will and calls on all his energies, he can even in this life arrive at total perfection; and the thought is also, on the contrary, that if he relaxes in point of energy, falls behind, and begins to sin, he can cast himself out of the state of grace into which he was first taken up. He can again become a godless person and be eternally lost. And just as both these ideas come up out of the same heresy of the will and the work of man in sanctification, so too they are both supported by the same fear. The thought is that when the perseverance of the saints is taught the moral life suffers damage, the energy and exertion of the believer will lack incentive, and that a premium will be put upon godless living by the proposition: once lost, always lost!

If, however, we should in maintaining this doctrine of the perseverance of the saints seek all our strength in the will and the ability of man, we should lose all ground under our feet and have to doubt the steadfastness of every believer. For all saints have only a small beginning of the perfect obedience; according to the testimony of their own conscience, they are still inclined to all evil and they falter daily in many things; each moment they sin and forfeit the grace which is granted them. If the whole matter depended upon themselves, not a single believer would persevere to the end. The opponents of the confession of the perseverance of the saints can only escape these inferences and conclusions by making a distinction between one kind of sins and another. Inasmuch as all believers still become guilty of all kinds of transgressions of the law of God these opponents really ought to teach that the defection of the saints is not only possible but that it actually is the case for all believers. When, on the contrary, they nevertheless hold that some, many, or even the most of the believers, preserve this grace and persevere in it, they can hold to this only by making some kind of distinction between mortal sins and forgiveable sins and that it is only through the first and not through the second kind that grace can be lost.

To do this, however, is to introduce a highly dubious distinction into the doctrine of sin, for the various sins do not stand alongside of each other in discrete independence, but they all issue from a single impure source; consequently all lead to death, and are also, but for the blasphemy against the Holy Spirit, forgivable by the grace of God which is in Christ Jesus. Moreover, who can himself determine, or what priest can determine for anyone else, whether in a given instance he has become guilty of a so-called mortal or of a forgivable sin, and whether he has therefore forfeited grace or still preserves it. Transgressions which human beings often regard as petty and small are sometimes great in the eyes of God who searches the heart and tries the reins; and the sins which a merciless world regards as disgraceful are judged very differently by Him who knows all circumstances and conditions. The result, then, could only be that the believer lives in constant dread that he have committed a so-called mortal sin and have forfeited grace, or that in a false security he is depending upon the judgment of a priest.

We put an end to all these doubts and uncertainties immediately when we think of the perseverance of the saints not as an accomplishment of the human will, but as a work of God which from beginning to end is effected by God Himself. We put an end to all the doubts and uncertainties if, in other words, we regard the perseverance of saints as a preservation of God before it can become a human perseverance. Scripture leaves no doubt at all about this, but gives us in the work of the Father, the Son, and the Spirit, in connection with the covenant of grace and all its benefits, a multitude of evidences.

The Father has chosen the believers in Christ from before the foundation of the world (Eph. 1:4), ordained them to eternal life (Acts 13:48), conformed them to the image of His Son (Rom. 8:29); and this election is immutable (Rom. 9:11 and Heb. 6:17) and in time brings with it the calling, the justification, and the glorification (Rom. 8:39). Christ, in whom all the promises of God are yea and amen (2 Cor. 1:20), died for those who were given Him by the Father (John 17:6, 12), in order that He might give them eternal life and not lose one of them (John 6:39 and 10:28). The Holy Spirit, who regenerates them, remains eternally with them (John 14:16), and seals them unto the day of redemption (Eph. 4:30). The covenant of grace is sure and confirmed with an oath (Heb. 6:16-18 and 13:20), as unbreakable as a marriage (Eph. 5:31-32) and as a testament (Heb. 9:17). And by virtue of that covenant, God calls His elect, writes His law in their hearts, and puts His fear there also (Heb. 8:10 and 10:14ff.). He does not let them be tempted above their ability to withstand (1 Cor. 10:13), establishes and completes the good work which He has begun in them (1 Cor. 1:9 and Phil. 1:6), and preserves them for the future of Christ in order to make them partakers of the heavenly inheritance (1 Thess. 5:23 and 1 Peter 1:4-5). By way of His intercession with the Father, Christ is always active on their behalf in order that their faith may not fail (Luke 22:32), that they may be preserved from the evil one in the world (John 17:11 and 20), may be altogether saved (Heb. 7:25), receive the forgiveness of sins (1 John 2:1), and one day all be with Him and see His glory (John 17:24). And, finally, the benefits of Christ in which the Holy Spirit causes them to share, are all without repentance (Rom. 11:29), and are mutually and inseparably related to each other: he who is called is justified and glorified (Rom. 8:30); he who is received as a child of God is an heir of eternal life (Rom. 8:17 and Gal. 4:7); he who believes has everlasting life immediately (John 3:16). And that life, because it is eternal, cannot be lost; it is a life which cannot sin (1 John 3:9) and which cannot die (John 11:25-26).

But as in the case of sanctification, the preservation of the believers is applied and worked out in such a way in the believers that they themselves also persevere in grace which is given them of God. God never uses force, but deals with man in a reasonable way. In regeneration He imparts new potentialities and so transforms the will which was rebellious that it is rebellious no longer. And in that same spiritual way He keeps on working in the believers after the initial regeneration; He does not in a false sense make them passive, but arouses them, rather, and causes them to walk in the good works prepared for them. In doing this He makes use of the Word as His means.

He never ceases admonishing them to persevere to the end,[46] to remain in Christ, in His word and His love,[47] to watch and be sober,[48] to preserve the faith and to remain faithful unto death.[49] He warns them against high-mindedness and in the event of apostasy threatens

---

46. Matt. 10:22; 24:13; and Rom. 2:7-8.
47. John 15:1-10; 1 John 2:6, 24, 27; 3:6, 24; and 4:12ff.
48. Matt. 24:42; 25:13; 1 Thess. 5:6; and 1 Peter 5:8.
49. Col. 1:23; Heb. 2:1; 3:14; 6:11; and Rev. 2:10 and 26.

them with heavy punishment;[50] but He also attaches rich promises of reward to the sanctification and perseverance.[51] In fact, in the persons of David and Peter we are given examples of deep defection, and in such persons as Hymeneus and Alexander (1 Tim. 1:19-20 and 2 Tim. 2: 17-18), Demas (2 Tim. 4:10), and others (Heb. 6:4-8 and 2 Peter 2:1) we are given examples, by way of warning, of a total apostasy.

But all these warnings and admonishments do not prove that the truly sanctified can fall away. For of those examples named last in the paragraph above the statement of John holds that they went out from the church, but that they were not in their heart of it (1 John 2:19). And the persons of David and Peter show us very plainly that God does not forsake them in their falling off but on the contrary preserves them and leads them back to the confession of guilt and to repentance. They are examples given us for admonishment, but also for comfort, so that we too, if through weakness we should fall into sin, need not doubt the grace of God nor remain in sin, but strengthen ourselves with the thought that we have an eternal covenant of grace with God. And it is in the way of that covenant that He causes us to walk through His word and Spirit. Whoever teaches the possibility of the falling away of the saints does injustice to the faithfulness of God, makes the salvation and the perseverance dependent upon the human effort and accordingly changeable and uncertain, and does violence also to the unity and maturation of the spiritual life. Such a person must take the position that this life can again and again be definitively broken off and again and again be begun anew. But he who believes the perseverance of the saints has his starting point and resting point in the grace of God, glories in God's fidelity, and at the same time maintains the coherence of the spiritual and the eternal life. For, although in the life of the believer, so long as the old man continues to live in him, there is all kinds of change and vacillation, this new life is nevertheless indestructible; the seed which God has planted remains in him (1 John 3:9).

This certainty of perseverance, however, is so far from exciting in believers a spirit of pride, or of rendering them carnally secure, that on the contrary it is the real source of humility, filial reverence, true piety, patience in every tribulation, fervent prayers, constancy in suffering and in confessing the truth, and of solid rejoicing in God; so that the consideration of this benefit should serve as an incentive to the serious and constant practice of gratitude and good works, as appears from the

50. John 15:2; Rom. 11:20-22; Heb. 4:1; 6:4-8; 10:26-31; and 2 Peter 2:18-22.
51. Matt. 5:12; 6:4; 10:22; 16:27; 24:13; 25:21ff.; Rom. 2:7; Rev. 2:7; 22:12 and elsewhere.

testimonies of Scripture and the example of the saints (Canons of Dort, V, 12).

* * * * *

If this precious fruit is to be produced, the preservation of the saints must be believed as God wants it to be believed. Is this, then, the reason why God has revealed it in His word, namely, that we should accept it as a doctrine and should protest to others: This is sound teaching and pure truth? Indeed, God willed and intended this also in His revelation, for truth in itself has already great worth. But this is nevertheless not the only reason, and it is not the main reason. For if we embrace the preservation of the saints with a true faith, we are confessing also that God still continues to work in this way with His children. The preservation of the saints is not an historical truth, is not a fact which took place somewhere at some time in the past; it is not a scientific truth like the sum of a column of figures or the product of multiplication; but it is, rather, an eternal truth, a truth to which God binds Himself from age to age and from generation to generation, a reality in the midst of which we live, which God calls into being and which He maintains in the life of all His children.

In this sense he only can believe the preservation of the saints who knows himself to be the object of it and who knows its reality by experience. And it is then self-evident that anyone who so believes the preservation — including also his own preservation — cannot make this confession an occasion for the flesh anymore than a person in whom Christ by a true faith has been planted can fail to bring forth fruits of gratitude.

Something else follows from this too. If the preservation of the saints is a work of God which He continuously carries out in the heart and life of all believers, then it follows that in time in the consciousness of these believers a firm assurance of this reality also develops. If there is no such thing as a preservation of the saints, then no believer can even for a moment ever have perfect assurance of his salvation, for he will be living in constant fear lest on the morrow or another day he lose the grace of God by some grave sin. But if God preserves His own, then the believer not only can have a firm assurance of this fact in his heart, but he may have it also and he must have it; for without such an assurance of salvation the preservation of the saints would lose all its value for the practical life of the believers. Of what use would the doctrine of the preservation of the saints be to the children of God if they could never come to know with certainty that they are His children! The preservation of the saints and the assurance of salvation therefore are inseparably connected with each other; without the first the second would not be possible, and the second makes the first a real support to the believers and a comfort to their hearts.

All the saints who come to our attention in the Old and the New Testament are, accordingly, partakers of such a certainty. Not Abraham alone (Gen. 15:6 and Rom. 4:18ff.), nor Jacob (Gen. 49:18), nor David (2 Sam. 22:2ff. and Habak. 3:17-19), but also all the believers whose circumstances are described by the psalmists, proverb writers, and the prophets. They often live in profound misery, are oppressed by their enemies, persecuted, and taunted: Where is now your God? You trusted in the Lord, that He should deliver you![52] Sometimes despair masters their soul as though God had forgotten them and in His wrath denied them access to His mercies.[53] They also acknowledge the justice of God's judgments, confessing their sins.[54] Nevertheless, God is their Father, and they are His people, the sheep of His pasture.[55] He cannot forsake them for His Name's sake, for the sake of His covenant (Ps. 79:8-9). His anger endures but a moment; in His favor is life (Ps. 30:5). He does not deal with them according to their sins, nor reward them according to their iniquities (Ps. 103:10). He forgives their trespasses and covers their sins (Ps. 32:1). The Lord is their rock and their bulwark, their fortress and high tower, their shield and the horn of their salvation, their light and their joy, and their one and all (Ps. 18:2 and 73:25 and elsewhere).

The tone in which the apostles and the believers of the New Testament speak of their salvation is just as sure and certain. There is no question of doubt. They know that God did not spare His own Son, but delivered Him up for them all and will now freely give them all things (Rom. 8:32), that they are justified by faith, have peace with God, and that no one can lay anything to their charge (Rom. 5:1 and 8:33), that they have been begotten again unto a lively hope and have passed from death into life,[56] that they have received the Spirit of adoption as children, and that this Spirit testifies with their spirit that they are children of God (Rom. 8:15-16).

And this their knowledge has bearing not only on the present, on that which they now are, but extends also in the future to that which they shall be. For whom God has known, called, and justified, him He has also glorified (Rom. 8:30). If they are children, they are also heirs (Rom. 8:17). They have in the faith already received eternal life, and they cannot lose it (1 John 3:9 and 5:1). They have been

52. Psalm 22:9; 42:4; and 71:11.
53. Psalm 10:1, 11ff.; 13:2; 28:1; 44:10ff.; 77:8ff. and elsewhere.
54. Ps. 51:5; Neh. 9:33; Dan. 9:14 and elsewhere.
55. Ps. 95:7; 100:3; Isa. 63:16; and 64:8.
56. 1 Peter 1:3; James 1:18; and 1 John 3:14.

begotten again unto a living hope, and are kept by the power of God unto salvation (1 Peter 1:3-5). The good work begun in them will be performed until the day of Jesus Christ (Phil. 1:6). In short, they have been sealed with the Holy Spirit as security and guarantor until the day of the promise.[57]

More force and influence would issue from the believers if they always stood in the firm assurance of this faith. But they are often less than sure of their own cause; how can they then give an eloquent witness, and provoke the world to jealousy by their joyous testimony? In the Roman Catholic Church this assurance is even denied to the faith; the believer can be absolutely certain of his salvation only through a special revelation such as is the portion of the few only. All other believers have nothing better than a surmise, a hope, a probability. And Rome thinks that this fact is not a disadvantage but an advantage in that it makes for a profitable anxiety and serves as an incentive to sanctification. Hence, too, the Roman Christian does not depend upon the testimony of the Holy Spirit in his own heart, but upon the pronouncement of the priest, upon the assurance which the Church gives him for his salvation. And in general this gives him a high confidence.

The Reformation, however, had a very different idea of justification and faith, and thus also of the assurance of salvation. For Rome, faith is simply the approbation of the teaching of the Church; justification consists of the pouring in of the supernatural grace, and its function is to equip man once more to do good works and so to earn eternal life. From its very nature, therefore, faith cannot give anyone a certainty concerning his salvation; to the extent any such certainty is possible it must be inferred from love, from good works, and it cannot therefore ever be absolute certainty but must remain a weaker or stronger intimation or hope. But the Reformation recognized an independent significance in justification, saw in it the restoration of man's relationship to God, and it thus had to see in faith something more and something different than a sheer consent to the truth. That further thing was a personal confidence of the heart in the grace of God in Christ Jesus.

This faith carried assurance with it. But the Lutherans and the Remonstrants regarded this assurance as relevant only to the present. The believer can be absolutely certain that now, as of the moment, he is a believer, but he cannot be sure that he will always believe and therefore that he will actually be saved. The Reformed churches, however, included the future also in the pale of the certainty; and that is why the search after the assurance of salvation occupies so large a place in the life of the saints. In the first period, when there was a quicken-

---

57. Rom. 6:23; 2 Cor. 1:22; 5:5; Eph. 1:13; and 4:30.

ed, powerful life of belief, such a deliberate search was not necessary; men lived and spoke out of the abundance of the heart, as is so plainly evident in our confessions, forms, and prayers. But when the faith waned, there followed the reflection upon the faith and the search for its earmarks. And instead of then finding certainty, people became more and more involved in the entanglements of doubt. The certainty of the faith cannot be obtained by any process of reasoning or by any inference. This is something which issues only from faith itself. When the faith, therefore, pines away and goes into hiding, the certainty also leaves the heart and cannot be revived by any artificial means.

The Canons of Dort put this very beautifully: "The elect in due time, though in various degrees and in different measures, attain the assurance of this their eternal and unchangeable election, not by inquisitively prying into the secret and deep things of God, but by observing within themselves with a spiritual joy and holy pleasure the infallible fruits of election pointed out in the Word of God — such as — a true faith in Christ, filial fear, a godly sorrow for sin, a hungering and thirsting after righteousness, etc."

So reads Article 12 of the First Head of the Canons, and in Articles 9 and 10 of the Fifth Head, we read further: "Of this preservation of the elect to salvation and of their perseverance in the faith, true believers in themselves may and do obtain assurance according to the measure of their faith, whereby they surely believe that they are and ever will continue true and living members of the Church, and that they have the forgiveness of sins and life eternal. This assurance, however, is not produced by any peculiar revelation contrary to or independent of the Word of God, but springs from faith in God's promises, which He has most abundantly revealed in His Word for our comfort; from the testimony of the Holy Spirit, witnessing with our spirit that we are children and heirs of God; and lastly from a serious and holy desire to preserve a good conscience and to perform good works."

The assurance of salvation is not, accordingly, something which is added to the life of faith from without, but something, rather, which blossoms up out of that life of faith itself. Hence, the assurance differs "according to the measure of the faith." In this life, the believers must battle against various carnal doubts, and are sometimes grievously tempted, and hence they do not always feel this full assurance of faith, and certainty of persevering (Compare the Canons, V, 11).

But all this does not take away from the fact that the saving faith, such as Scripture describes it and the Reformation restored it, is not in its inner nature certainty, and that this certainty becomes stronger in proportion to the extent that the faith becomes stronger. Such faith is not opposed to knowledge, but it is opposed to all doubt whatsoever.

Doubt does not come up out of the new man but out of the old; it does not come up out of the Spirit but out of the flesh. The faith says yea and amen to all the promises of God, embraces those promises, and leans upon them. As it does this, and in proportion to the extent that it does so, the refugee confidence of the faith becomes sure confidence, and it gives the believer the freedom to apply all of those promises of God to himself and to appropriate them; the growing confidence becomes a sure confidence that not to others only but to *me* also the forgiveness of sins, eternal righteousness and salvation have been given of God, out of pure grace, and solely for the merits of Christ.

Such a confidence extends also, not through a piece of rationalization but according to its own nature and being, to the future. That were surely a strange faith which should say: Now I am a child of God but I do not know whether I shall still be that tomorrow! If the faith be real and powerful, it naturally rejoices: The Lord is my Shepherd: I shall not want; even though I should pass through the valley of the shadow of death, I should fear no evil, for Thou art with me. Thy rod and Thy staff they comfort me. And the faith rejoices and testifies thus, not because it relies upon itself, but because it relies upon the promises of God. Among those promises are these: I will be your God, now and eternally; I have loved you with an eternal love, and will never forsake you or leave you. The faith, in other words, that is no assurance for the present and for the future does violence to the truth of God's promises and the faithfulness of His love.

To this consideration, in the second place, must be added the testimony of the Holy Spirit. The Holy Spirit is the great, almighty Witness of Christ, who testifies of Christ in our hearts, brings us to the point of faith in His name, and causes us to know the things which are given us of God in Christ.[58] But that Spirit of Christ at the same time causes us to know ourselves, not only in our guilt and impurity, but also in our fellowship with Christ and our portion in Him. After He has first convicted us of sin, righteousness, and judgment, and, as the Spirit of faith (2 Cor. 4:13), has worked the faith in us, He follows up His work by assuring us of the faith. He becomes a Spirit of adoption as children (Gal. 4:6), a Spirit such as is suitable to children and lives in children (Rom. 8:15), and one who makes us know that we are children.

He does that in various ways. He does it by testifying with our spirit that we are children of God (Rom. 8:16); by powerfully driving us to the joyous confession: Abba, Father (Rom. 8:15); by giving us

---

58. John 15:26; 16:13-15; 1 Cor. 12:3; 2 Cor. 4:3-6 and elsewhere.

peace with God and by shedding the love of God abroad in our hearts (Rom. 5:1 and 5); by quickening a new life in us, progressively leading us in our Christian life, and filling our souls with a joy unknown before;[59] and He does all this — to say nothing of other things besides — to seal us unto the day of redemption.

The phrase *to seal*, in reference to persons or matters (letters and the like) sometimes means to place them outside the reach of anyone else, to preserve them from harm;[60] sometimes it is used to prove particular persons or witnesses valid and authoritative, to establish them.[61] In this last sense the believers are sealed with the Holy Spirit as guarantor unto the day of redemption.[62] The Holy Spirit who has been given to the believers, who has planted the faith in them and who continuously sustains it, who testifies to them, and leads them, and the like, He it is who seals their salvation. In and through all this He proves to be guarantor and security to the believers in order that they may be preserved unto the day of redemption and may inherit the heavenly blessedness. For that Spirit will never depart from them, but remain eternally with them (John 14:16). And he who has the Spirit, he is Christ's, is His property (Rom. 8:19), and is preserved by Him unto eternity (John 17:24). Christ in heaven and the Holy Spirit on earth are surety for the salvation of the elect, and seal this in the hearts of the believers.

These two ways, along which the assurance of salvation comes to be in the believers, are really not two separate ways, and do not run in parallel lines alongside of each other, but they are one way being viewed from differing points of view. After all, the Holy Spirit does not operate and testify and seal the believers alongside of or outside of the faith, but does these things always through the means of the faith. And that faith is not a dead faith, but a living faith; it reveals its essence and proves its power in good works.

Hence we can speak of these good works, as joining the faith in God's promises and the testimony of the Holy Spirit, and as deserving attention, in the third place, as a means by which God assures the believers of their adoption as children in Christ (Heidelberg Catechism, Question 86; Canons of Dort, V, 10). But we must carefully note that in seeking for assurance we cannot begin with these good works, that the faith can never firmly lean or rest upon them, and that still less can they

---

59. Rom. 8:10-11; 14:17; and 15:13.
60. Deut. 32:34; Cantc. 4:12; Isa. 8:16; 29:11; Dan. 6:17; 12:4; Ezek. 9:1-6; Matt. 27:66; Rev. 5:5-6; 7:1-4; 20:3; and 22:10.
61. Esther 3:12; 8:8; 1 Kings 21:8; Neh. 9:38; Jer. 32:10; John 3:13; 6:27; Rom. 4:11; and 1 Cor. 9:2.
62. Rom. 8:32; 2 Cor. 1:22; 5:5; Eph. 1:13; and 4:30.

be performed by us with a view to our achieving the assurance of salvation by means of them. For all good works are imperfect, and they are more or less perfect in proportion to the extent that they issue from a stronger or weaker faith. But to the extent that they do issue from a true faith, they can serve as aids to our assurance. Just as faith proves and illustrates itself in good works, so the faith is also confirmed and strengthened by them. And when men thereupon see our good works, they glorify the Father who is in heaven.

XXIII

The Church of Christ

All the rich benefits which Christ gives to His believers on earth receive their fulfillment and their crown in the glorification which accrues to them in part upon death but only in its fulness after the day of judgment. But this benefit of glorification is one which we cannot yet discuss, because we have first to pay some attention to the way in which, or the route along which, Christ brings the benefits of calling and regeneration, faith and repentance, justification and adoption as children, renewal and sanctification, into being in His believers on earth, and sustains and reinforces them. We have already noted that He grants all those benefits by means of His Word and His Spirit, but have still to see that He also grants them also only in the fellowship which binds all the believers together. He does not distribute them to single individuals, nor to a small group of persons, but He gives them out to a great multitude, to the whole of the new humanity, which was chosen in Him by the Father from before the foundation of the world (Eph. 1:4).

The believer, therefore, never stands apart by himself; he is never alone. In the natural world every human being is born in the fellowship of his parents, and he is therefore without any effort on his own part a member of a family, of a people, and also of the whole of mankind. So it is also in the spiritual sphere. The believer is born from above, out of God, but he receives the new life only in the fellowship of the covenant of grace of which Christ is the Head and at the same time the content. If by virtue of this regeneration God is his Father, the church may in a good sense be called his mother. In the world of heathendom also there is no believer or no gathering of believers except by way of the mission which the church of Christ sends them. From the first moment of his regeneration, therefore, the believer is, apart from his will and apart from his own doing, incorporated in a great whole, taken up into a rich fellowship; he is member of a new nation and citizen of a spiritual kingdom whose king is glorious in the multitude of his subjects (Prov. 14:28).

This fellowship is a powerful support to every particular believer. We ought to be so strong that we would not doubt and would not fear even though we were quite alone, and even though there were, according to Luther's statement, as many devils as there are tiles on the roof. For if God be for us, who shall be against us; if the Lord be with us what can man do to us?[1] But as a general rule we are not equal to such independence, isolation, and solitude. There are special instances, it is true, in which a person is called upon to follow the voice of the Lord, to break with his total environment, and to take issue with his whole generation; and when that is necessary God grants a special grace and extraordinary power such as, for example, He gave to an Abraham, a Moses, and an Elijah. But even then the solitude comes hard. Elijah complained that he alone was left of the faithful (1 Kings 18:22 and 19:10), and Paul was sad at heart when at the end of his life he saw himself forsaken of everyone (2 Tim. 4:10). A human being is a companionable creature, and he does not like being alone.

Election comprises a very great multitude out of all generations, languages, people, and nations. True, it is personal and individual also and has specific human beings known to God by name as its object, but it selects these in such a way and combines them in such a way that they altogether can form the temple of God, the body and bride of Christ. The purpose of the election is the creation of an organism, that is, the redemption, renewal, and glorification of a regenerated mankind which proclaims the excellences of God and bears His name upon its forehead. When God carries out this election in time, He does this only by way of the covenant of grace; and He never in that covenant includes anyone in independence from all the others, but in that one person He at the same time calls in his family and generation. He did so for Adam, Noah, and Abraham, and He does so still for everyone whom He transfers from the service of the world to His fellowship; He establishes His covenant with such a one and his seed and He confirms it from generation to generation.

To this organic activity of God there is in the heart of all believers a social tendency, a longing for fellowship, which responds to it. On the one hand, there is no power in the world which so greatly divides people, and on the other hand there is no power which so greatly binds people together. Outside of Christianity, however, the religious fellowship almost always coincides with the unity of a tribe or people; in other words, religion is apparently not strong enough without tribal support to stand on its own feet. And hence there is not in heathendom a church in the proper sense of that word. But in Christendom this is very different.

It is true that in Israel the nation and the church, generally taken, were coextensive, but from the very beginning the national unity depended more upon the religious unity than vice versa. The marvelous birth of Isaac serves as evidence of this; the covenant of grace creates a peculiar people with Abraham as bearer. In this patriarch God as the

---

1. Ps. 56:12; 118:6; and Rom. 8:31.

516   *Our Reasonable Faith*

Omnipotent One makes nature serviceable to grace. Hence it is that in the Old Testament the God of the covenant, the people of Israel, and the land of Canaan are so intimately interrelated. Israel owes its nationality and unity to the fact that God has chosen it;[2] and Canaan is the land of the Lord (Lev. 25:23 and 1 Sam. 26:19) given to Abraham and his seed as their inheritance out of free grace.[3] Ruth gave expression to this fact when, returning to the land of Judah with her mother-in-law, she said: Where thou goest, I will go, and where thou lodgest, I will lodge; thy people is my people, and thy God my God. And it was for this reason, too, that when the people more and more fell away, and were finally led away into captivity and dispersed, there nevertheless remained a remnant which was faithful to God and His service and which, in the midst of the mass of the people, was the true Israel, the true seed of Abraham.[4] And as these saints separate themselves from the ungodly, they are mutually attracted to each other and are fortified by each other's fellowship.[5]

This separation was continued and completed in the New Testament. After John the Baptist with his preaching of repentance and forgiveness of sins had prepared the way, Jesus himself began His ministry and directed His ministry at first to the people of Israel. He taught in Galilee and Judaea, in the cities and villages, and went through the country doing good and healing all that were oppressed of the devil (Acts 10:38). But He soon learned from experience that the people under the leadership of the Scribes and Pharisees wanted to hear nothing of His Messiahship and of His spiritual kingdom; the longer He ministered the more antagonistic this people became, and it finally delivered Him up to crucifixion. The more this end approached the more Jesus therefore spoke of the cities of Chorazin, Bethsaida, and Capernaum (Matt. 11:20 ff.), of the Pharisees and Scribes (Matt. 23:13 ff.), of Jerusalem and her children (Matt. 23:37), of the people of Israel (Matt. 21:19 ff. and Luke 23:28 ff.), of the city and of the temple (Matt. 24), and over these all He pronounced His awful judgment. Israel rejected its Messiah; hence others were to come in its place.

At first it was only the little circle of disciples who confessed Jesus as their Lord; but this confession bound them into such a unity that, after the Master had left them also, they continued with one accord in prayer and supplication (Acts 1:14). On the Day of Pentecost they were clothed with power from on high and they received in the Holy Spirit an independent principle of life which emancipated them from

2. Ex. 19:5; Deut. 4:20; and 7:6.
3. Gen. 12:7 and Lev. 20:24.
4. Amos 5:15; Isa. 1:9; 4:3; 8:18 and elsewhere.
5. Ps. 1:1; 16:3; 22:23; 26:4-12; 35:18; 40:10; 66:16; 122:1ff.; and 133:1ff.

every national bond and organized them into a peculiar fellowship in the world, quite independent of any people or country. The pouring out of the Holy Spirit gave the church of Christ its independent existence.

* * * * *

The gathering of believers which confesses Jesus as their Lord was from the very beginning designated by the name of communion or church. The Hebrew Old Testament was already in possession of two words for the gatherings of the people of Israel, but it made no real distinction between the two. The Jewry of the later period seems however to have distinguished the two terms in such a way that the first designated the church in its actual situation, and the second the church in its ideal condition, that is, as a gathering of people called by God to His salvation. The first word was translated into the Greek by the word *synagogue,* the second by the word *ecclesia.* The distinction which had obtained already among the Jews contributed to the eventuality that Christians gave their preference to the second word. The Christian church, after all, was that gathering of believers which came into the place of the old Israel and which actualized the thought of God's elective love.

When the Jews and the Christians went their separate ways for good and all, the usage gradually developed of calling the gathering of Jews by the name *synagogue* and that of the Christians by the name *ecclesia* (community of believers or church), and this usage has remained in force up to the present day. Originally no such difference of force characterized the two terms. In James 2:2 (and Heb. 10:25) the word *synagogue* is used for the gathering of the Christian church, and in Acts 7:38 (and Heb. 2:12) the word *ecclesia* is used to refer to the gathering of the people of Israel. In fact, in Acts 19: 32, 39, and 41 the latter term is used for a general popular meeting. But the separation of the Jews and the Christians played into the hands of different meanings for the two terms.

The disciples of Jesus at Jerusalem, after Pentecost too, continued often to meet in the temple or in one of the subsidiary buildings,[6] in order to keep the hallowed hours of prayer of the Jewish moral code and at the same time to preach the gospel to the people. This preaching of the apostles, on the day of Pentecost and long after, was richly blessed. Thousands were added to the church who were saved.[7] But then a persecution broke out which culminated in the stoning of Stephen as the first martyr (Acts 6:8 — 7:60), and the disciples at Jerusalem dispersed throughout the lands of Judaea and Samaria and going as far as Phoenicia and Cyprus and Antioch (Acts 8:1 and 11:19). By the preaching of

---

6. Acts 2:46; 3:1; and 5:12.
7. Acts 2:41; 2:47; 4:4; 5:14; and 6:7.

the disciples there in a number of places many Jews were won to the faith, and many churches were established; these churches enjoyed peace for a time and were greatly multiplied.[8] It speaks for itself that these Jews who became Christians continued for a long while to nurse the hope that the whole people of Israel would turn to the Lord (Acts 3:17-26). But that hope disappeared more and more; gradually the center of gravity came to shift from the Jewish-Christian to the Gentile-Christian church.

Already during the period of Jesus' life there were a few proselytes from the Greeks who had come up to worship at the feast, and who expressed the desire to see Jesus (John 12:20 ff.). Among the members of the church at Jerusalem there were also certain Grecians (Acts 6:1) who very probably, like Stephen, entertained a more liberal idea of the relationship of Christians to the temple and the law (Acts 6:13 and 14). In the dispersion the disciples from Jerusalem proclaimed the gospel also to the Samaritans (Acts 8:5 ff.), to the chamberlain from Ethiopia (Acts 8:26 ff.), to the Roman centurion Cornelius (Acts 10), and to the Greeks in Antioch (Acts 11:20).

All these events were preparations for the great mission work which Paul, together with Barnabas, at the behest of the Holy Spirit and after the church at Antioch had laid their hands upon them, set about to accomplish (Acts 13:2ff.). In this mission work Paul followed the rule that he direct his appeal first to the Jews.[9] But when these, as they usually did, despised his preaching, he turned to the Gentiles.[10] It was a great grief to him and a continuous sadness that his brethren according to the flesh were offended by the cross of Christ and sought to establish their own righteousness (Rom. 9:2). He never left off his efforts to excite them to jealousy and to save some of them (Rom. 11:14). And there was a remnant according to the election of grace. Paul himself being the living evidence of it (Rom. 11:1-5).

But the fact was not to be denied that blindness was in part come to Israel until the fulness of the Gentiles should come in (Rom. 11:25). The branches of the live tree have been broken off by reason of unbelief, and in their place the branches of the wild olive tree have been grafted in (Rom. 11:17-24). There is a difference between the Israel according to the flesh and the Spirit.[11] The church of Christ is now the true seed of Abraham, the people and the Israel of God.[12] Those among the Jews

---

8. Acts 8:4, 14, 25; 9:31, 35, and 38.
9. Acts 13:5 and 14; compare Rom. 1:16; 2:9; 3:1; 9:3; 11:13ff.; 1 Cor. 1:22ff.; and 9:20.
10. Acts 13:46; 17:17; 18:4, 6; and 28:25-28.
11. Rom. 2:28-29; 9:8; and 1 Cor. 10:18.
12. Acts 15:14; Rom. 9:25-26; 2 Cor. 6:16-18; Gal. 3:29; 6:16; Heb. 8:8-10; James 1:1, 18; 1 Peter 2:9; and Rev. 21:3, 12.

who reject the Christ are not the true Jews; they are not of the circumcision but of the concision (Phil. 3:2); they are unruly and vain talkers and deceivers and persecuters of the believers (1 Thess. 2:14-16 and Titus 1:10-11). The Jews who molest the church at Smyrna say that they are Jews but they are not that, but are rather a synagogue of Satan (Rev. 2:9 and 3:9). Thus it was that the Jews and the Christians went their separate ways. Although the confessors of Jesus were at first still regarded as a sect of the Jews (Acts 24:5, 14 and 28:22), they were given their own name at Antioch, the name of Christians (Acts 11:26). A distinction began to be made between the gathering of Jews and the gathering of Christians, and linguistically this led to calling the first regularly by the name of *synagogue* and the second by that of *ecclesia* (community of believers or church).

The word *ecclesia* was translated church in our Bibles, and was first used by Christ himself for the multitude of His confessors (Matt. 16:18 and 18:17). There is nothing strange about this if only we remember that the Hebrew word employed by Jesus occurs repeatedly in the Old Testament and was generally known. The new thing about it is that Christ applied it to the circle of His disciples and so declared that His church will supplant that of the people of Israel. Besides, Jesus does not use the term to designate a gathering of believers in a particular place, but includes in its compass all those who by the word of the apostles sometime believe in Him. He uses it as comprehensively as possible. It was only later, in accordance with the development of the church, that the word took on a more specific sense.

In Acts 2:47, 5:11, 8:1, and 11:22 the name church is applied to the local gatherings of believers at Jerusalem. At the time the church at Jerusalem was virtually the only one. Very probably there were some disciples living here and there also, in Judaea, Samaria and Galilee, and who later, when the persecution had broken out in Jerusalem and the disciples were dispersed, constituted a point of contact for the mission work among the Jews. But a gathering of believers, a church, existed at first in Jerusalem only. When, however, such gatherings also took place elsewhere through the preaching of the Word by the disciples, the term church was also applied to these local groups. The church at Jerusalem was not an organization which formed branches of itself elsewhere; rather, there grew up alongside of this church other gatherings of believers also called churches.

Thus, for example, there is mention made of the church at Antioch (Acts 11:26 and 13:1), and of churches at Lystra, Derbe, and the surrounding country (Acts 14:23). Paul continually applies the name of church to each of the gatherings of believers in Rome, Corinth, Ephesus, Philippi, Colosse, and elsewhere, and he also in accordance with this practice speaks in the plural of the churches that are in the territory of Galatia (Gal. 1:2) and Judaea (Gal. 1:22). Nor is that all. The believers living in a particular locality soon began to meet regularly, sometimes daily (Acts 2:46), but regularly in time on Sunday.[13] But they did not have their own church building — presumably the word *assembly* in James 2:2 is the first New Testament instance of a reference to a particular place; hence they had to come together in some house of a brother or sister which was suitable for the purpose.

In Jerusalem they first gathered for some time still in the temple,[14] but in addition to this they also had special meetings (Acts 1:14 and 2:42) in the homes of some of their fellows (Acts 2:46 and 5:42). So it happened that at first the house of Mary, the mother of John Mark (Acts 12:12) and later that of James (Acts 21:18) became the center of the ecclesiastical life of Jerusalem. Because the church was large, it divided into groups and came together in the same house at different times, or in different houses at the same time. This practice was followed also in other places, in Thessalonica (Acts 17:11), Troas (Acts 20:8), Ephesus (Acts 20:20), Corinth (1 Cor. 16:19), Colosse (Philemon 2), Laodicea (Col. 4:15), and Rome (Rom. 16:5, 14 and 15). It is remarkable that all of these various home-churches or house-churches were definitely given the name of church.[15] The one was not subordinated to another, but each of them was independent, having the same rights as the others.

Nevertheless they were all one. Jesus had spoken of all of His disciples taken together as His church (Matt. 16:18 and 18:17), and the apostles talk in the same way of the body of believers, Paul especially doing so. The church taken in its entirety is the body of Christ, and He is their head.[16] The church is the bride of the Lamb adorned for her husband,[17] the house and the temple of God built by the apostles on the foundation of Christ (1 Cor. 3:10-16), or, according to another application of the same figure, built up on the foundation of the prophets and apostles, Christ Himself being the cornerstone and the believers the living stones.[18] The church is a chosen generation, a royal priesthood, an holy nation, a peculiar people, called to show forth the praises of Him who has called it out of darkness into His marvelous light (1 Peter 2:9).

With an eye to the glorious virtues which the apostles ascribe to the church, some observers have wanted to make a distinction between

---

13. 1 Cor. 16:2; Acts 20:7; and Rev. 1:10.
14. Acts 2:1, 46; 3:11; 5:12, 20, and 42.
15. Rom. 16:5; 1 Cor. 16:19; Col. 4:15; and Philemon 2.
16. Eph. 1:22-23; 4:15; and Col. 1:18, 24.
17. Eph. 5:32; 2 Cor. 11:2; and Rev. 21:2.
18. Eph. 2:20-22; 1 Tim. 3:15; 1 Peter 2:5; and Rev. 21:3.

the empirical and the ideal church. But such a Western distinction is foreign to the New Testament. When the apostles, following in the example of Christ, speak so gloriously, especially in John 14-17, of the church, they are not thinking of something which exists in the abstract or in thought only, nor of an ideal which we are to follow after and which we will probably never attain. They always have in mind, rather, the whole and the actual church, that body of which the gatherings of believers in the various localities and countries and the various times are the particular revelations. Those revelations, it is true, are all of them very defective still — and to this the apostles in all their letters testify; but they are revelations nevertheless of a reality lying behind them, actualizations of a counsel of God carrying itself out from generation to generation.

In that counsel or decree God sees the whole church of Christ before Him in its perfection; in Christ who purchased it with His blood, the church lies contained as the fruit in the seed. In the Holy Spirit, who takes everything from Christ, lies the root of its existence and the guarantee of its fulfillment. The church is therefore not an idea or an ideal, but a reality which is becoming something and will become something because it is already something. Thus it is that the church continues in constant change; it was being gathered from the beginning of the world, and it will be gathered until the end of the world. Daily there depart from it some who have fought the fight, kept the faith, earned the crown of righteousness, and who constitute the church triumphant, the church of the firstborn and the spirits of just men made perfect (Heb. 12:23). And daily new members are added to the church on earth, to the militant church here below; they are born in the church itself or are brought in by the work of missions.

These two parts of the church belong together. They are the vanguard and rearguard of the great army of Christ. Those who have preceded now form round about us a great cloud of witnesses; during their lives they made their confession of faith and thus admonished us to faithfulness and patience. Without us they could not become perfect, and without them we could not be perfect (Heb. 11:40). Only all the saints together can fully grasp the greatness of the love of Christ and be filled with all the fulness of God (Eph. 3:18-19). History will continue, therefore, until we all have come to the oneness of the faith and the knowledge of the Son of God, to a perfect man, to the measure of the stature of the fulness of Christ (Eph. 4:13).

* * * * *

That the apostles, in ascribing such wonderful characteristics to the church as a whole, do not have an idea or an ideal in mind, but a reality, is indicated most clearly by the fact that they speak in the same way about each local church and even of each individual believer. The local church at Corinth, for example, is, despite its many errors and defects, called the temple of God, the dwelling place of His Spirit, and the body of Christ (1 Cor. 3:16 and 12:27, and just so we read also concerning each believer that his body is a temple of the Holy Spirit and that in body and spirit he belongs to God (1 Cor. 6:19-20). All of them together, the church in its entirety, each local church, and every individual believer, share the same benefits, partake of the same Christ, are in the possession of the same Spirit, and by that Spirit are led to one and the same Father.[19] There is a difference in the measure of grace which Christ grants to each of His believers (Rom. 12:6 and Eph. 4:7); there is a difference of gift, administration, operation, and working (1 Cor. 12:4-6). But this difference is no impediment to the unity of believers, but, rather, fosters and strengthens it.

If the church is really an organism, a living body, this implies that it comprises many and various members, each of whom receives his own name and place, his own function and calling inside the whole. If they were all one organ, one member, where were the body? (1 Cor. 12:19). For as the body is one, and has many members, and all the members are members of that one body, so it is for the church (1 Cor. 12:12). Every member of the church, accordingly, receives from Christ his own gift, modest or small as it may be, and with that gift he is to serve not himself but the church. According to the nature of the gift which each has received, he must minister to the brethren, as a good steward of the manifold grace of God (1 Peter 4:10). He did not receive his ability for himself but to profit withal (1 Cor. 12:7), to the edification of the church (1 Cor. 14:12), to the care of others even as they care for him.

In its rich variegation, therefore, the church of Christ remains a *unity*. That is to say not merely that there has always been but one church and there will always be but one; it means to say also that this church is always and everywhere the same, having the same benefits, privileges, and goods. The unity is not one which accrues to the church from the outside, which is imposed upon it by force, that is called into being by contractual arrangement, or is temporarily organized against a common enemy. It does not even come up out of the social instincts of the religious life. It is a unity, rather, which is spiritual in character. It depends upon and has its foundation and example in the unity which exists between the Father and Christ as Mediator (John 17:21-23). It is a unity which comes up out of Christ as the vine who gives rise to all the branches and who nourishes them (John 15:5), as the head in whom

---

19. 1 Cor. 8:6; Eph. 2:18; and 4:3-6.

the whole body has its growth (Eph. 4:16); and it is brought into being by that one Spirit with whom we are all led to one Father.[20] The love of the Father, the grace of the Son, and the fellowship of the Holy Spirit are the portion of every believer, of every local church, and of the church in its entirety. In this consists its profound and immutable unity.

This unity continues to be very defective and imperfect in the church here on earth. Just as the church itself, so its unity too is still in the process of becoming; it is present all the while but it is gradually worked out and applied. Jesus prayed for it (John 17:21), and the apostle Paul presented it as something that would be accomplished in full only in the future (Eph. 4:13). Nevertheless, it is no mere play of the imagination, without any basis in reality. On the contrary, it exists, and is come to expression more or less in the life of the church; it is present not only in the invisible but also comes to expression in the visible manifestation of the church. In the church at Jerusalem it revealed itself in this way that all the brothers and sisters after being taken up into the church by baptism, persevered in the doctrine of the Apostles, in fellowship, in the breaking of bread, and in prayers (Acts 2:42), that they were all of one heart and of one soul and shared what was needed with each other (Acts 2:44 and 4:32-35). When churches were founded later on in other places too this unity of the believers continued.

All the same the church by reason of the various backgrounds and customs of the Christians who stemmed from the Jews and those who stemmed from the Gentiles encountered a big impediment to this unity; often the two groups stood sharply opposed to each other in the frequently mixed churches, and sometimes, often, in fact, there was outright conflict between the two. Even Peter proved himself weak at a given moment in that conflict at Antioch and brought down Paul's reprimand upon his head (Gal. 2:11-14). But the apostle of the Gentiles who was a Jew to the Jews and became all to all kept the great goal of unity steadily before his eyes and in all the church admonished to love and peace. They were all, he said, one body, they all had one Spirit, one Lord, one baptism, one faith, one God and Father above all and in all (Eph. 4:4-6). Nor did they all have to be precisely alike, for a body assumes difference of members, and each was to serve the whole with his particular abilities (1 Cor. 12:4ff.) and they had to honor each other's liberty (Rom. 14). By the death of Christ the middle wall of partition was broken, and those two, the Jews and the Gentiles, were reconciled with each other, and made to be a new man (Eph. 2:14ff.). In the confession of Christ as Lord they were one (1 Cor. 12:3), and

---

20. 1 Cor. 12:13; Eph. 2:18; and 4:4.

they all stood committed to one duty, namely, to do all things to the glory of God.[21] And Paul was blessed in this his work; the opposition between the two gradually disappeared, and the unity of the church was preserved.

But later the church of Christ was divided by all kinds of heresy and schism in the successive centuries. At the present time its multitudinous denominations and sects present a most lamentable spectacle of disunity. Still, something of the old unity can still be seen, inasmuch as all Christian churches are still separated from the world by one and the same baptism, in the confession of the twelve Articles of Faith still continue in the doctrine of the apostles, and, be it in very different forms, still join in the breaking of bread and in prayers. The church is in its unity an object of faith; even though we cannot see it, or cannot see it as plainly as we should like to see it, it exists now and it will some time be perfected.

The same holds true of another characteristic of the church, namely, its *holiness*. From the beginning the only access to the church was by way of faith and repentance; whoever repented was baptized and received the forgiveness of sins and the gift of the Holy Spirit (Acts 2:38). Although Jesus Himself did not baptize (John 4:2), and although the apostles as a rule did not do it either (Acts 10:48 and 1 Cor. 1:14-17), baptism was administered to all who wanted to belong to the church. But this baptism was all the while understood in its oneness of the visible sign and the invisible spiritual significance, as being at once a laying aside of the filthiness of the flesh and the answer of a good conscience towards God (1 Peter 3:21), and it was accordingly set over against the circumcision as a ceremony which had now become vain. Viewed in this way, baptism was in very fact a preservation, like that of the ark which spared Noah (1 Peter 3:20-21), a dying and being raised again with Christ (Rom. 6:3-4), a washing away of sins (Acts 22:16), a break with the world and an entrance into a new fellowship.

Thus baptism implied an entirely different attitude towards the world; and it required great courage for a person to subject himself to this and to join the church of Christ. For not only did that church consist to a large extent of simple and ordinary people (1 Cor. 1:25-29) but one also had often to suffer disdain and oppression. At first this enmity and persecution came from the side of the Jews, be it the authorities,[22] or the people who, as was more than once the case, urged the Gentiles on to opposition and uproar.[23] Sometimes too the Gentiles on their own initiative were antagonistic to the Christians, but this was

---

21. Rom. 14:6-8; 1 Cor. 10:31; and Col. 3:17.
22. Acts 4:1ff.; 5:17ff.; 6:12ff.; 9:1ff.
23. Acts 9:23ff.; 13:50; 14:2; 17:5 and elsewhere.

an exception, and the government was for the most part not indisposed towards the Christians.[24]

The persecution of the church from the side of Rome first began under Nero in the year 64. Hence it was that the Christians looked for protection rather than persecution from the Roman authorities,[25] recognized in the Roman government an authority ordained of God, and encouraged people to subject themselves to its law and to pray for its welfare.[26]

As for the social life, the apostles advised that the believer ought not leave his or her spouse (1 Cor. 7:12 and 1 Peter 3:1), but that in marrying he should do it as in the Lord (1 Cor. 7:39 and 2 Cor. 6:14). They advised that everybody, whether servant or maidservant, continue to abide in the same calling with which he was called (1 Cor. 7:20), that believers ought not to withdraw altogether from contact with unbelievers (1 Cor. 5:10), that believers could accept invitations to a banquet, but that for the sake of conscience and the example, they should refrain from eating of an offering made to an idol (1 Cor. 10: 27, 28; 8:12; and 10:20). Further the apostles taught that the believers should live in peace and love with all men, with the enemy also,[27] and that they should regard no thing as unclean in itself, since every creature of God is good (Rom. 14:14 and 1 Tim. 4:4).

This relationship of the church to the world is, accordingly, a relationship of freedom, and is altogether free from every false and unnatural abstinence or withdrawal; but it can be this only so long as the church is conscious of its calling and so long as it walks in holiness before the face of God. The church is holy, is a holy people, and the believers are holy persons or saints (Rom. 1:7 and 1 Cor. 1:2) for they are altogether and each for himself temples of the Holy Spirit (1 Cor. 3:16-17 and 6:19); by that Spirit they are washed and sanctified in Christ Jesus,[28] and they are, therefore, to shun and to do battle to the death against all sins, all works of the flesh, all worldly desires,[29] and, on the contrary, are to exercise all the virtues and to support all that is good.[30] It is a life of love that the Christians must lead (Eph. 5:2) for love is the greatest of all the virtues (1 Cor. 13:13), the bond of perfection (Col. 3:14), and the fulfillment of the law (Rom. 13:10).

And discipline is a means given to the church by Christ so that the church may preserve this its holy character. Such discipline must be

24. Acts 17:9; 18:17; 19:35ff.; 21:32; and 23:17ff.
25. Acts 16:37; 22:25; 25:10; and 2 Thess. 2:7.
26. Rom. 13:1-7; 1 Tim. 2:2; Tit. 3:1; and 1 Peter 2:13-17.
27. Rom. 12:14, 17; 13:10; Gal. 6:10; Col. 4:5; 1 Thess. 3:12; 2 Peter 1:7.
28. John 17:17, 19; 1 Cor. 1:2; 6:11; and Eph. 26:27.
29. Gal. 5:19; Col. 3:5; and Hebr. 12:1 and 4.
30. Gal. 5:22; Phil. 4:8; Col. 3:12; Titus 2:14 and elsewhere.

exercised not merely in secret, say, by one brother over against another,[31] but in the event of public sins it must also be applied by the church to its members.[32] How much of this holiness was still missing in the apostolic time the various epistles all report, and later ages frequently gave rise to a profound religious and moral decay. But after the lapse and decay the Spirit of Christ again and again caused a revival and renewal to take place. This holiness of the church is also a characteristic which Christ earned for the church and which He works out, in and through the church.

And, finally, there is the characteristic of catholicity or universality which belongs to the church. This characteristic appears by name first of all in a post-apostolic piece of writing, and the intention was to declare that, over against all kinds of heresy and schism the true church is the one which obeys the bishop and remains with the main body since the whole, universal catholic church is the one in which Christ is. Later all kinds of other explanations were attached to the name; people came to understand by it that the church is spread out over the whole world, that from the beginning to the present day it includes all believers of all time, and that, sharing as it does in all truth and grace, it is an adequate means of salvation for all. These explanations are not mistaken, if only in thinking of the church one does not think merely of one ecclesiastical organization, the Roman Catholic one, for example, but takes it to refer to the Christian church which reveals itself in all the churches together and in very differing degrees of purity and soundness. For that church is in very fact a catholic church. Even in the Old Testament the mother-promise was made to Adam and Eve and thus to the whole human race. And if later on the conditions of the times led to the selection of a particular people in Abraham to serve as the bearer of revelation, that revelation nevertheless was and remained intended for all mankind. In Abraham's seed all the generations of the earth were to be blessed (Gen. 12:2). And prophecy kept its eye steadily fixed upon this general destination of redemption.[33]

When Christ entered upon His ministry, it is true that He addressed Himself only to the lost sheep of the house of Israel (Matt. 15:24), but the kingdom which He preached was nevertheless catholic, was quite free of any national limitations, and stood open to all who believed and repented (Mark 1:15). He says that if the Jews reject His gospel, the children of the kingdom will be cast out, and that many shall come from the east and the west, and shall sit down with Abraham, Isaac, and Jacob (Matt. 8:11-12). He Himself must like a grain of wheat fall into

31. Matt. 18:15-22; 1 Thess. 5:14; and Heb. 10:24.
32. Matt. 18:17; 1 Cor. 5:5; 2 Cor. 2:5-10; and Titus 8:10.
33. Joel 2:32; Micah 4:1-2; Zeph. 2:11; and Isa. 25:6-10.

the ground and die, but afterwards He will bring forth much fruit (John 12:24). He has other sheep besides Israel, and these He must also bring, in order that they may be one fold under one shepherd (John 10:16 and 11:52). After His resurrection He enjoins it upon His disciples that they preach the gospel to all creatures and make all nations to be His followers (Matt. 28:19 and Mark 16:15). And the apostles have carried out this mandate; they went out as His witnesses, both in Jerusalem and in the whole of Judaea and Samaria and to the uttermost parts of the earth (Acts 1:8).

It is remarkable that, although Jesus speaks continuously of the kingdom of heaven and only a few times of the church, the apostles to the contrary mention the kingdom of God comparatively seldom and speak in detail of the church of Christ. An explanation can be given for this, however.

The kingdom of heaven of which Jesus speaks is, after all, in the first place not a gathering of people, a commonwealth of citizens, but a composite of spiritual goods and blessings, a treasure (Matt. 13:44), a pearl (Matt. 13:45), righteousness, peace, and joy in the Holy Spirit (Matt. 6:33 and Rom. 14:17). That kingdom is of heaven, and it now comes down with Christ to the earth, for in Him the Father distributes all those blessings and those goods (1 Cor. 1:30 and Eph. 1:3). The Father has appointed the kingdom to Him and He in His turn appoints it to His disciples (Luke 22:29). He does this now already on earth; when through the Spirit of God He casts out devils, that is evidence that the kingdom of God has come (Matt. 12:28), and this kingdom keeps on coming when it shares itself and all its treasures by way of faith (Luke 17:21); this kingdom makes progress as a tree which grows up, and as a leaven which leavens the whole loaf (Matt. 13:31-33), and it will in all its fulness be distributed in the future upon the return of Christ.[34]

This kingdom, understood in this way, is nevertheless, from the first coming of Christ until His second coming given to people, to such as are born again of water and the Spirit, and who believe in the name of Christ (John 1:12-13 and 3:3-5). That is why it is represented in the figure of a seed which is planted in the ground in order to bring forth fruit, or in the figure of a net which, being cast into the sea, gathers all kinds of fish (Matt. 13:24 and 46). And the apostles are the fishers who go out with that net and gather men in order to cause them to share in the present and future blessings of the kingdom (Matt.4:19).

While Jesus is thus preaching the gospel of the kingdom and is explaining the nature, character, and development of that kingdom, His

---

34. Matt. 5:3ff.; 6:10; Luke 12:32; Acts 14:22; 1 Cor. 15:24-28; 2 Thess. 1:5 and elsewhere.

apostles have been called and qualified by Him to gather the church by means of that gospel of the kingdom — the church which shares in the treasures of the kingdom and will some day fully receive and enjoy them all. The word of the kingdom fixes our attention especially upon the treasures, the goods, the blessings which are distributed through the   Father in Christ; in distinction from that the church makes us think of the gathering of people who have received these goods and who are moving towards the full enjoyment of them. In other words, the church is in Christ the owner, possessor, preserver, distributor, and heir of the kingdom of God. That is its treasure and its glory; it has no other value. What Peter once said the church can in its way repeat after him: Silver and gold have I none, but such as I have I give thee: in the name of Jesus Christ of Nazareth, rise up and walk (Acts 3:6).

Because all the treasures of the kingdom which the church possesses are spiritual in kind, and do not consist of gold or silver, of power and might, but of righteousness, peace, and joy through the Holy Spirit, the characteristic quality of catholicity accrues to the church. The church is not bound to a land or a people, to a time or a place, to any given generation, to money and property; it is independent of all earthly distinctions and contrasts. It brings the gospel to all creatures, and that gospel is always and only the gospel, a joyous tiding which is suitable and necessary for all people, in all times, under all circumstances, for all conditions. The kingdom of God is in opposition to nothing except to sin.

* * * * *

From the very beginning this church thought of as a gathering of believers had a particular organization. Every organization of human beings must, in order to avoid confusion and dissolution, and in order to be adequate to the purpose for which it was established, have regulations governing its gatherings and activities. The church of Christ is also subject to this general law of human society. God is not a god of confusion, but a God of peace: He laid down ordinances for all His creatures, and He intends that in the churches also everything take place decently and in order (1 Cor. 14:33 and 40). And such a laying down of regulations is the more necessary for the life of the church because God wants to use it for a specific purpose. After all, the church, so long as it exists on earth, is still imperfect; each of its members and all of the members together must constantly be fighting against sin and following after holiness; at all times these people require instruction, guidance, direction, strengthening, comfort, admonishment, and chastisement. And not that only, but the church must also reproduce itself from generation to generation; it does not always have the same members, since it daily loses those who are transferred to the triumphant church, and is constantly augmented by new members who are nurtured in it, and who must be introduced into the life of the church. Besides, it has received the mandate from Christ to preach the gospel to the whole world and to all creatures. Inside itself, therefore, as well as outside, it has a holy and heavy calling to carry out.

When God lays this mandate upon the church He at the same time gives it the qualifications and equipment to carry it out. He arranges things in such a way and gives the church such gifts, powers, and administrations, as equip it to carry out the task which He lays upon its shoulders. He gave the church, as Paul expresses it, apostles, evangelists, pastors, and teachers in order that these might carry out the work of the ministry in the church, and so build up the body of Christ, and effect the perfecting of the saints; and this whole series of arrangements must therefore remain in force until the purpose is achieved and all together have come to the unity of the faith and the knowledge of God, to the perfect man, to the measure of the stature of the fulness of Christ (Eph. 4:11-13). In other words, the church as a gathering of believers has, with a view to the calling which it must fulfill on earth, received from Christ a particular institution, a peculiar arrangement of gifts and powers, offices and services, through which it can respond to its vocation. This institution of laws and regulations was not added to the church later, but was present in it from the beginning. Because not everything can be discussed at one and the same time, it is necessary first to discuss the church as a gathering of believers, and afterwards to speak of the regulations governing its life and operations. But it may not be inferred from this that the first was in effect for some time before the second came to be, and that it existed without the second. God immediately established the church on earth in such a way as its place and task in the world demanded.

But, although there is no temporary difference between the two there is a difference. That becomes apparent from the fact that the institution which was given the church changed remarkably in the course of the ages. From the time of Paradise there were believers on the earth, and they also undoubtedly came together in meeting with each other. We read in Genesis 4:26 that in the days of Enoch men began to call upon the name of the Lord, and no doubt this is a statement of the facts that in the days of the Cainites the Sethites separated themselves and gathered in meeting around the confession of the Lord's name. From that time on, therefore, there was public worship. It consisted for the most part of preaching, sacrifice, and prayer. But for the rest there was still little mention made of organization. The church at that time had its center in the family. In the patriarchal period the father was the king and also the priest of his family; he carried out the circumcision (Gen. 17: 23), and made the sacrifices (Gen. 22:2 and 26:1).

When the law was given on Sinai, and God established His covenant with His people, a big change took place. At that time a particular institution of the priesthood and of the Levites was instituted. A definite place and time was designated for the sacrifices. The offerings themselves were distinguished from each other and arranged in a definite order. And everything bearing on the sacred persons, times, places, and actions was strictly regulated and prescribed in detail. The law was a yoke which was heavy to bear (Acts 15:10), but it was necessary at that time in order to sharpen the sense of sin, to arouse the need for forgiveness, to shed light on the significance and necessity of sacrifices, and so to lead the way to Christ.

Nevertheless there grew up underneath and alongside of this official, legal prescription yet another organization of the religious life of Israel. We must remember that the people lived through the whole of Canaan and even to some extent on the other side of the Jordan. It speaks for itself that only a comparatively small part of this people could go up to Jerusalem for the great feasts. Besides all of them were strictly obliged to keep the Sabbath, and this they all celebrated in their own dwelling places. It lies ready to hand, and is very probable, that on such days the believers held religious meetings and joined in meditation on the law, and in song, and prayer. In Acts 15:21 we accordingly read that Moses from old times had in every city those that preached him, and that he was read in the synagogues every Sabbath day.

The origin of these synagogues is unknown to us, but it is certain that it goes far back; and during and after the captivity, when the Jews were dispersed through all lands and often lived far removed from their fatherland and the temple, that those synagogues got a new and rich significance. In every place where Jews lived a synagogue was built, and thither at specific times, on the Sabbath, on feast days, and also on days of the week, the Jews gathered to give expression to a common confession, to join in prayer, to listen to the reading of a portion of the law and the prophets, and also to an independent discourse (Luke 4:21), and to receive the blessing of the priest. The rule of the church was given to a college of elders to whom were delegated the right of carrying out discipline and of excommunication and who governed various parts of the service, and who regulated the religious services.[35] Among the officers was the treasurer, who received the gifts given for mercy, and a minister (Luke 4:20) who had to bring out the Holy Scriptures and return them again. This whole regulation governing the synagogues

---

35. Mark 5:22, 35ff.; Luke 8:49; and 13:14.

was of the greatest importance for the religious life of the Jews, and in various ways it formed also the example for the organization of the Christian church.

Jesus had the habit of visiting these assemblies in the synagogues (Luke 4:16), and He subjected Himself for the rest also to the maintenance of the whole Mosaic law and thus fulfilled all righteousness (Matt. 3:15). Nevertheless He came in order that by thus keeping the law He might fulfill it and so place a different burden on the shoulders of His disciples from that of the hard yoke of the law. This different burden was soft and light and gave rest to their souls (Matt. 11:29-30). He preached the gospel of the kingdom of God and gathered disciples around Him who acknowledged Him as their Master and who were gradually led deeper and deeper into the knowledge of His person and work.

Among this circle of disciples, Christ, with an eye to the twelve tribes of Israel (Matt. 19:28) chose twelve of their number to whom He also gave the name of Apostles (Luke 6:13). The seriousness and the importance of this choice becomes apparent from the fact that He made it after a night which He had spent upon the mountain alone in prayer with God (Luke 6:12). Humanly speaking so very much of the future of the kingdom of God depended upon this choice. The name of apostle, which He gave to each of the twelve disciples, means *ambassador,* or messenger, or missionary, and was not uncommon in those days. Among the Jews those men who were sent out from Jerusalem to collect the money for the temple were designated very probably by the name *apostles.* In the New Testament Jesus Himself is called apostle (Heb. 3:1), and also Barnabas (Acts 14:4 and 14), and it may be that here or there some other servant of the gospel was also so designated. But soon the name of apostle was limited to the twelve who were chosen by Jesus, and to Paul who later was in a particular way called to be an apostle to the heathen.[36]

The immediate purpose of this choice of the apostles was that they should be with Jesus, and that they should be sent out by Him to preach and to heal the sick (Mark 3:14-15). According to Matthew 10:1 ff. (Mark 6:7 ff. and Luke 9:1 ff.) Jesus did thus send them out to the various villages and cities of Galilee. By this mission Jesus undoubtedly meant to bring the gospel to the Jews whom He could not Himself reach, but at the same time He was preparing His apostles for their future vocation. And that future calling was none other than this, that after Jesus' ascension, they should come forward as His witnesses in the midst of the world and build His church upon that testimony. He

---

36. Acts 1:2; 2:37; Gal. 1:17; 1 Cor. 9:5; 15:7; Rev. 2:2; 18:20; and 21;14.

equipped them for this in a particular way by His going in and out with them and by His teaching, by letting them be the witnesses of His words and works, of His life and passion, of His death and especially, too, of His resurrection,[37] and by promising to send them the Spirit of truth, who would lead them in all truth, comfort them, and remain with them eternally.[38] Together with this preparation He gave them a particular power, namely the power to preach and to teach, in a particular way to heal all sorts of sick people, to administer baptism and the Lord's Supper, to exercise discipline, and to open and close the kingdom of heaven by forgiving or refusing to forgive sins.[39] The apostles were servants of Christ and stewards of the mysteries of God (1 Cor. 4:1).

Among the apostles Peter occupied the first place. He was the son of Jonas, a fisherman in Bethsaida (John 1:43-44), and he had married already at Capernaum before the time that Jesus learned to know him (Mark 1:21, 29). His name originally was Simon, but it was immediately at Jesus' first meeting with him augmented by the name of Cephas, or Peter, meaning rock (John 1:42). This name was an expression of his nature, of his enterprise, his independence, his openheartedness and his steadfastness. Thus we learn to know him during Jesus' life. He was the first to be chosen among the apostles (Mark 3:13), and he took the part of their representative and spokesman. His steadfastness had to undergo a hard proof during the passion of Christ, and it succumbed in his terrible denial. But raised and restored again by Jesus (Luke 22:32 and John 21:15 ff.), he could fortify his brethren the better for it (Luke 22:32). Hence it was that after Jesus' ascension he soon assumed the leadership again; he did this at the choosing of Matthias (Acts 1:15 ff.), at the preaching on Pentecost (Acts 2:14 ff.), at the work of performing miracles (Acts 3:6), at the defense of the church before the council (Acts 4:8 ff.), at the judgment pronounced upon Ananias and Sapphira (Acts 5:4ff.), at the visitation-journey to Samaria (Acts 8:14), at the preaching of the gospel to the heathen (Acts 10:1 ff.), and at the gathering or synod held at Jerusalem (Acts 15:7 ff.).

The Roman Catholics argue from all of these circumstances that Peter enjoyed a higher rank than the other apostles and that in Rome later on he was the first pope. There is, however, no basis for this. It is true that he was the first and foremost among his kind, but he had neither any rank nor any power above them. The other eleven were apostles quite as well as he. The power of preaching and teaching, of adminis-

---

37. Acts 1:8, 22; 2:32; 3:15 and elsewhere.
38. John 14:17; 15:26; 16:17; and 20:23.
39. Matt. 16:19; 18:18; 28:19; and John 20:23.

tering baptism and the Lord's Supper, of opening and closing the kingdom of heaven was not given to him alone (Matt. 16:19), but was also given to the other apostles.[40] As a matter of fact, after Acts 15 Peter withdraws into the background so that we know only these further things about him: that he was in Antioch (Gal. 2:11) and in Babylon (1 Peter 5:13), and that he later died in Rome as a martyr (John 21:18-19). Thereupon he makes way for Paul who, on the one hand, calls himself the least of the apostles (1 Cor. 15:9), but who, on the other hand, wants to be their inferior neither in rank, office, power, nor work,[41] and who even reprimands Peter in Antioch (Gal. 2:11).

We read in Matthew 16:18 that Jesus, after Peter's courageous and clean-cut confession of His Messiahship, addresses him as follows: Thou art Peter, and upon this rock shall I build my church. In saying this, Jesus has in mind not so much the person of Peter, nor even the confession which he has just made apart from his person, but has in mind rather the confessing Peter (Peter as confessor, and more specifically Peter as confessor of Christ in the name of all His apostles). And Peter was not such a confessor alone: the other apostles were that also, so that the church was not built upon Peter alone, but upon the apostles altogether (Eph. 2:20 and Rev. 21:14). The apostolate is and remains the foundation of the church; there is no communion with Christ except through communion with them and their word (John 17:20 and 1 John 1:3).

* * * * *

These apostles stood at the head of the church in Jerusalem immediately after Jesus' ascension, and they formed as it were the consistory of that church. All power resided with them. They had received it, not from the church, but from Christ Himself. But it was a power, as Peter himself later described it, designed to shepherd the flock of God and to exercise supervision over it, not by force, but willingly, not for unlawful gain, but from a ready mind, not as being lords over God's heritage, but as being examples to the flock (1 Peter 5:2-3). The apostolate stands above the church, but it is at the same time intended for the service of the church and for its profit. The apostolate has been instituted for the sake of the church (Eph. 4:11-12). We see this plainly in the church at Jerusalem. The apostles lead in the gatherings of the believers (Acts 1:15), they preach and baptize (Acts 2:38), they maintain the purity of the truth, and continue steadfast in the breaking of bread, and in the fellowship and prayers (Acts 2:42). They do signs and wonders (Acts 2:43), they distribute the gifts among the poor brothers and

---

40. Matt. 18:18; 28:19; and John 20:23.
41. 1 Cor. 15:10; 2 Cor. 11:23ff.; and 12:11.

sisters (Acts 4:37 and 5:2). At first there was no other office in the church but that of the apostles. They did everything that is being done nowadays by the teachers and the pastors, and by the elders and deacons.

But this condition could not long continue. When the church spread itself out, and particularly when churches were added outside the pale of Jerusalem in Judaea, Samaria, Galilee, and later also in the pagan world, counsel and help had to be supplied. That took place in two ways: for all the churches regarded as a unit, and for each church in particular.

The several churches which gradually grew up outside Jerusalem in other cities and villages were not subordinate to the church at Jerusalem but came to stand independently alongside of it. We are justified in calling the church at Jerusalem the mother church to the extent we mean by this that it was the first church, and that the other churches came into being through its missionary effort. But this designation is mistaken if we mean by it that the other churches stood in a relationship of dependency to the one at Jerusalem. In that sense there is and can be no such thing as a mother church, for each church, even the smallest and meanest, owes its origin and existence solely and directly to Christ and His Spirit, even though these make use of missions as the means. Every church is, accordingly, a church of Christ, and is not a subdivision or branch of another church, be it in Jerusalem, in Rome, or elsewhere. However, even though the churches which gradually grew up in Palestine and outside of the country were sister churches and not daughters of the church at Jerusalem they all without distinction and in the same sense remained dependent and subject to the authority of the apostles.

The apostles were much more than a local consistory; they were and they remained the consistory of the whole Christian church wherever it was established. The moment, therefore, that Samaria had accepted the word of God, the apostles sent Peter and John there to pray for the believers, to lay their hands upon them in reception of the gift of the Holy Spirit and further to preach the word among them (Acts 8:13-25). Later Peter went through the circuit of all the new churches in Judaea, Samaria, and Galilee in order to strengthen them and to foster the mutual fellowship of them all (Acts 9:31-32). So it was that the churches did not stand alongside of each other loosely, and that they were not abandoned to their own destiny and whim; instead these churches retained the foundation and center of the apostolate.

But this brought about a state of affairs in which the work of the apostles grew apace. A division of labor as well as an increase of workers became necessary. The division of labor took place when at the convention in Jerusalem it was with mutual approbation of all agreed that the apostles should go to the Jews at Jerusalem and that Paul should go to the Gentiles (Gal. 2:6-9). Naturally this division of labor was not so strictly intended that Paul could never again address his appeal to the Jews, or that the apostles in Jerusalem could never again work with the Gentiles. Paul continued to be concerned first of all with the people of his own nation and race, whom he loved so tenderly, and Peter, John, and James, according to their letters, were also active among the Christians gained from the Gentiles. Nevertheless this was a division of work which laid out general boundaries, and which gave to both parties some relief and some freedom of effort.

To this we must, in the second place, add the consideration that the apostles took on co-laborers, persons who stood by them in their variegated activities. Such persons were Barnabas (Acts 13:2), Mark and Luke (Acts 12:25; 13:5, and Philemon 1, 24), Timothy (Rom. 16:21 and 1 Thess. 3:2), Titus (2 Cor. 8:23), and Silas (Acts 15:40).[42] Sometimes these persons, like Philip (Acts 5:8, 40 and 21:8), were called evangelists (Eph. 4:11 and 2 Tim. 4:5). Besides, the apostles also received help from the prophets, persons who held no particular office but who received a special gift from God. Such were Agabus (Acts 11:28 and 21:10) and the daughters of Philip (Acts 21:9). These also assisted in enlightening the church and in building it up in the truth.[43]

All of these offices — that of apostles, prophets, and evangelists — have vanished to the extent that their incumbents have died and they from the nature of the case have not been supplanted by any others. They were necessary in that unusual time when the church had to be established on earth. But their work has not been idle in the Lord. For, in the first place, they did indeed build the church upon the one foundation of Jesus Christ (1 Cor. 3:11), and in the second place their testimony lives on in the books of the New Testament, in the gospels and the epistles, in the Acts and the Revelation, lives on, indeed, in the whole church up to this day. By reason of this testimony the church is able in all times to persevere in the doctrine of the apostles, in the fellowship, in the breaking of bread and in prayers (Acts 2:42). The word of the apostles, first spoken and thereupon written down, sustains and guarantees the unity of the church not only as it lies spread out over the whole world but also as it spans the ages.

Just as the apostles in their work of ruling the church as a whole received the help of the extraordinary offices of prophets and evangelists, so also in the care of each local church they were supported by the service of elders and deacons. We must remember that the apostles were at first themselves the distributors of the gifts of mercy (Acts 4:37 and

---

42. Compare Rom. 16:9; Phil. 2:25; 4:3; and Col. 4:10-11.
43. 1 Cor. 12:28; 14:4; Eph. 4:11.

5:2). But when the church became perceptibly larger, they could no longer carry out this work themselves. On the occasion of a dispute which arose in the church about the daily service, the apostles proposed that seven men, full of the faith and of the Holy Spirit, be chosen for the ministration of the tables (Acts 6:1-6). There has always been a considerable difference of opinion about whether or not this is an account of the institution of the office of deacon. It is not impossible that the office of these seven men, instituted by the apostles in Acts 6, originally comprised more service and work than the later office of deacons comprised. Nevertheless we read plainly that the apostles reserved for themselves the ministration of the word and the service of prayers (Acts 6:4), and that the seven new men were charged with the service of the tables, that is, with the regulation of everything bearing on the common mealtimes or feasts — usually concluded with the celebration of the Holy Supper — and with the distribution to the poor of what had been contributed to the feasts by the believers, and of what remained afterwards in the way of food, drink, and money.

In other churches too the office of deacon was instituted. We read of deacons in Philippi (Phil. 1:1), and at Ephesus.[44] In 1 Timothy 3:8ff. Paul sums up the qualifications which a deacon must be able to satisfy. The apostles at Jerusalem had done so also. They came to the church with the proposal that seven men be chosen, and they indicated the required abilities and the nature and function of the office. Thereupon the church selected them. But in the end it is again the apostles who by the laying on of hands delegate the office to them.

Alongside of the deacons the elders take their place. We are told nothing about the origin of this office. But when we recall that among the Jews a government by the eldest, whether in civic life or in the synagogues, was common practice, there is nothing surprising in the fact that from among the other members of the church some should be chosen to carry the responsibility of supervision and discipline. We read of them first of all in passing in Acts 11:30 where they receive the gifts which Barnabas and Saul brought with them for the brethren living in Judaea, and in Acts 15:2 ff. they share in the gathering which was called into being for the regulation of the mission work among the Jews and Gentiles.

This office of the elders, too, was quickly introduced into other churches. Paul and Barnabas had elders chosen in every church which they founded on their missionary journeys (Acts 14:23; compare 21:18). We find them in Ephesus (Acts 20:28), and in Philippi (Phil. 1:1). In these instances they are called bishops. In 1 Corinthians 12:28 we find

---

44. 1 Tim. 3:8; compare Rom. 12:8 and 1 Cor. 12:28.

them referred to perhaps under the name of governments, and in Ephesians 4:11 we meet them as pastors and teachers.[45] In 1 Timothy 3:1ff. and Titus 1:6-9 Paul indicates their qualifications, and in Titus 1:5 he requests Titus to designate elders in each church. These elders were charged with the supervision of the church,[46] and were, even within the apostolic period, distinguished as those who ruled and those who besides labored in the ministration of the word and the teaching of the truth.[47] It may be that Diotrephes, who according to 3 John 9 occupied the first place in the church, but who abused his power, and that the angels of the seven churches (Rev. 2:1-8) are also teachers of the kind who, in distinction from their fellow elders, labored in the word, and thus occupied a unique and significant place.

* * * * *

Such was the simple government which the apostles developed for the rule of the church. The offices which they instituted are few in number. Really those offices are but two: that of elder and that of deacon, be it that the first can be subdivided into teaching and ruling elder. These offices were actually ordained by the apostles; they laid down the duties and qualifications for them, but in the selection of the persons they reckoned with the church, and, once chosen in this way, they introduced them into the office by means of the laying on of hands. There was no such thing as a dominating power. Since Christ alone is the head of the church (Eph. 1:22), the one Master (Matt. 23:8-10), and Lord,[48] there can never arise in the church any single power which co-exists alongside of or over against His power, but only such as He himself has delegated and as remains limited by Him.

That was true of the extraordinary offices of apostle, evangelist, and prophet in that first period, instituted as they were in that first period before the establishment of the church in the world. They received their office and their power from Christ and not from the church, though they had to apply that power which they were given to the service of the church (Matt. 20:25-27 and I Peter 5:3). The same is true, and in an even stronger sense, of the ordinary offices which still exist in the church. The pastors and teachers, the elders and deacons also owe their office and their authority to Christ who instituted these offices and who continuously sustains them, who gives the persons and their gifts, and who has them designated by the church (1 Cor. 12:28 and Eph. 4:11).

---

45. 1 Thess. 5:12; 1 Cor. 16:15-16; Rom. 12:8; Heb. 13:7; 1 Peter 5:1; James 5:14-16; 1 Tim. 4:14; 5:17-22; and Titus 1:5-9.
46. Acts 21:28; Eph. 4:11; and 1 Peter 5:2.
47. 1 Tim. 5:17; Heb. 13:7; 1 Peter 4:11; and 1 Tim. 3:2 (apt to teach).
48. John 13:13; 1 Cor. 8:6; and Phil. 2:11.

But this gift and this authority are given them in order that they employ them for the benefit of the church and work with them to the end of the perfecting of the saints (Eph. 4:12). The office was instituted in order that thus the church should persevere in the teaching of apostles and in fellowship, in the breaking of bread and in prayers (Acts 2:42).

But this whole regulation or government, simple and beautiful as it was, was already distorted and denatured very soon after the apostolic period. First to come up was the office of the bishop, the so-called episcopacy. In the New Testament, and also in certain of the writings of the post-apostolic period, the names of elder (presbyter) and of overseer (bishop) were still used to designate one and the same person. The role of overseer, namely that of supervision and discipline, was the definition of the task given to the chosen eldest (or elders).[49]

But at the beginning of the second century a distinction was in some churches already being made between the two: the overseer or bishop was raised high above the elders and deacons in rank, and was regarded as the bearer of a particular office, as successor to the apostles, as preserver of purity of doctrine and as the cornerstone of the church. This was, of course, to enter upon the hierarchical road, and it led on the one hand to depriving the elders and deacons of all their independence and to degrading the believers to the level of mere immature lay persons, and on the other hand to raise the bishops and priests high above the church and, among them, to raise the bishop of Rome to the role of prince of the whole church. As the successor to Peter this bishop of Rome was supposed to bear the keys of the kingdom, to be the vice-regent of Christ on earth, and as pope to be clothed in matters of faith and life with Divine, infallible power.

This development of priestly rule in the church of Christ was countered at every step which it made in advance by opposition and impediment. But it was only at the Reformation that this conflict grew so strong that Christendom from that time on was torn into two great divisions. Some of these, such as the Anabaptists, then fell into a further extreme and held that every form of office, authority, or power was in conflict with the church of Christ. Others, such as the Anglican Church in England, broke the connecting bond with the pope in Rome, but kept the episcopacy in force. The Lutherans restored the office of preaching but they give the rule of the church and the care of the poor quite entirely into the hands of the civic authority. All kinds of propositions for the polity of the church came to exist alongside of each other. And to this day there is no less difference of opinion in the various Christian

49. Acts 20:17; compare Acts 20:28; Titus 1:5, 7; and 1 Peter 5:1-2.

denominations about church polity than there is about the confession of the church.

To Calvin goes the honor that, while doing battle against the Roman priestly hierarchy, he restored the offices of elder and deacon as well as that of the preaching office. Through him the church once received its own terrain and its own independent function. He fought bitterly and for years for the independence of the church, for the free exercise of its discipline, for the maintenance of purity in the ministration of the Word and Sacraments. In thinking of the church he did not think in the first place of the offices of that church, of the church as institute, but he saw in it above all a gathering or communion of believers who by their confession and walk had to prove themselves to be God's people, and who were all personally anointed of Christ to be prophets, priests and kings. The church is at once the mother and the community of believers. It is something different and something more than a crowd coming together in one place on Sunday to hear the preaching; it is a community or communion which during the week also makes its influence felt both towards the inside and the outside. The preaching office is but one of the offices; alongside of it there is the office of elder which must also through personal house visitation, supervision, and discipline, have its work to do; and there is, further, the office of deacon, which must show mercy to the poor and the sick; and, finally, there is the office of doctor or teacher whose function it is to develop the truth, and to instruct and defend it.

And while each church is independent, and owes its founding and existence, its gifts and power, its offices and ministrations solely to Christ, it is also intimately related to all the churches which stand with it on the same basis. It was so in the apostolic age. Every church, no matter how small or mean, was a church of Christ, His body and temple; but every church was also, from the very beginning, without ever making a decision or judgment about it, taken up into a spiritual unity with all other churches. All the churches together constituted one church (Matt. 16:18); all of them were subject to the authority of the apostles, who by their word laid the foundations of the whole church (Eph. 2:20). They are all together one in life and confession, and they all have one baptism, one faith, one Spirit, one Lord, one God and Father who is above all and in all (Eph. 4:3-6). They maintain fellowship with each other by means of travelling members (for example, Aquilla and Priscilla)[50] by reciprocal greetings,[51] and by serving each other with the gifts of love.[52] They also exchanged letters which the

---

50. Acts 18:2, 18; Rom. 16:3; and 2 Tim. 4:19.
51. Rom. 16:16; 1 Cor. 16:20; 2 Cor. 13:12; and elsewhere.
52. Acts 11:29; 1 Cor. 16:1; 2 Cor. 8:1; 9:1; and Gal. 2:10.

apostles sent them (Col. 4:16), and they made a beginning in difficult cases to deliberate on some matters together and to take common decisions (Acts 15).

Of all forms of church order, the presbyterian system as it was restored by Calvin, corresponds best to that of the apostolic time.

*   *   *   *   *

All the ministrations and offices which Christ instituted into His church are centered in the Word. He gave His disciples no worldly power (Matt. 20:25-27), nor priestly lordship (1 Peter 5:3), for they are all spiritual persons (1 Cor. 2:10-16), anointed by the Holy Spirit (1 John 2:20), and together forming a royal priesthood (1 Peter 2:9). The endowments and the offices have only this end that those who receive them serve one another by means of them in love (Rom. 13:18 and Gal. 5:13). The weapons of their warfare are purely spiritual in character (2 Cor. 10:4); they consist of the girdle of truth, the breastplate of righteousness, the shield of faith, the helm of salvation, and the sword of the Spirit (Eph. 6:14-17).

For this reason the Word is also the only earmark by which the church of Christ can be known in its truth and purity. It was by the Word that all true members of the church were reborn and brought to faith and repentance, purified and sanctified, gathered and established; and they in turn are called to preserve that Word (John 8:31 and 14:23), to study it (John 5:39), thereupon to prove the spirits (1 John 4:1), and to shun all those who do not teach this Word.[53] The Word of God is in very fact, to use the expression of Calvin, the soul of the church.

This Word of God was not given exclusively to the church as institute, to the office-bearers, but to all believers (John 5:39 and Acts 17:11), in order that with patience and comfort of the Scriptures they should have hope (Rom. 15:4) and in order that they should mutually teach and admonish each other.[54] Rome has done violence to this but the Reformation put the Bible back into all hands and so made it possible for the family and the school, for science and art, for society and the state, and for each individual believer, to have access to this source of teaching and instruction. In addition God provided for an official service of the Word. He gave and continues to give the church pastors and teachers[55] who are to minister the Word in public and in homes (Acts 20:20), to give it as milk to the immature and as meat to the

---

53. Gal. 1:8; Tit. 3:10; and 2 John 9.
54. Rom. 12:7-8; Col. 3:16; and Heb. 10:24-25.
55. 1 Cor. 12:28; Eph. 4:11; 1 Tim. 5:17; and 2 Tim. 2:2.

mature members of the church;[56] they are to do this in harmony with the needs of particular people and particular times, of each church and of each believer in particular.[57] In other words, the service of the Word includes its preservation, translation, interpretation, dissemination, defense, and its proclamation to all men; thus the church remains built up on the foundation of the apostles and prophets (Eph. 2:20), and is, as it should be, the pillar and ground of the truth (1 Tim. 3:15).

The Word has its confirmation in the sacraments which are signs and seals of the covenant of grace and which therefore serve for the strengthening of the faith. In the Old Testament God employed for this purpose the circumcision (Gen. 17:7) and the passover (Exod. 12:7ff.). Both signs had a spiritual significance, for the circumcision was a seal of the righteousness of faith (Rom. 4:11), and of the circumcision of the heart (Deut. 30:6 and Rom. 2:28-29). And the passover, as a sin offer and sacrificial meal point to Christ (John 1:29, 36 and 19:33, 36). Accordingly, too, both of them were fulfilled in the passion and death of Christ (Col. 2:11 and 1 Cor. 5:7) and were supplanted in the New Testament therefore by baptism (Matt. 28:19) and the Holy Supper (Matt. 26:17). These two signs, universally known as the sacraments (mysteries: 1 Cor. 4:1) are, without Biblical warrant, augmented with a further five sacraments (confession, penance, marriage, ordination, and last unction) and with countless ceremonies besides, and are not to be regarded as spatially and materially containing the grace of God within themselves, but are, rather, reminiscences and confirmations of the grace which God through the Holy Spirit gives to the hearts of His believers. Those two sacraments have the whole covenant of grace with all of its benefits, in other words, they have Christ Himself as their content, and accordingly they cannot convey those benefits except by the way of faith. They were, accordingly, instituted for the believers and assure these believers of their portion in Christ. They do not precede the Word but follow it; they have not the power to grant a particular grace which cannot be given by the Word nor be accepted by faith; rather, they are based on the institution of the covenant of grace on God's part and the confirmation of that covenant of man's part.

Specifically, baptism is a sign and seal of the benefit of forgiveness (Acts 2:38 and 22:16) and of regeneration (Titus 3:5), a being incorporated into the fellowship with Christ and His Church (Rom. 6:4). Therefore baptism is ministered not only to such adults as have been won for Christ through the work of missions, but to the children

---

56. 1 Cor. 3:2; Heb. 5:12; and 1 Peter 2:2.
57. Acts 20:20, 27; 2 Tim. 2:15; and 4:2.

of believers also, for they together with their parents are included in the covenant of grace,[58] belong to the church (1 Cor. 7:14), and have been taken up into fellowship with the Lord.[59] And when these children grow up, and by public confession personally acquiesce in that covenant, and have come to the years of discretion, and can distinguish the body and blood of the Lord (1Cor. 11:28), then they are called together with the whole church again and again to proclaim the Lord's death till He come, and so strengthen themselves in the fellowship with Christ. For, although baptism and the holy supper have the same covenant of grace as their content, and although both give assurance of the benefit of the forgiveness of sins, the holy supper differs from baptism in this regard that it is a sign and a seal, not of incorporation into but of the maturation and strengthening in the fellowship of Christ and all His members (1 Cor. 10:16:17).

To this ministration of the Word and sacrament the exercise of discipline must finally be added, and the service of mercy. Discipline which is also sometimes called the power of the keys and which was first given to Peter (Matt. 18:18 and John 20:20) and then to the whole church in its official organization,[60] consists of the fact that the church through its office-bearers says to the righteous in the name of the Lord that it will be well with him, and to the ungodly that they shall harvest the fruit of their doings (Isa. 3:10-11). The church does this generally and publicly in the ministration of the word at every gathering of believers. The church does it particularly and personally in official house-visitation. In the Reformed Churches this has come to supplant the Roman confession, and it is based on apostolic example.[61] And the church exercises such discipline also, finally, in particular admonishments directed to stiff-necked persistence in sin, and the excommunication from the fellowship.[62]

But while the church in Christ's name in this way cares for the sacraments of the Lord and puts sinners outside of its fellowship, it also pities with great compassion all the poor and the sick, and it offers them what they need for their spiritual and bodily destitution. Christ Himself did this (Matt. 11:5), and His disciples commanded that it be done.[63] The members of the church are told that they must contribute to the needs of the saints (Rom. 12:13), must make the distribution in simplicity, showing mercy with cheerfulness (Rom. 12:8), must visit the

---

58. Gen. 17:7; Matt. 18:2-3; 19:14; 21:16; and Acts 2:39.
59. Eph. 6:1; and Col. 3:20.
60. Matt. 18:17; 1 Cor. 5:4; and 2 Thess. 3:14.
61. Matt. 10:12; John 21:15-17; Acts 20:20; and Heb. 13:17.
62. Matt. 18:15-17; Rom. 1:16-17; 1 Cor. 5:2; 5:9-13; 2 Cor. 2:5-10; 2 Thess. 3:6; Titus 3:10; 2 John 10; and Rev. 2:2.
63. Matt. 5:42-45; 6:1-4; 25:34ff.; Mark 14:7; and elsewhere.

widows and orphans in their affliction (James 1:27), must offer up prayers for the sick in the name of the Lord (James 5:14), and in general must bear one another's burdens and so fulfill the law of Christ (Rom. 12:15 and Gal. 6:2).

Faith and love are the strength of the church of the Lord; and to these two is added hope. In the midst of a world which does not know where it is going and which often because of discouragement and despair lapses into decay, the church issues its glad hope. I believe the forgiveness of sins, the resurrection of the body, and eternal life.

XXIV

Eternal Life

The end and destination of all things, like their beginning and being, are enveloped in an impenetrable mist to the searching reason of man. Whoever tries to arrive at these mysteries by seeking light from science must sooner or later come to the acknowledgment of a scholar of modern times: What the end and purpose of history is, I do not know and nobody knows.

Nevertheless new ventures are constantly being made to supply an answer to these vexing questions, or else to obliterate the questions themselves and to root them out of the heart of man. It is not so long ago that many scholars took this position. Materialism was then the fashion and it proclaimed loudly that death marked the end of everything, and that belief in immortality was a piece of folly. One of their spokesmen declared openly that belief in an existence beyond the grave was the last enemy which had to be combatted by science and which, if possible, had to be subdued. This visible and tangible world, then, was the only one that exists; and of this world no one can speak of an origin or an end, because it meandered on in an eternal maze. The practical result of this superficial and comfortless doctrine was that it declared every effort to take account of eternity futile and recommended that men enjoy as much of this sensuous life as possible. Let us eat and drink, for tomorrow we die!

There are still a good many who think and act in this way; but there has nevertheless come about a change of direction. Upon closer investigation the questions about eternity did not seem to be so foolish and futile. Nor did they seem so easy to answer as had at first been thought. The study of the religions of the various peoples brought to light the fact that belief in immortality is common to all men and is present even among the most barbarian and primitive tribes. A Dutch scholar, who gained immense reputation in this area of learning, testified a few years back that we find the sense of immortality everywhere, among all peoples. and on every level of civilized development, if only no philosophical speculations have undermined it, or if no other causes have suppressed it. And he said further that this sense of immortality is everywhere connected with religion. Indeed, all the tribes and peoples

544

act on the conviction that man is by nature immortal, and that it is not immortality that must be proved, but death that cannot be explained. Death is everywhere felt to be something unnatural. According to the belief of many peoples it is the work of antagonistic spirits. These hold, in other words, that there was a time when death did not exist and an undisturbed and unbroken life was the portion of mankind.

Concerning the condition of souls after death the pagan world comes with very different representations. Some peoples hold that the souls remain with the bodies in the graves, that they continue to have fellowship with the living, exercise influence upon them, and can also appear to them. Others judge that all the souls after death come together in one great realm of death where they live a pale and ghostly existence, or also sink away entirely into unconsciousness and sleep. The thought is very widespread, too, that the souls, after having laid aside the human body, immediately go into another body and, depending upon what they have already done and how they have already lived on earth, take on the body of a tree, of one or another animal, of a human being, or of some higher creature. And, finally, the notion of immortality also expresses itself frequently in this form that the good and evil confront a different destiny after death and continue their existence in different places. In proportion to the extent that one thinks differently of the condition and status of the souls after death, the ceremonies at the burial or cremation of the bodies, and the ministrations tendered the deceased differ also. Sometimes the whole religion of pagan peoples practically assumes the form of worshipping the ancestors. Often the pagan view is limited to the condition of the souls after death; but sometimes it happens too that the vision is broader and that the end of the world falls within their purview. And then the expectation continually reappears that the good will sometime be victorious over the evil, the light over darkness, and the heavenly forces and powers over those upon the earth and under the earth.

All of these pagan representations, which have been subdued by Christianity or purged by it, have come back in modern times and have found adherents by the thousands. Materialism could after a brief period satisfy so few that some swung over to the opposite extreme. Man remains the same, his heart does not change, and he cannot live without hope. That souls continue to live after death, that they make appearances and revelations to those who remain behind, that immediately upon death, according to their conduct on earth before, they assume another body and develop themselves further in it: all this is now in many circles being welcomed as new wisdom and as the highest wisdom. As a matter of fact, in some instances, the deceased are again being called upon, worshipped, and feared; the worship of spirits, or spiritism, is coming back in the place of the service of the one and true God.

It is a particularly remarkable sign of the time that this worship of spirits is intimately connected with the doctrine of evolution. At first one might think this connection a strange one. How can anyone who accepts the development of man out of an animal believe in a continued existence of souls after death? But, upon second thought, this connection proves to be a very simple and natural one. For if in the past the living could come up out of the dead, and the soul out of matter, and the human being out of the animal, why should it then be impossible that in the future the human being should develop himself much further and higher, not on earth, only, but also hereafter on the other side of the grave? If life could come up out of death, death can also lead to a higher level of life. If an animal could become a man, man might also be able to become an angel. That one idea of evolution seemed to make everything possible and to explain everything.

But at the very moment that this house of cards was being carefully constructed, and this hope entertained, the foundation on which it all rested began to totter.

The fact is that the proponents of the theories of immortality and of evolution want to hear nothing of the scriptural doctrine concerning death and the grave, concerning judgment and punishment. Death is in their judgment not a penalty for sin, but only a transitional means to a higher and better life. There is no judgment in death except in this sense that everybody must bear the consequences of his willing and doing. There remains no place for a hell inasmuch as everybody is caught up in the process of evolution and that everybody must therefore, sooner or later, after a longer or shorter period of error and straying, come out at the right point. Asked then whether such a thing as eternal life is possible, a life of undisturbed blessedness and glory, these proponents are suddenly condemned to silence. They have so long been conducting the argument against the Christian doctrines of death and the grave, of judgment and punishment, and have so long delighted in the disappearance of these doctrines, that they forgot to ask the question whether, with the extinction of these, the hope of an eternal life, and of an everlasting blessedness did not also fall away. The moment that question is propounded, it becomes clear that in the heat of the battle the hope of an eternal life somehow got lost. With the same knife that was used to cut away all fear out of the heart of man all hope was also cut away.

So much is certain that if evolution is the one, all-commanding law of the world and of mankind, of the here and now and of the future, then the hope of an eternal life is robbed of every certain basis. The thought that in the end everything will come out satisfactorily is itself already a guess, and it is one which finds no support in Scripture and the conscience, in nature and in history. But assume for a moment that this guess were correct: then this were a condition which could never remain so. For the same law of development which had been operative before and which brought about this new condition would continue to operate and cause the human being to enter a different condition. In the theory of evolution there is nowhere a resting point, nowhere an end or a purpose; the blessedness which according to the expectation of many it is going to bring, is always in process of changing. No such thing is possible, then, as an eternal, blessed life. Hence it is that some, convinced of the impossibility of a resting place, have again called in the ancient, pagan doctrine of the eternal return of all things, and now present this notion as the solution to the world problem. If the now existing world has reached the apex of its development, it must again collapse and begin everything anew. After the flood of the tide comes the ebb, and the ebb will again cause a flood; after the development comes the retrogression, which newly brings about a development. And so on endlessly. There is only such a thing as time; there is no eternity. There is only movement; there is no rest. There is only a becoming; there is no being. There is only the creature; there is no creator who is and who was and who shall be.

All this confirms the word of Scripture that those who are without Christ, aliens from the commonwealth of Israel, and strangers from the covenants of promise, have no hope and are without God in the world (Eph. 2:12). They can guess, it is true, and wish, and indeed they never cease doing so; but they have no solid basis for their hopes. They lack the certainty of the Christian hope.

*   *   *   *   *

The moment, however, we turn to Israel we are led into a very different mentality. The Old Testament never speaks of the so-called immortality of the soul, and does not come with a single piece of evidence of it; but it nurtures ideas of life and death which can be found nowhere else and which put the future in a very different light.

In Scripture death is never the equivalent of annihilation or of not-being; to die and to be dead is there used as a contrast to the whole life, the rich life, and the full life which was man's portion originally in the fellowship with God here on earth. Hence, when man dies it is not only his body but his soul also that is affected. The whole man dies and in both body and soul he then exists in the state of death; he no longer belongs to the earth but is an inhabitant of the realm of the dead (Sheol), a place which is thought of as being in the depths of the earth, even be-

neath the waters and the foundations of the hills.[1] True, the deceased
still have an existence there, but this existence is no more worthy of the
name of life, and is like a non-existence.[2] They are weak and powerless
(Ps. 88:5 and Isa. 14:10), live in silence,[3] and in a land of darkness
(Job 10:20-21) and decay (Job 26:6 and 28:22). All that bears the
name of life ceases there; God and men are no longer seen there (Isa.
38:11): the Lord is no more praised there, nor thanked (Ps. 6:5 and
115:17); His excellences are no longer proclaimed there and His wonders are no more seen, (Ps. 88:11-13). The dead have no knowledge,
they have no wisdom and no science, they do no work and have no share
in all that takes place under the sun.[4] It is a land of oblivion (Ps.
88:13). It was thus that death was sensed by the saints in Israel: as a
total banishment from the realm of life and light. And over against this,
life was thought of as a fulness of well-being and salvation. Life was
not thought of in an abstract, philosophical manner as a kind of naked
existence. By its very nature life comprised a fulness of blessings: the
fellowship of God first of all, but then too, the fellowship of His people,
and the fellowship of the land that the Lord had given to His people.
Life in the full, rich existence of man in the unity of his soul and body,
in the unity with God and in harmony with his surroundings — all this
it includes, and also blessedness and glory, virtue and happiness, peace
and joy. If man had remained obedient to God's command, he would
have tasted of this rich life and would not have seen death (Gen. 2:17).
Then there would have been no division between his body and soul, and
the bond would not have broken which related him to God, to the human
race, and to the earth. Man, then, would have lived on eternally, in the
rich fellowship in which at the beginning he was placed. As man he
would in the oneness and fulness of his being have been immortal.

And if because of sin death has made its entrance into the world, God
nevertheless in grace renews the fellowship with man, and sets up His
covenant with Israel. In this covenant that full communion is re-esta-
blished in principle. That covenant, as it existed in the Old Testament,
comprised the fellowship with God but consequently also the fellowship
with his people and with his country. The fellowship with God is the
first and most important benefit of the covenant; without it there really
can be no talk about life. God bound Himself to Abraham and his seed
in covenant, saying: I will be a God unto thee and the God of thy

1. Num. 16:30; Deut. 32:22; Job 26:5; Ps. 63:10.
2. Job 7:21; 14:10; and Ps. 39:13.
3. Job 3:13, 18; Ps. 94:17; and 115:17.
4. Job 14:21; Eccles. 9:5, 6, and 10.

seed (Gen. 17:7). He led Israel out of Egypt and at Sinai He entered into covenant obligation with it.[5]

Hence for the people of Israel and for every member of that people there is no joy except in the fellowship with the Lord. The ungodly did not understand this, broke the covenant, and looked for life and peace in their own ways. They left the fountain-head of the living waters and hewed themselves cisterns, broken cisterns, which held no water (Jer. 2:13). But the saints knew that such was life and they gave expression to it in their prayer and their song. The Lord was the portion of their inheritance, their rock and fortress, their shield and high tower (Ps. 16:5 and 18:2). His lovingkindness was better to them than life (Ps. 63:3). He was their highest good, besides whom there was none in heaven or upon earth to desire (Ps. 73:25). Even though they might be forsaken of everyone and pursued by their enemies and subdued by them, in Him they leaped up and rejoiced, and they had joy in the God of their salvation (Habak. 3:18). In this fellowship with God they were able to transcend all the misery of this earthly life, and also the fear of the grave, the dread of death and the darkness of Sheol. It may be that the ungodly experience temporary prosperity, but in the end they perish (Ps. 73:18-20). Their way leads straight to death (Prov. 8:36 and 11:19), but for the saints the fear of the Lord is the spring of life (Prov. 8:35 and 14:27). He often delivers them in this life, but He also has power over the realm of death; with His Spirit He is present there also (Ps. 139:7-8). There is nothing that is hid from Him, not even in the hearts of the children of men.[6] The Lord destroys and makes alive; He can descend into the abyss and come up out of it again.[7] He can take Enoch and Elijah up to Himself without their death (Gen. 5:24 and 2 Kings 2:11), and He can give life back to those who have died.[8] In fact, He can destroy death, and by raising those who have died from death completely triumph over it.[9]

But even though it be true that the believers of the Old Testament realized to a lesser or greater extent that the fellowship of the Lord could not be destroyed, nor even temporarily broken off, by death, by the descent into the grave, and by remaining in the state of death, they nevertheless for the most part lived in a different climate of thought. They felt so very different about these things than we do. When we think of the future we almost exclusively think of our own death and the assumption of our soul in heaven. But the Israelites had an idea of life

---

5. Ex. 19:5; 20:2; Ezek. 16:8.
6. Job 26:6; 38:17; Prov. 15:11.
7. Deut. 32:39; 1 Sam. 2:6; 2 Kings 5:7.
8. 1 Kings 17:22; 2 Kings 4:34; and 13:21.
9. Job 14:13-15; 19:25-27; Hos. 6:2; 13:14; Isa. 25:8; 26:19; Ezek. 37:11-12; and Dan. 12:2.

which was much richer than ours. For them the awareness of the fellowship with God was connected with the fellowship with His people and His land. The true, full life was the victory over *all* separation; it was the restoration and confirmation of that rich fellowship in which man was originally created. The covenant had been established by God not with one person but with His people and also with the land that He had given His people as an inheritance. Hence death was fully overcome and life altogether brought to light only when, as in the future, the Lord would Himself come to dwell among His people, purge it of all unrighteousnesses, grant it the victory over all its enemies, and cause it to live safely in a land of prosperity and peace. Hence the eye of faith among the saints of Israel was comparatively rarely directed to the end of one's own personal life. His view as a general rule included much more; it included also the future of his country and his people. He felt himself to be always a part of the whole, a member of the family, the race, the tribe, the nation, the nation with whom God had established His covenant, and which therefore He could never forsake or destroy. And in the future of that people the believer in Israel found his own future assured; his immortality and eternal life had their guarantee in his portion in the theocracy. It might be that the Lord's wrath would last for a day: a whole life of His loving-kindness would ensue upon it. The present might suggest that God had forgotten His people and that their right had passed Him by, but after the chastisement God would return and raise up a new covenant which would never be broken. The yearning of Israel's saints stretched out to that future with all the longing of their soul; they were a people of hope; and the promise of the Messiah was the core of their expectations.

All of those expectations had their ground and foundation in the covenant which God had set up with His people. Even the law of that covenant that Israel, when it was disobedient to the voice of the Lord and proceeded to walk in its own ways, would be severely punished by the Lord and visited with all kinds of plagues. Precisely because the saints of Israel had been chosen out of all the generations of the earth, He would punish them for all their iniquities (Amos 3:2). But this chastisement would be temporary; after it was completed the Lord would again have compassion upon His people and cause it to share in His salvation.[10]

For the Lord cannot forget His covenant (Lev. 26:42). He chastises His people with restraint and forsakes it but for a little while.[11] He loves His people with an eternal love (Micah 7:19 and Jer. 31:3 and 20), and the covenant of His peace will not be removed (Isa. 54:10).

10. Lev. 26:42ff.; Deut. 4:29ff.; 30:1-10; and 32:15-43.
11. Isa. 27:7ff.; 54:7-8; and Jer. 30:11.

He is obligated to His own name, to His glory among the Gentiles, to redeem His people at the end of the period of penalty and to cause it to triumph over all its enemies.[12]

Accordingly a "day of the Lord" is coming, a great and terrible day,[13] in which the Lord will have compassion upon His people and will wreak His vengeance upon His enemies. The kingdom which He will establish at that time does not come into existence by way of a gradual development through the moral power of the people; rather, it comes from above, out of heaven, and is brought down to the earth by the anointed of the Lord. The promise of such an Anointed One goes back through the history of Israel and of all mankind to the oldest times. Already in Paradise the conflict between the seed of the woman and the seed of the serpent is announced, and the victory is promised to the former (Gen. 3:15). Abraham is told that in him all the generations of the earth will be blessed (Gen. 13:3 and 26:4). Judah is praised above his brothers, because out of him Shiloh shall come, whom all the nations will obey (Gen. 49:10).

But this promise takes on a particularly solid form when David is appointed to be the king over all Israel and is told that his house will be permanent in all eternity (2 Sam. 7:6 and 23:5). Prophecy thereupon works out this promise in greater detail. The ruler through whom God will establish His kingdom will be born out of David's royal house at Bethlehem (Micah 5:1-2). He shall come up as a rod out of the stem (Isa. 11:1-2), as a branch out of David.[14] He shall grow up in poverty of circumstance (Isa. 7:14-17), be meek and lowly, riding upon the foal of an ass (Zech. 9:9), and as the suffering servant of the Lord He will bear the iniquities of His people (Isa. 53). And yet this humble son of David is at the same time David's Lord (Ps. 110:1 and Matt. 22:43), the Anointed or Messiah, the true king of Israel, who combines with His royal worth also the prophetic and priestly abilities.[15] He is the ruler to whom all nations will be subjected (Gen. 49:10 and Ps. 2:12), and He shall bear the name Immanuel, the Lord our righteousness, wonderful, counsellor, the mighty God, eternal Father, and Prince of Peace.[16]

The kingdom which this Messiah will come to establish is a kingdom of righteousness and peace, and will bring with it a treasure of spiritual and material blessings. The psalms and prophets are full of the glory of that Messianic kingdom. Through His Anointed the Lord will

---

12. Deut. 32:27; Isa. 43:25; 48:9; and Ezek. 36:22.
13. Joel 2:11, 31; and Mal. 4:5.
14. Isa. 4:2; Jer. 23:5-6; 33:14-17; Zech. 3:8; and 6:12.
15. Deut. 18:15; Ps. 110; Isa. 11:2; 53:1ff.; Zech. 5:1ff.; 6:13; Mal. 4:5 and elsewhere.
16. Isa. 7:14; 9:5; and Jer. 23:6.

cause His people to return out of captivity, and together with this return will at the same time grant them the true repentance of heart. True, they will not all come back, nor all turn unto the Lord; and many will perish in the judgment that will come to His people also.[17] Nevertheless there will be a remnant according to the election of grace.[18] And this remnant will be a holy people to the Lord, to whom He will be faithful in all eternity.[19] He will raise up a new covenant with them, will forgive their sins, will cleanse them of all uncleanness, grant them a new heart, write His law in their hearts, pour out His Spirit over them and Himself dwell in the midst of them.[20]

All kinds of spiritual benefits not only, but also all kinds of material blessings will come with that kingdom. There will be no more war; the swords will be changed to plowshares, and the spears to pruning hooks, and they shall all sit down in peace under their own vine and fig tree. The land will be uncommonly productive; animals will be given a different nature than they had before; the heaven and the earth will be renewed; there will be no more sickness, nor sorrow and weeping, and death will be swallowed up in victory. The Israelites who have died will also share in these blessings in that they will be raised from the dead (Isa. 26:19 and Dan. 12:2), and the heathen nations will in the end acknowledge that the Lord is God and will glory in Him.[21] The nation of the saints will receive the lordship over all the nations of the earth (Dan. 7:14, 27), and the anointed king of David's house will reign from sea to sea and from the rivers to the ends of the earth.[22]

* * * * *

The fulfillment of all these Old Testament promises had its beginning when Christ appeared in the flesh; for in His person and through His work that kingdom of heaven was established on earth which had been expected throughout the ages. By His blood He confirmed the new and better covenant which the Lord would set up with His people in the last days; and on the day of Pentecost He sent that Spirit of grace and of prayer out into the church which would lead it in all the truth and perfect it up to the end. But what the prophecy of the Old Testament comprehended in one large figure, broke up into various parts later on. One thing and another came into being alongside of it. It was actualized not in a moment or a day but through a long period of time and piece by

---

17. Amos 9:8-10; Hos. 2:3 and Ezek. 20:33ff.
18. Isa. 4:3; 6:13; Jer. 3:14; Zeph. 3:20; Zech. 13:8-9.
19. Hos. 1:10; 2:15; Isa. 4:3; and 11:9.
20. Joel 2:28; Isa. 44:21ff.; 43:25; Jer. 31:31; Ezek. 11:19; 36:25ff. and else-where.
21. Jer. 3:17; 4:2; 16:19; Ezek. 17:24 and elsewhere.
22. Ps. 2:8; 22:28; and 72:8 ff.

piece. More specifically, we are taught by the New Testament that the one coming of the Messiah which was anticipated by the prophets must be separated into a first and a second coming. In accordance with prophecy, the Messiah had to come for the purpose of redemption and judgment, for the redemption of His people and the judgment of His enemies. But when this prophecy comes to fulfillment it becomes evident that each of these purposes requires a particular coming of the Christ.

After all, Jesus repeatedly during His stay on earth gave expression to the fact that He was now come to seek and to save that which was lost (Luke 19:10), in order to serve and to give His soul a ransom for many (Matt. 20:28), not to condemn the world but to save it.[23] But at the same time He states plainly and powerfully that He through the light which He sheds abroad brings a judgment and a division into the world (John 3:19 and 9:39), and that He will sometime return to judge the living and the dead (John 5:22 and 27-29). It is true that He must be crucified and put to death, but thereupon He will be raised again and ascend back to heaven (Matt. 16:21 and John 6:62) in order at the end to come again, to gather all peoples before Him and to reward each according to his doing.[24]

There is, accordingly, a big difference between these two comings of the Lord. At the first Christ appeared in the weakness of the flesh, in the form of a servant, to suffer and to die for the sins of His people (Phil. 2:6-8), and at the second He will manifest Himself to all in great power and glory as a King who goes out conquering and to conquer.[25] Nevertheless, both of these comings of the Lord are closely interrelated. The first paves the way for the second because according to the idea of Holy Scripture and the basic law of the kingdom of heaven it is only the passion that can lead to the glory, the cross that can lead to the crown, and the humiliation that can lead to the exaltation (Luke 24:26).

At His first coming Christ laid the foundation, and at His second He brings the completion of the building of God; the first is the beginning and the second is the end of His work as Mediator. Because Christ is a perfect Savior, who brings not only the possibility but also the actuality of salvation, He cannot and may not and will not rest before those who are His own have been bought by His blood, been renewed by His Spirit, and brought where He is, there to be the spectators and sharers of His glory (John 14:3 and 17:24). He must give those whom the Father has given Him the eternal life (John 6:39; and 10:28), He must present His church without spot or blemish or anything of the kind to the

---

23. John 3:17; 12:47; and 1 John 4:14.
24. Matt. 16:27; 24:30; 25:32 and elsewhere.
25. Matt. 24:30; Rev. 6:2; and 19:11.

Father (Eph. 5:27), and transfer the Kingdom to Him after it has been wholly completed and fulfilled (1 Cor. 15:23-28).

Because the first and second coming of Christ are so intimately related to each other, and because the one would not for a moment be thinkable without the other, Holy Scriptures place very little emphasis on the length or shortness of the time that must elapse between the two. In Scripture the temporal connection is far behind the material connection in importance. The time which intervenes between the two is often presented as being very short. The believers of the New Testament are living towards the end of the ages (1 Cor. 10:11), in the last times (1 Peter 1:20), in the last time (1 John 2:18). They have only a little while left to suffer (1 Peter 1:6 and 5:10), for the day is approaching (Heb. 10:25 and 37), the future is drawing nigh (James 5:8), the time is at hand (Rev. 1:3 and 22:10, the judge is standing at the door (James 5:9), and Christ is coming quickly (Rev. 3:11 and 22:7 and 20). Paul regarded it as not improbable that he and his contemporaries would live to see the return of Christ (1 Thess. 4:15 and 1 Cor. 15:51).

In saying these things, Scripture does not give us any specific instruction concerning that interim, for it tells us plainly elsewhere that the day and the hour is hid from men and angels and that it has been fixed by the Father in His own power (Matt. 24:36 and Acts 1:7). Every effort to calculate the moment of that future is unwarranted and unfruitful (Acts 1:7), for the day of the Lord will come as a thief in the night at an hour which men do not know.[26] As a matter of fact, that day cannot come until the gospel has been preached to all peoples (Matt. 24:14), until the kingdom of heaven has leavened all things (Matt. 13:33), and until the man of sin has appeared (2 Thess. 2:2 ff.). The Lord has a different norm for measuring time than we; one day is to Him as a thousand years and a thousand years as a day. His apparent postponement is long-suffering which would not that any should be lost, but rather that all should come to repentance (2 Peter 3:8-9).

But what the Holy Scriptures want to teach us by these various utterances concerning the intervening period between Christ's comings is that the two stand in the closest of relationships with each other. The work which the Father has given Christ to do is one work; and that work extends into all the ages and comprises the whole history of mankind. It was begun in eternity; it was continued in time; and it will again end in eternity. The brief period in which Christ lived in the body on earth is but a tiny portion of the ages over which He has been appointed Lord and King. That which He achieved during that period by His passion and death He applies in the church through His Word and

---

26. Matt. 24:42-44; 1 Thess. 5:2, 4; 2 Peter 3:10; Rev. 3:3; and 16:15.

Spirit from the time of His ascension on, and He completes it at His second coming. Indeed, He ascended into heaven in order to be the nearer to His own, to be constantly more intimately related with them, and always to come nearer them. The time which elapses between His first and His second coming is in fact a continuous coming of Christ to the world.

Just as in the days of the Old Testament He had His coming in the flesh heralded by all kinds of manifestations and activities, so He is now busy preparing His return in order to judge and divide — a judgment and a division which He brings into being by His Word and Spirit in the world of men. It is a continuous coming of Christ, that of which the believers of the New Testament are witnesses. They see the Son of Man sitting at the right hand of the power of God and coming upon the clouds of heaven (Matt. 26:64). They see His coming in the preaching of His Word and in the operation of His Spirit (John 14:18-20 and 16:16, 19 ff.). It is not true to say that Christ came once to the earth, but rather that He comes continuously, that He is the coming one and the one who will come (Heb. 10:37 and Rev. 1:4 and 8).

For these reasons the believers of the New Testament look forward with great longing to Christ's return. Just as the saints of the Old Testament, so those of the New thought and spoke comparatively seldom about their personal end in death. All their expectations were directed on the return of Christ and the fulfillment of the kingdom of God. They were very conscious of the fact that they were living in the day of the fulfillment, in that day which the prophecy of the Old Testament had represented as the great illustrious day of the Lord, and which extends from the ascension to the return of Christ. The nearness of this return, as they thought of it, is but another expression of the absolute certainty with which they awaited it. Their strong faith is the root of their unwavering hope.

In His sojourn with His disciples Jesus spoke a great deal about faith and love and little about hope, for what mattered most then was that their attention be fixed on His person and work. But He gave out many promises concerning His resurrection and ascension, His sending of the Spirit, and His return in glory. Through the passion and death of Christ the disciples were for a period crestfallen and disappointed in their expectations, but by His resurrection they were reborn to a living hope (1 Peter 1:3 and 21). Christ Himself was now their hope, the object and the content of all their expectations (1 Tim. 1:1). For when He returns He fulfills all His promises and grants to His confessors the perfect salvation and the eternal life. Therefore they live in hope, and expect continuously the blessed hope and appearing of the glory of their great God and Savior Jesus Christ (Titus 2:13). And this expectation is shared by the whole of a groaning creation, subject as it is to vanity; it also longs to be liberated from the bondage of corruption into the freedom of the glory of the children of God (Rom. 8:21).

Nevertheless, even though the believers of the New Testament have virtually all of their attention fixed upon the return of Christ, certain details are given in the New Testament which shed some light upon the status which death has in their estimation. According to the Roman Church comparatively few saints and martyrs can by their good works achieve so much on earth that upon death they are immediately taken up into heaven. The great majority of the believers, according to this view, must upon death spend a shorter or longer period in Purgatory in order there to pay the temporal penalties which they have earned by their sins and which in their earthly life they could no more satisfy.

Purgatory is therefore not a place of repentance, in which the unbelievers and the ungodly are still given the opportunity to be saved, for the unbelievers and the ungodly go directly to hell. It is not really a place of purging and sanctification either, for the believers who go there cannot achieve any new excellences or merits there. Rather, it is singly and solely a place of punishment, where the believers, who on the one hand are blessed and on the other hand are poor souls, are so long punished by material fire that the measure of their temporal penalties is satisfied. In addition to a militant church upon earth, therefore, and a triumphant one in heaven, there is according to Rome a passive or suffering church in Purgatory. One can aid those who are there by means of prayers, good works, abstinence and especially through offerings of the mass; and inasmuch as those in Purgatory are ahead of the believers and nearer salvation, these, like the angels and the saints in heaven, can be called upon for aid and assistance.

Because there were many who did not understand this Roman confession properly, they have often glorified it extravagantly and made use of the doctrine of Purgatory to plead for a continuing purging of the believers after death. Such people could not understand that believers who up to their hour of dying were imperfect and prone to all evil should immediately upon death be delivered of all sin and ready for heaven. And others went even much farther. They applied the notion of evolution to the life hereafter also, and they represent the matter in this way that all people without distinction continue the straight line of life on the other side of the grave which they had begun on earth and perhaps also in an earlier existence. Death is then not a breaking off of this life and a penalty for sin but simply the transition from one kind of existence to another, such as that when the caterpillar becomes the butterfly. And this evolution, the thought is, will continue so long until everything is set right again or returns to nothingness.

But Holy Scripture knows nothing of all these comfortless teachings. It sets forth everywhere that this earth is the only place for repentance and purging. It nowhere mentions anything about any preaching of the gospel on the other side of the grave, neither in Matthew 12:32, nor in 1 Peter 3:18-22, nor in 1 Peter 4:6. Death as the penalty for sin represents a total break with life here on earth, and at the last judgment the interim period gets no consideration. The judgment is concerned solely with what happened in the body, whether it be good or whether it be evil (2 Cor. 5:10). But for those who believe in Christ both the death and the judgment lose all their terror; for in the fellowship with God, through Jesus Christ our Lord, death is no longer death. The covenant which God sets up with His own in grace guarantees the perfect salvation and eternal life. God is not a God of the dead, but of the living (Matt. 22:32). Whoever believes in Christ shall live, though he have died, and whoever lives and believes in Him shall not die in eternity (John 11:25-26), and he shall not come into judgment for he has passed over from death into life (John 5:24).

Hence it is that the believers upon death are immediately taken up with Christ in heaven in their souls. If the justification and the sanctification were the work of man, which he achieved through his own strength or through the strength of a supernatural grace poured into him, then this could not be understood, namely, that he could achieve this work in the short span of this life. Hence it is that those who think thus must hit upon the idea of a Purgatory and of a continuing purgation after this life. But Christ has fulfilled everything for His own. He not only bore the penalty for them, and not only earned the full forgiveness of all their sins, but He also fulfilled the law in their place and brought eternal life in its incorruptibility to light. He who believes is immediately delivered from the wrath of God and is the inheritor of eternal life. In that very moment he is ready for heaven. If he must remain on earth that is not because he must still perfect himself and through good works earn eternal life; it is, rather, for the sake of the brethren, in order that they walk in good works which God has prepared (Phil. 1:24 and Eph. 2:10). Even the suffering which such a person must often still bear upon earth is not a punishment and is not a penalty, but is a fatherly chastisement which serves for his nurture (Heb. 12:5-11); it is a filling up of that which is behind of the afflictions of Christ in his flesh for His body's sake, which is the church, to build and to establish it in the truth (Col. 1:24).

On the basis of the perfect work of Christ, therefore, heaven stands open for the believers immediately upon their death. They do not have to suffer penalties for their sins in any Purgatory anymore, for Christ has fulfilled all and achieved all. According to the parable in Luke 16 the poor Lazarus immediately upon his dying is carried into Abraham's bosom by the angels in order there, in fellowship with Abraham, to enjoy the eternal blessedness. When Jesus died on the cross He committed His own spirit into the hands of His Father, and He promised beforehand to the murderer that he would that day be with Him in Paradise (Luke 23:43 and 46). The first Christian martyr, Stephen, while he was being stoned cried out to the Lord Jesus and prayed Him to receive his spirit (Acts 7:59). Paul is certain that he when he is unbound from the body will be with Christ and dwelling in the Lord (2 Cor. 5:8 and Phil. 1:23). According to Revelation 6:8 and 7:9 and elsewhere, the souls of the martyrs and of all the saved in heaven are present before the throne of God and before the Lamb, clothed with long white clothes and having palm branches in their hands. For blessed are the dead who die in the Lord from this time on; they rest from their labors which they have done on the earth, and their works do follow them (Rev. 14:13 and Heb. 4:9); and they live and reign with Christ all the while up to His return (Rev. 20:4 and 6).

* * * * *

Although the believers upon their death immediately become sharers of the heavenly blessedness according to their soul, still their condition is in a certain sense still a preliminary one and a still imperfect one. After all, their bodies are still in the grave and are there subject to decay; soul and body are still separated and do not share in the eternal blessedness in union with each other. Taken as a whole therefore, the believers in this interim period find themselves still in the state of death, just as Jesus after His death and before His resurrection continued in that state, even though His soul had been taken up into paradise. Accordingly, the believers in that state are called those who are asleep in Christ or have died in Him;[27] their dying is called a sleeping (John 11:11 and 1 Cor. 11:30) and a seeing of corruption (Acts 13:36). All this goes to prove that the intermediate state is not yet the final state. Since Christ is the perfect Savior, He is not content with the redemption of the soul, but effects also the redemption of the body. The kingdom of God, therefore, will be completed only when He has put down all rule and authority and power, has put all enemies under His feet, and has conquered the last enemy, death (1 Cor. 15:24-26).

Both in heaven and on earth, accordingly, there is a yearning for that future in which the last blow will have been struck and the perfect victory have been achieved. The souls of the martyrs in heaven call out with a loud voice, How long, O Lord, holy and true, dost Thou not

---

27. 1 Thess. 4:14, 16 and 1 Cor. 15:18.

judge and avenge our blood on them that dwell on the earth (Rev. 6:10)? And the Spirit and the bride on earth say, Come, Lord Jesus, yea, come quickly (Rev. 22:17)! And not that only, but Christ Himself prepares for His own coming, prepares for it both on earth and in heaven. In the house of His Father He prepares a place for His own, and when He will have prepared it, He will come again and take His own unto Him, in order that they too may be where He is (John 14: 2-3). And on earth He rules as king, by His grace in the church, by His power in the world, until He has gathered all His elect and subdued all His enemies (1 Cor. 15:25). He does not rest, but works always, and in His work He gives expression to it also: See, I come quickly, and my reward is with me, to give every man according as his work shall be (Rev. 22:12, 20).

The history of the world which intervenes between Jesus' ascension and return is a continuous coming of Christ, a progressive gathering of His church on earth, a continuing subjection of His enemies. Often we do not see it, we do not understand it, but Christ is in very fact the Lord of times, the king of the ages; He is the Alpha and the Omega, the beginning and the end, the first and the last (Rev. 22:13). Because the Father has loved the Son, He created the world in Him, He elected the church, and all those who are given Him, to behold His glory with Him (John 17:24).

The completion of the kingdom of God is therefore not the result of a gradual development of nature, nor a product of human effort. For, even though the kingdom of heaven is like a mustard seed, like a leaven, and like a grain of corn, it nevertheless grows without the knowledge and contribution of men (Mark 4:27). Paul may plant and Apollos may water, but it is God alone who gives the increase (1 Cor. 3:6). Scripture knows nothing of a self-sufficient nature and an autonomous man; always it is God who keeps the world in force and who makes history. And especially as the end approaches, He will in an extraordinary way intervene in history and by the appearance of Christ cause it to stand still and to have time pass over into eternity. That will be an awful event when Christ, sent by the Father (Acts 3:20 and 1 Tim. 6:15) will appear on the clouds of heaven. Just as on His leaving the earth He was taken up into heaven, so upon His return will He come back from heaven to earth (Phil. 3:20). At His ascension a cloud removed Him from the sight of His disciples; and on the clouds of heaven, spreading themselves out as a great chariot of victory underneath Him He will return to the earth (Matt. 24:30 and Rev. 1:7). It was in the form of a servant that He appeared on the earth the first time, but the second time He will come with great power and glory (Matt. 24:30), as a King of kings and as a Lord of lords, seated upon a white horse, a sharp sword proceeding from His mouth and surrounded by His angels and saints.[28] And He will be heralded by the voice of an archangel and the trumpet of angels.[29]

In order to give us an impression of the majesty and glory in which Christ will appear, Scripture does and must make use of words and images which we can comprehend. And it is often difficult for us to make a distinction between the reality itself and the representation which is given of it. But so much is certain: Christ is coming again, the same Christ who was born of Mary, who suffered under Pontius Pilate, who died, was buried, and ascended into heaven; but He will return in glory to judge the living and the dead. He that descended is the same also that ascended up far above all heavens, that He might fill all things (Eph. 4:10). He who demeaned and humiliated Himself is the same whom God highly exalted, and who has received a name above every name, that in the name of Jesus every knee should bow and every tongue confess that He is Lord to the glory of the Father (Phil. 2:6-11). He who was once sacrificed to bear the sins of many shall appear the second time without sin to those who are expecting Him unto salvation (Heb. 9:28). This Maranatha is the comfort of the church; He who loved the church from eternity and gave Himself up for her unto death, will return to take her to Himself and cause her to share His glory forever. The Savior and the Judge of the church is one and the same person.

This comfort of the believers is, however, remarkably modified by the so-called Chiliasts, who are the proponents of the pre-millenial doctrine. They make a distinction in the return of Christ between a first and a second return. At the first return Christ will subdue the anti-Christian forces, will bind Satan, will raise up the dead of the believers, will gather the church, particularly the church of a penitent Israel and will then in and through this church rule over the nations. After this kingdom has existed for a longer or shorter time and Satan has again been loosed, Christ will return once more to raise up all men from the dead, to pronounce judgment upon them, and to establish the perfected kingdom of God upon the new earth.

By this distinction between two kinds of Christ's return, the end of world history is postponed a long time. When Christ, then, returns upon the clouds of heaven, the end of the ages has not yet come, but only a preliminary period of lordship and power, of spiritual and material blessings, a period of which the Chiliasts themselves can only with difficulty form a definite idea, and concerning whose duration there is great difference of opinion among them.

---

28. Matt. 25:31; 1 Thess. 3:13; and Rev. 19:14.
29. Matt. 24:31; 1 Cor. 15:52; and 1 Thess. 4:16.

The fundamental error of this Chiliastic departure from the truth lies in a mistaken conception of the relation between the Old and the New Testament. The choice of Abraham and his seed did not have as its purpose to place the people of Israel at some time in the future, or even in the perfected kingdom of heaven, at the head of all the nations, but rather to bless all the generations of the earth in Him who was the true seed of Abraham.[30] Israel was chosen not at the expense of mankind, but for the benefit of mankind. Accordingly, when Christ appeared on earth, all the promises of the Old Testament began to be fulfilled in His church. Those promises are not throughout the dispensation of the New Testament merely lying there staticly awaiting fulfillment, but they are constantly being fulfilled from the first coming of Christ to His return. Not only is Christ in His person the true prophet, priest, and king, the true servant of the Lord, and not only is His offering the true sin-offering, the true circumcision, the true Passover,[31] but His church is also the true seed of Abraham, the true Israel, the true people of God, the true temple, and the real Zion. All the blessings of Abraham and all the promises of the Old Testament accrue to the church in Christ and in the course of the centuries are carried out there.[32]

But just as the life of Christ can be separated into a state of humiliation and a state of exaltation, so too His church and every believer in particular cannot enter the kingdom of glory except through the school of suffering. There is no separate suffering church in Purgatory, as Rome maintains, but the suffering church is the same as the militant church here on earth. Nowhere does the New Testament open up to the church of Christ the prospect that they will once more in this dispensation enjoy power and lordship. On the contrary, a disciple is not greater than his master nor a servant than his lord; if they have persecuted Jesus, will they not persecute His followers (John 15:19-20)? In the world they shall have tribulation (John 16:33). And only in the coming age will they receive eternal life (Mark 10:30), for if they suffer with Christ they shall also be glorified with Him (Rom. 8:17). As a matter of fact the New Testament repeatedly gives expression to the thought that towards the end of time wickedness will increase, and apostasy become more rampant.[33] What precedes the day of Christ is the great apostasy, the revelation of the man of sin, of anti-Christ (2 Thess. 2:3ff.); this anti-Christ it is true will have been prepared for by many false prophets and false Christs,[34] but in the end he will

---

30. Gal. 3:16; Gen. 12:3; and Gal. 3:8 and 14.
31. Rom. 3:25 and 1 Cor. 2:11 and elsewhere.
32. Rom. 9:25-26; 11:17; 2 Cor. 6:16-18; Gal. 3:14, 29 and elsewhere.
33. Matt. 24:37ff.; Luke 17:26ff.; and 18:8.
34. Matt. 7:5; 25:5, 24; 1 John 2:22; and 4:3.

himself appear, and will concentrate all his power in a world-kingdom (the beast coming up out of the sea or the abyss in Rev. 11:7 and 13: 1-10), which is supported by false religion (the beast out of the earth of Rev. 13:11-18), will establish his seat in Babylon (Rev. 17 and 18), and will from that point make his last desperate attack upon Christ and His kingdom.

But by His appearance in glory (Rev. 19:11-16) Christ puts an end for good and all to the power of the beast out of the sea and out of the earth (Rev. 19:20), and also subdues Satan. This last event, however, has two aspects: first Satan will be seized and bound as the tempter of Christian peoples (Rev. 20:1-3; compare 12:7-11); thereafter he will be bound as tempter of the nations dwelling in the four corners of the earth (Rev. 20:7-10). Meanwhile the believers who have remained faithful to the testimony of Jesus and the word of God even unto death will live and reign with Christ in heaven as kings all the while (a period symbolically represented as a thousand years: Rev. 20:3,4, 6-7), during which Satan has been driven from the nations among which the church is spread out, and during which Satan is busy organizing a new power against the kingdom of Christ in the midst of the heathen peoples.[35] The first resurrection consists of this living and reigning with Christ; the other dead, who have followed the beast and his image do not live and rule, but the first kind do and these do not have to fear the second death, the punishment of hell; they are now already priests of God and of Christ (Rev. 20:6), and after the resurrection and the judgment of the world they are taken up as citizens into the New Jerusalem.

*   *   *   *   *

The resurrection of the dead follows upon the appearance of Christ. Although this resurrection of the dead is also sometimes generally ascribed to God (1 Cor. 6:14 and 2 Cor. 1:9), it is nevertheless more specifically the work of the Son to whom the Father gave life in Himself (John 5:26), who is Himself the resurrection and the life (John 11:25), and who received the authority by the voice of His mouth to raise all the dead from the grave (John 5:28-29). All this plainly teaches, here as well as elsewhere,[36] that there will be a resurrection of all men, of the unjust as well as of the righteous.

Nevertheless there is a big difference between the two. The resurrection of the former is an evidence of the power and righteousness of Jesus Christ; that of the latter is a manifestation of His mercy and grace. The former consists merely of a rejoining of soul and body and takes

---

35. Rev. 20:4; compare 2:26; and 3:21.
36. Dan. 12:2; Matt. 10:28; Acts 24:15; and Rev. 20:12-13.

place for the judgment (John 5:29), but the second is a resurrection unto life, a quickening of the whole man, a renewal of soul and body both in the fellowship and through the Spirit of Christ.[37] It does not follow from this that the two resurrections will differ in point of time, that the resurrection of the righteous will precede by a longer or shorter time that of the unrighteous; but it does follow that the nature and character of the one differs greatly from that of the other. Only the first is a blessed resurrection and has its cause and surety in the resurrection of Christ; Christ is the first fruits, the first-born of the dead; thereupon follow those who are in Christ, at His coming (1 Cor. 15:20-23).

In that resurrection the unity of the person, both according to soul and body, is preserved. How this is possible through the awful catastrophe of death we do not know. Hence it is that many reject the resurrection of the body and maintain that after death the soul takes on another body, be it a human or animal body, a more refined or a coarser material body. But in so doing, these people forget that the preservation of the unity of the soul, though it may be in another kind, at bottom runs into the same tremendous difficulties; hence, many teach the immortality of the soul only in the sense that the spirit of man lives on, but without any preservation of the unity of his consciousness. But this is to forfeit immortality altogether, for if self-awareness and memory are completely broken off at death, the person who lives on is no longer the same as the one who lived on earth.

This self-consciousness of the human being, however, includes the possession of a body as well as a soul. The body is not a prison of the spirit, but belongs to the essence of man. That is why it is redeemed just as well as the soul by Christ, the perfect Savior. The whole man was created after the image of God and the whole man was corrupted; hence the whole man is redeemed from sin and death by Christ, is re-created after God's image, and is ushered into His kingdom. But the body which the believers receive at the resurrection corresponds to the earthly body, not in external form, in accidental characteristics, in material quantity, but only in essence. It is not a natural, but a physical body. It is raised above sexual life (Matt. 22:30), above the need for food and drink (1 Cor. 6:13). It is immortal, incorruptible, spiritualized, and glorified (1 Cor. 15:42-44), and it is conformed to the body of Christ as it was after His resurrection (Phil. 3:21).

The resurrection is followed by the judgment. From the very beginning, since God established enmity, there is a great division among people between the seed of the woman and the seed of the serpent (Gen.

---

37. John 5:29; Rom. 8:8; and Phil. 3:21.

3:15). In the Old Testament this division ran on between Seth and Cain, Shem and Japheth, Israel and the nations, and in Israel itself ran between the children of the promise and the children of the flesh. When Christ came upon earth He confirmed and sharpened this distinction, even though His first coming did not have the purpose of condemning but rather of saving the world (John 3:17). By His word and by His person He brought judgment, and a separation among men (John 3: 19-21). It is a judgment which continues up to the present time, and it culminates in the last judgment. There is in very fact a judgment which goes through the history of all peoples, generations, families, and persons. If the secret places of the heart of man were known to us, we should know even more about that and be more deeply convinced of it. Nevertheless the history of the world is not *the* final judgment. Too much iniquity goes unpunished for that, too much goodness unrewarded, and our consciences could not be satisfied with the present dispensation on that score. The head and the heart of mankind, the reason and conscience, the philosophy and religion, the whole history of the world calls for a last, righteous, and definitive judgment.

It is towards such a judgment that we, according to the testimony of Scripture, are moving. It is appointed to man once to die, and after that the judgment (Heb. 9:27). Although God alone is the Law-giver and Judge of all men,[38] the last judgment is nevertheless more specifically conducted by Christ to whom the Father has delegated it because He is the Son of man.[39] The judgment of the living and the dead is the completing of His work as Mediator, the last step in His exaltation. From that judgment it will become manifest that He has perfectly fulfilled all things which the Father gave Him to do, that He has put all His enemies under His feet, and has perfectly and eternally redeemed His whole church.

But when Christ proceeds to judge, we know too what kind of judgment it will be: merciful and gracious and at the same time absolutely just. For He knows the nature of man and all that is in him; He knows the secret places of the heart and detects all evil and falling away in it, but He sees also the smallest beginning of faith and of love which is present there. He does not judge according to appearances and does not respect the person, but He judges according to truth and righteousness. Using law and gospel as norm, He will judge the works of man (Matt. 25:35 ff.), the words of man (Matt. 12:36), and the thoughts of man (Rom. 2:16 and 1 Cor. 4:5), for nothing remains hid and everything is revealed (Matt. 6:4 and 10:26). For all who can say with Peter: Thou knowest all things, Thou knowest

---

38. Gen. 18:25; Ps. 50:6; Isa. 33:22; and James 4:12.
39. John 5:22; Acts 10:42; 17:31; and Rom. 14:9.

that I love Thee, this judgment is a source of comfort. But for all who did not want this Christ to be their King, it is a cause of fear and awful terror.

For this judgment brings with it a perfect and eternal separation between man and man. Just as among Israel there were those who said: "The Lord shall not see, neither shall the God of Jacob regard it," and who further said, "Every one that doeth evil is good in the sight of the Lord, and He delighteth in them"; or, "Where is the God of judgment?" (Mal. 2:17), so there are now also those who flatter themselves with the thought that there is no last judgment, that the possibility of repentance remains open after this life and after the conclusion of world history also, and that thus in the long run all men, and even the devils, will come to share in salvation, or that the ungodly who continue to harden themselves in sin will eternally be annihilated.

Both conscience and Scripture alike, however, must take issue with these vain imaginations. In the night of judgment two men will be lying on one bed, and the one shall be taken and the other left: two women will be grinding at the mill: the one shall be taken, and the other left; two people will be working in the field: the one shall be taken and the other left (Luke 17:34-36). The righteous shall go in to eternal life, but the ungodly will be given over to eternal pain (Matt. 25:46). There is a heaven of glory, but there is also a Gehenna, a hell, where the worm does not die and the fire is not extinguished (Mark 9:44), where there is weeping and gnashing of teeth (Matt. 8:12), where darkness and corruption and death reign to eternity (Matt. 7:13; 8:12; and Rev. 21:8). It is the place where the wrath of God will be revealed in all of its terror.[40]

Nevertheless there will be a big difference between the eternal punishment which comes to all the wicked — a difference of gradation or degree. The heathen who did not know the Mosaic law, but who sinned against the law which was known to them by nature, will also be lost without that law (Rom. 2:12). It will be more tolerable for Sodom and Gomorrah, Tyre and Sidon in the day of judgment than for Capernaum and Jerusalem (Matt. 10:15 and 11:22 and 24). Those who knew the will of the Lord and did not do it shall be beaten with double stripes (Luke 12:47). Even among evil spirits a distinction is made in the degree of their evil (Matt. 12:45). Hence everyone will receive his reward according to his doing.[41] The judgment will be so perfectly just that no one will be able to criticize it in any regard; his own conscience will have to approve it altogether. Just as Christ here on earth fights with no other weapons than with spiritual ones, so on

40. Rom. 2:8; 9:22; Heb. 10:31; and Rev. 6:16-17.
41. Matt. 16:27; Rom. 2:6; and Rev. 22:12.

the day of judgment He will by His Word and judgment justify Himself in the consciences of all men.

We know that He is the Faithful and True, who conducts His warfare in no other way than in righteousness; the sharp sword which proceeds out of His mouth is the sword of the Word (Rev. 19:11, 15, and 21). Hence at the end of time, whether willingly or unwillingly, every knee shall bow in the name of Jesus and every tongue confess that Christ is Lord to the glory of God the Father (Phil. 2:11). The punishment of the wicked is not in itself the final purpose, but the glory of God which in the victory of Christ is manifested over all His enemies. The sinners will be consumed out of the earth, and the wicked will be no more. Bless thou the Lord, O thou my soul. Hallelujah (Ps. 104:35).

* * * * *

After the final judgment and the banishment of the wicked there follows the renewal of the world. Holy Scriptures often speak of this in very strong language and tell us that the heaven and the earth will vanish like smoke, will become old as a garment, and that God thereupon will create new heavens and a new earth.[42] Nevertheless, we are not in this connection to think of an absolutely new creation. It is true that the present heaven and earth will in their present form pass away (1 Cor. 7:31) and that these, like the ancient earth which was destroyed by the flood, will be burned and purged by fire (2 Peter 3:6, 7, and 10). But just as man himself is recreated by Christ indeed, but is not annihilated and thereupon created again (2 Cor. 5:17), so too the world in its essence will be preserved, even though in its form it undergoes so great a change that it can be called a new heaven and new earth. The world in its entirety, too, moves on to the day of its great regeneration (Matt. 19:28).

And in this new creation God will then establish His kingdom. For Christ has completed the work that was given Him as Mediator to do; He has reigned so long as King that He has put all His enemies under His feet and has raised to life all those whom the Father has given Him. True, even after that, He will in eternity remain the head of the church, the One who gives them His glory to behold and who fills them with His fullness (John 17:24 and Eph. 1:23). Nevertheless, His work of redemption has run its course; He has fulfilled the kingdom and now transfers it to God and the Father in order Himself then as Mediator to be subjected to Him who has subjected all things, in order that God may be all and in all (1 Cor. 15:24, 28).

---

42. Ps. 102:27; Isa. 34:4; 51:6; 65:17; 66:22; Matt. 24:35; Heb. 1:11-12; 2 Peter 3:10, 12-13; 1 John 2:17; and Rev. 21:1.

That kingdom comprises heaven and earth, and brings a bounty of spiritual and physical blessings with it. Not only the Old Testament, but also the New, plainly teaches that the saints shall inherit the earth (Matt. 5:5). The whole creation will sometime be delivered from the bondage of corruption into the glorious liberty of the children of God (Rom. 8:21). The heavenly Jerusalem which is above and which designates the city where God dwells with His people, will return to earth (Rev. 21:2). And in this new Jerusalem in the immediate presence of God, there is no longer any sin, any sickness, or death, but glory and incorruptibility rule also in the material world.[43] This, too, is a revelation of the eternal, holy and blessed life, which all the citizens of that city share in the fellowship of God.[44]

In that kingdom too there will be variation and change within the oneness of the fellowship. Small and great will be there (Rev. 22:12), and the first and the last (Matt. 20:16). Each person will there receive his own name and his own place (Rev. 2:17) in accordance with the works of faith and love which he has done on earth. For he who sows sparingly, shall also harvest sparingly, and he who sows bountifully, shall also harvest bountifully (2 Cor. 9:6). There is reward in heaven for all the persecution which the disciple of Jesus has borne for His sake, and for every deed which he has done in His name (Matt. 5:12 and 6:1, 6, 18). In proportion as a person has been faithful in using the talents given him he will in the kingdom of God receive greater honor and lordship (Matt. 25:14ff.). Even the cup of cold water which in the name of a disciple is given to one of His little ones, will not be forgotten in the day of judgment; He crowns and rewards the good works which in and through Himself He brought into being through His own. Thus all, it is true, share in the same blessings, the same eternal life, and the same fellowship with God. But there is nevertheless a difference among them in brilliance and glory. In proportion to their faithfulness and zeal, the churches receive from their Lord and King a different crown and reward (Rev. 2-3). There are many, many mansions in the one house of the Father (John 14:2).

By this difference of rank and place and task the communion of the saints is enriched. Just as the harmony of a hymn is enhanced by the quality of the voices, and the beauty of light is multiplied in the richness of its colors and tints, so Christ will one time be glorified in the multitude of His saints, and He will become wonderful in the thousands times a thousand who believe in His name. For all the inhabitants of the New Jerusalem will behold God's face, and will bear His name upon their foreheads. And all together they will raise the song of

---

43. 1 Cor. 15:42-44; Rev. 7:16-17, and 21:4.
44. 1 Cor. 13:12; 1 John 3:2; Rev. 21:3; and 22:1-5.

Moses before the throne, and the song of the Lamb, and each in his own way will proclaim the great works of God: Great and marvelous are Thy works, Lord God Almighty; just and true are Thy ways Thou king of saints. Who would not fear Thee, and glorify Thy name (Rev. 15:3-4)?

For of Him and through Him and to Him are all things, to Him be the glory forever! Amen.